F

OREST
PRODUCTS
AND WOOD
SCIENCE

THIRD EDITION

AN INTRODUCTION

WITHDRAWN

FOREST PRODUCTS AND WOOD SCIENCE

THIRD EDITION

AN INTRODUCTION

JOHN G. HAYGREEN
AND JIM L. BOWYER

DRAWINGS BY **KAREN LILLEY**

IOWA STATE UNIVERSITY PRESS / AMES

JOHN G. HAYGREEN has served on the faculties at Auburn University, University of Minnesota, Colorado State University, and Michigan State University. He was involved in teaching and research in wood science and product technology from 1956 until his retirement in 1990. During that period he served as the first head of the Department of Forest Products at the University of Minnesota and as the associate dean of the School of Forestry at Auburn University. Dr. Haygreen received his B.S. degree from Iowa State University and his M.S. and Ph.D. degrees from Michigan State University. He is a past president of the Society of Wood Science and Technology and the Forest Products Society and a fellow in the International Academy of Wood Science. He is author of three patents and over 60 research papers dealing with the drying, mechanical behavior, and utilization of lumber and panel products. Since retirement he has remained active as a litigation consultant and an alternate member of the American Lumber Standards Committee.

JIM L. BOWYER is director of the Forest Products Management Development Institute, an entity of the Department of Forest Products at the University of Minnesota. He previously served as head of the Department of Forest Products from 1984 until 1995. Dr. Bowyer received a B.S. degree in forestry from Oklahoma State University, an M.S. degree in forest products from Michigan State University, and a Ph.D. in wood science and technology from the University of Minnesota. He has served as president of the Society of Wood Science and Technology and Forest Products Society and is a fellow of the International Academy of Wood Science. He also serves on the Scientific Advisory Board of the Temperate Forest Foundation and on the Board of Directors of the Tropical Forest Foundation. Dr. Bowyer has authored more than 100 articles dealing with various aspects of forest products production and use and is a frequent speaker on related topics.

© 1982, 1989, 1996 Iowa State University Press, Ames, Iowa 50014
All rights reserved

♾ Printed on acid-free paper in the United States of America

Authorization to photocopy items for internal or personal use, or the internal or personal use of specific clients, is granted by Iowa State University Press, provided that the base fee of $.10 per copy is paid directly to the Copyright Clearance Center, 27 Congress Street, Salem, MA 01970. For those organizations that have been granted a photocopy license by CCC, a separate system of payments has been arranged. The fee code for users of the Transactional Reporting Service is 0-8138-2256-4/96 $.10.

First edition, 1982, through three printings
Second edition, 1989, through three printings
Third edition, 1996

Library of Congress Cataloging-in-Publication Data

Haygreen, John G.
    Forest products and wood science: an introduction / John G. Haygreen and Jim L. Bowyer; drawings by Karen Lilley.—3rd ed.
        p. cm.
    Includes bibliographical references and index.
    ISBN 0-8138-2256-4
    I. Bowyer, Jim L. II. Title.
  TA419.H34 1996
  674—dc20   96-15734

Last digit is the print number: 9 8 7 6 5 4 3 2

CONTENTS

WOOD PROPERTIES AND MODIFICATION OF QUALITY

**THE TECHNOLOGY OF MAJOR
FOREST PRODUCTS**

**WOOD AS A FUEL AND
INDUSTRIAL RAW MATERIAL**

PREFACE

THIS BOOK was written as a textbook for an introductory study of wood as an industrial raw material. It is intended to assist the student in understanding the physical and chemical nature of wood, important wood properties, and the nature of major wood products.

The text is designed primarily for two types of students: those who intend to pursue careers in wood science or forest products and those in forestry who receive exposure to the forest products field through only one or two product-oriented courses. The book also provides an appropriate introduction to wood products for students of materials science and construction materials. It is prepared for the student with no previous knowledge of the wood science/forest products field. In all sections the objective is to present pertinent information in a concise manner, avoiding detail and technical terminology wherever possible.

The book is divided into four parts. Part 1 introduces the nature of wood and bark and the trees that produce them. Part 2 deals with the physical properties of wood, relating these properties to the chemical and structural characteristics covered in Part 1. The subject of Part 3 is major forest products; basic manufacturing processes and product properties are discussed. The book is concluded in Part 4 with a look at wood in the global raw materials picture, including use of wood as a source of energy. Environmental implications of wood use are also examined.

Although it was recognized that most students beginning an introductory forest products course will have a knowledge of basic botany, Part 1 is written to permit understanding by those without a botany background. Throughout Part 1, features of wood that are useful in identification of timbers are highlighted. The subject of wood identification is not addressed, however, since several good texts are available that deal with this subject.

The authors wish to express sincere thanks to the following reviewers for their suggestions: Kent T. Adair, Terry L. Amburgey, Donald G. Arganbright, H. Michael Barnes, Thomas E. Batey, Jr., B. Alan Bendtsen, Dwight W. Bensend, Arthur B. Brauner, Ben S. Bryant, Honorio Carino, Gilbert L. Comstock, Harold

A. Core, John B. Crist, Robert W. Erickson, David W. French, Roland O. Gertjejansen, Irving S. Goldstein, Hans M. Gregersen, Bruce Hoadley, Judson G. Isebrands, Philip O. Larson, E.A. McGinnes, Thomas M. Maloney, Kenneth J. Muehlenfeld, Wayne K. Murphey, Helmuth Resch, Irving B. Sachs, John F. Senft, Craig E. Shuler, Richard A. Skok, Otto Suchsland, Edward Sucoff, Richard J. Thomas, Ed Williston, John I. Zerbe, and Steven C. Zylkowski.

Special thanks are extended to Simo Sarkanen for extensive assistance in revising Chapter 3, and to John Crist and Ron Teclaw of the U.S. Forest Service, John P. Limbach of Ripon Microslides, Inc., and Elisabeth Wheeler and North Carolina State University for their extensive photographic contributions.

J.G. Haygreen
J.L. Bowyer

INTRODUCTION

■ **AS WE NEAR** the beginning of the 21st century, the world population is growing at an unprecedented rate. The mid-1995 figure of 5.7 billion is expected to double or more within the next century. In addition to population, world economies are also growing rapidly; with the exception of Africa, economic activity is expanding globally at a significantly greater rate than population.

Growth of world population and affluence translates to rapidly rising consumption of raw materials. Demand is increasing for materials used in providing shelter, fuel, clothing, communication, packaging, and durable and nondurable goods of all kinds.

An examination of currently used raw materials shows that wood is a principal material, both domestically and globally. On a worldwide scale, the industrial use of wood approximates that of cement and steel and far exceeds plastic; the total harvest volume, which includes wood used for fuel and for industrial purposes, exceeds the volume of all principal materials *combined* (Table I.1). The same is true in the United States.

Given its dominant role in today's raw materials picture, it is clear that wood will continue to play a major role in fulfilling human needs through the 21st century and beyond. Moreover, in view of the inherent advantages of wood, it is likely that its importance as a raw material will increase. Among the many advantages of wood are the following:

Table I.1. Comparison of annual world production of various raw materials

	Billion tonnes	Billion m^3
Roundwood	2.1	3.5
Industrial roundwood	1.0	1.7
Cement	1.1	1.0
Steel	0.8	0.1
Plastics	0.09	0.08
Aluminum	0.02	0.007

Source: Schultz 1993.
Note: From FAO (1991) and German Federal Statistics Office (1990, 1991).

1. *Wood is an extremely versatile raw material.* It can be sawn into lumber, sliced into veneer, chipped into particles, separated into fiber, ground into flour, or broken into basic chemical constituents. In addition, it is strong yet light-weight, is a good insulator, and will last indefinitely if used correctly. The technological opportunities to serve human needs are accordingly great.

2. *Wood can be processed to finished products with the input of very little energy.* At a time when society is seeking ways to harness energy from the sun, wood is a prime example of a product produced entirely from converted solar energy. Little additional energy is needed to produce useful products from wood. Furthermore, much of this additional energy is provided by forest and wood manufacturing residues. As a result, forest products manufacturing industries are increasingly becoming energy self-sufficient, drawing little from the nation's supply of largely imported energy resources.

3. *The production and use of wood result in less-detrimental impacts to the environment than is the case with alternative materials—metals, plastics, and cements.* In large part due to the comparatively lower energy consumption associated with production of wood products, the environmental advantages of wood are many.

4. *The product of harvest—wood—is renewable.* The renewable nature of forests and wood ensures that, with proper forest management, society can be assured of an indefinite supply of raw material as well as sustainable forest ecosystems.

When considering developments related to the use of wood, it may be helpful to briefly review the history of the use of forests and wood in this country. Clawson (1979) provides an interesting discussion of the growth of forestry and forest products in the United States. More recently MacCleery (1993) describes the role of forests and forestry in American history. His paper should be read by all interested in forests and forestry. MacCleery points out that until about 1900 the area of forestland in the United States was continuously decreasing. By 1920, land clearing for agriculture and community settlement had largely ceased, due to improved farming technology and the adoption of the internal combustion engine that greatly reduced the need for draft animals and associated pastureland. The clearing of forests dropped dramatically. The forestland area in the United States is now stable, covering approximately 68–70% of the area occupied by forests in the year 1600.

Wood produced through U.S. forest growth has exceeded the amount harvested in every year since about 1940. In 1992 net forest growth exceeded harvest by 31%. The growth in volume in our forests is estimated to be three and one-half times greater today than it was in 1920. Figure I.1 shows an estimate of the trends in standing sawtimber volume from 1800 to 1992; note that standing timber volume has been rising steadily for the past five decades. The average volume of standing timber per acre in U.S. forests is almost one-third greater today than it was in 1952. Thus, the often-heard belief of the public that the forests of this country are disappearing is contrary to what is actually happening.

The healthy growth/harvest situation in U.S. forests does not mean that the industry has no resource problems. Economic availability is, of course, more critical to the forest products industry than gross physical supply. Environmental and aesthetic concerns of the public limit availability particularly on public lands.

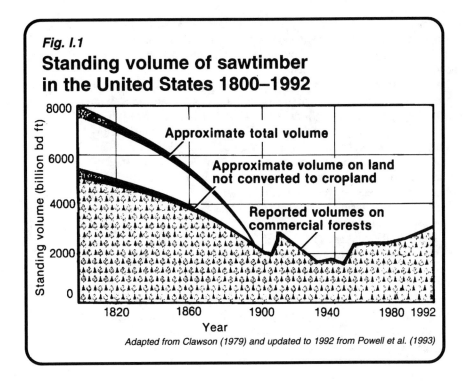

Fig. I.1

Standing volume of sawtimber in the United States 1800–1992

Adapted from Clawson (1979) and updated to 1992 from Powell et al. (1993)

Concerns over endangered species, wetland preservation, and old-growth stands have become political issues. Furthermore, the nature of the resource that is available for harvest is changing toward an increasing proportion of small, more-rapidly grown trees. All of these provide challenges to the wood using industry.

One of the great challenges for the future centers is the need to modify product and production technology to permit use of the type of wood now growing in the forests and available for harvest. Softwoods are in relatively tight supply in many regions, but most regions have species of hardwood that are underutilized, although the small size and low quality of many of these hardwoods are a problem. Technological developments outlined in this text and as summarized in Chapter 18 have made possible the utilization of more and more of this material; yet ongoing progress in this area will be needed. A related challenge involves the need for development of technologies for economically growing and utilizing nonforest fiber such as those from short-rotation intensive-culture tree farms or from more-traditional agriculture.

The size structure of forest products industries presents a second challenge. Production in some sectors of the forest products industry, e.g., hardwood lumber, is dominated by small firms. It is difficult for such firms to rapidly adopt increasingly sophisticated technological improvements and to develop integrated processes affording complete use of the tree. The large firms in the industry have the potential to utilize all of the material removed in harvesting. Under an ideal utilization system, a tree can be cut and subdivided, with each portion of the stem being used to produce the highest-value product possible. Larger manufacturing complexes are well on the way to achieving complete utilization, aided by the fact that many have sufficient power and heat requirements to justify the large capital investment required for wood and bark burners and boilers. Some smaller firms are moving to catch their larger counterparts in technical sophistication. Those that cannot may pass from the scene.

A third issue or problem faced by the forest products industry is the need for increasing productivity and efficiency in the use of all resources, human as well as material. One important need is to improve the technical competence of those who use wood within their industries, i.e., homebuilders, furniture manufacturers, contractors, architects, and others. All must become better educated with respect to use of wood. There are many opportunities to conserve wood products by improved product or building design. In some cases one type of wood-based material can be used more effectively than another. In still other situations less material can be used if the design is improved, or if greater attention is given to designing for product durability over time.

A major factor in the solution of the latter two problems is the availability of personnel with a sound knowledge of wood. The industry needs foresters who understand the properties and potential uses of alternative species they may plant and who can foresee how the management plans they develop will affect the wood produced. Forest products specialists and wood scientists who have the training to modify processes to suit the changing quality of timber, and who can develop new products to serve the needs of consumers, will continue to be sought by large and small firms alike. Young people knowledgeable about wood and how to properly use it will also be increasingly needed in industries using wood products.

Some major technological developments of the past that have been of great importance in broadening the wood resource base are the development of pulping processes suitable for hardwoods and development of wood composite products technology to the point that structural particleboards from hardwood are now an alternative to softwood plywood. These and other advancements have been accomplished through the efforts of researchers and production engineers, many of whom have come from academic backgrounds in wood science or forest products.

Those interested in the science and technology of wood should be aware that this field has been clearly separated from related disciplines only in recent decades. Compared to the profession of forestry, wood science and technology is in its infancy. Engineering, product design, and fundamental research on wood prior to the 1940s was carried out primarily by professionals who were trained as engineers, chemists, or foresters but who later devoted their careers to working with wood. Gradually the academic programs of a number of universities have broadened in scope recognizing forest products (under a number of names including wood technology, wood science, wood engineering, forest products, and wood utilization) as a distinct and separate area of study.

The birth in 1947 of the technical society of the forest industries, the Forest Products Society (FPS), could be claimed as the date at which this field began to be recognized as something different from forestry or engineering. As a technical society, the major role of FPS is the publication and dissemination of research and technical information as well as the advancement of technology in the forest products industries. Today FPS has over 3000 members worldwide. Another society, the Society of Wood Science and Technology (SWST), likewise has as one of its goals the advancement of the science of wood. SWST is a professional society that acts primarily as the professional home for researchers and technologists qualified for membership by academic training or professional experience. Membership in both of these organizations can be of great help in building and maintaining competence in the areas of specialization within forest products.

The growing world demand for affordable supplies of materials for building, furniture, packaging, paper, and consumer goods of all kinds ensures the future importance of wood-based industries. This demand, coupled with the productive capacity of forestlands and the relatively low environmental impact of wood products production and use, should assure a student interested in wood that this field can provide both a significant career opportunity and an exceptional avenue for contributing to the betterment of society.

REFERENCES AND SUPPLEMENTAL READINGS

Clark, T.D. 1984. The Greening of the South. Lexington, KY: Univ. of Kentucky Press.

Clawson, M. 1979. Forests in the long sweep of American history. Science 204:1168–1174.

Crocker, T.C., Jr. 1987. Longleaf pine—a history of man and a forest. USDA For. Ser. Forest Rept. R8-FR7.

MacCleery, D.W. 1993. American Forests—A History of Resiliency and Recovery. Forest History Society Issues Series.

Office of Technology Assessment. 1983. Wood use—U.S. competitiveness and technology. U.S. Congr. OTA-ITE-210.

Powell, D., J. Faulkner, D. Darr, Z. Zhu, and D. MacCleery. 1993. Forest Resources of the United States, 1992. USDA Forest Service, Gen. Tech. Rep. RM-234.

Revkin, A. 1990. The Burning Season. Boston: Houghton Mifflin Press.

Schultz, H. 1993. The development of wood utilization in the 19th, 20th, and 21st centuries. Forestry Chronicle 69(4):413–418.

USDA Forest Service. 1988. The South's fourth forest—alternatives for the future. For. Ser. Forest Resource Rept. No. 24.

_____. 1991. The conditions and trends of U.S. forests. USDA For. Ser. Rept. 28.

1

The nature of wood

AN UNDERSTANDING of wood—its appearance, properties, and potential for conversion to various products—first requires an understanding of its physical and anatomical structure and chemical composition, which are covered in this section of the book.

Chapter 1 deals with differences in types of trees and wood produced by them as well as the development and function of cambial layers in woody plants. Growth processes are presented only conceptually. The intent here is to provide a basis for comprehending the cellular and chemical nature

▶

of wood and the ways in which forestry practice can affect this.

The cellular and subcellular structures of normal mature wood are examined in Chapters 2 through 5. Chapter 6 is devoted to variations in wood form traceable to age and environmental effects. In Chapter 7, the nature of bark is discussed. Structural features that are important in wood identification are covered, but no attempt is made to explain how woods are separated. This topic is considered but one of many important subjects in the field of wood science and technology and is thus left to other texts.

■

1

Tree growth and production of woody tissue

■ **TREES** are complex organisms. Originating through vegetative propagation or from sexually fertilized eggs that become tiny seed-encased embryos, trees grow to be one of nature's largest living organisms.

Like humans, trees are delicate when young and typically grow vigorously when given proper nutrition and a suitable environment. As juveniles, they form tissues that differ from those formed in mature trees. They respire. They require a balanced intake of minerals to maintain health. They metabolize food, but unlike humans they also synthesize their own foods. If wounded, they react quickly to effect healing. As age progresses, vigor is maintained for a lengthy period but then begins to wane. Life processes eventually slow to the point that the tree has difficulty healing wounds and warding off disease. Finally, the tree dies.

The focus of this book is not on the growth process but on an important product of growth: wood. However, a brief study of the process of wood formation provides a useful basis for a study of wood itself.

Wood is formed by a variety of plants, including many that do not attain tree stature. A *tree* is generally defined as a woody plant 15–20 ft (4–6 m) or more in height and characterized by a single trunk rather than several stems. Plants of smaller size are called shrubs or bushes. Species that normally grow to tree size may occasionally develop as shrubs, especially where growth conditions are adverse. Because of the size attained, wood produced by plants of tree stature is useful for a wider range of products than wood from shrubs and bushes. For this reason, wood produced by trees is emphasized.

Classification of woody plants ■

Woods, and the trees that produce them, are divided into two categories: hardwoods and softwoods. Hardwood and softwood trees are botanically quite different. Both are included in the botanical division spermatophytes (Table 1.1), meaning they produce seeds. They are, however, in different botanical subdivisions. Hardwoods are in the subdivision angiospermae and softwoods are in the gymnospermae subdivision. *Angiosperms* are characterized by production of seeds within ovaries, whereas *gymnosperms* produce seeds that lack a covering layer.

Table 1.1. Trees in the vegetable kingdom

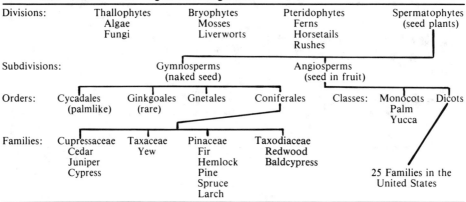

Needlelike leaves characterize *softwood* trees. Such trees are commonly known as evergreens, since most remain green the year around, annually losing only a portion of their needles. Most softwoods also bear scaly cones (inside which seeds are produced) and are therefore often referred to as *conifers*. Included in the softwood group in the Northern Hemisphere are the genera *Pinus* (pine), *Picea* (spruce), *Larix* (larch), *Abies* (fir), *Tsuga* (hemlock), *Sequoia* (redwood), *Taxus* (yew), *Taxodium* (cypress), *Pseudotsuga* (Douglas-fir), and the genera of those woods known commonly as cedars (*Juniperus, Thuja, Chamaecyparis,* and *Libocedrus*).

In contrast to softwoods, *hardwoods* are angiosperms that bear broad leaves (which generally change color and drop in the fall in temperate zones) and produce seeds within acorns, pods, or other fruiting bodies. Referring again to Table 1.1, note that angiosperms are subdivided into monocotyledons and dicotyledons. Hardwood-producing species fall within the dicotyledon class. Hardwood genera of the Northern Hemisphere include *Quercus* (oak), *Fraxinus* (ash), *Ulmus* (elm), *Acer* (maple), *Betula* (birch), *Fagus* (beech), and *Populus* (cottonwood, aspen). Included in the monocotyledon class are the palms and yuccas. Many of the roughly 2500 species of palms produce relatively large-diameter fibrous stems, which are strong if left in the round condition but tend to fall apart when cut into lumber. Paper can be made from the fiber.

Not only do hardwood and softwood trees differ in external appearance, but the wood formed by them differs structurally or morphologically. The types of cells, their relative numbers, and their arrangements are different, the fundamental difference being that hardwoods contain a type of cell called a *vessel element*. This cell type occurs in most hardwoods but very seldom in softwoods. All hardwoods do not, incidentally, produce hard, dense wood. Despite the implication in the names hardwood and softwood, many softwoods produce wood that is harder and more dense than wood produced by some hardwoods. Balsa wood, for example, is from a hardwood species.

Distribution of hardwoods and softwoods ■

Hardwood species occur in every major region of the United States. They predominate in the East, forming an almost unbroken forest from the Appalachians westward to the Great Plains. Across the Plains, the trees that line rivers, streams, and ponds are hardwoods. Farther west, the perpetually green softwoods that cover the Rockies are frequently interrupted by patches of white-stemmed aspen and other hardwoods. In the far West, hardwoods grow in valleys below softwood-covered mountains. On a worldwide basis also, hardwoods predominate. They are found in most areas of the world (Table 1.2). Tropical forests are almost exclusively hardwoods. In total, hardwood growing stock has been estimated to exist in volumes almost double that of softwoods.

Table 1.2. Land area of world forest resources by region and type

Region	Softwood Forests		Hardwood Forests		Combined Softwood and Hardwood Forests	
	Land area	Percent of world total	Land area	Percent of world total	Land area	Percent of world total
	(millions of ha)		(millions of ha)		(millions of ha)	
North America	400	30.5	230	13.4	630	20.8
Central America	20	1.5	40	2.3	60	2.0
South America	10	0.8	550	32.0	560	18.5
Africa	2	0.2	188	10.9	190	6.3
Europe	107	8.2	74	4.3	181	6.0
Former Soviet Union	697	53.0	233	13.6	930	30.6
Asia	65	5.0	335	19.5	400	13.2
Oceania	11	0.8	69	4.0	80	2.6
Total World	1,312	100.0	1,719	100.0	3,031	100.0

Source: Sedjo and Lyon (1990).
Note: The values in this table indicate areas of closed forests; more open savannah-type areas were not included.

Softwoods occur naturally throughout the Northern Hemisphere and sporadically in the Southern Hemisphere. With the help of humans, many Northern Hemisphere species are found today in many regions of the southern part of the world. In the continental United States, softwoods dominate forests of the deep South, the far North, the mountainous West, and the extreme Northwest (Fig. 1.1). Softwoods also are predominant in the mountains and coastal regions of Alaska.

Fig. 1.2
Typical woody cell of softwood

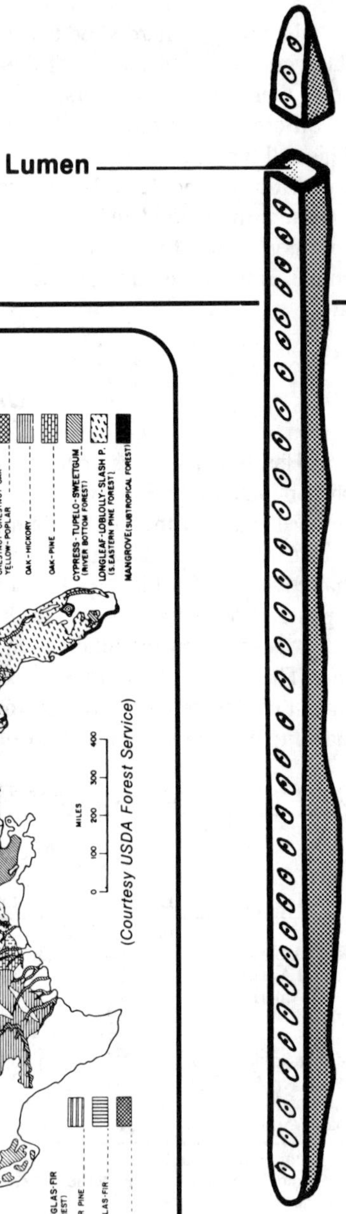

Lumen

Fig. 1.1
Forest vegetation of the continental United States

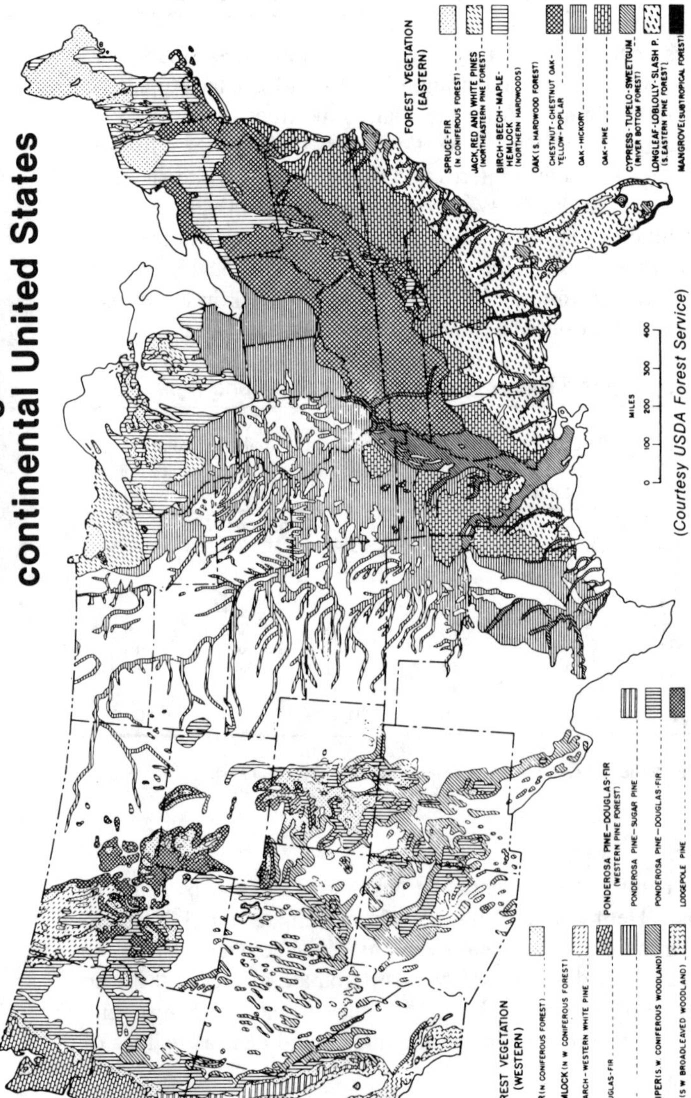

FOREST VEGETATION
(EASTERN)

SPRUCE-FIR
(N CONIFEROUS FOREST)

JACK, RED AND WHITE PINES
(NORTHEASTERN PINE FOREST)

BIRCH-BEECH-MAPLE-
HEMLOCK
(NORTHERN HARDWOODS)

OAK (S. HARDWOOD FOREST)

CHESTNUT-CHESTNUT OAK-
YELLOW-POPLAR

OAK-HICKORY

CYPRESS-TUPELO-SWEETGUM
(RIVER BOTTOM FOREST)

LONGLEAF-LOBLOLLY-SLASH P.
(S. EASTERN PINE FOREST)

MANGROVE (SUBTROPICAL FOREST)

MILES

0   100   200   300   400

(Courtesy USDA Forest Service)

FOREST VEGETATION
(WESTERN)

SPRUCE-FIR (N. CONIFEROUS FOREST)

"CEDAR"-HEMLOCK (N. W. CONIFEROUS FOREST)

WESTERN LARCH-WESTERN WHITE PINE

PACIFIC DOUGLAS-FIR

REDWOOD

PINYON-JUNIPER (S. W. CONIFEROUS WOODLAND)

CHAPARRAL (S. W. BROADLEAVED WOODLAND)

PONDEROSA PINE-DOUGLAS-FIR
(WESTERN PINE FOREST)

PONDEROSA PINE-SUGAR PINE

PONDEROSA PINE-DOUGLAS-FIR

LODGEPOLE PINE

In the United States about 100 wood-producing and commercially important species reach tree size; only about 35 of these are softwoods. Roughly the same is true of Europe. However, throughout the world, and particularly the tropical regions, the number of wood-producing species of tree size exceeds 10,000. Of these, the number of softwoods is small—only about 500. The wet tropics are particularly rich in species; several hectares may contain several hundred species. The large number of species complicates efforts to fully utilize the tropical rain forest. Despite considerable research to determine properties, use potential, and processing technology, work has been completed on only a relatively small number of species. Today, approximately 2500 tree species have commercial importance.

Wood—A collection of small cells ∎

A close look at wood shows it to be made up of tiny cells or fibers that are so small they generally cannot be seen without a magnifying glass or microscope. Illustrated in Figure 1.2 is a type of cell that makes up most of the volume of a softwood such as white fir; the cell has a hollow center (*lumen*), is closed at the ends, and is perforated with openings in the sidewall.

Figure 1.3 shows how a tiny block of white fir would look if magnified. Unmagnified, this block would occupy only about 1/50,000 cm³. Rays, which are composed of a number of individual ray cells and provide for horizontal movement of moisture in a standing tree, can be seen cutting across the near left (radial) surface; rays in an end view can be seen on the right vertical (tangential) surface.

In Figure 1.3 note that the three different surfaces of the block—labeled transverse (cross section), radial, and tangential—look quite different (see also Fig. 2.1). A cross-sectional or *transverse* surface is formed by cutting a log or piece of lumber to length, while radial and tangential surfaces result from cutting along the grain. A *radial* surface is made by cutting longitudinally along the radius of a round cross section. Tangential surfaces result from cutting perpendicular to a radius. The names transverse, radial, and tangential are frequently encountered in the study of wood science.

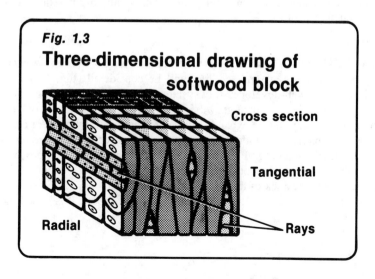

Fig. 1.3
Three-dimensional drawing of softwood block

Cross section

Tangential

Radial

Rays

Basic processes in tree growth ■

PRODUCTION OF WOOD AND BARK. Wood (*xylem*) is found inside a covering of bark, which is composed of an inner layer (*phloem*) and an outer protective layer (*outer bark*). As a tree grows, it adds new wood, increasing the diameter of its main stem and branches. Bark is also added in the process of growth to replace that which cracks and flakes off as the stem grows larger.

Like all green plants, a tree can manufacture its own food through the process of photosynthesis, which takes place in the leaves. It needs only water (from the soil), carbon dioxide (from the atmosphere), and light (from the sun) to do this. Water, along with nutrients, is taken up by the roots and moved through the outer part of the xylem up to the leaves. Carbon dioxide is taken in through tiny openings in leaf surfaces. With the help of the sun, water and air are combined in the presence of chlorophyll to make sugars that provide energy to the growing tree. Some sugars are used in making new leaves, some in making new shoots, and some in making new wood. A part of the sugar moves to special locations in the wood or to the roots where it is stored for later use; a part is consumed through respiration. Sugars used in making new wood move down a tree through the phloem.

Sugar is transported throughout the tree in the form of *sap*, a solution containing various sugars and water as well as growth regulators and other substances. The term sap is also used to refer to the mineral-rich water that is taken up by roots and moved upward through the outer portion of the xylem.

A thin layer between the xylem and phloem produces new xylem and phloem tissue. This layer, called the *cambium,* completely sheaths the twigs, branches, trunk, and roots, meaning that a season of growth results in a new continuous layer of wood throughout the tree (Fig. 1.4).

Since sap moves down the tree through the phloem but is necessary for food in the cambium, a way is needed for it to travel horizontally toward the center of the tree. *Wood rays* provide for this horizontal movement. Rays also function in storing carbohydrates and may serve as avenues of horizontal transport for stored materials from near the center of the tree outward following periods of dormancy.

Figure 1.5 illustrates the relative position of various portions of a tree stem. Careful examination should help in gaining an understanding of the relationship between various layers of tissue.

DEVELOPMENT OF A YOUNG STEM. To begin a study of the development process, growth of a young pine seedling will be considered (Fig. 1.6). The seedling shown has a well-developed root system and crown typical of a 5- to 6-year-old tree. With the beginning of growth in early spring, buds at the tip of each branch (and root) swell as tissue expands through formation and growth of cells. These regions in which cells divide repeatedly to form new cells are called *meristematic regions*. Highlighted in Figure 1.6 is an expanding bud at the apex of a young pine. Buds of similar appearance occur at the tip of each branch. The meristematic zone at the apex of the main stem is of special significance since it controls to some extent the development of branches and shoots; it is called the *apical meristem.*

Fig. 1.4
New growth occurs as a sheath
covering the main stem, branches, and twigs

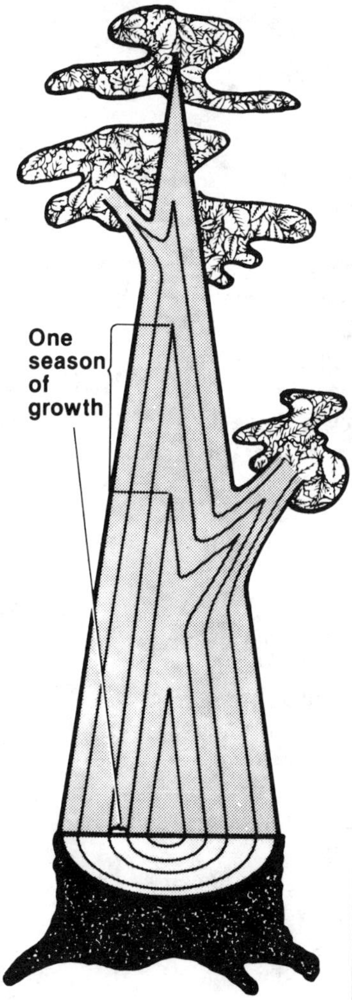

One season of growth

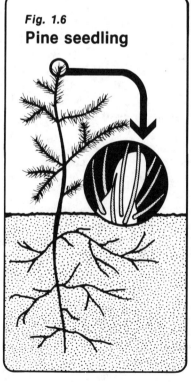

Fig. 1.5
Parts of a mature tree stem

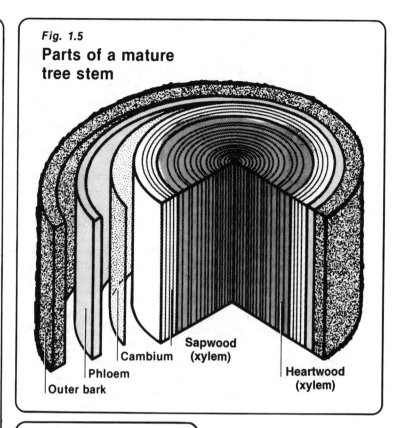

Outer bark

Phloem

Cambium

Sapwood (xylem)

Heartwood (xylem)

Fig. 1.6
Pine seedling

Cell division at the apical meristem serves to lengthen the main stem. New cell production at this location is followed by cell elongation resulting in height growth. As the stem is built through production of new cells during growth periods, the terminal bud moves upward, leaving new and expanding cells behind. Thus a spike driven into a tree at, for example, 2 m above ground level will remain 2 m off the ground regardless of the height to which the tree grows.

Cell production at the stem tip and subsequent cell lengthening are followed by a sequence of changes as newly formed cells mature. This entire process is explained below using a representation of a section of a growing stem tip that shows various tissue layers (Fig. 1.7). The student should be cautioned that Figure 1.7 and the accompanying discussion present a greatly simplified picture of the actual growth process.

New cells are produced in the several layers of cells in the area designated as section I. Soon after formation, these newly formed cells begin to differentiate with changes in size, shape, and function. Tissue at the outer edge of the young stem forms an *epidermis* composed of one layer of cells which have thick, wax (cutin)-covered outer walls that serve as protection from moisture loss. Nearer the center of the stem, cells undergo a developmental process, changing size and shape to eventually form an unbroken ring about the stem center. This region is called the *procambium* and is the precursor of a new meristematic region that develops a bit later. At the very center of the stem, cells develop differently yet, forming a layer dissimilar to the wood that will later surround it. This is the *pith*. The pith, procambium, and epidermis can be seen in section II of Figure 1.7.

The process of change continues. The procambium reaches a maximum size (lower edge of section II); then cells that make it up undergo further differentiation. As depicted in section III, inner cells of the procambium continue to undergo change to become similar to xylem, which will form later. Cells of the outer portion of the procambium assume characteristics similar to phloem, formation of which will also follow. These two new tissue layers are called *primary xylem* and *primary phloem*. The transformation to primary xylem or primary phloem continues until eventually a ring of procambium tissue only one to several cells in width remains (sections IV–V).

As a final step in the developmental process that began at the stem apex, the remaining ring of procambial tissue becomes active, its cells dividing repeatedly to form xylem and phloem. Vascular cambium (or simply cambium) is the name given to this meristematic layer.

The new lateral meristem, the vascular cambium, is considered of secondary origin since it forms after the terminal meristem. Xylem and phloem cells produced in this new meristem are thus correctly called *secondary xylem* and *secondary phloem* respectively. It is interesting to note that in monocotyledons (palms) all procambial cells typically differentiate into primary xylem or phloem, leaving no vascular cambium. These plants, therefore, do not produce secondary xylem and phloem.

Once formed at a given location in the tree, the vascular cambium remains active throughout the life of the tree (or tree part). Because new cell formation in the cambium serves to increase stem diameter, the very large stature attained by mature trees is traceable to cell division in the cambium.

The stem depicted in section V of Figure 1.7 would be about 1 year old.

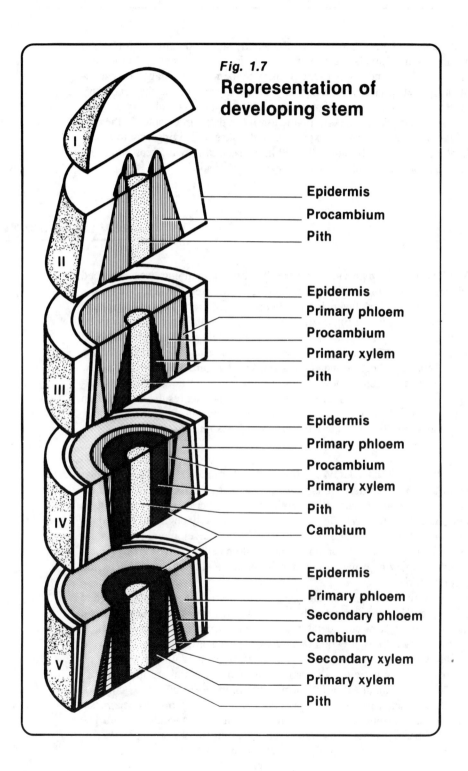

Fig. 1.7
Representation of developing stem

Epidermis
Procambium
Pith

Epidermis
Primary phloem
Procambium
Primary xylem
Pith

Epidermis
Primary phloem
Procambium
Primary xylem
Pith
Cambium

Epidermis
Primary phloem
Secondary phloem
Cambium
Secondary xylem
Primary xylem
Pith

Note that the tissue layers that sheathed the woody stem soon after its formation have become thinner; this is because of compression forces resulting from diameter expansion. The same is true of the primary phloem. At this stage of stem development, no cell division occurs in any of the layers outside the secondary phloem. Because of this, the circumference of these layers cannot keep pace with the expanding stem diameter. As explained in more detail in Chapter 7, the epidermal layer fractures with stem expansion and flakes off, giving way to a new outer bark layer. Eventually (normally within the second growing season) all tissue originally formed outside the secondary phloem is shed.

Vascular cambium ■

COMPOSITION. In the previous section, the vascular cambium was described as consisting of a one- to several-cell-width ring of meristematic cells. An artist's conception of a cambium layer that has been isolated from surrounding wood and bark tissue is shown in Figure 1.8. Two kinds of cells can be seen to make up the cambium layer. The long, slender cells are called *fusiform initials;* these divide repeatedly to form either new *cambial initials* or new xylem and phloem cells (Fig. 1.9). The short, rounded cells shown in Figure 1.8 are *ray initials;* division of these create either new xylem or phloem rays or new ray initials. Division parallel to the stem surface in a tangential plane that results in formation of either xylem or phloem cells is called *periclinal division.* Production of new initials by radial partitioning is termed *anticlinal division.*

DEVELOPMENT AND GROWTH OF XYLEM AND PHLOEM. Periclinal division of a fusiform initial results in formation of two cells, one of which remains meristematic and a part of the cambium. The other cell becomes either a xylem or phloem *mother cell.* The mother cell immediately begins to expand radially and may itself divide one or more times before developing into a mature xylem or phloem element. Maturation of new xylem cells involves growth in diameter and length, with growth accompanied by thickening of the cell walls and finally lignification.

It should be noted that not all types of cells grow in both diameter and length. For example, longitudinal cells formed in late summer by pines, spruces, and other softwoods grow considerably in length but little in diameter. Vessel elements that characterize hardwood (*broadleaf*) species grow little or may even shrink slightly in length but may expand up to 50 times in diameter.

Two consecutive periclinal divisions of a fusiform initial are illustrated in Figure 1.10. Beginning at (a), a fusiform initial prepares to divide, as chromosomes split, and then separate. In (b), a cell plate begins to form and becomes a new cell wall at (c). Both cells begin to grow in diameter (d) and length (e). The innermost cell becomes part of the xylem, pushing outward the other portion that remains part of the cambium. In (f), the cycle begins again.

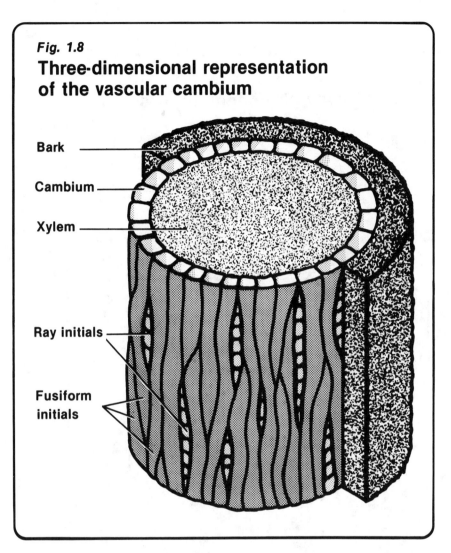

Fig. 1.8

Three-dimensional representation of the vascular cambium

Bark

Cambium

Xylem

Ray initials

Fusiform initials

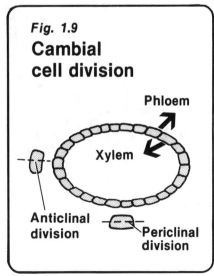

Fig. 1.9

Cambial cell division

Phloem

Xylem

Anticlinal division

Periclinal division

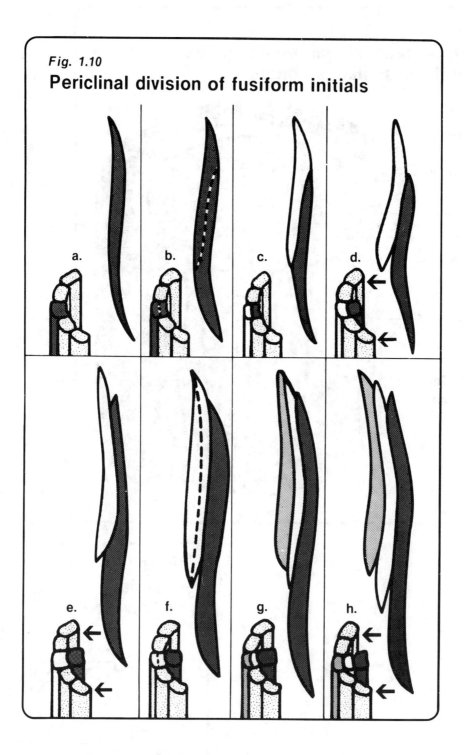

Fig. 1.10

Periclinal division of fusiform initials

a.

b.

c.

d.

e.

f.

g.

h.

Early in the growing season, new cell production in primary meristems at stem tips occurs rapidly. Intervals of only 8–18 hr between successive divisions in the primary meristems of white cedar (*Thuja*) have been reported (Zimmermann and Brown 1971, p. 78). This rate diminishes as the season progresses. Cambial initial division typically commences later than division at the apical meristems, and once initiated, division occurs relatively slowly. (See the section Duration of Cambial Activity in Temperate Regions for an explanation of this phenomenon.) Bannan (1955) found in experiments with northern white cedar (*Thuja occidentalis*) that successive cambial divisions occurred about once weekly (each 7 days) in the early spring. Zimmermann and Brown (1971), after working with the same species, agreed with the finding of a 7-day interval. They found, however, that the rate of division increased several weeks into the growing season. Only three to four cambial initial divisions were noted in the first few weeks of activity, after which the rate increased to one division per 4- to 6-day interval during the period of most-rapid earlywood formation. Wilson (1964), on the other hand, found a 10-day interval between successive divisions of cambial initials during earlywood formation in white pine.

The process of periclinal division of cambial initials is again illustrated in Figure 1.11; subsequent development of new cells is also depicted. In 1.11A, the one-cell-wide cambium (C), with mother cells (M) adjacent on either side, can be seen sandwiched between the xylem (X) and phloem (P). Line 1 of 1.11B shows the appearance of cells in and near the cambial zone during a period of cambial activity. To the left of the cambial initial are two xylem mother cells and one cell of mature secondary xylem. To the right of the cambial initial is one phloem mother cell and a secondary phloem cell. Looking now at line 2, which represents the cambial zone a short time later, the xylem mother cell nearest the cambium has divided to form two mother cells. The xylem mother cell farthest from the cambium has begun to enlarge (E). No activity is noted on the phloem side of the cambium or in the cambium itself. By line 3, one of the xylem mother cells formed in the previous period has divided again. The other has begun to enlarge. Although no cambial activity is noted in this period, outward movement of the cambium and phloem cells has occurred as the result of new cell formation through division of a xylem mother cell. At the stage of activity illustrated by line 4, the cambial initial has divided; a portion of the initial remains in the cambium, and the other half becomes a xylem mother cell. Enlargement of yet another xylem mother cell has begun. Growth of the innermost mother cell has ceased and cell wall thickening has begun. This cell (X_1) is mature and cannot divide further. To the outside of the cambium, the phloem mother cell seen earlier has divided into two cells, one of which has begun to enlarge. This sequence of events is repeated again and again as growth continues.

Figure 1.11 and the previous discussion describe the cambium as being one cell in width. However, the research of Catesson (1984) suggests that any of the cells in the cambial zone can, given the proper stimulus, either divide to form new cells or differentiate into vascular tissue. This raises the possibility that specific initials may be frequently replaced as the initials themselves differentiate to become cells of the xylem or phloem.

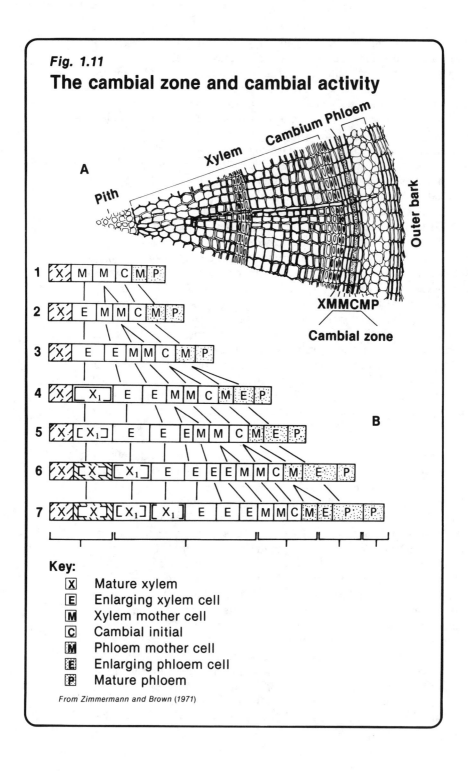

Fig. 1.11
The cambial zone and cambial activity

Key:
- ☒ Mature xylem
- 🅴 Enlarging xylem cell
- 🅼 Xylem mother cell
- 🅲 Cambial initial
- 🅼 Phloem mother cell
- 🅴 Enlarging phloem cell
- 🅿 Mature phloem

From Zimmermann and Brown (1971)

EXPANSION OF THE CAMBIAL LAYER. As a tree expands in diameter, the cambium is pushed progressively outward. Thus the cambium must expand in circumference to remain an unbroken layer around the stem. Such growth of the cambium is achieved in several ways, the most important of which is anticlinal division of fusiform initials.

Anticlinal division of a fusiform initial (see Fig. 1.9) results in two cells, both of which remain in the cambium. Assuming that the new cells survive, they begin to grow in length almost immediately. After a short rest, the new meristematic cells may divide again, either periclinally or anticlinally.

As with new initials that result from periclinal division, survival of new fusiform initials formed anticlinally is dependent upon availability of adequate nutrition. Availability of nutrition is, in turn, dependent upon proximity to rays. A fusiform initial without sufficient ray contact may die or further divide to form one or more ray initials (Zimmermann and Brown 1971, p. 74). Undernourished cells may also fail to redivide, then mature as xylem or phloem cells. Initials in the process of failing in this manner have been called *declining initials* (Philipson et al. 1971, p. 26). Bannan (1960) reported that only 20% of new cambial initials formed in rapidly growing northern white cedar remained as part of the cambium. The figure was 50% for slower-growing trees. The fact that ray contact is needed for survival and normal development means that long cells, which nearly always have adequate contact, survive while very short cells nearly always decline. There is evidence that very small fusiform initials usually decline even where ray contact is extensive (Philipson et al. 1971). This mechanism ensures that fusiform initials will maintain a long average length, even in periods of rapid growth (Panshin and de Zeeuw 1980).

In addition to expansion through an increase in the number of fusiform initials, the cambium also expands through an increase in the length of these cells. The length of initials progressively increases over time so that the length of functioning initials in a mature tree is much greater than those present at the seedling to sapling stage. In one study of white pine, initials at age 60 were found to be four to five times longer than those present in the first year of growth.

Other factors leading to circumferential expansion of a cambium are diameter growth of fusiform and ray initials and increases in the number of ray initials (Bailey 1923).

DURATION OF CAMBIAL ACTIVITY IN TEMPERATE REGIONS. During cold winter months the vascular cambium is inactive. In the spring, reactivation occurs, apparently in response to hormonal signals at the stem tips and possibly in the roots as well. An increase in average temperature to about 7°C (the precise temperature varying by species) or higher is apparently the most important of several factors leading to the onset of cell division.

Initiation of growth means production of new cells at the stem apices and, in addition, growth stimulators or *auxins* such as indole-3-acetic acid (IAA). IAA plays an important role in reinitiating activity in the cambium as it travels downward (with sap) to growth sites (Avery et al. 1937; Wareing 1951, 1958; Wareing et al. 1964; Digby and Wareing 1966; Thimann 1972). Other compounds linked to growth stimulation are gibberellic acid (GA)—at least in hardwoods—and ethylene. Some have suggested that growth stimulating compounds may have direct and specific roles in the process of cambial cell division, with IAA or closely related compounds linked to stimulation of cambial cell replication and xylem production, and gibberellin linked to production of phloem (Roberts et al. 1988).

Since IAA is produced in the buds, developing shoots, and leaves and movement is downward from that point, cambial growth begins in the spring at the top of a stem and moves toward the base (Little and Savidge 1987). In a large softwood, cambial activity may begin at the top of the tree 2–6 weeks before the cambium is reactivated at the base of the trunk (Digby and Wareing 1966; Zimmermann and Brown 1971, pp. 75–76). Much the same is true in diffuse-porous hardwoods (Eames and MacDaniels 1947, pp. 155–56). However, in ring-porous hardwoods, cambial activity may begin almost simultaneously throughout a tree (Priestley 1930; Priestley and Scott 1933). Hardwoods are classified as ring- or diffuse-porous depending upon the distribution of vessels in a cross section. Woods that form very large diameter vessels part of a year and smaller ones thereafter are called *ring-porous*. Woods forming vessels of the same size throughout the year are classed as *diffuse-porous*.

Shoot extension, which normally begins earlier than diameter growth, typically ceases earlier. In fact, height growth often occurs rapidly in the spring over a period of only 7–10 weeks and then ceases altogether (Kozlowski et al. 1991). Cambial growth, on the other hand, ordinarily continues more slowly and over a much longer period, sometimes extending into the early fall (Kienholz 1934; Reimer 1949).

As the latter part of the growing season approaches (mid-July to October, depending upon latitude) the rate of cell division in the cambium slows and then ceases as cells again become dormant. The precise mechanisms causing the onset of dormancy are not known, but as noted by Kozlowski et al. (1991), the decreasing *photoperiod* (length of day) in late summer in middle to high latitudes is a certain indicator of the coming of autumn and winter, and many species cease shoot growth and develop resting buds in response to short days. Freezing and near-freezing temperatures have also been reported to induce dormancy. However, shoots of many woody plants stop growing before seasonal temperatures are low enough to stop growth and days are short enough to promote dormancy (Kramer and Kozlowski 1979). Moreover, experiments in which trees are artificially exposed to long days have shown that shoot growth in some species can be prolonged, but not indefinitely. Wareing (1956) found, for example, that Scotch pine and sycamore maple eventually reached a dormant state even in the presence of continuous light.

The fact that many tree species reach a dormant state even in the absence of photoperiod or temperature variation indicates that other, perhaps more-complex mechanisms play a role in cessation of growth. There is considerable evidence that development and subsequent breaking of dormancy is related to the presence of relative quantities of growth stimulators, or auxins, and growth inhibitors such as abscisic acid (Nitsch 1957; Larson 1964; Kramer and Kozlowski 1979). Experimentation has shown high concentrations of growth inhibitors in terminal meristems during periods of dormancy and much lower concentrations during initiation of growth (Wareing 1958; Wareing and Phillips 1970).

The ages of both the tree part and the tree itself have been noted to have an effect upon the duration of seasonal growth activity. It has been reported that in both cases, the greater the age, the shorter the duration of cambial activity

(Eames and MacDaniels 1947). More recently, shoot growth has been reported to occur over a longer period in young trees than in older ones (Kozlowski 1971).

DURATION OF CAMBIAL ACTIVITY IN TROPICAL REGIONS. In the tropics, where rainfall tends to be evenly distributed throughout the year and when temperatures are constantly mild, cambial activity in trees may be continuous (Oppenheimer 1945; Lanner 1964; Kozlowski et al. 1991); such trees are often characterized by a lack of distinct growth rings (Jacoby 1989). However, intermittent cambial activity is more common, leading to periodic or annual growth rings (Kramer and Kozlowski 1979; Worbes 1989; Zimmerman and Brown 1971). Growth/dormancy cycles may occur one to five times each year in these locations (Tomlinson and Longman 1981). The same growth pattern has been found in trees from temperate zones that have been transplanted in the tropics (Romberger 1963). Formation of well-defined growth rings appears to be most closely associated with seasonal variation in rainfall (Ogden 1981), although moderate seasonality of temperature can also induce dormancy and growth ring formation (Jacoby 1989).

REVIEW

A. Terms to define or explain:
1. Tree
2. Xylem
3. Phloem
4. Sap
5. Angiosperm
6. Gymnosperm
7. Pith
8. Meristematic
9. Mother cell

B. Questions or concepts to explain:
1. Explain the difference between the origin of primary and secondary xylem.
2. Know the sequence of events leading up to development of the vascular cambium.
3. Understand the difference between periclinal and anticlinal division of fusiform initials. Know the products of each type of division.
4. Explain the stages of development of a xylem mother cell from the time of formation to maturity.
5. Draw a cross section of a woody stem that is several years old, indicating the various layers of tissue that would be present. Be able to explain why some layers that were present in the first year are missing.
6. Know the means by which a cambium can increase in diameter and understand why diameter expansion is necessary.
7. Understand the basic function of rays. Know the primary direction of flow along the rays.
8. Given the fact that long fibers are preferred for manufacture of high-strength papers, explain why a mill manufacturing such paper would be more interested in chips obtained from outer slabs of a log (from a sawmill) than from the portion of the log near the pith.

REFERENCES AND SUPPLEMENTAL READING

Avery, G.A., Jr.; Burkholder, P.R.; and Creighton, H.B. 1937. Production and distribution of growth hormone in shoots of *Aesculus* and *Malus* and its probable role in stimulating cambial activity. Am. J. Bot. 24:51–58.

Bailey, I.W. 1923. The cambium and its derivative tissues. IV. The increase in girth of the cambium. Am. J. Bot. 10:499–509.

Bannan, M.W. 1955. The vascular cambium and radial growth in *Thuja occidentalis* L. Can. J. Bot. 33:113–184.

———. 1960. Ontogenic trends in conifer cambium with respect to frequency of anticlinal divisions and cell length. Can. J. Bot. 38:795–802.

———. 1962. The vascular cambium and tree-ring development. In Kozlowski, T.T. Tree Growth. New York: Ronald Press, pp. 6–9.

Catesson, A.M. 1984. La dynamique cambiale. Ann. Sci. Nat. Bot. Biol. Veg. 6:23–43.

Digby, J., and Wareing, P.F. 1966. Ann. Bot. NS. 30:607–622.

Eames, A.J., and MacDaniels, L.H. 1947. An Introduction to Plant Anatomy, 2d ed. New York: McGraw-Hill.

Jacoby, G.C. 1989. Overview of tree-ring analysis in tropical regions. IAWA Bull. 10(2):99–108.

Kienholz, R. 1934. Leader, needle, cambial, and root growth of certain conifers and their relationships. Bot. Gazette 96:73–92.

Kozlowski, T.T. 1971. Growth and Development of Trees, Vol. 1. New York: Academic Press.

Kozlowski, T.T.; Kramer, P.J.; and Pallardy, S.G. 1991. The Physiological Ecology of Woody Plants. San Diego: Academic Press.

Kramer, P.J., and Kozlowski, T.T. 1979. Physiology of Woody Plants. New York: Academic Press.

Lanner, R.M. 1964. Temperature and the diurnal rhythm of height growth in pines. J. For. 62(7):493–495.

Larson, P.R. 1964. Some indirect effects of environment on wood formation. In Formation of Wood in Forest Trees, ed. M.H. Zimmermann. New York: Academic Press, pp. 345–365.

Little, C.H.A., and Savidge, R.A. 1987. The role of plant growth regulators in forest tree cambial growth. Plant Growth Regulation 6:137–169.

Nitsch, J.P. 1957. Growth response of woody plants to photoperiodic stimuli. Proc. Am. Soc. Hortic. Sci. 70:512–525.

Ogden, J. 1981. Dendrochronological studies and the determination of tree ages in the Australian tropics. J. Biogeog. 8:405–420.

Oppenheimer, H.R. 1945. Cambial wood production in stems of *Pinus halapensis*. Palest. Bot. Rehovot. Ser. 5:22–51.

Panshin, A.J., and de Zeeuw, C. 1980. Textbook of Wood Technology, 4th ed. New York: McGraw-Hill, p. 70.

Philipson, W.R.; Ward, J.M.; and Butterfield, B.G. 1971. The Vascular Cambium. London: Chapman and Hall, p. 29.

Phillips, I.D.J., and Wareing, P.F. 1958. Studies in the dormancy of sycamore. I. Seasonal changes in growth substance content of the shoot. J. Exp. Bot. 9:350–364.

Priestley, J.H. 1930. Studies in the physiology of cambial activity. III. The seasonal activity of the cambium. New Phytol. 29:316–354.

Priestley, J.H., and Scott, L.I. 1933. Phyllotaxis in the dicotyledon from the standpoint of developmental anatomy. Camb. Philos. Soc. Biol. Rev. 8:241–268.

Reimer, C.W. 1949. Growth correlations in five species of deciduous trees. Butler Univ. Bot. Stud. 9:43–59.

Roberts, L.W., Gahan, P.B. and Aloni, R. 1988. Vascular Differentiation and Plant Growth Regulators. New York: Springer-Verlag, p. 24.

Romberger, J.A. 1963. Meristems, growth, and development of woody plants. USDA For. Serv. Tech. Bull. 1293.

Sedjo, R.A., and Lyon, K.S. 1990. The Long Term Adequacy of World Timber Supply. Washington D.C.: Resources For The Future.

Thimann, K.V. 1972. The natural plant hormones. In Plant Physiology, Vol. 6B, ed. F.C. Steward. New York: Academic Press, pp. 3–145.

Tomlinson, P.B., and Longman, K.A. 1981. Growth phenology of tropical trees in relation to cambial activity. In Age and Growth Rate of Tropical Trees, ed. F.H. Bormann and G.P. Berlyn. Yale Univ. Sch. For. Environ. Stud. Bull. 94, pp. 7–19.

Wareing, P.F. 1951. Growth studies in woody species. IV. The initiation of cambial activity in ring-porous species. Physiol. Plant. 4: 546–62.

_____. 1956. Photoperiodism in woody plants. Ann. Rev. Plant Physiol. 7:191–214.

_____. 1958. The physiology of cambial activity. J. Inst. Wood Sci. 1:34–42.

Wareing, P.F., and Phillips, I.D.J. 1970. The Control of Growth and Differentiation in Plants. New York: Pergamon Press.

Wareing, P.F., Haney, C.E.A., and Digby, J. 1964. The role of endogenous hormones in cambial activity and xylem differentiation. In The Formation of Wood in Forest Trees, ed. M.H. Zimmermann. New York: Academic Press, pp. 323–344.

Wilson, B.F. 1964. A model for cell production by the cambium of conifers. In The Formation of Wood in Forest Trees, ed. M.H. Zimmermann. New York: Academic Press, pp. 19–36.

Worbes, M. 1989. Growth rings, increment and age of trees in inundation forests, savannas and a mountain forest of the neotropics. IAWA Bull. 10(2):109–122.

Zimmermann, M.H., and Brown, C.L. 1971. Trees: Structure and Function. New York: Springer-Verlag.

Macroscopic character of wood

A NUMBER of features of wood can be detected by casual observation and are termed *macroscopic* since a microscope is not needed for detection. Macroscopic characteristics of wood are of interest because they often give clues to conditions under which wood was grown, provide an indication of physical properties, and serve as an aid in wood identification.

Three distinct surfaces of wood

Illustrated in Figure 2.1 is a wedge-shaped piece of wood as it would appear if cut from a round cross section. Notice that the macro features of the cross-sectional, radial, and tangential surfaces appear quite different (see also Fig. 1.3).

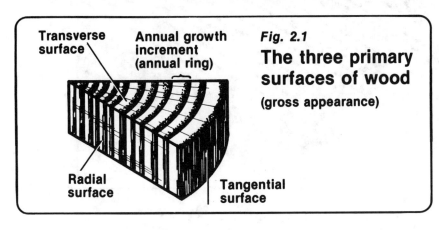

Transverse surface

Annual growth increment (annual ring)

Radial surface

Tangential surface

Fig. 2.1
The three primary surfaces of wood
(gross appearance)

Wood differs not only in appearance, depending upon the direction from which it is viewed, but (as will be explained a bit later) in physical properties as well. Thus in a solid wood product such as lumber, boards are classified by the surface of wood that corresponds to the widest face (Fig. 2.2).

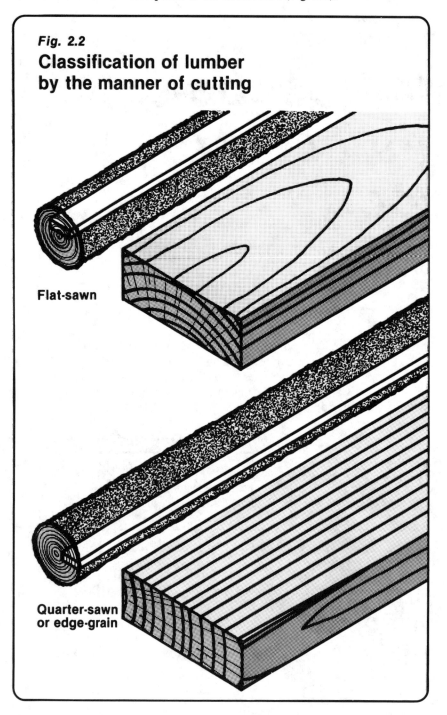

Fig. 2.2
Classification of lumber by the manner of cutting

Flat-sawn

Quarter-sawn or edge-grain

Growth rings ■

ANNUAL RINGS

Appearance. The seasonal nature of growth was indicated in Chapter 1. Growth in temperate zones was characterized as proceeding rapidly in early spring and slowing in late summer before ceasing in the fall. For reasons explained in succeeding paragraphs, this kind of growth pattern results in different kinds of wood being formed in various seasons of the year; alternating bands of wood formed early and late in a growing season mark annual growth limits.

Figure 2.3 is a photograph of a magnified thin cross section of redwood. At this magnification it is easy to see why wood formed in the latter part of a growing season appears different to the unaided eye than that formed early in the year. The latewood tissue is of greater density, being composed of cells of relatively small radial diameter, with thick walls and small lumens. It is this tissue that forms the darker-colored portion of the growth ring. Illustrations of portions of earlywood and latewood cells are presented in Figure 2.4.

Fig. 2.3
Latewood cells appear as distinct bands
Transverse view of redwood (*Sequoia sempervirens*). ×85

Bark⟶

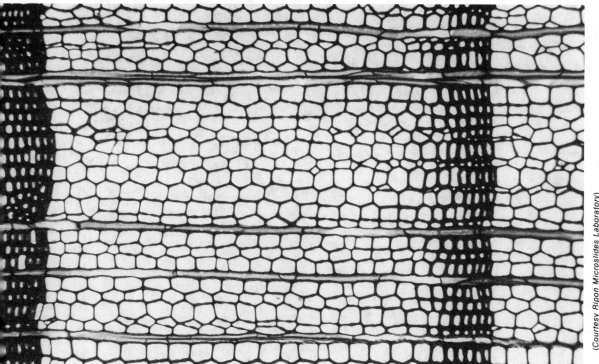

(Courtesy Ripon Microslides Laboratory)

(Reproduced with permission from North Carolina Agric. Res. Serv. Bull. 474, 1986)

Fig. 2.4

Earlywood and latewood cells of a softwood

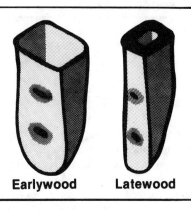

Earlywood   Latewood

Annual growth rings do not always appear as distinct alternating bands of earlywood and latewood. Some hardwoods, for example, form large-diameter pores early in a growing season and much smaller, and usually fewer, pores later in the year (Fig. 2.5); such woods are called *ring-porous*. Other woods exhibit little variation in cell structure across a growth increment, thus forming rings that are difficult to detect. Since the pores are about the same size throughout the growth ring, these woods are termed *diffuse-porous*. A diffuse-porous hardwood having indistinct rings is pictured in Figure 2.6.

Fig. 2.5

Ring-porous hardwood

Transverse view of southern red oak (*Quercus falcata*). ×30

Bark→

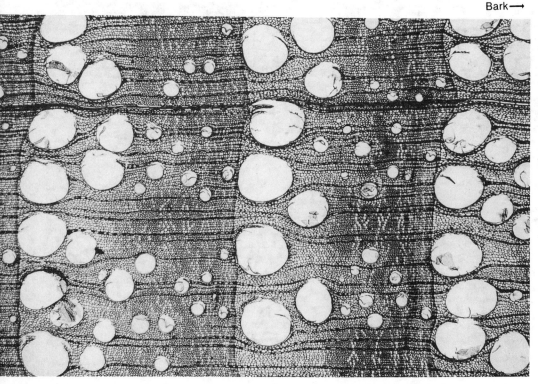

Fig. 2.6
Diffuse-porous hardwood
Transverse view of yellow poplar (*Liriodendron tulipifera*). ×80

Bark ⟶

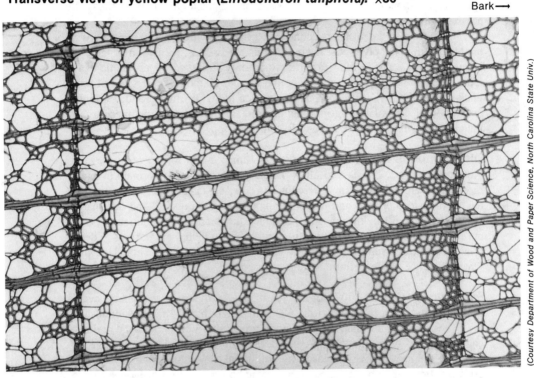

(Courtesy Department of Wood and Paper Science, North Carolina State Univ.)

Formation. Scientists have sought to explain the causes of earlywood and late-wood formation for over 100 years and the riddle is not completely solved. Strong evidence does exist, however, indicating that earlywood and latewood formation is related to photosynthate availability and presence of auxins.

A number of investigators have concluded that two major characteristics of *latewood*—relatively small radial diameter and thick cell walls—develop independently of each other (Zimmermann and Brown 1971, p. 96). The formation of large-diameter cells, characteristic of *earlywood*, is apparently dependent upon an abundance of soil moisture (Kozlowski et al. 1991). Development of thick cell walls, on the other hand, is related to a plentiful supply of photosynthate.

Using the deciduous softwood larch as an example, spring finds the tree with swollen buds but no leaves. Sugars used in the growth process come from storage sites in the roots and elsewhere. As new needles emerge and begin to produce photosynthate, they also begin to grow in size. At the same time, a flush of shoot growth at the apical meristems is typically under way. Thus most available sugars at this time of the growing season are consumed in building new shoots; little photosynthate is left for thickening walls of cells produced by the cambium. Later in the growing season, factors such as drought, low temperature, and short-ened daylight hours provide less-favorable growing conditions, resulting in a reduced rate of new cell production and development of cells of lesser radial diameter. By this time, the growth of shoots and development of new needles have largely ceased. Thus most of the photosynthate produced by the now full-grown needles is available for cell wall synthesis. Small-diameter and thick-walled cells are the result.

The effect of late-season abundance of photosynthate is less obvious in hardwoods than in softwoods. In ring-porous hardwoods, formation of large-diameter vessels early in the season is commonly followed by production of a more-compact latewood having fewer and smaller diameter vessels and of more thick-walled fibers. Diffuse-porous hardwoods likewise often produce a higher proportion of fibers late in a growing season, and these are sometimes radially flattened as well (Zimmermann and Brown 1971, pp. 91–93).

Discontinuous rings. *Growth rings* sometimes fail to form around the complete cross section. This is a result of the cambium remaining dormant in one or more places around the stem. *Discontinuous rings* are occasionally found in trees having one-sided crowns and in heavily defoliated, suppressed, and overmature trees (Kramer and Kozlowski 1979). The fact that the discontinuous rings do occur indicates that caution should be used when using increment borings to determine tree age; borings from several locations around a stem should be used where presence of discontinuous rings is suspected.

False rings. Occasionally, normal seasonal growth is interrupted by events such as drought, late frost, or defoliation by insects or hail. If these result in slowing or cessation of terminal growth, auxin production will be reduced and may cause latewood-type cells to be produced. If events causing slow growth are followed in the same growing season by conditions favorable to growth, normal growth patterns may be resumed, accompanied by production of large and thin-walled earlywood cells. Casual observation of an annual ring formed under such circumstances will show two rings to have formed in a single year. The ring thus created is called a *false ring* (Fig. 2.7). It is possible for several of these to form in a given year (Esau 1965). Such rings may form throughout the length of a stem, but more commonly they are restricted to upper regions of the crown.

False rings of conifers can usually be distinguished from normal growth rings by examining latewood to earlywood transition (Panshin and de Zeeuw 1980). Normal growth rings are characterized by an abrupt change in cell size and wall thickness from the last-formed latewood of one seasonal ring to the earlywood of the next (Fig. 2.7A). False rings exhibit a gradual change in cell character on both sides of the false latewood, resulting in a double gradation (Fig. 2.7B).

Heartwood and sapwood

Trees were defined in Chapter 1 as one of nature's largest living organisms. Some of them are frequently described as being nature's oldest living creations as well. Indeed, one bristlecone pine growing in the White Mountains of California is estimated to be earth's oldest living resident at a ripe old age of about 4600 years.

Fig. 2.7
Normal vs. false growth rings
Transverse view of cypress (*Taxodium distichum*).

Bark→

A. Normal ring

Bark→

B. False ring

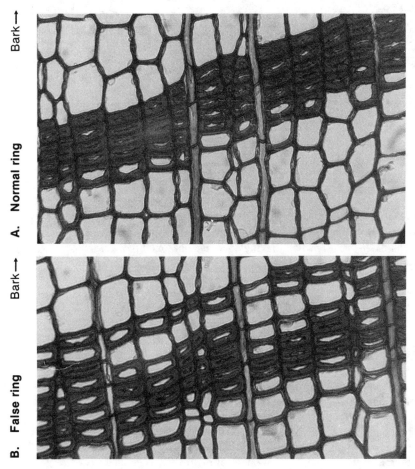

An estimate that a living organism is almost 5000 years old is impressive, but it can also be misleading. Plant tissue seldom remains alive longer than several years, even when part of an old bristlecone pine. This apparent contradiction is explained by the fact that new cells are continually being produced while others cease functioning. Even cambial initials are periodically replaced. It has been estimated that living cells of a tree may comprise as little as 1% of its total bulk (Mirov and Hasbrouck 1976). The longevity of trees such as the bristlecones provides evidence that wood will last indefinitely if conditions are favorable.

Examination of a stem cross section often reveals a dark-colored center portion surrounded by a lighter-colored outer zone (Fig. 2.8). The dark center area is known as *heartwood*, the lighter tissue as *sapwood*. It is in the sapwood that the living cells are found. Sapwood tissue also serves to conduct water upward in a living tree. Heartwood no longer functions physiologically but provides mechanical support to the tree.

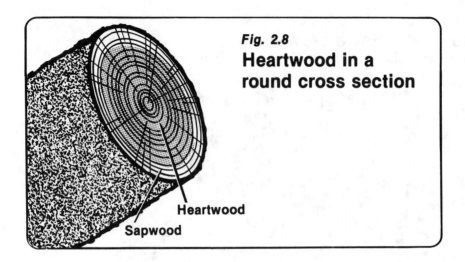

Fig. 2.8
Heartwood in a round cross section

Heartwood
Sapwood

FORMATION OF HEARTWOOD. Perhaps no term relating to wood has more mystery associated with it than the word *heartwood*. A typical belief is that because heartwood is older than sapwood, having aged and seasoned more slowly, it is better. Heartwood is reputed to be heavier, stronger, more highly figured, and more resistant to decay than sapwood. Some of these notions are true, but others are not. Before an understanding can be gained of what properties heartwood does and does not have, and why, it is first necessary to know what heartwood is.

When a tree or tree part is young and growing vigorously, it often contains no heartwood. After a number of years, however, heartwood typically begins to form near the center of a stem. The most common age at which transformation from heartwood to sapwood occurs is reported to be 14–18 years (Hillis 1987). Once initiated, the transformation of sapwood into heartwood occurs continuously. In general, the number of rings of sapwood is directly related to the size of the crown of the tree (Hazenburg and Yang 1991; Yang and Hazenburg 1991). This means that the number of sapwood rings tend to increase early in the life of a tree (i.e. heartwood is either lacking or expanding in size at a rate slower than the rate of tree diameter growth); once attainment of maturity, crown closure, or other stimulus reduces the size of the crown, the formation of heartwood may exceed one ring per year, thus reducing the number of sapwood rings. The boundary between heartwood and sapwood does not necessarily follow the growth rings.

In Chapter 1, formation of new cells by the cambium was discussed. Recall that for a time these cells retain the ability to further subdivide, then they lose this capacity as thickened and lignified cell walls form. Death of most cells follows cell wall thickening and is marked by the disappearance of nuclei and protoplasm (Esau 1965). However, some cells (from 5 to 40% of those that comprise sapwood) retain their protoplast; these are specialized storage cells known as *parenchyma cells* and occur both as longitudinal and ray cells (Kollmann and Côté 1968). The living cells of the sapwood carry on metabolic processes such as respiration and digestion. Deeper toward the stem center, metabolic rates and enzymatic activity decline and the few remaining living cells begin to fail. The cytoplasm begins to change chemically, with a reduction in starches, sugars, and

wood. When this occurs, it is from the presence of significant amounts of extractives.

Several other properties such as low hygroscopicity and a reduced fiber saturation point (see Chapter 8) might be listed, but note that strength does not appear on the list. There is no difference in the strength of heartwood and sapwood, with one relatively rare exception. In some instances, as in redwood, western redcedar, and black locust, considerable amounts of infiltrated material may somewhat increase the weight of wood and its resistance to crushing.

Rays ∎

Recall that *rays* provide an avenue by which sap can travel horizontally in either direction from the phloem layer. Virtually all woods contain rays. In some hardwoods such as oak, rays are quite large and readily visible in a cross section (Fig. 2.9). In softwoods and a number of hardwoods, rays are very narrow and in some cases difficult to see even with a magnifying glass (Fig. 2.10). Many highly valued hardwoods used for paneling and furniture and in other decorative ways are characterized by distinct ray patterns on radial and tangential surfaces (Fig. 2.11). These are often helpful when identifying wood species.

In addition to contributing to wood figure, rays also have an effect upon wood properties. Rays, for example, restrain dimensional change in the radial direction, and their presence is partially responsible for the fact that upon drying, wood shrinks less radially than it does tangentially. Rays also influence strength properties since they constitute radially oriented planes of weakness. Because of this effect upon strength, splitting may occur along rays in veneer-slicing operations if the veneer knife is improperly oriented. Splitting can also develop along rays when wood is dried.

A close look at a ray layout on a cross section (Fig. 2.9) reveals that rays extend from the cambium and bark inward. Few rays can be traced to the stem center. Further observation shows that the distance between rays remains relatively constant in growth rings near the pith and outward.

Review of the way in which rays form helps to explain why rays are arranged as they are. Ray cells are produced by division of ray initials in the cambium. Ray initials, in turn, arise either from division of other ray initials or from an unequal division of a fusiform initial. An undernourished or unusually small product of cell division will invariably fail to redivide (and mature as a xylem or phloem cell) or it will reduce to become a ray initial. Since the cause for inadequate nourishment is lack of proximity to rays, uniform spacing of rays is methodically assured. As soon as the distance between rays begins to increase, chances decrease that a cell midway between them will obtain sufficient nutrients and thus develop normally.

The fact that most rays can be traced from the xylem to the cambium and into the phloem is traceable to permanence of the cambium. Initials, once formed, continue to divide, while the cambium of which they are a part moves outward. A ray will be terminated (and thus not connect with the cambium) only if the ray initials that formed it fail and are not replaced by new ones.

transition zone of some species, the translocation of a considerable amount of primary metabolites from the sapwood to the transition zone is required to form the high levels of extractives found in some heartwoods" (Hillis 1987, p. 187).

From the preceding discussion, it is evident that the basic cell structure is unchanged in the transformation to heartwood and that the primary change is the presence of extractable chemicals. Recognition of this fact is important in understanding differences in properties of heartwood and sapwood. One structural change sometimes associated with heartwood formation in softwoods is aspiration of bordered pits in tracheids. Pit structure and aspiration is covered in Chapter 3.

PROPERTIES OF HEARTWOOD. As the differences between heartwood and sapwood are almost totally chemical, the presence of these chemicals is primarily responsible for giving heartwood its unique properties, a number of which are discussed below:

1. *Heartwood may be darker in color than sapwood.* This occurs when some extractable compounds are dark in color. In some woods, heartwood and sapwood show no color difference; this does not necessarily mean an absence of heartwood but may simply indicate that no dark-colored extractives have formed. Hardwoods exhibit a wider range of heartwood coloration than softwoods.

2. *Heartwood may be highly decay- and insect-resistant.* When woods are naturally resistant to decay and insects, it is because some of the extractives are toxic or at least repellent to decay fungi and insects; this is the case with woods like cypress, redwood, and most cedars. The heartwood of many woods does not contain fungus-repelling extractives, and such heartwood is no more decay-resistant than sapwood. Because decay resistance is imparted by chemicals that occur only in heartwood, sapwood of all species is readily susceptible to decay.

3. *Heartwood may be difficult to penetrate with liquids* (such as chemicals used to help preserve it). When this is the case, it is the result of (a) the presence of extractable oils, waxes, and gums that may serve to plug tiny passages in cell walls; (b) closure of cell-to-cell passageways in softwoods through slight rearrangement of tiny membranes in the passageways (called *pit aspiration*); or (c) blocking of pores in hardwoods by movement of parenchyma cell sacs into vessel lumens (called *tyloses*) (see Chapter 5). Similar structures, known as *tylosoids,* develop in the resin canals of softwoods during the transition to heartwood. When a wood is both susceptible to decay and difficult to penetrate, its usefulness for certain applications is limited. Douglas-fir is an example of a wood not highly resistant to decay; furthermore, its heartwood is difficult to treat for improved durability.

4. *Heartwood may be difficult to dry.* Drying difficulties are generally traceable to the same factors that inhibit penetration.

5. *Heartwood may have a distinct odor.* When it does, this is usually due to the presence of aromatic extractive compounds. Most cedars contain pungent smelling compounds.

6. *Heartwood may have a slightly higher weight per unit volume than sap-*

Fig. 2.10
Rays in some hardwoods are hard to see even under magnification.
Transverse view of red gum (*Liquidambar styraciflua*). ×30

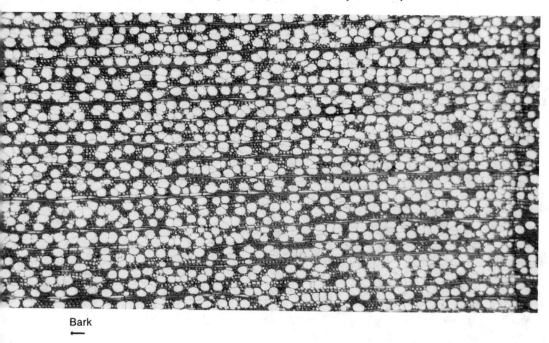

Bark
←

Fig. 2.11
Distinct ray patterns in hardwoods

 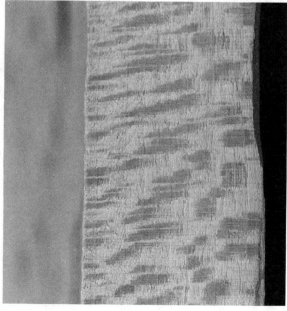

A. Tangential view of sugar maple
(*Acer saccharum*). ×3

B. Radial view of sycamore
(*Platanus occidentalis*). ×3

Fig. 2.9

Large rays of oak are readily visible even without magnification.

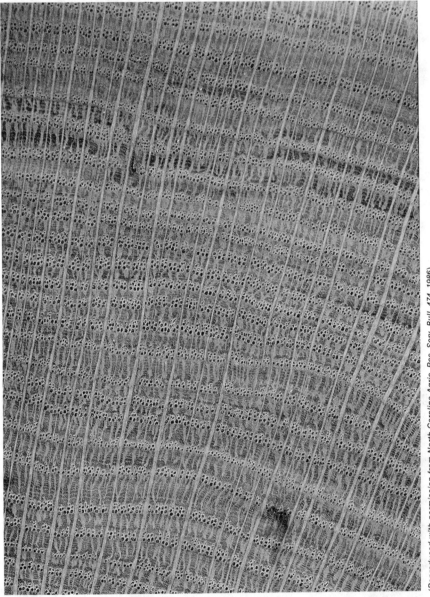

(Reproduced with permission from North Carolina Agric. Res. Serv. Bull. 474, 1986)

Grain orientation ▮

The direction parallel to the long axis of most of the long tapered fibers of wood is called the *grain direction*. Fibers are normally oriented as illustrated in Figure 2.12, with their length essentially parallel to the long axis of the stem. Not uncommon, however, is fiber arrangement at a slight angle to the stem axis rather than precisely parallel to it. In fact, angled grain orientation may be the rule rather than the exception (Beals and Davis 1977). Occasionally, the deviation from parallel is large, resulting in an obvious spiraling grain pattern. This kind of grain orientation can significantly affect wood properties.

SPIRAL GRAIN. Trees in which fibers are spirally arranged about the stem axis (Fig. 2.13) are said to have *spiral grain*. This condition is apparently caused by anticlinal division in which new cambial cell formation occurs in one direction only, i.e., walls formed during fusiform initial division consistently slant the same way (Bannan 1966).

When logs exhibiting spiral grain are sawn, the lumber formed has a grain direction that is not parallel to the board length. Such lumber is said to have slope of grain (see Fig. 10.15); it is typically low in strength and stiffness and may tend to twist as it dries. Planing of such lumber to a high-quality surface may also be difficult.

INTERLOCKED GRAIN. In some trees, grain may spiral in one direction for several years, then reverse direction to spiral oppositely (Fig. 2.14). Wood produced in this way is said to have *interlocked grain*.

Reversing spiral grain is evidently genetically controlled, occurring very frequently in some species and seldom if at all in others. Woods with interlocked grain, such as elm, are difficult to split and thus are recognized as woods for the do-it-yourself firewood splitter to avoid. Wood with this characteristic may also shrink longitudinally upon drying and/or warp unpredictably. Occurrence of interlocked grain is occasionally considered desirable from an appearance standpoint. Alternating grain directions cause light to reflect in varying patterns across radially cut wood, giving what is known as a ribbon stripe figure. When well developed, this feature can add considerably to the value of veneer.

Knots ▮

The seasonal addition of new wood results in progressive layering over previously produced wood. As new growth increases the diameter of the main stem, branch bases become more and more deeply embedded.

Examination of Figure 2.15 shows the living branch extending to the pith, the point at which most branches originate. The base of the branch is cone shaped, appearing as a tapered wedge when sectioned. This arises from the fact that the cambium, which sheaths branches and the main stem, moves ever farther

Fig. 2.12
Straight-grain orientation

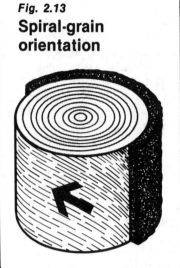

Fig. 2.13
Spiral-grain orientation

Fig. 2.14
Reversing spiral grain
(interlocked grain)

from the embedded branch base as the main stem grows larger, preventing further diameter increase at this location. Since main stem and branch growth are simultaneous, incorporation of living branches into the main stem results in knots that are an integral part of the surrounding wood. Such knots do not become loose or fall out upon drying and are called *intergrown* or *tight knots*.

When a branch dies, its cambial layer also dies, stopping diameter growth throughout its length. The cambial layer of the main stem or bole continues to grow, however, slowly encasing the dead branch in the process. Knots formed in this way are not an integral part of the surrounding wood and if included in lumber may fall out as drying takes place. These are called *loose* or *encased knots*.

Embedded branch stubs are usually free of surrounding bark. This was explained by Eames and MacDaniels (1947), who wrote: "As the base of a [living] branch is buried by the formation of new xylem on the main axis, the phloem tissues about its insertion are forced outward ... so that the base of the branch is stripped of its phloem. In small branches in which the increase in diameter is relatively small as compared with that of the main axis ... this stripping is most marked. In this process the phloem tissues are thrown up into folds which often appear as concentric rings about the base of the partly buried branch." A similar process takes place in larger branches.

When branches are lost from a stem, the surrounding cambium layer gradually overgrows the area (similar to the growth depicted in Fig. 2.16) and within a few years begins to produce clear, knot-free wood. In some species, dead

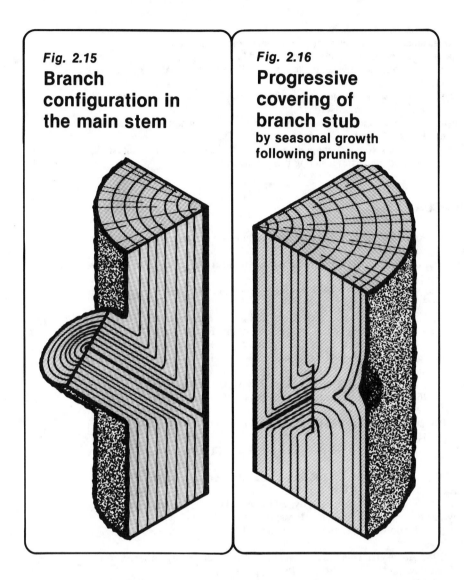

Fig. 2.15
Branch configuration in the main stem

Fig. 2.16
Progressive covering of branch stub
by seasonal growth following pruning

branches are persistent, so clear wood is not produced for many years after the lower branches on the tree die. Artificial pruning is sometimes used on valuable trees. The results of pruning are illustrated in Figure 2.16.

REVIEW

A. Terms to define or explain:
 1. Discontinuous ring
 2. Heartwood
 3. Straight grain
 4. Intergrown knot
 5. Loose knot

B. Questions or concepts to explain:
   1. Distinguish among transverse (cross-sectional), radial, and tangential surfaces.
   2. Explain the difference between earlywood and latewood.
   3. Discuss the difference between the terms growth ring and annual ring (refer back to Chapter 1).
   4. List properties that are unique to heartwood, including reasons for variation in heartwood and sapwood properties.
   5. Illustrate the appearance of rays on the three surfaces of wood and explain why rays are arranged as they are.
   6. Discuss deviations from straight grain orientation that can occur and point out differences in wood properties resulting from this variation.

REFERENCES

Bannan, M.W. 1966. Spiral grain and anticlinal division in the cambium of conifers. Can. J. Bot. 44:1515–1538.

Beals, H.O., and Davis, T.C. 1977. Figure in wood: An illustrated review. Auburn Univ. Agric. Exp. Sta. Bull. 486.

Eames, A.J., and MacDaniels, L.H. 1947. An Introduction to Plant Anatomy, 2d ed. New York: McGraw-Hill, pp. 156–165.

Esau, K. 1965. Plant Anatomy, 2d ed. New York: John Wiley & Sons, pp. 249–250.

Frey-Wyssling, A. 1963. Cytology of aging ray cells. In The Formation of Wood in Forest Trees, ed. M.H. Zimmermann. New York: Academic Press, p. 457.

Hazenburg, G., and H.C. Yang. 1991. Sapwood/heartwood width relationships with tree age in balsam fir. IAWA Bull. 12(1):95–99.

Hillis, W.E. 1987. Heartwood and Tree Exudates. New York: Springer-Verlag.

Hillis, W.E. 1968. Chemical aspects of heartwood formation. Wood Sci. Tec. 2(4):241–259.

Huber, B. 1956. Die Gefässleitung. In Encyclopedia of Plant Physiology, ed. W. Ruhland. Vol. 3, pp. 541-581.

Koch, P. 1972. Utilization of the Southern Pines, Vol. 1. USDA For. Serv. Agr. Handb. 420.

Kollmann, F.F.P., and Côté, W.A., Jr. 1968. Principles of Wood Science and Technology, Vol. 1. New York: Springer-Verlag, p. 55.

Kozlowski, T.T.; Kramer, P.J.; and Pallardy, S.G. 1991. The Physiological Ecology of Woody Plants. San Diego: Academic Press, Inc., pp. 258, 268–269.

Kramer, P.J., and Kozlowski, T.T. 1979. Physiology of Woody Plants. New York: Academic Press.

Larson, P.R. 1962. Auxin gradients and the regulation of cambial activity. In Tree Growth, ed. T.T. Kozlowski. New York: Ronald Press, pp. 97-117.

Mirov, N.T., and Hasbrouck, J. 1976. The Story of Pines. Bloomington: Indiana Univ. Press, p. 16.

Panshin, A.J., and de Zeeuw, C. 1980. Textbook of Wood Technology, 4th ed. New York: McGraw-Hill, pp. 20–22.

Rudman, P. 1966. Heartwood formation in trees. Nature 210(5036):608–610.

U.S. Forest Products Laboratory (USFPL). 1987. Wood Handbook: Wood as an Engineering Material. USDA For. Serv. Agr. Handb. 72.

Wheeler, E.A.; Pearson, R.G.; LaPasha, C.A.; Zack, Z.; and Hatley, W. 1986. Computer-aided wood identification. N.C. Agr. Res. Serv. Bull. 474.

Yang, K.C., and Hazenberg, G. 1991. Rleationship between tree age and sapwood/heartwood width in Populus tremuoloides Michx. Wood and Fiber Sci. 23(2):247-252.

Zimmermann, M.H. 1983. Xylem Structure and the Ascent of Sap. New York: Springer-Verlag.

Zimmermann, M.H., and Brown, C.L. 1971. Trees: Structure and Function. New York: Springer-Verlag.

3

Composition and structure of wood cells

AS A BUILDING MATERIAL wood is one of the simplest, most easily used products; it can be cut and shaped with ease and fastened readily. At the same time, wood is one of our most complex materials. It is made up of tiny cells, each of which has a precise structure of tiny openings, membranes, and intricately layered walls. The ease with which wood is converted to a product and maintained depends upon practical knowledge of its structure. The cellular nature of wood was introduced in Chapters 1 and 2. In this chapter the molecular composition of wood cells is discussed.

Chemical components

Wood is composed principally of carbon, hydrogen, and oxygen. Table 3.1 details the chemical composition of a typical North American wood and shows carbon to be the dominant element on a weight basis. In addition, wood contains inorganic compounds that remain after high-temperature combustion in the presence of abundant oxygen; such residues are known as *ash*. Ash is traceable to the occurrence of incombustible compounds containing elements such as calcium, potassium, magnesium, manganese, and silicon. The fact that domestic woods have a very low ash content, particularly a low silica content, is important from the standpoint of utilization; woods having a silica content of greater than about

0.3% (on a dry weight basis) dull cutting tools excessively. Silica contents exceeding 0.5% are relatively common in tropical hardwoods and in some species may exceed 2% by weight.

Table 3.1.   Elemental composition of wood

Element	% dry weight
Carbon	49
Hydrogen	6
Oxygen	44
Nitrogen	Slight amounts
Ash	0.1

The elemental constituents of wood are combined into a number of organic *polymers* (*poly* meaning many, *mer* denoting unit): cellulose, hemicellulose, and lignin. Table 3.2 shows the approximate percent of dry weight of each in hardwood and softwood. Cellulose, perhaps the most important component of wood, constitutes slightly less than one-half the weight of both hardwoods and softwoods. The proportion of lignin and hemicellulose varies widely among species and between the hardwood and softwood groups.

Table 3.2.   Organic constituents of wood

Type	Cellulose	Hemicellulose	Lignin
		(*% dry weight*)	
Hardwood	40–44	15–35	18–25
Softwood	40–44	20–32	25–35

Source: Kollmann and Côté (1968), pp. 57, 65.
Note: Pectins and starch commonly compose approximately 6% of the dry weight.

CELLULOSE. *Photosynthesis* is the process by which water and carbon dioxide are combined, employing the energy from sunlight to form glucose and other simple sugars, with oxygen as a by-product (Fig. 3.1). As indicated in Chapter 1, these sugars are used by trees to make leaves, wood, and bark.

Cellulose is manufactured directly from units of glucose. As a first step in the process, a tree transports glucose to processing centers located at branch and root tips (apical meristems) and to the cambial layer that sheaths the main bole, branches, and roots. Then the glucose molecules ($C_6H_{12}O_6$) are joined together end to end in a complicated process that results in the elimination of a water molecule for each chemical linkage formed between neighboring units. The ensuing linear long-chain polymer, cellulose ($C_6H_{10}O_5$)$_n$, has a degree of polymerization, *n,* which may be as large as 30,000. The structural relationship between glucose and cellulose is formally depicted in Figure 3.2.

Cellulose is a material with which people are somewhat familiar. Cotton, for example, is 99% pure cellulose. Fine writing papers are also manufactured largely from the cellulosic fraction of wood. Although it is a carbohydrate, cellulose is not a source of food for humans or most animals. In cellulose, the glucose units are interconnected through linkages involving a β spatial arrangement of chemical bonds around the participating carbon atom adjacent to the ring oxygen. As a point of interest, the glucose residues of the *polysaccharide* (saccha-

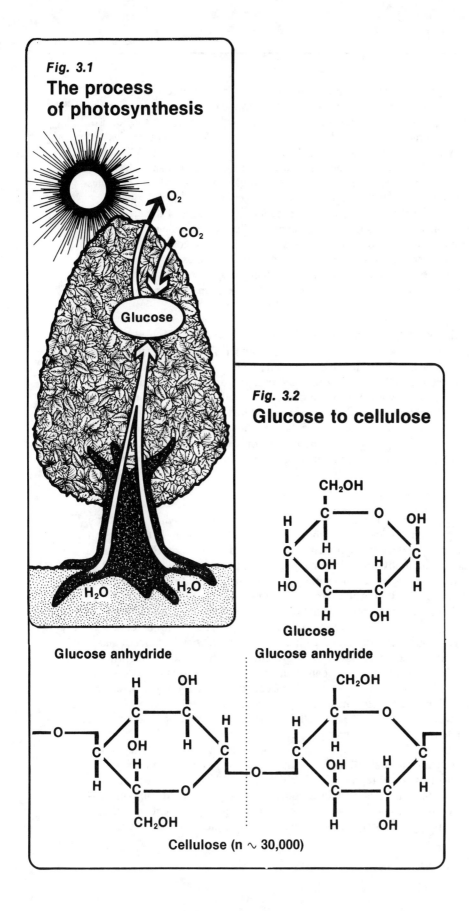

Fig. 3.1
The process of photosynthesis

O_2

CO_2

Glucose

H_2O H_2O

Fig. 3.2
Glucose to cellulose

CH_2OH

Glucose

Glucose anhydride   Glucose anhydride

CH_2OH

CH_2OH

Cellulose (n $\sim$ 30,000)

ride meaning sugar unit) starch are identical in every respect except one: they incorporate an α (actually, the mirror image of β) arrangement of bonds around the corresponding carbon atom in each monomer. Though cellulose in the form of wood or cotton has as much food value as sucrose, cellulose cannot be digested by humans since the enzymes in body fluids can hydrolyze α but not β linkages. However, certain animals (ruminants) are able to utilize cellulose as food because they maintain intestinal colonies of microorganisms that produce enzymes known as cellulases, which convert cellulose to metabolically useful glucose.

At this point it is important that the reader have an idea of the size of the material being discussed. After reading about a cellulose molecule made of up to 30,000 glucose units, a very large structure might be envisioned. While large from a molecular viewpoint, the longest cellulose molecules are about 10 microns (μm) (1/1000 cm) in length and about 8 angstroms (Å)(1/10,000,000 cm) in diameter, still too small to be seen even with the use of an electron microscope.

HEMICELLULOSE. While glucose is the primary sugar produced in the process of photosynthesis, it is not the only one. Other six-carbon sugars, such as galactose and mannose, and five-carbon sugars, such as xylose and arabinose, are also manufactured in the leaves. These and other sugar derivatives such as glucuronic acid, along with glucose, are used in synthesizing lower molecular weight polysaccharides called *hemicelluloses*. Most of the hemicelluloses are branched-chain polymers, in contrast to the straight-chain polymer cellulose, and generally are made up of sugar units numbering only in the hundreds (i.e., the degrees of polymerization are in the hundreds rather than thousands or tens of thousands).

LIGNIN. Lignin is a complex and high molecular weight polymer built upon phenylpropane units (Fig. 3.3). Although composed of carbon, hydrogen, and oxygen, lignin is not a carbohydrate nor even related to this class of compound. It is, instead, essentially phenolic in nature. Lignin is quite stable and difficult to isolate and occurs, moreover, in a variety of forms; because of this, the exact configuration of lignin within wood remains uncertain.

Lignin occurs between individual cells and within the cell walls. Between cells, it serves as a binding agent to hold the cells together. Within cell walls, lignin is very intimately associated with cellulose and the hemicelluloses and it gives rigidity to the cell. Lignin is also credited with reducing dimensional change with moisture content fluctuation and has been said to add to wood's toxicity, thus making it resistant to decay and insect attack. The rigidity provided by lignin is an important determinant of wood properties. Recollection of the very soft nature of cotton (almost pure cellulose) is an indication of how nonrigid wood would be without a stiffening ingredient.

In its native form, lignin is only very lightly colored. However, even the mildest treatments available for removing lignin from wood cause appreciable degradation of its structure, resulting in a deepening of its color. Thus chemical pulps (see Chapter 16) that contain residual lignin require considerable bleaching to make them white in color. Since the pulping process used in making newsprint involves mechanical separation of fibers, and not lignin-removing

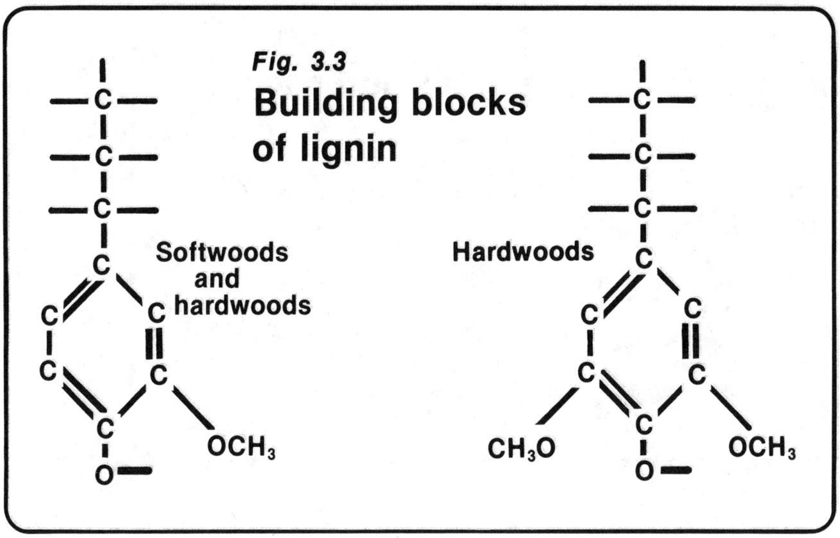

Fig. 3.3
Building blocks of lignin

Softwoods and hardwoods

Hardwoods

treatments, only a light brown color develops, which is readily removed by light, lignin-preserving bleaching. However, when the lignin present in newsprint is exposed to air, particularly in the presence of sunlight, the resulting lignin derivatives tend to become yellow or brown with age. Consequently, newsprint has a notoriously short longevity due to its high lignin content; it is also coarse, bulky, and of low strength since the fibers are difficult to bond to one another because of their inherent stiffness.

Cell wall ■

CHEMICAL STRUCTURE. Recall that a tree is sheathed by a thin cambial layer, which is composed of cells capable of repeated division. New cells produced to the inside of this sheath become new wood, while those moved to the outside become part of the bark.

A newly formed wood cell is encased in a thin, membranelike and pectin-rich wall called a *primary wall,* and the cell is filled with fluid. *Pectins* are complex colloidal substances of high molecular weight that upon hydrolysis usually yield galacturonic acid and small amounts of arabinose and galactose. The precise structure of pectin is not completely understood. In a process that may take several weeks to complete, the cell enlarges and the cell wall gradually thickens as biopolymers produced within the cells are progressively added to the inside (lumen side) of the wall (Fig. 3.4). Eventually, the fluid filling the cell is lost and the cell has a thickened wall, consisting of primary and secondary wall layers and a hollow center (Fig. 3.4d). Successive arrangements of biopolymer assemblies are responsible for the gradual thickening of a cell wall. But what are these *biopolymers*? They are the three distinct types of macromolecule described earlier—cellulose, hemicellulose, and lignin.

Fig. 3.4
Stages in development of a wood cell

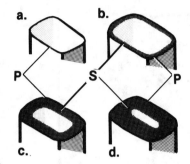

a. b.

P   S   P

c. d.

Longitudinal cells in cross section: (a) new cell has only ultrathin primary wall (P); (b) cell enlarges, then wall thickens as secondary wall (S) forms to inside of primary; (c), (d) wall continues to thicken with buildup of deposits

The building of biopolymers on the inner surfaces of the cell wall is not haphazard; it occurs in a very precise fashion. Cellulose, for example, is not incorporated into the cell wall as individual molecules but rather as intricately arranged clusters of molecules. For example, the long-chain cellulose molecules are synthesized from anhydroglucose (actually glucose attached to a mononucleotide) in many specific locations at the inner surface of the cell wall itself. As these chains lengthen, they aggregate laterally in a well-defined way with their immediate neighbors, which are also growing, to form crystalline domains in a unit cell configuration (Fig. 3.5). The native cellulose crystal lattice is held together by intermolecular hydrogen bonds and dipolar interactions in an arrangement which is so stable that the individual chains cannot be dissolved in anything, short of being chemically modified.

Fig. 3.5
Unit cell configuration of cellulose

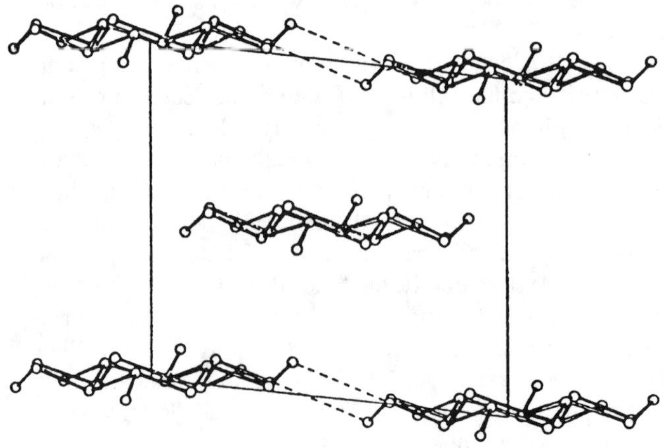

From Woodcock (1979)

A number of studies of wood, with some dating back three decades, have determined that the highly crystalline networks of cellulose are united into larger structures within the wood cell wall. These structures are known as *microfibrils*. Because of the difficulty of isolating cellulose that is part of a heavily lignified woody cell wall, researchers have focused on cells that can be more easily studied. One such kind of cell is that of the green algae, valonia, that has unlignified cell walls in which cellulose is organized into microfibrils. Other work has been done with the bacterium *Acetobacter xylinum* and the primary walls of tobacco leaf epidermal cells. Findings have been correlated with measured sizes of wood microfibrils to develop models of the cellulose structure in wood.

Fujita and Harada (1991) described cellulose microfibrils in a very straightforward manner, describing them as consisting of a "core crystalline region of cellulose surrounded by the paracrystalline [less highly ordered] cellulose and short chain hemicellulose." Ruben et al. (1989) proposed a more-specific structure based on their studies of tobacco leaf cells and *A. xylinum*. Their work indicates that the extent of each crystalline domain is confined to just nine cellulose chains, which together may be viewed as a *subelementary fibril* 18Å in width. Three such subelementary fibrils are wound in a lefthanded triple-helical fashion around one another to form an *elementary fibril* that is 37Å wide. These elementary fibrils then aggregate into microfibrillar bundles with some assistance from hydrogen bonding in which hemicellulose plays a role.

Later work led to the observation that electron micrograph analyses of microfibrils of valonia showed cellulose to be highly crystalline; furthermore there did not appear to be any subunits in these microfibrils corresponding to elementary or subelementary fibrils (Fujita and Harada 1991). There is some speculation that the triple-stranded structures typify microfibrils in the primary cell wall, whereas microfibrils in the *secondary cell wall* are highly crystalline arrays of straight cellulose chains (Ruben et al. 1989). In any case, it is clear that longchain cellulose molecules are arranged within the cell wall in a rather precise fashion and are combined into larger structures, the microfibrils.

What, then, of the hemicellulose and lignin? The hemicelluloses, probably somewhat selectively, interact through hydrogen bonding with the cellulose and have been implicated in the aggregation of elementary fibrils into microfibrils. Hemicelluloses, for example, are known to sheath the microfibrillar bundles (Stamm 1964; Jane et al. 1970). Moreover, the hemicelluloses are chemically linked to lignin *macromolecules* and thus fulfill a particularly important function in maintaining cohesion between the architectural building materials of the wood cell wall. The way in which lignin is incorporated into the cell wall represents another area of disagreement among scientists. The longstanding view is that lignin is deposited between microfibrils during and after the wall thickening process. A more-recent view (Goring 1977) is that lignin is placed in a lamellar configuration between the microfibrils (Fig. 3.6): it appears to occupy its allocated space in the form of undulating two-dimensional sheets with thicknesses of 16–20Å. Although the precise nature of lignin continues to elude researchers, it is known that the aromatic rings tend to lie parallel to one another within the wood cell wall. Yet neither lignin nor its chemical derivatives have ever been coaxed into a crystalline form from solution, while cellulose and many of the hemicelluloses crystallize quite readily.

In summary, the secondary layer of the wood cell wall can be viewed as a laminated filamentary composite. The cellulose molecules provide the struc-

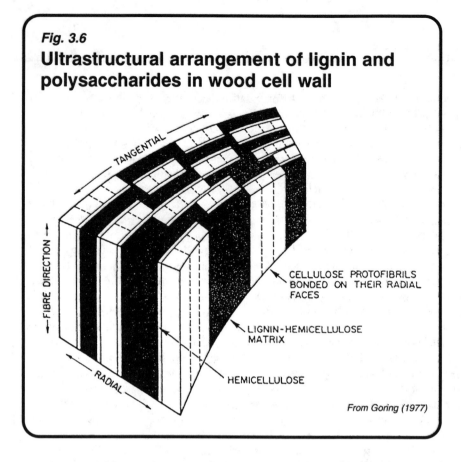

Fig. 3.6

Ultrastructural arrangement of lignin and polysaccharides in wood cell wall

TANGENTIAL

FIBRE DIRECTION

RADIAL

CELLULOSE PROTOFIBRILS
BONDED ON THEIR RADIAL
FACES

LIGNIN-HEMICELLULOSE
MATRIX

HEMICELLULOSE

From Goring (1977)

turally reinforcing network. These are embedded in a matrix composed also of hemicelluloses and lamellar lignin "sheets" which are partly bound to one another through chemical bonds. There is, however, more to the story, and the part to come is no less important.

LAYERING. The primary wall, described previously as being pectin rich, later becomes heavily lignified. The primary wall is also reinforced with a more-or-less random network of microfibrils. This random arrangement contrasts with the very organized microfibril pattern in the secondary wall.

The first few microfibrils that are synthesized as the secondary wall starts to form are laid down in a particular way; they are spiraled around the cell interior, with the long axes of the microfibrils nearly perpendicular to, or 50°–70° from, the long axis of the cell. After a few layers form in this way, the orientation begins to change; microfibrils spiral about the cell at a much smaller angle to the cell axis, varying from 10° to 30°. Just prior to final development of the cell, a change in orientation again occurs, with the last several layers arranged similarly to the first few layers, i.e., 60°–90° to the long axis. Thus the secondary part of a cell wall has three more-or-less distinct layers (Fig. 3.7). For purposes of discussion, these layers are numbered according to the order in which they are formed: S-1, S-2, S-3. Study Figure 3.7 carefully. This intricate structure of the cell wall is the key to the behavior of wood. Note that the S-2 layer is much thicker than the others. The S-1 and S-3 layers in a softwood are on the order of 4–6 layers of clustered microfibrils, or *lamellae*, thick, while the number of lamellae comprising the S-2 may vary from 30 to 40 in thin-walled earlywood cells to 150 or more in latewood cells (Kollmann and Côté 1968, p. 26). In an earlywood cell, these proportions would translate to thicknesses of about 0.1 µm for S-1 and S-3 layers and 0.6 µm for the S-2. Because the S-2 layer is much thicker, this wall layer has the greatest effect on how the cell behaves.

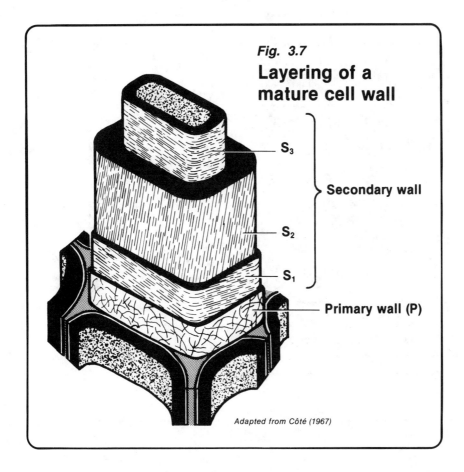

Fig. 3.7

Layering of a mature cell wall

S₃

Secondary wall

S₂

S₁

Primary wall (P)

Adapted from Côté (1967)

Many investigators believe microfibrils to be organized into larger units. These units, called *macrofibrils*, are thought to be aggregations of several hundred microfibrils. Whether microfibrils actually combine to form macrofibrils or not, it is clear that various layers of the secondary wall are built up as a series of uniformly thick sublayers or lamellae. Moreover, microfibril angles in the cell wall change gradually from lamella to lamella, rather than abruptly as might be inferred from Figure 3.7.

A look at the distribution of biopolymeric components in the various wall layers will conclude this discussion of cell wall organization. It is important to recognize that cellulose, hemicellulose, and lignin all occur in each layer of the cell wall. This is illustrated in Figure 3.8, which was derived from chemical analysis of various cell wall layers of coniferous woods. Note that cellulose is present in only small amounts in the compound middle lamella, increasing as a proportion of the dry weight of the cell wall through the center portion of the S-2 layer. Lignin, on the other hand, is the dominant component between cells, with the concentration as a proportion of the cell wall decreasing as the lumen is approached. Considerable disagreement exists as to the proportion of lignin in the compound middle lamella. Figure 3.8 shows that although the largest concentration of lignin is in the middle lamella, the extreme thinness of this layer means that most of the overall quantity of lignin is found in the secondary wall.

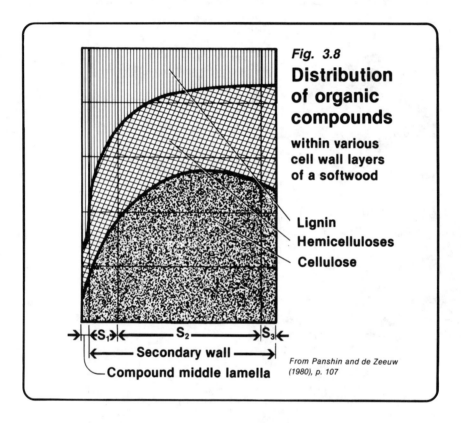

Fig. 3.8
Distribution of organic compounds
within various cell wall layers of a softwood

Lignin
Hemicelluloses
Cellulose

S_1 S_2 S_3
Secondary wall
Compound middle lamella

From Panshin and de Zeeuw (1980), p. 107

CELL WALL SCULPTURING. Wood cells that function primarily in the storage and conduction of food materials are known as *parenchyma*. These cells typically form thin secondary walls and are the last to remain functional prior to heartwood formation. Other kinds of cells, in contrast, serve principally as avenues of conduction in the living tree; these often form thick secondary walls and thus are important in providing mechanical support to stems in which they occur.

Pitting. All types of cells are characterized by secondary wall layers that are not continuous. Instead, walls are interrupted by regions in which the secondary portion of the wall is lacking. Known as *pits*, these regions generally appear quite different in parenchyma as compared to other kinds of cells.

Normally, pit placement in one cell is exactly matched by the position of pits in adjoining cells. Pits thus tend to occur as matched pairs.

Since pit regions are areas of the cell wall that lack secondary thickening, they are, in effect, thin spots in the cell wall. As such, these areas are much more readily penetrated by fluids and gases than are unpitted zones; thus *pit pairs* are the primary avenues of cell lumen-to-lumen transport (Fig. 3.9).

Pits that mark the walls of parenchyma cells are called *simple pits*. Pitting between two ray parenchyma cells is illustrated in Figure 3.10. Because both cells in this figure are of the parenchyma type, the pits shown form a simple pit pair. Note that whereas secondary wall material is lacking in the pit zone, the primary walls of the two adjacent cells remain. The primary walls and the thin layer of intercellular material that separates them form the *pit membrane*.

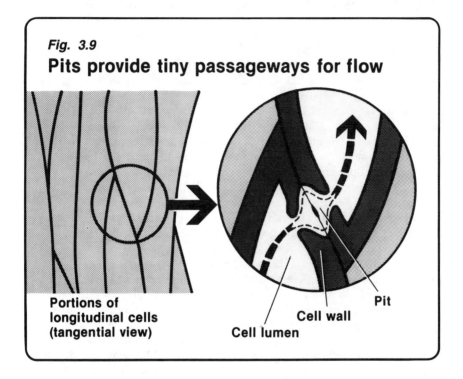

Fig. 3.9

Pits provide tiny passageways for flow

Portions of longitudinal cells (tangential view)

Cell lumen

Cell wall

Pit

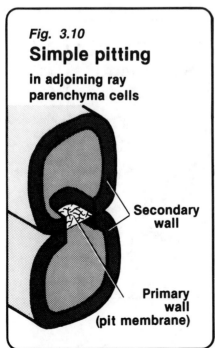

Fig. 3.10

Simple pitting

in adjoining ray parenchyma cells

Secondary wall

Primary wall (pit membrane)

The type of pit typifying non-parenchyma cells is shown in Figures 3.11 and 3.12. This is called a *bordered pit,* so named because the pit aperture appears to be surrounded by a border when viewed frontally. Rather than a simple gap in the secondary part of the wall, a bordered pit is a conical depression in the secondary wall that is concave toward the middle lamella and has an opening leading to the cell lumen at the depth of the depression. A pair of this kind of pits, typical of those connecting two conductive cells, is shown in highly magnified profile view in Figure 3.13B. In this view, secondary walls are seen to overarch the primary wall, forming a pit cavity. As in simple pits, the primary walls of adjacent cells form a pit membrane. When storage (parenchyma) and conductive cells are in contact, each cell usually forms simple and bordered pits respectively. The resulting pit pair is termed *half-bordered* (Fig. 3.13C).

In a softwood, the pit membrane between two bordered pits differs from that separating a simple or half-bordered pit pair. In the latter two kinds, the pectin-rich and microfibril-reinforced primary wall remains unmodified within the pit zone. The common primary walls separating two softwood bordered pits are, however, changed considerably as pits are formed.

Bordered pit formation apparently begins prior to the start of S-1 layer formation with the development of a ring of cellulose on the primary wall. This ring defines the outer boundary of the pit. Then, as secondary wall formation commences, the pit membrane undergoes modification. The membrane center becomes thickened through accumulation of densely packed and sometimes circularly arranged microfibrils. This thickening is called the *torus*. The area surrounding the torus is named the *margo*, and it too becomes different from the normal primary wall. A net of radially arranged microfibrils may form over the existing primary wall, connecting the torus to the pit exterior. At about the same time, the pectin matrix of the compound middle lamella enzymatically decomposes, leaving a more or less open network (Fig. 3.14). Finally, secondary wall thickening is completed through successive development of microfibrillar layers, thus forming the arch or conically shaped wall structure (Wardrop 1964).

Bordered pits are structurally similar in hardwood and softwood species except that the membranes are quite different. Membranes of all pit combinations in hardwoods are similar to those characterizing simple and half-bordered pit pairs in softwoods. Hence, no torus develops and there is no dissolution of portions of the primary wall. In such an unmodified wall, it has been reported that no openings are visible, even at magnifications of ×100,000 (Kollmann and Côté 1968, p. 31). In comparison, filtration experiments with softwood bordered pit membranes have shown openings approximating 0.2 μm in size in the reinforced microfibril network (Liese 1954).

It has long been conjectured that pit regions substantially reduce fiber strength, a notion that is not generally substantiated by scientific observation (Mark 1967, p. 47). Bailey (1958) noted that bordered pits, which characterize stem-strengthening and fluid-conducting cells, appear to be configured to provide the maximum exposure of thin, readily penetrable wall area, with only minimal reduction in secondary wall reinforcement. Microfibril buildup around pit areas may also help to reduce the effect of pits upon wall strength.

The pits dotting the cell wall cause local variation in the normal

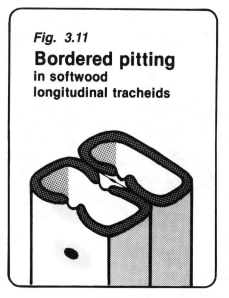

Fig. 3.11

Bordered pitting
in softwood
longitudinal tracheids

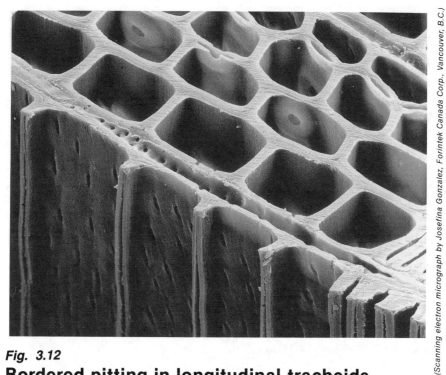

(Scanning electron micrograph by Josefina Gonzalez, Forintek Canada Corp., Vancouver, B.C.)

Fig. 3.12

Bordered pitting in longitudinal tracheids

Radial/transverse view of Sitka spruce (*Picea sitchensis*). ×400

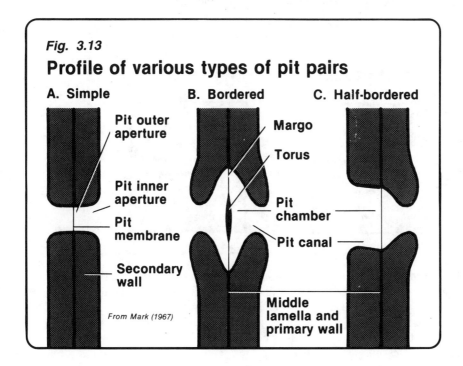

Fig. 3.13

Profile of various types of pit pairs

A. Simple   B. Bordered   C. Half-bordered

Pit outer aperture

Margo

Torus

Pit inner aperture

Pit membrane

Pit chamber

Pit canal

Secondary wall

From Mark (1967)

Middle lamella and primary wall

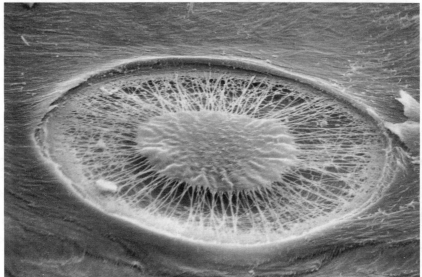

(Scanning electron micrograph by Crist and Teclaw)

Fig. 3.14
Bordered pit membrane
Red pine (*Pinus resinosa*). ×4300

S-1, S-2, and S-3 microfibril orientation discussed earlier. Figure 3.15 illustrates how microfibrils curve around the pit regions (Mark 1967, p. 13). This variation in orientation is known to affect directional shrinkage properties of wood.

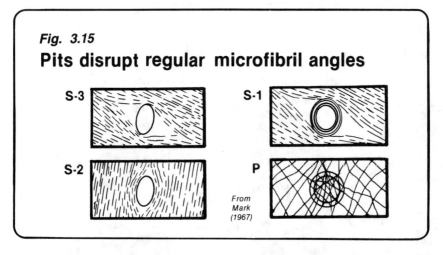

Fig. 3.15
Pits disrupt regular microfibril angles

S-3   S-1

S-2   P

From Mark (1967)

Spiral thickening. In some woods, formation of the S-3 layer is followed by development of spirally arranged ridges of microfibril bundles on the lumen side of the secondary wall. Such ridges are distinctly separate from the S-3 layer, as evidenced by the fact that they are relatively easily detached from it (Wardrop 1964), and they only rarely parallel the S-3 microfibril orientation. These ridges are termed *spiral thickenings* (Fig. 3.16).

Spiral thickenings occur in cells of relatively few softwoods and thus, when present, are a valuable clue to a wood's identity. In hardwoods, spiral thickening is relatively common. While helically arranged thickenings may form throughout the length of a cell, this feature in other cells may be restricted to only the tips or center portions. As location of thickenings is often consistent within a given species of wood, this factor can also be of diagnostic significance.

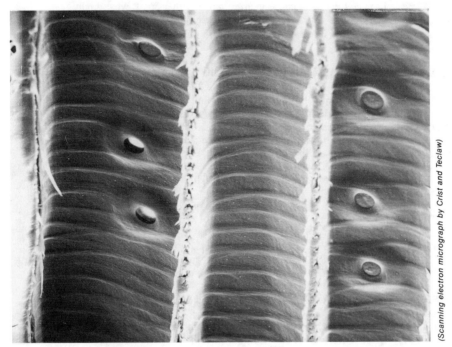

(Scanning electron micrograph by Crist and Teclaw)

Fig. 3.16
Spiral thickening in longitudinal tracheids
Douglas-fir (*Pseudotsuga menziesii*). ×830

REVIEW

A. Terms to define or explain:
  1. Carbohydrate
  2. Micron
  3. Polymerization
  4. Crystallites
  5. Parenchyma
  6. Torus
  7. Spiral thickening
  8. Primary wall
  9. Microfibril
  10. Elementary fibril
  11. Subelementary fibril

B. Questions or concepts to explain:
  1. What are the principal biopolymeric components in wood and the approximate proportions of wood made up of each? How do softwoods and hardwoods differ in this regard?
  2. Describe the essential characteristics of cellulose, hemicellulose, and lignin.
  3. How are the biopolymeric components structurally incorporated into the cell wall?

    4. What is the function of pit pairs in adjacent wood cells? Which kinds of pitting connect different types of cells?

    5. What are pit membranes? What is the nature of such membranes?

C. Food for thought:

    1. Knowing the orientation of microfibrils in the S-2 layer of a cell, what would be the effect on cell dimensions if these microfibrils were to somehow move more closely together?

    2. Assuming that water molecules could gain access to sites between microfibrils in the S-2 layer of the cell wall and cause them to move farther apart, what might happen if this process were not restrained? Along these lines, what might be one function of the S-1 and S-3 layers of the cell wall?

REFERENCES AND SUPPLEMENTAL READING

Atalla, R.H. 1990. The structures of cellulose. In Materials Interactions Relevant to the Pulp, Paper, and Wood Industries: Proceedings: Materials Research Society Symposium, D.F. Caulfield, J.D. Passaretti, S.F. Sebcznski, eds., Vol. 197, pp. 89–98.

Bailey, I.W. 1958. The structure of tracheids in relation to the movement of liquids, suspensions, and undissolved gases. In The Physiology of Forest Trees, ed. I.V. Thimann. New York: Ronald Press, pp. 71–82.

Côté, W.A., Jr. 1967. Wood Ultrastructure—An Atlas of Electron Micrographs. Seattle: Univ. of Washington Press.

Fujita, M., and Harada, H. 1991. Ultrastructure and formation of wood cell wall. In Wood and Cellulosic Chemistry. Hong, D. N.-S., Shiraishi, N., eds. New York: Marcel Dekker, pp. 3–57.

Goring, D.A.I. 1977. A speculative picture of the delignification process. In Cellulose Chemistry and Technology. ACS Symposium Series, 48, pp. 273–277.

Jane, F.W.; Wilson, K.; and White, D.J.B. 1970. The Structure of Wood. London: Adam and Charles Black, p. 170.

Kollmann, F.F.P., and Côté, W.A., Jr. 1968. Principles of Wood Science and Technology, Vol. 1. New York: Springer-Verlag.

Liese, W. 1954. Der Feinbau der Hoftüpfel im Holz der Koniferen. Proc. Int. Conf. Electron Microscopy, London, pp. 550–554.

Mark, R.E. 1967. Cell Wall Mechanics of Tracheids. New Haven, Conn.: Yale Univ. Press.

Meier, H. 1964. General chemistry of cell walls and distribution of the chemical constituents across the walls. In The Formation of Wood in Forest Trees, ed. M.H. Zimmermann. New York: Academic Press, pp. 137–151.

Okamura, K. 1991. Structure of cellulose. In Wood and Cellulosic Chemistry. Hong, D.N.-S., Shinaishi, N., eds. New York: Marcel Dekker, pp. 89–112.

Panshin, A.J., and de Zeeuw, C. 1980. Textbook of Wood Technology, 4th ed. New York: McGraw-Hill, pp. 93–96.

Ruben, G.C. and Bokelman, G.H., and Krakow, W. 1989. Triple-stranded left-hand helical cellulose microfibril in *Acetobacter xylinum* and in tobacco primary cell wall. In Plant Cell Wall Polymers—Biogenesis and Biodegradation. ACS Symposium Series 399, pp. 278–298.

Stamm, A.J. 1964. Wood and Cellulose Science. New York: Ronald Press, p. 31.

Wardrop, A.B. 1964. The structure and formation of the cell wall in xylem. In The Formation of Wood in Forest Trees, ed. M.H. Zimmermann. New York: Academic Press, pp. 87–134.

Woodcock, C. 1979. The x-ray crystallographic analysis of the structure of native ramie cellulose. MS thesis. SUNY College of Environmental Science and Forestry.

4

Softwood structure

■ **SOFTWOODS** have traditionally been the mainstay of the wood products industry in North America, and these woods continue to be extremely important today. The homogeneous, straight-grained, and light-weight softwood is preferred for construction lumber and plywood. Tall, straight-boled softwoods are used for poles and pilings. Because they are typically composed of long fibers, softwoods are also a premium raw material in the manufacture of strong papers. A knowledge of the physical nature of softwood xylem is basic to an understanding of wood and wood products. The structural characteristics of this important group of woods are examined in this chapter.

The xylem of softwoods is quite simple. Most species have no more than four or five different kinds of wood cells, and only one or two of these occur in appreciable numbers. Because of this simplicity and uniformity of structure, softwoods tend to be similar in appearance.

Longitudinal tracheids ■

CONFIGURATION. The great majority of softwood volume, 90–95%, is composed of long, slender cells called *longitudinal tracheids.* Such cells are oriented parallel to the stem axis (Fig. 4.1). Longitudinal tracheids are about 100 times greater in length than in diameter and are rectangular in cross section (Fig. 4.2). Tracheids have hollow centers (lumens) but are closed at the ends, and their shape is blunt or rounded radially and pointed tangentially. The pits in tracheids are normally bordered. A longitudinal tracheid can be visualized by thinking of a soda straw, pinched shut at both ends. In this way the straw is similar in both appearance and relative proportions to a longitudinal tracheid. The tracheid is much smaller, however, averaging only 25–45 µm in diameter and 3–4 mm in length.

As explained in Chapter 2, the softwood cells formed early in a growing season differ from those formed later in the year. A review of earlywood and late-wood differences is perhaps best accomplished by looking at one radial file of tracheids representing 1 year of growth. Thin-walled earlywood cells with rela-

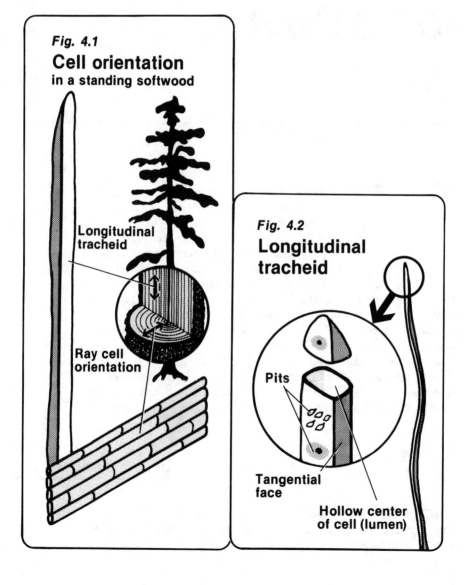

Fig. 4.1
Cell orientation
in a standing softwood

Longitudinal tracheid

Ray cell orientation

Fig. 4.2
Longitudinal
tracheid

Pits

Tangential face

Hollow center of cell (lumen)

tively large radial diameters are seen to the right in Figure 4.3; thicker-walled and smaller-diameter cells are seen to the left. The abrupt change from thin- to thick-walled cells depicted in the figure is characteristic of only some softwood species such as the hard pines, larch, and Douglas-fir. In these woods, latewood is sharply delineated from the earlywood part of the ring. In other species such as true fir and hemlock, the transition in wall thickness and radial diameter progresses gradually from early- to late-formed wood. Rings in these woods are less clearly defined than in those having abrupt transition. Abrupt and gradual transition in growth rings is shown in Figure 4.4.

PITTING. Again referring to Figure 4.3, most of the numerous pits that mark the radial cell walls are of the bordered type. Such pits typify tracheid-to-tracheid linkages, and thus their location is usually matched with a pit in an adjacent longitudinal tracheid. The rows of small, lemon drop–shaped pits mark the points at which ray parenchyma cells contact the longitudinal tracheids.

The characteristics of the softwood bordered pit membrane were outlined in Chapter 3. Recall that the softwood pit membrane in most species has a thickened central torus surrounded by a microfibrillar network known as the margo. At least one softwood species—western redcedar—lacks tori in bordered pit membranes.

The typical softwood bordered pit membrane is the source of several significant use-related problems: a shift in the membrane from its normal central position can result in both drying and treating difficulties. Because the membrane is flexible, it can shift to one side of the pit cavity, resulting in the blocking of the aperture by the impenetrable torus (Fig. 4.5). A pit in this condition is said to be aspirated. Wood with aspirated pits is resistant to penetration by protective chemicals such as creosote or CCA (chromated copper arsenate). Such wood also dries slowly. Drying can, in fact, be the cause of pit aspiration from differences in pressure that may develop on different sides of pit membranes (Tsoumis 1964; Hart and Thomas 1967). Once aspiration occurs, it is apparently a permanent condition (Jane et al. 1970, p. 282); hydrogen bonding between the torus and the over-

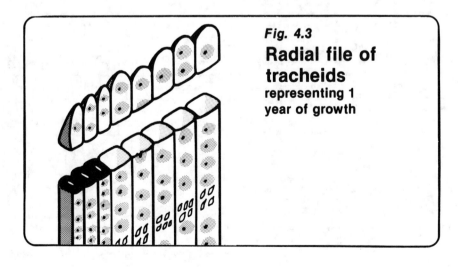

Fig. 4.3
Radial file of tracheids
representing 1 year of growth

Fig. 4.4

Earlywood to latewood transition in softwoods

Bark ⟶

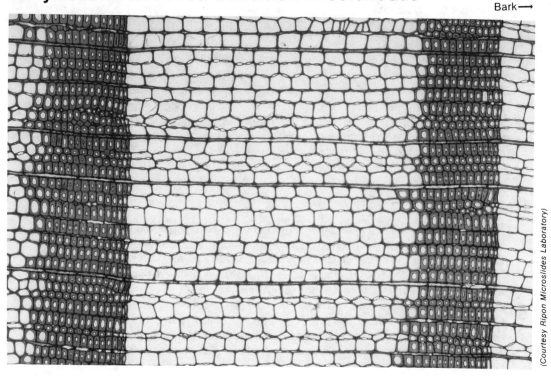

(Courtesy Ripon Microslides Laboratory)

A. Abrupt transition in transverse view of western larch (*Larix occidentalis*). ×85

B. Gradual transition in transverse view of balsam fir (*Abies balsamea*). ×85

Bark ⟶

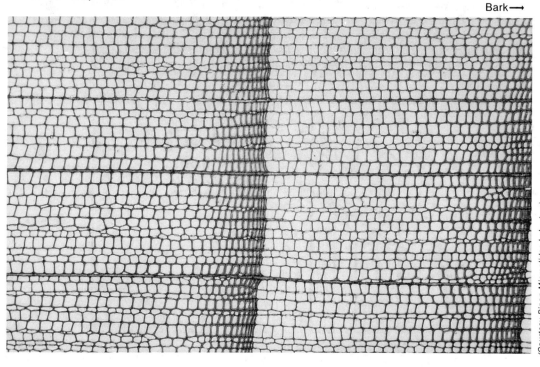

(Courtesy Ripon Microslidas Labortory)

Fig. 4.5

Aspirated pits in pine

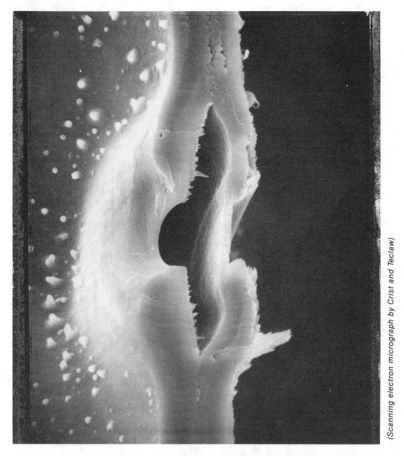

(Scanning electron micrograph by Crist and Teclaw)

A. Sugar pine (*Pinus lambertiana*). Cross section of pit. ×4000

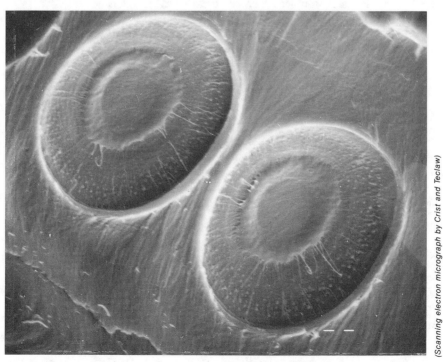

(Scanning electron micrograph by Crist and Teclaw)

B. Red pine (*Pinus resinosa*). ×2800. Tori are blocking inner apertures of pits; rim of outer apertures are in foreground.

arching secondary wall can fix the position of the membrane.

Pit aspiration happens as a result of liquid tensions that can occur in standing trees or in processed wood that is being dried. A situation that results in aspiration, for example, is one in which there is a closed system of water under tension in the lumen on one side of a bordered pit and an air/water-filled lumen, with resulting meniscus at the air/water interface, in the other (Hart and Thomas 1967). Evaporation in any part of the system or transpirational pull on the closed-water system can produce sufficient liquid tension to cause pit aspiration. Hart and Thomas reported that aspiration is always toward the closed-water system side of the membrane. Aspiration can also occur in zones characterized by air/water-filled lumens on both sides of pit pairs. In this case, evaporation from one or both lumens can create a pressure differential, causing deflection of pit membranes toward the lower air pressure side. Although the kinds of situations described above can occur in functioning sapwood, pit aspiration is much more common during the transition from sapwood to heartwood. This at least partially explains why sapwood of some species, such as Douglas-fir, is readily penetrated by treating chemicals, while little or no penetration can be achieved in heartwood of the same piece. Nonpenetrability of heartwood may also result from a buildup of encrusting materials in the margo, rendering pit membranes progressively less porous over time.

Pit aspiration develops more frequently in earlywood (characterized by large pits) than in latewood (characterized by small bordered pits). This explains why end-grain penetration of treating chemicals often extends for some distance along the grain in latewood zones, whereas adjacent earlywood zones are free of the chemicals.

Crossfields are areas where longitudinal tracheids contact ray parenchyma. Half-bordered pits form at these locations, and the bordered portion that marks the tracheids is of quite unique form. Crossfield bordered pit apertures, when viewed radially, vary in shape from lemon drops, to cat's eyes, to extended slits, to an expansive windowlike form (Figs. 4.2, 4.3, 4.6). The type, size, and number of crossfield pitting is fairly consistent within a species; thus, this feature is quite useful in determining the identity of softwood timbers. A microscope is needed to view crossfield pitting.

Other longitudinal cells ∎

In some softwood species, such as fir and hemlock, the longitudinal tracheid is commonly the only kind of longitudinal cell present. In other species, including redwood, the cedars (genera *Juniperus, Libocedrus, Chamaecyparis,* and *Thuja*), and the pines, several other kinds of cells make up minor portions of the volume.

LONGITUDINAL PARENCHYMA. A small portion of the volume of some softwoods is composed of longitudinally oriented parenchyma cells. When mature, these cells have the same general shape as longitudinal tracheids, although they often subdivide a number of times along their length prior to forming secondary walls. The result is that mature parenchyma usually occur as longitudinal

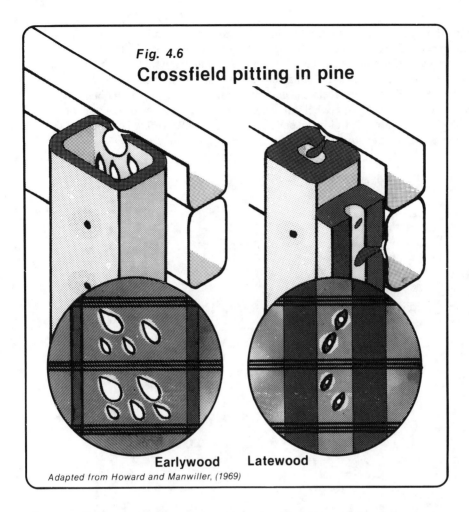

Fig. 4.6
Crossfield pitting in pine

Earlywood **Latewood**

Adapted from Howard and Manwiller, (1969)

strands of short cells butted end-to-end in series. The thin-walled and simple pitted parenchyma account for as much as 1 or 2% of the volume of some softwoods.

EPITHELIUM. Structures known as resin canals are found in certain softwood species. They are consistently found in the genera *Pinus* (pines), *Picea* (spruce), *Larix* (larch), and *Pseudotsuga menziesii* (Douglas-fir); this is one other feature that assists in the identification of softwoods. Normal longitudinal resin canals are always accompanied by horizontal canals, which occur in some of the rays.

A *resin canal* is an intercellular space surrounded by specialized parenchyma cells that secrete resin into the canal. This resin is believed to play an important role in the healing of damaged tissue and in repelling attack by insects or other would-be invaders. A cut through the inner bark of pine, for example, begins a flow of resin to the wound area and may even be accompanied by production of new resin-producing cells near the wound (Mirov and Hasbrouck 1976, p. 36).

Longitudinal resin canals arise following cell formation in the cambium and are formed through separation at the adjoining corners of several undifferentiated longitudinal cells. Cells that surround the space then fail to develop like the surrounding tracheids, forming a series of crosswalls and remaining thereafter thin walled; these units are the resin-secreting cells and are known as *epithelial cells* (Esau 1965). Radially oriented resin canals form similarly. Several longitudinal resin canals with surrounding epithelium are shown in the transverse view of ponderosa pine in Figure 4.7. Epithelial cells may be thin walled (*Pinus*) or thick walled (*Larix, Picea, Pseudotsuga*).

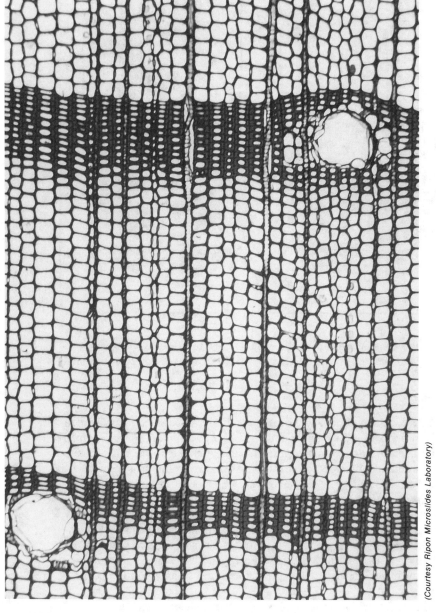

(Courtesy Ripon Microslides Laboratory)

Fig. 4.7

Resin canals characterize some softwoods
Transverse view of ponderosa pine (*Pinus ponderosa*). x85

Production of resin canals in response to injury or other traumatic events is not restricted to those genera that produce resin canals of the normal type. Although the tendency to produce traumatic canals is greater in some woods than in others, resin canals of this type may occasionally occur in almost any of the softwoods. Hemlock (*Tsuga*), redwood (*Sequoia*), and true fir (*Abies*) are examples of woods that do not exhibit canals of the normal type but commonly form resin canals in response to injury.

Because the presence or absence of resin canals is used in wood identification, occasional development in some species could hamper use of this feature for this purpose if it were not possible to distinguish between normal and traumatic canals. Fortunately, it is relatively easy to distinguish the difference. Although traumatic canals form in exactly the same way as normal ones (i.e., through postcambial separation of the middle lamella of adjacent cells), they are usually larger and often occur in tangential bands at the start of the growth ring. Traumatic canals, moreover, rarely occur in both longitudinal and radial orientation in the same piece of wood. Traumatic resin canals are pictured in Figure 4.8.

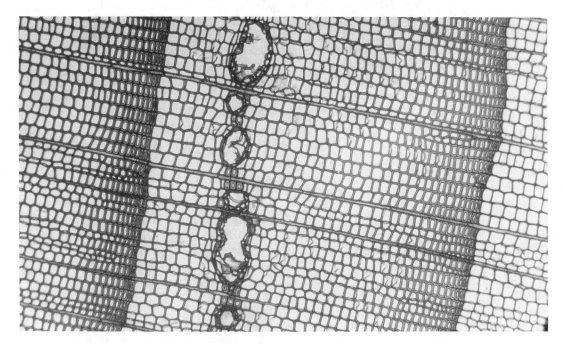

Fig. 4.8

Traumatic resin canals
Transverse view of incense cedar (*Librocedrus decurrens*). ×80

Uniformly narrow rays characterize softwoods except where horizontal resin canals are present. Viewed tangentially, softwood rays are from one to many cells in height but are usually only one cell wide (*uniseriate*). Rays of redwood are typically two cells in width (*biseriate*). In Figure 4.9 a typical softwood ray is shown in contact with the radial row of cells depicted earlier.

The cells composing softwood rays may be either ray parenchyma or ray tracheids. *Ray tracheids* are similar to longitudinal tracheids in that they have thick cell walls and bordered pits. In the hard pines (ponderosa, lodgepole, jack, red, and southern), ray tracheids form secondary walls that are locally thickened in the vicinity of pits. The ridgelike thickenings look much like teeth extending into the lumen. Such tracheids are called *dentate ray tracheids* (Fig. 4.10). Ray cells of the parenchyma type, on the other hand, may be either thin or thick walled. Very thin walled *ray parenchyma* commonly form no pitting, while simple pits typically perforate the thicker walled variety of ray parenchyma cells.

An individual ray may be composed entirely of parenchyma, entirely of tracheids, or of both ray parenchyma and ray tracheids. A close-up of a uniseriate softwood ray (Fig. 4.11A) shows it to be composed of both ray parenchyma and ray tracheids. Another uniseriate ray might be entirely ray parenchyma or ray tracheids. Uniseriate rays that are constructed entirely of ray parenchyma or entirely of ray tracheids are termed homogeneous. A heterogeneous uniseriate ray contains both ray tracheids and ray parenchyma.

In Figure 4.11B, a special kind of ray is shown that occurs only in some woods. Thick-walled and dentate tracheids are seen on the upper and lower mar-

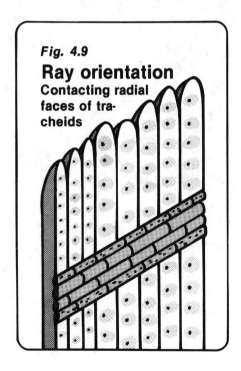

Fig. 4.9

Ray orientation
Contacting radial
faces of tra-
cheids

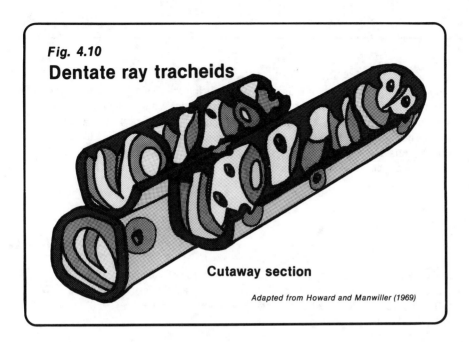

Fig. 4.10
Dentate ray tracheids

Cutaway section

Adapted from Howard and Manwiller (1969)

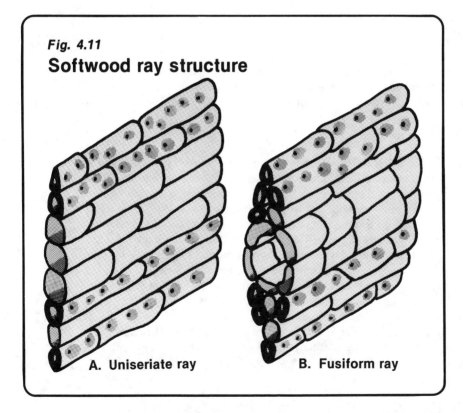

Fig. 4.11
Softwood ray structure

A. Uniseriate ray

B. Fusiform ray

gins, bracketing rows of ray parenchyma. A resin canal and surrounding epithelium can be seen in the center. Numerous pits can be seen connecting ray cell to ray cell; these are bordered pairs between ray tracheids, simple pairs between ray parenchyma (of the thickened variety), and half-bordered pairs between ray parenchyma and ray tracheids. Pitting on the ray sidewalls connects pits to longitudinal cells. Note that the ray is not uniseriate, appearing swollen at the center where the resin canal and accompanying epithelium occur. When a ray contains a resin canal, it is known as a *fusiform ray*. As shown in Figure 4.11B, a fusiform ray normally contains both ray tracheids and ray parenchyma in addition to epithelial cells. Depending upon the species, the ray tracheids may or may not be of the dentate type. In woods that contain them, only about 1 ray in 20 has the fusiform configuration.

Wood identification ■

For those interested in learning how to identify the wood of various species, several excellent texts are available that deal with this subject, see Kribs (1968), Edlin (1969), Jane et al. (1970), Core et al. (1979), Panshin and de Zeeuw (1980), Desch (1981), and Hoadley (1990).

Summary ■

A convenient way of reviewing the structure of softwoods is to study a three-dimensional block of a species that exhibits all the features listed earlier. A carefully drawn representation of southern pine (Fig. 4.12) will serve this purpose.

TRANSVERSE SURFACE (I). Examination of the transverse surface of Figure 4.12 reveals numerous longitudinal tracheids in cross section. Portions of two growth rings are shown. Latewood tracheids of one annual growth layer lie to the left (1); these are followed to the immediate right by earlywood (2-2a) and latewood (3-3a) of the succeeding annual ring. Transition in zone 3-3a is relatively abrupt. A row of tracheids visible at 4-4a are traceable to an anticlinal division of a fusiform initial that occurred when the position indicated by 4 marked the outer extremity of the xylem and the position of the tangentially oriented cambium. Bordered pits that have been sectioned transversely are pictured at A, B, C, and D; the pit labeled B has been sectioned below the pit apertures, while pits at A and C are sectioned through the torus and pit apertures.

A resin canal, pictured at 5, is surrounded by short, thin-walled epithelium (E). Thin-walled longitudinal parenchyma (F) lie to the outside of the epithelial cells. A transversely sectioned row of ray tracheids can be seen at 6-6a.

RADIAL SURFACE (II). Numerous conically shaped bordered pits dot the radial surface of longitudinal tracheids, marking locations of matching pits in adjacent rows of tracheids. Earlywood tracheids are bluntly tapered in this view, while end walls of the narrower latewood are more angular.

A longitudinally sectioned uniseriate and heterogeneous ray composed of

Fig. 4.12
Three-dimensional representation of distinct-ring softwood

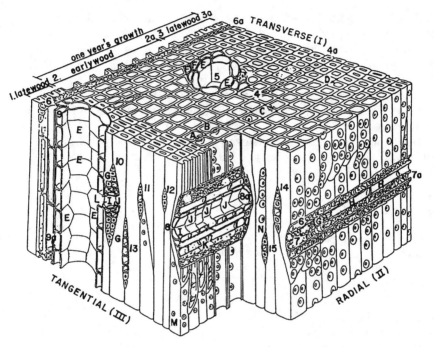

Transverse surface (I). *1,* latewood of one growth ring; *2-2a,* earlywood; *3-3a,* latewood of growth ring formed subsequent to *1; 4-4a,* row of longitudinal tracheids initiated by earlier anticlinal division of cambial initials at *4; 5,* longitudinal resin canal; *6-6a,* row of sectioned ray tracheids; *A,B,C,D,* bordered pits; *E,* epithelial cell; *F,* longitudinal parenchyma.

Radial Surface (II). *7-7a,* sectioned uniseriate ray; *8-8a,* sectioned fusiform ray; *G,* dentate ray tracheid; *H,* ray parenchyma; *I,* transverse resin canal; *J,* ray epithelial cells; *K,* ray tracheid.

Tangential Surface (III). *9-9a,* longitudinal parenchyma strand; *10,* fusiform ray; *11, 13, 14, 15,* uniseriate heterogeneous rays; *12,* homogeneous ray composed of ray tracheids; *E,* epithelial cells; *G,* ray tracheid; *H,* ray parenchyma; *I,* transverse resin canal; *J,* ray epithelium; *L,* opening connecting longitudinal transverse resin canals; *M,* longitudinal tracheid (latewood); *N,* longitudinal tracheid (earlywood).

From Howard and Manwiller (1969)

both ray tracheids (G) and ray parenchyma (H) is shown at 7-7a. A sectioned fusiform ray is at 8-8a. This ray is built around a resin canal (I) and contains short, bricklike epithelial cells (J), ray parenchyma, and ray tracheids. An unsectioned ray tracheid is at (K).

TANGENTIAL SURFACE (III). To the extreme left of the tangential surface a septated longitudinal parenchyma cell is visible (9-9a). This is adjacent to a large longitudinal resin canal, which is surrounded by epithelium (E). An opening can be seen connecting transverse and longitudinal resin canals (L).

A fusiform ray at 10 exhibits ray tracheids (G), ray parenchyma (H), ray epithelium (J), and a large-diameter transverse resin canal (I). Uniseriate heterogeneous rays are shown at 11, 13, 14, and 15. A homogeneous type ray, composed of ray tracheids, is seen at 12.

Longitudinal tracheids appear sharply tapered tangentially rather than rounded as in radial view. Pitting is sparse but can be seen in occasional tracheids at M (latewood) and N (earlywood).

REVIEW

A. Terms to define or explain:
   1. Softwood
   2. Resin canal
   3. Traumatic resin canal
   4. Uniseriate ray
   5. Ray tracheid
   6. Dentate ray tracheid
   7. Parenchyma strands

B. Questions or concepts to explain:
   1. Softwood xylem is mostly composed of one kind of cell. What kind of cell is this, and what proportion of softwood xylem is made up of these cells?
   2. Aspirated pits can present special problems to the wood products manufacturer. What are aspirated pits and how do they affect wood processing?
   3. Woods are sometimes described as having abrupt transition. What does this mean?
   4. What portion of the cambium is made up of epithelial cells? Explain your answer (be careful on this one).
   5. The function of resin canals is still somewhat open to question. What is thought to be an important function of resin canals?
   6. Softwood rays may contain both ray tracheids and ray parenchyma. How do these cell types differ? What name is given to a ray that contains both tracheids and parenchyma?
   7. The terms *fusiform initial* and *fusiform ray* sound similar but refer to quite different things. What is a fusiform ray? A fusiform initial?
   8. Do all softwoods have crossfields? Of what significance are crossfields?

REFERENCES AND SUPPLEMENTAL READINGS

Core, H.A.; Côté, W.A., Jr.; and Day, A.C. 1979. Wood Structure and Identification, 2d ed. Syracuse, N.Y.: Syracuse Univ. Press.

Desch, H.E. 1981. Timber, Its Structure, Properties, and Utilization, 6th ed. Forest Grove, Oreg.: Timber Press.

Edlin, A.L. 1969. What Wood Is That? New York: Viking Press.

Esau, K. 1965. Plant Anatomy, 2d ed. New York: John Wiley & Sons, pp. 62, 254.

Hart, C.A., and Thomas, R.J. 1967. Mechanism of bordered pit aspiration as caused by capillarity. For. Prod. J. 17(1 I):61–68.

Hoadley, R.B. 1990. Identifying Wood. New Town, Conn.: The Taunton Press.

Howard, E.T., and Manwiller, F.G. 1969. Anatomical characteristics of southern pine stemwood. Wood Sci. 2(2):77–86.

Jane, F.W.; Wilson, K.; and White, D.J.B. 1970. The Structure of Wood. London: Adam & Charles Black.

Kribs, D.A. 1968. Commercial Foreign Woods on the American Market. New York: Dover.

Meylan, D., and Butterfield, B.G. 1972. Three Dimensional Structure of Wood: A Scanning Electron Microscope Study. Syracuse, N.Y.: Syracuse Univ. Press.

Mirov, N.T., and Hasbrouck, J. 1976. The Story of Pines. Bloomington: Indiana Univ. Press.

Panshin, A.J., and de Zeeuw, C. 1980. Textbook of Wood Technology, 4th ed. New York: McGraw-Hill.

Tsoumis, G. 1964. Light and electron microscope evidence on the structure of the membrane of bordered pits in tracheids of conifers. In Cellular Ultrastructure of Woody Plants, ed. W. A. Côté, Jr. Syracuse, N.Y.: Syracuse Univ. Press, pp.305–307.

5

Hardwood structure

■ **THE WOOD** formed by hardwoods is much different than that produced by softwoods. Softwoods have a uniform arrangement of a few cell types and therefore are often without a distinctive appearance. Hardwoods, on the other hand, are composed of widely varying proportions of markedly different kinds of cells and are thus often uniquely and even spectacularly figured. Because of the unique figure possessed by many hardwood species, their woods are widely used for furniture, paneling, and other decorative purposes.

Differences between hardwood and softwood xylem ■

It was mentioned in the introduction that softwoods are uniform in structure, whereas hardwood structure is complex. This and other differences are summarized below:

1. Softwoods are composed of a few significant cell types—hardwoods of many (Fig. 5.1). Long cells known as *longitudinal tracheids* compose 90–95% of the volume of softwoods. *Ray cells* (either ray tracheids or ray parenchyma) constitute the remainder of softwood xylem. Although a few other types of cells may occur, they make up an insignificant part of the volume of softwoods. Hardwoods are composed of at least four major kinds of cells (Table 5.1); each of

Table 5.1. **Major hardwood cell types**

Cell type	Proportion of xylem volume accounted for by cell type*
	(%)
Fiber tracheid†	15–60
Vessel element	20–60
Longitudinal parenchyma	0–24
Ray parenchyma	5–30

* Within a species the relative proportion of various cell types is quite consistent. Among species and species groups (genera) the mix of various kinds of cells is pronounced.

† Included in this category are several kinds of cells: variations of true fiber tracheids and transition elements between fibers and vessel elements or between fibers and longitudinal parenchyma.

these may constitute 15% or more of the volume of hardwood xylem.

2. Only hardwoods contain vessels, a structure composed of *vessel elements*. Specialized conducting cells known as vessel elements occur in significant volume in most hardwoods but seldom occur in softwood xylem. The nature of vessel elements is discussed in the next section.

3. Wide rays of some hardwoods contrast with the uniformly narrow rays of softwoods (Fig. 5.2). Except for fusiform rays, softwood rays are one cell (or occasionally two) in width when viewed tangentially. Collectively, ray cells comprise about 5–7% of the total softwood volume. Hardwood rays range in width from 1 cell to 30 or more in some species. These rays can constitute more than 30% of the volume of hardwood xylem, the average being around 17%.

4. Straight radial rows of cells characterize softwoods; they are generally not found in hardwoods (Fig. 5.3). Softwood cells are aligned in straight radial rows in parallel form, with straight spokelike rays; each row of cells is formed by a single fusiform initial in the cambium. Hardwood rays are seldom aligned in straight radial rows, nor are other hardwood elements. Distortion from a purely radial orientation occurs in the vicinity of large vessel elements.

It is important to note that a summary of hardwood-softwood differences does not include any reference to the relative hardness of the wood produced. Many softwoods produce wood that is harder and denser than wood produced by some hardwoods.

Longitudinal cells

Although longitudinal cells of hardwoods vary considerably in size and general configuration, all these different cell types can be produced by a single fusiform initial in the cambium. Newly produced cells appear quite similar. The differences between types develop during the process of cell maturation.

VESSEL ELEMENTS—UNIQUE CELLS OF HARDWOODS. Several differences exist between hardwood and softwood xylem, but the fundamental anatomical difference is that hardwoods contain specialized conducting cells called vessel elements. This cell type is found in virtually all hardwoods, rarely in softwoods. The wood of a few dicotyledons does not contain vessels; however, the number and economic importance of species exhibiting this feature are small. Vessel elements are generally much larger in diameter than other types of longitudinal cells. Figure 5.4 compares the size and shape of a softwood tracheid, a typical hardwood fiber, and a hardwood vessel element. Note that vessel elements are shorter than hardwood and softwood fibers but larger in diameter. The short length of vessel elements is traceable to the fact that they often do not grow in length during the maturation process and may become even shorter than the cambial initials from which they were produced (Jane et al. 1970). Normally, a number of vessel elements link end to end along the grain to form long tubelike structures known as *vessels*. Such vessels are seldom arranged in a precise parallel and vertical alignment; instead, within a growth ring, vessels form a network with considerable tangential variation from a straight vertical orientation. This arrangement ensures that each branch of the crown receives water from many different roots, providing a safety feature against crown damage from the loss of one or more roots (Zimmermann 1983).

Vessel arrangement. Because of their large diameter, vessels often appear as holes when viewed in cross section; in this view they are often referred to as *pores*. Both size and arrangement of pores are used to classify hardwoods for purposes of identification. Figure 5.5A is a drawing of a magnified cross section of a hardwood. Only the vessels and rays are illustrated. Vessels of large diameter are concentrated in the earlywood, with vessels of much smaller diameter in the latewood. This type of wood is called ring-porous because the earlywood vessels form a visible ring in a tree cross section. Figure 5.5B shows a hardwood that has pores of uniform size distributed fairly evenly across the growth ring. This wood is classified as diffuse-porous. The majority of hardwoods are diffuse-porous, but in northern temperate regions some of the most valuable woods, such as oak (*Quercus* spp.), ash (*Fraxinus* spp.), and pecan (*Carya illinoensis*), are ring-porous. When hardwoods are sawn into lumber, the lengthwise sectioning of vessels results in a distinctive scratchlike pattern on radial and tangential surfaces. Sectioning of large earlywood vessels in ring-porous woods forms a very deep and sometimes spectacular pattern of vessel scratches (*vessel lines*) that is interrupted by latewood regions having little texture. Photographs of ring- and diffuse-porous woods are shown in Chapter 2 (Figs. 2.5, 2.6). Look ahead to Figure 5.19 for an artist's conception of a three-dimensional diffuse-porous hardwood.

The lack of radial alignment of cells in hardwoods has been mentioned. Recall that all types of longitudinal cells arise from the same fusiform initial in the cambium. Remember also that all longitudinal cells are quite similar in size and shape immediately after formation. Since nothing occurs to disrupt alignment, newly formed hardwood xylem cells tend to be arranged in neat radial files corresponding to the initials that produced them. During the maturation process, however, cells begin to change, eventually assuming the characteristics of the mature units. In the case of vessel elements, one of these characteristics is a large diameter. Thus cells that will mature to become vessels begin marked diameter growth, expanding from 2 to 50 times their original diameter. Other cells expand little in cross section. This diameter growth of vessel elements pushes cells out of radial alignment. Follow the path of rays around the large earlywood vessels

Fig. 5.1

Principal cell types of hardwoods and soft-woods

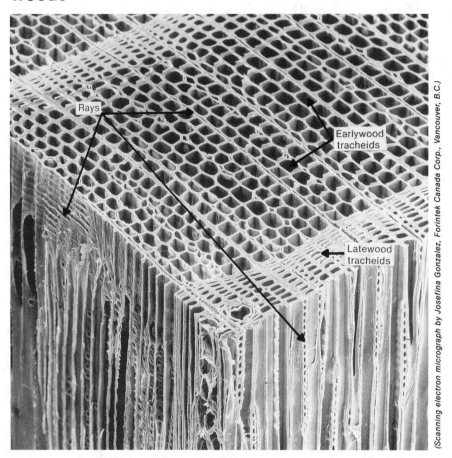

Rays

Earlywood
tracheids

Latewood
tracheids

(Scanning electron micrograph by Josefina Gonzalez, Forintek Canada Corp., Vancouver, B.C.)

A. Softwood: Sitka spruce (*Picea sitchensis*). ×75

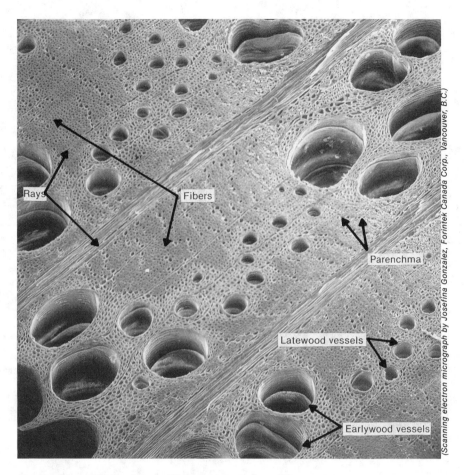

Rays

Fibers

Parenchma

Latewood vessels

Earlywood vessels

(Scanning electron micrograph by Josefina Gonzalez, Forintek Canada Corp., Vancouver, B.C.)

B. Hardwood: Red oak (*Quercus* spp.). ×55

A. Western larch (*Larix occidentalis*). ×85

B. Quaking aspen
(*Populus tremuloides*). ×80

C. Sugar maple (*Acer saccharum*). ×100

Fig. 5.2

Narrow rays of softwood (A) vs. narrow to broad rays of hardwoods (B,C). Tangential view.

(Courtesy Ripon Microslides Laboratory)

79

Fig. 5.3

Straight rays of softwood (A) and meandering rays of hardwood (B). Transverse view.

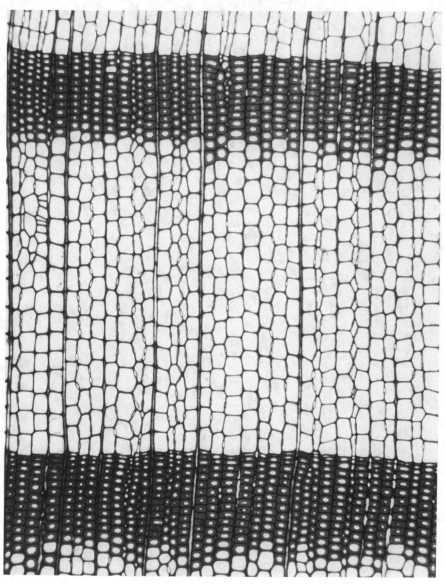

A. Western larch (*Larix occidentalis*). ×85

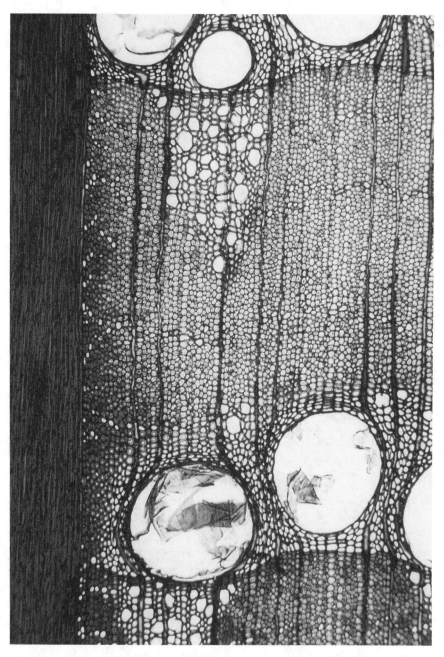

B. White oak (*Quercus alba*). ×85

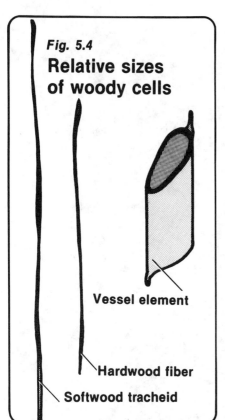

Fig. 5.4

Relative sizes of woody cells

Vessel element

Hardwood fiber

Softwood tracheid

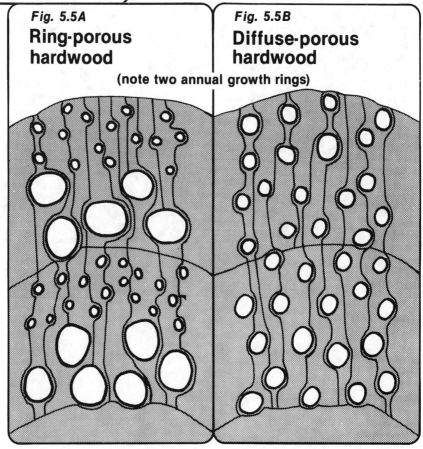

Fig. 5.5A

Ring-porous hardwood

Fig. 5.5B

Diffuse-porous hardwood

(note two annual growth rings)

pictured in Figure 5.3; it is evident that the meandering ray pattern is caused by vessel growth.

End-to-end connection of vessel elements. Vessels are uniquely suited to serve as avenues of conduction. Relatively small and membrane-divided pit pairs connect other cells such as fiber tracheids end to end. Common end walls of longitudinally linked vessel elements are, however, perforated by unrestricted holes. To facilitate discussion about this feature, names are given to the common vessel element end walls (*perforation plates*) and the holes in them (*perforations*).

Perforations develop near the end of the cell maturation process. Certain enzymes contained in the protoplast of developing vessel elements (such as cellulase) are apparently responsible for this dissolving of portions of the perforation plates (Roelofsen 1959). Some rearrangement of cell wall material may also be involved in formation of perforations (Frey-Wyssling 1959). It is interesting to note that perforations do not develop in a random fashion; instead, they form in one of several definite patterns, as depicted in Figure 5.6. A photograph of scalariform perforations is shown in Figure 5.7.

Within a given species, the pattern of perforations is commonly the same in all perforation plates. Because of this, the nature of vessel perforations is often useful as an aid in the identification of hardwood timbers. Perforation plates invariably slope at an angle toward the radial. This surface should be examined microscopically to determine the type of perforation.

Side-to-side connection of vessels. Lateral communication from vessel to vessel is provided by numerous pairs of bordered pits. Closely packed bordered pits are depicted in Figure 5.8A,B. A third type of intervessel pitting can be seen in Figure 5.8C. As is the case with perforation plates, the shape and arrangement

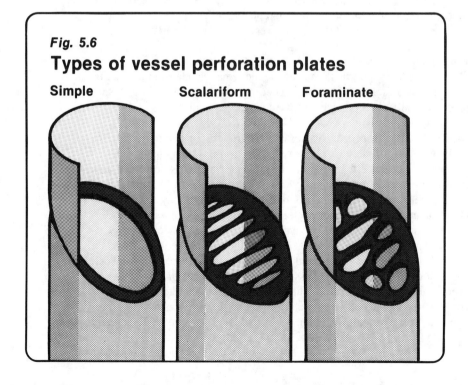

Fig. 5.6

Types of vessel perforation plates

Simple   **Scalariform**   **Foraminate**

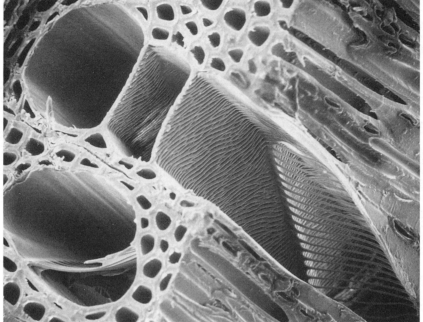

(Scanning electron micrograph by Crist and Teclaw)

Fig. 5.7

Scalariform perforation
In vessel of white birch (*Betula papyrifera*). ×400

of vessel-to-vessel pitting is often consistent within a given species and can be of assistance in wood identification. Photographs of adjacent vessels are presented in Figures 5.9 and 5.10, in which intervessel pitting is clearly visible.

Connections between vessels and other cells. Vessels often occur adjacent to fiber tracheids, longitudinal and ray parenchyma, or other kinds of cells. Although fiber tracheids and vessels are sometimes not linked by pitting, other kinds of cells typically form pits where they contact vessel elements.

Tyloses—Their significance. *Tyloses* are outgrowths of parenchyma cells into the hollow lumens of vessels. They commonly form in many hardwoods as a result of wounding and effectively act to prevent water loss from the area around damaged tissue (Zimmermann 1983). Tyloses also form in a number of species during the transition from sapwood to heartwood and may also develop as a result of infection from fungi or bacteria, or drought.

Just prior to tylosis formation, enzymatic action partially destroys membranes in vessel-to-parenchyma pit pairs. At about the same time, the cytoplasm of the parenchyma cells begins to expand with protrusion of the parenchyma cell membrane through pit pairs into the vessel lumen; this protrusion is called a *tylosis*. Several studies have indicated that a special membranelike meristematic layer forms in parenchyma cells, completely encasing the cytoplasm, prior to tylosis formation. This layer, known as the protective layer, is believed to actually

Fig. 5.8
Vessel-to-vessel pitting arrangements
A. Alternate pitting B. Opposite pitting C. Scalariform pitting

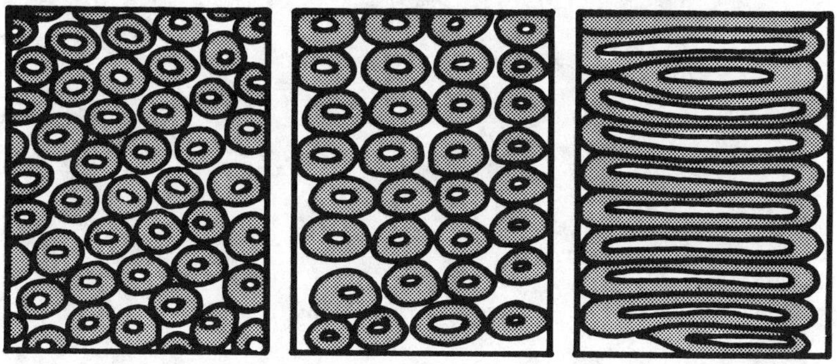

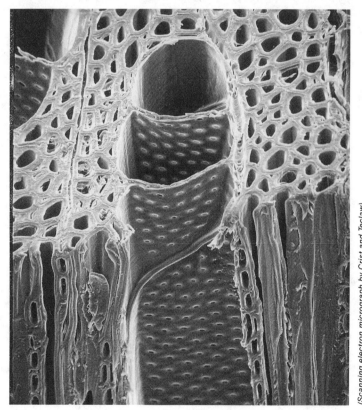

(Scanning electron micrograph by Crist and Teclaw)

Fig. 5.9
Abundant vessel-to-vessel pits
Tangential view of *Populus* spp. ×450

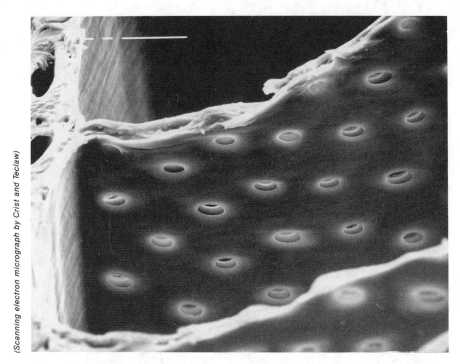

(Scanning electron micrograph by Crist and Teclaw)

Fig. 5.10
Highly magnified bordered pits in adjacent vessels
***Populus* spp.** ×1750

form tyloses (Schmidt 1965; Meyer and Côté 1968). The membrane forming the tylosis may remain quite thin, or the walls may thicken in much the same way that they do in developing cells. Pits may even form where one tylosis contacts another (Foster 1967).

Tyloses are significant in that they partially or often completely block the vessels in which they occur, a situation that can be either detrimental or beneficial depending upon the use to which the wood is put. The existence of tyloses in the heartwood vessels of white oak, and the relative lack of them in red oak, (Fig. 5.11) is the reason white oak is preferred in the manufacture of barrels, casks, and tanks for the storage of liquids. White oak heartwood, with its tightly plugged vessels, is almost universally used in the manufacture of whiskey barrels, for example, whereas the open-vesseled red oak is avoided for this use. In contrast to this beneficial feature of tyloses, wood in which they are well developed may be difficult to dry or to impregnate with decay-preventive or stabilizing chemicals. A radial view of thick-walled tyloses in hickory is shown in Figure 5.12.

FIBERS. The term *fiber* is often used in a general way to refer to all wood cells isolated in pulping processes. However, in the context of wood morphology, the

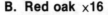

Fig. 5.11

Tyloses fill earlywood vessels of white oak (A), not red oak (B)

A. White oak ×16   **B. Red oak** ×16

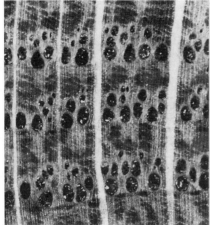 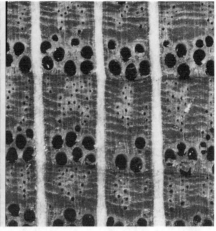

(Courtesy Department of Wood and Paper Science, North Carolina State University).

term *fiber* refers to a specific cell type. Thus fibers, or fiber tracheids as they are more properly called, are long, tapered, and usually thick-walled cells of hardwood xylem. A casual look suggests a great similarity to the longitudinal tracheids of softwoods; but closer examination reveals several significant differences.

Figure 5.4 shows hardwood fibers to be considerably shorter than softwood tracheids. The softwood tracheids average 3–4 mm in length; hardwood fibers, in contrast, have an average length of less than 1 mm. That fact explains why softwood tracheids are often preferred as raw material for paper manufacture. Fiber length is an important determinant of paper strength; thus, long fibers are a necessary ingredient of kraft paper used for unbleached paper products such as corrugated cartons and grocery bags.

Hardwood fibers tend to be rounded in cross section as compared to the nearly rectangular shape of softwood tracheids (Fig. 5.13). However, fibers are sometimes flattened radially in last-formed latewood in much the same way that latewood tracheids are in softwoods. Fibers are also characteristically very thick walled and have bordered pits with less-developed borders than softwood tracheids (Esau 1965, p. 239).

Although hardwood fibers and softwood tracheids are similar, the function of the fiber is more specialized. Longitudinal tracheids of softwoods serve as primary avenues of conduction while also being almost totally responsible for the strength of the wood of which they are a part. A high proportion of thin-walled earlywood tracheids is invariably related to low wood strength. The situation is somewhat different in hardwoods, where two kinds of longitudinal cells—fibers and vessel elements—are common. Most conduction occurs through the specialized vessels, leaving the thick-walled fibers the primary function of mechanical support. Fibers are most highly specialized as supporting elements in those

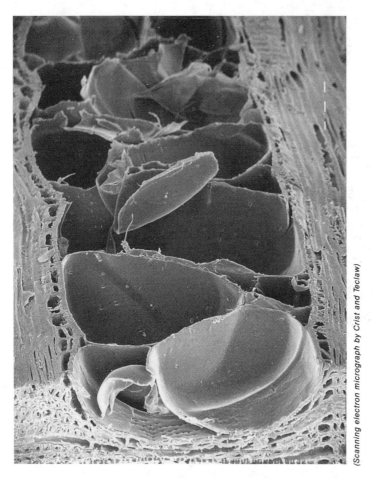

(Scanning electron micrograph by Crist and Teclaw)

Fig. 5.12
Tyloses in vessel
Hickory (*Carya* spp.). ×170

woods that have the most specialized vessel members (Esau 1965, p. 239). Density, and thus strength, of hardwoods is therefore generally related to the portion of wood volume occupied by fibers relative to that accounted for by vessels. As a general rule, the higher the proportion of thick-walled fibers, the higher the strength.

The walls of fiber tracheids are marked by pits of the bordered type. Fiber-to-fiber pit pairs are normally bordered, while fiber-to-parenchyma pitting is typically half-bordered. A variation of the fiber, known as a *libriform fiber,* is marked by simple, rather than bordered, pits. Libriform fibers occur in considerable numbers in some species. Fibers and vessels are seldom connected by pit pairs.

LONGITUDINAL PARENCHYMA. Parenchyma cells are thin-walled storage units. In hardwoods, such cells occur in the form of long, tapered longitudinal

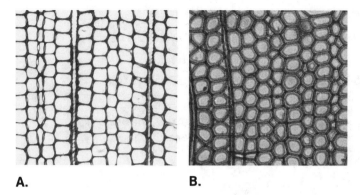

A.   **B.**

Fig. 5.13
Softwood tracheids (A) and hardwood fibers (B) in transverse view

cells; short, brick-shaped epithelium around gum canals (in only a few species); and ray cells. The longitudinal form of parenchyma is often divided into a number of smaller cells through the formation of crosswalls during the process of cell maturation (Fig. 5.14).

Parenchyma cells on occasion are thin walled to the point that no secondary wall forms. Since a *pit* is defined as a gap in the secondary wall, a cell with an unthickened wall is therefore unpitted. Pits do form in parenchyma cells that form thickened walls, and in accordance with rules set forth in Chapter 3, simple pit pairs connect cells of the parenchyma type. Pitting "rules" are often broken where thickened parenchyma contact vessels or fibers; in this case, the pit pairs formed are usually half-bordered but may be of the simple or bordered type (Esau 1965, p. 239).

Whereas *longitudinal parenchyma* is relatively rare in softwood species (no more than 1–2% of the volume of those woods in which it does occur), the longitudinal form of parenchyma is often quite significant in hardwoods. Certain species of hardwoods contain no longitudinal parenchyma. Some domestic hardwoods may, however, have up to 24% of their volume made up of longitudinal parenchyma cells; this figure may even exceed 50% for a few tropical hardwoods (Panshin and de Zeeuw 1980, p. 186). In these woods, the longitudinal parenchyma is commonly arranged into definite and unique patterns that are readily visible in a transverse section (Fig. 5.15). Since both the proportion and arrangement of longitudinal parenchyma are genetically reproduced, this kind of cell is often of value in the identification of hardwood timbers.

Gum canals occur in a few hardwoods and are similar to resin canals of softwoods. The hardwood canals are sometimes lined with parenchymatype epithelial cells.

OTHER KINDS OF LONGITUDINAL CELLS. In addition to vessels, fibers, and longitudinal parenchyma, other kinds of longitudinal cells occur in a few hardwoods, contributing to the variable nature of this group of woods. These other cells are mostly transition elements between major cell types and as such

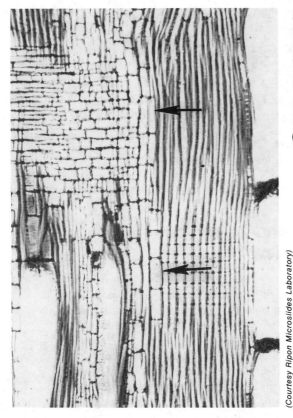

Fig. 5.14

Longitudinal strand parenchyma

Radial view of Honduras mahogany (*Swietenia macrophylla*). x85

(Courtesy Ripon Microslides Laboratory)

have features typical of each kind of cell to which they are related.

An example of a transition element is a *vascular tracheid;* this cell has a shape like a vessel element, but it lacks perforations in the end walls, having instead bordered pits in this location similar to those found in fibers. Another kind of cell known as a *vasicentric tracheid* looks much like parenchyma in cross section, yet it is covered with numerous bordered pits.

Rays ∎

As listed in the summary of hardwood-softwood differences, hardwood rays range in width tangentially from 1 to 30 or more cells. Softwood rays in comparison are generally 1 or, rarely, 2 cells in width. Also, unlike softwoods, the cells of hardwood rays are all of the parenchyma type (although two distinct types of ray parenchyma are formed).

RAY SIZE. Hardwoods characterized by very large rays, such as oak, exhibit distinctive ray patterns on both tangential and radial faces (Fig. 5.16); such rays

Fig. 5.15

Parenchyma configurations occurring in hardwoods as seen in transverse view

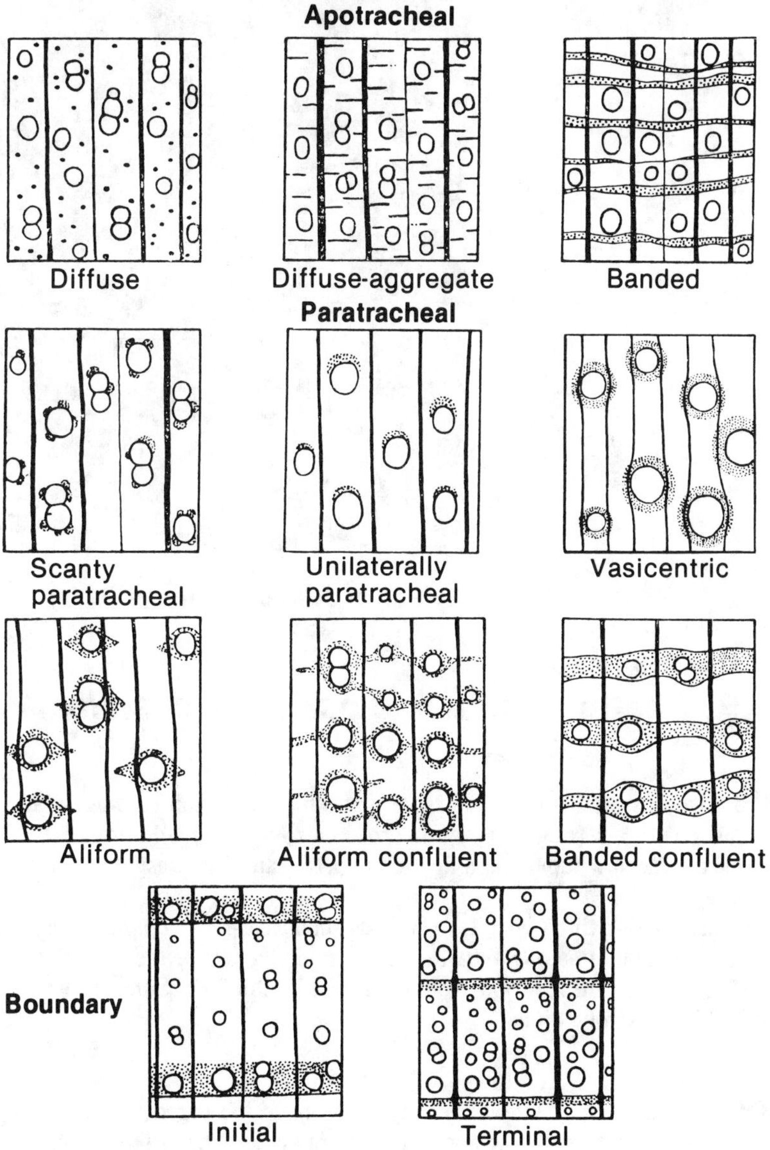

Apotracheal

Diffuse

Diffuse-aggregate

Banded

Paratracheal

Scanty
paratracheal

Unilaterally
paratracheal

Vasicentric

Aliform

Aliform confluent

Banded confluent

Boundary

Initial

Terminal

From Jane et al. (1970)

A. Radial surface (unmagnified)

Fig. 5.16
Ray patterns in white oak (*Quercus alba*)

often add to a wood's aesthetic appeal. Note that a highly magnified tangential view of this wood (Fig. 5.16D) reveals numerous narrow rays in addition to the wide ones; the rays seen without magnification in 5.16A and C represent only the largest of these.

Not all hardwoods exhibit wide rays. Woods such as aspen (*Populus tremuloides*) and cottonwood (*Populus deltoides*) have rays that are of the uniseriate type only (Fig. 5.2B). These woods totally lack a visible ray pattern unless viewed under high magnification.

TYPES OF RAY CELLS. Although all ray cells are of the parenchyma type, there are, nonetheless, different types of hardwood ray cells. The difference is in cell shape or configuration.

The ray parenchyma cells of hardwoods are sometimes almost square when viewed radially, but more commonly such cells have a rectangular shape. In most woods these rectangular ray cells lie so that the long dimension is perpendicular

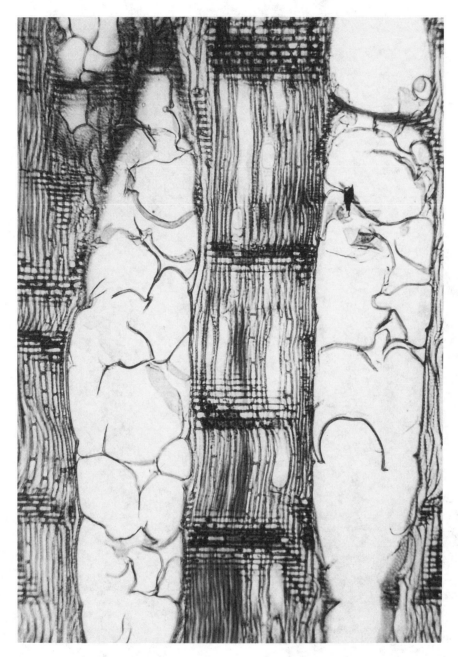

B. Radial surface (×85)

C. Tangential surface (unmagnified)

D. Tangential surface (×85)

(Courtesy Ripon Microslides Laboratory)

to the axes of longitudinal cells (Fig. 5.16C). Since ray cells arranged in this way appear to be lying down, they are said to be *procumbent*. In some hardwood species, part of the rectangularly shaped ray cells appear to stand on end with their long axes parallel to the grain direction (Fig. 5.17); these cells are logically called *upright ray cells*. Upright or *square ray cells* usually occur along the upper and lower margins of rays.

The significance of ray cell configuration is that this feature can be used in wood identification since upright and square ray cells occur as a constant feature in only some species. An example is provided by cottonwood and willow—two easily confused species. Positive identification is based upon the fact that rays of willow consistently have upright cells along the margins, whereas cottonwood rays do not.

In some hardwood species, the rays tend to be arranged into definite, tangentially oriented tiers. In these woods, rays in each layer are roughly the same

(Reproduced with permission from North Carolina Agric. Res. Serv. Bull. 474, 1986)

Fig. 5.17
Upright ray cells on ray margins
Radial view of Andiroba (*Carapa guianensis*). ×200

Fig. 5.18

Storied rays on tangential surface of Sapele
(*Entandrophragma cylindricum*).

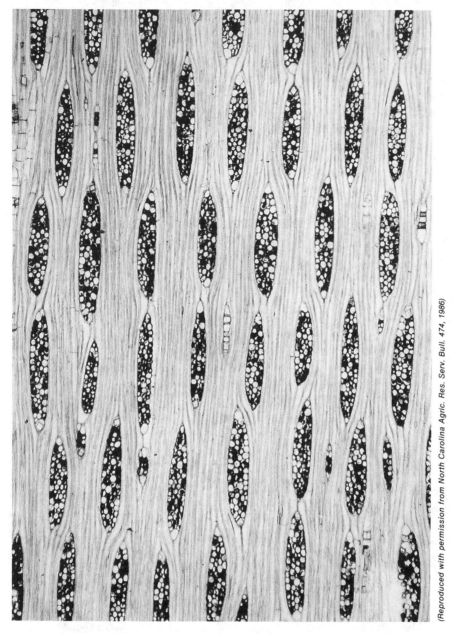

(Reproduced with permission from North Carolina Agric. Res. Serv. Bull. 474, 1986)

A. Tangential view. ×50   Rays occur in a definite tier arrangement.

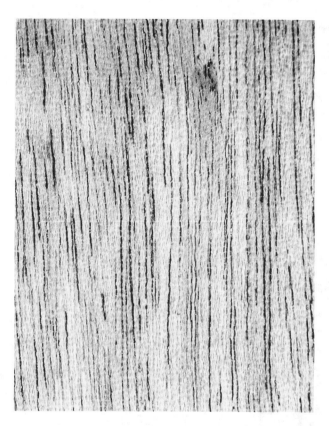

B. Rays show up as ripple marks on unmagnified tangential surface.

height, and all begin and end at about the same levels along the grain (Fig. 5.18A). Such woods are said to have *storied rays,* and they often exhibit a readily visible banded pattern on tangential surfaces (Fig. 5.18B). A storied cell arrangement is not restricted to ray cells. Almost any type of hardwood cell can occur in storied arrangement, and the resulting pattern is often similar to that produced by storied rays. This pattern will show on both tangential and radial surfaces, while that from storied rays will be seen only on the tangential. Storying of elements is primarily of interest for wood identification.

Wood identification ■

As with softwoods, no discussion of hardwood identification is included in this text. For a listing of books that deal with this subject, the student is referred to Chapter 4.

Summary ■

A three-dimensional drawing of a diffuse-porous hardwood is presented in Figure 5.19 and will be used as a means of reviewing structural features of hard-

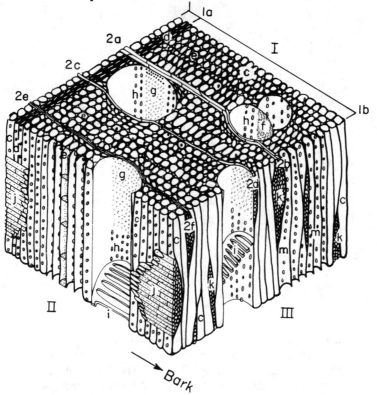

Fig. 5.19

Three-dimensional representation of diffuse-porous hardwood

Transverse view. I. *l-la*, latewood; *la-lb*, earlywood of succeeding growth ring; *c*, earlywood fiber; *d*, latewood fiber; *e*, longitudinal parenchyma; *f*, vessel-to-vessel pitting; *g*, vessel-to-ray parenchyma pitting; *h*, vessel-to-fiber pitting; *2a-2b, 2c-2d, 2e-2f*, rays.

Radial view. II. *c*, earlywood fiber; *d*, latewood fiber; *e*, longitudinal parenchyma; *g*, vessel-to-ray parenchyma pitting; *h*, vessel-to-fiber pitting; *i*, perforation plate between vessel elements; *j*, ray composed of procumbent ray parenchyma.

Tangential view. III. *c*, fibers; *i*, perforation plate between vessel elements; *k*, rays in end view; *m*, fiber-to-fiber pitting (bordered).

Birch (Betula spp.)

woods. The figure is drawn to the same scale as the softwood block depicted in Figure 4.12.

TRANSVERSE SURFACE (I). Portions of two annual growth rings appear on the transverse surface (Fig. 5.19). The latewood of one growth ring can be seen at the left (1-1a) followed at the right by a portion of the earlywood of the succeeding growth layer (1a-1b). Growth rings in this case are delineated by a difference in wall thickness and radial diameter between earlywood fibers (c) and latewood fibers (d); latewood fibers have thicker walls, and in the outermost part of the growth ring these cells are flattened radially.

Thin-walled longitudinal parenchyma can be seen in cross section (e). Ray parenchyma is much in evidence, with three rays visible in cross section (2a-2b, 2c-2d, 2e-2f).

Vessel-to-vessel pitting can be seen (f), as can vessel-to-ray parenchyma pits (g) and pitting between vessels and fibers (h).

RADIAL SURFACE (II). Several radially sectioned vessels are visible on this surface, revealing the perforated plates between vessel elements (i). Also visible are earlywood and latewood fibers (2c, d).

A ray (j) is seen to be made entirely of procumbent ray parenchyma. Pitting of ray cells can be seen as small dots on sidewalls and as gaps in common end walls.

TANGENTIAL SURFACE (III). Rays appear in the end view on the tangential surface (k), providing an opportunity to judge ray size. The rays in this wood are not in a storied arrangement and thus begin and end at different levels along the grain. Rays vary from two to five cells in width.

A long, hollow vessel appears on the tangential surface, interrupted by a perforated remnant of the plates marking the ends of individual vessel elements (i). Between vessels and rays are thick-walled fibers (c). Note the small bordered pits connecting adjacent fibers (m). Because the cut forming the tangential face was made through a transition area between earlywood and latewood, no fibers of the type found in 1-1a are seen on this surface.

REVIEW

A. Terms to define or explain:
1. Hardwood
2. Vessel
3. Vessel element
4. Ring-porous
5. Diffuse-porous
6. Fibers
7. Upright ray cell
8. Procumbent ray cell
9. Storied rays

B. Questions or concepts to explain:
1. A furniture salesperson points out a desk made totally of northern hardwoods, implying that because of this it is superior to a competitor's desk constructed with comparable workmanship but made of a softwood species. Assuming that the desk

is, in fact, made of hardwoods, does this mean that it is a superior product to the softwood desk?

2. Furniture is often advertised as being constructed of fine hardwoods. What is meant by this? Why are fine hardwoods widely preferred for use in furniture?

3. The xylem of hardwood species is quite different from that of softwoods. In what ways do hardwood and softwood xylem differ?

4. End-to-end connection of fibers is quite different from the type of communication between elements making up a given vessel. What is the difference, and of what significance is this difference?

5. The presence or absence of tyloses in a wood has an effect upon the types of products for which it may be used. What are tyloses, and how do they affect utilization?

6. Although hardwood fibers and softwood tracheids appear somewhat similar, there are major differences. What are they, and which is the most important from the standpoint of utilization?

7. What types of parenchyma cells occur in hardwoods? Of what significance is hardwood parenchyma?

8. Ray flecks characterize radial surfaces of many hardwoods, even when care is taken to ensure that a precise radial face is formed. Why do rays appear as flecks instead of radially aligned stripes on such surfaces?

REFERENCES AND SUPPLEMENTAL READING

Esau, K. 1965. Plant Anatomy, 2d ed. New York: John Wiley & Sons.

Foster, R.C. 1967. Fine structure of tyloses in three species of the Myrtaceae. Aust. 3. Bot. 15(1): 25–34.

Frey-Wyssling, A. 1959. Die pflanzliche Zellwand. Berlin:Springer-Verlag.

Jane, F. W.; Wilson, K.; and White, D.J.B. 1970. The Structure of Wood. London: Adam & Charles Black, p. 108.

Meyer, R.W., and Côté, W.A., Jr. 1968. Formation of the protective layer and its role in tyloses development. Wood Sci. Technol. 2(2):84–94.

Panshin, A.J., and de Zeeuw, C. 1980. Textbook of Wood Technology, 4th ed. New York: McGraw-Hill.

Roelofsen, P.A. 1959. The plant cell wall. In Handbuch der Planzenanatomie, Band 3, Part 4.

Schmidt, R. 1965. The fine structure of pits in hardwoods. In Cellular Ultrastructure of Woody Plants, ed. W.A. Côté, Jr. Syracuse, N.Y.: Syracuse Univ. Press.

Wheeler, E.A.; Pearson, R.G.; La Pasha, C.A.; Zack, Z.; and Hatley, W. 1986. Computer-aided wood identification. N.C. Agr. Res. Bull. 474.

Zimmermann, M.H. 1983. Xylem Structure and the Ascent of Sap. New York: Springer-Verlag.

6

Juvenile wood, reaction wood, and wood of branches and roots

■ **THE FIRST FIVE** chapters deal only with the formation, composition, structure, and gross features of wood formed in the main stem of mature, upright trees. The character of wood in young trees, in trees that are leaning rather than vertical, and in branches and roots is considerably different from the normal wood of the mature *bole*. Such wood commonly has properties that affect the ways it may be processed and utilized.

Wood formed in the early (or juvenile) stages of a tree's existence is called *juvenile wood*. That produced in response to tipping of a tree stem is termed *reaction wood*. It is tempting to characterize juvenile and reaction woods as abnormal; yet one (and usually both) of these types of wood occurs in virtually every tree.

Branchwood and *rootwood* properties are increasingly important as more emphasis is being placed on maximizing use of all material in a tree. Thus a working knowledge of wood must include an awareness of these variations in wood form.

101

Juvenile wood ■

A young tree is somewhat analogous to a young child—it grows vigorously, requires a balanced nutritional diet for normal development, is subject to being "bullied" or suppressed by its peers if it is weak, and tends to heal quickly if injured. And like a child, its characteristics are not always considered desirable in relation to those of adults (Fig. 6.1). In the case of a young tree, the wood produced is different (and often viewed less favorably) than that of adult trees.

In Chapter 1 it was noted that an undefined mass of tissue known as the pith marks the stem center, and this region is surrounded by a thin layer of primary xylem. Both the pith and primary xylem are wholly formed in the first year of the life of a stem, and both types of tissue differ from secondary xylem produced later by the cambium. An important point is that secondary xylem produced for the first 5–25 years is different from secondary xylem produced after this juvenile period.

Juvenile wood has been defined as secondary xylem produced by cambial regions that are influenced by activity in the apical meristem (Rendle 1960). This definition serves to explain why there is typically a gradual transition in wood properties between juvenile and mature wood. Juvenile wood is less likely to

Fig. 6.1
Many juvenile wood characteristics are undesirable

form in the outer portions of stem cross sections because as the cambium in a given location continues to cause diameter expansion, it also becomes progressively farther from and therefore less subject to the influence of the apical meristem.

By most measures, juvenile wood is lower in quality than mature wood; this is particularly true of the softwoods. In both hardwoods and softwoods, for example, juvenile wood cells are shorter than those of mature wood. Mature cells of softwoods may be three to four times the length of juvenile wood cells, while the mature fibers of hardwoods are commonly double the length of those found near the pith (Dadswell 1958). In addition to differences in cell length, cell structure differs as well. There are relatively few latewood cells in the juvenile zone, and a high proportion of cells have thin wall layers. The result is low density and a corresponding low strength in comparison to adult wood. In conifers of the United States, density is typically 10–15% lower in the juvenile core, with strength of such material reported to range from only slightly lower to commonly 15–30% and as much as 50% less than normal mature wood for some strength properties (Bendtsen 1978). These reductions appear mild when compared to findings of Senft et al. (1986). In a study of 60-year-old Douglas-fir, they found an average specific gravity difference of 32% when wood formed in the first 15 years was compared to wood formed thereafter. Moreover, though they found the average strength of mature wood to be about 40–60% higher than that of juvenile wood, differences as high as several hundred percent were found when comparing stiffness of the first several growth rings to rings formed much later. Large differences have been found in southern pine as well. In 36-year-old loblolly pine, McAlister and Clark (1991) found juvenile wood to have 76% the density, only 39% the stiffness (MOE), and 54% of the bending strength (MOR) (see Chapter 10) than mature wood from the same trees. Spectacular differences were also found in a study of plantation-grown Caribbean pine. In this material, density was found to be only about 50% that of wood from forest-grown trees, with stiffness as little as 26% of published values for the species (Boone and Chudnoff 1972).

Again comparing juvenile and adult woods, there appears to be a greater tendency for spiral grain in juvenile wood (Noskowiak 1963; Zobel et al. 1972). Within the cell, the microfibril angle in the S-2 part of the secondary wall is characteristically greater in juvenile wood. This kind of secondary wall microfibril orientation also occurs in compression wood that commonly develops in juvenile wood zones. As indicated in Chapter 3, the large S-2 microfibril angle causes a high degree of longitudinal shrinkage and a corresponding decrease in transverse shrinkage; along-the-grain shrinkage of juvenile wood has been reported to average from three times that of mature wood (McAlister and Clark 1992) to 9 or 10 times as much as mature wood (Boone and Chudnoff 1972; Senft et al. 1986). Several investigators have noted, however, that not all juvenile wood shows excessive longitudinal shrinkage and that pieces may actually increase in length upon drying, possibly due to growth stresses (Koch 1972, p. 298–299; McAlister and Clark 1992). Large fibril angles are also associated with low tensile strength (Page et al. 1972; Krahmer 1986). In addition, veneer produced from juvenile wood has been found to be rougher and to contain more splits and deeper lathe checks, producing greater thickness variation (Kellogg and Kennedy 1986).

The kinds of differences indicated in the previous paragraphs often translate to problems when using juvenile wood. For example, a comparison of lumber yield by grade from rapidly versus more slowly grown loblolly pine of the same diameter (20 versus 50 years old respectively) showed rapidly grown logs to yield only one-fifth to one-half as much high-grade dimension lumber as more slowly grown materials (Fight et al. 1986). In another study of slash pine, the value of lumber obtained from 20-year-old, 14.3-in. diameter trees was only 66% of the value obtained from 50-year-old, 15.1-in. diameter trees (MacPeak et al. 1990). Another study resulted in the observation that unless juvenile wood is separated from mature wood, there is a considerable loss in efficiency in utilizing lumber from fast-grown trees when attempting to use reliability-based design, particularly when stiffness is a critically important factor (Tang and Pearson 1992). Senft et al. (1985) reported, moreover, that juvenile wood is a matter of "obvious concern to construction in general and to the laminating industry in particular," due both to low strength and high longitudinal shrinkage. Considering all these factors—reduced strength, occurrence of spiral grain, a high degree of longitudinal shrinkage, and problems in use—juvenile wood is generally undesirable when used in many wood products (Table 6.1).

As a raw material for high-grade and high-strength paper, juvenile wood has long been regarded as inferior. However, it has been viewed with less disfavor by pulp and paper specialists as more has become known about it. The bad reputation of juvenile wood is based partially on the fact that its lignin and hemicellulose content is higher than that of mature wood and the cellulose content lower. The high proportion of lignin results in lower pulp yields, since chemical pulp-

Table 6.1. *Some wood properties of juvenile wood compared to mature wood*

Wood property	Juvenile wood	Mature wood
Specific gravity (green)	0.42[a]	0.48
	0.40	0.53[b]
Density (kg/m³)	427.2[a]	489.2
Fiber length (mm)	2.98[a]	4.28
	1.28[c]	2.68
Cell wall thickness (μm)	3.88[a]	8.04
Lumen size (μm)	42.25[a]	32.78
Cell diameter (μm)	50.01[a]	48.86
S-2 layer fibril angle (°)	55[d]	20
	28[e]	10
	37[f]	7
Longitudinal shrinkage, green to 12%	0.57[g]	<0.10
moisture content (% of green dimension)	0.9[c]	<0.10
Breaking strength or MOR (psi)	7,770[h]	10,660
	4,924[b]	9,147[b]
Stiffness index or MOE (10^6 psi)	1.12[h]	1.75
	.594[b]	1.549[b]
Compression strength parallel to the grain index	100[i]	124

[a]Data for 11-year-old (juvenile) vs. 30-year-old (mature) loblolly pine from Zobel and Kellison (1972) as presented by Bendtsen (1978).

[b]Data from test of juvenile and adult wood of 36-year-old loblolly pine, McAlister and Clark (1991).

[c]Based upon tests of Caribbean pine by Boone and Chudnoff (1972).

[d]Information from Dadswell (1958) for coniferous woods.

[e]Information from Dadswell (1958) for hardwoods.

[f]Figures for Douglas-fir as reported by Erickson and Arima (1974).

[g]Data for loblolly pine from Pearson and Gilmore (1971).

[h]Figures for Douglas-fir from Senft et al. (1986).

[i]Data based upon tests of plantation-grown conifers (Olson et al. 1947) vs. published figures for forest-grown trees of the same species. The comparison here is between small, fast-grown trees (with strength values assumed to be 100) and wood of the same specific gravity from larger, forest-grown trees.

ing processes separate wood fibers by dissolving away lignin. The outcome, in addition to lower yields, is higher chemical consumption in the pulping process and up to a 10% increase in manufacturing costs (Zobel and Kellison 1972). Yields of turpentine and possibly tall oil by-products of *kraft pulping* (see Chapter 16) are also reported lower when processing juvenile wood (Foran 1984; Mc-Kee 1984), and pulp from juvenile wood has been reported to be of low strength. However, juvenile wood looks better when results of recent investigations are reviewed. Several investigators have found, for example, that paper from juvenile wood has low tear strength (as much as 30% lower than paper made from adult wood) but unusually high burst and folding strength (Posey 1964; Gooding and Smith 1972; Semke 1984). *Burst strength* is measured by applying gradually increasing fluid pressure to a small area of the surface of a paper sheet and measuring the force required to rupture the sheet. Other researchers (Barefoot et al. 1964; Zobel et al. 1978) found that wood from the juvenile core produced paper with a higher tensile strength. Hatton (1993) and Hatton and Gee (1994), working with second-growth jack and lodgepole pine and bleachable-grade kraft pulps, confirmed earlier findings regarding strength; they noted that paper made of juvenile wood and topwood pulps (see branchwood topic later in this chapter) exhibits better interfiber bonding than paper made of mature wood pulp. Both of these studies concluded that finer fibers from juvenile wood will provide new opportunities to tailor-make pulps with specific properties sought by papermakers. Jackson and McGraw (1986) commented on the reasons for different strength properties in juvenile wood pulps. They pointed out that the thinner cell walls of juvenile wood result in tighter packing of fiber in a paper sheet, with more contact between adjacent fibers. The result is higher sheet density and higher tensile and burst strength. Tear strength, on the other hand, is directly and negatively influenced by a short fiber length.

Many problems associated with use of juvenile wood in pulp and paper manufacture develop because the juvenile material is processed under conditions designed for mature wood. Crist (1976) commented on this, recalling an observation that "you can't cook a steak from an old bull with one from a young bull and expect both to be cooked to a 'T'." He went on to say that juvenile wood is more "tender" than mature wood. *Cooking* refers to the practice in chemical pulping operations of placing wood in a chemical solution and subjecting the mixture to a combination of heat and pressure. This process softens and/or dissolves lignin.

When juvenile wood is cooked under the severe conditions necessary for mature wood, pulp yield and strength suffer. Yet when cooked alone under conditions tailored for it, the pulp yield and strength from juvenile wood should improve. Numerous studies support this notion (Bella and Hunt 1973; Hunt and Keays 1973; Barker 1974; Jett and Zobel 1975), with findings that indicate little difference in properties of juvenile and mature wood pulps when each are produced under ideal conditions. Ideal treatments for juvenile wood are, incidentally, generally less energy intensive than traditional ones, since cooking times required for juvenile wood are shorter and energy requirements for beating are lower (Laundrie and Berbee 1972; Einspahr 1976). *Beating* involves the forced movement of softened wood fibers through a narrow gap between an apparatus like a paddle wheel and a bedplate. As they pass through the gap, the fibers are subjected to a beating or pounding action that flattens and unravels them, increasing potential for fiber-to-fiber bonding in a paper sheet. A more-recent report (Hatton and Cook 1992) recommended chipping of juvenile and mature wood separately, with chips then combined in different ratios to produce kraft pulps with a wide range of properties. The difference between this and previous approaches is that rather than seeking ways to make juvenile and mature wood pulp the same, Hatton and Cook acknowledge differences between juvenile and mature wood pulps and seek to take advantage of these differences in designing various types of paper.

All of the preceding discussion refers to the use of juvenile wood in paper made from chemical pulps. When mechanical pulps are considered (see Chapter 16), the situation is much different. Because lignin is retained along with cellulose and hemicellulose after mechanical pulping (meaning that high lignin content does not adversely affect yield), and because low-density woods produce a more-satisfactory mechanical pulp than woods of high density, juvenile wood is quite suitable for use in production of mechanical pulps. Carpenter (1984) indicated, in fact, that "low density wood containing relatively large amounts of juvenile wood and springwood is *preferred* to denser wood."

A question that has drawn increasing attention of researchers in recent years is what effect juvenile wood might have on the properties of wood composite products such as particleboard, flakeboard, and fiberboard. Composite products technology offers an opportunity for production of greater quantities of large-dimension structural materials without the need to use large-size trees as raw material. In an extensive study of 144 trees from three locations in Georgia and Arkansas, Pugel et al. (1989, 1990) found flakeboard, standard particleboard, and fiberboard panels made of juvenile wood to have comparable strength and durability to otherwise identical composite panels made of mature wood. However, both thickness swelling and linear expansion—two undesirable properties—were significantly greater in the juvenile wood panels.

Juvenile wood is difficult to identify by casual observation, especially in softwoods, although several normal characteristics are sometimes modified. In hardwoods, vessels of juvenile wood are often smaller and arranged differently from those in mature wood. Ring-porous woods may, for example, have juvenile wood that tends to be diffuse-porous. Another normally consistent feature that becomes variable in juvenile wood is the type of vessel plate perforations (Jane et al. 1970). Scalariform perforations have been reported in the juvenile wood of species that normally have simple vessel plate perforations.

There is typically no sharp demarcation between juvenile and mature wood. Instead, a gradual transition in properties occurs from the tree center outward. Bendtsen (1978) explained this well when he wrote: "Wood in the first formed rings has the lowest specific gravity, shortest fibers, largest fibril angles, and so forth. In successive rings from the tree center, the specific gravity increases, fibers become longer, and so on. The rate of change in most properties is very rapid in the first few rings; the later rings gradually assume the character of mature wood." Figures 6.2 and 6.3 illustrate this gradual change in wood properties.

The substantial amounts of reaction wood often occurring within the juvenile region contribute to the lack of a well-defined juvenile wood zone. One study of southern yellow pine showed the juvenile wood region to contain 42% reaction wood in comparison to only 7% in the surrounding mature wood (North Carolina State College 1957).

Because of the gradual change in wood properties, it is unclear as to where juvenile wood ends and adult wood begins. The location of this boundary de-

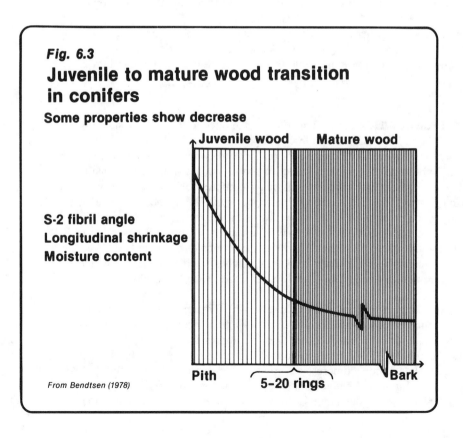

Fig. 6.2

Juvenile to mature wood transition in conifers
Many properties show gradual increase

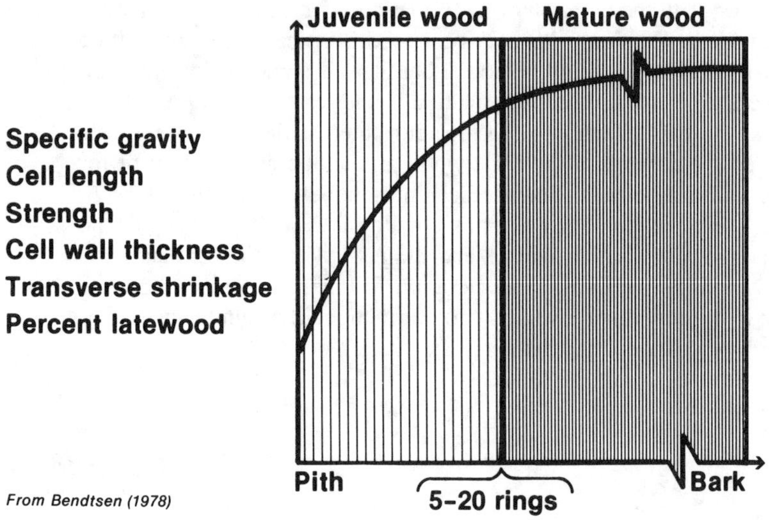

Juvenile wood   Mature wood

Specific gravity
Cell length
Strength
Cell wall thickness
Transverse shrinkage
Percent latewood

Pith   5–20 rings   Bark

From Bendtsen (1978)

Fig. 6.3

Juvenile to mature wood transition in conifers
Some properties show decrease

Juvenile wood   Mature wood

S-2 fibril angle
Longitudinal shrinkage
Moisture content

Pith   5–20 rings   Bark

From Bendtsen (1978)

pends, furthermore, upon the property or properties used to define the zone (Ab-del-Gadir and Krahmer 1993). For example, a property such as cell length may reach maturity before another feature such as cell wall thickness. Nonetheless, researchers are in general agreement that juvenile wood predominates in the first 5–20 growth rings, with the duration of its formation affected by several factors, including geographic location, site and genetic differences, and silvicultural practices (Peszlen 1995). It should be noted that there is some evidence to indi-cate that the period of juvenile wood formation is shorter near the upper part of a tree than near the base. Yang et al. (1986) attributed such findings to a rela-tionship between the duration of juvenile wood production and the year of for-mation of the cambial initials. Some researchers believe that stimulation of growth (through fertilization, irrigation, or silvicultural treatment) during the pe-riod of juvenile wood formation will extend the juvenile period (Larson 1969; Megraw and Nearn 1972). Growth acceleration following the juvenile period does not result in reinitiation of juvenile wood formation. The significance of this observation will be discussed in Chapter 12.

Reaction wood ■

A reaction is a response to a triggering event. *Reaction wood* was appropri-ately named. This special kind of wood may be formed if the main stem of a tree is tipped from the vertical (Fig. 6.4). It can also arise following the deflection of a lateral stem (or branch) from its normal orientation.

Reaction wood formed in hardwoods differs from that formed in softwoods. In softwoods, it is termed compression wood and in hardwoods, tension wood. In both, however, the function of reaction wood is the same: to bring the stem or branch back to the original position.

COMPRESSION WOOD. If sufficient force is applied to the top of a standing pole, it will bend (Fig. 6.5). The side of the pole toward which the top is bent tends to become shorter as the result of an induced compression stress. Con-versely, the other side of the pole is stretched slightly as it is subjected to tension stress. In softwoods, reaction wood forms on the compression side (or underside) of a leaning stem. Thus the name *compression wood.* This name, incidentally, refers only to the position in which softwood reaction wood is formed and does not imply that it forms as a result of compression stress. Compression wood also forms almost universally in branches, where it functions to maintain branch an-gle. An exception is a species with drooping branches, such as spruce, in which there is a conspicuous absence of compression wood (Timell 1973c).

Properties. Compression wood is of interest to the forest products technologist because its properties are considerably different—and in virtually every case less desirable—than those of normal mature wood. Compression wood tracheids, for example, are about 30% shorter than normal (Spurr and Hyvärinen 1954; Din-woodie 1961). In addition, compression wood contains about 10% less cellulose and 8–9% more lignin and hemicellulose than normal wood (Côté et al. 1966). These factors reduce the desirability of compression wood for pulp and paper

Fig. 6.4
A leaning tree such as this one produces considerable reaction wood.

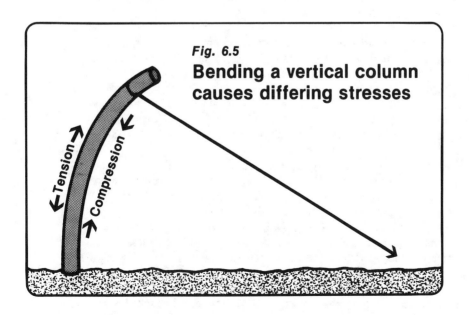

Fig. 6.5
Bending a vertical column causes differing stresses

Tension

Compression

manufacture. Watson and Dadswell (1957), obtained a 27% lower sulfite pulp yield and a 17% lower sulfate pulp yield from compression wood than from normal wood. Dadswell and Wardrop (1960) indicated that compression wood not only yields less cellulose but produces low-strength pulp, especially when subjected to the sulfite chemical pulping process. Sulfite pulp from compression wood was said by Timell (1973c) to be clearly less desirable than normal wood pulp, but use of the kraft (sulfate) process with compression wood was reported to yield an only slightly inferior product. Timell further noted that satisfactory groundwood pulp cannot be made from compression wood, apparently because of the high lignin content. (Groundwood, sulfite, and kraft pulping methods are described in Chapter 16.) Barefoot et al. (1964) acknowledged the adverse effects of compression wood on pulp quality but tempered this observation by pointing out that compression wood fibers vary from a mild to a severe form. Mild forms of compression wood were found to have a detrimental effect upon tear strength but not upon other paper properties.

Compression wood is highly undesirable in lumber or other solid wood products. A major concern when using compression wood in solid form is the longitudinal shrinkage that occurs upon drying. Longitudinal shrinkage is commonly 1–2% (compared to 0.1–0.2% for normal wood) and may be as great as 6–7%. The results of this extreme longitudinal shrinkage are shown in Figure 6.6. Compression wood is higher in density than normal wood of the same species; its density is commonly 10–20% and sometimes as much as 40% higher. Because of the higher density, it might be expected that compression wood also would have higher strength than normal wood. However, compression wood is about equal in strength to normal mature wood of the same species. If material of similar density is compared, the relatively dense compression wood is inferior in most strength properties compared to normal wood. This is a disadvantage for many structural applications, since the most-valuable woods are those having a high strength-to-weight ratio; many products such as tool handles, boat masts, and ladders require low weight as well as strength. Understandably, such abnormal properties make it desirable to eliminate compression wood from the raw material going into most solid wood products.

Identification. Compression wood is relatively conspicuous and can often be identified visually when looking at smooth surfaces. It is especially noticeable in a transverse view. While compression wood may be apparent on a smooth cross section, detection on the rough-cut end of a log (required if this defect is to be identified in a sawmill) is more difficult. One study, in which 680 logs were sawn after a visual search for compression wood by an expert, showed that visual attempts to identify compression wood in rough-cut logs were unreliable (Hallock 1969).

A stem cross section containing significant amounts of compression wood often has exceptionally wide growth rings on the lower or compression side of the leaning stem, with much narrower rings to the opposite side of the pith. The pith, as a result, is nearer to the upper side of the stem, which causes it to be eccentric (Fig. 6.7). In addition, the wide growth rings contain a high proportion of latewood, and the contrast between earlywood and latewood is often less distinct than in normal mature wood. This latter characteristic is normally evident on radial and tangential faces of surfaced lumber and is the primary means used to detect compression wood in a mill setting.

At the microscopic and submicroscopic levels, more differences between

Fig. 6.6
Longitudinal shrinkage
can cause
spectacular results.

Fig. 6.7
Eccentric cross section of spruce (*Picea* spp.)
exhibiting compression wood.

normal and compression wood become evident. Viewed longitudinally, tips of compression wood tracheids are bent and folded. In cross section, these cells are rounded rather than rectangular and have pronounced intercellular spaces between them. Analysis of the walls of compression wood tracheids shows only S-1 and S-2 layers to the inside of the primary wall, with the slope of microfibrils in the S-2 layer about 45 degrees from the vertical. This large S-2 microfibril angle results in great longitudinal shrinkage (Wardrop and Dadswell 1950). Deep, helically arranged checks extending from the lumen mark this S-2 layer.

Before leaving the topic of compression wood, a few words are in order regarding *opposite wood*, a term used to describe wood formed on the opposite side of the stem from compression wood. This wood is reported to have significantly different characteristics than normal wood (Timell 1973a,b; Timell 1986, pp. 1969–1998; Tanaka and Koshijima 1981; and Siripatanadilok and Leney 1985). Some similarities to compression wood have been reported such as high microfibril angles—in some cases as large as, or larger than, the angles of the compression wood side of the same tree. Opposite wood of softwoods differs from compression wood in having a lower lignin content, higher cellulose content, and cells having thick, highly lignified S-3 layers.

Those interested in a comprehensive discussion of compression wood, its formation, structure, properties, chemistry, and uses, will find the three-volume series by Timell (1986) to be extremely enlightening.

TENSION WOOD. *Tension wood* is reaction wood of the hardwood species. It forms on the upper or tension side of leaning stems.

Properties. Like compression wood, tension wood properties are quite different from those of normal mature wood. They are not all undesirable, however, and the usefulness of tension wood might best be described by a proverbial good news–bad news tale. With respect to pulp and paper manufacture, for example, the bad news is that tension wood has long been considered a less-desirable raw material than normal wood. It requires special care in pulping, and pulp containing large amounts of tension wood produces weaker paper than normal pulp (Jayme and Harders-Steinhäuser 1953). Tensile and burst strengths appear to be most affected (Dadswell et al. 1958). The good news is that tension wood pulp strength compares favorably to that of normal wood after it is subjected to a refining treatment (Isebrands and Parham 1974; Parham et al. 1976). The good news gets better: The cellulose content of tension wood is higher than normal. The higher cellulose content, together with a 5–10% increase in density over normal wood, results in slightly improved chemical pulp yields (Casperson et al. 1968).

Tension wood is especially well suited for both dissolving and mechanical pulps. It is desirable for dissolving pulps because it gives high pulp yields. *Dissolving pulp* is a very pure pulp made by removing residual hemicellulose and lignin from a chemical pulp. It is used in making cellulose products such as cellophane, rayon, and nitrocellulose. For this use, individual fiber strength is unimportant. Compared to normal wood, *mechanical pulping* of tension wood yields higher-strength pulp and is easier to accomplish since the proportion of lignin in tension wood is lower (Scaramuzzi and Vecchi 1968). Recall that compression wood is difficult to pulp mechanically because of a high lignin content.

In the manufacture of solid wood products, there is little good news associated with the presence of tension wood. Tension wood tends to produce a fuzzy surface upon sawing or surfacing, particularly when processed green (Fig. 6.8). This causes saws to overheat and makes satisfactory finishing difficult. Satisfactory machining is also more difficult to achieve with tension wood (Schumann and Pillow 1969). Upon drying, tension wood shows a decided tendency to collapse irreversibly (Dadswell 1958; Jane et al. 1970). *Collapse* is the cave-in or flattening of wood cells during drying, often resulting in severely distorted wood surfaces. (More information about this drying defect can be found in Chapter 8.) Tension wood also shrinks excessively along the grain, although to a lesser extent than compression wood. Longitudinal shrinkage of tension wood is usually 1% or less. This degree of longitudinal shrinkage may seem insignificant, but any amount of dimensional change along the grain can create problems. For instance, a change of only 0.5% can mean about 0.25 in. of shrinkage for each 4 ft (or 0.6 cm/0.8 m) of length. Warp or twist sometimes results when tension wood is present along only one side or edge of a board.

Fig. 6.8
**Sawing through tension wood zones can result
in formation of fuzzy surfaces.**

The strength of tension wood generally compares unfavorably to that of normal mature wood. Most measures of strength are less than in normal wood of similar density, and this is particularly true of compression strength parallel to the grain. In an air-dry condition, tension wood is slightly higher in impact bending strength than normal wood (Panshin and de Zeeuw 1980). Because of limited research comparing tension wood and normal wood strength and conflicting find-ings, Tsoumis (1968) indicated that caution is advisable where strength is im-portant. He said that because of erratic strength properties "tension wood in wooden structures should be viewed with concern analogous to compression wood, especially if strength of the structure is of primary importance."

Identification. Tension wood is not easy to detect visually, making removal during wood-processing operations difficult. A clue to its presence in a log is the shape of the cross section and/or the arrangement of rings within it. As in com-pression wood, stems containing tension wood often have wider rings in the re-action wood zone than on the opposite side of the pith, which results in an ellip-tical shape (Fig. 6.9). Other indications of the presence of tension wood are the fuzzy surfaces produced during sawing or planing, a lustrous sheen that appears on machined surfaces of some species, and a darker color that characterizes ten-sion wood of some tropical hardwoods. Unfortunately, none of these are totally reliable indicators of tension wood. Detection is further complicated because ten-sion wood zones are seldom totally composed of tension wood tissue. Such tis-sue occurs in a mixture with normal cells, with the proportion of tension wood depending upon the degree of lean in a stem. Efforts to find better ways of de-tecting tension wood continue.

Positive identification of tension wood is possible when laboratory methods are available. Examination under a microscope reveals that tension wood con-tains fewer and smaller vessels and fewer rays than normal wood (Scurfield

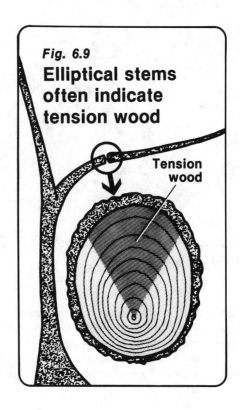

Fig. 6.9
Elliptical stems often indicate tension wood

Tension wood

1973). Tension wood fiber walls are often quite thick, with very small lumens, and secondary wall layers are commonly only loosely connected to the primary cell wall. In Figure 6.10B, thick-walled tension wood fibers of *Populus* surround a vessel; loosely attached secondary walls, dislodged in cutting, protrude from cell lumens. The loosely connected secondary wall provides positive evidence of tension wood and also at least partially explains the reason for several tension wood properties. Cells with loosely attached secondary walls have also been reported in the opposite wood of hardwoods (Hamilton et al. 1985). Thick and loosely attached secondary walls of fibers are responsible for heating of saws during processing and for the fuzzy surfaces that often remain. The soft walls are difficult to cut cleanly, and cutting forces can result in tear-out of fiber bundles from below the surface being formed. Thick fiber walls are also one cause of lower strength in paper made from tension wood fiber. These rigid cells do not easily bend and flatten within the paper and thus fiber-to-fiber bonding is hindered.

The thick and loosely attached secondary wall of tension wood fibers is almost pure cellulose of highly crystalline organization. Because this layer contains little lignin, it is soft or gelatinlike, rather than stiff like other wall layers, and thus is called a gelatinous (or G) layer. In addition to being almost pure cellulose, the G layer is composed of microfibrils arranged nearly parallel to the cell axis, varying only about 5 degrees (Preston and Ranganathan 1947; Côté and Day 1965). A highly magnified view of a G layer is shown in Figure 6.11. The highly cellulosic gelatinous layer is the reason for high yield upon chemical pulping of tension wood.

Careful analysis of tension wood fiber walls shows variability in the sequence of layering. In some cells, the S-2 and S-3 portions of the cell wall are missing and the G layer lies to the inside of the primary (P) and S-1 cell wall layers, giving a P, S-1, G configuration. Other tension wood fibers are ordered P, S-1, S-2, G or P, S-1, S-2, S-3, G (Dadswell and Wardrop 1955). Apparently, the cell wall configuration is dependent upon the stage of development of a particular cell at the time of stem tilting (Scurfield 1973). Cells that have formed S-1 and S-2 layers of the secondary wall will immediately stop normal development if the stem leans and will shift to G-layer development.

Compression wood shrinks longitudinally because of the large microfibril angle in the S-2 wall layers of longitudinal tracheids. This is not the case in tension wood, which exhibits a normal S-2 orientation in cells having this layer but has longitudinal orientation of microfibrils in the thick G layer. Tension wood shrinks longitudinally because the loosely attached G layer does not provide shrinkage restraint as the S-2 layer in normal wood does. Wood shrinks when microfibrils move more closely together as water molecules leave the cell wall. A cell wall layer in which most of the microfibrils are oriented perpendicularly to the cell axis, such as the S-1 layer, will tend to shrink longitudinally as water is lost. This tendency is counteracted in a normal cell by the thick and firmly attached S-2 layer, which does not shrink longitudinally. (For a more complete discussion of why and how wood shrinks, see Chapter 8.)

Fig. 6.10

Normal hardwood fibers vs. tension wood fibers

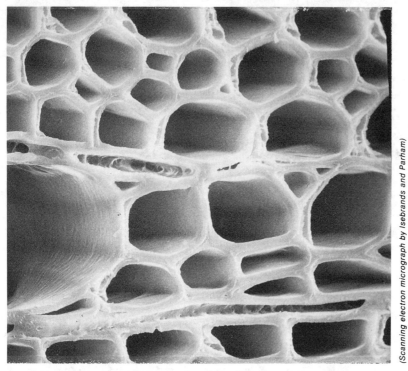

(Scanning electron micrograph by Isebrands and Parham)

A. Normal poplar (*Populus* spp.) in cross section. ×800

B. Tension wood fibers surround a vessel in xylem of poplar (*Populus* spp.). ×1600

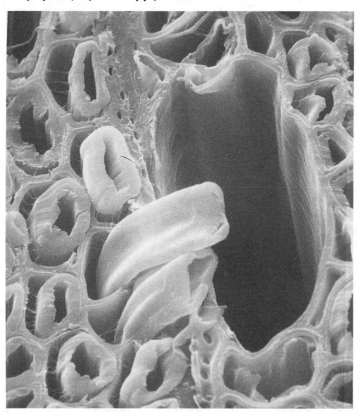

(Scanning electron micrograph by Isebrands and Parham)

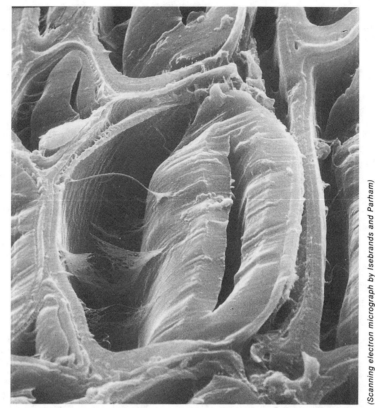

(Scanning electron micrograph by Isebrands and Parham)

Fig. 6.11
Thick gelatinous layer of tension wood fiber detached from the underlying secondary wall. ×2800. Note the transition of the flat microfibril angle in the secondary wall to the longitudinal orientation in the gelatinous layer.

FORMATION OF REACTION WOOD. A number of investigators have considered how reaction wood brings about redirection of a leaning stem. There are at least two major factors to consider: (1) The sequence of events that triggers the development of reaction wood and (2) the mechanics of stem straightening. Regarding mechanics, it appears that stem-straightening forces are brought about by a combination of rapidly developing reaction wood on one side of the stem, which pushes the stem the opposite direction, and cell expansion or contraction of the reaction wood itself resulting from higher or lower lignin content, respectively (Timell 1986).

The question of what triggers reaction wood formation is not yet solved. Scientists who first looked into stem adjustment believed that reaction wood formed as a result of induced compression or tension stress (Metzker 1908), and much of the early experimentation supported this theory (Wardrop 1964). Stress as a cause of reaction wood formation was later conclusively discounted by studies indicating that gravity played a decisive role. This was demonstrated effectively in an experiment in which young stems were bent into complete loops prior to the growing season and then examined after a period of growth (Ewart and Mason-Jones 1906; Jaccard 1938). Growth of softwood stems under these conditions resulted in formation of compression wood along the lower edges of the uppermost part of the loops where there was indeed compression stress (Fig. 6.12a). At the bottoms of the loops, however, compression wood formed on the lower, or tension, side. Precisely the opposite results were obtained in tests with hardwoods (Fig. 6.12b). In a related experiment, pine stems were bent, but tipped sidewise so that all parts of the stems were oriented horizontally (Burns 1920). These circumstances led to formation of compression wood at neither the compression nor the tension face of the bent stem but on the lower side (Fig. 6.13). These results make it tempting to conclude that the force of gravity plays an important role in reaction wood formation, a view that was accepted by early researchers. However, as pointed out by Timell (1986), it has long been known that if branches of conifers are bent upward, compression wood forms on the upper side, forcing them down again. Thus, it appears that mechanisms leading to reaction wood formation are quite complex; as yet, these are not understood.

Clues as to how reaction wood formation is induced are provided by experimentation with growth regulators. It has been shown that artificially induced auxins such as indole-acetic acid (IAA) and gibberellic acid cause formation of compression wood (Wershing and Bailey 1942; Fraser 1952; Wardrop and Davies 1964). It has also been shown that injection of IAA in one side of a vertical softwood stem causes it to tilt away from the injection site (Wardrop and Davies 1964). These findings, coupled with the observations that leaning softwood stems have higher concentrations of auxins at the lower side than at the upper side (Onaka 1949), indicate that auxin concentrations may play a role in compression wood formation. Něcesaný (1958) and Westing (1968) also found that auxin concentrations are associated with tension wood formation. They noted that concentrations of auxin served to inhibit formation of tension wood.

Reaction wood has been found in nonleaning stems of loblolly pine (Zobel and Haught 1962), yellow poplar (Taylor 1968), and several species of *Populus* (Krempl 1975). Tsoumis (1968) explained this by pointing out that very young trees may be tipped, form tension wood, and recover to the vertical position. He also indicated that reaction wood can form in trees that are tilted by wind action but not permanently displaced. Thus gravity appears to play a key role in reaction wood formation even in nonleaning trees. Gravity may not, however, be the only environmental factor leading to reaction wood formation. Observations of tropical trees suggest that tension wood may serve to direct crowns toward openings in a dense jungle canopy (Panshin and de Zeeuw 1980). There is also mounting evidence that reaction wood formation is associated with fast growth (Tsoumis 1952; Isebrands and Bensend 1972; Isebrands and Parham 1974; Crist et al. 1977; Timell 1986, p. 1696).

What triggers auxin production upon tipping of stems and how these substances move to specific locations in the stem are other unsolved riddles. Regardless of the trigger/transport mechanisms, it is clear that the system is sensitive and that events occur quickly. Stem displacements as small as 2 degrees can cause compression wood formation, with the amount of reaction wood formed directly related to the angle of lean. Studies have also shown reaction wood to

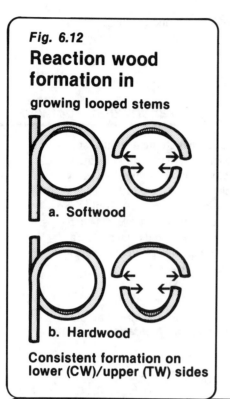

Fig. 6.12

Reaction wood formation in

growing looped stems

a. Softwood

b. Hardwood

Consistent formation on lower (CW)/upper (TW) sides

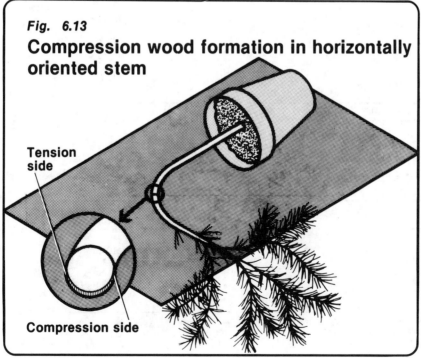

Fig. 6.13

Compression wood formation in horizontally oriented stem

Tension side

Compression side

begin developing in as short a period as 24 hours (Kennedy and Farrar 1965). In a more-recent study (Yoshizawa et al. 1992), changes in cell structure were not observed until the fourth day after stem inclination.

Branchwood, rootwood ■

Ever greater demand for wood and wood products has stimulated interest in finding new sources of wood. An important development arising from this interest is the total-tree (or whole-tree) concept developed in the 1960s and early 1970s by Hakkila (1971), Keays (1971a,b,c), Koch (1973), Young (1964, 1974), and others. Whereas traditional methods of harvest involve removal of only the main stem, which is trimmed of the top and branches, *total-tree harvest* is characterized by gathering of main stems, branches, twigs, leaves, and even roots. Tables 6.2 and 6.3 indicate increases in yield of 60–100% and greater over conventional methods of harvest through removal of total trees.

Table 6.2. Weight distribution (ovendry basis) of above- and below-ground parts of three 22-year-old, 7.7-in., unthinned, plantation-grown slash pine trees cut in central Louisiana

	Weight fraction		
Portion of tree	Total tree	Aboveground parts	Bark-free stem to 4-in. top (DOB)*
		(%)	
Bark-free stem	58.5	70.2	100.0
Roots and stump (roots to a 3-ft radius)	16.5	19.8	28.2
Stem bark to 4-in. top	12.5	15.0	21.4
Top (with bark)	5.0	6.0	8.5
Needles	4.0	4.7	6.7
Branches (with bark)	3.5	4.2	5.9
Total	100.0		

Source: Koch (1973).
* DOB = diameter outside bark.

Table 6.3. Weight distribution (ovendry basis) of above- and below-ground parts of 6- to 10-in. naturally grown red maple

Portion of tree	Total tree	Aboveground parts	Bark-free stem to 4-in. top (DOB)*
		(%)	
Bark-free stem	50.1	64.6	100.0
Roots and stump (with bark)	22.4	28.9	44.8
Stem bark to 4-in. top	7.7	9.9	15.3
Top (with bark)	5.3	6.8	10.6
Branches (with bark and leaves)	14.5	18.7	29.0
Total	100.00		

Source: Adapted from Young et al. (1963, 1965).
* DOB = diameter outside bark.

Harvesting of all aboveground segments of trees became reality in the late 1960s and early 1970s with the development in the United States of mobile units with capabilities of on-site chipping of entire trees. This system provided for the collection of chips in semitrailers for movement to processing centers (see Fig. 18.7). Tractor-mounted shearing devices, developed at about the same time, ensured maximum removal of aboveground tree parts; this equipment produced stumps only 2–6 in. (5–15 cm) in height.

Mechanized stump-removal equipment came on the scene in 1973–74, with almost simultaneous development in Finland and the United States. The Finnish system focused upon removal of stumps following harvest of aboveground segments (Fig. 6.14). In contrast, prototype equipment developed for use in southern pine forests of the United States was designed to remove roots at the same time as the main stem (Fig. 6.15).

Although yield can be greatly increased by whole-tree operations, there has been concern about the nature or quality of material harvested. The properties of branchwood and rootwood differ from each other and from wood of the main stem, so manufacturing processes may need to be modified to accommodate these variable components.

BRANCHWOOD. From a utilization viewpoint, one of the most-significant differences between material from branches and from that of the main stem is that branches have a much higher proportion of bark. This is especially true of those less than 1 in. (2.5 cm) in diameter (Table 6.4). Because bark has markedly different properties than wood (see Chapter 7) and often picks up considerable dirt during harvest, the use of branches for fiber or particle products requires caution. Considerable process modification may be necessary. Processes to separate wood and bark are not yet perfected or widely used.

Table 6.4. Bark as a proportion of the dry weight of various tree parts

Portion of tree	White pine	Red maple
	(%)	
Merchantable bole	18.7	13.3
Unmerchantable top	16.8	16.6
Branches larger than 1 in.	21.1	20.7
Branches smaller than 1 in.	71.6	71.2
Stump	20.8	11.9
Roots larger than 4 in.	17.5	10.5
Roots 1–4 in.	18.5	19.9
Roots less than 1 in.	54.4	50.7

Source: Adapted from Young et al. (1965).
Note: For trees approximately 8 in. diameter at breast height (4.5 ft from ground level).

Aside from the bark, *branchwood* itself differs from wood of the bole. This can make wood identification as well as utilization difficult. Some kinds of cells are more abundant in branchwood than they are in the wood of the main stem. In hardwood branches, vessels and rays are more numerous than in the bole, with

Fig. 6.14
Stump removal in Finland follows aboveground harvest

Fig. 6.15
Puller-buncher
harvests southern pine complete with taproot attached.

fibers present in lesser numbers. Softwoods that normally have resin canals also exhibit this feature in branchwood, although canals in branches are both smaller in diameter and more numerous. Softwood branches also characteristically have a higher than normal ray volume.

Narrow growth rings typify both hardwood and softwood branch material, and longitudinal cells are generally both shorter and of lesser diameter than those in the main stem (Tsoumis 1968). In studies of a number of hardwoods, fiber length in branchwood was found to average 25–35% less than wood of the main stem (Manwiller 1974; Taylor 1977; Phelps, et al. 1982); similar results have been obtained for softwoods (Brunden 1964; Lee 1971).

Early literature indicates that branchwood is generally higher in specific gravity than *stemwood* (Fegel 1941; Jane et al. 1970). More-recent work suggests, however, that this relationship is species dependent. Branches of softwoods tend to be 5–20% lower in specific gravity than bolewood (Brunden 1964; Phillips et al. 1976; Pugel et al. 1989), while specific gravity of hardwood branches ranges from higher in some species (Hamilton et al. 1976; Taylor 1977) to lower or the same in others (Taylor 1977).

Products made from branchwood have different properties than those made of main stemwood. Particleboard made of Douglas-fir branchwood was, for example, shown to have lower stiffness and breaking strength in bending and lower strength retention after aging than board made from bolewood (Lehmann and Geimer 1974). *Particleboard* is a product composed of wood particles that have been sprayed or mixed with an adhesive, 2–8% of the dry weight, and compressed to a desired thickness. Stiffness and breaking strength of boards made entirely of branch material were only 30–65% that of composite panels, depending upon whether branches were small—less than 1 in. (2.5 cm) diameter—or large, respectively. A more-recent study (Pugel et al. 1989) using loblolly pine branches showed stiffness of flakeboard, standard particleboard, and fiberboard panels to be 10–20% less than identical panels made of main stemwood. However, with the exception of flakeboard, breaking strength and internal bond (a measure of the tensile strength of the panel core) were equal or better in the panels made of branchwood. Particleboard manufactured from logging slash (including branches, twigs, needles, and cones) was found to have considerably lower strength than board made of conventional materials when using the same percent of adhesive (Boehner and Gertjejansen 1975).

A number of investigations have assessed the suitability of branch material for wood fiber products. Timell (1986, p. 1876) noted that the major disadvantage of using treetops as a source of pulp is that they consist almost entirely of juvenile wood and, in the case of softwoods, have a high content of compression wood as well. Kraft pulp from branchwood requires less beating time and has lower strength than pulp made from wood of the merchantable bole (McKee 1960; Worster and Vinje 1968). One study of western hemlock showed that paper from kraft branch pulp had 20–25% lower tear strength and 40–45% lower burst and tensile strength than paper made from wood of the main stem (Keays and Hatton 1971). Little work has been done to determine the suitability of branchwood for pulping processes other than kraft. Studies do suggest, however, that relatively good-quality mechanical or chemimechanical pulp can be obtained from this material (Keays 1971a).

Low pulp strength is not the only reason why branchwood is looked upon with disfavor by papermakers. Branchwood is also a less-desirable raw material because of nonuniformity of chip sizes and high proportions of bark. The configuration of branches and twigs, along with higher bark fractions, results in decreased yield and a higher proportion of rejects in the form of oversized material such as slivers, chunks, or uncooked knots that remain after pulp is passed through a series of screens (Hunt and Hatton 1975). Tests of hardwoods showed pulp yields from branch material to be virtually the same as yields from bolewood when yield was expressed in terms of pulp weight divided by the weight of chips entering the digester. Yield from branch material was far lower, however, when unacceptable chips produced in the chipping operation were considered. Over 50% of branchwood chips were rejects, compared to about 22% for chips from the main stem (Young and Chase 1966). Rejection in this case was based upon nonuniform chip size.

One wood fiber product for which branchwood appears to be an entirely suitable raw material is *hardboard*, a high-density product made from mechanically ground pulp by compressing a fiber mat under heat and pressure. A number of U.S. mills currently use branches mixed with normal wood for hardboard manufacture.

In summary, branchwood is an acceptable raw material, although for some products it is less desirable than stemwood. Because of the significant potential for increased yield when tops and branches are used, process modifications will probably be made wherever possible to accommodate this material. Although use of branchwood as a fuel is significant and is likely to continue, utilization of branch material in a mixture with traditionally used pulp chips is also likely to increase, as is use of branchwood in making composite panels.

ROOTWOOD. Young et al. (1965) generated interest in utilization of roots as a source of fiber by publicizing the fact that the stump/root systems of white pine and red maple contain an amount of fiber equivalent to 32–39% of the fiber volume in the main stem. Koch (1972, 1974) later demonstrated that southern pine typically produced a carrotlike taproot which when combined with the stump contained 20–25% as much fiber as the main stem. Koch also was instrumental in the development of root-harvesting equipment (Fig. 6.15) designed for use in sandy soils of the southern United States (Koch and Coughran 1975). Wider utilization of roots is likely; yet, problems remain to be solved. Roots are dirty and often difficult to clean, and dirt can plug or cause excessive wear of expensive pulp mill equipment. Dirt can also dull knives or saws when cutting the final product. Another complicating factor is bark, which (as in branches) makes up a large portion of the small-diameter material (Table 6.4).

Rootwood is structured quite differently from either branchwood or wood of the main stem. Wood of softwood roots exhibits relatively few resin canals, a smaller ray volume than that of the main stem (Fegel 1941), and exceptionally large-diameter cells. Length of cells is apparently highly variable. Rootwood cells are reported by some to be as long or longer than those found in the main stem (Gerry 1915; Dinwoodie 1961; Fayle 1968), while others report that they are shorter (Fegel 1941; Eskilsson 1969). Manwiller (1972) studied tracheids in stumps and roots of southern pine and found them to be about one-third larger in diameter and one-third longer than tracheids of the stump. Walls of the root tracheids were significantly thinner. Davis and Hurley (1978), in contrast, found tracheids of southern pine roots to be about 10% shorter than tracheids in the stem. Frequent occurrence of compression wood and spiral grain, the lack of a well-defined pith (Koch 1972), and high fibril angles in cell walls (Koch 1974) also appear to be characteristic of southern pine roots.

Comparing xylem of hardwood roots to that of the main stem, the vessels and parenchyma of roots occur in greater than normal quantity, while fiber volume is low. Cell size varies as well, with abnormally large diameters and long fibers. Vessels are variously reported as abnormally large in diameter as compared to stemwood (Tsoumis 1968) to unusually small (Cutler 1976). Ring-porous characteristics and tyloses are often lacking in roots.

Specific gravity of rootwood of hardwoods is reported to be low in relation to that of the bole (Fegel 1941; Young et al. 1965). Several tests of southern pine also show low specific gravity of roots (Howard 1973, 1974; Koch 1974; Davis and Hurley 1978), although experimentation with roots of northern softwoods suggests abnormally high specific gravity levels (Fegel 1941; Young et al. 1965). Chemical analysis of slash pine roots showed the cellulose content lower than that in the main stem, with lignin and extractive content correspondingly higher (Howard 1973) (Table 6.5).

Table 6.5. *Chemical composition of various parts of slash pine trees*

Tree part	Chemical compound				
	Cellulose*	Hemicellulose*	Lignin*	Extractives†	Ash†
Bark	23.7	24.9	50.0	13.0	0.9
Needles	42.6	22.3	37.7	26.2	2.4
Branches	36.9	33.7	35.0	13.6	1.2
Top	41.5	31.2	32.5	11.0	0.8
Roots	44.6	25.6	31.3	11.7	1.6
Stem	51.1	26.8	27.8	9.1	0.3

Source: Adapted from Howard (1973).
*Expressed as a percentage of extractive-free ovendry weight.
†Expressed as a percentage of unextracted ovendry weight.

Because of low specific gravity and a reduced cellulose fraction, Koch (1974) concluded that southern pine roots would give slightly lower kraft pulp yields than stemwood. He also predicted inferior pulp properties because of the high fibril angles. This was confirmed by Davis and Hurley (1978), who obtained a kraft pulp yield (as a percent of ovendry wood) of 54.1% from stumps and roots of loblolly pine compared to 56.8% from bolewood. Strength tests showed burst and tensile strength in paper made from stump and root pulp to be about 3% higher, while tear strength was 19% less. For other softwoods, kraft pulping tests of root and stump wood have shown strength values to be low in relation to pulp made from the bole. Tear, burst, tensile, and fold strength values have been found to be 3–20%, 10–17%, 15%, and 18% lower, respectively, for root pulp than for pulp made from wood of the bole (Eskilsson 1969; Keays and Hatton 1971). Conclusions were that chemical pulp of acceptable quality was obtainable from roots but that process modifications would be necessary to utilize this material economically.

In tests of northern hardwoods, Young and Chase (1966) found kraft pulp yield from roots to be lower than from bole material. As with branchwood, the difference was relatively small when pulp yield was expressed as a percent of chip weight entering the digesters but became quite significant when losses resulting from unacceptable chips were considered as well (Table 6.6). These tests showed rootwood pulp from maple to be significantly inferior to pulp of main stemwood in tensile, burst, and tear strengths. However, rootwood properties for birch were comparable to those of the main stem pulp.

Table 6.6. Chipping/pulping results for red maple and white birch pulps

	Birch			Maple		
Operation	Roots	Bole	Branches	Roots	Bole	Branches
Chipping*						
% Acceptable chips†	32.4	75.2	44.6	52.4	80.9	50.2
% Rejected chips	67.6	24.8	55.4	47.6	19.1	49.8
Cooking†						
% Acceptable pulp	45.1	46.2	47.8	36.4	49.8	48.2

Source: Young and Chase (1966).
* Yield based on wood charged to chipper.
† Acceptable chips are those that meet industry standards for size. Small material (fines) is undesirable for many pulping processes.
† Yield based on weight of dry chips charged to digester.

Rootwood has also been evaluated as a raw material for the manufacture of structural flaketype particleboard (Howard 1974). Root material of slash pines was found difficult to flake because of high fibril angles in the secondary walls that resulted in a high proportion of flakes with distorted grain and rough surfaces and in a board with high surface porosity and poor adhesion. Ingrown dirt pockets also caused rapid dulling of flaker knives. The low specific gravity of rootwood resulted in slightly higher stiffness and a nearly doubled internal bond strength compared to board made of bolewood. All other strength properties were reported comparable, while dimensional stability was found to be slightly decreased. Low density is an advantage in manufacturing particleboard, as will be explained in Chapter 15.

Before concluding this discussion of the potential for root utilization, it should be pointed out that roots have been used for years as fuel and as a source of chemical extractives. A process for extracting turpentine, rosin, and pine oils from pine stumps was commercialized in 1909 and is considered to mark the beginning of the naval stores industry in the United States (Panshin et al. 1962). Several such plants continue in operation today, although the total volume of stumps and roots used by this industry is miniscule compared to the volume that could be harvested.

REVIEW

A. Terms to define or explain:
  1. Reaction wood   3. Compression wood   5. Opposite wood
  2. Juvenile wood   4. Tension wood

B. Questions or concepts to explain:
  1. How common is juvenile wood (i.e., in approximately what proportion of trees is it found)?

2. Stimulated growth and short rotations are methods frequently discussed by foresters as means of meeting increased demands for wood. For what wood products might these practices cause problems? What limits to growth rate and length of rotation do these potential problems suggest?

3. When present in a solid wood product such as lumber, juvenile wood is a serious defect. How might the manager of a sawmill modify the process to minimize the effects of juvenile wood in the product?

4. Because juvenile and reaction woods are generally undesirable in wood products, their separation from mature wood might be a good idea. For a separation plan to be practical, however, identification of abnormal wood must be fast and based upon visual characteristics. What features would allow easy identification of juvenile wood? Compression wood? Tension wood?

5. How can compression wood be distinguished from normal wood under a microscope? Based upon chemical analysis? What about tension wood?

6. Can pulp and paper manufacturing processes be modified to minimize adverse effects of using juvenile wood? Compression wood? Tension wood?

7. Why does compression wood shrink along the grain as it dries? Why does longitudinal shrinkage occur in tension wood?

8. If compression wood occurs along only one edge of a board, what will the board look like if it is dried without restraint?

9. Other than semipermanent tipping of a stem, what other conditions can result in reaction wood formation?

10. What is thought to happen within a leaning stem prior to the onset of reaction wood formation? How quickly does reaction wood production begin after tipping of a tree?

11. How does the wood of branches differ from wood of the merchantable bole? Chemically? Structurally?

12. Does the wood of branches differ from that of roots? In what ways?

13. From the standpoint of a paper or particleboard mill supervisor, what features of rootwood and branchwood might cause concern? Why?

14. To what extent might the yield of wood fiber per acre of forest harvested be increased through the gathering of branches? Unmerchantable tops? Roots?

REFERENCES

Abdel-Gadir, A.Y., and Krahmer, R.L. 1993. Estimating the age of demarcation of juvenile and mature wood in Douglas-fir. Wood and Fiber Science 25(3):242–249.

Andersson, S.; Hansen, R.; Jonsson, Y.; and Nylinder, M. 1978. Harvesting systems for stumps and roots—A review and evaluation of Scandinavian techniques. In Complete Tree Utilization of Southern Pine, ed. C. W. McMillin. Madison, Wis.: Forest Products Research Society, pp. 130–145.

Barefoot, A.C.; Hitchings, R.G.; and Ellwood, E.L. 1964. Wood characteristics and kraft paper properties of four selected loblolly pines. I. Effect of fiber morphology under identical cooking conditions. TAPPI 47(6):343–356.

Barker, R.G. 1974. Papermaking properties of young hardwoods. TAPPI 57(8):107–111.

Bella, I.E., and Hunt, K. 1973. Kraft pulping of young trembling aspen from Manitoba. Can. J. For. Res. 3(3):359–366.

Bendtsen, B.A. 1978. Properties of wood from improved and intensively managed trees. For. Prod. J. 28(10):61–72.

Boehner, A.W., and Gertjejansen, R.O. 1975. Effect of three species of logging slash on properties of aspen planer shavings particleboard. For. Prod. J. 25(12):36–42.

Boone, R.S., and Chudnoff, M. 1972. Compression wood formation and other characteristics of plantation grown *Pinus caribaea*. USDA For. Serv. Res. Pap. ITF–13.

Brunden, M.N. 1964. Specific gravity and fiber length in crown-formed and stem-formed wood. For. Prod. J. 14(1):13–17.

Burns, G.P. 1920. Eccentric growth and the formation of red wood in the main stem of conifers. Vt. Agric. Exp. Stn. Bull. 219.

Carpenter, C.H. 1984. The mechanical pulping of southern pine containing relatively large amounts of spring and juvenile fiber. In Utilization of the Changing Wood Resource in the Southern United States. North Carolina State Univ., pp.124–146.

Casperson, G.; Jacopian, V.; and Phillipp, B. 1968. Influence of different cooking processes on the ultrastructure of poplar reactionwood. Sven. Papperstidn. 71(13/14):482–87. (Ger. Abstr. in Weiner, J., and Roth, L. 1970. Biblio. Ser. 184, Suppl. 2. Inst. Pap. Chem.)

Côté, W.A., Jr., and Day, A.C. 1965. Anatomy and ultrastructure of reaction wood. In Cellular Ultrastructure of Woody Plants, ed. W.A. Côté, Jr., Syracuse, N.Y.: Syracuse Univ. Press, pp. 391–418.

Côté, W. A., Jr; Day, A.C.; Simson, B.W.; and Timell, T.E. 1966. Studies of larch arabinogalactin. I. The distribution of arabinogalactin in larch wood. Holzforschung 20(6):178–192.

Crist, J.B. 1976. Utilization advantages of material produced in maximum fiber yield plantations. Intensive plantation culture—Five years research. USDA For. Serv. Gen. Tech. Rep. NC-21.

Crist, J.B.; Dawson, D.H.; and Nelson, J.A. 1977. Wood and bark quality of juvenile jack pine and eastern larch grown under intensive culture. Proc. TAPPI Biol.-Wood Chem. Conf., pp. 211–216.

Cutler, D.E. 1976. Variation in root wood anatomy. In Wood Structure and Biological and Technological Research, ed. P. Baas, A.J. Bolton, and D.M. Catling. Leiden, Netherlands: Leiden Univ. Press.

Dadswell, H.E. 1958. Wood structure variations occurring during tree growth and their influence on properties. J. Inst. Wood Sci. 1:11–33.

Dadswell, H. E., and Wardrop, A.B. 1955. The structure and properties of tension wood. Holzforschung 9(4):97–104.

_____. 1960. Recent progress in research on cell wall structure. Proc. 5th World For. Congr., vol. 2, pp. 1279–1288.

Dadswell, H.E.; Wardrop, A.B.; and Watson, A.J. 1958. The morphology, chemistry and pulping characteristics of reaction wood. In Fundamentals of Papermaking Fibers, ed. K Bolam. London: British Paper and Board Makers Association, pp. 187–229.

Davis, B.M., and Hurley, D.W. 1978. Fiber from a southern pine root system? In Complete Tree Utilization of Southern Pine, ed. C.W. McMillin. Madison, Wis.: Forest Products Research Society, pp. 274–276.

Dinwoodie, M.J. 1961. Tracheid and fibre length in timber—A review of literature. Forestry 34(2):125–144.

Dyer, R.E 1967. Fresh and dry weight, nutrient elements, and pulping characteristics of northern white cedar. Me. Agric. Exp. Stn. Tech. Bull. 27.

Einspahr, D.W. 1976. The influence of short-rotation forestry on pulp and paper quality. II. Short-rotation hardwoods. TAPPI 59(11):63–66.

Erickson, H.D., and Arima, T. 1974. Douglas-fir wood quality studies. II. Effects of age and stimulated growth on fibril angle and chemical constituents. Wood Sci. Tech. 8(4):255–265.

Eskilsson, S. 1969. Fiber properties in the spruce root system. Cellul. Chem. Tech. 3(4):409–416.

Ewart, A.C.J., and Mason-Jones, A. 1906. The formation of red wood in conifers. Ann. Bot. Lond. 20:201–203.

Fayle, D.C.E. 1968. Radial growth in tree roots. Univ. Toronto Fac. For. Tech. Rep. 9:183.

Fegel, A.C. 1941. Comparative anatomy and varying physical properties of trunk-, branch-, and rootwood of certain northeastern trees. N.Y. State Col. For., Syracuse Univ. Tech. Publ. 55.

Fight, R; Snellgrove, T.; Curtis, R.; and Debell, D. 1986. Bringing timber quality considerations into forest management decisions: A conceptual approach. In Douglas-fir:

Stand Management for the Future, C. Oliver, D. Hanley, and J. Johnson, eds. Seattle: Univ. of Washington Press.

Foran, C.D. 1984. Wood quality, a pulp mill perspective: Case studies of the impact of juvenile wood usage on by-products recovery. In Utilization of the Changing Wood Resource in the Southern United States. North Carolina State Univ., pp.231–242.

Fraser, D.A. 1952. Initiation of cambial activity in some forest trees in Ontario. Ecology 33(2):259–273.

Gerry, E. 1915. Fiber measurement studies: Length variations; where they occur and their relation to the strength and uses of wood. Science 61(1048):179.

Gooding, J.W., and Smith, W.H. 1972. Effects of fertilization on stem, wood properties, and pulping characteristics of slash pine (*Pinus elliottii* var. *elliottii* Engelm.). Proc. Symp. Effect of Growth Acceleration on the Properties of Wood, Madison, Wis., E1–19.

Hakkila, P. 1971. Branches, stumps, and roots as future raw material source. In Forest Biomass Studies, ed. H. Young. Orono: Univ. of Maine Press.

Hallock, H. 1969. Sawing to reduce warp of lodgepole pine studs. USDA For. Serv. Res. Pap. 102.

Hamilton, J.R.; Cech, F.C.; and Shurtliffe, C.E. 1976. Estimating bole specific gravity from limbs of mature black cherry and northern red oak trees. Wood Fiber 7(4):281–286.

Hamilton, J.R.; Thomas, C.K.; and Carvell, K.L. 1985. Tension wood formation following release of upland oak advance reproduction. Wood Fiber Sci. 17(3):382–390.

Hatton, J.V. 1993. Kraft pulping of second-growth jack pine. TAPPI 76(5):105–113.

Hatton, J.V., and Cook, J. 1992. Kraft pulps from second-growth Douglas fir: Relationships between wood, fiber, pulp, and handsheet properties. TAPPI 75(1):137–144.

Hatton, J.V,. and Gee, W.Y. 1994. Kraft pulping of second-growth lodgepole pine. TAPPI 77(6):91–102.

Howard, E.T. 1973. Physical and chemical properties of slash pine tree parts. Wood Sci. 5(4):312–317.

_____. 1974. Slash pine rootwood in flakeboard. For. Prod. J. 24(6):29–35.

Hunt, K., and Hatton, J.V. 1975. Full forest utilization. II. Quality and kraft pulp yield of eastern Canadian hardwoods. Pulp Paper Mag. Can. 76(1):97–102.

Hunt, K., and Keays, J.L. 1973. Short-rotation trembling aspen trees (*Populus tremuloides* Michx.) for kraft pulp. Can. J. For. Res. 3(2):180–184.

Isebrands, J., and Bensend, D. 1972. Incidence and structure of gelatinous fibers within rapid-growing eastern cottonwood. Wood Fiber 4(2):61–71.

Isebrands, J., and Parham, R.A. 1974. Tension wood anatomy of short rotation *Populus* spp. before and after kraft pulping. Wood Sci. 6(3):256–265.

Jaccard, P. 1938. Eccentric increment and anatomical-histological differentiation of wood. Berl. Schweiz. Bot. Ges. 48:491–537.

Jackson, M., and Megraw, R.A. 1986. Impact of juvenile wood on pulp and paper products. In Juvenile Wood—What Does It Mean to Forest Management and Forest Products? For. Prod. Res. Soc., Proc. 47309.

Jane, F.W.; Wilson, K.; and White, O.J.B. 1970. The Structure of Wood. London: Adam & Charles Black.

Jayme, G., and Harders-Steinhäuser, M. 1953. Tension wood and its effect in poplar and willow wood. Holzforschung 7(213):39–43.

Jett, J.B., and Zobel, B.J. 1975. Wood and pulping properties of young hardwoods. TAPPI 58(1):92–96.

Keays, J.L. 1971a. Complete-tree utilization—An analysis of the literature. III. Branches. Can. Dep. Fish. For. Inf. Rep. VP-X-71.

_____. 1971b. Complete-tree utilization—An analysis of the literature. IV. Crown and slash. Can. Dep. Fish. For. Inf. Rep. VP-X-77.

_____. 1971c. Complete-tree utilization—An analysis of the literature. V. Roots and stump-root system. Can. Dep. Fish. For. Inf. Rep. VP-X-79.

Keays, J.L., and Hatton, J.V. 1971. Complete-tree utilization studies: The yield and quality of kraft pulp from the components of *Tsuga heterophylla*. TAPPI 54(I):99–104.

Kellogg, R.M., and Kennedy, R.W. 1986. Practical applications of wood quality relative
to end use. In Douglas-fir: Stand Management for the Future, C.D. Oliver, D. Hanley, and J. Johnson, eds. Univ. of Washington.

Kennedy, R.W., and Farrar, J.L. 1965. Tracheid development in tilted seedlings. In Cellular Ultrastructure of Woody Plants, ed. W.A. Côté, Jr. Syracuse, N.Y.: Syracuse
Univ. Press, pp. 419–453.

Koch, P. 1972. Utilization of the Southern Pines, Vol. 1. USDA For. Serv. Agr. Handb.
420, pp. 535–574.

_____. 1973. Whole tree utilization of southern pine advanced by developments in me-
chanical conversion. For. Prod. J. 23(10):30–33.

_____. 1974. Harvesting southern pine with taproots can extend pulpwood resource sig-
nificantly. J. For. (May).

_____. 1976. Harvesting southern pine with taproots can extend pulpwood resource sig-
nificantly. Proc. Applied Polymer Symp. 28, pp. 403–420.

Koch, P., and Coughran, S.J. 1975. Development of a puller-buncher for harvesting southern pines with taproot attached. For. Prod. J. 25(4):23–30.

Krahmer, R.L. 1986. Fundamental anatomy of juvenile wood and mature wood. In Juvenile Wood—What Does It Mean to Forest Management and Forest Products? For.
Prod. Res. Soc., Proc. 47309.

Krempl, H. 1975. Differences in proportion of tension wood in various poplar species.
Holzforsch. Holzverwert. 27(6): 131–137.

Larson, P.R. 1969. Wood formation and the concept of wood quality. Yale Univ. Sch. For.
Bull. 74.

Laundrie, J.F., and Berbee, J.G. 1972. High yields of kraft pulp from rapid-growth hybrid
poplar trees. USDA For. Serv. Res. Pap. FPL-186.

Lee, P.W. 1971. Physical properties of the stem, branch, root, and topwood of pitch pines
grown in Korea. Seoul Natl. Univ. For. Bull. 8, pp. 35–45.

Lehmann, W.F., and Geimer, R.L. 1974. Properties of structural particleboards from Douglas-fir residues. For. Prod. J. 24(10):17–25.

MacPeak, M.D.; Burkart, L.F.; and Weldon, D. 1990. Comparison of grade, yield, and
mechanical properties of lumber produced from young fast-grown and older slow-
grown planted slash pine. For. Prod. J. 40(1):11–14.

Manwiller, E.G. 1972. Tracheid dimensions in rootwood of southern pine. Wood Sci.
5(2):122–24.

_____ . 1974. Fiber lengths in stems and branches of small hardwoods on southern pine
sites. Wood Sci. 7(2):130–132.

McAlister, R.H., and Clark, A. 1991. Shrinkage of juvenile and mature wood of loblolly
pine from three locations. For. Prod. J. 42(7/8):25–28.

_____. 1992. Effect of geographic location and seed source on the bending properties
of juvenile and mature loblolly pine. For. Prod. J. 41(9):39–42.

McKee, J.C. 1960. The kraft pulping of small diameter slash pines. TAPPI
43(6):202A–204A.

_____. 1984. The impact of high volumes of juvenile wood on pulp mill operations and
operating costs. In Utilization of the Changing Wood Resource in the Southern
United States. North Carolina State Univ., pp. 178–182.

Megraw, R.A., and Nearn, W.T. 1972. Detailed DBH density profiles of several trees from
Douglas-fir fertilizer/thinning plots. Proc. Symp. Effect of Growth Acceleration on
the Properties of Wood, Madison, Wis., G1–24.

Metzker, K. 1908. Konstruktionsprinzip des sekundaren Holzkorpers. Naturwiss. Z. For.
Landwirtsch. 6:249–274.

Něcesaný, V. 1958. Effect of β-indolacetic acid on the formation of reaction wood. Phy-
ton 11:117–127.

North Carolina State College. 1957. First annual report. N.C. State-Ind. Coop. For. Tree
Improv. Program.

Noskowiak, A.F. 1963. Spiral grain in trees—A review. For. Prod. J. 13(7):266–77.

Olson, R.A.; Poletika, N.V.; and Hicock, H.W. 1947. Strength properties of plantation-grown coniferous woods. Conn. Agric. Exp. Stn. Bull. 511.

Onaka, F. 1949. Studies on compression and tension wood. Wood Res. Kyoto No. 1.

Page, D.H.; El-Hosseiny, F.; Winkler, K.; and Bain, R. 1972. The mechanical properties of single woodpulp fibers. I. A new approach. Pulp Pap. Mag. Can. 73(8):72–76.

Panshin, A.J., and de Zeeuw, C. 1980. Textbook of Wood Technology, 4th ed. New York: McGraw-Hill.

Panshin, A.J.; Harrar, E.S.; Bethel, J.S.; and Baker, W.J. 1962. Forest Products—Their Sources, Production, and Utilization. New York: McGraw-Hill.

Parham, R.A.; Robinson, K.W.; and Isebrands, J.G. 1976. Effects of tension wood on kraft paper from a short-rotation hardwood (*Populus* "Tristis #1"). Inst. Pap. Chem. Tech. Pap. Ser. 40.

Pearson, R.G., and Gilmore, R.G. 1971. Characterization of the strength of juvenile wood of loblolly pine (*Pinus taeda* L.). For. Prod. J. 21(1):23–30.

Peszlen, I. 1995. Juvenile wood characteristics of plantation wood species. Abstract XX IUFRO World Congress, Finland. IAWA Journal 16(1):14.

Phelps, J.E.; Isebrands, J.G.; and Jewett, D. 1982. Raw material quality of short-rotation, intensively cultured *Populus* clones. I. A comparison of stem and branch properties at three spacings. IAWA Bull. 3(3/4):193–200.

Phillips, D.R.; Clark, A. III; and Taras, M.A. 1976. Wood and bark properties of southern pine branches. Wood Sci. 8(3):164–69.

Posey, C.E. 1964. The effects of fertilization upon wood properties of loblolly pine (*Pinus taeda* L.). N.C. State Coll. Sch. For. Tech. Rep. 22.

Preston, R.D., and Ranganathan, V. 1947. The fine structure of the fibers of normal and tension wood in beech (*Fagus sylvatica* L.) as revealed by X-rays. Forestry 11(1):92–97.

Pugel, A.D.; Price, E.W.; and Hse, C.Y. 1989. Composites from southern pine juvenile wood. Part I. For. Prod. J. 40(1):29–33.

_____. 1990. Composites from southern pine juvenile wood. Part II. For. Prod. J. 40(3):57–61.

Rendle, B.J. 1960. Juvenile and adult wood. J. Inst. Wood Sci. 5:58–61.

Scaramuzzi, G., and Vecchi, E. 1968. Characteristics of mechanical pulp from poplar tension wood. Cellul. Carta 19(2):3–12.

Schumann, D.R., and Pillow, M.Y. 1969. Effect of tension wood on hard maple used for manufactured parts. USDA For. Serv. Res. Pap. FPL–108.

Scurfield, G. 1973. Reaction wood: Its structure and function. Science 179:647–655.

Semke, L.K. 1984. Effect of juvenile pine fibers on kraft paper properties. In Utilization of the Changing Wood Resource in the Southern United States. North Carolina State Univ., pp. 160–177.

Senft, J.F.; Bendtsen, B.A.; and Galligan, W.L. 1985. Weak wood: Fast grown trees make problem lumber. J of For. 83(8):477–484.

Senft, J.F; Quanci, M.J.; and Bendtsen, B.A. 1986. Property profile of 60-year-old Douglas-fir. In Juvenile Wood—What Does It Mean to Forest Management and Forest Products? For. Prod. Res. Soc. Proc. 47309.

Siripatanadilok, S., and Leney, L. 1985. Compression wood in western hemlock (*Tsuga heterophylla*). Wood Fiber Sci. 17(2): 254–265.

Spurr, S.H., and Hyvärinen, M.J. 1954. Wood fiber length as related to position in the tree and growth. Bot. Rev. 20(9):561–575.

Tanaka, E, and Koshijima, T. 1981. Characterization of cellulose in compression and opposite woods of a *Pinus densiflora* tree grown under the influence of strong wind. Wood Sci. Tech. 15(4):265–273.

Tang, Y., and Pearson, R.G. 1992. Effect of juvenile wood and choice of parametric property distributions on reliability-based beam design. Wood and Fiber Sci. 24(2):216–224.

Taylor, F.W. 1968. Variation of wood elements in yellow poplar. Wood Sci. Tech. 2(3):153–165.

_____. 1977. A note on the relationship between branch- and stemwood properties of selected hardwoods growing in the mid South. Wood Fiber 8(4):257–261.

Timell, T.E. 1986. Compression Wood in Gymnosperms, Vol. I, II, and III. Berlin: Springer-Verlag.

_____. 1973a. Studies on opposite wood in conifers. I. Chemical composition. Wood Sci. Tech. 7(1):1–5.

_____. 1973b. Studies on opposite wood in conifers. II. Histology and ultrastructure. Wood Sci. Tech. 7(2):79–91.

_____. 1973c. Ultrastructure of the dormant and active cambial zones and the dormant phloem associated with formation of normal and compression wood in *Picea abies* (L.) Karst. State Univ. N.Y. Tech. Publ. 96.

Tsoumis, G. 1952. Properties and effects of the abnormal wood produced by leaning hardwoods. Yale For. Sch. (unpublished).

_____. 1968. Wood as Raw Material. New York: Pergamon Press.

Turner, L.M. 1936. Root growth of seedlings of *Pinus echinata* and *Pinus taeda*. J. Agric. Res. 53:145–149.

Wardrop, A.B. 1964. The reaction anatomy of arborescent angiosperms. In The Formation of Wood in Forest Trees, ed. M.H. Zimmermann. New York: Academic Press, pp. 405–456.

Wardrop, A.B., and Dadswell, H.E. 1950. The nature of reaction wood. II. The cell wall organization of compression wood tracheids. Aust. J. Sci. Res. 5B(1):1–13.

Wardrop, A.B., and Davies, G.W. 1964. The nature of reaction wood. VIII. The structure and differentiation of compression wood. Aust. J. Bot. 12(1):24–38.

Watson, A.J., and Dadswell, H.R. 1957. Papermaking properties of compression wood from *Pinus radiata*. Appita 11:56–70.

Wershing, H.F., and Bailey, I.W. 1942. Seedlings as experimental material in the study of "redwood" in conifers. J. For. 40(5):411–414.

Westing, A.H. 1968. Formation and function of compression wood in gymnosperms. II. Bot. Rev. 34(1):51–78.

Worster, H.E., and Vinje, M.G. 1968. Kraft pulping of western hemlock tree tops and branches. Pulp Pap. Mag. Can. 69(14):57–60.

Yang, K.C.; Benson, C.A.; and Wong, J.K. 1986. Distribution of juvenile wood in two stems of *Larix laricina*. Can. J. For. Res. 16(5):1041–1049.

Yoshizawa, N.; Satoh, I.; Yokota, S.; and Idei, T. 1992. Response of differentiating tracheids to stem inclination in young trees of *Taxus cuspidata*. IAWA Bull. 13(2):187–194.

Young, H.E. 1964. The complete tree concept—A challenge and an opportunity. Proc. Soc. Am. For., pp. 231–233.

_____. 1974. Complete tree concept: 1964–1974. For. Prod. J. 24(12):13–16.

Young, H.E., and Chase, A.J. 1966. Pulping hardwoods? Try sulfate process on branches, roots. Pulp Pap. 40(27):29–31.

Young, H.E.; Gammon, C.; and Hoar, L.E. 1963. Potential fiber from red spruce and red maple logging residues. TAPPI 46(4):256–259.

Young, H.E.; Hoar, L.E.; and Ashley, M. 1965. Weight of wood substance for components of seven tree species. TAPPI 48(8):466–469.

Zobel, B.J., and Haught, A.E., Jr. 1962. Effect of bole straightness on compression wood of loblolly pine. N.C. State Coll. Sch. For. Tech. Rep. 15.

Zobel, B.J., and Kellison, R.C. 1972. Short rotation forestry in the southeast. TAPPI 55(8): 1205–1208.

Zobel, B.J.; Jett, J.B.; and Hutto, R. 1978. Improving wood density of short-rotation southern pine. TAPPI 61(3):41–44.

Zobel, B.J.; Kellison, R.C.; and Kirk, D.G. 1972. Wood properties of young loblolly and slash pines. Proc. Symp. Effect of Growth Acceleration on the Properties of Wood, Madison, Wis., M1–22.

Wood properties and modification of quality

PART 2 covers the properties of wood that are important for solid and composite wood products. The effects of moisture and its relationship to dimensional stability are basic concerns when using any forest product. The most-important physical characteristic of wood is its density; thus, its measurement and its relationship to other properties will be discussed. The strength properties of wood are of primary consideration when wood is used as a building or construction material. The explanation of mechanical (strength) properties should provide an understanding of these characteristics, which

▶

are important to wood engineers and architects in the design of wood structures.

Knowledge of the agents that can cause deterioration of wood is particularly vital for those who will be involved in the distribution and use of forest products building materials. Wood structures can be designed to avoid decay and insect attack if users understand the causes of deterioration.

Students interested in the growth of wood and the management of forests for wood production will find the discussion of silvicultural practices to be particularly important. They also need to recognize the importance of moisture, density, and strength of wood when evaluating the forest management practices that may affect these properties.

Part 2 is not an exhaustive discussion of the physical properties of wood. Many topics, such as the relationship of wood to light, sound, heat, and electricity, are not addressed. Its purpose is to provide an overview of the most-important characteristics of wood. More-detailed study of these subjects must be left to other courses and appropriate textbooks.

■

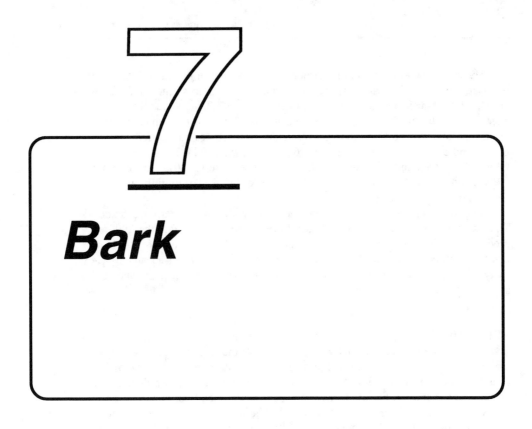

Bark

ALTHOUGH the focus of this textbook is on wood and its utilization, several other components of the tree are both abundant and increasingly valuable. One of these materials is bark, a by-product of wood products manufacture. In 1991 approximately 51 million m³ (or about 16.626 million metric tons, dry weight basis) of bark was delivered to U.S. mills as part of sawlogs, pulpwood bolts, and wood chips. To provide an idea of just how much material this is, it has been calculated that this amount of bark would fill a train of railcars 11,200 km long, which would extend almost two and one-half times the distance from New York to Los Angeles (estimates adapted from Corder 1976). Once considered an expensive and irritating disposal problem, bark is now widely used as an industrial fuel, soil amendment, and ground cover and is a possible source of chemical feedstocks. Most pulp and paper mills, sawmills, and plywood plants today burn all their bark to produce energy to run the plant. This is discussed in Chapter 17.

Structure

In comparison to wood, the cellular structure of bark has received relatively little attention by botanists and wood anatomists. However, though there is still some disagreement as to the precise function of and relation between various bark elements, a generally accepted model of bark structure has evolved. Based

135

on early work by German scientists Holdheide and Huber in the early 1950s and by Esau (1950) and Chang (1954a,b), several investigators, including Esau (1964, 1965), Martin and Crist (1970), and Howard (1971), advanced the knowledge of bark structure considerably. Contributions to the current understanding of bark structure were also made by researchers Hossfeld and Kaufert (1957), Grillos and Smith (1959), Roth et al. (1960), Srivastava (1963, 1964), Whitmore (1963), Northcote and Wooding (1968), Nanko and Côté (1980), Trockenbrodt (1990), and others. The discussion that follows is a synopsis of findings and conclusions of these scientists.

The term *phloem* was used interchangeably with bark in earlier chapters. This usage will now be modified slightly in recognition of the fact that phloem produced by the vascular cambium composes only the inner part of the bark layer. As will be explained, the origin of the outer, rough bark is traceable to activity of a second cambium, called phellogen, that forms subsequent to and outside the true vascular cambium.

INNER BARK. Secondary phloem is a product of the same cambial initials that divide to form cells of the xylem (wood). Because of the common parentage, several types of phloem cells are quite similar to those in the wood. Other types of cells that form from division of these initials are unique to the phloem. The anatomical structure of bark is consequently more complex than that of wood.

Consider the phloem of a softwood. Like the wood, softwood phloem may contain longitudinal and ray parenchyma cells as well as longitudinal and ray epithelial cells. All of these parenchymatous cells are thin walled and generally quite similar to the parenchyma of wood, although they are often shorter and usually unlignified. Cells that are similar to ray tracheids of the xylem (called *albuminous cells*) also occur in softwood bark. A major difference between the structure of wood and bark is that the longitudinal tracheids, which make up some 95% of the volume of softwood xylem, are totally lacking in the phloem. There are, instead, abundant elements known as sieve cells and, in most species, phloem fibers and stone cells (also called sclereids or brachysclereids).

Sieve cells are similar in shape to longitudinal tracheids of the xylem although somewhat shorter; and like tracheids, these cells are a primary avenue of conduction. The similarity ends there, however, as sieve cells have little structural function because walls seldom lignify or form secondary layers. Moreover, movement of fluids through sieve cells occurs only while protoplasm fills the lumens; tracheids lose their protoplasm prior to assuming a conductive role.

Because sieve cells lack secondary wall layers, such cells commonly do not form *pits* (pits, remember, are defined as gaps in a secondary cell wall). Walls of sieve cells are, however, marked by depressed and ultrathin areas, called *sieve areas*, that are perforated by small pores. The pores in adjacent cells are normally aligned, allowing cell-to-cell connection of protoplasm.

Phloem fibers are long, slender, thick walled, and often heavily lignified cells that resemble latewood tracheids of the xylem. These cells serve as structural·elements. From the standpoint of conventional wood products manufacture, phloem fibers appear to constitute the most potentially useful bark fraction. Unfortunately, these fibers compose only a small portion of the bark of some softwood species (usually less than 10% by volume) and are not found at all in the pines.

Sclereids are thick-walled, often irregularly shaped, and highly lignified cells (Fig. 7.1) that typically arise from differentiation of phloem parenchyma cells. They often occur in clusters within the bark.

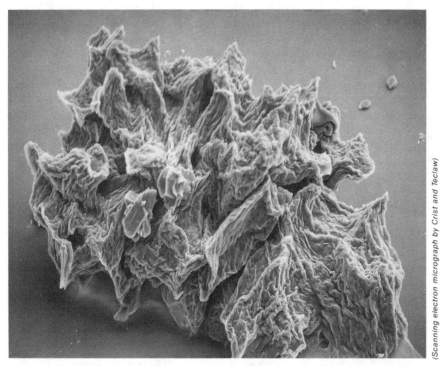

(Scanning electron micrograph by Crist and Teclaw)

Fig. 7.1
A stone cell or brachysclereid
isolated from the bark of red oak (*Quercus* spp.). ×770

Although they compose a small portion of bark, sclereids can cause problems when bark constitutes a significant portion of a pulp mixture. Because they have thick, highly lignified walls, they resist pulping chemicals and can cause accelerated wear of equipment as well as problems with paper drainage, thickness control, and coating.

The inner bark of hardwood species is very similar to that of softwood. Longitudinal and ray parenchyma and phloem fibers occur in hardwood bark, as do cells known as *sieve tube elements*, which are much like the sieve cells of softwood bark, although the hardwood elements have a more-definite structure. They are also comparable to the vessel elements of hardwood xylem, being similarly shaped and arranged end to end with other sieve tube elements. Like vessels, these cells are primary avenues of conduction. Pore-marked end walls called *sieve plates* permit unbroken strands of cytoplasm to extend from sieve cell to sieve cell.

One curiosity of hardwood inner bark is a longitudinal parenchymatous element known as a *companion cell*. Cells of this type are always paired with sieve tube elements and are apparently formed at the same time by the same cambial initials. Companion cells are thought to play a role in regulating functions of the sieve tube elements. A summary of bark elements is presented in Table 7.1.

Table 7.1. Analogous elements of bark and wood in hardwoods and softwoods

Angiosperms (hardwoods)		Gymnosperms (softwoods)	
Phloem or outer bark element	Xylem element	Phloem or outer bark element	Xylem element
Longitudinal			
Sclereids	None	Sclereids	None
Phloem and bark fibers	Tracheids and fibers	Phloem and bark fibers	Tracheids
Sieve tube elements	Vessels	Sieve cells	
Companion cells			
Parenchyma	Parenchyma	Parenchyma	Parenchyma
	Epithelial cells	Epithelial cells	
Transverse			
Ray parenchyma	Ray parenchyma	Ray parenchyma	
		Albuminous cells	Ray tracheids
		Epithelial cells	Epithelial cells
Periderm			
Phellem	None	Phellem	None
Phellogen	None	Phellogen	None
Phelloderm	None	Phelloderm	None

Source: Martin and Crist (1970).

As is the case with softwood bark, the phloem fibers of hardwood constitute the potentially most useful portion of the bark. Hardwood barks, however, contain even fewer fibers than bark of softwood and generally are less than 5% phloem fibers by volume. Table 7.2 presents pulping data for hardwood bark. Note that when the pulp is screened, usable fiber ranges from 0 to 10% of original whole bark entering the process. About a 50% usable xylem fiber yield is normally obtained after kraft pulping of wood.

Table 7.2. Pulp and fiber yield from bark

Species	Pulp yield (bark)	Usable bark fiber*	Sclereids remaining*
		(%)	
Quaking aspen	34	10	1.0
Sugar maple	34	3	0.2
White birch	36	0	0.7
Northern red oak	28	5	0.2
Southern red oak	31	4	0.1
Northern white oak	35	3	0.2
Southern white oak	37	3	0.1

Source: Einspahr and Harder (1976).
*Usable bark fiber and sclereids remaining are the fibers and sclereids retained on the 60- and 100-mesh screens.

The inner bark of both softwood and hardwood is quite thin, ranging from about 0.5 to 15 mm in thickness. This layer, or part of it, serves as the pathway by which sap moves down the tree from the leaves. Esau (1965) estimated that only the most-recently produced layer of bark, a layer some 0.2–0.3 mm thick, functions in this way. Lev-Yadun (1991) uses the term *conducting phloem* to describe phloem that has open pores and is thus able to provide an avenue for conduction. Other cells may die, collapse, or develop closed pores. Movement in the inner bark is occasionally upward, especially in the early spring.

Distinct annual rings of phloem are reported in some species, whereas growth rings in the phloem of other species are either missing or indistinct. In species such as birch or alder that do form distinct rings of phloem, the first part of each ring is rich in sieve tube elements, with more parenchyma in the portion formed later (Huber 1958).

OUTER BARK. A young stem is encased in a layer of primary and secondary phloem, which in turn is covered by a thin epidermis. Because the epidermis is not meristematic and thus cannot grow in size as the tree expands, this layer fractures and peels from the tree, usually in the first year. Before this happens, however, a new meristem forms in the bark and immediately begins to produce a new layer of stem-protecting cells.

The new bark meristem develops from parenchyma cells of the cortex or occasionally from parenchymatous cells of the epidermis itself. A cylinder of such cells only one cell wide becomes meristematic and begins dividing periclinally (tangentially) to form new tissue. This cylinder of cells is called the cork cambium or *phellogen*. As is the case with the vascular cambium, tissue is produced both toward the outside and the inside (pith side) of the phellogen. The result is a three-layered region, a *periderm*, near the stem exterior.

Cells composing a periderm are quite unlike cells of the inner bark (Fig. 7.2). Cells of the outer layer (or *phellem*) are flattened radially; short; and square, hexagonal, or even sprocket shaped tangentially. Walls are thin to very thick, and it is reported that the thin-walled phellem cells tend to be heavily suberized (wax impregnated), whereas the thicker walled elements lignify but lack suberin. This lignified and suberized phellem takes the place of the epidermis in protecting the stem against moisture loss and also serves as a shock-absorbing layer. The innermost layer of the periderm, the *phelloderm*, also contains cells that are square to hexagonally shaped in tangential view and usually, but not always, flattened radially. These provide additional protection against moisture loss. Other cells of the phelloderm are thin walled and greatly expanded in cross section; these are thought to provide thermal protection. A photograph of a periderm (Fig. 7.3) clearly shows the layers described above.

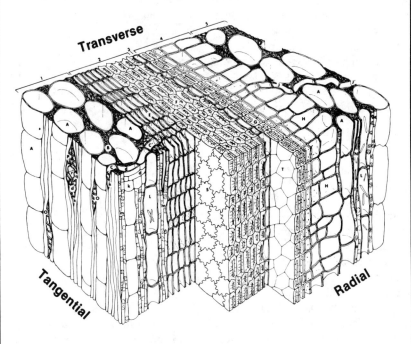

Fig. 7.2

Representation of pine bark

Transverse

Tangential

Radial

1. **Obliterated phloem**
2. **Phellem**
3. **Phellogen**
4. **Phelloderm**
5. **Obliterated phloem (newer layer than #1)**

Transverse view. *1.* – Obliterated phloem: *A*, expanded parenchyma; *B*, crushed sieve cells; *C-C′*, uniseriate ray; *d*, ray parenchyma. *2.* – Phellem: *E*, thin-walled cork (slightly distorted); *F*, thick-walled phellem with pit canals. *3.* – Phellogen (cork cambium). *4.* – Phelloderm: *G*, thickened unexpanded phelloderm with simple pits; *H*, expanded thin-walled phelloderm. *5.* – Newer layer of obliterated phloem: *J-J′*, inner portion of ray *C-C′*.

Radial view. *k*, albuminous cells of ray; *L*, longitudinal parenchyma with styloid crystals; *m*, sieve areas of sieve cells; *N*, sieve cell containing crystals.

Tangential view. *O*, uniseriate rays; *P*, fusiform ray; *q*, epithelial cells; *r*, horizontal resin canals; *TP*, thick-walled phellem; *T*, irregular polygonal phelloderm arrangement.

From Howard (1971)

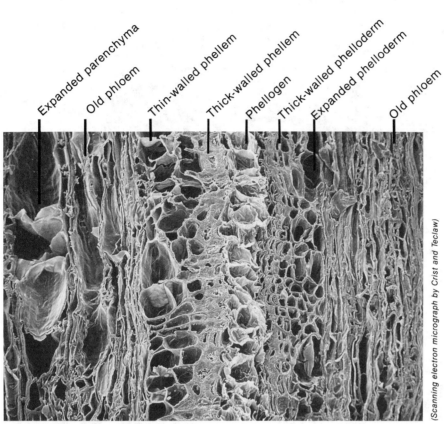

Expanded parenchyma · Old phloem · Thin-walled phellem · Thick-walled phellem · Phellogen · Thick-walled phelloderm · Expanded phelloderm · Old phloem

(Scanning electron micrograph by Crist and Teclaw)

Fig. 7.3
Scanning electron micrograph of periderm region
Red pine (*Pinus resinosa*). ×150

In some species the periderm formed in the first year continues to function for a number of years. In rare cases it may function for the life of a tree. Long-lived periderms are typical of smooth-barked species such as maple and beech. Far more common than smooth bark, however, is rough, ridged, and scaly bark. In these trees a periderm typically functions for only a short time (1–2 years) before being replaced by a new one. Almost invariably, the secondary and subsequent periderm layers form in short, overlapping segments rather than developing as a complete cylinder (Fig. 7.4). These layers are readily visible in the bark of some species (Fig. 7.5).

New periderm-producing phellogen layers form from parenchyma cells of the secondary phloem. Secondary phloem is pushed outward as new phloem is produced by the vascular cambium. At the same time, very thin-walled sieve cells or sieve tube elements become crushed, and some phloem parenchyma cells expand greatly in diameter. This activity results in a rearrangement of bark elements; during this process some parenchyma cells unite into short tangential bands and become meristematic.

Formation of a new periderm cuts off ray contact with the older periderm to

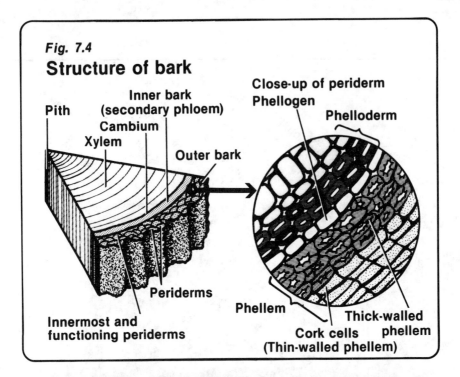

Fig. 7.4
Structure of bark

Pith
Xylem
Cambium
Inner bark (secondary phloem)
Outer bark
Periderms
Innermost and functioning periderms

Close-up of periderm
Phellogen
Phelloderm
Phellem
Cork cells (Thin-walled phellem)
Thick-walled phellem

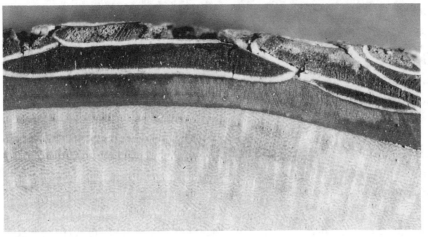

Fig. 7.5
Periderms are clearly visible in bark of American elm (*Ulmus americana*).

(Courtesy Department of Wood and Paper Science, North Carolina State Univ.)

the outside. Because the energy supply is cut off, all tissue outside the innermost periderm is dead. The names *outer bark* and *rhytidome* are both used to refer to all tissue outside the last-formed (functioning) periderm. Included in the outer bark are old periderms and crushed phloem tissue (Fig. 7.4).

Outer bark ranges from relatively thin (1.3–2.5 cm) in some species such as aspen to quite thick (0.3 m or more) in species such as coast redwood and Douglas-fir. Regardless of bark thickness, the bark is never as thick as the pith-to-cambium thickness of xylem beneath it. This is because (1) the vascular cambium produces far more xylem than phloem cells (on the order of 3–10 times more xylem than phloem in softwoods and hardwoods respectively) and (2) thin-walled and unlignified bark cells are crushed during outer bark formation, and (3) outer bark is periodically sloughed from the tree.

Appearance ∎

As Sandved (Sandved et al. 1993) recorded in a series of spectacular photographs, the outer appearance of tree barks differs remarkably from species to species, forming highly contoured and sometimes quite colorful patterns. While barks may appear little different to the casual observer, the nature of bark within a species is often sufficiently unique to allow identification of trees using this feature alone.

The barks of some trees appear green in color. This coloration is sometimes more than cosmetic. Some trees in arid regions, for example, lose their leaves during extended dry periods, thereby preventing excessive moisture loss through transpiration. Those that have green bark, which is traceable to a chlorophyll-rich layer beneath a thin outer covering, are able to continue production of photosynthate even without a canopy of leaves, enhancing chances for survival. This ability is similar to that of desert cacti.

Chemical composition ∎

The lignin content of bark is much higher than that of wood, and the polysaccharide or sugar content is correspondingly lower (Table 7.3). The extractive-free cellulose portion of bark is only 20–35% compared to 40–45% for wood. This provides a partial explanation for the low pulp yields noted in Table 7.2.

Table 7.3. Proximate composition of ash-free wood and bark

	Softwoods		Hardwoods	
	Wood	Bark	Wood	Bark
	(%)		(%)	
Lignin*	25–30	40–55	18–25	40–50
Polysaccharides†	66–72	30–48	74–80	32–47
Extractives†	2–9	2–25	2–5	5–12

Sources: Harkin and Rowe (1971), Harun and Labosky (1985).
*The lignin that is part of bark is somewhat different from the lignin of xylem, the methoxyl content of bark lignin being only about one-half that of xylem lignin.
† Percentages are of extractive-free material.

Because minerals that are important to physiological functions of the tree tend to become concentrated in bark tissue, the ash content of bark is usually higher than that of wood. *Ash content* is defined as the weight of residue remaining, expressed as a percentage of moisture-free weight of wood, after high-temperature burning in the presence of abundant oxygen. (See Chapter 3.) Windborne soil or sand particles that may be trapped in rough outer bark contribute to a high ash content. The ash content of wood is generally less than 0.5%, while that of the bark of softwoods and hardwoods averages 2% and 5%, respectively (Corder 1976). Occasionally, the ash content of bark is quite high; levels up to 20% of dry weight have been reported. Ash levels are significant when considering use of bark as a fuel since high temperature causes formation of slag and clinkers in boilers through melting and fusing of ash.

Extractive content (based on successive extractions with benzene, 95% alcohol, and hot water) of bark is high compared to wood, commonly amounting to 15–26% of unextracted bark weight compared to 2–9% for wood. Bark extractives include various starches, resins, and waxes. A major portion of the extractable chemicals, one-fourth to one-half by weight, is tannic acid, a chemical often used as a component of well-drilling muds to help control viscosity and gel strengths. *Tannic acid* is also used as a tanning agent in the making of leather and as an important additive in the manufacture of inks and dyes. Tannin currently used in most industrial processes such as leather manufacture is chemically synthesized rather than extracted from tree bark. Tannin used in well-drilling mud is, however, often obtained from this source.

A chemical product of bark that continues to have great importance today is *latex*, a polyterpene produced in the inner bark of a number of species of trees and other plants. Today, most natural rubber is made from the latex produced by several species of trees that are cultivated in plantations; the most common is the Brazilian rubber tree (*Hevea brasiliensis*) that is cultivated not only in Brazil and other parts of South and Central America, but also in large areas of Asia as well. Latex production is stimulated by scoring the bark with a machete and then collecting the milky latex—the same material found in the stem of a dandelion. This is later cleaned, dewatered, and dried for shipment to rubber products manufacturers. Over 40% of the rubber produced in the world today is natural rubber made from latex; the rest is butyl rubber, produced from petroleum, natural gas, coal, coke, and even grain.

Water-soluble extractives of most barks range from moderately to highly acidic, with pH values ranging from about 3.5 to 6 (Bollen 1969; Murphey et al. 1970; Martin and Gray 1971). Bark extract is usually more highly acidic than extract from wood of the same species. The acidic nature of bark may require some modifications in processing methods where it is to be used. For example, Chow (1971) reported that resin used in making particleboard would likely require a change in formulation if significant amounts of highly acidic bark were incorporated. Acidity of bark extractives has been variously reported to pose a problem for use of bark as a potting medium, soil amendment, or ground cover. Studies indicate, however, that poor plant performance in some instances is due to low nitrogen content of bark or low nitrogen availability because of nitrogen consumption by bark-destroying fungi rather than to low pH. This kind of situation can be corrected by use of supplemental nitrogen.

Moisture content ■

The moisture content of bark is comparable to that of wood and often exceeds 100% of the ovendry weight. It is calculated by dividing the weight of water present by the moisture-free weight of bark (see Chapter 8). The difference in moisture content between inner and outer bark is considerable (Table 7.4), with an abrupt change between the two layers in some species (Fig. 7.6). Thus the moisture content of whole bark is largely dependent upon the ratio of inner to outer bark. Moisture content is extremely important where use for fuel is considered.

Table 7.4. Moisture content of inner and outer bark of various species

Species	Moisture content	
	Inner bark	Outer bark
Douglas-fir	133	80.3
Hemlock	134	65.2
Silver fir	77.4	39.6
Yellow cedar	145	79.4
Sitka spruce	112	55.3
Redcedar	88.5	37.4
White pine	118	75.3
Grand fir	81	51.4
Lodgepole pine	128	42.2
Ponderosa pine	77.8	21
Western larch	98.6	44
White spruce	104	50
Engelmann spruce	121	60.5
Southern pine	232	27.5
Alder	87.8	66
Black cottonwood	130	77.4
Birch	67.7	22.5
Broadleaf maple	134	70.1
Black cherry	119	41.9
Aspen	121	93.4

Source: Smith and Kozak (1971), except for southern pine (Martin 1963).

Note: Based on samples taken at 1 and 4.5 ft (0.3 and 1.4 m) aboveground.

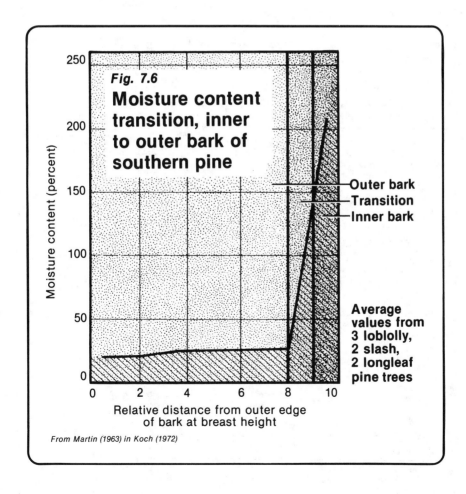

Fig. 7.6
Moisture content transition, inner to outer bark of southern pine

Outer bark
Transition
Inner bark

Average values from 3 loblolly, 2 slash, 2 longleaf pine trees

Moisture content (percent)

Relative distance from outer edge of bark at breast height

From Martin (1963) in Koch (1972)

BARK VOLUME. The ability to calculate bark volume has become more important as the value of bark has increased. Estimation of the quantity of phloem fiber that may appear in a given volume of pulp or computation of the likely contribution of a log shipment to bark fuel requirements at the industrial boiler are examples of situations where accurate measurement of volume is needed. The volume of bark relative to wood is dependent upon species and stem diameter and upon bark thickness. It is possible to estimate bark thickness in standing trees of various diameters by using regression equations such as those in Table 7.5. For example, the *double bark thickness* (DBT) of red oak at a point having a 12-in. *diameter outside bark* (DOB) can be calculated using the following equation:

$$DBT = 0.187 + (0.065 \times DOB) = 0.187 + (0.065 \times 12) = 0.967 \text{ in.}$$

where both DBT and DOB are expressed in inches. When calculating bark thickness in centimeters, the formula $DBT = 0.475 + (0.065)(DOB)$ should be used; DOB should be in centimeters in this case.

Bark thickness of the same species at a 20-in. diameter outside bark is:

$$DBT = 0.187 + (0.065 \times 20) = 1.48 \text{ in.}$$

Note in Table 7.5 that bark thickness is directly proportional to stem diameter in all cases (as indicated by positive regression coefficients).

Table 7.5. Regression of double bark thickness on diameter outside the bark

Species	Constant	Regression coefficient
Western redcedar, coastal*	0.434	0.025
Western redcedar, interior*	0.303	0.041
Yellow cypress*	0.243	0.030
Douglas-fir, coastal*	−0.234	0.139
Douglas-fir, interior*	−0.403	0.170
Alpine fir*	0.051	0.058
Western hemlock, coastal*	0.305	0.044
Western hemlock, interior*	0.043	0.086
Eastern hemlock†	0.183	0.083
Loblolly pine†	0.642	0.086
Lodgepole pine*	0.073	0.039
Ponderosa pine*	0.208	0.103
Eastern white pine†	0.018	0.103
Western white pine*	0.107	0.049
Engelmann/white spruce*	0.149	0.044
Sitka spruce*	0.394	0.009
Red alder*	0.156	0.044
Ash†	0.381	0.048
Trembling aspen*	0.103	0.065
Basswood†	0.048	0.052
Beech†	0.000	0.020
White birch*	0.132	0.051
Yellow birch†	0.145	0.034
Black cottonwood*	0.064	0.081
Hard maple†	−0.058	0.034
Soft maple†	−0.054	0.048
Red oak†	0.187	0.065
Yellow poplar†	0.092	0.083

* J. G. H. Smith and Kozak (1967).
† Adapted from McCormack (1955) using supplemental data from Forbes (1956) and Koch (1971).

Once double bark thickness is known, either from use of the previous equation or by direct measurement at the ends of a log, *bark volume* (BV) as a percentage of *total volume* (TV) of wood plus bark can be calculated (Dobie and Wright 1975):

$$\text{BV as \% of TV} = \frac{\text{DOB}^2 - \text{DIB}^2}{\text{DOB}^2} \times 100$$

where DOB is diameter outside bark, DIB is *diameter inside bark,* and DIB = DOB − DBT.

Similarly, bark volume can be calculated as a percentage of wood volume (WV):

$$\text{BV as \% of WV} = \frac{\text{DOB}^2 - \text{DIB}^2}{\text{DIB}^2} \times 100$$

Continuing the previous example for red oak, double bark thickness at a 12-in. diameter was found to be 0.967 in., so

DIB = 12.00 − 0.97 = 11.03 in.

$$\text{BV as \% of TV} = \frac{(12)^2 - (11.03)^2}{(12)^2} \times 100 = \frac{144 - 121.67}{144} \times 100 = 15.5\%$$

By repeating this procedure at various points along the length of merchantable logs and averaging the results, average bark volumes for various species can be obtained.

Since most bark contains numerous fissures and voids, bark volume percentages, calculated as shown previously, should be adjusted downward to allow for this factor. Using figures such as those presented in Table 7.6, the oak bark volume as a percentage of total wood volume becomes

$$(\text{BV as \% of TV}) \times 1 - \left(\frac{\% \text{ void volume}}{100}\right) = 15.5 \times (1 - 0.203)$$
$$= 12.35\% = \text{adjusted BV}$$

Table 7.6. Void volumes of bark for various species

Species	Bark void volume*
	(%)
Hardwoods	
Ash	13.5, 22.9
Elm	25.1
White oak	22.9
Red oak	11.1, 20.3
Sweet gum	23.7, 30.5
Tupelo gum	18.2, 20.9
Willow	22.4
Softwoods	
Douglas-fir	27
Western larch	28
Ponderosa pine	26

Source: For hardwoods, Cassens (1976); for softwoods, Krier and River (1968).
*Values for ash, red oak, sweet gum, and tupelo gum are given for two Mississippi delta sites in Louisiana. Bark on one of the sites had consistently lower void volumes, which accounts for the two values listed for each for these species.

Unfortunately, void volumes have been calculated for relatively few species and thus estimation of this factor may be necessary.

Although bark thickness typically decreases with increased height in a stem, the proportion of bark often increases with increased height position. Likewise, bark volume usually increases as tree diameter decreases (Table 7.7). In very small branches and twigs, bark may compose more than 70% of the dry weight (see Table 6.4).

Table 7.7. Bark volume

Wood	Diameter of tree		Number of growth rings	Bark volume based on wet log volume
	(in.)	(cm)		(%)
Spruce	4.2	10.7	62	12.06
	8.7	22.1	112	9.26
Fir (true)	4.5	11.4	38	10.0
	8.4	21.3	65	9.4
White birch	3.9	9.9	46	14.5
	8.3	21.1	68	9.5
Yellow birch	4.2	10.7	74	10.1
	9.3	23.6	92	9.3
Beech	4.2	10.7	63	6.9
	8.9	22.6	125	6.1
Sugar maple	4.1	10.4	67	13.5
	7.8	19.8	114	18.0

Source: Harkin and Rowe (1971).

SPECIFIC GRAVITY. Bark of some species has a significantly higher weight per unit volume than the wood. In other species the opposite is true (Table 7.8). Relative specific gravity of inner versus outer bark is also highly variable, with that of outer bark sometimes higher, sometimes lower. Specific gravity of woody materials is calculated by dividing the moisture-free weight of wood, or bark, by the weight of water that would occupy the same volume (see Chapter 9). Increased specific gravity of outer bark caused by compression of dead bark and formation of thick-walled phellem cells is offset by leaching of water-soluble extractives, incipient flaking and scaling, and development of expanded phelloderm cells. Chapters 8 and 9 should be consulted for information on how to convert specific gravity values and moisture content data to bark weights per unit volume.

When bark is ground to a powder before specific gravity is measured (thus removing all void spaces), the values of all barks are virtually the same, and they are essentially the same as the specific gravity of wood measured in the same way. The specific gravity of ground material is about 1.5. This characteristic is discussed in more detail in Chapter 9.

Table 7.8. Comparative specific gravity of wood and bark

	Specific gravity (green volume)			
Species	Wood§	Inner bark	Outer bark	Whole bark‖
Alder*	0.37	0.52	0.62	0.56
Quaking aspen†	0.38	0.40	0.55	0.50
White birch†	0.49	0.57	0.54	0.56
Black cherry*	0.47	0.41	0.77	0.48
Black cottonwood*	0.31	0.41	0.44	0.43
Sugar maple†	0.59	0.69	0.49	0.54
Northern red oak†	0.56	0.53	0.71	0.65
Southern red oak†	0.60	0.72	0.74	0.73
Northern white oak†	0.62	0.60	0.47	0.53
Southern white oak†	0.68	0.69	0.47	0.56
Balsam fir†	0.36	0.32	0.42	0.38
Douglas-fir*	0.45	0.45	0.43	0.44
Western hemlock*	0.42	0.45	0.56	0.50
Western larch*	0.48	0.43	0.35	0.37
Jack pine†	0.43	0.15	0.43	0.34
Ponderosa pine*	0.38	0.36	0.34	0.34
Red pine†	0.46	0.15	0.27	0.24
White pine*	0.35	0.31	0.54	0.49
White spruce*	0.37	0.45	0.50	0.47

* Smith and Kozak (1971).
† Einspahr and Harder (1976).
† Lamb and Marden (1968).
§ Figures corresponding to data from Smith and Kozak and Lamb and Marden were obtained from USFPL (1987).
‖ For Smith and Kozak data, whole bark specific gravity derived by weighting specific gravity for each bark layer by thickness reported for each.

Strength ■

Bark is low in strength compared to wood. Tests by Murphey and Rishel (1977) show considerable differences in the strength of various barks (Table 7.9). The stronger barks, such as hickory, were determined to be very fibrous, whereas low-strength barks tended to have a nonfibrous or conglomerate character. For all species listed in Table 7.9, the compressive strength of bark is far below that of wood stressed parallel to the grain. In some cases, however, values for bark do exceed values for xylem of a different species.

Table 7.9. Mean strength in compression parallel and perpendicular to the longitudinal axis of the tree of mature xylem, phloem, and rhytidome for several species

	Compression parallel (psi)			Compression perpendicular (psi)		
Species	Mature xylem	Phloem	Rhytidome (outer bark)	Mature xylem	Phloem	Rhytidome (outer bark)
Basswood	4730	2000	1200	370	1420	1540
Beech	7300	1100	1030	1010	1540	2390
Elm	5520	2940	1250	690	2630	1910
Hickory	9100	5250	4800	1800	3010	7050
Honey locust	7500	1020	1740	1850	1400	3380
Soft maple	6540	2680	1490	1000	2750	2110
Red oak	6760	1220	1930	1010	1640	2990
White oak	7440	1360	1500	1070	1840	1800
Yellow poplar	5540	1420	900	500	1310	1090
Black willow	4100	1600	1350	430	850	1000

Source: Adapted from Murphey and Rishel (1977); figures for mature xylem are from USFPL (1987).

Because bark strength is generally markedly less than that of wood, significant amounts of bark are seldom used for applications in which high strength is important. When whole tree chips or topwood containing bark are used as raw material for manufacture of a structural product, care must be taken to limit the proportion of bark. An indication of the effect of bark upon strength is provided by data for structural panels made of 100% bark, pressed to a density of 40 lb/ft^3 (640 kg/m^3) and bonded with urea formaldehyde resin (Table 7.10). Commercial standards governing similar products made from wood specify a minimum bending strength of 1600 psi (lb/in.^{2}) and minimum stiffness of 250,000 psi. Note that it is possible to achieve minimum standards in many cases by using high resin levels (5–6% resin is normally used). Other examples of the effect of bark in various products are presented in Chapter 6.

Table 7.10. Strength values for bark boards with a density of 40 pounds per cubic foot made with urea resin

Species	Bending strength (MOR)* resin content		Stiffness (MOE)* resin content	
	5%	10%	5%	10%
	(psi)		*(1000 psi)*	
Basswood	940	2060	104	199
Beech	450	2100	117	312
Black birch	850	400	55	88
Eastern redcedar	1620	1530	197	189
Red elm	710	1260	75	141
White elm	690	1550	84	161
Hemlock	1710	2110	278	318
Hickory	1700	2760	100	190
Black locust	3230	1650	282	138
Red oak	2390	2390	214	219
White oak	1040	1030	97	78
White pine	1370	2420	164	280
Black walnut	1990	2600	214	290

Source: Adapted from Murphey and Rishel (1977).
Note: To convert from pounds per square inch to SI units (Pascals) multiply values by 6.895 × 10^3.
*See Chapter 10 for an explanation of the terms MOR and MOE.

REVIEW

A. Terms to define or explain:

1. Secondary phloem	7. Phellem
2. Sieve cell	8. Phelloderm
3. Phloem fiber	9. Sclereids
4. Sieve tube element	10. Rhytidome
5. Periderm	11. Bark void volume
6. Phellogen	12. Double bark thickness

B. Questions or concepts to explain:
1. What is the difference between inner and outer bark? Structural differences? Functional differences?
2. How does a periderm layer form? For what period of time does a periderm typically function?
3. What are the characteristics of periderms in trees having rough outer bark? In trees characterized by smooth bark?
4. Why are the bark layers invariably thinner than the layers of wood they cover?
5. Of what practical importance are the ash and extractive contents of barks? Of other materials?

REFERENCES

Bollen, W.B. 1969. Properties of tree barks in relation to their agricultural utilization. USDA For. Serv. Pac. Northwest For. Range Exp. Stn. Res. Pap. PNW77.

Cassens, D.L. 1974. Bark properties of eight western softwoods. For. Prod. J. 24(4):40–45.

_____. 1976. Physical characteristics of bark of several delta hardwoods. La. State Univ. Wood Utilization Note 28.

Chang, Y.P. 1954a. Bark structure of the North American conifers. USDA Tech. Bull. 1095.

Chang, Y.P. 1954b. Anatomy of common North American pulpwood bark. TAPPI Monogr. 14.

Chang, Y.P., and Mitchell, R.L. 1955. Chemical composition of common North American pulpwood barks. TAPPI 38(5):315–320.

Chow, P. 1971. The degree of acidity of selected hardwood barks from the Midwest. In Techniques of Processing Bark and Utilization of Bark Products, ed. J. Mater. For. Prod. Res. Soc. Bark Comm. Publ.

Corder, S.E. 1976. Properties and uses of bark as an energy source. Oreg. State Univ. For. Res. Lab. Pap. 31.

Crist, J.B. 1972. Periderm morphology and thick-walled phellem ultrastructure of longleaf pine (*Pinus palustris* Mill.). Ph.D. diss., Virginia Polytechnic Inst. and State Univ.

Dobie, J., and Wright, D.M. 1975. Conversion factors for the forest-products industry in western Canada. West. For. Prod. Lab. Inf. Rep. VP-X-97.

Einspahr, D.W., and Harder, M.L. 1976. Hardwood bark properties important to the manufacture of fiber products. For. Prod. J. 26(6):28–31.

Esau, K. 1950. Development and structure of the phloem tissue. II. Bot. Rev., 16:67–114.

_____. 1964. Structure and development of bark in dicotyledons. In the Formation of Wood in Forest Trees, ed. M.H. Zimmermann. New York: Academic Press, pp. 37–50.

_____. 1965. Plant Anatomy, 2d ed. New York: John Wiley & Sons, p. 302.

Forbes, R.D. 1956. Forestry Handbook. New York: Ronald Press, pp. 1–3.

Grillos, S J., and Smith, F.H. 1959. The secondary phloem of Douglas-fir. For. Sci. 5:377–378.

Harkin, J.M., and Rowe, J.M. 1971. Bark and its possible uses. USDA For. Serv. For. Prod. Lab. Res. Note FPL–091.

Harun, J., and Labosky, P., Jr. 1985. Chemical constituents of five northeastern barks. Wood Fiber Sci. 17(2):274–280.

Hossfeld, R.L., and Kaufert, F.H. 1957. Structure and composition of aspen bark. For. Prod. J. 7(12):437–439.

Howard, E T. 1971. Bark structure of the southern pines. Wood Sci. 3(3):134–48.

Huber, B. 1958. Anatomical and physiological investigations on food translocation in trees. In The Physiology of Forest Trees, ed. K.V. Thimann. New York: Ronald Press, pp. 367–379.

Koch, C.B. 1971. Thickness and specific gravity of inner and outer bark of red oak and yellow poplar. Wood Sci. 3(4):214–17.

Koch, P. 1972. Utilization of the southern pines, Vol. 1. USDA For. Serv. Agri. Handb. 420, pp. 467–533.

Krier, J.P., and River, B.H. 1968. Bark residues: A model study for quantitative determination. Univ. Mont. Sch. For. Bull. 35.

Lamb, F.M., and Marden, R.M. 1968. Bark specific gravities of selected Minnesota tree species. For. Prod. J. 18(9):76–82.

Lev-Yadun, S. 1991. Terminology used in bark anatomy. IAWA Bull. 12(2):207–209.

McCormack, J.F. 1955. An allowance for bark increment in computing tree diameter growth for southeastern species. USDA For. Serv. Southeast For. Exp. Stn. Pap. 60.

Martin, R.E. 1963. Thermal and other properties of bark and their relation to fire injury of tree stems. Ph.D. diss., Univ. of Michigan.

_____. 1969. Characterization of southern pine barks. For. Prod. J. 19(18):23–30.

Martin, R.E., and Crist, J.B. 1970. Elements of bark structure and terminology. Wood Fiber 2(3):269–279.

Martin, R.E., and Gray, G.R. 1971. pH of southern pine barks. For. Prod. J. 21(3):49–52.

Murphey, W.K., and Rishel, L.E. 1977. Properties and potentials of bark as a raw material. Pa. State Univ. Agri. Exp. Stn. Prog. Rep. 363.

Murphey, W.K.; Beall, F.G.; Cutter, B.E.; and Baldwin, R.C. 1970. Selected chemical and physical properties of several bark species. For. Prod. J. 20(2):58–59.

Nanko, H., and Côté, W.A., Jr. 1980. Bark structure of hardwoods grown on southern pine sites. Renewable Materials Institute Ser. 2. Syracuse, N.Y.: Syracuse Univ. Press.

Northcote, D.H., and Wooding, F.B.P. 1968. The structure and function of phloem tissue. Sci. Prog., Lond. 56 :35–58.

Roth, L.; Saeger, G.; Lynch, F.J.; and Weiner, J. 1960. Structure, extractives, and utilization of bark. Inst. Pap. Chem., Bibliogr. Ser. 191.

Sandved, K.J.; Prance, G.T.; and Prancer, A.E. 1993. Bark: The Formation, Characteristics, and Uses of Bark around the World, Portland: Timber Press, Inc.

Smith, J.H.G., and Kozak, A. 1967. Thickness and percentage of bark of the commercial trees of British Columbia. Univ. British Columbia Fac. For. Pap.

_____. 1971. Thickness, moisture content, and specific gravity of inner and outer bark of some Pacific Northwest trees. For. Prod. J. 21(2):38–40.

Srivastava, L.M. 1963. Secondary phloem in the Pinaceae. Univ. Calif. Publ. Bot. 36:1–142.

_____. 1964. Anatomy, chemistry, and physiology of bark. In International Review of Forestry Research, J. Romberger and P. Mikola, eds. New York: Academic Press, pp. 203–277.

Trockenbrodt, M. 1990. Survey and discussion of the terminology used in bark anatomy. IAWA Bulletin 11(2):141–166.

U.S. Forest Products Laboratory (USFPL). 1987. Wood Handbook: Wood as an Engineering Material. USDA For. Serv. Agri. Handb. 72.

Whitmore, T.C. 1963. Studies in systematic bark morphology. IV. The bark of beech, oak, and sweet chestnut. New Phytol. 62:161–169.

Yang, K.C., and Hazenburg, G. 1991. Relationship between tree age and sapwood/heartwood width in *Populus tremuloides* Michx. Wood and Fiber Science 23(2):247–52.

SUPPLEMENTAL READING

Chow, P. 1976. Properties of medium-density, dry-formed fiberboard from seven hardwood residues and bark. For. Prod. J. 26(5):48–55.

Einspahr, D.W., and Harder, M.L. 1980. Increasing hardwood fiber supplies through improved bark utilization. TAPPI 63(19): 121–124.

Emanuel, D.M. 1976. Hydromulch: A potential use for hardwood bark residue. USDA For. Serv. Res. Note NE-226.

Galezewski, J.A. 1977. Method of making cellular materials from red oak bark. For. Prod. J. 27(12):21–24.

Gartner, J.B., and Williams, D.J. 1978. Horticultural uses for bark—A review of current research. TAPPI 61(7):83–86.

Gartner, J.B.; Meyer, M.M., Jr.; and Saupe, D.C. 1971. Hardwood bark as a growing media for container-grown ornamentals. For. Prod. J. 21(5):25–29.

Hall, J.A. 1971. Utilization of Douglas-fir bark. USDA For. Serv. Pac. Northwest For. Range Exp. Stn. Misc. Rep.

Harder, M.L.; Einspahr, D.W.; and Parham, R.A. 1978. Bark fibrous yield for 42 pulpwood species. TAPPI 61(11):121–122.

Hemingway, R.W. 1981. Bark: Its chemistry and prospects for chemical utilization. In Organic Chemicals from Biomass, ed. I.S. Goldstein. Boca Raton, Fla.: CRC Press, pp. 189–248.

Holdheide, W., and Huber, B. 1952. Ähnlichkeiten und unterschiede im Feinbau von Holz und Rinde. Holz-loer kst. 10: 263-268.

Koch, C.B., and Hall, C.S. 1978. Utilization of hardwood bark for production of semi-durable bark-board. W. Va. For. Notes 2 :5–38.

Lightsey, G.R.; Mitchell, J.W.; and Travis, J. 1976. Bark as trickling-filter dewatering medium for primary sludge. For. Prod. J. 26(12):17–21.

McGovern, J. N.; Zehner, C.E.; and Boyle, J.B. 1977. Investigations of bark residues for livestock bedding. For. Prod. J. 27(7):29–34.

Martin, R.E., and Crist, J. 1968. Selected physical-mechanical properties of eastern tree barks. For. Prod. J. 18(11):54–60.

Mater, J., ed. 1974. Technological options in bark utilization. For. Prod. Res. Soc., Madison, Wis. Proc. P-73/74-11.

_____. 1977. Utilizing bark and wood residues to solve technical problems. For. Prod. Res. Soc., Madison, Wis. Proc. P-77-20.

Mater, J., and Mater, M.H. 1976. Technology of utilizing bark and residues as an energy and chemical resource. For. Prod. Res. Soc. Bark Comm. Proc. P-75/76-15.

Panshin, A.J., and de Zeeuw, C. 1980. Textbook of Wood Technology, 4th ed. New York: McGraw-Hill, pp. 49–53.

Rishel, L.E.; Blankenhorn, P.R.; and Murphey, W.K. 1980. A note on the flexural properties of bark board. Wood Fiber 11(4):233–236.

Sarles, R.L., and Emanuel, D.M. 1977. Hardwood bark mulch for revegetation and erosion control on drastically disturbed sites. J. Soil Water Conserv. 32 :209–214.

Tsoumis, G. 1968. Wood as a Raw Material. New York: Pergamon Press, pp. 110–121.

Wood and water

WATER is a natural constituent of all parts of a living tree. In the xylem portion of the stem, water commonly makes up over half the total weight. Stated another way, the weight of water in green wood is commonly equal to or greater than the weight of dry wood substance. When the tree dies or a log is processed into lumber, veneer, or chips, the wood immediately begins to lose some of its moisture to the surrounding atmosphere. If drying continues long enough, the dimensions and the physical properties of the wood begin to undergo change. Some water remains within the structure of the cell walls even after wood has been manufactured into lumber or other wood-based products.

The physical and mechanical properties, resistance to biological deterioration, and dimensional stability of any wood-based product are all affected by the amount of water present. Since almost all properties of wood and wood products are affected by water, it is important to understand the nature of water in wood and how it is associated with its microstructure and properties. Chapter 8 is devoted to this subject and in addition covers some practical aspects of wood drying and dimensional change. For satisfactory use of wood as a raw material, these relationships must be clearly understood.

Location of water in wood ■

Water in green or freshly harvested wood is located within the cell wall and in the cell lumen. The amount of water within the cell wall structure of a living tree remains essentially constant from season to season, although the amount of water in the lumen may vary. The water in the lumen may contain dissolved food materials produced by photosynthesis as well as inorganic compounds. This solution is commonly referred to as *sap*.

When wood is dried during manufacture, all the liquid water in the cell lumen is removed. The cell lumen always contains some water vapor, however. The amount of water remaining in the cell walls of a finished product depends upon the extent of drying during manufacture and the environment into which the product is later placed. After once being removed by drying, water will recur in the lumen only if the product is exposed to liquid water. This could result from placing wood in the ground or using it where it is in contact with rain or condensation.

Figure 8.1 may help in visualizing the location of water in a wood cell. As long as there is any liquid water remaining in the lumen, the wall of the cell will be saturated; i.e., it will contain as much water as it physically can adsorb. (See following discussion.) Most physical properties of wood (other than weight) are not affected by differences in the amount of water in the cell lumen. For example, if the lumen is one-fourth full of liquid water, the cell (and the wood) will have the same strength as when one-half full.

The green cell is illustrated in Figure 8.1A. As green wood begins to dry, water is first removed from the lumen. When wood is dried to the extent that all the water in the lumen is removed, water begins to leave the cell wall. Almost all wood products used in buildings, or where there is no contact with the ground, contain water in the form shown in Figure 8.1B.

The point at which all the liquid water in the lumen has been removed but the cell wall is still saturated is termed the *fiber saturation point* (FSP). This is a critical point, since below this the properties of wood are altered by changes in moisture content. If dry wood is used where it has no contact with a source of liquid water, the amount of water in the wood will always be less than the FSP.

Nature of water in wood ■

To simplify discussion, the liquid water found in the lumen of wood is often referred to as *free water*. The water within the cell wall is called *bound water*. This is an appropriate description, since the free water is relatively easy to remove and so is the first to be lost in the drying process. Bound water is held more tightly because of surface adsorption within the wood structure. The lower the moisture content below the FSP, the more tightly bound is the remaining water.

The water within the cell wall, bound water, is held by *ad*sorption forces,

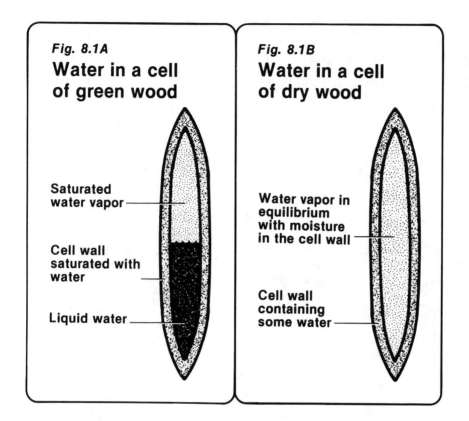

Fig. 8.1A
Water in a cell of green wood

Saturated water vapor

Cell wall saturated with water

Liquid water

Fig. 8.1B
Water in a cell of dry wood

Water vapor in equilibrium with moisture in the cell wall

Cell wall containing some water

which are physicochemical in nature. This is not to be confused with the *ab-sorption* that takes place, for example, when a noncellulose sponge soaks up water. *Absorption* results from surface tension forces. *Adsorption,* in contrast, involves the attraction of water molecules to hydrogen-bonding sites present in cellulose, hemicellulose, and lignin. This hydrogen bonding occurs on the hydrogen side of the OH or hydroxyl group found throughout the chemical elements of wood. Figure 8.2 illustrates where water molecules are held to a segment of a cellulose molecule by hydrogen bonding. The left-hand side of this figure illustrates monomolecular adsorption of water onto the cellulose; the right-hand side shows polymolecular adsorption. In saturated green wood, as many as five or six water molecules may be attracted to each accessible sorption site.

In Chapter 3 the submicroscopic structure of wood was discussed. Recall that the groupings of long-chain molecules in the cell wall contain crystalline and amorphous regions. In the crystalline regions, it is believed that the OH groups of adjacent cellulose molecules are mutually bonded, or cross-linked. Therefore, there are no sites to hold water within the crystallites. Within the amorphous or disordered regions, however, the hydroxyl groups are accessible for adsorption of water. The location of water molecules in relation to the cellulose molecules is illustrated in Figure 8.3.

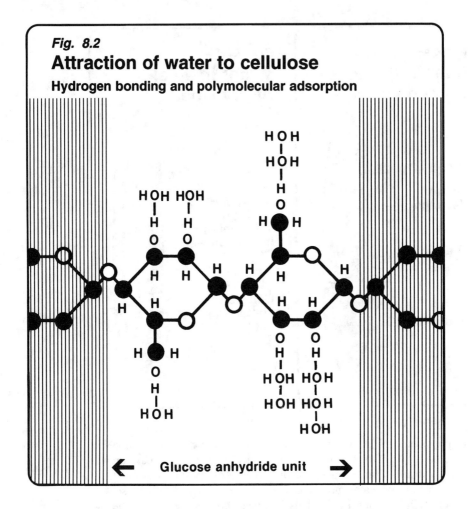

Fig. 8.2
Attraction of water to cellulose
Hydrogen bonding and polymolecular adsorption

← **Glucose anhydride unit** →

Calculating moisture content ■

The amount of water in wood or a wood product is usually expressed as the moisture content. *Moisture content* (MC) is defined as the weight of the water expressed as a percentage of the moisture-free or *ovendry* (OD) weight of the wood. The term weight rather than mass is employed throughout this book to conform to general usage. Thus

$$\% \text{ MC} = \frac{\text{weight of water}}{\text{OD weight}} \times 100$$

Note that because the denominator is the dry weight, not the total weight, the moisture content calculated in this way can be over 100%. In the pulp and paper industry, other practices are used to calculate moisture content, as will be discussed later.

One of the most reliable methods of determining the moisture content is to weigh the wet sample, dry it in an oven at 103 ± 2°C to drive off all water, and

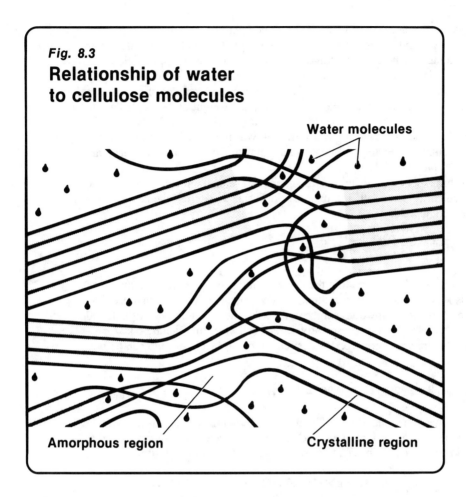

Fig. 8.3

Relationship of water to cellulose molecules

Water molecules

Amorphous region   **Crystalline region**

then reweigh it. The details of this ovendry method are described in American Society for Testing and Materials (ASTM) Standard D 2016. When using the *ovendry method,* the moisture content is computed as follows:

$$\% \text{ MC} = \frac{\text{weight with water} - \text{OD weight}}{\text{OD weight}} \times 100$$

An example may help illustrate how moisture content is calculated. A block of green redwood has a total weight of 970 g. After oven-drying, the weight is 390 g. What was the moisture content when the weight was 970 g?

$$\% \text{ MC} = \frac{970 - 390}{390} \times 100 = 149\%$$

If a similar block of wood with the same ovendry weight is partially dried until the weight drops to 540 g, what is the moisture content?

$$\% \text{ MC} = \frac{540 - 390}{390} \times 100 = 38\%$$

Note that when calculating the moisture content, the amount of water is expressed as a percent of the weight of the dry wood. This method of calculating moisture content is the accepted standard for all lumber, plywood, particleboard, and fiberboard products in the United States and in most of the world. In the pulp and paper industry and when wood is used as a fuel, the amount of moisture is often expressed as a percent of the total weight, i.e., weight of wood plus water. When the wet weight basis is used in this text it is indicated as % MC (wet basis). This is a good practice for you to follow whenever dealing with moisture content calculations. Examples of calculating moisture content on a wet basis are given in Chapter 17.

The basic equation for moisture content can be manipulated to forms that are convenient to use in other situations. For instance, solving the equation for ovendry weight yields

$$\text{OD weight} = \frac{\text{green weight}}{1 + (\% \text{ MC}/100)}$$

This form is useful for estimating the dry weight of green wood when the green weight is known and moisture content has been obtained from a small sample. Example: A load of pulpwood weighs 32,200 lb. The moisture content is found to be 90% by oven-drying representative cross sections from several bolts. An estimate of the dry weight of wood is desired so that the yield of pulp can be predicted.

OD weight = 32,200/(1 + 0.90) = 16,947 lb

In another situation, 400 ft^3 of lumber is to be shipped at a moisture content of 19%. The ovendry weight of a cubic foot of this species (volume measured at 19%) is known to be 47 lb. The total weight of the shipment is desired.

Green weight = OD weight $\times$ (1 + % MC/100)

so

Green weight = (47 $\times$ 400)(1 + 0.19) = 22,372 lb

Consider a situation where 40,000 bd ft of lumber, weighing 3800 lb per 1000 bd ft (MBF) when green, is to be shipped. The shipping cost is $3 per 100 lb. The lumber is estimated to average 60% MC when green. How much money would be saved in shipping cost if this lumber were dried to 15% MC prior to shipping?

OD weight/MBF = 3800/1.60 = 2380 lb
Weight at 15% MC/MBF = 2380 $\times$ 1.15 = 2730 lb
Weight savings/MBF = 3800 − 2730 = 1070 lb
Total weight savings = 40 MBF $\times$ 1070 lb/MBF = 42,800 lb
Savings in shipping cost = 428 $\times$ 3 = $1284

Measuring moisture content ■

The determination of moisture content during manufacture and subsequently to verify conformance to commercial standards is generally accomplished by the ovendry method, described in the preceding section, or by the use of electrical moisture meters, which have the advantage of being relatively simple and direct. Other methods of determining moisture content are sometimes used for research purposes where high precision is required. Such methods are outlined in ASTM D 2016.

The major disadvantages of the ovendry method are (1) that it is a destructive test requiring that a sample be cut from the piece; (2) it can take up to several days to complete; and (3) a few species contain volatile components other than water that can be driven off in the drying process, resulting in an incorrectly high moisture indication. However, for most species of lumber and for a wide variety of wood products, the ovendry method is a more-reliable indication of moisture content than that obtained by using meters or other nondestructive methods.

A variety of electrical meters are available to measure the moisture content of lumber, chips, and particles. Although meters are generally less precise than the ovendry method, their instant readout, ease of operation, and nondestructive nature make them well suited for industrial applications.

The most commonly used hand-held meter for lumber is the *resistance-type moisture meter,* which measures the electrical resistance between pins driven into the wood. This type of meter indicates the moisture content based upon the relationship shown in Figure 8.4. Insulated pins can be used to make it possible to measure the resistance between the tips of the pins and therefore to determine the moisture content at different depths. Moisture meters of the resistance type are generally reliable in the 6–30% moisture content range. Since the electrical resistance of wood varies with temperature, corrections must be made if the wood temperature is significantly different from the calibration temperature indicated by the manufacturer. Also, corrections for species are often necessary, since extractives do influence resistance. Above the FSP, electrical resistance meters give only a qualitative measure of moisture content, so other methods should be used when dealing with green wood.

Some electric meters are based upon the effect moisture has on the behavior of wood as a capacitor when placed in a high-frequency field. The capacitance of wood varies with the density and moisture content. These meters measure the dielectric constant or power loss of the sample. Such meters must be calibrated for each species to account for density differences. The effective range of 0–30% for capacitance/power-loss meters is only slightly greater than for the resistance-type meters. These meters have electrodes that may contact the surface of the lumber or veneer but no pins need be driven, a particular advantage in valuable woods or when greater speed of measurement is needed. However, the proper use of species corrections is more critical with these meters than with resistance meters. Several types of hand-held meters are shown in Figure 8.5.

A number of types of meters used widely in the wood products manufacturing industry measure the moisture content of veneer, particles or fibers that are bulk-piled or on conveyors. The continuous measurement may be accomplished by measuring the water content with a neutron gauge and the total mass with a

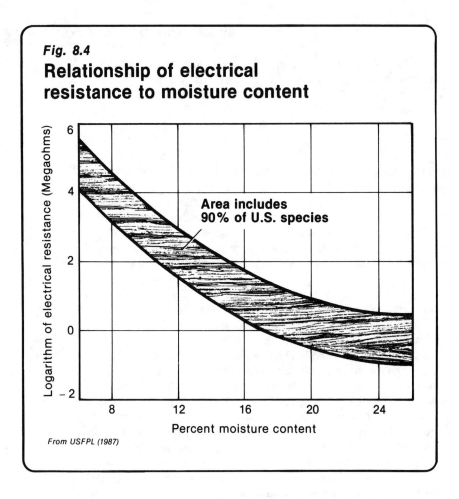

Fig. 8.4

Relationship of electrical resistance to moisture content

From USFPL (1987)

gamma radiation gauge. Wood moisture can also be measured by a microwave power absorption method. Some of these moisture measuring systems are suitable for automatically controlled production processes. Such systems can provide moisture content information to a data file monitoring output of a production line or provide input to a microprocessor used to control the drying process.

Relation of moisture content to the environment ■

Because of the adsorptive nature of wood, it has the ability to remove water vapor from the surrounding air until it is in moisture equilibrium with the air. Thus wood is called a *hygroscopic material.* If wood is in equilibrium with the surrounding environment and the air then becomes drier, it will lose water (or desorb) until it again comes into equilibrium. The term *sorption* is applied to the combined or general phenomena of adsorption and desorption.

The moisture content of wood in equilibrium with a water vapor environment will be less than the FSP. Below the FSP, the forces holding the water to the wood become greater as the moisture content decreases. As wood approaches the

Fig. 8.5
Several types of hand-held moisture meters.

(Courtesy McCarthy Products Co. and Univ. of Minnesota)

dry condition, less polymolecular adsorption and more monomolecular adsorption is involved.

Stamm (1957) stated that monomolecular water is found in wood that is in equilibrium with relative vapor pressure (relative humidity) of 0.2 or less. Between relative vapor pressures of 0.2 and 0.9, most water is held by polymolecular adsorption. Between 0.9 and 0.99, it is believed that some water is held in preexisting capillaries by condensation. Authorities disagree on the extent of capillary-condensed water in wood.

The relationship between the relative vapor pressure in the environment and the moisture content of wood in equilibrium with that environment is not linear. This results from the different ways in which bound water is held. The graph of this relationship at a constant temperature is called a *sorption isotherm*. Isotherms developed for white spruce in 1931 by Seborg and Stamm, two of the first wood scientists, illustrate the shape of the curve that is typical of most species and most wood products (Fig. 8.6). Three curves are shown: desorption, adsorption, and cyclic desorption-adsorption. These show that if a piece of wood has desorbed to an equilibrium point, it may attain a moisture content as much as 3% higher than if it had adsorbed at the same relative vapor pressure. Above a relative vapor pressure of about 0.5, the initial desorption curve of green wood is slightly above that of a previously dried piece.

The difference between the desorption and adsorption curves is referred to as *hysteresis* or lag effect. Hysteresis is common to many types of physicochem- ical phenomena. A rather simplistic view of this complex phenomenon, but one that may help to visualize the dynamic nature of the water-wood equilibrium process, is as follows. In the green condition, the hydroxyl groups of the cellu- losic cell wall are satisfied by water molecules, but as drying occurs these groups move closer together, allowing the formation of weak cellulose-to-cellulose bonds. When adsorption of water then occurs, fewer sorption sites are available for water than was the case originally. Those interested in a thorough discussion of sorption, isotherms, and hysteresis should study Stamm (1964) or Skaar (1972).

In situations where a wood product is subjected to alternating high- and low-humidity conditions, the moisture content will approach the middle curve of Figure 8.6. There is a species effect; a few vary markedly from the typical val- ues shown in 8.6. The general shape of the sorption isotherm for all species is similar, however. The FSP indicated in Figure 8.6 is about 31% moisture content. Thirty percent is a value often used as a typical FSP for wood. Higgins (1957) demonstrated that the FSP varies widely. He also found that the hysteresis effect was considerably greater in some species than in others. One cause of variation in the FSP is the presence of extractives. Species generally high in extractives have a relatively low FSP. The extractives occupy some sites in the cell wall that would otherwise attract water.

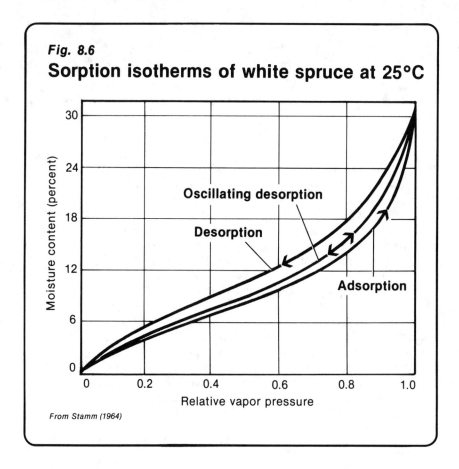

Fig. 8.6
Sorption isotherms of white spruce at 25°C

From Stamm (1964)

Table 8.1. The fiber saturation point of several species

Species	Fiber saturation point
	(% *MC*)
Southern yellow pine	29
Sitka spruce	28
Western redcedar	18
Redwood	22
Teak	18
Rosewood	15

Source: Higgins (1957).

Temperature also has an effect on wood-water relationships. The general relationship is illustrated in Figure 8.7. Note that this temperature effect is relatively small. In addition to this real time effect, high temperatures also have a permanent effect on the wood itself. Wood that has been subjected to temperatures in excess of 100°C for long periods becomes less hygroscopic; i.e., it equalizes at a lower moisture content than normal wood. This is one of the reasons that products such as fiberboard and particleboard have a lower moisture content in any constant environment than do solid wood products. These products are often subjected to temperatures in excess of 150°C during manufacture.

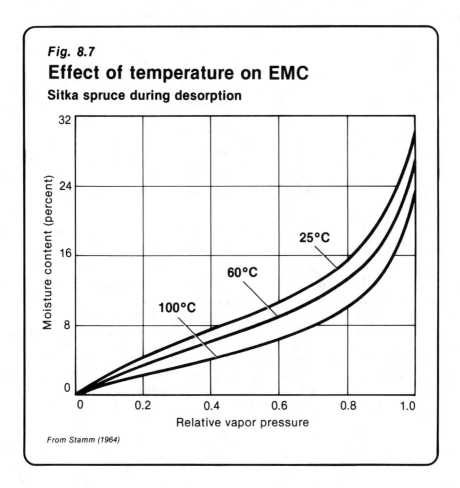

Fig. 8.7
Effect of temperature on EMC
Sitka spruce during desorption

From Stamm (1964)

The moisture content that wood or a wood-based product attains when in an environment of constant temperature and humidity is termed the *equilibrium moisture content* (EMC). Considerable time is required before large pieces of wood will come into equilibrium, i.e., reach their EMC.

It is assumed for most applications and manufacturing considerations that wood attains the same EMC under any given temperature and relative humidity condition. This is done while acknowledging woods variability in sorption and FSP characteristics. A table prepared from data for Sitka spruce is presented in the Wood Handbook (USFPL 1987). Used throughout much of the world to estimate the EMC, it is condensed in Table 8.2.

Table 8.2.   Percent moisture content of wood in equilibrium with dry-bulb temperatures and relative humidity conditions

Dry bulb		Relative humidity							
°F	(°C)	20%	30%	40%	50%	60%	70%	80%	90%
30	(−1)	4.6	6.3	7.9	9.5	11.3	13.5	16.5	21.0
50	(10)	4.6	6.3	7.9	9.5	11.2	13.4	16.4	20.9
70	(21)	4.5	6.2	7.7	9.2	11.0	13.1	16.0	20.5
90	(32)	4.3	5.9	7.4	8.9	10.5	12.6	15.4	19.8
110	(43)	4.0	5.6	7.0	8.4	10.0	12.0	14.7	19.1
130	(54)	3.7	5.2	6.6	7.9	9.4	11.3	14.0	18.2
150	(66)	3.4	4.8	6.1	7.4	8.8	10.6	13.1	17.2
170	(77)	3.0	4.3	5.6	6.8	8.2	9.9	12.3	16.2

Source: Adapted from USFPL (1987).

Note that at 70°F (21°C) the moisture content of wood subjected to relative humidities from 30 to 70% will vary from 6.2 to 13.1%. This is the range of humidity conditions to which most wood is subjected in use. It is therefore the range of moisture content that is normal for wood used indoors where it is protected from contact with water.

Wood products such as plywood and particleboard tend to have slightly lower EMCs than the raw wood from which they are produced. This is because of the effect of heat treatment and also because of the addition of resins, coatings, and sizing materials, which in themselves are usually less hygroscopic than wood. The less the extent of reconstitution involved in the manufacturing process the less the effect on the EMC. For example, plywood and laminated wood products generally have EMC characteristics similar to wood or lumber while fiber and particle products may exhibit considerably different characteristics. Table 8.3 shows EMC values for a softwood plywood, a particleboard, a tempered hardboard, and a decorative laminate as compared to that of solid wood. If accurate EMC information is needed when dealing with a specific forest product, a laboratory determination should be made. Even products of the same type will vary in EMC because of differences in the raw materials used and in the manufacturing process.

Table 8.3. *Equilibrium moisture content of typical forest products at 70°F (21°C)*

Relative humidity	Wood	Softwood plywood	Particle-board	Oil-treated hardboard	High-pressure laminate
(%)			(% MC)		
30	6.0	6.0	6.6	4.0	3.0
42	8.0	7.0	7.5	4.6	3.3
65	12.0	11.0	9.3	6.9	5.1
80	16.1	15.0	11.6	9.5	6.6
90	20.6	19.0	16.6	10.8	9.1

Source: Heebink (1966).

Moisture content of green wood ∎

The moisture content of green wood is important because of its direct relation to the weight of logs and green lumber. Therefore, it is of concern to those who design harvesting and transport equipment, purchase wood on a weight basis, or must ship or transport green wood.

The moisture content of green wood varies considerably among species. Note that among species shown in Table 8.4, the moisture content of heartwood ranges from 33 to 98% and that of sapwood from 44 to 249%. The values in Table 8.4 should be considered as only general indications. Within any species there is considerable variation depending upon the location, age, and volume of the tree. In softwoods the average green moisture content tends to decrease as a tree grows older. There can be a 30% difference in the moisture content of southern pines over 45 years of age compared to trees under 25 years of age (Koch 1972).

Table 8.4. *Moisture content of green wood*

Species	Moisture content	
	Heartwood	Sapwood
	(%)	
Hardwoods		
White ash	46	44
Aspen	95	113
Yellow birch	74	72
American elm	95	92
Sugar maple	65	72
Northern red oak	80	69
White oak	64	78
Sweetgum	79	137
Black walnut	90	73
Softwoods		
Western redcedar	58	249
Douglas-fir	37	115
White fir	98	160
Ponderosa pine	40	148
Loblolly pine	33	110
Redwood	86	210
Eastern spruce	34	128
Sitka spruce	41	142

Source: USFPL (1987).

Within a single tree there is typically a considerable variation in moisture content. The differences between sapwood and heartwood (Table 8.4) are one source of such variation. When wood in the bole of a tree undergoes change from sapwood to heartwood, the amount of moisture in the cell wall may decrease as a result of deposition of extractives. These tend to take the place of water molecules associated with cellulose and hemicellulose. Some extractives may also be left in solution or suspension in the water found in the lumen of the heartwood cells.

Hardwoods generally have only small differences in moisture content between sapwood and heartwood. This contrasts markedly to softwoods, where the moisture content of sapwood is usually much higher than heartwood, often by a factor of three to four. Softwoods have a lower overall moisture content as they grow older because the percent of sapwood volume declines. If you are lost in the woods and forced to build a fire from green wood, try burning the heartwood of a softwood, not a hardwood!

For most design or total weight estimates, the moisture contents of green wood given in Table 8.4 should be adequate. A more complete listing can be found in Table 2.1. Many trade associations and railroads publish lists of weights, by species, for green and dried products such as lumber and poles. Such information may be useful, but if the actual moisture content can be measured, a more-accurate estimate of green weight can be made by using procedures described in Chapter 9.

If green weight is to be used as the basis for purchasing logs or pulpwood, it would be advisable to conduct an on-the-site study of the green moisture content. The effect of the size of the logs or bolts and the season of the year should be determined. The goal of most weight-scaling procedures is to pay a fixed amount per unit of dry wood. Occasionally, adjustments to the price per unit weight may be made for defects, for small diameters, or for the degree of seasoning of the wood.

Little information has been published regarding the seasonal variation of the green moisture content, although many firms and associations have compiled such data. Koch (1972) reported that in southern pine the moisture content of increment cores is higher during midwinter than in summer. In Minnesota, where aspen pulpwood is often purchased by weight, some mills use a weight of 4800 lb during the winter as the equivalent of a cord and 4600 lb as the conversion factor during the summer, reflecting a higher moisture content in the winter. For some other species, a higher moisture content is reported in the summer months.

Shrinking and swelling ■

As wood loses moisture below the FSP, i.e., loses bound water, it shrinks. Conversely, as water enters the cell wall structure, the wood swells. Shrinking and swelling is a completely reversible process in small pieces of stress-free wood. In wood panel products such as fiberboard and particleboard, however, the process is often not completely reversible. This results, in part, from the compression that wood fibers or particles undergo during the manufacturing process.

In large pieces of solid wood, swelling or shrinking may not be completely reversible because of internal drying stresses.

Shrinking of the cell wall, and therefore of the whole wood, occurs as bound-water molecules escape from between long-chain cellulose and hemicellulose molecules. These chain molecules can then move closer together. The amount of shrinkage that occurs is proportional to the amount of water removed from the cell wall. Swelling is simply the reverse of this process. Since the S-2 layer of the cell wall is generally thicker than the other layers combined, the molecular orientation in this layer largely determines how shrinking occurs. In the S-2 layer most of the chain molecules are oriented more or less parallel to the long axis of the cell. Thus both transverse dimensions decrease as these molecules move closer together. For the same reason, the length of the cell is not greatly affected as the cell wall substance shrinks or swells.

In reaction wood and other abnormal wood, the orientation of the microfibrils in the S-2 layer is often at a significant angle from the cell axis. Therefore, as the wood dries there is a measurable shortening of the cell; consequently, longitudinal shrinking occurs. Longitudinal shrinkage in such abnormal wood can be as great as 3% when going from the FSP to the ovendry condition. A 2 × 4-in. stud 8 ft long for the wall of a home would shrink almost 3 in. in length when drying from its FSP to EMC condition if it were manufactured from such material. Fortunately, such lumber is rarely encountered.

Shrinking and swelling are expressed as a percentage of dimension before the change occurred. Thus

$$\% \text{ shrinkage} = \frac{\text{decrease in dimension or volume}}{\text{original dimension or volume}} \times 100$$

$$\% \text{ swelling} = \frac{\text{increase in dimension or volume}}{\text{original dimension or volume}} \times 100$$

The longitudinal shrinkage of normal wood is negligible for most practical purposes. This is one of the characteristics that makes lumber and lumber products such useful building materials. If this were not so, the change of moisture content during use could be disastrous. Usually, some longitudinal shrinkage does occur in drying from the green to the ovendry condition, but this amounts to only 0.1–0.2% for most species and rarely exceeds 0.4%.

From an idealized "soda-straw" concept of wood, one might visualize that the radial and tangential dimensions would shrink or swell the same amount. However, tangential shrinkage is greater than radial shrinkage by a factor between 1.5 and 3.0. Several anatomical traits are believed responsible for this differential, including presence of ray tissue, frequent pitting on radial walls, domination of summerwood in the tangential direction, and differences in the amount of cell wall material radially versus tangentially. The average transverse shrinkage values of a number of domestic and imported species are shown in Table 8.5. These values are good guidelines to use for estimates of dimensional behavior; however, the actual shrinkage of individual pieces in service may vary significantly from these averages.

Variation in the shrinkage of different samples of the same species under the same conditions results primarily from three factors:

Table 8.5. Shrinkage values of wood from green to ovendry moisture content

Species	Radial	Tangential	Volumetric
		(%)	
Domestic hardwoods			
White ash	4.9	7.8	13.3
Quaking aspen	3.5	6.7	11.5
Yellow birch	7.3	9.5	16.8
American elm	4.2	9.5	14.6
Sugar maple	4.8	9.9	14.7
Northern red oak	4.0	8.6	13.7
Black walnut	5.5	7.8	12.8
Imported hardwoods			
Apitong	5.2	10.9	...
Balsa	3.0	7.6	...
Mahogany	3.0	4.1	...
Teak	2.5	5.8	...
Khaya (African mahogany)	2.5	4.5	...
Softwoods			
Western redcedar	2.4	5.0	6.8
Coast Douglas-fir	4.8	7.6	12.4
White fir	3.3	7.0	9.8
Western hemlock	4.2	7.8	12.4
Loblolly pine	4.8	7.4	12.3
Sitka spruce	4.3	7.5	11.5

Source: USFPL (1987).

* % Shrinkage = $\frac{\text{change in dimension}}{\text{green dimension}} \times 100$

1. *The size and shape of the piece.* This affects the grain orientation in the piece and the uniformity of moisture through the thickness.

2. *The density of the sample.* The higher the density of the sample, the more it will tend to shrink.

3. *The rate at which the sample is dried.* Under rapid drying conditions, internal stresses are set up because of differential shrinking. This often results in less final shrinkage than would otherwise occur. In contrast, however, some species shrink more than normal when dried rapidly under high-temperature conditions due to the collapse of some cells.

Shrinking of lumber during the manufacturing process is significant and must be considered when determining the size of the piece to saw from a log. For example, if a nominal 2 × 10-in. Douglas-fir plank is to be sawn from a log, it must be expected that it will shrink about 0.05 in. in thickness and 0.4 in. in width when it is dried to 15% MC. Since the final dry and surfaced size of that piece must be at least 1.50 × 9.25 in. to meet softwood lumber standards, adequate shrinkage allowance must be provided. Allowance must also be made for sawing variability and surfacing. Some softwood sawmills use a target sawing size of 1.8 × 9.9 in.

The amount of shrinkage is generally proportional to the amount of water removed from the cell wall. This suggests that higher-density species should shrink more per percent moisture content change than lower-density species. This is generally the case. Note that high-density woods lose a greater amount of water per percent moisture content change. As an example, sugar pine contains about 0.34 g ovendry wood substance per cm³, while the same volume of long-leaf pine contains about 0.54 g dry wood substance. If each of these woods loses 10% MC, the sugar pine will lose 0.034 g water per cm³, but longleaf pine will lose 0.054 g per cm³. The normal volumetric shrinkage, green to ovendry, for sugar pine is 7.9%, while that for longleaf pine is 12.2%. In this example, there is a close relationship between the amount of water lost per unit of moisture content change and the resulting shrinkage.

Often, there is a much less direct relationship between the mass of water removed and the resulting shrinkage than in the above example. One would expect, based upon the density difference, that black walnut containing 0.55 g dry wood substance/cm³ would shrink more than eastern cottonwood containing 0.40 g wood/cm³. However, the average green to ovendry volumetric shrinkage of walnut is only 12.8% compared to 13.9% for cottonwood. A major factor that tends to mask the effect density has upon shrinking and swelling is the presence of extractives, which tend to lower the FSP and bulk the cell wall. Because of this, the heartwood of some species is more dimensionally stable than the sapwood.

The relationship between shrinkage and moisture content is essentially linear. Figure 8.8 shows the shape of the curve for southern pine. This near linearity makes it relatively simple to estimate shrinkage between any two moisture contents if the green to ovendry shrinkage values for the wood are known. The rationale for such a calculation is shown in Figure 8.9, which illustrates the shrinkage expected in the tangential dimension of loblolly pine when dried from 15 to 8% MC. The rate of tangential shrinkage for this species is 7.4/30, or 0.25% shrinkage per percent of moisture content change. This assumes that the FSP is 30%, a reasonable assumption in most situations. Since the moisture content change is 7%, the total shrinkage expected is about 7 × 0.25, or 1.75%. If the piece were dried from the FSP (30%) to 8% MC, the predicted shrinkage would be 22 × 0.25, or 5.5%. Note that when drying from a higher moisture content, such as 50% to 8%, the predicted shrinkage would also be 5.5%, since it is assumed that shrinkage does not commence until the wood is dried to the FSP. The estimate of radial shrinkage from 15 to 8% MC would equal 4.8/30 × 7, or 1.1%.

In actual practice, the shrinkage of a board may commence before the average moisture content drops below the FSP. This is a result of shrinking in the surface layers of wood that have dried while the core was still wet. However, this need not be considered in general practice when estimating shrinkage as described above.

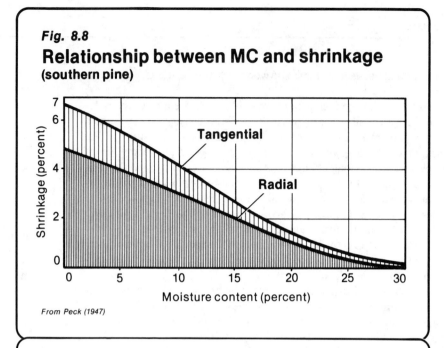

Fig. 8.8

Relationship between MC and shrinkage
(southern pine)

From Peck (1947)

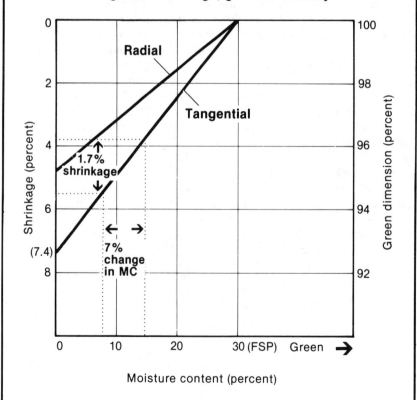

Fig. 8.9

Estimating shrinkage and change in size
**for loblolly pine with 4.8% radial
and 7.4% tangential shrinkage, green to ovendry**

Dimensional changes and environmental conditions ∎

It follows from the previous discussion that wood used where the humidity fluctuates, as it does in almost all use situations, will continually change moisture content and therefore dimension. If humidity changes are small, these dimensional changes will not be noticed and will have no impact on satisfactory use. Even large fluctuations in humidity may have little effect if these conditions last for only short periods (hours or days) and the wood does not have time to come to the new EMC. Problems can arise, however, when a wood product is used under humidity and temperature conditions that cycle over long periods of time if the user of that product has not anticipated changes in dimension.

For the most trouble-free use of wood, the goal should be to fabricate it at the moisture content it will average during that application. Of course, this is not always possible. Framing lumber for light-frame wood buildings, as an example, is commonly manufactured at from 15 to 19% MC, a moisture content that is 5–10% above that to which it will eventually equilibrate in most areas of the United States. This is usually not a problem, because small changes in the dimensions of studs, rafters, and floor joists are not noticeable. The U.S. standards for the manufacture of softwood lumber (ALSC, 1994) specify a small percentage of shrinkage in use, which is to be considered acceptable. If green framing lumber is used, however, the dimensional changes may be large enough to cause problems such as cracked plaster, nail popping in gypsum walls, noisy floors, and distortion of wall surfaces.

For interior uses such as furniture and millwork, it is much more critical for satisfactory performance to use lumber at the proper moisture content. The objective in drying wood to be used in such products is to dry to a moisture content that is within the range of the EMCs experienced in service. Heated spaces in winter may experience EMC conditions as low as 1–3%, while under air-conditioning in summer, the same species may have EMC conditions of 11–13%. As a result, the recommended moisture content for wood to be used indoors is 6–8%. For demanding situations, where dimensional changes could obviously cause problems, the designer or user should carefully consider the moisture content of the lumber being used, the species, the conditions of use, and the amount of dimensional change that should be expected.

The following examples illustrate the type of cases deserving careful consideration. These will also serve to show procedures that can be used for estimating dimensional changes.

EXAMPLE 1: A gymnasium floor was constructed with wood strip flooring nailed tightly in such a way that essentially no cracks or spaces were left between the strips. The size of the gymnasium was 50×120 ft, with the strip floor laid parallel to the long axis of the gym. The flooring was of hard maple (sugar maple) dried to a uniform 6% MC. The flooring was nailed to 2×4-in. wood nailer strips attached by mastic to a concrete slab. Less than 1 in. of space for expansion was left between the wood strip floor and the concrete block wall. Unfortunately, the wood floor was nailed before the concrete floor had completely dried. Under these conditions, the moisture content of the maple increased to about 9%.

Within a short time after the floor was installed, it began to buckle; i.e., ridges began to develop where the strip flooring raised and pulled off the nailers. What was the source of the problem and how could it have been avoided? The buckling was the result of transverse swelling in the floor that was restrained at the edges so it could not remain flat. The only way for the flooring to accommodate swelling was to move upward or buckle.

The contractor could have anticipated this problem by estimating the amount of swelling that might be involved. Assuming that the wood would swell the average of the radial and tangential values (see sugar maple, Table 8.5), it would swell (4.8% + 9.9%)/2, or 7.4%, in going from an ovendry condition to the FSP. In this situation, the moisture content changed only 3%, so the anticipated swelling would be 3/30 or 10% of the total possible swelling. This then would amount to 0.1 × 7.4, or 0.74%. The total swelling that could be anticipated across the 50-ft-wide (600-in.) gym is 600 × 0.74%, or 4.4 in. Since this potential swelling is considerably greater than the expansion space available, a problem of this type should have been foreseen. The problem could have been prevented by being sure the concrete floor was adequately dry before laying the wood floor, thus avoiding the 3% moisture pick-up.

EXAMPLE 2: Rough-sawn western hemlock lumber paneling ¾ in. thick by 7¼ in. wide, with square edges, was used as paneling in an office building. When installed, the pieces were nailed as close together as possible. Cracks between the individual pieces were not over ¹⁄₁₆ in. and were not considered objectionable in view of the rough-natural appearance of the wall. The lumber was stored in the basement of the building for 2½ months during the summer prior to installation. During the that time it equilibrated to the 70°F and 70% relative humidity (RH) conditions. After the paneling was installed, the conditions in the heated building during the winter averaged 70°F and 20% RH. If the paneling was flat sawn (the width of the face in the tangential plane), what width of crack could be expected between each piece after shrinking had occurred down to the lower EMC condition?

EMC @ 70°F and 70% RH = 13.1% MC (see Table 8.2)
EMC @ 70°F and 20% RH = 4.5% MC
% MC change = 13.1 − 4.5 = 8.6%
Shrinkage green to OD = 7.8% (see Table 8.5)
% Shrinkage expected = 8.6/30 × 7.8 = 2.2%
Shrinkage per piece (average width of cracks) = 2.2% × 7.25 in. = 0.16 in.

In the real-life situation, the cracks averaged about 0.12 in. The difference between the 0.12-in. shrinkage actually encountered and the 0.16-in. estimate was probably because some of the pieces were not flat sawn. Therefore, some radial as well as tangential shrinkage was experienced. These cracks were considered unacceptable, and a large claim was filed against the building materials supplier. The fault lay with the contractor, who stored the material in the humid environment prior to installation.

EXAMPLE 3: A large Douglas-fir timber (8 × 12 in. actual size) was used as a mantle over a fireplace. The timber extended across the entire end wall of the room and the ends of the timber were plastered into the adjacent walls. Solid-sawn timbers cannot be purchased dry. In this case, the timber was green (actually about 45% MC) when installed. The radial face of the timber was in the 12-in. dimension, and the 8-in. dimension was the tangential surface of the wood. During a normal year, the conditions in the house averaged 70°F and 30% RH. How much could it be expected that this timber would shrink in use, i.e., how big a gap in the plaster would develop at each end of the mantle?

EMC @ 70°F and 30% RH = 6.2% MC
% MC change through which shrinkage would occur = 30 − 6.2 = 23.8%
% Radial shrinkage green to OD = 4.8%
% Tangential shrinkage green to OD = 7.6%
% Radial shrinkage green to 6.2% MC = 23.8/30 × 4.8 = 3.8%
% Tangential shrinkage green to 6.2% = 23.8/30 × 7.6 = 6.0%
Radial shrinkage = 3.8% × 12 in. = 0.46 in.
Tangential shrinkage = 6.0% × 8 in. = 0.48 in.

Thus a gap about ½ in. wide could be expected to develop at each end of the mantle where it was plastered into the wall. In the actual situation these cracks measured about ⅜ in. wide. The moisture gradient and drying stresses in this large timber restricted the total shrinkage.

EXAMPLE 4: A wooden dowel manufacturer normally dries the northern red oak dowel blanks to 8% MC prior to turning them to the desired diameter. One purchaser of dowels was very concerned that they be round. Thus specifications called for dowels that were round within 0.02 in. when at 8% MC. This purchaser was less concerned with the actual diameter of the dowels. During the manufacture of a shipment of ¾-in. diameter dowels for this customer, the manufacturer had a problem with the dry kiln, and the blanks were dried only to 11% MC. If the dowels were turned at this moisture content, could the manufacturer be confident that the dowels would meet the out-of-round specification of 0.02 in. when they dried further to 8% MC?

% Radial shrinkage = 4% (green to OD) (see Table 8.5)
% Tangential shrinkage = 8.6% (green to OD)
% MC change = 11 − 8 = 3%
% Actual radial shrinkage expected = 3/30 × 4 = 0.4%
Radial shrinkage = 0.4% × 0.75 in. = 0.003 in.
Tangential shrinkage = 0.86% × 0.75 in. = 0.0065 in.

Therefore, the dowels will be out-of-round by only about 0.003 in. (0.0065 − 0.0030) after they have redried. Thus there appears to be no problem in meeting this specification if the dowels are, in fact, round immediately after machining.

These examples illustrate some practical uses for knowledge of the EMC and shrinkage behavior of wood. Although these procedures give only an estimate of what will actually occur, this is often sufficient to avoid costly and wasteful problems in manufacture and use.

Dimensional changes in veneer, fiber, and particle panel products ■

The shrinking and swelling characteristic of wood shown in Table 8.5 and used in the examples above are determined from measurements on small samples 2.5 cm square and 10 cm long. Such samples are cut so that the radial or tangential dimension to be measured is in the 10-cm dimension of the specimen. Because of the small size of the specimen and the fact that it is only 2.5 cm long in the longitudinal direction, drying occurs rapidly and uniformly throughout the sample. This avoids a large moisture content gradient from surface to center that could cause internal stresses. Therefore the shrinking/swelling values obtained are those exhibited under unrestrained conditions.

The dimensional stability characteristics of most lumber products correspond closely to these unrestrained values for wood. Products such as solid wood furniture, millwork, laminated beams, and construction lumber all behave in a similar way in regard to *radial, tangential,* and *longitudinal shrinking.* Forest products produced from veneer, particles, and fiber, in contrast, have unique dimensional behaviors under moisture change. These differences from solid wood result basically from three causes: (1) the degree of restraint to swelling provided by one element in the product to other elements in the product; (2) the degree of compression or crushing the wood elements (veneer, particle, or individual fibers) undergo during the manufacture of the product; (3) and the effect adhesives and other additives have on the ability of the elements to respond dimensionally to moisture change. In some cases these additives bulk the cell walls to some degree, thus lowering the EMC of the wood itself. Each of these factors is discussed below.

Plywood is produced by gluing together veneers, generally ⅛ in. or less in thickness, in such a way that in alternate layers (veneers) the longitudinal direction is at 90° to the adjacent layer. Construction of three-ply plywood is shown in Figure 8.10. If the veneers are not glued together, they can shrink or swell as normal wood. However, when glued into plywood, the face veneers restrain swelling of the core veneer in its transverse direction, while the core restrains the swelling of the faces in their transverse direction. As a result, plywood is a very dimensionally stable product in the plane of the panel. It exhibits much less dimensional change in either direction than normal radial or tangential characteristics of the species. It will shrink or swell slightly more, however, than the normal longitudinal change for the species. Dimensional changes in plywood, even though small, do occur. It is therefore advisable to leave a gap between adjacent 4 × 8-ft sheets when covering a wall or floor. Manufacturers supply specific instructions in this regard.

The second factor affecting the swelling characteristics of wood-based panel products is the amount of compression the product undergoes during manufacture. The thickness swelling or shrinking of plywood with moisture change is about the same as that of normal solid wood, since little compression occurs. However, in some cases, thickness swelling in plywood may be slightly more than normal wood if excessively high pressures occurred during the pressing process. Wood that is compressed will tend to partially recover its original dimension when rewet.

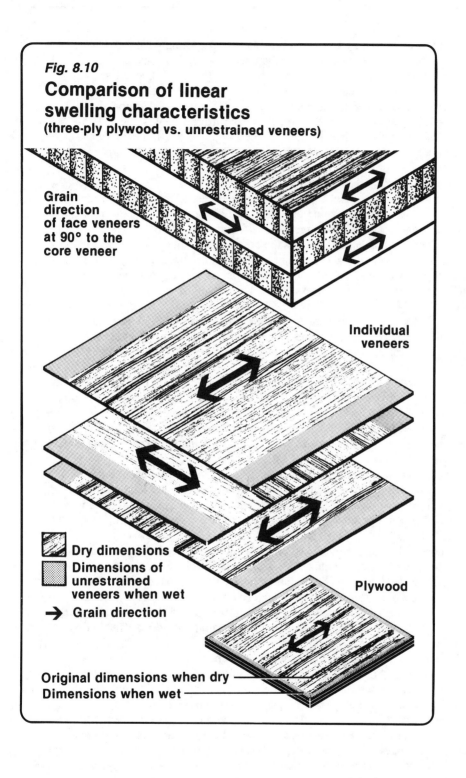

Fig. 8.10

Comparison of linear swelling characteristics
(three-ply plywood vs. unrestrained veneers)

Grain direction of face veneers at 90° to the core veneer

Individual veneers

Dry dimensions

Dimensions of unrestrained veneers when wet

→ Grain direction

Plywood

Original dimensions when dry

Dimensions when wet

A dent in wood furniture can often be removed by steaming. The crushed wood tends to recover its original shape. Much the same thing can happen to an entire panel of particleboard. In the manufacture of particleboard, small shavings, flakes, or wafers of wood are sprayed with droplets of a synthetic resin adhesive. These particles are compressed from 1.2 to 2.0 times their original density, and simultaneously the resin is cured. If such a product is subjected to steaming or other moisture content increases, the wood will swell in the normal way, and in addition the crushed particles will tend to return to their original thickness. For this reason compressed wood–based panel products often exhibit greater thickness swelling than normal wood.

The third factor is the amount of additives in the product. Synthetic resin adhesives and waxes are the most-common additives. The wax (or size) is intended to provide resistance to liquid water pick-up. Wax does not bulk the cell wall or change the ultimate EMC but rather helps the product shed liquid water, making it water-repellent. Synthetic adhesives can, however, alter the recovery of the crushed particles or fibers. Generally, the greater the amount of adhesives used to manufacture a panel product, the less the thickness swelling response to moisture pick-up.

Not only are the wood elements in a product held more tightly when more resin is used, but some resin may penetrate into the cell walls and provide a degree of *bulking,* or replacement of water molecules. Figure 8.11 shows this effect in a wafer-type particleboard. The A board was made with 3% phenolic resin, and boards B and C were made with 10% phenolic resin. In the case of board B, 7% of the total 10% resin was applied to green particles so that the resin could more easily enter the cell wall structure. In board C, all the resin was applied to dry particles. Note the difference in thickness between board types when wet and also how much of the swelling was irreversible, i.e., remaining after the panels were redried.

Figure 8.12 shows the dimensional change in the plane of the panel in this same experiment. Note that after moisture cycling, the panel was actually smaller in the plane of the panel than it had been. This type of behavior is often found in particle- and fiberboard products. Generally, this effect is so small that it is not noticeable.

Most fiber and particle products are manufactured under commercial or industry standards, which place limits on the swelling properties. Specific property limitations in the standards vary depending upon use of the product. For example, in the commercial standards for particleboard, limits are set on *linear swelling* (in the plane of the panel), ranging from 0.25 to 0.55%. There is no specification as to thickness swell. In the product standard for *hardboard* (a high-density wood fiber product), there are limits for thickness swell ranging from 8 to 30% but no specification as to linear swelling. Users of wood-based products should obtain data on dimensional characteristics of the specific product they are to use from the manufacturer. Products of the same type but from different manufacturers can vary considerably in this regard. Dimensional changes can almost always be accommodated by proper design, which considers whether the product is to be used for furniture, case goods, residential construction, or millwork. If dimensional changes are not anticipated, however, problems can arise.

Since plywood is a relatively stable product and its dimensional characteristics cannot be easily altered by manufacturing variables, there are no specifica-

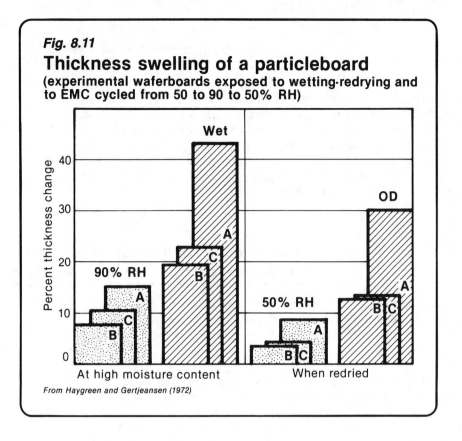

Fig. 8.11

Thickness swelling of a particleboard
(experimental waferboards exposed to wetting-redrying and to EMC cycled from 50 to 90 to 50% RH)

From Haygreen and Gertjeansen (1972)

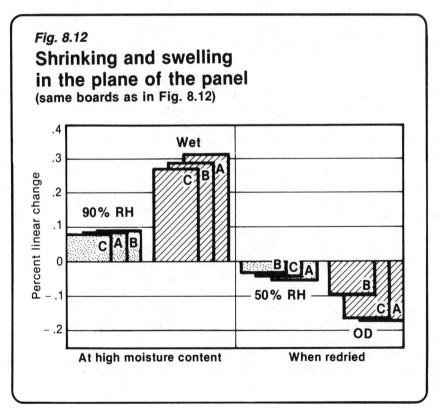

Fig. 8.12

Shrinking and swelling in the plane of the panel
(same boards as in Fig. 8.12)

tions in the plywood product standard as to dimensional stability. However, O'Halloran (1975) provided some helpful guidelines. He pointed out that about 0.2% of shrinking or swelling may occur for each 10% change in the relative humidity. Hygroscopic expansion of plywood consists of a uniform percentage of swelling or shrinking across the width or length or the panel plus an edge effect, which is independent of panel size. For a typical panel the edge effect is about 0.002 in. for each 10% increase in relative humidity.

Means of reducing moisture-induced dimensional change in wood products ∎

There are several means of reducing dimensional change of wood resulting from changes in moisture content. None of these can entirely eliminate dimensional change, but some come very close. Four approaches to reducing dimensional change are as follows:

1. *Preventing moisture sorption by coating the product.* This is a common but not completely effective method. Coatings include pigmented paints, clear finishes, synthetic resin of other types, and metallic paints. None of these will completely prevent the movement of water vapor but will slow the rate of diffusion. Some are effective in preventing the pick-up of liquid water. Proper coatings may be sufficiently effective to prevent dimensional problems in exterior siding and panel materials. It should be understood that regardless of the coating, coated wood will eventually attain the same EMC as uncoated wood if exposed for an adequate period.

2. *Preventing dimensional change by restraint that makes movement difficult or impossible.* The problem with this approach is that internal pressures are built up if wood attempts to swell but is prevented form doing so. These pressures may result in distortion of shape. The buckling of plywood on a roof or wall, which can occur if panels are not properly spaced, is an example of a response to swelling pressure. The restraint method can be used successfully, however, in some situations. For example, particleboard underlayment will exhibit little linear dimensional change if glued to the plywood subfloor beneath it. In this case, the swelling stresses in the particleboard are much less than the strength of the plywood itself.

3. *Treating wood with material that replaces all or part of the bound water in the cell wall* is a commercial means of stabilization. Such treatments are applied to wood when it is still green. The treating material remains within the cell wall as the wood is dried. This bulks the cell wall, retaining it in a partially swollen condition. The reduction in shrinkage from such treatments varies from about 30 to 90%. These treatments add up to 35% of the weight of the product, are generally expensive, and may adversely affect finishes applied to the final product. Thus they are used only for special products.

Several effective methods of treatment based upon this principle of bulking, i.e., replacing water molecules in the cell wall with other materials, have been developed. One of the first successful applications of this approach utilized phenol formaldehyde resin, which impregnated the cell wall. The resulting product was termed Impreg. Another product, polyethylene glycol (PEG), is used to stabilize a wide variety of wood products from wood carvings to gunstocks. PEG is a waxy substance that, when dissolved in water, can impregnate the wood. A simple soak is ordinarily used for treatment with PEG.

4. *Treating wood to produce mutual cross-linking of the hydroxyl groups in the cell wall* has been used experimentally with success. *Cross-linking* reduces the hygroscopicity of wood by reducing the bonding sites for water in the cell wall. Although not being used commercially today, means of accomplishing cross-linking are being studied.

Moisture movement during the drying process ∎

The movement of water in wood during drying takes place as mass movement of liquid water or diffusion of individual water molecules. Diffusion involves both bound water in the cell walls and vapor in the lumen.

Diffusion is a phenomenon that occurs as water moves from an area of higher concentration to one of lower concentration. Thus, to have diffusion occur, there must be a moisture gradient or a vapor pressure gradient across the cell walls. The rate of diffusion is related to the temperature, the steepness of the moisture gradient across the cells, and the characteristics of species that determine the ease with which diffusion can occur. The rate of diffusion in a species can be expressed as the diffusion coefficient. Diffusion through individual cells occurs only below the FSP, since above that level the walls are saturated and thus no moisture concentration gradient exists as a driving force. Above the FSP, free water moves out of wood as a result of surface drying and capillary forces. At that stage of drying, wood can be thought of as a series of partially filled tubes, with water evaporating from one side.

The rate at which lumber dries is determined by the rate at which water is removed from the surfaces and the rate of mass movement to the surface, i.e., diffusion. In the initial stages the rate of drying is often controlled by surface evaporation and in later stages by the diffusion characteristics.

In some species the structure of wood inhibits the mass movement of liquid water. Such woods are referred to as *impermeable.* Tyloses, aspirated pits, and deposition of extractives on pit membranes are examples of wood features that inhibit movement of water. In woods with these structures, the movement of water must be principally by diffusion; thus, drying is an extremely slow process. Redwood, white oak, and walnut are a few of the species having relatively impermeable heartwood. Sapwood is generally *permeable* in all species. Other species such as western hemlock and aspen contain pockets or localized zones that are impermeable. After drying, these latter woods may still contain wet spots. These impermeable wet areas are subject to drying defects if extreme care is not exercised in the drying process.

Using an analogy between electrical conduction and diffusion, Stamm (1964) developed the theoretical transverse drying diffusion coefficients shown in Figure 8.13. Note the over tenfold increase in the rate of diffusion by raising the temperature from 50° to 120°C.

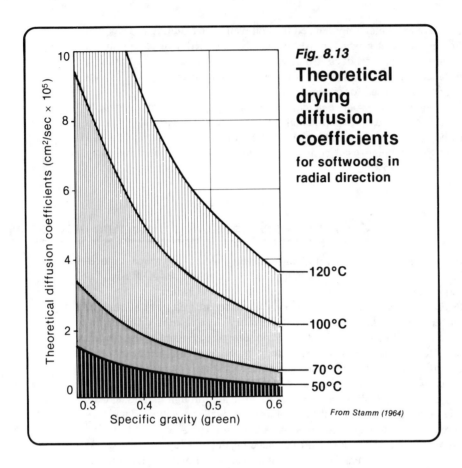

Fig. 8.13

Theoretical drying diffusion coefficients

for softwoods in radial direction

Theoretical diffusion coefficients (cm²/sec × 10⁵)

Specific gravity (green)

— 120°C
— 100°C
— 70°C
— 50°C

From Stamm (1964)

A variety of treatments to increase the movement of water through wood, i.e., increase permeability or diffusion, have been developed, but none has found wide commercial application. Erickson et al. (1966) found that freezing redwood lumber prior to drying improved drying performance. Application of hygroscopic chemicals such as urea, sodium chloride, and calcium chloride alters the moisture gradient and permits an increased rate of drying for some species. However, when so treated, the wood retains a hygroscopic surface layer that can cause problems in use. Presteaming of wood has been found to be beneficial in some cases. Unfortunately, a universally effective means of improving liquid water movement and/or diffusion is yet to be found.

Methods of drying lumber and other solid wood products ■

Most lumber, whether hardwood or softwood, is dried in some type of dry kiln. Modern kilns provide a controlled temperature and humidity environment and are equipped with fans to force air circulation and ventilation. Conventional kilns operate at temperatures up to about 100°C, while high-temperature kilns widely used to dry softwood lumber operate above the boiling point of water.

These latter kilns can dry some species in a period of one or two days. The lumber in such a kiln is dried in air that has been heated by steam coils or directly by the addition of combustion gases from a gas-, oil-, or wood residue–fired burner. Figure 8.14 illustrates the main elements in a typical cross-ventilated kiln heated by steam.

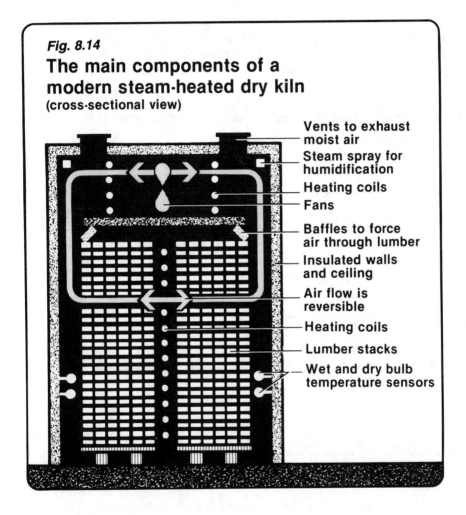

Fig. 8.14

The main components of a modern steam-heated dry kiln
(cross-sectional view)

Vents to exhaust moist air

Steam spray for humidification

Heating coils

Fans

Baffles to force air through lumber

Insulated walls and ceiling

Air flow is reversible

Heating coils

Lumber stacks

Wet and dry bulb temperature sensors

Drying in a conventional kiln progresses through a series of temperature and relative humidity steps designed to dry the wood gently while it is at a high moisture content. After the free water has been removed, more severe drying conditions are imposed to maintain an adequate rate of drying. The series of temperature and humidity conditions imposed on the lumber during drying is referred to as a *kiln schedule*. Most hardwood schedules are controlled according to the moisture content of the lumber; thus, changes in the drying conditions are made when the moisture content drops to predetermined levels. Softwoods are more-frequently dried by a time schedule, i.e., drying conditions are changed at predetermined times.

Two contrasting moisture content schedules for drying 1-in. hardwood lumber are shown in Table 8.6. Note the differences in temperature and relative humidity at each moisture content level for the difficult-to-dry white oak as compared to the easily dried basswood. These schedules are from recommendations in the *Dry Kiln Operator's Manual* (Simpson 1991), which is widely used as the guide to kiln drying. A more recent publication, *Drying Eastern Hardwood Lumber* (McMillen and Wengert 1978), is also available. Kiln drying schedules for southern pine are provided by Denig et al. (1993). Table 8.7 from this latter publication shows high-temperature drying times for two thicknesses of southern pine. After gaining experience with species and thicknesses they commonly dry, many firms develop their own drying schedules.

Table 8.6.   Kiln drying schedules for drying 1-in. basswood and white oak lumber

Basswood			White oak		
	Kiln conditions			Kiln conditions	
Moisture content	Tempera-ture	Relative humidity	Moisture content	Tempera-ture	Relative humidity
(%)	(°F) (°C)	(%)	(%)	(°F) (°C)	(%)
Above 60	160 (71)	58			
60	160 (71)	43			
50	160 (71)	31	Above 40	110 (43)	87
40	160 (71)	21	40	110 (43)	84
35	160 (71)	21	35	110 (43)	75
30	170 (77)	24	30	120 (49)	62
25	170 (77)	24	25	130 (54)	35
20	180 (82)	26	20	140 (60)	25
15	180 (82)	26	15	180 (82)	26

Source: USDA For. Serv. (1961).

Table 8.7.   Approximate schedules for high-temperature drying of southern yellow pine

Thickness (in.)	Width (in.)	Time (hr)	Dry-bulb temperature (° F)	Wet-bulb temperature (° F)
1	4–10	14–18	230	180
1.75	4–10	22–26	240	180

Source: Denig et al. (1993).

Since an entire kiln load of lumber can be destroyed by drying it too aggressively, care must be employed when developing new schedules. Means of optimizing drying operations, minimizing degrade, and maximizing the rate of drying are discussed by Holmes (1989), Ziegler (1988), Rice et al. (1994), and Carter and Sprague (1989). Industry trends in the drying practices for hardwoods and softwoods are summarized by Armstrong and Pahl (1994).

Some lumber is still air dried, but more commonly, air drying is used as a preliminary step to kiln drying. This can greatly lower drying costs, particularly for difficult-to-dry species that may take many weeks to kiln dry. The energy cost of drying lumber is high; thus, economies such as air drying may be advantageous. For refractory species of hardwoods, i.e., those that are difficult to dry without degrade, kiln drying may require over 6.5 million Btus of energy per 1000 bd ft of lumber. This amounts to about 70% of all the energy used in the manufacture of this lumber.

Lumber may be air dried without subsequent kiln drying at small mills not possessing kilns and in regions of the United States where the ambient humidity is normally very low, such as the Southwest and the Rocky Mountain states. Air drying may be satisfactory if adequate time is taken and if the drying specifications to be met are not too rigorous. From the user's standpoint, a disadvantage of air drying is that it may not be possible to reach the lower moisture content required for some applications. From the manufacturer's standpoint, air drying has the disadvantage of requiring a large and costly inventory in the drying yard. Also, degrade is more difficult to control than in a kiln. Air-drying times vary from a month under ideal conditions for easy-to-dry woods to a year or more for refractory woods dried under more-difficult conditions.

The amount of energy required to evaporate water from wood is shown in Figure 8.15. Although the heat of vaporization varies slightly with the temperature, in the range of normal drying temperatures it is about 1000 Btu/lb water evaporated. To accomplish drying below the FSP, the heat of wetting must be supplied as well as the heat of vaporization. The total actual energy required to dry wood is much greater than the sum of the heats of wetting and vaporization. Heat loss in the kiln resulting from venting of water vapor, air leakage, radiation, conduction losses through the kiln wall, and the use of steam to provide humidity control are also involved. The total amount of energy consumed in conventional kilns generally varies between 1600 and 3000 Btu/lb water evaporated.

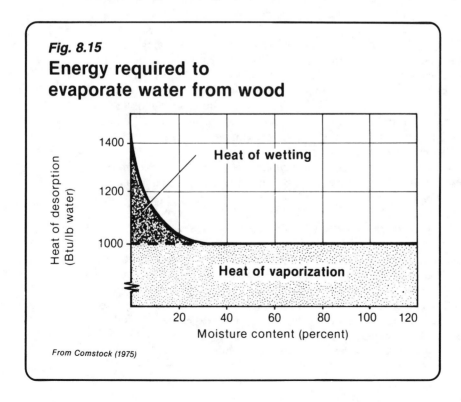

Fig. 8.15

Energy required to evaporate water from wood

From Comstock (1975)

A new drying system, *dehumidification drying,* is gaining use in North America. It was first used commercially in Europe; to date it has been used principally for the drying of hardwoods. The primary difference between this and a conventional kiln is that water is removed as condensate on refrigerated coils rather than by venting the moist air to the atmosphere. Since energy loss from venting is eliminated and heat from the compressor of the refrigeration unit is used to heat the kiln, the dehumidification drying method appears to offer some economies in energy use. Early installations of this type of kiln had the disadvantage of being slower than conventional kiln drying, but improvements are reducing this limitation. Since the energy used is in the form of electricity, this drying system does not adapt itself easily to the utilization of heat generated from mill residues.

A number of other methods have been used experimentally, and in a few instances commercially, for drying solid wood products. These may have advantages for special situations but are generally more expensive and less predictable than kiln drying. Wood scientists and industry engineers are actively engaged in work to improve drying practices. Some nonconventional drying methods have been studied. They include the following:

1. *Immersing wood in a heated organic liquid.* Liquids such as fuel oil or perchloroethylene are heated, raising the temperature of the wood above the boiling point of water, thus driving off the moisture.

2. *Vapor drying.* This method uses an organic liquid with a boiling point above 100°C. The drying chamber contains the wood and the organic vapor. The condensation of these vapors on the wood heats the wood rapidly, driving out the water, which is then separated from the solvent vapor in a condenser and separator.

3. *Radiofrequency dielectric heating.* This approach to drying involves placing wood between two electrodes and subjecting the material to an electric field oscillating at high frequency. Being polar, water molecules in wood rotate in the alternating field, thus generating heat. In woods that dry easily, the internal temperature tends to rise only slightly above the boiling point until the free water is gone. However, in impermeable woods, the temperature may rise to destructive levels. A variation of this process is the combination of microwave energy with hot-air impingement drying.

4. *Combination of radio frequency heating and vacuum drying.* Lumber is heated dielectrically at 7–9 MHz while it is in a chamber in which a partial vacuum has been created. In this way, water will boil at a lower pressure, speeding the drying process. Such kilns, capable of drying 10,000 bd ft of lumber, have been built and good results reported (Wengert and Lamb 1982).

5. *Press drying.* Wood is press dried by placing it between two heated platens. Heat transfer is by conduction from metal to wood and therefore is very rapid. This technique works well on thin pieces of easy-to-dry species. It is used commercially for high-quality veneer, but only one commercial application for lumber has been reported. This drying method can be combined with high pressures to produce a densified product. Figure 8.16 shows experimental results of simultaneously drying and densifying two species of pine. In one sample shown, phenolic resin was added to increase dimensional stability.

Fig. 8.16

**Normal and densified loblolly and Norway pine.
Specific gravity of the samples is indicated.**

Drying of veneer, particles, and fibers ■

The major difference in principle between drying veneer and lumber is that veneer, being very thin, develops a limited moisture gradient. Therefore, the drying stresses and impermeable zones that cause problems in the drying of lumber are not the limiting factors in veneer drying. Other considerations, such as the glueability of the surface, may dictate how fast and at what temperature veneer can be satisfactorily dried.

Veneer driers consist of a means of conveying the veneer through a heated chamber where temperatures range from 150 to 260°C. In older roller driers, air is circulated in a manner similar to that in a dry kiln. This type of drier is still in wide use for hardwood veneer. Most plants built in recent years utilize jet driers. These are also called impingement driers since a curtain of air at velocities of 2000–4000 fpm is directed against the surface of veneer. The high velocity produces turbulent air on the surface of the veneer. This eliminates the laminar boundary layer that slows down heat and moisture transfer under ordinary drying conditions.

Most particle- and fiberboard plants utilize a high-speed drying system of some sort because of the large tonnage of material to be dried; one plant in the United States dries 2 million lb wood/day. In common use are driers of two types: drum driers and tube driers. *Rotating drum driers* are the most common type used in particleboard plants. The wood particles make one, two, or three passes from one end of the drier to the other and then are discharged. Inlet temperatures of such driers can be as high as 870°C when wet furnish is being dried but is reduced to about 260°C or lower to reduce the fire hazard if dry planer shavings are involved.

Drying wood particles at temperatures above the burning point of about 230°C is possible as long as moisture is present in the wood. Drier control systems must be designed to ensure that dried wood is not present in the preliminary high-temperature stages of the drier. The particle movement through these driers is controlled by air velocity. The finer particles, which dry faster, are blown more rapidly through the drum and therefore are exhausted before reaching the combustion point.

The drying of fibers for dry-process fiberboard production can be accomplished in *tube driers*. The fibers are introduced into a stream of gas heated from 200° to 320°C. These driers may have a second stage operating at a lower temperature. Moisture is often flashed off in a few seconds; thus, effective feed and temperature control systems are critical to avoid fires.

The moisture content to which fiber- or particleboard particles are dried for the manufacture of panel products depends upon the specific product, the amount of water added with the resin and wax size, and the pressing cycle. Generally, the wood furnish is dried to between 4 and 8% MC. Precise control is necessary, since a moisture content 2% higher than desired can cause blows or internal explosions in the panels when the press is opened. A moisture content 2% below the desired level can cause poor bonds and therefore will reduce mechanical properties.

REVIEW

A. Terms to define or explain:
1. Moisture content
2. Fiber saturation point
3. Equilibrium moisture content
4. Resistance-type moisture meter
5. Sorption
6. Kiln schedule
7. Polymolecular adsorption of water on cellulose
8. Free water
9. Bound water
10. Hysteresis
11. Linear swelling
12. Longitudinal shrinkage
13. Dry kiln
14. Bulking agent
15. Cross-linking for stabilization
16. Dehumidification drying
17. Press drying

B. Questions or concepts to explain:
1. Be able to calculate the moisture content from green and dry weights.
2. Be able to estimate the weight of products at any moisture content, knowing the present weight and moisture content.
3. Be able to estimate the shrinking or swelling in any principal direction when wood changes from one moisture content to another.
4. Be able to estimate the dimensional change that would occur if the environmental conditions change.
5. Be able to estimate the equilibrium moisture content for wood at any temperature and relative humidity.
6. Discuss factors affecting the rate at which lumber dries.
7. Discuss the importance of using wood at the proper moisture content.

REFERENCES AND SUPPLEMENTAL READINGS

American Lumber Standards Committee. 1994. American Softwood Lumber Standard. PS 20-94.

Armstrong, J.P., and Pahl, T.L. 1994. Changes in the kiln-drying practice of the forest products industry in West Virginia: 1982 to 1992. W.V. For. Prod. J. 44(9):54–56.

Carter, L., and Sprague, M. 1989. Improve lumber drying by analyzing kiln environment. For. Ind. 116(7):12–15.

Comstock, G. 1975 Energy requirements for drying. Proc. For. Prod. Res. Soc. Energy Symp. Denver, Colo.

Denig, J.; Hanover, S.J.; and Hart, C.A. 1993. Kiln drying southern pine lumber. NC State Univ. Coop. Ext. Ser. Pub.

Erickson, R.W.; Haygreen, J.G.; and Hossfeld, R. 1966. Drying prefrozen redwood. For. Prod. J. 16(8):57–65.

Haygreen, J.G. and Gertjejansen, R.O. 1972. Influence of the amount and type of phenolic resin on the properties of a wafer-type particleboard. For. Prod. J. 22(12):30–34.

Heebink, B.G. 1966. Thoughts on the term EMC. Soc. Wood Sci. Tech. Log. (Nov.):1–3.

Higgins, N.C. 1957. The EMC of selected native and foreign woods. For. Prod. J. 7(10):371–77.

Holmes, S. 1989. Optimizing grade recovery in lumber drying. For. Ind. 116(7):15–20.

Koch, P. 1972. Utilization of Southern Pines, vols. 1 and 2. USDA For. Ser. Agric. Handb. 420, Chap. 8, 20.

Lewis, D.C. 1990. Dehumidification kilns let small mills dry lumber. For. Ind. 117(5):39–40.

McMillen, J.M. and Wengert, E. M. 1978. Drying eastern hardwood lumber. USDA For. Ser. Agric. Handb. 528.

O'Halloran, M.R. 1975. Plywood in hostile environments. Amer. Plywood Assoc. Res. Rep. 132.

Peck, E.G. 1947. Shrinkage of wood. USDA For. Prod. Lab. Rept. 1650.

_____. 1955. Moisture content of wood in use. USDA For. Prod. Lab. Rept. 1655.

Rice, R. W.; Howe, J.L.; Boone, R.S., and Tschernitz, J.L. 1994. A survey of firms kiln drying lumber in the U.S. For. Prod. J. 44(7/8):55–62.

Seborg, C.O., and Stamm, A.J. 1931. Sorption of water by paper making materials. Ind. Eng. Chem. 23:1271

Simpson, W.T. 1991. Dry Kiln Operator's Manual. USDA For. Ser. Agric. Handb. 188.

Skarr, C. 1972. Water in Wood. Syracuse Univ. Press. Syracuse, N. Y.

Spalt, H.A. 1958. Fundamentals of water vapor sorption by wood. For. Prod. J. 8(10):288–295.

Stamm, A.J. 1957. Adsorption in swelling vs. non-swelling systems. TAPPI 40(9):761–764.

_____. 1964. Wood and Cellulose Science. New York: Ronald Press.

U.S. Forest Products Laboratory. 1987. Wood Handbook: Wood as an Engineering Material. USDA For. Ser. Agric. Handb. 72.

Virginia Polytechnic Institute and State University. 1979. Proc. Symp. Wood Moisture Content, Temperature and Humidity Relationships.

Wengert, E.M., and Lamb, F.M. 1982. Hardwood drying tests new methods. For. Ind. (Jan.):21–22.

Ziegler, G.A. 1988. Addressing the basics of successful lumber drying. For. Ind. (Jul.):6–10.

Specific gravity and density

THE SPECIFIC gravity of wood is its single most important physical property. Most mechanical properties of wood are closely correlated to *specific gravity* and *density*. In general discussions, the terms *specific gravity* and *density* are often used interchangeably. However, as will be discussed later, these terms have precise and different definitions although they refer to the same characteristic. The strength of wood, as well as its stiffness, increases with specific gravity. The yield of pulp per unit volume is directly related to specific gravity. The heat transmission of wood increases with specific gravity as well as the heat per unit volume produced in combustion. The shrinking and swelling behavior of wood is also affected, although the relationship is not as direct as in the case of strength properties. It is possible to learn more about the nature of a wood sample by determining its specific gravity than by any other single measurement. Perhaps it is for this reason that density was the first wood property to be scientifically investigated.

Wood is a cellular material. The cellular structure gives wood many of its unique properties. The density of wood is directly related to its porosity, i.e., to the proportion of the *void volume*. A piece of sugar pine with a density of 23.4 lb dry wood substance/ft³ includes about 25% cell wall material and 75% voids (principally lumen space) by volume. In contrast, white oak with a density of 46.8 dry lb/ft³ has a void volume of about 50%. When considering the density of wood, it is helpful to visualize the void volume with which it corresponds. One can visualize why a block containing 50% void volume will resist crushing to a

191

much greater extent than a block from a different species with 75% void space.

The physicomechanical properties of wood are determined by three characteristics: (1) the porosity or proportion of void volume, which can be estimated by measuring the density; (2) the organization of the cell structure, which includes the microstructure of the cell walls and the variety and proportion of cell types (the organization of the cell structure is principally a function of the species); and (3) the moisture content. The effect of bound water on the properties of wood was discussed in Chapter 8. In the use and engineering of wood materials, it is important to keep these three characteristics in mind.

Two physical properties, density and specific gravity, are used to describe the mass of a material per unit volume. These properties are commonly used in connection with all types of materials. *Density* (D) is defined as the mass or weight per unit of volume. It is usually expressed in pounds per cubic foot (lb/ft³) or kilograms per cubic meter (kg/m³). In the International System of Units the pound is a unit of mass, not force.

Specific gravity (SG) is the ratio of the density of a material to the density of water. It is also referred to as *relative density*. With most materials the weight and the volume are determined under the same conditions. However, a dilemma exists when these characteristics are used for a hygroscopic material such as wood. Since both the weight and the volume vary with changes in moisture content, how should density and specific gravity be determined?

A word of caution is in order when discussing wood density. There is no universally accepted procedure for calculating the density of wood. However, it is a good practice to calculate density (the mass per unit volume) by determining the mass and the volume at the same moisture content. The moisture content at which the density is determined should be mentioned whenever providing density information. Density is frequently expressed in green weight and green volume when the use will be to calculate weights for transportation or construction. Unfortunately, you will find in practice and in the literature that density is sometimes calculated in other ways using the mass and volume at different moisture contents. Therefore, whenever wood density is discussed, it is a good practice to be sure of the basis of the calculation. You should always calculate density using mass and volume at the same moisture content even though others may not always do so.

Specific gravity is always calculated using ovendry weight or mass. Volume can be determined at any moisture content, but that moisture content must be specified. Because of this recognized standard procedure, confusion about the basis of the calculation is avoided. Specific gravity is defined in physics as *the ratio of the density of a material to the density of water at 4°C*. Water has a density of 1 g/cm³ or 1000 kg/m³ at that standard temperature. A modification of this definition for wood, as mentioned above, is that the mass is always determined in the ovendry condition. Specific gravity has no units since it is a ratio. In the metric system, specific gravity can be visualized by thinking of it as grams of dry wood substance per cubic centimeter. For example, OD (0% MC) wood with a specific gravity of 0.5 (SG @ 0% MC) has 0.5 g of dry wood substance per cm³ or 500 kg/m³. In the English system, water has a density of 62.4 lb/ft³. Therefore, the density of wood with a specific gravity of 0.5 (SG @ 0% MC) is 0.5 × 62.4, or 31.2 lb/ft³.

The advantage of using the metric system is that the calculation of specific gravity is simplified because 1 cm³ of water weighs precisely 1 g. Specific gravity can thus be calculated directly by dividing the ovendry weight in grams by the volume in cubic centimeters. When using these two metric units for ovendry wood, the density (D) and specific gravity (SG) are numerically the same. Why isn't this true at other moisture contents?

Common units used for density = g/cm^3, kg/m^3, lb/ft^3

$$D = mass/volume \qquad \text{(at any given moisture content)}$$

$$SG = \frac{OD\ mass/volume}{density\ of\ water} \qquad \text{(volume at any given MC)}$$

Density of water = 62.4 lb/ft^3, 1 g/cm^3, 1000 kg/m^3

The following example clarifies the difference between density and specific gravity using the methods of calculation in both the English and the metric systems. Suppose that a block of wood has the following measurements at three moisture contents:

		Green	@ 12% MC	Ovendry
Volume—English:		0.0777 ft^3	0.0738 ft^3	0.0706 ft^3
	metric:	0.00220 m^3	0.00209 m^3	0.00200 m^3
Mass—English:		3.97 lb	2.47 lb	2.20 lb
	metric:	1.800 kg	1.120 kg	1.000 kg

The density and specific gravity of that block can be calculated and expressed correctly in any of the following ways:

$$D\ (OD\ weight\ and\ volume) = \frac{1.000\ kg}{0.00200\ m^3} = 500 kg/m^3$$

or

$$= \frac{2.20\ lb}{0.0706\ ft^3} = 31.2\ lb/ft^3$$

$$D\ (green\ weight\ and\ volume) = \frac{1.800\ kg}{0.00220\ m^3} = 818\ kg/m^3$$

or

$$= \frac{3.97\ lb}{0.0777\ ft^3} = 51.5\ lb/ft^3$$

$$D\ (weight\ and\ volume\ @\ 12\%) = \frac{1.120\ kg}{0.00209\ m^3} = 535\ kg/m^3$$

or

$$= \frac{2.47\ lb}{0.0738\ ft^3} = 33.5\ lb/ft^3$$

$$SG\ (green) = \frac{1.000\ kg}{0.00220\ m^3} \div 1000\ kg/m^3 = 0.454$$

or

$$= \frac{2.20 \text{ lb}}{0.0777 \text{ m}^3} \div 62.4 \text{ lb/ft}^3 = 0.454$$

$$\text{SG (12\% MC)} = \frac{1.000 \text{ kg}}{0.00209 \text{ m}^3} \div 1000 \text{ kg/m}^3 = 0.478$$

or

$$= \frac{2.20 \text{ lb}}{0.0738 \text{ ft}^3} \div 62.4 \text{ lb/ft}^3 = 0.478$$

$$\text{SG (OD)} = \frac{1.000 \text{ kg}}{0.00200 \text{ m}^3} \div 1000 \text{ kg/m}^3 = 0.500$$

or

$$= \frac{2.20 \text{ lb}}{0.0706 \text{ ft}^3} \div 62.4 \text{ lb/ft}^3 = 0.500$$

The *total weight* of a wood product is, of course, the sum of the weight of the wood substance plus the moisture. As explained above, when density is calculated this total weight should be used as the numerator in the equation while when specific gravity is calculated it is standard practice to use the ovendry (OD) weight as the numerator. This difference is particularly significant when dealing with green wood. Consider this example: a cubic foot of green lumber has a weight of 42.0 lb at 50% MC, a weight of 53.2 lb at 90% MC, and an ovendry weight of 28.0 lb. The density at 50% MC is 42.0 lb/ft³ and 53.2 lb/ft³ at 90% MC, while the specific gravity is 0.45 at both moisture contents. The specific gravity is the same at both moisture levels because the volume is constant above the FSP. Even though there is some difference in specific gravity at different moisture levels below the FSP this difference is small compared to the change in density with moisture content. This is an important distinction in the use of specific gravity rather than density when studying wood properties.

Effects of moisture content

Density and specific gravity can be calculated at any moisture content desired. Density decreases as moisture content decreases, but below the fiber saturation point (FSP) the specific gravity of a sample increases as the moisture content decreases. This occurs because the dry weight remains constant while the volume decreases during drying. The greater the volumetric shrinkage, the greater the difference between the green and the ovendry specific gravity.

The following example illustrates the effect of volumetric change. Sample A has a green weight and volume of 800 g and 1000 cm³. When ovendry, the weight is 500 g. This sample undergoes 12% volumetric shrinkage in going from green to ovendry, so the dry volume is 880 cm³. For sample A

SG (green)   = 500/1000 = 0.50
SG (ovendry) = 500/880 = 0.57

Sample B has the same green weight and volume and the same ovendry weight as sample A. It shrinks only 6% in volume when drying, however, so the ovendry volume is 940 cm³. Therefore, for sample B

    SG (green)   = 500/1000 = 0.50
    SG (ovendry) = 500/940   = 0.53

Although the green specific gravity of A and B are the same, the OD specific gravity differs by 0.04.

Figure 9.1 shows the typical relationship between specific gravity and moisture content. This figure makes it simple to convert from green specific gravity to specific gravity at any moisture content. This figure is based upon an average volumetric shrinkage value for each density.

If the actual volumetric shrinkage of a species is known, it is more accurate

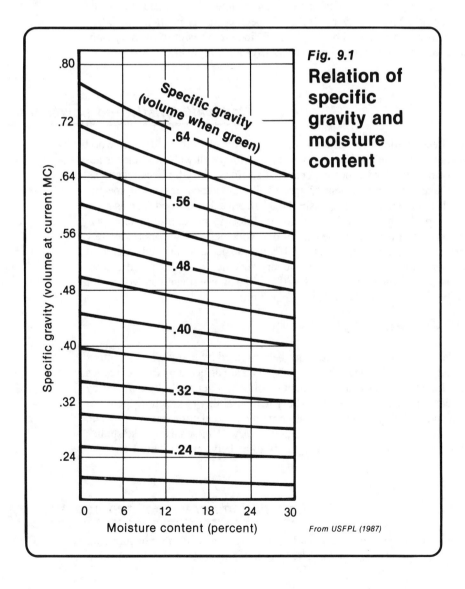

Fig. 9.1
Relation of specific gravity and moisture content

From USFPL (1987)

to calculate the new specific gravity using the following relationship than to use Figure 9.1:

$$SG_{X\% \, MC} = SG_{gm} / \left(1 - \frac{\% \text{ volume shrinkage to X\% MC}}{100} \right)$$

In the United States, specific gravity is commonly computed at either the green, ovendry, or 12% MC condition. The use of the green SG as a fundamental property has the advantage of being more reproducible because the wood is fully swollen and in its natural unstressed condition. The green specific gravity is often used in studies of silvicultural practices, when estimating shipping weights of logs and pulpwood, and for estimating yields of pulp.

The amount of shrinkage that occurs when any sample of wood is dried is affected somewhat by the size and shape of the piece and the means of drying. Therefore, specific gravity values based upon volumes determined below the FSP are likewise affected. Nevertheless, OD specific gravity is often used when wood products are to be tested below the FSP since it is easier to ovendry samples than to equilibrate them to a predetermined moisture level.

Cell wall density and porosity ■

The direct relationship between the proportion of void volume in wood (*porosity*) and density exists because the density of dry cell wall substance is approximately the same for all species. That is, if sections of void-free cell wall material were taken from a low-density species like basswood, tested for specific gravity, and compared to results of a similar test from a dense wood such as hickory, the two specific gravity values would be almost identical. For general purposes it can be assumed that the density of dry wood cell walls is approximately 1.5 g/cm³, i.e., the specific gravity is 1.5. If a wood species contained no cell lumens or other voids, it would have an ovendry specific gravity of 1.5. If it were 50% porous, its specific gravity would be 0.75. The approximate void volume of wood can be calculated by the following equation:

$$\% \text{ void volume} = [1 - (SG_{OD} / 1.50)] \times 100$$

The density of cell wall material has been studied by many wood scientists since the early 1900s. The density values observed are affected by the techniques employed. In determining cell wall density, volume is generally determined by displacement of a fluid. Different fluids vary in their ability to penetrate the voids in the wall and in their physical association with chemical components of wood, so it is to be expected that these measurements vary. In most cases these studies have determined the cell wall specific gravity to be between 1.45 and 1.54.

Calculations of weight and buoyancy ■

The weight of wood products can be easily estimated if the moisture content and specific gravity are known. The weight of the product should be calculated by using the specific gravity that corresponds as closely as possible to the moisture content of the product at that time.

Weight = volume × specific gravity × density of water × [1 + (% MC/100)]

EXAMPLE: 10 m³ (353 ft³) of mahogany (*Khaya* sp.) is shipped at an average moisture content of 40%. The average green specific gravity of African mahogany is known to be 0.43. What is the estimated weight?

Weight   = 10 m³ × 0.43 × 1000 kg/m³ × 1.40 = 6020 kg

or

= 353 ft³ × 0.43 × 62.4 lb/ft³ × 1.40 = 13,260 lb

Similar calculations have been performed for a series of moisture contents and specific gravities and the results compiled in Table 9.1. The densities in this table are based upon the weight and volume at the same moisture content.

Table 9.1.   Total density of wood

% MC	Specific gravity				
	0.30	0.40	0.50	0.60	0.70
			lb/ft³ (kg/m³)		
0	18.7	25.0	31.2	37.4	43.7
	(300)	(400)	(500)	(599)	(700)
10	20.6	27.5	34.3	41.1	48.1
	(330)	(440)	(550)	(659)	(770)
20	22.5	30.0	37.4	44.9	52.4
	(360)	(481)	(599)	(719)	(839)
40	26.2	34.9	43.7	52.4	61.2
	(420)	(559)	(700)	(839)	(980)
60	30.0	39.9	49.9	59.9	69.9
	(481)	(639)	(799)	(960)	(1120)
80	33.7	44.9	56.2	67.4	78.6
	(540)	(719)	(900)	(1080)	(1260)
100	37.4	49.9	62.4	74.9	87.4
	(599)	(799)	(1000)	(1200)	(1400)

Note: Total density is based upon the weight and volume at the moisture content indicated.

The following examples illustrate the application of density calculations to wood and wood products.

EXAMPLE 1:   White ash has an ovendry specific gravity of 0.60 and a green specific gravity of 0.55. What percent of the total volume of dry wood is made up of cell wall substance?

% solid wood substance by volume = 0.60/1.50 = 40%

What will be the weight of 1 m³ of this wood if the moisture content is 38%?

Weight = 1 m³ × 0.55 × 1000 kg/m³ × 1.38 = 759 kg

Recall that total weight = ovendry weight × [1 + (% MC/100)].

What will be the moisture content of this wood if it is completely saturated with water (all voids filled)?

> % void volume = 100 − [(0.60/1.50) × 100] = 60%
> Void volume per cubic centimeter = 0.60 cm³
> Mass of water per cubic centimeter when filling all voids = 0.60 cm³ × 1 g/cm³ = 0.60 g
> Saturated MC = 0.60 g/0.60 g × 100 = 100%

At what moisture content will a log of white ash have zero buoyancy (just float)? Recall Archimedes's principle—the force buoying up a body immersed in a liquid is equal to the weight of the liquid displaced by the body. There is also an equal force exerted downward on the liquid by the body.

> Mass of OD wood per cubic centimeter of green wood = 0.55 g
> Total mass per cubic centimeter for zero buoyancy = 1 g/cm³
> Weight of water per cubic centimeter for zero buoyancy = 1 g − 0.55 g = 0.45 g
> % MC = 0.45/0.55 = 82%

EXAMPLE 2:   A shipment contains 80 ft³ of ponderosa pine lumber. The moisture content as measured by an electrical meter averages 12%. The average specific gravity of ponderosa pine at 12% MC as indicated in Appendix Table A.5 is 0.40. What is the estimated weight of the lumber?

> Weight = 80 ft³ × 0.40 × 1.12 × 62.4 lb/ft³ = 2236 lb

What will be the specific gravity of this ponderosa pine at the ovendry condition and when green? (Refer to Fig. 9.1.)

> OD specific gravity = approximately 0.42
> Green specific gravity = approximately 0.38

Effects of extractives and inorganic materials on specific gravity ■

Wood often contains measurable quantities of extractives and infiltration materials including terpenes, resins, polyphenols such as tannins, sugars, and oils as well as inorganic compounds such as silicates, carbonates, and phosphates. These materials are located to a large extent within the cell wall, where they are deposited during the maturation of the secondary wall and during heartwood formation. The heartwood has a higher concentration of these materials than the sapwood; therefore, the density of heartwood is often slightly higher than that of sapwood.

The amount of extractives in wood varies from less than 3 to over 30% of the ovendry weight. Obviously, the presence of these materials can have a major effect upon the density. In some species, including pine, it has been shown that the presence of extractives contributes significantly to the variability observed in the specific gravity. The specific gravity of wood from which extractives have been removed tends to be more uniform than if the weight of extractives is included. In research work it is often desirable to determine the density of the wood without the extractives. Both water and organic solvents are used for extraction when determining extractive-free density. Some of the bulking effect is lost when extractives are removed, so in addition to the loss of weight, the sample tends to show greater dimensional change with moisture fluctuations.

Methods of determining specific gravity ∎

The volume at a given moisture content and the weight of the ovendry sample are necessary for the calculation of specific gravity. In most cases, the dry weight is found by oven-drying the sample, as would be done when finding the moisture content. However, since high temperature may drive off some of the extractives in addition to the water, it is sometimes desirable to determine the moisture content by a distillation method that involves condensing and weighing the vapor driven off.

The volume of the wood sample being tested may be obtained in a variety of ways. For a piece that is regular in shape, such as a section of lumber, the simplest method is to measure the dimensions as accurately as possible and calculate the volume. If the sample is irregular in shape, such a tree cross section or a wood chip, the volume can be obtained by the displacement method. The equipment to do this is illustrated in Figure 9.2. The scale or balance records the weight of the fluid displaced. This value can then be converted to a volume by dividing by the density of the fluid used. The displacement procedure using water as the fluid works well with green material since little water is sorbed by the wood. However, when dry wood is immersed, the sample must be coated with wax or paraffin so that water will not penetrate the block and produce an erroneously low volume determination. Use of a high–surface tension nonwetting fluid avoids the wetting problem with dry samples, but since many such fluids present safety hazards, the use of water and a waxy coating is usually more convenient.

A third method of determining volume involves use of a graduated cylinder as shown in Figure 9.3. In this case the volume is the difference between the fluid level before and after immersion. This is a quick and simple technique but involves the same problem for dry samples as the displacement method.

The details of these and other methods of determining the specific gravity of wood-based materials are discussed in ASTM Standard D 2395.

Relationship of density to rate of growth ∎

Intuition or common sense might suggest that wood density should decrease if the rate of growth of a tree increases. This is not necessarily or even usually the case. When wood density is related to growth rate, the response depends on the species and the range of growth rates involved. Other factors such as age, vitality of the tree when the wood was produced, and location of wood in the tree are more-closely correlated to density than is the rate of growth. The only species groups in which density is closely related to growth rate are the ring-porous hard-

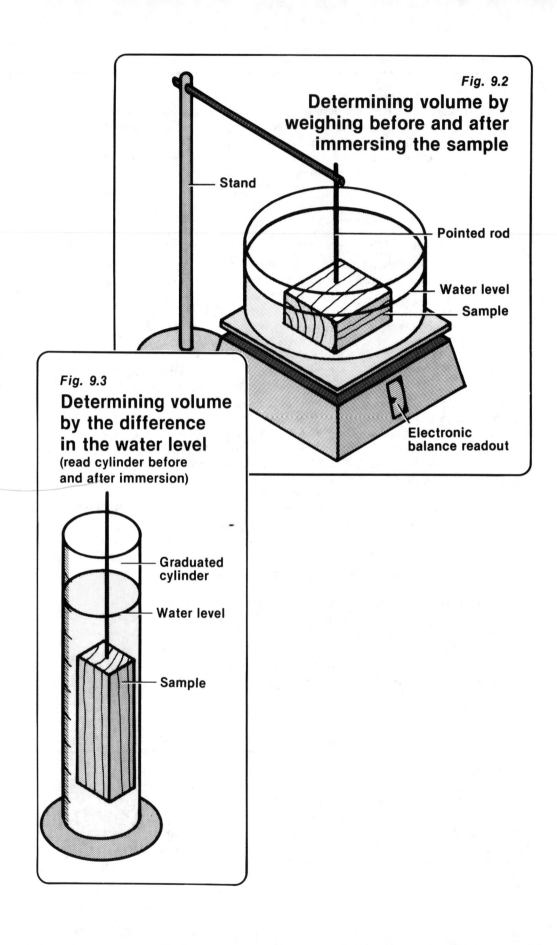

Fig. 9.2
Determining volume by weighing before and after immersing the sample

Stand

Pointed rod

Water level

Sample

Electronic balance readout

Fig. 9.3
Determining volume by the difference in the water level
(read cylinder before and after immersion)

Graduated cylinder

Water level

Sample

woods. In these species the density tends to increase as the growth rate increases. Softwoods and diffuse-porous hardwoods do not exhibit a consistent relationship between wood density and growth rate.

The rate of growth is used to estimate density (and thus strength) in the grading of several types of lumber products. Hickory tool handles are often graded based upon the number of growth rings per inch. The fewer the growth rings per inch, the higher the density and, therefore, the higher the grade. Ash shovel and hoe handles and implement parts can be graded based on the number of growth rings per inch. A handle with 30 or more rings per inch cannot be relied upon to perform satisfactorily under heavy use.

Although the density of softwoods is not related to growth rate, density is directly related to the percentage of latewood in a growth ring. There is generally a large difference in density between earlywood and latewood. In southern pine, the specific gravity of the earlywood is less that one-half that of latewood (0.28 versus 0.70)(Koch 1972). For this reason, relatively wide latewood zones indicate relatively high density. Since the strength of wood increases with density, wide growth rings exhibiting a low proportion of latewood may be of concern in products where strength is important.

Because of the desirability of a high percentage of latewood, a so-called *density rule* is sometimes applied in the grading of southern pine, Douglas-fir, and western larch lumber. Such lumber may be graded as Dense if it averages 6 or more growth rings per inch and if it contains one-third or more latewood. The requirement of at least 6 rings per inch reduces the chance of using juvenile wood, which has poor strength and dimensional properties. Material graded Dense carries engineering strength values 15–30% higher than normal lumber. Southern pine structural lumber containing 15% or less latewood is deemed to be exceptionally light and is excluded from the top three grades.

Most research directed to the question of the relationship between growth rate (or rings/inch) and density has been conducted in conjunction with studies on fertilization, irrigation, genetic improvement, or other intensive silvicultural practices. This is discussed in more detail in Chapter 12.

Variability of wood density ■

Wood density varies greatly within any species because of a number of factors. These include location in a tree, location within the range of the species, site condition (soil, water, and slope), and genetic source. However, the user of a wood or lumber product has no control or knowledge of where the particular tree was cut, in what part of the tree the product originated, or if the tree was normal or overmature. The user is concerned primarily with the variability that may be encountered in the density of the product, regardless of its source. This expected variability is important to understand. This knowledge is needed, for example, (1) in estimating the variability in the strength of a wood product, (2) in establishing a procedure for purchase of wood on a weight basis, and (3) in estimating the amount of pulp to be obtained per unit volume of raw wood.

Generally, the specific gravity of most species in North America has a *coefficient of variation* (COV) of about 10%. To estimate the range of wood densities one might normally encounter in any such species, the COV is multiplied by the average density (specific gravity) and by 1.96 (to include 95% of a normally distributed population). This figure is then added and subtracted from the mean. For example, the average green specific gravity of black cherry as indicated in Appendix Table A.5 is 0.47. Therefore, the range of density to be expected in black cherry is approximately $0.47 \pm (10\% \times 0.47 \times 1.96) = 0.47 \pm 0.09 = 0.38$ to 0.56. Wood users frequently question the quality of material they purchase if it has a specific gravity that differs from the average value published in the *Wood Handbook* (USFPL 1987) (Appendix Table A.5) or in trade association literature. It should be understood that such differences are to be expected because of variability. Table 9.2 shows the average and the range of green specific gravity for some important species in the United States, assuming a 10% COV. Figure 9.4 shows the variability encountered in the specific gravity of a Douglas-fir gluelaminated beam.

Table 9.2. *Range of specific gravity for important species*

Species	Average green specific gravity	Normal* range of specific gravity
Softwoods		
Douglas-fir (coast)	0.45	0.36–0.54
Loblolly pine	0.47	0.38–0.56
Longleaf pine	0.54	0.43–0.65
Ponderosa pine	0.38	0.31–0.45
Western hemlock	0.42	0.34–0.50
Western white pine	0.35	0.28–0.42
White fir	0.37	0.30–0.44
Hardwoods		
Black walnut	0.51	0.41–0.61
Northern red oak	0.56	0.45–0.67
Quaking aspen	0.35	0.28–0.42
Southern red oak	0.52	0.42–0.62
Sugar maple	0.56	0.45–0.67
Sweetgum	0.46	0.37–0.55
White ash	0.60	0.48–0.72
Yellow poplar	0.42	0.34–0.50

* Assuming a 10% COV.

Comprehensive lists of species and average specific gravities are found in Appendix Tables A.5, A.6, and A.7. These list important woods grown in the United States, tropical countries, and Canada, respectively. Appendix Table A.5 indicates the specific gravity both at 12% MC and when green, while Tables A.6 and A.7 provide only the green specific gravity.

Relatively limited information is available on the variability of density in tropical species. In some instances, as with balsa, it has been found that the COV is considerably higher than 10%. It is unfortunate that much of the literature accessible to potential users, describing the density and properties of woods imported into the United States, includes only average density and strength values, with no measure of variability. This situation is improving as forest products research expands worldwide and computer databases become available.

The variability in density of major softwood species in the United States became of considerable concern in the 1960s and early 1970s. This arose in large part because of questions regarding the properties of structural timbers and ply-

Fig. 9.4
**Variation of specific gravity between laminants
in a Douglas-fir glulam beam.**

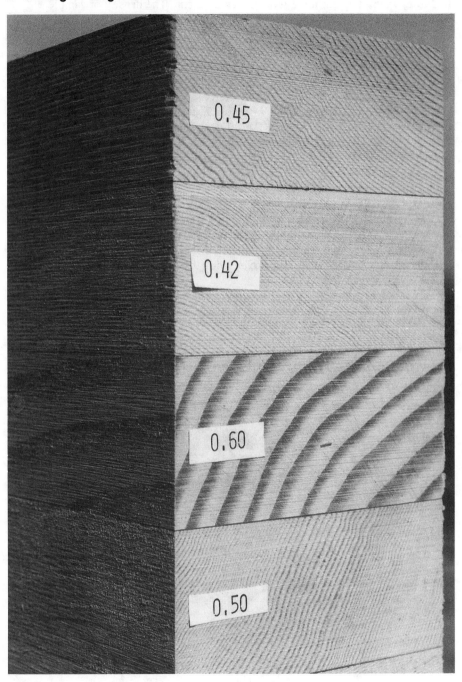

wood produced from smaller second-growth timber. Large-scale wood density surveys were carried out by the U.S. Forest Service to determine regional and tree-to-tree variability in southern pines and the major western softwoods. About 25,000 trees were sampled in the western survey alone. The density of sample trees was determined from increment cores taken at breast height. From these cores and analyses of selected whole trees, regressions were developed to predict average whole-tree densities. These studies provided new insights into the variability of these species and led to new strength values being assigned to lumber of several species.

Some of the results of the southern and western wood density (specific gravity) surveys are shown in Figures 9.5, 9.6, and 9.7 and Table 9.3. The three specific gravity values indicated in Figure 9.5 for each survey region are from data taken from loblolly pine in three diameter classes. Note that these averages varied from 0.45 to 0.57 over the range. The variability found in the density of Douglas-fir (Fig. 9.6) is almost as great. This information on Douglas-fir verified the lower strength values assigned to material produced in the interior southern region.

Consistent increases in the specific gravity of Douglas-fir with tree age is shown in Figure 9.7. The western density survey also involved the other major western species. These findings are summarized in Table 9.3. Compare the range of specific gravity measured in this survey with that estimated using the assumption of a 10% COV.

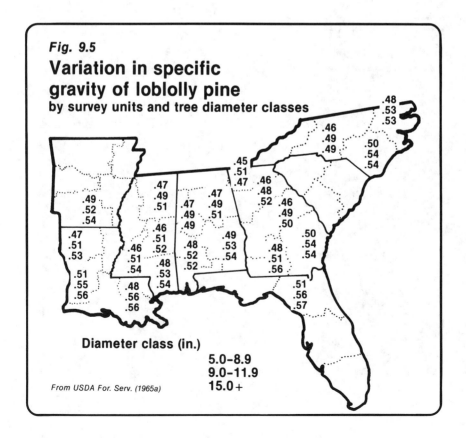

Fig. 9.5

Variation in specific gravity of loblolly pine
by survey units and tree diameter classes

Diameter class (in.)
5.0–8.9
9.0–11.9
15.0+

From USDA For. Serv. (1965a)

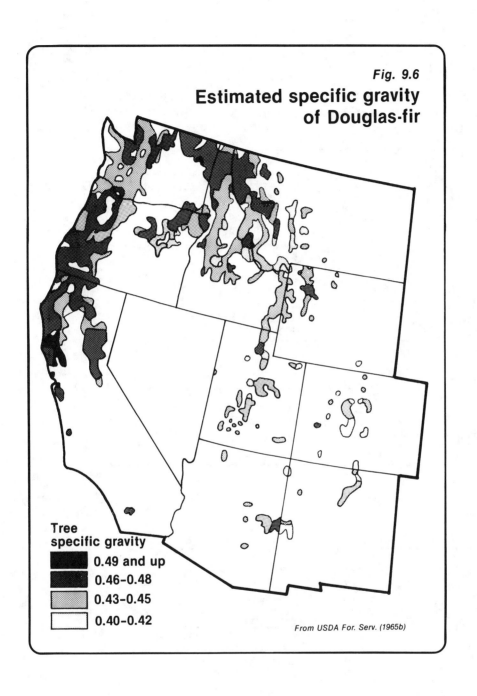

Fig. 9.6
Estimated specific gravity of Douglas-fir

Tree specific gravity
- 0.49 and up
- 0.46–0.48
- 0.43–0.45
- 0.40–0.42

From USDA For. Serv. (1965b)

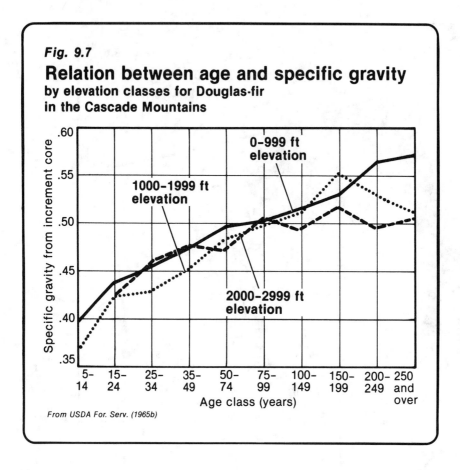

Fig. 9.7

Relation between age and specific gravity
by elevation classes for Douglas-fir
in the Cascade Mountains

From USDA For. Serv. (1965b)

Table 9.3. *Specific gravity data for 15 western species*

Species	Mean estimated tree specific gravity	Range of estimated tree specific gravity	Number of trees sampled	Wood Handbook average green specific gravity
Douglas-fir	0.45	0.33–0.59	9133	0.45
White fir	0.37	0.26–0.54	2150	0.37
California red fir	0.36	0.31–0.46	840	0.36
Grand fir	0.35	0.24–0.55	862	0.35
Pacific silver fir	0.40	0.28–0.55	330	0.40
Noble fir	0.37	0.26–0.44	158	0.37
Western hemlock	0.42	0.30–0.52	1040	0.42
Western larch	0.48	0.38–0.54	678	0.48
Black cottonwood	0.31	0.28–0.40	120	0.31
Ponderosa pine	0.37	0.27–0.54	5337	0.38
Sugar pine	0.34	0.28–0.45	299	0.34
Western white pine	0.36	0.29–0.45	292	0.35
Lodgepole pine	0.38	0.26–0.55	3516	0.38
Engelmann spruce	0.35	0.23–0.58	1789	0.33
Western redcedar	0.32	0.27–0.42	504	0.31

Source: Maeglin and Wahlgren (1972); USFPL (1987).

Sources of variation in specific gravity ■

Many factors, including site, climate, geographic location, and species, affect the specific gravity of wood. Since many of these occur in combination, it is difficult to separate the independent effects. There is a great deal of scientific literature dealing with these relationships, the inconsistencies of which indicate their complex interactions.

Site-related factors such as moisture, availability of sunlight and nutrients, wind, and temperature can affect specific gravity. These are in turn determined to a large extent by elevation, aspect, slope, latitude, soil type, stand composition, and spacing. All these factors can affect the size and wall thickness of the cell and thus the density. Species differ greatly, however, in their sensitivity to these factors.

It is common for density to vary significantly within a tree. Figure 9.8 shows the variation found within young yellow poplar in West Virginia. Note that the density was found to vary from 0.36 to 0.42 at various heights of the tree and from 0.37 to 0.40 at different distances from the pith at selected heights. In many species, butt logs tend to have a higher density than logs cut from higher in the main stem. However, in some woods such as tupelo gum and yellow cypress the wood near the base of the tree may be lighter than normal wood. Generally, in softwoods the density decreases with height in the tree and increases with dis-

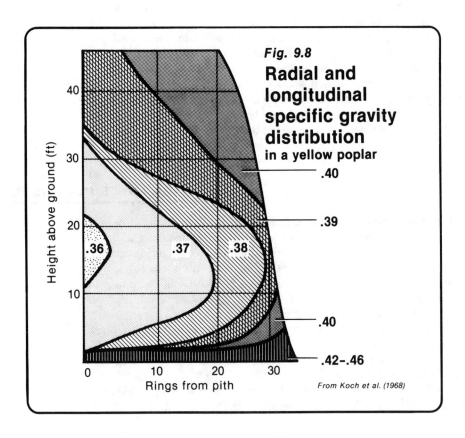

Fig. 9.8

Radial and longitudinal specific gravity distribution

in a yellow poplar

.40

.39

.36   .37   .38

.40

.42–.46

From Koch et al. (1968)

Height above ground (ft)

Rings from pith

tance from the pith. In large softwood logs, the density often increases outward from the pith and then reaches a fairly constant level.

Juvenile wood, reaction wood ■

As explained in Chapter 6, the density of juvenile wood is usually less than that of mature wood, and such wood has a correspondingly lower strength. Strength may be of concern when the portion of a log near the pith is utilized for lumber or veneer. Another problem in the utilization of juvenile wood is the tendency to exhibit abnormally high longitudinal shrinkage. In lumber such shrinkage results in excessive warp making the product unusable for most applications. This is less serious in plywood for reasons discussed in Chapter 14.

The specific gravity of compression wood, in contrast to juvenile wood, is generally greater than that of normal wood—up to 40% greater. This higher density can often be detected visually because of the higher proportion of summerwood; yet in some cases, the density of compression and normal wood may not differ significantly. Despite its usually higher density, compression wood is to be avoided in lumber products because of its high longitudinal shrinkage and erratic strength properties.

The commercial standards for ladder rails specifically exclude compression wood because of its unreliable strength and the tendency to exhibit *brash failure* (splinter-free fracture). Recognizing the influence of juvenility, the American Institute of Timber Construction limits the amount of pith-associated wood permitted in tension laminations of laminated beams. In higher-grade glulam beams, no more than one-eighth of the cross section can consist of such wood.

Tension wood, like compression wood, often possesses higher than normal specific gravity. However, some hardwoods with normal density often contain scattered groups of gelatinous fibers that could be termed tension wood. The effect of tension wood upon density is highly variable.

Density of forest products ■

The density of veneer, particle, and fiber products differs from the density of the wood raw material because of the weight of adhesives and other additives and the compression of the wood that occurs during the manufacturing process. Plywood is ordinarily only slightly denser than the wood from which it is produced—usually 5–15%. The pressure used to press plywood is intended only to provide good contact between the veneers and not to densify the wood, although a slight amount of densification does occur.

Particleboard, by contrast, is usually produced at a density of 1.2–1.6 times the density of the species used. Particleboard densities ranging from 39 to 55 lb/ft³ are common. Of this weight, 3–12% is the weight of the resin (adhesive) and wax used to impart water repellency.

Fiber products vary widely in density. Insulation board used for wall sheathing is produced at 10–30 lb/ft³, medium density board at 31–50 lb/ft³, and hardboard at 50–70 lb/ft³. These products may contain from 1 to 30% bonding resins and other additives to improve strength and water-resistant properties.

Metric practice ▪

The *International System of Units* (SI), used throughout most of the world, may someday be commonly used in the United States. This system is a modern version of the meter-kilogram-second-ampere system that was adopted by international treaty in 1935. SI units are recommended for wood science research, although presently much work is being reported in English measurements. In areas of applied technology such as product sizes, codes and standards, and engineering and structural design, most work in the United States is still based upon English units.

Wood scientists and technologists need to be able to work and think either in terms of meters and newtons or in feet and pounds. An excellent guide to the proper use of metric units is *Standard for Metric Practice,* E 380, published by the American Society for Testing and Materials. The following comments may aid in understanding metric units commonly encountered in forest products research. Table 9.4 contains conversions for some of the commonly used non-SI units.

One great advantage of SI is that only one base unit is used for each physical quantity. Base units include meter (m) for length, second (s) for time, and kilogram (kg) (not gram) for mass. All mechanical properties are then derived from the base units. Some derived units are given special names such as newton (N) for force, joule (J) for work or energy, and watt (W) for power. The SI units force, energy, and power are the same regardless of whether the process is mechanical, electrical, chemical, or thermal.

The use of the centimeter (cm) is discouraged in SI and should be avoided. However, use of the centimeter for length and cubic centimeter for volume will undoubtedly persist in wood research because of the ease of calculating specific gravity in these quantities.

Confusion about the definition of a *pound* is common when using the English system. This unit is used both as a mass and as a force unit, although properly it should be indicated as *pound-force* (lbf) when used in the latter sense. When used to indicate mass, the pound can be converted to kilograms. When indicating force, the pound should be converted to newtons (N), the unit of force in SI. A *newton* is the force resulting from a kilogram, i.e., kg × m/s².

For large quantities of material, the *ton* is often used in commerce as the unit of mass. A *long ton* is 2240 lb, a *short ton* 2000 lb, and a *metric ton* is 1000 kg. None of these terms are SI and when used, their definition should be given to avoid confusion. Note that the term *weight*, as commonly used, generally applies to mass. Because of the uncertainty as to whether mass or force is indicated, however, the use of the term weight is discouraged by SI. Nonetheless, it will undoubtedly remain in common practice and is used in this text as a unit of mass.

Many wood science references in the European literature use *kilogram-force* (kgf) or *kilopond* (kp) as the units of force. These have been replaced in SI with the newton (N). The newton is used for other derived units involving force.

Table 9.4.   Common non-SI to SI conversions

Non-SI unit	SI unit equivalent
Length	
foot	3.048×10^{-1} m (meters)
inch	2.540×10^{-2} m
mile (U.S. statute)	1.609×10^{3} m
Area	
acre	4.046×10^{3} m^2
hectare	1.000×10^{4} m^2
ft^2	9.290×10^{-2} m^2
in.^{2}	6.452×10^{-4} m^2
Volume	
ft^3	2.832×10^{-2} m^3
in.^{3}	1.639×10^{-5} m^3
board foot	2.360×10^{-3} m^3
Force	
kilogram-force	9.807 N (newtons)
kilopond	9.807 N
lbf	4.445 N
Mass	
pound (avoirdupois)	4.536×10^{-1} kg (kilograms)
ton (short)	9.072×10^{2} kg
ton (metric)	1.000×10^{3} kg
Moment	
lbf·in.	1.130×10^{-1} N·m (newton
lbf·ft	1.356 N·m meters)
Energy and work	
Btu	1.055×10^{3} J (joules)
ft·lbf	1.356 J
Density (mass per unit volume)	
lb/ft^3	1.602×10 kg/m^3
g/cm^3	1.000×10^{3} kg/m^3
Pressure or stress	
lbf/in.^{2} (psi)	6.895×10^{3} Pa (pascals)
kgf/m^2	9.807 Pa

Other SI symbols	
s	second
k	kilo or 10^3
M	mega or 10^6

For example, stress is expressed as newtons per square meter (N/m^2) and called a *pascal* (Pa); the unit of energy, a *newton meter* (N·m), is termed a *joule* (J); and the unit of power, called a *watt* (W), is a N·m/S.

For engineering purposes it is generally more convenient to work with *kilopascals* (kPa = 1000 Pa) than with pascals. It may be helpful to remember that 1 pound per square inch (psi) equals approximately 7 kPa. In some cases the use of *megapascals* (MPa) is convenient. Note that in SI the prefix M equals 10^6. In the English system M is often used to indicate 10^3, as in MSF (thousand square feet), another source of possible confusion. Also, the use of the terms such as *billion* and *trillion* should be avoided. In the United States billion means 10^9, but it means 10^{12} in most other countries.

The standard method for metric measurement of lumber utilizes the actual length, width, and thickness to calculate the cubic meter volume. The standard unit of lumber volume measurement in the United States is the *board foot* (bd ft), which is based upon nominal rather than actual measurements. This will be discussed in Chapter 13.

REVIEW

A. Terms to define or explain:
1. Density
2. Specific gravity (as applied to wood)
3. Void volume specific gravity
4. Porosity
5. Specific gravity of dry cell wall substance
6. Coefficient of variation
7. Density survey

B. Questions or concepts to explain:
1. Be able to calculate specific gravity.
2. Be able to calculate density in English and metric units.
3. Be able to estimate the proportion of void volume in wood.
4. Be able to estimate the weight of a lumber product from its volume, specific gravity, and moisture content.
5. Be familiar with the sources of information on specific gravity of U.S. and imported species.
6. Be able to calculate the moisture content at which wood will sink in water.
7. Be able to convert from specific gravity at one moisture content to that at a different one.
8. Know how to estimate the range of specific gravity of a species.
9. Know three procedures for determining the volume of a sample to determine the specific gravity.
10. Be able to estimate the moisture content of a wood sample when all voids are filled with water.
11. Explain the effect of moisture content on specific gravity.
12. Explain how specific gravity is related to growth rate in hardwoods and softwoods.
13. Describe the factors that may affect specific gravity within a species.

REFERENCES AND SUPPLEMENTAL READINGS

American Society of Testing and Materials. 1987. Standard test methods for specific gravity of wood and wood-based materials. ANSI/ASTM Vol. 4.09; D 2395.

Brown, H.P.; Panshin, A J.; and Forsaith, C.C. 1952. Textbook of Wood Technology, Vol 2. NY: McGraw-Hill, pp 1–22.

Kellogg, R.M., and Wangaard, F.F. 1969. Variation in the cell wall density of wood. Wood Fiber 1:180–204.

Koch, C.B.; Brauner, A.; and Kulow, D. 1968. Specific gravity variation within yellow poplar. W.V. Ag. Exper. Sta. Bull. 564T.

Koch, P. 1972. Utilization of southern pines, Vol 1. USDA For. Ser. Handb. 420. pp. 235–264.

Kollmann, F.P., and Côté, W.A., Jr. 1968. Principles of Wood Science and Technology. NY:Springer-Verlag, pp. 160–80.

Maeglin, R.R., and Wahlgren, H.E. 1972. Western wood density survey, Report No. 2. USDA For. Ser. Res. Pap. FPL-183.

Oberg, J.C. 1989. Impact of changing raw material on lumber and panel products. USDA S.E. For. Exp. Sta. Gen. Tech. Rpt. SE-63. pp.17–33.

Senft, J.F.; Bendtsen, B.A.; and Galligan, W.L. 1985. Weak wood-fast grown trees make problem lumber. J. For. 83(8):477–82.

Shepard, R.K., and Shottafer, J.E. 1992. Specific gravity and mechanical property relationships in red pine. For. Prod. J. 42(7/8):60–67.

———. 1990. Effect of early release on the specific gravity of black spruce. For. Prod. J. 40(1):18–24.

Stamm, A.J., and Sanders, R. 1966. Specific gravity of wood substance of loblolly pine as affected by chemical composition. TAPPI 49:397–400.

Thomas, R.J., and Kellison, R.C. 1989. Impact of changing raw material on paper manu-
    facture. USDA S.E. For. Exp. Sta. Gen. Tech. Rpt. SE-63. pp.33–47.
USDA Forest Service. 1965. Southern wood density survey, 1965 Status Report Res. Pap.
    FPL-26.
_____. 1965. Western wood density survey—Report No.1. Res. Pap. FPL-27.
U.S. Forest Products Laboratory. 1987. Wood Handbook. USDA For. Ser. Agric. Handb.
    72(3):12–15.
_____. 1972. Proc. Symp. Effect of Growth Acceleration on Properties of Wood, Madi-
    son, Wis.

10

Mechanical properties of wood

■ **THE STRENGTH** and resistance to deformation of a material are referred to as its mechanical properties. *Strength* is the ability of a material to carry applied loads or forces. Resistance to deformation determines the amount a material is compressed, distorted, or bent under an applied load. Changes in shape that take place instantaneously as a load is applied and are recoverable when the load is removed are termed *elastic deformation.* If the deformation, on the other hand, develops slowly after the load is applied, it is termed a *rheological* or *time-dependent* property.

Mechanical properties are usually the most important characteristics of wood products to be used in structural applications. A *structural application* is any use where strength is one of the primary criteria for selection of the material. Figure 10.1 shows two structural applications of wood. Structural uses of wood products include floor joists and rafters in wood-frame homes, power line transmission poles, plywood roof sheathing and subflooring, glue-laminated beams and decking in commercial buildings, particleboard flooring in mobile homes, steps and rails of wood ladders, sailboat masts, and frames of upholstered furniture.

The term *strength* is often used in a general sense to refer to all mechanical properties. However, since there are many different types of strength and elastic properties, it is important to be very specific about the type of mechanical property being discussed. A wood that is relatively strong with respect to one strength property may rank lower in a different property. The type of mechanical property

213

Fig. 10.1

Structural lumber products used as primary building elements

Courtesy USFPL (1974)

A. An experimental light-frame structure utilizing a system that connects the studs rigidly to the roof and floor.

Courtesy American Institute of Timber Construction (1971)

B. A building utilizing a three-hinge, glue-laminated arch.

most critical to any application is determined by the type of loading to which that product will be subjected. For example, in a floor joist the modulus of elasticity is very important because it determines the amount the joist will bend under a load and thus how solid the floor will feel. In the case of wood flooring, the side hardness determines the resistance to denting when under a concentrated load. Some of the most important mechanical properties of wood products are listed in Table 10.1. To appreciate the meaning of the various strength properties of wood, it is necessary to understand some basic definitions of engineering mechanics.

Table 10.1. Important mechanical properties of wood

Properties	How or where this property is important
Strength properties	
Bending strength (MOR)	Determines the load a beam will carry.
Compression strength parallel to the grain	Determines the load a short post or column will carry.
Compression perpendicular to the grain	Important in design of the connections between wood members in a building and at the supports for a beam.
Tension strength parallel to the grain	Important for the bottom member (chord) in a wood truss and in the design of connections between structural members.
Shear strength parallel to the grain	Often determines the load-carrying capacity of short beams.
Toughness	Measure of the amount of work expended in breaking a small specimen in impact bending.
Resilience	Measured by the amount of energy absorbed when a piece is bent within its elastic range.
Side hardness	Relates to the resistance to denting, as for flooring.
Tension perpendicular to the grain	Important in design of the connections between wood members in a building.
Work to maximum load	Measure of the energy absorbed by a specimen as it is slowly bent.
Elastic properties	
Modulus of elasticity	Measure of the resistance to bending, i.e., directly related to the stiffness of a beam, also a factor in the strength of a long column.
Modulus of elasticity parallel to the grain (Young's modulus)	Measure of the resistance to elongation or shortening of a specimen under uniform tension or compression.

Concepts of stress, strain, and flexure ■

Two basic concepts used throughout the study of mechanics are stress and strain. *Stress* is a distributed force per unit of area. A stress occurs where one member acts upon another to impose a force or transfer a load, such as a column supporting a beam. Stress also occurs internally within a body. Stress is usually expressed in psi (lb/in.^{2}) or in pascals (N/m^2). One psi equals 6895 pascals.

When an external force is applied to any body, internal stresses result. These stresses distort or deform the shape and size of the body. The change in length per unit of length in the direction of the stress is called the *strain*. Since strain is expressed in units of length divided by the length, it has no dimensions.

Figure 10.2 illustrates stress and strain in a wood test specimen under compression parallel to the grain. When a load of 8000 lb is applied to the specimen, an internal parallel-to-grain stress of 2000 psi is created throughout. The stress is uniformly distributed at all distances from the end; therefore, the total deformation of 0.0072 in. (6.0000 − 5.9928) is distributed uniformly along the 6-in. length. Since strain is change in length per unit of length, the strain is 0.0072 in./6 in. or 0.0012.

Strain will result whenever stress is applied to any solid body. If the stress applied does not exceed a level called the *proportional limit,* there is a linear relationship between the amount of stress and the resulting strain. The shape of a typical stress-strain curve for wood tested parallel to the grain is shown in Figure 10.3. Below the proportional limit the ratio of stress to strain, i.e., the slope of the line, is a constant value called the *modulus of elasticity* (MOE). In compression and tensile tests, this ratio is sometimes termed *Young's Modulus* to differentiate it from the MOE as determined by a bending test. In the example shown in Figure 10.2, the MOE is 1.67 million psi. Notice that the greater the stress required to produce a given strain, the greater the resistance to deformation and the higher the MOE of the material.

The concepts of stress and strain are quite simple in uniaxial tension and compression but become more complex in a beam (bending member). When a beam such as a wood floor joist is bent, the top half is stressed in compression and the bottom half is stressed in tension. The maximum stresses develop at the top and bottom surfaces of the beam. In simple beam analysis, it is assumed that the stresses vary in a linear manner from the top to bottom surface as shown in Figure 10.4. No tension or compression stresses occur at the center of a rectangular beam. This center plane, free of compression or tension, is termed the *neutral axis.*

In fact, the tensile and compressive stress distribution is not precisely as idealized as in Figure 10.4. The equal stress distribution above and below the neutral axis as shown is generally assumed and used for most engineering purposes. Actually, clear straight-grained wood is slightly stronger in tension than in compression, but lumber containing knots and grain deviation is usually stronger in compression than in tension.

Since no tensile or compressive stresses develop at the neutral axis of the beam, the length (AA in Fig. 10.4) of the neutral axis remains the same when the beam is bent. The top surface of the beam is compressed and the bottom surface is lengthened as a result of the compression and tension stresses. The beam then bends because of the tensile and compressive strains. The amount of bending at the midpoint of the beam is termed the *deflection.* The deflection that occurs when a beam is loaded depends upon the location and magnitude of the load, the length and size of the beam, and the MOE of the material. The higher the MOE of the material, the less a beam will deflect under a given load.

The MOE of wood materials is generally determined by use of a bending test since this test is relatively easy to perform. To do the test, the beam is center-loaded while the load and deflection are measured. From this data, the MOE can be calculated by use of its relationship with the beam size, span, load, and deflection. It is a simpler test to conduct and more closely related to most use situations than the MOE (Young's Modulus) as determined from a tensile or compressive test.

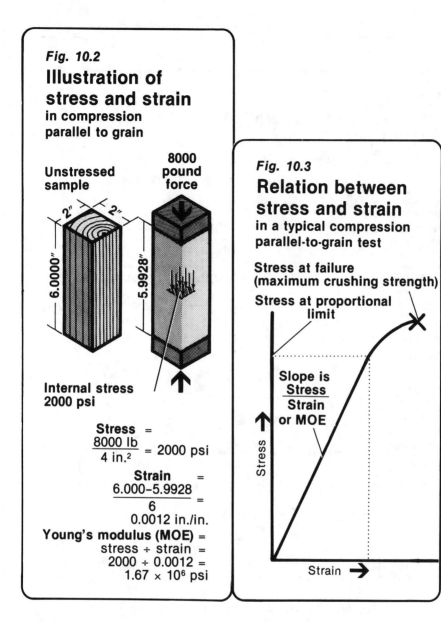

Fig. 10.2

Illustration of stress and strain
in compression parallel to grain

Unstressed sample

8000 pound force

2" 2"

6.0000"

5.9928"

Internal stress 2000 psi

Stress = $\dfrac{8000\ \text{lb}}{4\ \text{in.}^2}$ = 2000 psi

Strain = $\dfrac{6.000-5.9928}{6}$ = 0.0012 in./in.

Young's modulus (MOE) = stress ÷ strain = 2000 ÷ 0.0012 = 1.67×10^6 psi

Fig. 10.3

Relation between stress and strain
in a typical compression parallel-to-grain test

Stress at failure (maximum crushing strength)

Stress at proportional limit

Slope is $\dfrac{\text{Stress}}{\text{Strain}}$ **or MOE**

Stress

Strain →

For a test specimen loaded by a concentrated load at the center of its span and supported at its ends, the MOE can be calculated from the following formula:

MOE = $PL^3/48ID$ (psi)

where

P = the concentrated center load in pounds (below the proportional limit)
D = the deflection at midspan in inches resulting from P
L = the span in inches
I = moment of inertia, a function of beam size
   = (width × depth^3)/12 for beams with a rectangular cross section; units are inches^4.

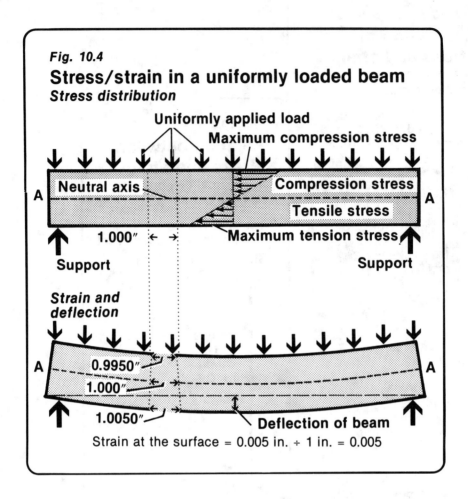

Fig. 10.4
Stress/strain in a uniformly loaded beam
Stress distribution

Uniformly applied load

Maximum compression stress

Neutral axis

Compression stress

Tensile stress

A   A

1.000"

Maximum tension stress

Support   Support

Strain and deflection

A   A

0.9950"

1.000"

1.0050"

Deflection of beam

Strain at the surface = 0.005 in. ÷ 1 in. = 0.005

If the MOE of the beam is known, this same equation can be solved for *D* to predict the amount of deflection that results from a concentrated load applied at midspan.

The MOE for wood ranges from about 0.5×10^6 psi to 2.8×10^6 psi. The engineer or structural designer uses the MOE of the product he or she is using to determine the required size of the beam. To do so, he or she must consider the deflection that is considered acceptable, the span of the beam, and the load that it will be carrying. Several examples may help illustrate how the MOE can be calculated and how knowledge of the MOE can be used by the structural engineer.

EXAMPLE 1:   A $2 \times 2 \times 30$-in. clear dry specimen of red oak is supported near each end of its 28-in. span and loaded at the center in a universal testing machine. A gradually increasing load is applied, and when the load reaches 1500 lb (below the proportional limit), the deflection at midspan under the load measures 0.260 in. The MOE of this specimen can then be determined as follows:

$$\text{MOE} = \frac{PL^3}{48ID} = \frac{1500 \times 28^3}{48 \times (2 \times 2^3/12) \times 0.260} = 1{,}980{,}000 \text{ psi}$$

EXAMPLE 2:   Suppose a 3-in.-square piece of red oak of the same type and quality as in example 1 is to be placed between two roof beams and a space heater weighing 3000 lb is to be hung from the center of the span. The *span* (the distance between the roof beams) is 50 in. How much will the 3 × 3-in. specimen deflect when the 3000-lb load is applied?

$$D = \frac{PL^3}{48\,(MOE)I} = \frac{3000 \times 50^3}{48 \times 1.98 \times 10^6 \times (3 \times 3^3/12)} = 0.58 \text{ in. deflection}$$

EXAMPLE 3:   A strip of particleboard 0.5 in. thick and 3 in. wide is loaded at midspan between supports 12 in. apart. When the load reaches 20 lb, the deflection is measured as 0.058 in. The MOE of the particleboard therefore is

$$MOE = \frac{PL^3}{48ID} = \frac{20 \times 12^3}{48 \times (3 \times 0.5^3/12) \times 0.058} = 397,000 \text{ psi}$$

EXAMPLE 4:   Suppose a strip of this same particleboard 10 in. wide is used for a bookshelf 24 in. long and that a book weighing 12 lb is placed in the center of the shelf. How much could you expect this shelf to bend?

$$D = \frac{PL^3}{48(MOE)I} = \frac{12 \times 24^3}{48 \times 397,000 \times (10 \times 0.5^3/12)}$$

$$= 0.084 \text{ in. deflection at the center}$$

In example 4 the deflection calculated is an estimate of the elastic deflection which would occur instantaneously if the piece were loaded as specified. If the weight was left on the shelf for a long period of months or years, some additional deflection might occur. This sagging of the shelf with time is an example of rheological or time-dependent behavior, in this case called *creep*.

The bending strength of solid wood and wood-based products is usually expressed in terms of the *modulus of rupture* (MOR). The MOR is calculated from the maximum load (load at failure) in a bending test, using the same testing procedure for determining the MOE. Using a test specimen with a rectangular cross section, the MOR is calculated from the following equation:

$$MOR = 1.5PL/bd^2 \text{ (psi)}$$

where

P = the breaking (maximum) load in pounds
L = the distance between supports (span) (inches)
b = the width of the beam (inches)
d = the depth of the beam (inches)

This equation is valid only when the rectangular beam is freely supported at both ends and is loaded at the center of the span; it can be used to estimate the stress (below the proportional limit) that develops on the top and bottom surfaces of a beam as a result of any given load. For instance, if P is a load below the proportional limit, the solution of the equation will give the compression and tension stress at the top and bottom surface of the beam. Consider these examples illustrating the use of the flexural stress equation.

EXAMPLE 5:   The same sample of red oak from example 1 is loaded to failure in a testing machine, using the procedure described. The breaking load is found to be 2100 lb. The MOR can then be calculated as follows:

$$\text{MOR} = \frac{1.5PL}{bd^2} = \frac{1.5 \times 2100 \times 28}{2 \times 2^2} = 11,025 \text{ psi}$$

EXAMPLE 6:   Suppose it is now of interest to determine the short-term load at which the 3×3 in example 2 would probably fail (break). This could be estimated as follows:

$$P = \frac{(\text{MOR})bd^2}{1.5L} = \frac{11,025 \times 3 \times 3^2}{1.5 \times 50} = 3969 \text{ lb}$$

EXAMPLE 7:   If this same 3×3 is loaded to only 3000 lb, as described in example 2, what would be the stress at the center of the span on the top and bottom surfaces of the beam? This can be determined using essentially the same equation as for the MOR, i.e.:

$$\text{Flexural stress} = \frac{1.5PL}{bd^2} = \frac{1.5 \times 3000 \times 50}{3 \times 3^2} = 8330 \text{ psi}$$

These examples are intended only to provide some insight into the application of a knowledge of mechanical properties. A wide range of equations and design considerations must be used by wood scientists and engineers to cover the many ways in which structural members are supported and loaded. To become proficient in wood structural design requires a knowledge of (1) the mechanical and moisture-related behavior of wood, (2) good civil engineering practice, and (3) building codes and standards. Books by Hoyle and Woeste (1989), Gurfinkel (1973), Madsen (1992), and Breyer (1980) describe in detail the engineering of wood structures.

The procedure for testing clear wood is specified by the American Society for Testing and Materials in the standard designated ASTM D 143. The standard procedures for testing wood-based panel products are described in ASTM D 1037. Figure 10.5 shows a piece of particleboard being tested to determine the internal strength by loading it at 45° to the plane of the specimen. This test method was developed by wood scientists at the University of Minnesota.

Fig. 10.5
**Testing the internal strength of a
particleboard using the Minnesota
shear test method.**

Shear stress and strain ■

Shear stress differs from tensile or compression stress in that it tends to make one part of a material slip past the material adjacent to it. Figure 10.6 shows a method of determining the *shear strength* of wood parallel to the grain. Wood is low in shear strength parallel to the grain but extremely high in shear strength across the grain. In fact, if an attempt is made to shear wood across the grain using the device illustrated in Figure 10.6, the wood will be crushed rather than sheared.

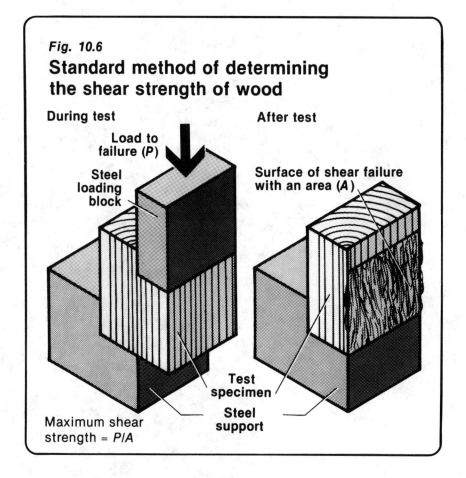

Fig. 10.6

Standard method of determining the shear strength of wood

During test   **After test**

Load to failure (*P*)

Steel loading block

Surface of shear failure with an area (*A*)

Maximum shear strength = *P/A*

Test specimen

Steel support

Shear stresses develop internally in wood beams, and thus shear strength is sometimes important in design. When beams are loaded, the various levels or layers tend to slip horizontally past each other as the beam bends. This can be visualized by considering a beam made of six 1-in.-thick boards that are nailed only at the center of the span, as shown in Figure 10.7. As this composite beam bends, the ends of the boards slip with respect to each other. If these boards were glued together to form a laminated beam, the slipping would be resisted and the beam would be much stiffer, but as a result shear stresses would develop internally in the beam. Such shear stresses are usually not high enough to be a factor in the engineering of light-frame wood beams such as rafters and floor joists. In large solid timber beams and laminated beams, however, the shear strength may be the limiting factor in how much load can be safely carried. In contrast to bending compression and tension stresses, which are maximum at the top and bottom surfaces of a beam, shear stresses are greatest in the center horizontal plane of the beam.

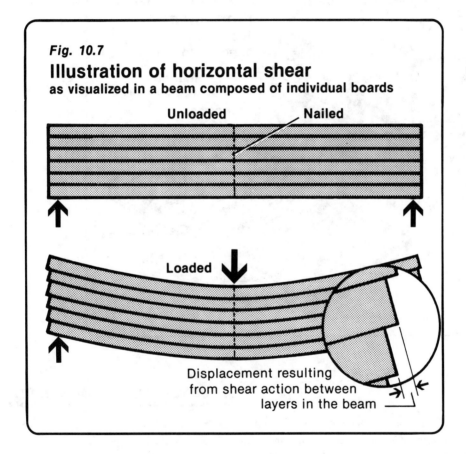

Fig. 10.7

Illustration of horizontal shear
as visualized in a beam composed of individual boards

Unloaded   **Nailed**

Loaded

Displacement resulting
from shear action between
layers in the beam

Another type of shear stress, sometimes termed *rolling shear,* is important in plywood components where veneers of wood are glued with the grain direction in adjacent pieces perpendicular to one another. Rolling shear is a stress that acts in the plane of the plywood panel. It is important in the engineering design of plywood-wood components such as stress-skin panels and box beams. In such products, rolling shear is developed at the point that the solid wood member is glued to the plywood. In solid wood products, shear strength parallel to the grain is important when designing the metal connections between structural elements.

Figure 10.8 illustrates the action of rolling shear in a stress-skin floor panel.

The wood cells at the glue line tend to roll (or so it can be visualized) when the stress is applied. This must be considered when engineering the component, because the rolling shear strength of wood is less than shear strength parallel to the grain.

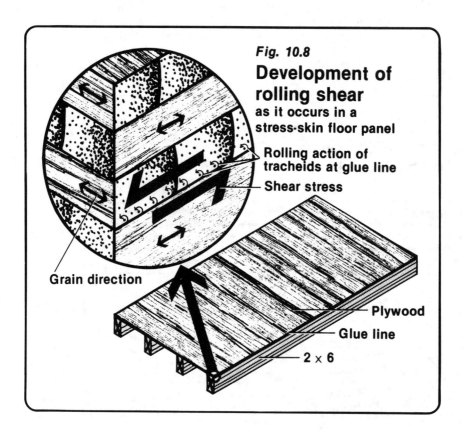

Fig. 10.8

Development of rolling shear
as it occurs in a stress-skin floor panel

Rolling action of tracheids at glue line

Shear stress

Grain direction

Plywood

Glue line

2 × 6

Anisotropic nature of wood ■

A material that has the same mechanical properties in each direction is termed *isotropic*. Many metals, plastics, and cement products are isotropic. In contrast, wood has drastically different properties parallel to the grain versus the transverse direction, and thus it is termed *anisotropic* (not isotropic). More specifically, wood can be considered as an *orthotropic* material, i.e., one that exhibits different properties in the three mutually perpendicular directions or axes.

The strength and elastic properties of wood are different in the longitudinal, tangential, and radial directions. However, the properties in the radial and tangential directions usually do not differ greatly. Since it is not possible to predict the radial-tangential grain orientation of lumber (i.e., whether flat-sawn or edgegrain lumber will be used), a common strength value for the tangential and radial direction is standard for engineering purposes. It is referred to as a *perpendicular-to-grain property*.

Figure 10.9 illustrates the maximum load a Douglas-fir 10 × 10-in. post could safely support if designed in the normal way (loaded *parallel* to the grain) and the amount it would be compressed under this load. This is compared to a post produced by stacking pieces sidewise (loaded *perpendicular* to the grain). The MOE of Douglas-fir parallel to the grain is 20 times as large as MOE perpendicular to the grain. This results in the greater change in length of the unusual post despite the fact that it can be loaded to only one-eighth the capacity of a normal post.

Forest products produced from cross-laminated veneers, particles, or fibers tend to be more isotropic than solid wood since the process of reconstitution randomizes the effect of grain direction. Panel products such as plywood have a major advantage over a solid wood panel since they possess strength in both direc-

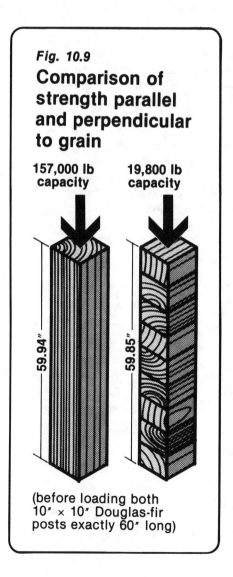

Fig. 10.9

Comparison of strength parallel and perpendicular to grain

157,000 lb capacity

19,800 lb capacity

59.94"

59.85"

(before loading both 10″ × 10″ Douglas-fir posts exactly 60″ long)

tions of the plane of the panel. Unfortunately, reconstitution also tends to reduce the maximum strength that can be attained as compared to the parallel-to-grain direction for solid wood. Because of the orthotropic nature of wood, it is not possible to subdivide wood into small, randomly oriented elements and reconstitute it to a product as strong in one direction as the original solid wood.

Products laminated parallel to the grain such as parallel-laminated veneer and glue-laminated beams are often stronger than a single piece of wood of the same size. This is largely because in the laminated product the knots and other defects are randomized and do not occur together; while in the single solid member the defects may proceed through the entire piece.

Relationship of strength to specific gravity ∎

As discussed in Chapter 9, the strength of wood is closely correlated with specific gravity (SG). It is possible to make a reasonably good estimate of strength based only upon specific gravity without knowing the species. In some developing countries, where grading rules for lumber are not highly developed or where many species are sawn and used interchangeably, the grading of structural lumber is based primarily upon specific gravity.

Mechanical properties are not all affected to the same degree by changes in specific gravity. Table 10.2 shows some strength-specific gravity relationships established at the U.S. Forest Products Laboratory. Note that properties such as MOE in bending and maximum crushing strength parallel to the grain increase linearly with specific gravity. The relationship for other properties is a power function. Thus some properties increase with specific gravity much more rapidly than others.

Table 10.2. Relationship between mechanical properties and specific gravities for softwoods

Property	Strength prediction from SG	Estimated strength at selected specific gravitites (SG @ 12% MC)			
		0.30	0.40	0.50	0.60
Bending					
MOR (psi)	$25600 \times SG^{1.05}$	7230	9780	12360	14970
MOE (10^6 psi)	$3.13 \times SG^{0.90}$	1.06	1.37	1.68	1.98
Compression parallel to the grain					
Maximum crushing strength (psi)	$14600 \times SG^{1.02}$	4270	5730	7200	8670
MOE 10^6 psi)	$3.72 \times SG^{0.91}$	1.24	1.62	1.98	2.34
Compression perpendicular to the grain					
Stress at proportional limit (psi)	$2540 \times SG^{1.65}$	348	560	809	1094
Side hardness (lb)	$3770 \times SG^{2.25}$	251	480	793	1194

Source: USFPL (1987).

It is sometimes necessary to compare test results from a single specimen to the published average strength values for that species. This can be done even if the specific gravity of the specimen varies from the published average for a species. It is possible to estimate the strength of a species at one specific gravity if the strength property at another specific gravity is known. The following relationship (USFPL 1944) may be used:

$$S_1/S_2 = (SG_1/SG_2)^n$$

where

S_1 = strength at specific gravity 1 (SG_1)
S_2 = strength at specific gravity 2 (SG_2)
n = exponent 0.25 greater than exponents shown in Table 10.2 for the strength–specific gravity relationship;

For example, the maximum crushing strength of longleaf pine at a specific gravity of 0.59 is known to be 8470 psi (obtained from Appendix Table A.5). The estimate of the strength at a specific gravity of 0.65 is

$$S_1/8470 = (0.65/0.59)^{1.25}$$
$$S_1 = 9560 \text{ psi}$$

Comparative strengths of important species ■

Although it is possible to estimate the strength of wood knowing only the specific gravity, more-precise information can be obtained by referring to data collected for that particular species. One of the most widely used sources of such information is tables from the *Wood Handbook* (USFPL 1987). These are reproduced as Appendix Tables A.5, A.6, and A.7 for your convenience. Another source of information on properties of U.S. and Canadian species is ASTM D 2555. In addition to the mean values, this ASTM standard also indicates the standard deviation of each property mean.

The data presented in Appendix Tables A.5, A.6, and A.7 show strength values for clear, straight-grained, defect-free wood at both the green and 12% MC conditions. These tables can be very helpful in making comparisons among species. Note that they contain information on the MOE and MOR in bending, shear strength parallel to the grain, and maximum crushing strength parallel to the grain. Other strength properties included in Appendix Table A.5 are *side hardness,* which is the force required to embed a 0.444-in.-diameter ball halfway into the side of a piece of wood; *impact bending,* which is the height of drop at which a 50-lb hammer will break a 2 × 2-in. beam supported on a 28-in. span; and work to maximum load, which also is a measure of the energy absorbed when a beam is broken in bending. In this latter case, the load is applied slowly in contrast to the impact load used in the 50-lb hammer drop test. You should become familiar with the type of information available in these tables, as this will enable you to answer many questions about the comparative properties of alternative species. Remember that these values are for clear straight-grained wood. Defects such as knots and slope of grain greatly reduce strength properties.

Following are some examples that illustrate the use of the clear wood strength values in Appendix Tables A.5, A.6, and A.7.

EXAMPLE 1:   A manufacturing plant has been producing interior furniture parts from American sycamore but is considering changing to sweetgum parts. The most important property for these parts is bending and screw-holding strength. Will sweetgum have adequate strength?

For wood at 12% MC, the information needed from Appendix Table A.5 is:

	Specific gravity	MOR (psi)
Sweetgum	0.52	12,500
Sycamore	0.49	10,000

Sweetgum should be satisfactory in bending strength since it is 25% stronger than sycamore, but remember that this comparison is valid only for clear wood. Will the grade (freedom from knots and slope of grain) be the same for the sweetgum as for the sycamore? Screw-holding strength is directly related to specific gravity, so sweetgum should be about 6% stronger than sycamore in this regard. Therefore, it appears that sweetgum would serve as well as sycamore with respect to these two properties.

EXAMPLE 2:   Inexpensive skateboards are being successfully manufactured from hackberry, but the manufacturer is considering the use of yellow poplar instead. The important properties are impact bending and work to maximum load. Will yellow poplar be an adequate substitute for hackberry?
The information needed from Appendix Table A.5 is

	Specific gravity	Impact bending (in.)	Work to maximum load (in. lb/in.^{3})
Hackberry	0.53	43	12.8
Yellow poplar	0.42	24	8.8

Since yellow poplar has significantly lower values in both properties it appears that this substitution would not be satisfactory.

EXAMPLE 3:   Two imported species, jarrah from Australia and keruing from Southeast Asia, are being considered for use as industrial flooring. The important properties for this use are side hardness and nailability. Which of these would appear to be better suited to this application?
Appendix Table A.6 indicates that

	Specific gravity (green)	Side hardness (@ 12% MC)
Jarrah	0.67	1910
Keruing	0.69	1270
Black maple	0.52	1180

Jarrah is clearly more resistant to denting than keruing, as indicated by the side hardness value. However, keruing has about the same side hardness as black maple, which is a common industrial flooring material. Therefore, it should be satisfactory in this regard. When considering imported species, it is wise to obtain data on properties from the region where the material is produced. This is advisable since much variability exists over the range of many of these species.

EXAMPLE 4:   A manufacturer of pool tables is using jack pine from Canada to produce the structural frame that holds the table top. The important properties are bending stiffness and compression perpendicular to the grain. A sales person is trying to convince the firm to use Canadian white spruce for this application.
Appendix Table A.7 provides the following information:

	Specific gravity (green)	MOE in bending (@ 12% MC)	Compression perpendicular to the grain (@ 12% MC)
Jack pine	0.42	1.48×10^6 psi	830 psi
White spruce	0.35	1.45×10^6 psi	500 psi

The white spruce possesses approximately the same MOE as the pine so would probably be satisfactory in terms of stiffness. However, the compression strength perpendicular to the grain is much less. Therefore, if this property is critical, it is doubtful that white spruce would be a suitable substitute.

These examples are much simpler than most situations faced by wood scientists and engineers. In actual cases, many other factors such as dimensional stability, machinability, weight, availability, and cost must also be considered. These professionals must also apply their judgment regarding the expected variability in the material to be delivered.

Allowable stresses ■

Although knowledge of the properties of clear defect-free wood may be sufficient to answer many questions, the engineer and wood scientist are more frequently involved in the use of structural lumber and laminated lumber products. These forest products contain knots, slope of grain, and other defects that reduce strength. These strength-reducing characteristics are considerations in the strength values used for the design of buildings and other wood structures. In addition, the weakening effect of continuous loading (long-term loading), natural variability within the species, effect of temporary overloading, and other uncertainties involved in manufacture and application must also be included for assurance of safety in the structural design. Strength values that have been adjusted to consider all these factors are referred to as *allowable stresses* (discussed below).

Procedures used for many years in the United States for deriving allowable stresses for lumber are detailed in ASTM Standards D 245 and D 2555. These procedures are complex when a group of species is sold under one name, e.g., southern pine. However, the general approach for a single species can be understood from the following equation, which explains the derivation of the *allowable bending stress* (F_b).

$$F_b = \frac{\text{average MOR} - 1.645s}{F_{DL}} \times F_{MC} \times F_{SR} \times F_S$$

where

> s = the standard deviation of the MOR (ASTM D 2555) (average MOR − 1.645s determines the lower 95% exclusion limit)
> F_{DL} = reduction factor for duration of load and a safety factor
> F_{MC} = moisture content correction factor (ASTM D 2555 provides green-strength values)
> F_{SR} = strength ratio to account for strength-reducing defects, i.e., knots, slope-of-grain, etc.
> F_S = correction factor for beam depth

It is important to distinguish between allowable stresses used by engineers to design structural members of a building and average strength values given in Appendix Tables A.5, A.6, and A.7. Allowable stress values for softwood lumber are published by the American Forest and Paper Association (AF&PA) and by the regional lumber associations and trade organizations. The AF&PA also publishes the National Design Specification, which details procedures for the design of wood structures.

In some cases the allowable stresses for lumber may be only a small percentage of the strength of clear wood. Table 10.3 compares clear wood strength with the allowable stresses of 2 × 10s for three important commercial species. Note that allowable MOE values are not reduced for variability and use conditions as are strength values, since no threat to safety would result from overestimating stiffness. The allowable MOE values are higher than average green values because of the effect of drying.

Table 10.3.   Comparison of average clear wood strength properties with allowable stresses used for structural design

Species and property	Strength of clear wood (green)	Property symbol	Allowable stress (green) of 2 × 10 dimension lumber	
			No. 1 grade	No. 2 grade
	(psi)		*(psi)*	*(psi)*
Coast Douglas-fir				
MOR	7700	F_b	1500	1250
MOE	1.56×10^6	E	1.8×10^6	1.70×10^6
Maximum crushing (compression parallel to the grain)	3780	F_c	1250	1050
Western hemlock				
MOR	6600	F_b	1200	1000
MOE	1.31×10^6	E	1.5×10^6	1.40×10^6
Maximum crushing (compression parallel to the grain)	3360	F_c	1000	850
Loblolly pine				
MOR	7300	F_b	1500	1050
MOE	1.40×10^6	E	1.8×10^6	1.40×10^6
Maximum crushing (compression parallel to the grain)	3510	F_c	1250	900

The grades of lumber shown in Table 10.3 are visually assigned by a lumber grader who must make a rapid judgment as to the strength-reducing defects present in each piece. Most structural lumber is graded in this way. Some lumber grades are determined by a machine that measures the stiffness of the lumber and correlates strength properties to the measured MOE. Such lumber is termed MSR (machine stress-rated lumber). Because of its higher cost, its use is limited mainly to highly engineered applications such as trussed rafters and floor trusses.

Variability of clear wood strength properties ■

Strength varies widely within and among species. There is a wide overlapping range of mechanical properties between hardwoods and softwoods used in the United States. Strengths of selected woods are shown in Table 10.4 to illustrate the range of properties that exist in important North American species.

Table 10.4. Average strength values at 12% MC for clear wood of selected species

Species	MOR Ave. psi	MOR Ratio*	Bending MOE Ave. 10^6 psi	Bending MOE Ratio	Maximum crushing parallel to the grain Ave. psi	Maximum crushing parallel to the grain Ratio	Compression perpendicular to the grain at proportional limit Ave. psi	Compression perpendicular to the grain at proportional limit Ratio
Hardwoods								
Quaking aspen	8,400	1.00	1.18	1.00	4250	1.00	370	1.00
Red alder	9,800	1.17	1.38	1.17	5820	1.37	440	1.19
Yellow poplar	10,100	1.20	1.58	1.34	5540	1.30	500	1.35
Southern red oak	10,900	1.30	1.49	1.26	6090	1.43	870	2.35
White ash	15,400	1.83	1.74	1.47	7410	1.74	1160	3.14
Sugar maple	15,800	1.88	1.83	1.55	7830	1.84	1470	3.97
Softwoods								
Eastern white pine	8,600	1.00	1.24	1.00	4800	1.07	440	1.07
Engelmann spruce	9,300	1.08	1.30	1.05	4480	1.00	410	1.00
Ponderosa pine	9,400	1.09	1.29	1.04	5320	1.19	580	1.41
White fir	9,800	1.14	1.49	1.20	5810	1.30	530	1.29
Coast Douglas-fir	12,400	1.44	1.95	1.57	7240	1.62	800	1.95
Longleaf pine	14,500	1.69	1.98	1.60	8470	1.89	960	2.34

*Ratio of strength to weakest species in the group.

Within any species there is a considerable variation in clear wood strength properties, which corresponds to the variation in density and to the density-strength relationship for that property. The coefficient of variation of selected strength properties is illustrated in Table 10.5. These coefficients were derived from tests conducted at the U.S. Forest Products Laboratory on green specimens of 50 species.

Table 10.5. *Average coefficient of variation for some properties of 50 species of clear wood*

Property	Coefficient of variation
	(%)
Static bending	
MOR	16
MOE	22
Compression parallel to the grain	
Maximum crushing strength	18
Shear parallel to the grain	14
Compression perpendicular to the grain	28

Factors affecting the strength of clear wood ■

MOISTURE CONTENT. As wood dries below the fiber saturation point, most strength and elastic properties increase. It might be expected that this would occur because as water is removed from the cell wall, the long-chain molecules move closer together and thus become more tightly bonded. The increase in strength begins to happen as the moisture level drops to slightly below the fiber saturation point—usually around 25% MC. The relationship between the moisture content and strength properties of white ash are shown in Figure 10.10.

An exponential relationship can be used to estimate the strength at any given moisture content, using the properties of green wood and wood at 12% MC given in Appendix Tables A.5, A.6, and A.7. This relationship is

$$P = P_{12} \times (P_{12}/P_q)^{-(M-12/M_p-12)}$$

where

P = the property at M% moisture content
P_{12} = the property at 12% MC (can be obtained from Appendix)
P_q = the property green (can be obtained from Appendix)
M_p is usually taken at 25%; the *Wood Handbook* (USFPL 1987) provides other values for a few selected species.

As an example, suppose the MOR of northern red oak at 6% MC is desired. Appendix Table A.5 gives the property at 12% MC and green as 14,300 and 8300 psi respectively. Therefore, the MOR at 6% MC would be approximately

$$P = 14,300 \times (14,300/8300)^{-(6-12)/(25-12)} = 14,300 \, (1.72)^{6/13} = \text{approx. } 18,400 \text{ psi}$$

The moisture-strength relationship varies considerably among species, so one should not rely heavily upon estimates of the type shown above or any others that generalize for all species. Another method for estimating a property value at an intermediate moisture content when the values at two other moisture levels are known is outlined in ASTM Standard D 2915.

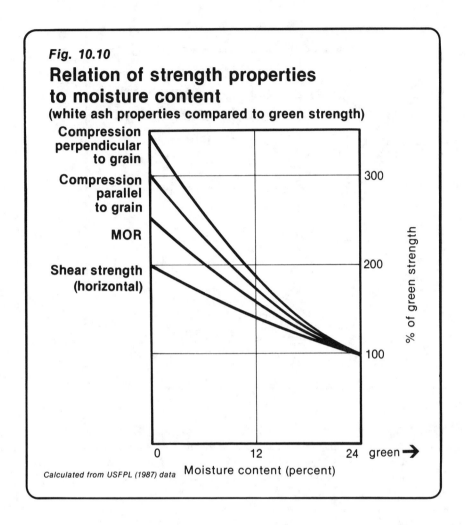

Fig. 10.10

Relation of strength properties to grain
to moisture content
(white ash properties compared to green strength)

Calculated from USFPL (1987) data Moisture content (percent)

TIME. The strength of wood does not decrease over time unless the product is subjected to the deleterious effects of microorganisms, high temperature, drastic moisture fluctuation, or strong chemicals. After centuries, changes do occur, but these are usually the result of environmental factors and not aging per se.

Some loss of strength will occur if aging is accompanied by continuous loading of the member. Most mechanical properties of wood are affected by the length of time the load is imposed. The longer a load is supported, the lower the load that can be safely carried. The relationship between stress level and time to failure for a variety of forest products is shown in Figure 10.11. Even if a load is small enough that there is no danger of ultimate failure, the member may continue to deflect or deform very gradually under the constant stress. A common example is the gradual sagging of a shelf heavily loaded with books. This phenomenon is known as *creep*.

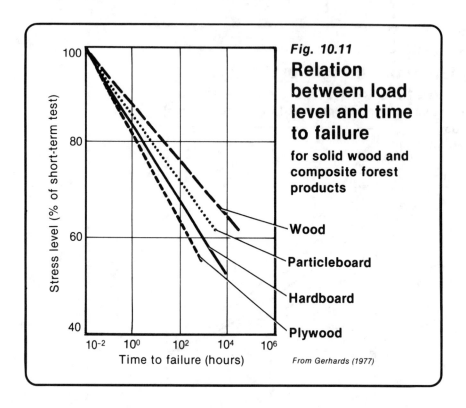

Fig. 10.11
Relation between load level and time to failure
for solid wood and composite forest products

Wood

Particleboard

Hardboard

Plywood

From Gerhards (1977)

It is believed that creep occurs at the molecular level from slippage in the relative position of the long-chain molecules in the cell wall. The bonding sites that hold water or are mutually satisfied in dry wood may shift or slide with respect to adjacent molecules when the whole matrix is placed under stress. The more water present within the wall, the more easily this slippage can occur. Alternate addition and removal of water from the bonding sites also creates an opportunity for slippage.

Creep most commonly shows itself as deflection in a wood beam after many years of loading. Creep can be troublesome in long wood beams such as headers over large doors or in long floor joists. Beams used in the green condition or at a high moisture content are particularly subject to creep. It has been shown that creep will be greatly accelerated under cyclic humidity conditions as compared to wood subjected to a constant environment. The most practical means of minimizing creep is to avoid overloading, use thoroughly dried material, and minimize moisture content fluctuation.

Creep can occur in any grain direction, but it occurs at much lower stress levels when the stress occurs in the transverse rather than the longitudinal direction. In particle and fiber products where the stresses act in the transverse grain direction within some of the small elements, creep is more evident than in solid wood materials. Figure 10.12 shows the results of an experiment to compare the rate of creep in particleboard and solid wood stressed parallel and perpendicular to the grain. The behavior of particleboard shows the effect of transverse stress resulting from the random orientation of particles.

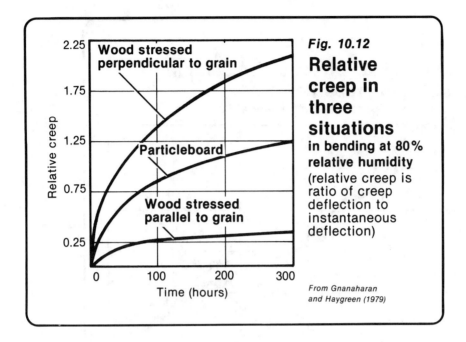

Fig. 10.12

Relative creep in three situations in bending at 80% relative humidity (relative creep is ratio of creep deflection to instantaneous deflection)

From Gnanaharan and Haygreen (1979)

In the derivation of allowable stresses, the strength of wood determined by standard short-term test methods is reduced about 38% to adjust it to a 10-year loading period. Ten years is considered the cumulative time that wood in a building is normally under nearly maximum loading. In situations where the load will be imposed permanently, the stress is reduced another 10% beyond the reduction for a 10-year load. When designing a structure for loads of shorter duration, such as snow or wind, engineers will increase the allowable stresses used in structural design.

TEMPERATURE. Most mechanical properties decrease when wood is heated and increase when it is cooled. This immediate temperature effect is shown in Figure 10.13 for wood at 12% MC and when ovendry. As long as temperatures do not exceed 100°C, there is little permanent loss of strength in the wood. Exposure to high temperatures for long periods can cause a permanent loss of strength. Generally, the higher the moisture content of the wood, the greater its sensitivity to high temperature. This point should be considered when extremely high kiln temperatures are used to dry critical structural members.

The effect that exposure to high temperature has on wood tends to be cumulative; i.e., the sum of short exposure times at a high temperature can often be as great as a single exposure of equal duration. There is one factor, however, that may result in short exposures being less severe; namely, the interior of the wood may not have adequate time to heat to the equilibrium temperature. In that case the deterioration would occur only on the surface. Nevertheless, anytime wood is to be used where it will continually be subjected to temperatures in excess of 100°C, consideration should be given to the loss of strength that may result.

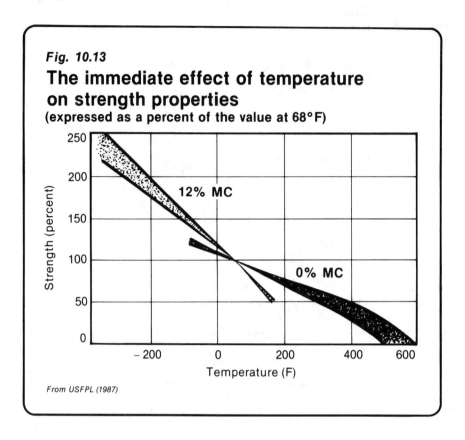

Fig. 10.13

The immediate effect of temperature on strength properties

(expressed as a percent of the value at 68°F)

From USFPL (1987)

Gerhards (1982) provides an extensive review of the research literature dealing with the effect of temperature and moisture content upon the strength of wood. He points out the importance of new research designed to find out why these factors affect wood as they do.

FATIGUE. The *fatigue* strength of a material is its ability to retain its strength when subjected to repeated severe loading. The beams in a railroad bridge are an example of an application where fatigue strength is important. In this case the beams are cyclically loaded each time the wheels of a rail car pass. This could occur millions of times in the life of a bridge. According to the *Wood Handbook* (USFPL 1987), clear straight-grained wood subjected to 2 million cycles of bending will retain 60% of its static strength. Cycling of stress may have a more severe effect when defects such as knots are present in the product or when slope of grain is involved. Most types of materials are subject to fatigue if repetitively stressed at a high level of loading. Only rarely, however, is the fatigue characteristic of wood an important factor in structural design because most structural wood members are not frequently stressed to the high levels assumed in the design of the structure.

EXPOSURE TO CHEMICALS. The strength of wood may be reduced by exposure to severe acidic or alkaline environments; yet, wood is more resistant than steel to acidic conditions. Chemical fertilizer and highway-salt storage buildings are often built from wood because of its ability to withstand corrosion and deterioration when in contact with these chemicals.

Chemical deterioration of the cell wall can result in loss of strength from hydrolysis of cellulose, oxidation by oxidizing agents, or delignification by alkalies. Softwoods tend to be more resistant to chemical deterioration than hardwoods. Woods that are less permeable to moisture movement tend to be more resistant since the chemicals take longer to penetrate. For this reason under conditions where chemical deterioration might occur, white oak is preferable to red oak, Douglas-fir heartwood to sapwood, and old-growth cypress to second growth. Cypress, Douglas-fir, southern pine, and redwood are often used where contact with acidic materials is expected.

A type of chemical deterioration can occur around iron or steel fasteners such as nails or bolts. When moisture is present in acidic woods or those that contain high extractive levels, particularly tannins, a chemical reaction produces iron salts. These salts promote localized weakening of the wood around the fastener and reduce the natural resistance of the wood to decay. This action may continue until the nail or other connector is badly corroded and eventually becomes loose in the wood. This effect is sometimes seen in old unpainted buildings where it is easy to pull nails from the lumber. When using nails in an exterior application with redwood, cedar, oak, or cypress, or when fabricating salt-treated lumber or plywood (such as CCA), it is always desirable to use special coated or stainless steel nails to avoid such problems.

Factors affecting the strength of lumber products ■

The strength of wood varies continuously with the moisture content fluctuations below about 25%. It would be very difficult, however, for structural engineers to consider the variable moisture content and induced variation in the strength of wood products in the design of a wood structure. To avoid this complication, the allowable stresses are established at a fixed moisture content. The allowable stresses of lumber, glue-laminated beams, and plywood are considered constant below some limiting moisture content. This limit (*maximum moisture content*) is 19% for softwood lumber and 16% for plywood and glue-laminated beams. If these moisture content limits are to be exceeded when the product is in use, the allowable stresses must be reduced. The reduction to be made when these moisture content limits are exceeded depends upon the product and the specific strength property involved. Reductions range from 3 to 40%.

In addition to the factors that affect the strength of the clear wood itself, three growth characteristics are very important to the strength of lumber. The effect of these characteristics is considered when deriving allowable stresses.

KNOTS. Knots are the most common wood characteristic that reduces the strength of lumber. The effect of a knot may in many cases be considered equivalent to that of a hole. In some cases the knot may have a greater effect than a drilled hole because of the distortion in the grain that accompanies it. The amount that a knot reduces strength depends not only upon the size of the knot but upon its location in the piece. A knot on the top or bottom edge of a beam is much more critical than the same knot located near the centerline. Recall that the maximum bending stresses occur on the top and bottom edges of a beam. Knots on the bottom edge of a beam are even more serious than on the top edge because a knot has a more drastic effect on tensile strength than it does on compressive strength. A good carpenter will inspect floor joists and place the largest knots on the top edge, not on the bottom.

The amount of strength loss from knots of various sizes is outlined in ASTM Standard D 245. Table 10.6 lists the percent of strength loss that results from knots in the center and on the edge of beams of several widths. Note the difference between the loss in strength for knots located in the center of the piece as compared to the edge. A 2-in. knot in a 2 × 8 will reduce the strength by 24% if in the center but by 43% if on one edge.

Table 10.6. Strength reduction in lumber resulting from knots and slope of the grain as shown in ASTM Standard D 245

Strength reduction from knots in the center of the wide face of a beam

Size of knot (in.)	Width of the beam (in.)			
	3½	5½	7½	9½
	(%)			
1	25	16	12	10
2	51	33	24	20
3	...	50	37	30

Strength reduction from knots on one edge of the wide face of a beam

Size of knot (in.)	Width of the beam (in.)			
	3½	5½	7½	9½
	(%)			
1	43	30	23	18
2	81	55	43	35
3	...	79	63	50

Strength reduction in bending and compression parallel to the grain resulting from slope of the grain

Slope of the grain	In bending	In compression
	(%)	
1 in 6	60	44
1 in 8	47	34
1 in 10	39	26
1 in 15	24	0
1 in 20	0	0

DECAY. Decay is generally prohibited in grades of lumber used for structural purposes (some localized types are permitted) because it is often impossible to estimate by visual inspection the extent to which decay has weakened the piece. By the time decay is apparent, the loss in strength may be severe. Impact strength deteriorates as a result of decay much faster than static strength. Figure 10.14 shows the zone of fracture from two toughness (small impact-bending) test specimens of Douglas-fir. The sapwood specimen on the left is normal, and the heartwood specimen on the right has a slight amount of decay. The splinter-free fracture on the right *(brash failure)* is typical of decayed wood. In this case the scaffold plank from which the specimen on the right was cut had its toughness reduced 85% by decay but looked normal to the user until failure occurred. It is important to be alert for decay when manufacturing lumber from large, overmature logs, where decay is occasionally encountered.

Fig. 10.14
Normal and brash failure of Douglas-fir toughness specimens. The brash character of failure resulted from decay.

Some grades of dimension lumber permit blue stain to be present. Blue-stain fungi do not cause a weakening of the wood. They live upon food materials in the cell lumen not upon the cell wall substance. One problem encountered with stain, however, is that it can occur in combination with decay and make the decay difficult to detect.

SLOPE OF THE GRAIN. *Slope of the grain* in lumber is expressed as the length in inches through which a 1-in. deviation in the grain occurs. Figure 10.15 shows three examples of how a slope of 1 in 8 could develop in a piece. The first two examples show how slope of grain can result from the way the lumber is cut from the log. Slope of the grain of this type is fairly easy to detect in a species that has distinct growth rings. Slope can also result from logs containing spiral grain. In this case, even though the growth rings appear parallel to the edges of the piece, the slope of the grain may be quite significant. The best way to visually detect this type of grain deviation is to look at resin streaks, surface checks, mineral stains, or other minor defects that tend to be oriented with the cells.

The strength of wood is affected whenever there is a slope of the grain greater than about 1 in 20. The percent of strength loss in bending and compression resulting from grain deviation is shown in Table 10.6. Tension strength has been found to be more severely affected by grain deviation than either bending or compression. All grades of structural lumber carry limitations to the slope of grain. These are especially strict for critical structural members such as ladder rails. Figure 10.16 shows broken ladder rails that failed as a result of excessive slope of the grain.

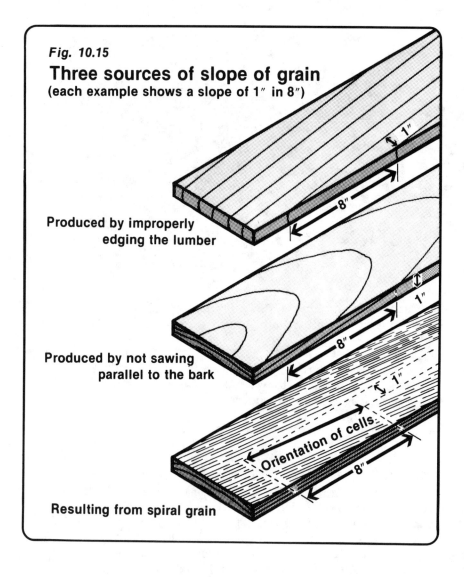

Fig. 10.15

Three sources of slope of grain
(each example shows a slope of 1″ in 8″)

1″

8″

Produced by improperly
edging the lumber

1″

8″

Produced by not sawing
parallel to the bark

1″

Orientation of cells

8″

Resulting from spiral grain

Fig. 10.16
**Slope of the grain contributed to the failure
in the side rails of these two wood ladders.**

REVIEW

A. Terms to define or explain:
1. Structural application
2. Stress
3. Strain
4. Pascal
5. Proportional limit
6. Modulus of elasticity (MOE)
7. Young's modulus
8. Modulus of rupture (MOR)
9. Shear strength
10. Rolling shear
11. Isotropic, anisotropic, and orthotropic
12. Side hardness
13. Impact bending strength
14. Allowable stresses
15. Creep
16. Rheological properties
17. Fatigue
18. Slope of the grain
19. Brash failure

B. Questions or concepts to explain:
   1. Explain the relationship between stress, strain, and MOE.
   2. Be able to calculate the MOE of a simple center-loaded beam.
   3. Be able to calculate the MOR for a center-loaded beam.
   4. Explain why plywood is less anisotropic than solid wood.
   5. Describe the general relationship between strength and specific gravity.
   6. Be able to estimate some major strength properties if only specific gravity is known.
   7. Be able to estimate strength of a species at one specific gravity if the strength at another is known.
   8. Know where to obtain information to compare the strength of various species.
   9. Explain the difference between average strength values and allowable stresses.
   10. Explain how strength properties are affected by moisture and be able to estimate strength at any moisture content from values when green and at 12%.
   11. Describe how strength properties are affected by time, temperature, and fatigue.
   12. Describe the major defects or growth characteristics that reduce the strength of lumber.

REFERENCES AND SUPPLEMENTAL READINGS

American Forest and Paper Association. 1995. National Design Specification for Wood Construction. Washington, D.C.
_____. 1995. Design Values for Wood Construction. Washington, D.C.
American Society for Testing and Materials (ASTM). 1987. Standard methods for establishing structural grades and related allowable properties for visually graded lumber. ASTM D 245.
_____. 1987. Standard methods of testing small clear specimens of timber. ASTM D 143.
_____. 1987. Standard methods for evaluating allowable properties for grades of structural lumber. ASTM D 2915.
_____. 1987. Evaluating the properties of wood-base fiber and particle panel materials. ASTM D 1037.
_____. 1987. Standard method for establishing clear wood strength values. ASTM D 2555.
Bodig, J. and Jayne, B.A. 1982. Mechanics of Wood and Wood Composites. New York: Van Nostrand Reinhold.
Breyer, D.E. 1980. Design of Wood Structures. New York: McGraw-Hill.
Gerhards, C.C. 1977. Effect of duration and rate of loading on strength. USDA For. Ser. Res. Pap. FPL-283.
_____. 1982. Effect of moisture content and temperature on the mechanical properties of wood. Wood and Fiber 14(1):9–36.
Gnanaharan, R. and Haygreen, J.G. 1979. Comparison of creep behavior of waferboard and that of solid wood. Wood and Fiber 11(3):155–70.
Gurfinkel, G. 1973. Wood Engineering. New Orleans: Southern Forest Products Association.
Hoyle, R.J., Jr., and Woeste, F.E. 1989. Wood Technology in the Design of Structures. Ames, IA: Iowa State University Press.
Karacabeyli, E. and Barrett, J.D. 1993. Rate of loading effects on the strength of lumber. For. Prod. J. 43(5): 28–36.
Koch, P. 1985. Utilization of Hardwoods Growing on Southern Pine Sites. USDA For. Ser. Handb. 605.
Kollman, F.P. and Côté, W. A., Jr. 1968. Principles of Wood Science and Technology. New York: Springer-Verlag.
Madsen, B. 1992. Structural Behavior of Timber. N. Vancouver, B.C.: Timber Engineering Ltd.
U.S. Forest Products Laboratory (USFPL). 1944. Design of wood aircraft. ANC Bull. 18.
_____. 1987. Wood Handbook. USDA For. Serv. Agric. Handb. 72.

11

Deterioration of wood products

■ **ONE KEY** to the satisfactory use of forest products as building materials is an understanding of the agents and conditions that can lead to decay or other forms of deterioration. Wood buildings, when properly designed and constructed, can serve satisfactorily for hundreds of years. Figures 11.1 and 11.2 show examples that are still in excellent condition after a century or more of service. However, as with any naturally produced organic material, wood may be subject to decay, fungal stains, insect infestation, fire, and surface weathering, all of which can cause the useful life of a building or a product to be greatly reduced.

There is no reason for wood deterioration to occur within a building where exposure to water can be controlled. Wood that is used out of doors, is subjected to rain, or has contact with the ground or to seawater will eventually decay or be attacked by marine borers or insects. Its service life, however, can be greatly extended by proper treatment or species selection. To avoid deterioration in buildings or to extend the life of wood materials used under severe conditions, those using wood products must understand the conditions under which deterioration develops and the preventive measures to be taken.

Biological agents are the major causes of wood deterioration. Deterioration can result from fungi that cause staining, softening, and decay; marine borers, mainly small mollusks and crustaceans; insects including termites, carpenter ants, and a variety of wood-boring beetles; and bacteria that cause minor deterioration in water-stored logs. The greatest financial losses from biodeterioration result from decay fungi. These agents of biological deterioration are most active

243

Fig. 11.1
Dean-Page Hall
Built about 1850 in Eufala, Alabama. An example of fine antebellum wood homes found throughout the South.

Fig. 11.2
Swedish home
This structure built about 350 years ago in Vimmerby, Sweden, was originally a log structure but was later covered with board siding.

in tropical climates but also develop, usually at a slower rate, in temperate and colder regions.

Fire is by far the most catastrophic and economically important form of nonbiological deterioration. Less-important nonbiological agents of wood deterioration include ultraviolet light and mechanical abrasion, which contribute to surface weathering; chemical agents such as strong acids or alkalies; and products of metal corrosion that can cause wood to deteriorate around nails or other metal fasteners.

Fungi ■

TYPES. Fungi causing deterioration of wood and other cellulosic materials are simple plants that contain no chlorophyll. Unable to produce their own food, fungi must derive their energy from other organic materials. The carbohydrate and lignin components of wood provide food for a wide range of fungi. The hyphae (mycelium) of the fungi secrete enzymes that break the carbohydrate materials, and sometimes lignin, into simple sugarlike compounds that can be metabolized for energy.

The fungi that degrade wood may be classified as decay, soft-rot, stain, or mold according to the type of degradation they cause. *Decay fungi* cause significant softening or weakening of wood, often to the point that its physical characteristics are completely destroyed. Wood so affected is referred to as rotten or decayed. *Soft-rot fungi* most often attack wood that is very wet and usually penetrate rather slowly. Soft-rots gradually degrade wood from the surface inward. *Staining fungi* that inhabit wood often create a bluish or blackish color and so are detrimental to its appearance and value; yet, they do not have a serious effect on the strength or the physical integrity of the wood. Molds and mildews occur only on exposed surfaces and may discolor products in use, such as house siding, but do not affect the strength.

Most decay fungi belong to the botanical class Basidiomycetes, named for the spore-bearing structure, the basidium. A few are Ascomycetes. Several hundred species of fungi may decay wood products in North America. The most common genera include *Poria, Gloeophyllum, Polyporus, Lentinus,* and *Coniophora.* The species in these genera vary widely as to the species of wood, moisture content, and temperature most conducive to their growth. Some are more likely to be encountered in buildings, some in unseasoned wood, others in posts or poles. The species of decay fungi found in living trees rarely infect wood products. A few, however, continue to grow in wood after it is harvested if the products are not thoroughly dried.

Decay fungi may be further classified as brown rots or white rots. The *brown rots* selectively attack the cellulose and hemicellulose of the cell, with little effect on the lignin. Wood seriously degraded by these fungi will have an abnormally brownish or reddish color. Brown-rotted wood develops checks perpendicular to the grain and when dried breaks into cubical pieces. Figure 11.3 shows a section from a large timber badly deteriorated by a brown-rot fungus. These fungi may attack all layers of the cell wall, but the cellulose-rich S-2 layer is often the first to be degraded. Up to two-thirds of the total wood substance may eventually be consumed by brown-rot fungi.

White-rot fungi have the ability to degrade both the lignin and cellulosic components of the cell although the lignin is usually utilized at a somewhat faster rate. *White rots* may change the color of wood only slightly but more often give it a bleached or whitish color. These fungi typically erode outward from the cell lumen by decomposing successive layers of the cell wall, much as a river erodes its bank. Thus the cell wall becomes progressively thinner. The wood does not tend to shrink, check, or collapse as is often the case with brown rots. White-rotted wood usually retains its shape but may eventually become a fibrous spongy mass. There is great variability in mode of action of white-rot fungi, and mycologists and forest products pathologists are attempting to better understand the mechanisms through which these fungi degrade wood substance.

Although most fungi can attack only wood in which moisture is already present, a few species known as *water-conducting fungi* have the ability to transport water to the wood material affected. Two species, *Poria incrassata* and *Serpula lacrymans,* are the best known of the water-conducting fungi. *S. lacrymans* is found in buildings in central and northern Europe and occasionally in the northeastern United States, while *P. incrassata* is found principally in the southeastern and northwestern United States. Water-conducting fungi have the ability to transport water in mycelial tubes to dry wood, thus placing it in a condition subject to biological deterioration.

Staining and mold fungi do not usually deteriorate the cell wall of wood but grow either on the surface or within the cell lumens, primarily of ray parenchyma. The dark color of *staining fungi* gives the wood a bluish or black-

Fig. 11.3
Douglas-fir timber destroyed by brown rot at the point it was in contact with a concrete wall.

ish tinge that can greatly reduce its value. The hyphae of *mold fungi* are colorless, so they do not discolor wood, but the spores produced by molds discolor wood surfaces. Stain and mold fungi belong to the Ascomycetes or Fungi Imperfecti (classes of higher fungi).

Since staining fungi and molds do not degrade the cell wall, they must live on food found within the lumen, mainly sugars and starch. For this reason they are found in ray parenchyma of sapwood. Molds and stains are particularly troublesome in freshly felled logs and recently sawn lumber where the surface is relatively wet and the sugar-starch content is still high. Figure 11.4 shows the development of blue stain in a log killed by insects. Note that the stain is limited to the sapwood.

Blue staining of freshly cut lumber can often be avoided by quickly drying the surface. This procedure prevents pigment formation that develops from germinating spores. In warm regions and with highly susceptible species such as southern pine, white pine, yellow poplar, and sweetgum, a fungicidal dip is often used to treat the lumber immediately after sawing. This is generally a good practice with all species of lumber that are not to be immediately kiln dried.

Molds and mildew can develop under high humidity on products in storage, in use conditions where the surface remains above 20–25% MC for a long period, or sometimes on painted surfaces. Fungicides may be incorporated into paint formulations to reduce this latter problem.

Soft-rot fungi belong to the Ascomycetes and Fungi Imperfecti. These organisms cause a gradual progressive degradation from the surface of wood inward. The effects are slower to develop and less apparent than decay or staining fungi. However, in some wet service applications, such as wood cooling towers

(Courtesy S. Sinclair)

Fig. 11.4
Blue stain in a southern pine killed by the southern pine beetle.

and hardwood transmission poles, failure of a structure has been found to be caused by soft rotters. These fungi often contribute to the surface weathering of wood exposed to wet exterior conditions. As will be discussed later, weathering also results from nonbiological agents of deterioration. In the early stages, soft rot differs from other decay in that it is usually a surface effect that can be removed by scraping. The decomposition of the cell wall is characterized by long cavities in the longitudinal direction entirely within the secondary wall.

NATURE OF A DECAY FUNGUS. A fungus is produced in a suitable host by germination of a spore, growth of segments of hyphae, or colonization from a nearby infection source. Long slender threads called *hyphae* grow in length along the surface of the wood and penetrate into it primarily through exposed end grain or cut ends of wood cells. Hyphae then go from cell to cell through pit pairs or through holes (bore holes) created in the cell wall. Many hyphae growing together are called *mycelium*. Figure 11.5 illustrates the spread of hyphae through the cells of wood. The mycelium grows within the wood, producing more-frequent bore holes and progressively degrading the cell wall. As growth continues, more and more wood material is consumed and the wood loses strength and weight. Fruiting bodies (*sporocarps*) eventually develop, producing large numbers of spores that are spread by wind or other agents. There is no practical way of isolating wood products from contact with spores. Thus to avoid infection, it is necessary to prevent the conditions that allow the spores to germinate and grow.

To use cellulose, hemicellulose, or lignin as food, fungi must be able to break down these cell constituents into simple molecules that can be metabolized. These biochemical changes are accomplished by the catalytic action of enzymes produced by the hyphae. In some cases, chemical hydrolytic action may also be involved. The enzymes are produced at the tips of the hyphae in the process of creating bore holes and also are produced along the sides of these vegetative elements. For enzymes to diffuse into the cell wall and for the breakdown products to enter the hyphae, it is necessary for some water to be present. Water is also needed for the breakdown process catalyzed by enzymes. Therefore, one of the best ways of preventing wood decay is to ensure that there is not enough water present to permit the enzymes to do their job.

CONDITIONS REQUIRED FOR DECAY. How much moisture is needed for decay to develop? Generally, there is very little danger of decay if wood is below the fiber saturation point. A few fungi are able to grow slowly at moisture contents slightly less than this. Some industry standards, such as those of the American Institute of Timber Construction, recommend that wood be treated with preservatives if it is to be used under conditions where it will be above 20% MC continuously. In most cases, buildings can be designed to avoid conditions where the moisture content of wood will exceed this amount. This is possible by proper use of ventilation, vapor barriers, and caulking to ensure that liquid water does not come in contact with wood.

Although there are other physiological requirements for the growth of fungi besides moisture, there is less chance to control them. Fungi grow most rapidly

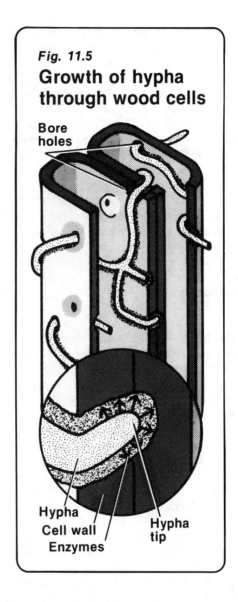

Fig. 11.5

Growth of hypha through wood cells

Bore holes

Hypha
Cell wall
Enzymes

Hypha tip

at temperatures in the range of 70°–90°F and are inhibited at temperatures below 32°F and above 100°F. Therefore, in tropical climates and within heated buildings in temperate climates, the temperature is ideal for the development of decay. When temperatures drop below 32°F, the fungi are not killed but simply become inactive or dormant. High temperatures, on the other hand, are sometimes used in drying and treating processes to sterilize wood, killing any fungi that may be present.

Fungi also require oxygen, but they can flourish on much less than normal atmospheric amounts. There is no practical way of sealing air out of a finished wood product to eliminate decay. However, logs in storage may be sprinkled with water to maintain the moisture content at a high enough level that there is not adequate oxygen for fungi to grow actively. Pieces of wood buried in the ground or submerged in water also do not have enough oxygen for decay to occur. On the other hand, wood sunk in rivers, lakes, or ponds may be affected by anaerobic bacteria, which can destroy the pit structure and greatly increase the permeability of the wood. This can result in drying and treating problems if the wood is used for lumber.

Fungi tend to prefer a somewhat acidic environment. The pH range of 4–6 is best for growth. Some fungi appear to have the ability to change the acidity of the wood slightly as they develop. As with other physiological factors, species of fungi vary considerably in regard to their preferred pH.

The food requirements of decay fungi are provided by the wood itself. There has been considerable research to find treatments for wood that change or remove certain components essential to fungal growth. One such procedure is to remove the thiamine, which is found in minute quantities in wood and is necessary for the growth of most fungi. Processes to alter the chemical makeup of the cellulosic fraction in wood to make it immune to the enzymes of fungi have also been studied. None of these approaches to wood preservation has as yet found practical application.

PREVENTING WOOD DECAY. There are three general approaches to preventing wood decay. Each is appropriate under certain situations.

First, where possible, the simplest approach is to keep the wood product dry. This is certainly the best and least expensive approach. If wood buildings in temperate regions of the world are properly designed to avoid condensation and leakage problems, the wood will last indefinitely. In wood buildings in temperate climates, the equilibrium moisture content (EMC) is never high enough to maintain the wood at 20% MC unless condensation or water leaks are present. Look at the EMC table (A.1) in the Appendix to see the high humidity required to produce such a moisture content. In tropical countries, where rainfall and humidity are high, it may not be possible to maintain wood buildings in an adequately dry condition to prevent decay. The avoidance of deterioration by maintaining a low moisture content is obviously not suitable for wood in contact with rain, the ground, or other damp materials such as concrete or stone.

Second, where it is not possible to keep wood dry, wood treated with chemicals that are toxic to fungi should be used. If the moisture content cannot be maintained at less than 20%, the use of preservative-treated material is the most practical way to avoid decay. Various chemical treatments are available. The level of treatment can be varied to suit the application and expected severity of the decay hazard. The American Wood Preservers Association has developed standards for pressure-treated wood to be used under a great variety of conditions.

Third, in a few cases rather than using preservative-treated wood, it may be possible to use naturally decay-resistant species. The practical problem with this approach is that only the heartwood of these species is resistant, and this resistance is greatest with old-growth timber. Woods like redwood and cypress are often used where a combination of decay resistance and natural appearance is desired. Appendix Table A.4 indicates the decay resistance of some woods grown in the United States. Note that all the commonly used construction woods—Douglas-fir, southern pines, firs, spruces, and hemlocks—have moderate to low resistance to decay. These species then must be treated to obtain a high degree of decay resistance. In turn, grades of lumber allowing only heartwood must be specified for use where natural decay resistance is needed. Because of the limited availability and high cost of naturally decay-resistant species in these grades, this approach is most suitable for applications where both durability and appearance are important. Such an application is the use of western red cedar or redwood for the construction of patio decks and privacy fences as shown in Figure 11.6.

The degree of natural resistance to decay exhibited by heartwood depends upon the nature and amount of fungitoxic extractives in the species. The amount varies considerably within a species, location in the tree, age, and rate of growth. Rapidly grown second-growth timber often has a lower extractive content and thus lower natural decay resistance than older slow-growth material.

PRESERVATIVE TREATMENTS AND STANDARDS. The requirements for an ideal wood preservative include the following: (1) toxicity to a wide range of wood-inhabiting fungi; (2) high degree of permanence (low volatility, resistance to leaching, chemical stability); (3) ability to penetrate wood readily; (4) resistance to corrosion by metals and resistance to injury of wood; and (5) economy. Preservatives used today in commercial practice meet most, though not all, of these requirements.

Wood preservatives in commercial use today are of two general types: *oil-soluble chemicals* and *waterborne salts*. The fundamental difference is the type

Fig. 11.6
Weathered unfinished red-wood privacy fence.

of liquid used to carry the toxic chemicals into the wood structure. Heavy oil preservatives have some advantage in uniquely wet-use situations, since in addition to being toxic to fungi, the liquid carrier retards liquid water movement. A serious drawback to the heavy-oil treatments is that the wood surface is oily and difficult or impossible to finish or paint. To overcome this problem, it is possible to use light organic solvents as the carrier for toxic compounds so that the wood may be painted after treatment. These solvents evaporate rapidly, leaving the wood with an untreated appearance.

When water is used as the carrier for moving preservative salts into wood, it may be necessary to redry the wood product after treatment. Often, however, lumber to be used outdoors in 2-in. and greater thicknesses is not redried. If not redried, the treated product will shrink in use, the same as green wood. Figure 11.7 shows a sound barrier along an interstate highway in Minneapolis, Minnesota, constructed with southern pine lumber treated with waterborne preservatives.

The most-commonly used types of oilborne preservatives are coal-tar creosote solutions, copper naphthenate, copper 8-quinolinolate (oxine copper), and a variety of biocides, including thiazoles, triazoles, carbamates, chlorothalonil, and substituted isothiazolones. It is important to realize that the oil carrier itself has no preservative value.

The waterborne preservatives in use in the United States include ammoniacal copper arsenate (ACA), acid copper chromate (ACC), chromated zinc chloride (CZC), *chromated copper arsenate* (CCA), ammoniacal copper zinc arsen-

Fig. 11.7
A wood wall treated with waterborne preservatives serves as a sound barrier in an urban area adjacent to an interstate highway.

ate (ACZA), chromated copper borate (CCB), inorganic boron, and alkylammonium compounds (also called quaternary ammonium compounds or quats) (Barnes and Murphy 1995). There are three types of CCA, which vary in the proportion of chromium oxide, copper oxide, and arsenic pentoxide they contain. Because of the higher cost of the petro-based carriers and the environmental concerns about the oilborne preservatives, the waterborne treatments, particularly CCA, are in much greater use (see Fig. 11.8). In 1990 three-fourths of treated wood utilized waterborne preservatives—mostly CCA. Production of treated wood in the United States in 1990 by product type is shown in Table 11.1.

Table 11.1. Production of treated wood in the United States, by product, 1990

	Volume Treated With				
Products	Creosote solutions	Oilborne preservatives	Waterborne preservatives	Fire retardants	All chemicals (1990)
			(1,000 cubic feet)		
Crossties	62,988	—	—	—	62,988
Switch and bridge ties	7,165	—	—	—	7,165
Poles	13,251	42,821	17,429	—	73,501
Crossarms	5	1,237	165	—	1,407
Piling	2,494	6	4,686	—	7,186
Fence posts	2,131	252	12,491	—	14,874
Lumber	2,595	721	319,853	4,409	327,578
Timbers	965	545	46,491	—	48,001
Plywood	—	48	9,317	2,908	12,273
Other products	1,598	964	27,244	859	30,665
All products (1990)	93,193	46,592	437,675	8,176	585,635

The effectiveness of a preservative treatment depends not only on the toxicity of the chemical to the species of decay fungi but upon how completely it has penetrated and how much is retained within the wood following treatment. Standards of the American Wood Preservers Association (AWPA) specify how deeply the preservatives must penetrate and the amount of preservative per unit of volume that must be retained in the wood.

Chemical retention is stated in treatment standards in terms of the weight of the chemical per cubic foot of wood retained after treating. In the case of creosote treatment, the total weight of the creosote is used to calculate the retention. In the case of CCA and other waterbornes, the weight of the chemical only, not the carrier, is used in the calculation of retention. Typical retention requirements for CCA-treated wood range from 0.25 lb/ft^3 (pcf) for aboveground exposure to 0.60 pcf for use in wood foundations. For creosote-treated poles and pilings, the retention requirements range from 8 pcf for building poles to 25 pcf for marine pilings. AWPA standards applicable to a variety of wood products are listed in Table 11.2

In 1993 the American Lumber Standards Committee (ALSC) became responsible for accreditation of inspection agencies who are qualified and who adhere to AWPA standards. Wood treating companies who conform to AWPA standards and who submit lumber to inspection by an authorized inspection agency may use the quality stamp of approval of that agency on their products. Utility

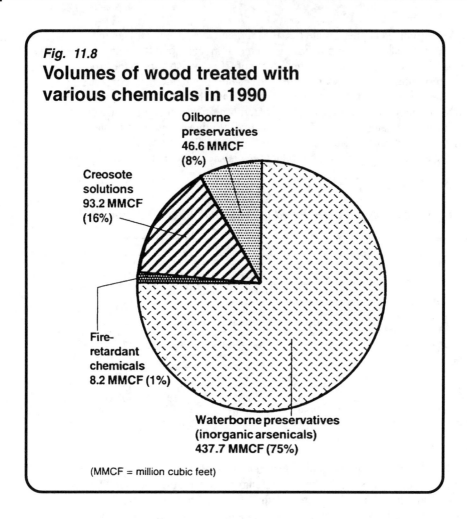

Fig. 11.8
Volumes of wood treated with various chemicals in 1990

Oilborne preservatives 46.6 MMCF (8%)

Creosote solutions 93.2 MMCF (16%)

Fire-retardant chemicals 8.2 MMCF (1%)

Waterborne preservatives (inorganic arsenicals) 437.7 MMCF (75%)

(MMCF = million cubic feet)

companies and railroads using treated poles and railroad ties for purposes other than building construction often utilize additional standards to ensure the quality of their products.

TREATING METHODS. Most treating processes involve the use of pressure to force the preservative into the wood. The wood to be treated is placed in a pressure retort where the preservative can then be added and pressure applied. With oilborne preservatives the preservative and the wood are often heated to increase penetration. A vacuum can be pulled prior to introduction of the preservative to remove the air from the cell lumen, allowing easier penetration of the treating oil. Many different vacuum pressure–time cycles are used depending upon the species, the type of preservative, and the amount to be deposited (retained) in the wood.

Some treating cycles are intended to leave the cell lumen filled with preservative for applications where the hazard of deterioration is high. These are termed *full cell processes*. In *empty cell processes* an attempt is made to remove

Table 11.2. American Wood Preservers Association standards for 1992

Standard	Wood Commodities
C1	All timber products, pressure treatment
C2	Lumber, timbers, bridge ties and mine ties, pressure treatment
C3	Piles, pressure treatment
C4	Poles, pressure treatment
C5	Posts, pressure treatment
C6	Crossties and switch ties, pressure treatment
C7	Incised (red, white, and yellow cedar) pole butts, thermal treatment
C8	Poles (western red and Alaska yellow cedar), full-length thermal treatment
C9	Plywood, pressure treatment
C10	Poles (lodgepole pine), full-length thermal treatment
C11	Wood blocks for floors and platforms, pressure treatment
C12	Poles (western larch), full-length thermal treatment
C14	Wood for highway construction, pressure treatment
C15	Wood for commercial-residential construction, pressure treatment
C16	Wood used on farms, pressure treatment
C17	Playground equipment treated with inorganic preservatives, pressure processes
C18	Material in marine construction, pressure treatment
C20	Structural lumber, fire-retardant pressure treatment
C22	Lumber and plywood for permanent wood foundations, pressure processes
C23	Pole building construction, pressure treatment
C24	Sawn timber piles used for residential and commercial building, pressure processes
C25	Crossarms, pressure treatment
C27	Plywood, fire-retardant pressure treatment
C28	Structural glued laminated members and laminations before gluing, pressure treatment
C29	Lumber to be used for the harvesting, storage and transportation of food stuffs
C30	Lumber, timbers and plywood for cooling towers, pressure processes
C31	Lumber used out of contact with the ground and continuously protected from liquid water
C32	Glue-laminated poles of southern yellow pine or coastal Douglas fir

excess oil once the preservative has been forced to the desired depth. These latter processes are typically used for telephone and power transmission poles. Figure 11.9 illustrates the pressure-time sequence used in the pressure-treating tank for one type of empty cell process, i.e., the Rueping process. In another empty cell process, the Lowry process, the tank is filled with preservative before any pressure is applied.

The thermal process is the major nonpressure treating method for wood to be used in ground contact. It consists of immersing wood successively in baths of hot and then cool liquid preservatives. The hot bath expands the air in the outer zones of the wood, and the cool bath then causes the air to contract, causing a partial vacuum in the wood. This process is often used in the western United States for butt-treating poles.

Nonpressure methods to apply preservatives are also used commercially, but these methods are applicable only for wood that will be used under conditions presenting only a light or moderate decay hazard. Such methods of application include brushing, dipping, and soaking. Dipping or soaking in preservatives is used extensively to protect millwork, such as windows. If the wood parts are machined prior to dipping, the preservative will be taken up by the end grain, the point where the decay hazard is greatest.

Different species vary greatly in their resistance to penetration by preservatives although the sapwood of almost all species is readily penetrated. Species that typically have a high proportion of sapwood are, therefore, easier to treat properly. Species that are very difficult to treat, like coast-type Douglas-fir, are sometimes incised to form passages for the preservative to penetrate more deeply

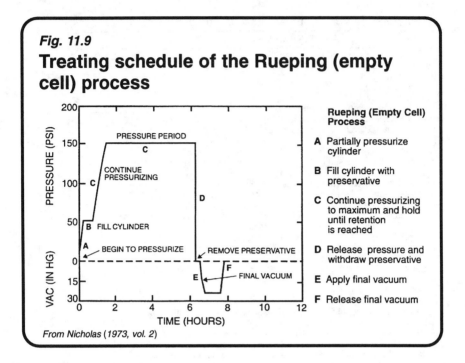

Fig. 11.9

Treating schedule of the Rueping (empty cell) process

Rueping (Empty Cell) Process

A Partially pressurize cylinder

B Fill cylinder with preservative

C Continue pressurizing to maximum and hold until retention is reached

D Release pressure and withdraw preservative

E Apply final vacuum

F Release final vacuum

From Nicholas (1973, vol. 2)

into the wood. Incising machines used for poles and lumber puncture the surface of wood with chisel-shaped points that expose end grain up to a depth of 1 in. (2.5 cm). In so-called refractory species, such as Douglas-fir and white oak, it is common that only the sapwood portion receives adequate treatment unless incising is used.

CONSIDERATIONS IN THE USE OF PRESERVATIVES. The cleanliness of the preservative treatment is obviously important for uses such a millwork, stadium seating, or residential decks. For other uses, such as railroad ties or bridge timbers, an oily surface may be desirable. The oily surface increases the resistance to weathering and thus increases service life. Tar on the surface of a pole used in a rural area likewise may be acceptable but would be objectionable if used where contact with people is likely. If cleanliness of the treated wood product is important, the preservative should be either waterborne or penta dissolved in a volatile carrier.

Deposits on the surface of treated wood can present problems in both gluing and painting. Such problems are more likely to be encountered with oil-type preservatives than with those that are waterborne. In some cases, such problems with paints and finishes can be overcome by surface sanding or washing with an appropriate solvent. For gluing, however, the wood should be surfaced and an adhesive must be selected that is compatible with the preservative and the exposure conditions.

Corrosion of metal fasteners, such as nails and truss plates, can be a problem in treated and untreated wood where the moisture content remains high. In addition to a loss of strength in the fastener itself, as a result of corrosion, there can be a chemical deterioration of the wood surrounding the fastener. Although heavy oil-type preservatives may retard corrosion somewhat, the waterborne salts do not. For applications as in wood foundations, CCA-treated wood systems should be fastened with stainless steel or hot-dipped galvanized nails. The inorganic fire-retardant salts present an even more difficult problem. Wood with these treatments will pick up moisture under high humidities, and this will accelerate the corrosion problem. Nonhygroscopic fire-retardant treatments suitable for use where high humidities are likely to be encountered are available.

The strength of wood products is sometimes affected by chemical treatments. The extent of strength loss, if any, is usually more determined by the conditions of preservative impregnation than by the chemical itself. High temperatures or high pressures used in the treating cylinders to force the liquid into the wood can have a detrimental effect upon strength. Oil-type preservatives undergo no chemical reaction with the wood that might affect strength, but waterborne salts do react to a slight degree. Such reaction is greater at higher temperatures and when higher levels of chromium are present.

The *National Design Specifications of the American Forest and Paper Association* provide wood strength and design information used by structural engineers. These specifications call for a 10% reduction in the strength of wood that has been pressure-impregnated with a fire retardant but do not require a strength reduction of decay protection treatments applied by approved processes.

Safety and Environmental Factors. Environmental impact and safety of preservatives are common concerns. Since all preservatives now in use have some toxicity to living protoplasm, care should always be exercised in the application and use of preservatives. Those who apply wood treating chemicals are more subject to harmful exposure than those who use treated wood. For this reason, many of the most effective wood preservatives are not available to the general public and may be used only by those trained and with proper equipment for safe application. It is important that those who handle wood preservatives minimize their direct exposure to these chemicals.

The Environmental Protection Agency (EPA) studied creosotes, penta, and waterborne preservatives and, after six years of discussion, issued a number of findings in 1984. Among their conclusions were that (1) preservatives play a significant role in conserving the U.S. timber resource by preventing premature decay; (2) the preservatives studied have the potential to adversely affect the health of people both through direct and indirect contact; (3) ways could be found to allow the continued use of these chemicals through tougher restrictions on handling and treating practices. As a result of these efforts, an agreement between the EPA and the wood-preserving industry included changes in industry practice to ensure protection of treating company personnel, the user, and the environment.

Marine borers ■

Wood used in contact with sea- or brackish water is subject to damage by marine borers. These small animals cause extensive damage to posts, pilings, and wooden boats. There are three types. Two, the *shipworms* (species *Teredo* and

Bankia) and the *pholads* (principally *Martesia*), are mollusks related to clams and oysters. The third type are crustaceans, principally species of *Limnoria*, *Chelura*, and *Sphaeroma*, which are related to crayfish.

The larvae of shipworms attach to the surface of wood and make only a small entry hole there. Once inside, they form irregular galleries (cavities) along the grain. As these organisms grow, the galleries become larger until the wood is completely honeycombed. The exterior of the wood remains intact. Figure 11.10 shows the damage caused by pholads and shipworms. Note that the galleries are lined with shell-like material. Shipworms often concentrate near the mud line on a post or piling and leave little exterior evidence of their presence until damage is severe.

The shells on the heads of shipworms grind away the wood to form the galleries. The rear portion of the body remains near the entry hole where it obtains water and gets rid of wastes. As the shipworm elongates and burrows deeper from the entry hole, it may reach a length of several feet.

The damage from pholads is similar to that from shipworms except that their borings tend to be shorter. They reach a length of up to 2.5 in. (6.4 cm). Pholads retain their clamlike bivalve appearance as they grow, while shipworms have a shell only on the head, with a long worm-shaped body behind.

Limnoria attack on wood pilings is less catastrophic than that of shipworms or pholads because it is more easily detected and occurs in the surface layer. The principal area of attack is wood exposed between high and low tides. Wave action can erode this infested portion of the pilings so that the effective diameter is continuously decreased and eventually results in an hourglass shape. The borings of *Limnoria* are small cylindrical channels less than ⅛ in. (0.3 cm) in diameter, which honeycomb the wood. The depth of penetration is apparently limited by oxygen requirements for respiration.

Preventing attack from marine borers by chemical treatment is possible but difficult. A few species of tropical hardwoods have natural resistance, but these woods are not generally available. No timbers native to North America possess such natural durability. Whenever wood with possible contact to marine borers is used, adequate and appropriate chemical treatment is a necessity. Without such treatment, destruction is often rapid and complete.

In warm coastal waters, the presence of *Limnoria* and pholads present a difficult preservation problem. Even heavy treatments of creosote are sometimes inadequate to provide complete protection. Dual treatments, first with ACA or CCA and then with creosote, have proved reasonably effective under such severe marine environments.

The rate at which leaching of the preservative occurs depends upon the water conditions and the temperature. Loss in stagnant water is less than in the currents in tidal basins. Loss also increases with increase in temperature. Thus, retentions that prove satisfactory in cool climates may be completely inadequate in the tropics.

Insects ■

Wood products in use throughout the world are subject to infestation by a wide variety of termites and beetles and by a few species of ants and bees. Some

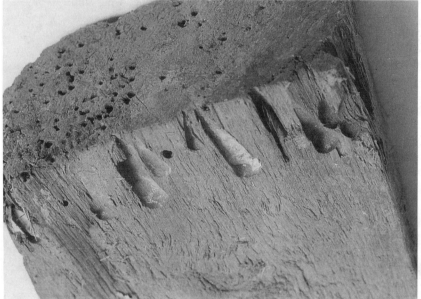

Fig. 11.10
The attack of shipworms and pholads on material exposed to marine environments. (*above*) Piling almost completely consumed by shipworms. The exterior shell still appears relatively sound however. (*below*) The end and exposed sawn surface of a timber attacked by pholads. This piece was stored in the Caribbean for only a short time prior to shipment to the United States.

insects, particularly termites and wood-destroying beetles, cause great financial loss and are of concern in wide areas of North America. A great number of other insects are important in specific regions of the world because of their damage to standing timber, logs, and wood products in use.

Termites have by far the greatest economic impact. Over 0.5 million dwelling units in the United States receive treatment for control of termites each year. *Subterranean termites* have been reported in every contiguous state in the United States but are relatively rare in the tier adjacent to Canada. They are most common and represent the greatest economic problem in California and the states bordering the Gulf of Mexico and the Atlantic Ocean from Texas to Virginia. Several types of termites, including about 60 species, are present, but the most important is the subterranean type. Also common are drywood termites, which are limited to an area within about 100 miles from the coast of California and from the Gulf and South Atlantic coasts, including all of Florida.

Subterranean termites live similarly to ants—in colonies in the ground. Most species have three specialized castes: workers, reproductives, and soldiers. They are sometimes incorrectly referred to as white ants. Termites differ from ants in that they do not have the narrow waist between the abdomen and thorax, and their two pairs of equal-size wings are connected to distinct wing stubs, which are apparent when the wings are lost.

Subterranean termites usually enter the wood from the ground or through *shelter tubes* they construct as a means to reach the wood. These termites use the wood both as a shelter and to obtain cellulose, their source of food. To avoid exposure to outside environments, they live entirely within the wood once a colony is established. Figure 11.11 illustrates a wood post destroyed by termites. The exterior showed no sign of its condition until failure occurred. Termites can attack sound wood but prefer that which has already been degraded by fungi. For the continued extension of subterranean termite infestation, these insects must maintain a reasonably high level of moisture. This moisture is brought from the ground to their sealed colonies.

(Courtesy T. L. Amburgey)

Fig. 11.11
Wood post that failed at the groundline principally from termites, although decay was also present.

Materials selection and building design should always be carried out with consideration for the severity of termite damage in the region. Protection against subterranean termites in areas of low or moderate attack can be accomplished by proper construction of foundations, sills, and floor slabs so that termites cannot reach the wood without being visually detected. Where termite problems are more common, the use of soil-treatment insecticides is recommended and in fact required by mortgage companies. The combination of soil treatment and proper construction with effective termite barriers will provide adequate protection in most temperate regions. Where extreme termite hazard exists, as in tropical regions, it may be desirable to use chemically treated lumber, plywood, and particleboard throughout the building. Fortunately, the chemicals that provide protection from termite attack are also effective against decay fungi. ACA, CCA, and coal-tar creosote are among the most effective and widely used wood treatments for termite protection.

Drywood termites, on the other hand, can enter exposed wood above the ground directly from the air. Once they have gained entry, they can live in wood with moisture contents as low as 5 or 6%. For this reason, it is difficult to isolate buildings from contact with these insects. Structures of wood in regions subject to drywood termite attack should be inspected regularly to see that all cracks and exposed wood are caulked or painted and that ventilation is screened to prevent termites from coming in contact with unpainted wood.

There are several types of wood-destroying beetles in North America including lyctid beetles (true powder-post beetles), anobiid beetles (false powder-post beetles), the furniture beetle, and long-horned borers. Table 11.3 lists common wood-destroying beetles and the types of material they typically attack—both hardwood and softwood, in the green or dry condition. Evidence of *powder-post beetles* is the presence of small exit holes and fine flourlike powder (frass) dropped from the holes, which vary in size from $\frac{1}{16}$ to $\frac{3}{16}$ in. (.16 to .50 cm) depending on the species. Figure 11.12 shows powder-post exit holes in American basswood.

Table 11.3. Wood-destroying beetles

Family	Common name	Material attacked*
Anobiidae	Furniture beetles	Old hardwood, old softwood
Lyctidae	True powder-post beetles	New hardwood
Bostrychidae	False powder-post beetles	New hardwood, new softwood doubtful
Cerambycidae	Long-horned borers	New softwood
Curculionidae	Weevils	Old softwood, old hardwood

Source: Williams (1973).
*Lumber less than 10 years old is considered to be new.

Care should be taken to avoid bringing lumber infested with powder-post beetles into a wood structure or a wood storage yard. Fumigation may be required to eliminate these pests. In regions where powder-post beetles are a serious problem, freshly cut lumber may be treated with insecticides to prevent attack.

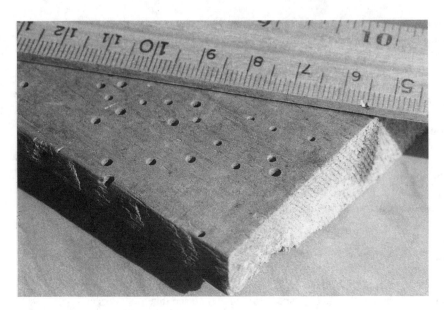

Fig. 11.12
Powder-post beetle attack on basswood lumber.

Heat and fire ■

When wood is heated above about 100°C, decomposition of the wood components takes place. If the temperature is between 100°–200°C, the decomposition will occur slowly. Water vapor will be driven off along with carbon dioxide and some carbon monoxide. The wood will gradually degrade or pyrolyze. *Pyrolysis* is heating in the absence of oxygen. If the temperature is raised above 200°C, more-rapid pyrolysis will begin to take place. Pyrolysis accelerates at from 260° to 350°C. At these temperatures, flammable gases are generated. When heated in the presence of oxygen (air), these gases can either ignite from an ignition source like a flame, or they will self-ignite if the temperature becomes high enough. Above about 270°C the rate of heat produced will be greater than the heat required to generate the gas, and the fire can support itself. Burning will continue as long as the wood can be maintained at a sufficiently high temperature.

In a burning piece of wood, the carbon char left after the volatile gases are driven off tends to increase in thickness with time but at a decreasing rate. Since wood and char are good thermal insulators, the rate of heat transfer to the interior wood decreases as the char thickens. Eventually, the heat transferred inward may be insufficient to produce and drive off flammable gases. If this occurs, the flame will die, and unless there is an outside source of heat, the piece will gradually cool. Because of this self-insulating behavior of burning wood, heavy members such as glue-laminated beams or solid-sawn timbers provide excellent fire resistance.

Building codes recognize three classes of wood buildings: heavy timber, ordinary frame, and light frame. The small 2 × 4-in. to 2 × 12-in. wood members commonly used in light frame buildings are subject to complete destruction by fire because of their small cross sections. Improved fire resistance ratings for light frame buildings can be obtained by use of gypsum board on both sides of walls and on ceilings. In cases where a greater level of fire resistance is needed, light frame members and other forest products can be treated with *fire retardants*.

The impregnation of wood with fire-retardant salts is used commercially to reduce surface flammability by reducing the production of flammable gases. Wood so treated will char and decompose but will not support combustion. Commonly used fire retardants incorporate combinations of zinc chloride, ammonium sulfate, and diammonium phosphate and boric acid; 2–5 lb of chemicals/ft^3 are required for proper protection. Most fire-retardant salts can be leached from the wood by water, so their use must be restricted to interior applications. High concentrations of inorganic salts result in treated materials being slightly more hygroscopic than normal wood at low humidities. This effect can become quite significant above about 65% relative humidity. Nonleaching fire-retardant treatments are now available and do not affect hygroscopicity. These can be used for exterior applications such as wood shingles.

The three major model building codes used in the United States permit fire retardant–treated lumber to be used in many building systems, which can then be rated as noncombustible. Some common applications for fire-retardant lumber include interior nonbearing walls in noncombustible-type buildings, exposed wood roof systems, and interior wall and ceiling paneling in buildings requiring a low (25 or less) flame-spread rating. The heat-release rate and the rate of flame spread are two of the most-important characteristics evaluated when determining the effectiveness of fire retardants.

Weathering ∎

The surface of wood exposed to outdoor conditions without the protection of paint or other finishes is subject to a surface roughening and degradation commonly termed *weathering*. The color of the wood turns to gray or silver (depending on the species), the cells at the surface are slowly broken down, and the surface is gradually eroded. Figure 11.13 shows the surface of a redwood board weathered for 8 years. This photograph clearly illustrates the difference in the weathering rate of latewood as compared to earlywood. Weathering is usually not a serious problem unless the effect on the appearance is considered detrimental. In some regions of the country, wood siding is often left unpainted or treated with a bleach to accelerate weathering to obtain a rough, gray, natural-looking architectural effect. However, in damp climates, blackish fungal stains may develop, which degrade the desired appearance. In such areas where blue-stain or surface molds commonly develop, a water-repellent treatment containing a fungicide can be used to inhibit development of such discoloration.

Weathering results from a combination of factors. Light, particularly the ultraviolet wavelengths, slowly degrades portions of the cell wall. Soft-rot fungi, which grow well in alternately wet and dry conditions, are also frequently involved. The alternate shrinkage and swelling of the surface layers produce stresses that can cause small fractures. Finally, the mechanical abrasion of wind

Fig. 11.13
**An unfinished redwood board showing the difference
in the rate of weathering of earlywood and latewood
after 8 years of exposure.**

and water gradually wears away the surface that has been degraded by these other mechanisms. If wood is left exposed to the elements and unfinished, it can weather at a rate exceeding 0.25 in. per century. Higher-density species generally weather at a slower rate, although they are more subject to surface checking and distortion.

REVIEW

A. Terms to define or explain:

1. Hyphae (mycelia)
2. Decay or rots
3. Staining (by fungi)
4. Brown rot
5. White rot
6. Oil-based preservatives
7. Waterborne preservatives
8. Natural resistance to decay
9. CCA
10. Shipworms
11. *Limnoria*
12. Pholads
13. Subterranean termite
14. Coal-tar creosote
15. Powder-post beetles
16. Termite shelter tubes
17. Fire-retardant treatments
18. Weathering
19. Pyrolysis

B. Questions or concepts to explain:
1. The mechanism by which decay fungi deteriorate wood.
2. Differences between brown, white, and soft rots.

3. Methods of preventing the decay of wood products.
4. Factors necessary for the growth of fungi and the extent to which these can be controlled.
5. The basic nature of stain and surface molds.
6. The relation of species and wood type to the natural decay resistance of wood.
7. Means of reducing the danger of subterranean termite infestation.
8. Other types of insects that attack wood and the means of reducing danger of infestation.
9. How wood is degraded by heat and fire.
10. The effect of fire on different types of wood buildings.
11. Causes of weathering of wood.
12. Means of controlling moisture content to prevent decay.
13. Retention you would expect with the Rueping versus the Lowry process.

REFERENCES AND SUPPLEMENTAL READINGS

Barnes, H.M. and Murphy, R.J. 1995. Wood preservation—The classics and the new age. For. Prod. J. 45(9):16–26.

Corbett, N.H. 1975. Micro-morphological studies on the degradation of lignified cell walls by Ascomycetes and Fungi Imperfecti. J. Inst. Wood Sci 14:18–29.

DeGroot, R.C. 1976. Your wood can last for centuries. USDA For. Serv.

Ericksson, K.L.; Blanchette, R.A.; and Ander, P. 1990. Microbial and Enzymatic Degradation of Wood and Wood Components. New York: Springer-Verlag.

Feist, W.C. 1990. Outdoor wood weathering and protection. Amer. Chem. Soc. Archeological Wood. Chap. 11.

Freas, A. 1982. Evaluation, maintenance and upgrading of wood structures. ASCE Comm. on Wood.

Gjovik, L.R., and Baechler, R.H. 1977. Selection, production, procurement and use of preservative-treated wood. USDA For. Ser. Gen. Tech. Rep. FPL-15.

Graham, R.D., and Helsing, G.G. 1979 Wood pole maintenance manual. Ore. State U. For. Res. Lab. Bull. 24.

Highley, T.L. 1989. Wood decay: New concepts and opportunities for control. AWPA Proc. Vol. 85. 71–77.

Highley, T.L., C.A. Clausen, S.C. Croan, F. Green III, B.L. Illman, J.A. Micales. 1994. Research on biodeterioration of wood, 1987–1992. USDA For. Ser. Res. Pap. FPL-RP-529.

Johnston, H.R.; Smith, V.K.; and Beal, R.H. 1972. Subterranian termites: Their prevention and control in buildings. USDA Home Bull. 64.

Koch, P. 1972. Utilization of Southern Pines. USDA For. Ser. Agric. Handb. 420, Vol. 2. 650–720.

Koch, P. 1985. Utilization of Hardwoods Growing on Southern Pine Sites. USDA For. Ser. Agric. Handb. 605, Vol. 2. 2268–2536.

LaFage. J.P., and Williams, L.H. 1979. Lyctid beetles—Recognition, prevention and control. La. State Univ. Agric. Exp. Sta. Circ. 106.

Micklewright, J.T. 1992. Wood Preservation Statistics—1990. Amer. Wood Pres. Assoc.

Milton, F.T. 1994. The preservation of wood—A self study manual for wood treaters. Pub. MI-6413-S. Univ. of Minn. Extension Ser.

Nicholas, D.D. 1973. Wood Deterioration and Its Prevention by Preservative Treatments. vol. 1 and vol. 2. Syracuse, N.Y: Syracuse Univ. Press.

Richardson, B.A. 1987. Wood Preservation. Construction Press, Lancaster, England.

Scheffer, T.C., and Cowling, E.B. 1966. Natural resistance of wood to microbial deterioration. Ann. Rev. Phytopathol.4:147–170.

Scheffer, T.C., and Verrall, A.F. 1973. Principles for protecting wood buildings from decay. USDA For. Ser. Res. Rept. FPL-190.

Verrall, A.F. 1965. Moisture content of wood in buildings. ASTM Spec. Tech. Publ. 385.

Walsh, M.R. 1985. Treated Wood: Bright spot in wood economy. For. Ind. 112(11):36–38.

Wilcox, W.W. 1968. Changes in wood microstructure through progressive stages of decay. U.S. For. Prod. Lab. Rep. 70.

_____. 1978 Review of literature on the effects of early stages of decay on wood strength. Wood Fiber 9(4):252–257.

12

Silvicultural practices and wood quality

■ **THE PRACTICE** of caring for and cultivating forest trees is known as *silviculture;* this activity is one of the responsibilities of the forester, whose objective is usually to accelerate growth. One method of increasing growth rate involves reduction of competition for available sunlight, nutrients, and water, which can be achieved through such practices as control of understory vegetation, thinning, or control of spacing between seedlings at the time of planting. Another approach is to add nutrients and water by fertilizing and irrigating. Growth rate of new forest stands can also be stimulated through genetic selection of seed or planting stock. Tremendous increases over natural growth rates are possible. Tables 12.1 and 12.2 contain data representative of a number of trials conducted to determine the effect of silvicultural treatments upon yield.

Table 12.1. Percentage increase in pulp weight obtainable in wood formed during the 4-year period after silvicultural treatment compared with the previous 4 years

Position in tree	Control	Thinned	Fertilized	Thinned and fertilized
Section between 9th and 10th branch whorl from top	55	184	214	104
Section between 13th and 14th branch whorl from top	22	41	59	51
Section between 17th and 18th branch whorl from top	29	37	53	63
Breast height (4.5 ft or 1.4 m from ground level)	34	62	59	100

Source: Parker et al. (1976).
Note: Figures are for 25-year-old Douglas-fir growing in British Columbia.

267

Table 12.2. Volume growth response of a 6-year-old quaking aspen stand following silvicultural treatment

Treatment	Relative volume growth after 3 years (9 years old)	Relative weight of new growth after 3 years (9 years old)
Control	100	100
Fertilizer*	116	118
Water†	163	156
Fertilizer plus water	244	219

Source: Einspahr et al. (1972).

* 1000 lb $N_{20}P_5K_{10}Ca_{10}Mg_2$ fertilizer applied per acre (or 1.12 metric tons/ha) in one application.

†5-7 in. (13-18 cm) additional moisture added per acre through overhead sprinkler system.

Measures of wood quality ∎

Before examining how silvicultural practices affect wood quality, it is necessary to explain the concept of quality. *Quality* can be generally defined as a measure of the characteristics of wood that influence properties of products made from it. Briggs and Smith (1986) put it differently, saying that "wood quality is a measure of the aptness of wood for a given use." A more-precise definition of quality can be elusive, since characteristics important in wood to be used for one product are often different from those for another product. In one case, quality may be measured in terms of density, uniformity of growth rings, and percent of knot-free wood, while in another instance, properties, such as proportion of latewood, cellulose yield, and the fiber-to-vessel ratio, may be primary quality indices. Larson (1969) provided insight into the matter of wood quality when he wrote: "During wood formation, numerous factors both inside and outside the tree lead to variation in the type, number, size, shape, physical structure, and chemical composition of the wood elements. Wood quality is the arbitrary classification of these variations in the wood elements when they are counted, measured, weighed, analyzed, or evaluated for some specific purpose. Wood quality is therefore a concept."

Although the concept of quality may be difficult to pinpoint, several factors influence the suitability of wood for a variety of purposes. These factors include density, uniformity of growth rings, fiber length, percent of clear bole, straightness of grain, proportion of heartwood, percentage of vessels (in hardwoods), and presence of juvenile and reaction woods.

DENSITY. As explained in Chapter 10, density of wood is a prime determinant of strength, and the strength/density relationship is direct. In general discussion, the term *density* refers to the same characteristic as specific gravity, i.e., the dry wood substance per unit of volume. (Chapter 9 discusses the technical difference.) Species that are usually high in density, such as Douglas-fir, larch, and southern yellow pine, are preferred for uses in which high strength is important. Lower-density species, such as white and sugar pine, hemlock, and true fir, may be used for light framing or lumber products in which dimensional stability or other characteristics are of more importance than strength.

Although high-density species are preferred where high-strength lumber products are required, it must be realized that density varies considerably within a given species (Figs. 12.1, 9.4). Trees (or even zones within a tree) that form the highest-density wood will be the most valuable to the producer of structural lumber products. Therefore, any practice that might cause wood to fall in the upper part of the density range for that species can increase its value as structural lumber. This is recognized, for example, in the grading rules for southern pine. On the other hand, conditions that cause wood density to fall into the lower density range also result in lower strength. Such wood has diminished value as structural material, although it may be easier to machine.

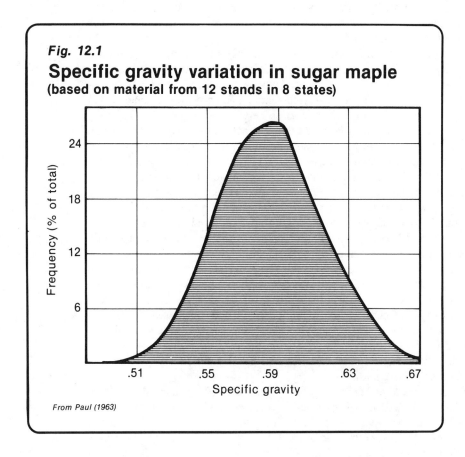

Fig. 12.1
Specific gravity variation in sugar maple
(based on material from 12 stands in 8 states)

From Paul (1963)

Species that produce relatively low- or medium-density wood are often preferred as raw material for pulp and paper manufacture over species that produce higher-density wood (see Chapter 16). However, the higher the density (based on ovendry weight), the greater the yield of pulp from a given volume of wood. Thus, the forest manager may be faced with the seemingly conflicting objectives of growing low-density species, such as spruce, cottonwood, or aspen, so that both volume per acre and density of wood are maximized.

Growth rate can significantly affect wood density. This is particularly true of ring- and semi-ring-porous hardwoods that tend to show greater density and hardness with increases in rate of growth.The width of earlywood in ring- and semi-ring-porous hardwoods tends to remain relatively constant regardless of the growth rate. In these woods, a slowing of diameter growth brings the rows of large pores closer together in successive annual rings (Fig. 12.2). Development of thick-walled latewood fibers and small-diameter vessels is minimized in ring-porous species when the growth rate is slow (Paul 1963). Therefore, within limits, the faster ring-porous hardwoods are grown, the denser (and thus stronger) they are. Jane et al. (1970) pointed out that this rule holds only within limits, because wood grown at an extremely fast rate may develop abnormally thin-walled fibers and/or an unusually high proportion of parenchyma cells. He estimated that maximum density and strength develop in mature wood when growth rings measure 6–10/in. (2.5–4.0/cm).

Softwoods with distinct growth rings (*distinct-ring softwoods*) produce wood characterized by bands of latewood that are clearly discernible from the bands of earlywood on either side. In such woods, latewood tracheids have distinctly thicker walls and smaller radial diameters than earlywood tracheids, and the change within a growth layer from one cell type to the next is typically abrupt. It was once commonly believed that distinct-ring softwoods decrease in density with an increase in growth rate, and numerous studies have supported this notion (Ciesler and Janka 1902; Wellwood 1952; Aldridge and Hudson 1958, 1959; Paul 1963). The explanation advanced for this relationship is that in distinct-ring softwoods the latewood remains relatively constant in width with varying rates of growth. Despite a longstanding acceptance of a fast-growth/low-density relationship in distinct-ring softwoods, a study published in 1947 refuted this notion. In that year Turnbull reported that density variations between plantation pines were traceable to an age effect rather than to growth rate. This result was later confirmed by Rendle and Phillips (1957), who studied samples taken from the outer portions of stems. The age effect is illustrated by a plot of density versus age for a typical forest-grown distinct-ring softwood (Fig. 12.3). Here, density increases rapidly through the juvenile period, then increases slowly and steadily through maturity. This pattern has also been observed in several diffuse-porous hardwoods. A variation of this relationship is one in which wood density declines slightly for several years following the juvenile period before tending to increase in successive growth rings.

Some 30 years after Turnbull's report, Bendtsen (1978) stated that the age effect had not been sufficiently considered by a number of investigators studying effects of growth rates upon density and cited several studies that substantiated this conclusion (Wardrop 1951; Spurr and Hsiung 1954; Spurr and Hyvarinen 1954; Dadswell 1958; Goggans 1961; Erickson and Arima 1974). He summarized reservations to the notion of a growth rate–density relationship in distinct-ring softwoods by pointing out that "problems arise when growth rate–wood property relations are studied independently from other factors that affect wood. For example, if the specific gravity of fast and slow growth pine trees of *similar diameter* is measured, the slow growth trees will generally have a higher specific gravity because of the consistent pattern of increasing density from pith to bark associated with age. If the age effect is ignored, growth rate can be wrongly interpreted as the causal factor of differing specific gravity. Actually, if the specific

Fig. 12.2
Slow growth (A) results in a higher proportion of large
vessels in ring-porous hardwoods than fast growth (B).
Red oak (*Quercus* spp.). ×4

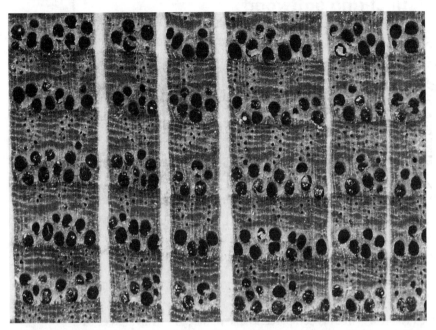

A. Slow growth

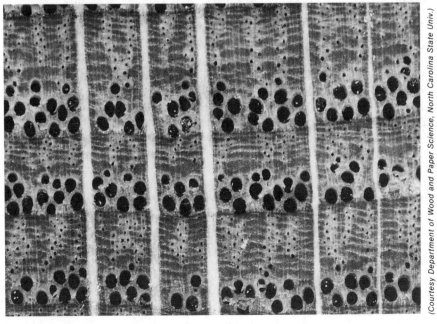

B. Fast growth

(Courtesy Department of Wood and Paper Science, North Carolina State Univ.)

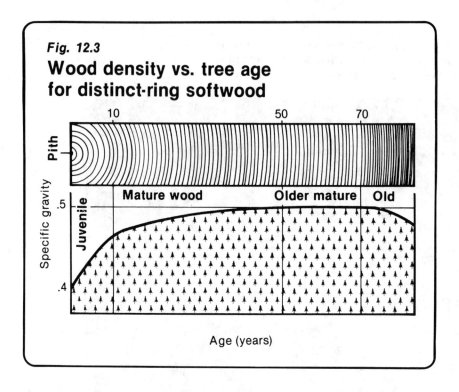

Fig. 12.3

Wood density vs. tree age
for distinct-ring softwood

gravity of the fast growth trees is compared to that of the slow growth trees over the same number of annual rings, counting from the pith, they tend to be similar." A number of subsequent studies have supported this observation (McKimmy and Campbell 1982; Taylor and Burton 1982; Barrett and Kellogg 1984; McKimmy 1986).

The density of diffuse-porous hardwoods and softwoods without distinct growth rings is sometimes affected by growth rate, but results are variable. Radcliffe (1953) reported no relationship between density and growth rate in sugar maple, while Paul (1963) found higher than normal density resulting from fast growth in the same species. Studies dealing with yellow poplar (*Liriodendron tulipifera*) also show mixed results. Paul (1957) compared specific gravity of old-growth and second-growth yellow poplar and found the faster-grown second-growth material to have an 8% higher specific gravity. More-recent studies by Thor and Core (1977) and Fukazawa (1984), however, indicated no relationship between growth rate and specific gravity. Experiments with trees of the genus *Populus* have also shown density occasionally to be higher than normal, unaffected, or lower than normal as a result of fast growth. In Fukazawa's work with diffuse-porous hardwoods, an age effect, rather than growth rate effect, was noted in wood density differences. Similar examples could be given for *indistinct-ring softwoods* such as the soft pines, firs, and hemlocks.

UNIFORMITY. Uniformity of growth rate has an effect upon wood structure and density variation both within and between growth rings. Larson (1967, 1969) indicated that lack of uniformity represents one of the greatest wood quality problems facing all wood-using industries. In the manufacture of pulp and paper, for instance, nonuniformity in wood density may result in losses from overprocessing of some components and/or underprocessing of others. Thus, strength and surface qualities of paper products may be difficult to maintain precisely. Use of uniform material, on the other hand, increases the probability of producing paper of uniformly high quality.

Uniform wood is desirable not only for manufacture of fiber products but for solid wood products as well. A case in point is a product like siding that must accept and then retain a coat of paint. Wood characterized by significant within-ring density variation (i.e., by bands of very dense latewood and alternate zones of low-density earlywood) often presents a problem when painted and exposed to the elements. The paint film tends to flake off after a period of weathering. The very dense wood shrinks and swells more than the lower-density wood, thus causing a relative movement between the paint film and wood surface. Such wood is also difficult to machine to a smooth condition because of differing hardness between earlywood and latewood bands. In addition to within-ring variation, variation between growth rings also causes problems in solid wood products. Difficulties traceable to the presence of juvenile and adult woods in the same timber are discussed in Chapter 6.

Uniformity of wood structure both within and between growth rings is determined to a great extent by growth rate and conditions under which growth occurs. Silvicultural treatments should therefore be prescribed with uniformity as well as density of wood in mind.

PROPORTION OF HEARTWOOD. In certain solid wood products, the proportion of heartwood is important. As explained in Chapters 2 and 11, heartwood of some species is less susceptible to attack by fungi and insects than sapwood and is often less penetrable by preservatives. In products designed for use where insects or decay are potential problems, resistance to attack by wood-destroying organisms significantly influences the value of wood. This is evidenced by the expensive all-heart grades of redwood and some cedars. Therefore, redwood, cedar, baldcypress, or other wood grown to produce naturally durable lumber for the siding, fence, or patio deck market should be managed with consideration of the effect upon heartwood formation. The proportion of heartwood can also be important in products where natural color patterns are desirable. A lack of well-developed heartwood in species such as walnut, cherry, or rosewood would negatively affect value.

As explained in Chapter 2, heartwood formation does not begin on average until a stem is 14–18 years of age. Once heartwood begins to form in species with naturally durable heartwood, the least durable forms first. Durability increases from the center of the tree outward until some degree of maturity is reached (Dadswell 1958). Moreover, the proportion of heartwood varies directly with tree age (Hillis and Ditchburne 1974). These relationships indicate that short *rotation ages* and/or very fast growth rates should be avoided where maximum production of heartwood (particularly durable heartwood) is desired.

FIBER LENGTH. Fiber length has an effect upon a number of pulp and paper properties, including tear resistance and tensile, fold, and burst strength. In most cases, long lengths are desirable.

In both hardwoods and softwoods, rotation age and growth-accelerating treatments such as fertilization and irrigation have an effect upon the average fiber length in a stem. Rotation age affects fiber length for two reasons. First, juvenile wood near the core is made up of shorter fibers than those in subsequently formed wood. Therefore, unless a stem is grown to a relatively large diameter, so as to minimize the proportion of juvenile wood, the average fiber length will be small. Second, fusiform initials of the cambium continue to grow in length for many years. The result is that with increased age, longer fibers are formed from these initials.

Fertilization and irrigation treatments affect fiber length differently in hardwoods than in softwoods. Numerous experiments with southern yellow pine have shown reduced fiber length as a result of intensive culture (Youngberg et al. 1963; Posey 1965; Klem 1968). In contrast, studies involving hardwoods almost invariably show longer fiber lengths after growth stimulation (Kennedy 1957; Kennedy and Smith 1959; Einspahr et al. 1972; Murphey and Bowier 1975; Maeglin et al. 1977). Whether it is the increase in growth rate resulting from intensive culture or plentiful nutrients and water that more greatly affects fiber length is uncertain. For example, findings correlating fiber length and growth rate (Bissett et al. 1951) are contradicted by more-recent studies that indicate little or no correlation (Zobel et al. 1961; Zobel et al. 1969).

While more information is needed, it is nonetheless clear that fiber length is affected by forestry practices. This factor should therefore be considered whenever product quality is significantly related to fiber length.

OCCURRENCE OF JUVENILE WOOD AND REACTION WOOD. The proportion of juvenile wood that develops in a stem is related to the growth rate at a young age. Softwood stems grown rapidly during the juvenile period will have a relatively high proportion of juvenile wood as compared to those grown more slowly early in the rotation period. Not only do wide rings near the stem center mean that a substantial amount of wood is formed during the normal juvenile period, but steps taken to stimulate growth at an early age may even cause an extension of the juvenile period (Larson 1969; Megraw and Nearn 1972; Zobel et al. 1972). This notion was later supported by Bryant (1984) when he observed that in slower-growing trees an optimum or high average density is reached at an earlier age than in more rapidly growing trees. Recent research suggests that the period of juvenile wood may be governed by more than simply genetics and growth rate (Kucera 1994; Peszlen 1995). Kucera, for example, hypothesized that the period of juvenile wood formation is closely linked to height growth, with transition to mature wood coinciding with slowing of height growth as crown closure occurs.

Bendtsen (1978) reported that the combined effects of early accelerated growth can be quite significant. He explained that it is not unusual for improved trees to reach sawtimber size in 15–25 years, depending upon species and locality of growth. He indicated that loblolly pine trees of that age may contain 75% or more juvenile wood. By contrast, trees of similar dimensions from a natural forest, growing more slowly, contain only a small fraction of juvenile wood when they reach merchantable size. Briggs and Smith (1986) described a theoretical 36-in.-diameter tree that had grown at a uniform rate of 30 rings per inch and had produced juvenile wood for the first 20 years. The wood of this 540-year-old tree would be less than 5% juvenile wood. In comparison, a 36-year-old, 36-in.-diameter tree grown at a uniform rate of two rings per inch would contain over 60% juvenile wood. Trees of the latter example will become increasingly common in the South over the next 30 years as fast-growing pine plantations replace slower-growing, naturally regenerated forests; in this region, it is inevitable that much more juvenile wood volume will be harvested in the future. In any event, timing of silvicultural treatments is obviously important if occurrence of juvenile wood is to be minimized.

Reaction wood formation is apparently also affected by growth conditions. As explained in Chapter 6, the juvenile core often contains an appreciable amount of reaction wood. Therefore, rapid growth at a young age not only increases the proportion of juvenile wood but reaction wood as well. Several investigators have reported reaction wood formation in rapidly grown wood even without lean in the stems (Pillow and Luxford 1937; Isebrands and Bensend 1972; Isebrands and Parham 1974; Crist et al. 1977). Timell (1986) stated that a connection between rapid growth and compression wood formation in conifers is not surprising and suggested a linkage to abundant supplies of auxin.

CELLULAR COMPOSITION. In the manufacture of pulp and paper from hardwoods, the relative proportions of vessels, fibers, and rays are important because ray cells and vessels (particularly large vessels) tend to be lost in the pulping process. Vessels that are retained sometimes cause difficulty with respect to surface quality of paper, since their shape is not conducive to development of strong intraelement bonds. "Picking" or lift-off of vessels from the paper surface during printing is one result (Allchin 1960). Any increase in the number or volume of vessels resulting from growth manipulation is then viewed as undesirable in pulp to be used for many kinds of paper products.

Although determinations have been made for only a few species, studies have generally indicated that the proportion of vessels and ray tissue is unaffected by growth acceleration treatments such as fertilization and irrigation (Einspahr et al. 1972; Saucier and Ike 1972). However, genetics have been shown to significantly affect the mix of various cell types; for example, Crist and Dawson (1975) showed 19% vessels in one clone of *Populus tristis* as compared to 30% in another. There may also be a relationship between genetic characteristics and associated growth rate; Ganchev (1971) found that clones exhibiting high growth rates tended to have fewer but larger vessels.

KNOTS. From the standpoint of sawlog and veneer log production, size and frequency of knots is perhaps the single most important aspect of quality. Knots greatly affect both appearance and strength, and because of this their occurrence is a primary factor in determination of log and lumber grades.

Although all trees produce branches (and thus knots), it is possible to minimize their development. A number of silvicultural practices can influence knot development, including spacing at the time of planting, timing of thinnings, treatments to accelerate rate of growth, and pruning. Selection and breeding of less-branchy trees is also a possibility.

Harris et al. (1975) noted the combined importance of density and size and frequency of knots in structural lumber and suggested that development of large knots could be compensated for by an increase in density. Working with *Pinus radiata,* they calculated that bending resistance can be maintained even when knot diameters increase 60% if a relatively modest 10% increase in density is also achieved. This work clearly indicates the importance of density to strength but illustrates the substantial effect of knots.

Boyce (1965) wrote that the largest percentage of top-grade lumber and veneer can be grown in the shortest possible time by concentrating cultural and genetic practices on the butt log. He also referred to comments by Krajicek (1959) and Brinkman (1955) indicating that treatment of the second log is more costly and difficult because it is higher from the ground and has more and larger branches. The concept that treatment to minimize knottiness should be concentrated on the butt log is generally accepted today.

GRAIN ORIENTATION. Grain orientation that is not parallel to the long axis of a stem often results in slope of grain in manufactured products. As explained in Chapter 10, this can drastically reduce strength. This kind of grain orientation also adversely affects machining properties and the nature of moisture-induced dimensional changes. Grain orientation that is not parallel to the pith, such as spiral grain (see Chapter 2), is thus to be avoided, if possible, in wood to be used for many kinds of products.

A number of investigators have noted an apparent connection between development of spiral grain and growth conditions. Fortunately, it appears that *intensive culture practices*, (see Intensive culture) and irrigation in particular, tend to reduce the occurrence of spiral grain (Boyd 1968; Smith et al. 1972; Brazier 1977). Pruning stems at an early age is also suspected of suppressing development of spiral grain (Noskowiak 1963). Because intensive culture apparently reduces grain deviation, this factor is a minor consideration when prescribing traditional silvicultural treatments. However, since growth conditions influence grain orientation, this relationship should still be considered when evaluating the merits of new techniques for accelerating growth.

CHEMICAL COMPOSITION. The portion of wood weight composed of cellulose, lignin, hemicellulose, and/or extractable compounds significantly affects pulp yields (Chapter 16). Consumption of *cooking liquor,* a chemical solution containing lignin-dissolving compounds used in chemical pulping of wood, and the potential for bleaching are also affected. Generally, it is desirable to have the largest possible fraction of cellulose coupled with minimal fractions of lignin and extractives.

Because acceleration of growth can affect the proportion of juvenile wood in a stem, this kind of activity can also affect chemical composition of a stem. Juvenile wood tends to be low in cellulose and high in lignin compared to mature wood. Acceleration of growth early in a rotation increases the proportion of juvenile wood and can thereby cause an undesirable reduction in the proportion of cellulose. But what happens if growth is accelerated after the juvenile period? Numerous investigations into this important matter have yielded conflicting results, and further work is needed to define the relationships more precisely.

There is some evidence that stand density may influence chemical composition of wood. For example, Shupe et al. (1995) found that lower stand densities yielded greater lignin, holocellulose, and alpha cellulose content of wood and that higher stand densities resulted in higher extractive content.

CONCEPTS OF WOOD QUALITY. A number of factors determine the suitability of wood for a specific end use: density, uniformity, proportion of heartwood, fiber length, occurrence of juvenile and/or reaction wood, cellular composition, presence of knots, grain orientation, and chemical composition. The combined effect of these factors determines wood quality; the importance of each is dependent upon intended use.

To the forester, the fact that quality is determined by a number of factors is matched in importance by the fact that silvicultural practices affect virtually all of them. The net effect of specific forestry practices upon wood quality is the subject of the following section.

Growth manipulation and wood quality ■

The amount of space in which a tree grows is an extremely important determinant of growth rate and thus of wood properties. The spacing between trees and the extent of surrounding vegetation define the degree of competition for such critical growth elements as nutrients, water, and sunlight. When competition is slight, crowns and root systems can develop fully because these critical elements are not limiting factors. On the other hand, when crowding occurs, trees must compete intensely for elements needed for growth. For example, consider sunlight-tolerant seedlings that have taken root in a clear-cut area. They first must compete with weeds and shrubs. Young trees that develop quickly have the best chance for survival. Others may remain stunted and eventually die. Trees that do become established face a new battle—with each other. If a large number of trees survive the first stage of competition with other vegetation, crown development will quickly fill the open space between trees. As competition for sunlight, nutrients, and moisture intensifies, growth of the entire stand slows. Despite the slow growth, slight differences in the rate of height extension will eventually begin to favor a few trees, giving them a significant advantage over their neighbors. This slight advantage is magnified as success in competition for sunlight improves growth rate even more. Suppressed trees are left further and further behind, and the weakest fails. Even the trees that grow fastest lose branches through natural pruning caused by limited light from lateral crowding; such crowding may eventually diminish the capacity for wood production.

The scenario described above serves to illustrate one role of the forester: to minimize the effects of competition and thus to maximize the rate of growth. For example, fertilization and irrigation can be applied so that critical elements are present even in densely stocked stands. Another approach to control of competition levels is manipulation of the stand to ensure that it is in balance with naturally occurring growth elements. By spacing trees widely at planting time and then controlling competing vegetation, early growth can be accelerated greatly (Table 12.3). Later, timely thinnings can reduce competition so that remaining stems continue to grow at a fast pace. Such techniques have been used successfully for centuries. But growth manipulation affects wood properties. The questions to be addressed now are what properties are affected, in what ways, and by how much.

Table 12.3. Merchantable volume and number of trees removed in thinning and residual after 10 years for a cottonwood plantation

| | Original stand | | | Wood removed in thinning | | | Residual stand | | | |
| | | | | | | | | | | Residual stand plus thinning volume |
Spacing	<5 in.	≥5 in.	Vol.	<5 in.	≥5 in.	Vol.	<5 in.	≥5 in.	Vol.	
(ft)	*(no. of trees)*		*(ft³)*	*(no. of trees)*		*(ft³)*	*(no. of trees)*		*(ft³)*	*(ft³)*
4 × 9	685	3	8	123	37	262	...	102	1474	1744
8 × 9	245	23	64	28	99	355	...	87	1458	1877
12 × 12	23	98	514	...	37	452	...	75	1770	2736
16 × 18	6	47	615	...	...	...	...	63	1782	2397

Source: Krinard and Johnson (1975).
Note: Only stems ≥ 5 in. (12.7 cm) measured for volume.

SPACING TREES AT PLANTING TIME. Assuming that nutrient and water availability is limited and maximum sunlight is desirable for growth, widely spaced trees will grow faster than crowded ones. When this relationship is combined with the knowledge that growth rate in some tree species is related to wood density, and properties such as strength and dimensional stability are closely correlated with wood density, it is easy to see how spacing of trees can affect wood properties.

By increasing growth rate, wide spacing of young ring-porous hardwoods tends to maximize density and thus strength of these trees. However, the effect of accelerated growth upon density of softwoods with distinct latewood is not as clear. For these species, then, the effect of wide initial spacing is open to question. Some would argue that density is decreased. Others would predict no effect, as discussed earlier. There are conflicting findings on the question of whether spacing affects the period of juvenile wood formation. Yang (1994), when working with white spruce, found more growth rings of juvenile wood at a 3.6 m × 3.6 m spacing than when trees were spaced more closely. He did not, however, find this effect in black spruce. Clark and Saucier (1989) studied juvenile to mature wood transition in southern pine under different plantation spacings and concluded that spacing had no effect on the age of transition. They did acknowledge that wide initial spacing (4.6 m × 4.6 m) led to a significantly larger juvenile core (16 cm) than a narrower spacing (a 1.8 m × 1.8 m spacing resulted in an 11-cm juvenile core). One point upon which research findings are in almost total agreement is that by maximizing ring width in the early years, the size of the juvenile core is also enlarged. Since juvenile wood is low in density, a large juvenile core will in itself reduce average stem density. Thus, although open-grown stands of distinct-ring softwoods will produce merchantable-size trees in a shorter time than dense stands, the average annual production of fiber per acre—or of woody biomass—will not necessarily be greater, since average density may be less.

Rapid early growth, resulting in a large core of juvenile wood, is an important consideration regardless of the species involved. Should a large juvenile core be developed so that later growth of mature wood occurs in the form of the largest possible cylinder? Or should early growth be subdued to minimize the size of the juvenile core? Although this point has been debated, no clear-cut answer has emerged. The answer appears to vary, depending upon management objectives and product alternatives. Kellogg and Kennedy (1986) shed some light on the spacing dilemma. They agreed that planting to an initial spacing such as 2.4 m and then thinning later would result in a minimal juvenile core. They also noted, however, that unless there was a commercial market for the thinned material, which in many regions there was not, the initial narrow spacing/thinning strategy made the remaining trees at least twice as expensive as planting to a wider spacing. One study of a situation in which a commercial market for thinnings was available (Clark et al. 1994) showed significant financial benefits from close initial spacing and late thinning. Loblolly pine, thinned at age 18 and at 5-year intervals thereafter to age 38, was shown to yield more than 60% No. 2 and better lumber when planted at a 1.8 m × 1.8 m spacing and later thinned to about 100 ft^2/acre, but less than 42% No. 2 and better when planted at 3.6 m × 3.6 m spacing and thinned to the same basal area.

One direct result of growth under wide spacing is that knots are larger and more prevalent than if growth occurs under crowded conditions; availability of light reduces natural pruning and tends to cause branches to attain relatively large diameters. Thus when harvesting and converting open-grown trees to solid wood products, more substance is wasted than when using wood from more densely grown stands.

An important effect of open growth on wood quality is that stems are more highly tapered than those that develop in closed stands. To understand this, it may be necessary to review Chapter 1 and the discussion about how growth is initiated in the spring. Auxins produced in the swelling buds move downward through the tree, progressively reinitiating cambial activity. In softwoods, the cambium in the upper part of the stem may become active as much as 3 weeks before the portion of the cambium near the base. Growth later ceases at about the same time throughout the stem. Thus, in a tall tree with active branches only at the top (i.e., in closed-stand conditions), more growth is added near the top each year than at the bottom. Formation of a cylindrical stem is the result. In contrast, trees grown in the open retain branches fully along their length, meaning that there is little lag time between onset of diameter growth in the crown and that near the base. Taper in such stems is perpetuated. Lumber yield as a percent of original log volume is invariably lower from highly tapered logs than from cylindrical logs of similar volume.

Wide spacing of trees in replanting of open areas can result in higher proportions of juvenile wood, larger and more frequent knots, and somewhat greater stem taper than that which develops with closer spacing. When growing trees for lumber production, it may be better from a wood quality standpoint to manage for relatively slow growth for the first 5–10 years, with steps taken to improve growth rate thereafter. The practical closeness of planting is largely dependent upon a combination of planting costs, later response to thinning, markets for material removed in the thinning process, and the future impact of quality considerations on the value of sawlogs and veneer logs.

THINNING. Trees remaining when surrounding trees are removed by thinning or partial cutting respond to the more-open environment by stimulated crown development and formation of wider growth rings along the bole. Effects upon growth are often dramatic. One study of slash pine in Georgia indicated the benefits of thinning. A yield of 28 cords/acre (251 m³/ha) was obtained at age 23 for a plot that had been thinned at age 3, as compared to a yield of less than 5 cords/acre (45 m³/ha) in an adjacent unthinned plot (Jones 1977). In addition to increased yield at harvest, another benefit of periodic thinning is that material normally lost through natural mortality is salvaged.

A note of caution is in order at this point with respect to results of thinning and other silvicultural treatments. Larson (1972) indicated that it was important to distinguish between very young and mature trees when measuring the results of silvicultural practices, pointing out that young and mature trees may react quite differently to the same treatments. An example of this is provided by Phelps and Chen (1991), who in working with white oak observed significantly higher diameter growth rates after thinning in intermediate-size trees but little change in codominant trees.

Because of the impact on crown development and growth rate, thinning may adversely affect some wood properties. These effects can be minimized, however, since much of the impact on wood properties is traceable to the timing of thinnings. Done early in the life of a stand, thinning can have the same result as wide spacing in a plantation. One effect of early thinning is an increase in the size of the juvenile core through greater ring width in this zone. Early thinning can also cause the juvenile period to be extended, resulting in a broader transition zone. To the extent that the proportion of juvenile wood in stems is increased as a result of thinning, wood can be expected to have lower density and strength, shorter fibers, higher longitudinal shrinkage upon drying, and a greater proportion of lignin. Delay of thinning until after the juvenile stage would avoid these problems.

Whether or not a tree is in the juvenile stage, thinning decreases the tendency for upward crown recession and may stimulate growth of existing branches as well as development of new ones. The results are increased knot development and stem taper. The tendency for resurgence of branch growth is most serious in very young softwood stands in which lower branches are still alive. In thick stands of pine, lower branches will usually be dead by the time pole size is attained. Since pine cannot regain lost lower branches, there is no chance of revitalizing branch growth by thinning; thus, trees can never revert to an open-grown form. The same is true of many hardwoods as well, but some species tend to produce new branches (called *epicormic branches*) in the lower stem if competition within a stand is reduced.

Middleton et al. (1995) addressed the issue of stem taper and knot development in a study of lodgepole pine and found that although lumber recovery increased in general with increasing tree diameter classes, lumber recovery was lowest in trees from stands containing few trees/ha; such trees were highly tapered and knotty. A significantly higher combination of lumber grade and yield was obtained from trees in medium-density stands (1000–1200 trees/ha) as compared to trees from a stand density class of 700 trees/ha.

Thinning has been found to have an effect upon the development of compression wood. Working with ponderosa pine, Barger and Ffolliott (1976) discovered that thinning or partial harvest cutting can substantially increase the incidence of compression wood in remaining trees. They found that compression wood was more likely to form in leaning stems following thinning than before this treatment. Because of this, they suggested that guidelines for thinning should reflect a critical appraisal of stem form irregularities and lean in residual trees.

The conditions under which thinning is employed can impact wood quality. Brazier (1977) reported that thinning in a very windy location, uneven thinning, or thinning on a steep slope can cause uneven crown development, a tendency for crooked boles, and even compression wood development.

Thinning can affect the percentage of latewood in subsequent growth rings, although the degree of effect depends upon the age and prior history of the stand as well as the degree of release (Larson 1973). Larson indicated, for instance, that thinning of a very dense and stagnated stand of distinct-ring softwoods can be expected to result in an immediate and substantial increase in growth accompanied by a marked decrease in the proportion of latewood and thus density (suggesting a strong growth rate–density relationship). On the other hand, several studies of the distinct-ring softwoods larch and pine indicated either no change or increase in the wood's specific gravity after thinning of older stands (Lowery and Schmidt 1967; Nicholls 1971; Choong and Fogg 1989; Moschler et al. 1989). In several of these studies, it was noted that reduced competition served to reduce late-season depletion of soil moisture, thereby prolonging the latewood portion of the growing season. Moschler et al. (1989) also observed that heavy thinning tended to decrease the density of earlywood and increase the density of latewood. The implication is that although overall wood density may change little, if at all, wood quality may be nonetheless negatively impacted by thinning due to a decrease in wood uniformity. The same effect has been noted in trees genetically selected for fast growth characteristics (see Genetic improvement and wood quality). An indication of the response of hardwoods to thinning is provided by a study involving ash, a ring-porous hardwood. In this case, specific gravity was found to increase only 1% as a result of thinning compared to that of wood taken from dense, unthinned stands (Paul 1963). The trees examined ranged from 50 to 65 years of age, with thinning done at age 30.

As outlined above, a strong argument can be made for delay of thinning until the juvenile period is completed if lumber or other solid products are to be produced from the resulting wood. This strategy avoids the development of an unduly large juvenile core and results in formation of uniformly dense mature wood. Delay of thinning also minimizes knot development in the lower bole. In contrast, in at least some species there appears to be a critical period for thinning beyond which release seems to have little stimulus on crown enlargement. Furthermore, by delaying thinning and restricting diameter growth at a young age, later growth will be formed over a smaller core. It might also be added that pulpwood quality is not necessarily decreased by rapid early growth. The forester must weigh these factors against wood quality considerations in establishing a thinning schedule.

FERTILIZATION AND IRRIGATION. Forestry practices discussed thus far—spacing trees at planting time, thinning, and control of understory vegetation—are designed to maximize potential for growth, given the limitations of a particular site. Another strategy that can be used to achieve increased rates of growth involves modification of the site through such cultural practices as fertilization, irrigation, and combinations of the two. The objective here is to improve site quality. Thinning, for example, reduces competition for available nutrients, water, and sunlight and concentrates growth on fewer stems. Application of fertilizer, on the other hand, stimulates growth by increasing the availability of nutrients generally, thereby enhancing crown development and the size of photosynthesizing surfaces. Both the size and number of leaves in the crown are affected. Because growth of all vegetation on the site is stimulated, it is usually necessary to employ thinning and/or understory control in conjunction with a fertilization program. Use of fertilizer may serve to improve the growth potential of an already productive site or bring a nonproductive or nutrient-deficient site into productivity. Similarly, irrigation can be used on moisture-deficient sites to improve growth potential. An example of the effects of fertilization and irrigation is presented in Table 12.2.

Effects of fertilization on wood quality. Foresters and users of wood have long been concerned about the effects of fertilizer and water application on wood quality. Larson (1973) lent some perspective to this concern, pointing out that these techniques simply improve the site. He went on to say that all too often, fast-grown trees from better sites were readily accepted whereas the quality of similar wood produced by improved growth conditions was questioned.

Changes in wood properties resulting from fertilization or irrigation-induced fast growth are similar to those occurring as a result of increased growth rate associated with other practices. Wood density, for example, is affected according to the general rules given earlier: fast growth may cause a density increase in ring-porous hardwoods and a variable effect upon density in other woods.

The impact of fertilization upon wood density of softwoods can be substantial. Posey (1965) found that fertilization of a loblolly pine (*Pinus taeda*) stand with 160 lb N, 80 lb P, 80 lb K/acre (179 kg N, 90 kg P, 90 kg K/ha) caused wood specific gravity to decrease from 0.48 to 0.39 and latewood to decrease from 47 to 36%. The almost 20% drop in specific gravity was sizable and represented a decrease of about 475 lb of wood fiber/cord of wood (90 kg/m³ solid wood). However, Posey's figures also showed that rate of growth increased almost 50%, with the result that the increased rate of growth more than compensated for the decrease in density. Similar results have been found in numerous studies dealing with fertilization of distinct-ring softwoods including Douglas-fir (Erickson and Lambert 1958; Siddiqui et al. 1972; Parker et al. 1976), slash pine (Williams and Hamilton 1961; Gooding and Smith 1972), red pine (Gray and Kyanka 1974), spruce (Klem 1964; Weetman 1971), and others. The average wood density loss noted in these studies was about 6–10%. Although such studies have clearly indicated an inverse relationship between fertilization and density in distinct-ring softwoods, the magnitude of density decrease resulting from large-scale application may have been overestimated. Losses of less than 2% have been realized in commercial fertilization of spruce in Sweden (Hagner 1967). Larson (1973) indicated that density decreases of this order may be more realistic, since fertilizer application rates on experimental plots are commonly higher than those recommended for commercial practices.

Zobel and Talbert (1984), after a review of findings by a number of investigators, found that heavy nitrogen fertilization, in particular, caused decreases in wood specific gravity. They also indicated that some species produced wood of very high specific gravity when grown on phosphorus-deficient sites; in this case, addition of phosphorus to the site resulted in a lowering of wood specific gravity to normal levels in subsequent growth. These observations are interesting since they raise the possibility of adjusting fertilizer formulations to achieve wood quality as well as growth rate objectives.

Klem (1974) commented on the effect of different fertilizer application rates, saying his work had shown that varying the types and amounts of fertilizers did not influence density of wood differently as long as treatments caused the same increase in growth rates. This statement implies that although density decreases associated with commercial use of fertilizer may be relatively small as compared to experimental sites, the cause is that the increase in growth rate relative to the potential is small as well.

The fertilization-density relationships discussed above are for trees that have passed the juvenile stage. For trees that are still in this stage, however, the impact of fertilization appears to be somewhat different. Fertilization still increases the growth rate, but with little or no impact upon wood density. This result was found in studies of slash pine (Smith et al. 1972) and Douglas-fir (Gladstone and Gray 1973). In the latter study, it was observed that although wood density did not decrease with increased juvenile growth, the normal upward trend in density during this period was not observed either. Thus the tendency for decreased wood density with increased growth rate appears to be offset in young trees by age-related increases in this property.

Along with a slight to significant decrease in density, fertilization has also been noted to cause greater within-ring uniformity of density, a phenomenon that Zobel and Talbert (1984) indicated was one of the most-desired benefits of fertilization. Gladstone and Gray (1973) found an increase in cell wall thickness of earlywood tracheids and a simultaneous thinning of latewood tracheid walls in fertilized red pine and Douglas-fir. The same phenomenon has been observed in other studies dealing with Douglas-fir (Megraw and Nearn 1972; Parker et al. 1976) and Japanese larch (Isebrands and Hunt 1975). Larson (1973) explained this by pointing out that there was a transition zone between the earlywood and latewood consisting of tracheids that were neither true earlywood nor true latewood but which most closely resembled earlywood cells. He indicated that the transition zone was broadened in response to accelerated growth, resulting in lower proportions of true latewood (and thus lower density) and a generally more uniform cell structure within the ring. Figure 12.4 illustrates this characteristic. Klem (1967) concluded that all wood properties become more uniform after fertilization.

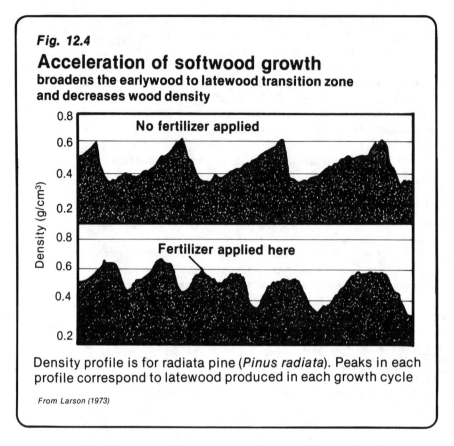

Fig. 12.4

Acceleration of softwood growth
broadens the earlywood to latewood transition zone
and decreases wood density

Density profile is for radiata pine (*Pinus radiata*). Peaks in each
profile correspond to latewood produced in each growth cycle

From Larson (1973)

Examination of Figure 12.4 shows that response to fertilization is greatest immediately following treatment. As time passes, within-ring density variation gradually returns to the pretreatment pattern. It appears that the effect of fertilization upon wood quality generally lasts only 3–5 years.

There is some disagreement as to whether fertilization of softwoods has an effect upon tracheid length; some investigators have found a 5–10% decrease (Posey 1965; Gray and Kyanka 1974), while others have noted a slight increase in the average length after fertilization (Manwiller 1972). Slight decreases in the *holocellulose fraction* (consisting of cellulose and the hemicelluloses) and small increases in extractive content of rapidly grown wood have also been reported.

The impact of fertilization on wood quality in hardwoods has been less widely investigated than effects upon softwoods. However, it appears that density is little affected by rapid growth induced by fertilizer. Studies with a number of diffuse-porous woods have shown no significant density effects from fertilizer treatments. The lack of any relationship has been noted in sycamore (Saucier and Ike 1972) and yellow poplar (Thor and Core 1977). Slight decreases in wood density have been observed in fast-grown quaking aspen (Kennedy 1968; Einspahr et al. 1972). The density of ring-porous woods tends to be slightly increased by fertilization, as it is by thinning. Slightly increased specific gravity in trees from fertilized stands has been shown in tests involving red oak (Szopa et al. 1977) and red oak and white ash (Mitchell 1972).

Investigations of fertilization effects upon hardwood quality have dealt with the impact upon vessel-to-fiber ratio, fiber length, and intrinsic values such as machining properties. A review of a number of such studies showed no change in vessel-to-fiber ratios and only a slight increase in the proportion of volume occupied by vessels, due to a tendency for rapid growth to slightly increase vessel diameter. Fiber lengths have been found to either remain unchanged or increase slightly.

As with thinning, fertilizer applied to young stands results in a large juvenile core because of increased ring width and extension of the juvenile period. Additionally, such treatment often increases the size of individual branches and delays natural pruning. Timing is therefore important when fertilizing, just as it is in thinning. Carmean and Boyce (1974) pointed out that although branch size was increased on better sites, the internode distance between branch whorls also increased. Thus if fertilization treatments are combined with a pruning program, log quality can be markedly improved.

Whereas the preceding discussion refers to experiments with fertilization, most of the relationships also apply to wood formed during irrigation or under the combined effects of fertilization and irrigation; i.e., irrigation results in moderate changes in cell dimensions, often results in increased uniformity of density, and can cause extension of the juvenile period. An exception is the effect of irrigation upon density levels. A number of studies have shown increases in the latewood percentage and thus density as a result of irrigation (Paul and Marts 1931; Chalk 1951; Posey 1965; Howe 1968). This increase is thought to be from reduced competition for soil moisture during late-season growth.

Effects of fast growth on product properties. A major consideration in the use of intensively grown wood is how it affects properties of products. In solid wood products, strength is important. Rapidly grown wood has been evaluated for this quality by several investigators. They found that although some aspects are diminished by accelerated growth, others are improved. For instance, in studies of wood from fertilized versus unfertilized red pine, Gray and Kyanka (1974) noted significant decreases in work to proportional limit and work to maximum load with accelerated growth (see Table 10.1, Fig. 10.3). They also found significant increases in modulus of elasticity (MOE) and only minimal changes in modulus of rupture (MOR) and *fiber stress at proportional limit* (fspl) in wood from fertilized trees. (The significance of these properties is discussed in Chapter 10.) These trees were 16 years of age at the time of treatment and 36 years at the time of harvest.

Other experimentation (Hsu and Walters 1975) revealed complex relationships between silvicultural treatments and strength in loblolly pine treated at age 18. For example, heavy fertilization of a wet plot yielded wood having a fspl of 3790 psi (26,000 kilopascals) as compared to 7120 psi (49,000 kPa) for wood from heavily fertilized but drier sites. The MOE and MOR were also affected. Strength values of wood from the fertilized but dry sites tended to slightly exceed accepted average strength values for the species involved. In contrast, strength figures determined for wood from wet fertilized sites were only about one-half the accepted values. However, no effect of treatment upon work to maximum load or work to proportional limit was found. This study further indicated that fertilization reduced the fspl, MOE, and MOR, whereas irrigation reduced only the MOE. Fertilization and irrigation together were noted to affect strength values more than either treatment individually.

Murphey and Brisbin (1970) also found that a combined fertilizer-irrigation treatment had a marked effect upon strength of red pine. The equivalent of 5 cm/wk (2 in./wk) of sewage plant effluent was found to adversely affect almost all mechanical properties, whereas a 2.5 cm/wk (1 in./wk) application showed no such effects. They concluded that adverse effects resulted from an abnormally high soil moisture content and recommended that excess irrigation be avoided with species sensitive to wet sites. Thus, strength of mature softwoods can be affected greatly by silvicultural treatment. The results are not always bad, however, and appear controllable with the proper treatment mix.

Because current grading rules for some lumber products limit maximum growth rates by specifying a minimum number of growth rings per inch, Koch (1972) urged caution in development of fast-growth southern pine (less than 3 rings/in., or 1.2 rings/cm). He suggested that mechanical properties as well as paint retention and gluing potential would be adversely affected by accelerated growth. He indicated that strength would be inadequate in wood used for small poles or squared timbers if harvesting was done too early, i.e., if rotation age was too short. Koch calculated that strength of large timbers would probably be adequate, although reduced, but said that such material would be too low in strength for use in the outer layers of large laminated beams. Senft (1985) points out that machine stress rating of lumber (see Chapter 13) efficiently culls that lumber with low density and low strength.

Probable difficulties in manufacturing plywood were also cited by Koch. This conjecture was later confirmed by MacPeak et al. (1987), who found unusually low yields of upper veneer grades and full-sheet veneers, and marginal stiffness in finished plywood in a mill trial involving logs from small-diameter, rapidly grown trees. Koch's concerns regarding lumber were substantiated by Fight et al. (1986). These investigators compared the lumber yield by grade from rapidly versus more slowly grown loblolly pine of the same diameter, 20 and 50 years old respectively. Results showed the proportion of lumber from rapidly grown logs that met dimension grade requirements for No. 2 and No. 3 common grades to be only one-fifth to one-half of that obtained from more slowly grown material. Most of these objections appear to be based upon occurrence of a large juvenile core in fast-grown material. In addition to the problems mentioned by Koch, the presence of juvenile wood is the cause of serious degrading losses in lumber because of warping upon drying. Longitudinal shrinking of juvenile zones causes a particularly high proportion of rejects when producing small lumber sizes.

Studies of machining properties of rapidly grown hardwoods have generally shown no adverse effects nor have significant detrimental effects upon strength been noted. In both hardwoods and softwoods, problems related to an expanded juvenile core and increased knottiness in wood grown quickly when young appear to be a serious concern when dealing with solid wood products. Other growth effects upon properties of solid products appear relatively minor. Regardless of the properties under consideration, it is generally acknowledged that growth rate–related changes in wood quality are less in hardwoods than in softwoods (Bendtsen 1978).

Pulp yields from wood produced under accelerated growth conditions are reported to be similar to yields from wood of more slowly grown trees. Effects of accelerated growth upon pulp quality have generally been found to be desirable. A study by Gladstone et al. (1970) dealing with loblolly pine indicated a 2–7% higher pulp yield from latewood as compared to earlywood. This finding led to suggestions that growth acceleration resulting in decreased quantities of latewood would cause similar reductions in yield. Subsequent pulping studies of fast-grown slash pine and Douglas-fir have shown pulp yields to range from 1% lower to 2% higher than slower-grown controls (Gooding and Smith 1972; Siddiqui et al. 1972; Parker et al. 1976). On the other hand, many pulp properties improved. Gooding and Smith (1972) found, for example, that paper produced from fertilized wood had higher density, burst factor, and tensile strength than that from unfertilized wood. This agreed with the earlier findings of Posey (1965). Posey's report of lower tear strength in paper from fertilized wood was confirmed by Gooding and Smith only for material taken from the basal portion of trees. Siddiqui and his co-workers reported no difference in paper properties between fertilized and unfertilized material except for tensile strength; again, the advantage in tensile strength favored the fertilized material. Silvicultural treatments involved trees that had passed the juvenile stage in all these studies. As indicated in Chapter 6, even juvenile material yields pulp with certain properties that are superior to those associated with mature wood. Juvenile pulps tend to exhibit higher burst and folding strength but lower tear strength and opacity than pulps made from adult wood. Even development of a large juvenile core, therefore, is not necessarily undesirable in material that is to be pulped. Experimentation with material from short-rotation, intensively cultured plantations has, in fact, shown that poplar trees harvested after only 3–5 years yielded satisfactory kraft pulp for use by itself or in a blend with softwood pulp from mature stands (Marton et al. 1968; Zarges et al. 1980; Phelps et al. 1985). These kinds of findings have led many people, including Snook et al. (1986), to suggest that pulpwood trees be grown as fast as economically feasible.

In conclusion, the impact of fertilization and irrigation upon wood product properties depends upon the products involved and the timing of silvicultural treatments. The most-serious problem associated with growth acceleration is an enlarged juvenile core. This problem is particularly important when solid wood products are involved. It is sufficiently serious that delays in growth-stimulating treatments until after completion of the juvenile period may be warranted. A practice of growing trees over a relatively long rotation so that the proportion of juvenile period in the stem is minimized may also be a good idea if solid products are the objective. Where trees are being grown for pulpwood, the importance of minimizing juvenile wood depends upon specific properties desired in the paper. Advantages of increases in the rate of wood production in many cases offsets disadvantages related to modified pulp properties.

PRUNING. Pruning is the practice of trimming branches from chosen portions of standing trees to reduce the occurrence of knots in subsequently produced wood. When a branch is removed from the bole of a tree, the sheath of new growth will eventually cover the stub, producing knot-free wood thereafter. Such wood has markedly higher value than knotty wood for solid wood products and veneer because of increased strength and improved appearance. Considerable improvements in lumber grade and veneer grade yields can result from pruning (Cahill 1991). It is employed only on a limited basis, however, because of the high cost.

It is perhaps obvious that branches should be trimmed as close to the bole as possible. The closer the cut, the sooner new growth will overtake and cover the stub. Calvert and Brace (1969) determined, for example, that pruning branches to produce 0.25 in. (0.6 cm) rather than 0.75 in. (1.9 cm) stubs would cut healing time in half (from 10 to 5 years). They also pointed out that 0.5 in. (1.3 cm) branch stubs were not uncommon where pruning was done more than 12 ft (3.7 m) from the ground.

Ideally, the knotty core of a tree should be as small as possible. As noted by Cahill et al. (1988), the size of the knotty core can be minimized by pruning of trees while they are young, a practice that also allows maximum growth of clear wood and produces small limb scars that heal quickly. However, several investigators have determined that pruning of larger trees yields the most-immediate payoff. Calvert and Brace (1969) recommended pruning only second-growth pine trees 8–10 in. in diameter and larger, pointing out that even slower-growing large trees tended to produce a greater volume of wood than faster-growing smaller ones. Brown (1965) had earlier come to a similar conclusion. Cahill et al. did not specify a minimum diameter for pruning treatment but did state that it was important from an economic viewpoint to concentrate treatments on trees that could be recognized as likely survivors until the time of harvest. This criteria in itself suggested a lower diameter limit for pruning that was above pulpwood size. Recommendations that pruning be restricted to larger trees must be tempered with the realization that many years pass before healing of pruning wounds occurs.

An example of the time required for healing was provided by Dimock and Haskell (1962), who found that 17 years of growth were required to produce clear, veneer-quality wood following pruning of 38-year-old Douglas-fir. Dobie and Wright (1978) evaluated quality of logs harvested 20 years after a thinning and pruning treatment. They found that severe grain distortions and brittle grain around pruning stubs caused lumber and veneer quality to be lower than untreated controls. Results such as this led Horton (1966) to urge waiting at least 40 years before harvesting pruned stems in order to balance wood quality benefits and harvesting costs.

The effectiveness of pruning depends on branch diameter, the method of cutting off branches, and the average length of branch stubs. Anderson (1951) found that pruning of branches with a saw led to considerably faster healing than when pruning was done with an axe. Several investigators reported better results from pruning small branches than from larger ones; healing was faster and pruning scars were less extensive when small branches were involved.

Because branch occurrence and the difficulty in achieving high-quality pruning increase with distance from the ground, it was suggested that pruning be concentrated on the lower 16 ft (4.9 m) (or butt log) of hardwood trees (Boyce 1965). After a study of conifers in New Zealand, Brown (1965) indicated that pruning of the butt log was clearly economical, that pruning of the third log clearly was not, and that the advisability of pruning the second log was marginal.

Pruning can affect wood quality indirectly. For example, when lower dead branches are cut, there is no effect upon tree growth. If pruning is flush with the bark, normal growth will quickly begin covering the stub. However, when green branches are removed in the pruning process, particularly if pruning is heavy, growth can be affected significantly. Larson (1969) indicated that heavy green pruning of softwoods can cause a decrease in the rate of height growth and wood production because of loss of photosynthesizing surface. This effect is serious, since rapid radial growth is needed to make the treatment economical. After heavy pruning, the size of remaining branches may markedly increase, and the earlywood to latewood transition may become more abrupt. Beneficial effects of heavy green pruning are an increase in the length of the clear bole and a decrease in bole taper (recall the cause of taper in stems). There is some question as to what constitutes heavy pruning. Mar: Møller (1960) stated that lower branches of conifers contributed little to growth and thus would not affect stem form or growth rate if removed. He indicated, however, that removal of one-fourth of the crown could diminish diameter growth. Others have indicated that up to one-third of the crown of coniferous species could be removed without affecting growth (Staebler 1963; Barrett 1968). Commenting on hardwoods, Kellison et al. (1982) indicated that the best way to prevent tree degrade was to thin and to prune lightly and frequently. They also suggested that only dead or declining branches be removed in pruning to prevent a reduction in tree growth. Whether frequent pruning is a sound strategy from an economic viewpoint is open to question.

It is likely that many of the effects of heavy green pruning noted in softwoods occur in hardwoods as well. These effects notwithstanding, a primary concern associated with pruning of hardwoods is the effect upon development of epicormic branching, a problem not encountered in softwoods. Epicormic branches are formed by reactivation of previously formed but inactive buds; thinnings or partial cuttings may cause them to reactivate. It has been found, however, that pruning of hardwoods usually results in a permanent reduction in the number of branches. It is apparently possible to avoid activation of epicormic buds by concentrating pruning on trees with fewer branches (McQuilkin 1975) and by scraping the area of the trunk from which branches were cut (Boyce 1965).

Pruning can thus significantly improve the quality of sawlogs and veneer logs. For maximum effectiveness, pruning should be concentrated on lower portions of larger trees that will not be harvested for some 30–40 years following treatment. Heavy pruning that removes a substantial portion of the green crown should be avoided.

Genetic improvement and wood quality ■

The field of genetics offers perhaps the greatest potential for improvement of wood yield and quality in the future. Over the past several decades, efforts in this area have concentrated on identifying trees in the natural forest that exhibit superior growth or form. Seeds have been collected from these trees and planted in nurseries to raise new generations of trees having many of the same characteristics. Vegetative propagation has also been employed in reproducing clones of certain species. A relatively recent development is the perfection of the technique of tissue culture, whereby a tiny portion of parent tissue is placed in a test tube with the proper chemical medium and grown to a small plantlet, which is then transferred to a nursery. Even more recent is the application of biotechnologies, including recombinant DNA technology, to the tree improvement field. Increasingly common in the literature are references to techniques such as gene transfer, protoplast fusion, and microinjection. These techniques are based upon the ability to identify *DNA fragments,* a single gene or group of genes that are responsible for certain tree or wood characteristics. Genes so identified and subsequently isolated are then multiplied and transferred to a host cell or cells, with cells thereby regenerated to form a plant. Such techniques offer opportunities for very rapid gains in tree improvement by bypassing the long developmental periods of woody plants. Spectacular gains are possible in the future.

As a follow-up to superior tree identification and production of seedlings from such trees, considerable effort has been invested in crossbreeding of selected tree progeny to develop trees that combine the best features of several superior trees. Wood quality characteristics are among the features upon which selection is based. Genetic selection of both hardwoods and softwoods has resulted in development of fast-growing trees that produce wood of normal to higher-than-normal density. It has been shown to be possible to breed for long fibers, high proportions of fibers relative to vessels, uniform density, amount of heartwood extractives, low proportions of lignin and juvenile wood, and minimal branch development. Even the tendency to produce spiral grain and cell wall microfibril angles has been shown to be heritable. In fact, recent research has determined that the large microfibril angle in juvenile wood of softwoods, which is a major factor in reduced stiffness and high longitudinal shrinkage of such wood, is also genetically controlled (Cave and Walker 1994; Ying et al. 1994). Cave and Walker observed, "Opportunities to improve wood quality through selection of juvenile material with a low microfibril angle are great and promise greater benefits than selection based on density." It has also been demonstrated that genetic selection can be used to reduce bark thickness, the number of sclereids, and other undesirable elements in the bark.

One of the terms used to express the potential for genetics in tree and wood improvement is *heritability.* As explained by McElwee (1963), heritability, which is expressed as a numerical value between 0 and 1, indicates the degree to which variation is determined by the parents. Thus a heritability of 1 for a given characteristic means that variability of that characteristic is determined entirely by parental origin. A heritability of 0 indicates variability in a characteristic to be totally governed by the environment, with no parental influence. To provide an indication of the potential for genetic selection in improvement of tree and wood properties, heritability values established experimentally for various tree and wood characteristics of pine species are presented in Table 12.4. Note that two factors—wood specific gravity and tracheid length—have very high heritability values. Latewood cell wall thickness and percentage of latewood, both of which are closely related to wood specific gravity, also rank high in heritability.

Although Table 12.4 indicates the relationship of various properties to parental influence, it does not give an idea of the magnitude of change possible through genetic selection. Even characteristics low in heritability can represent very significant opportunities for improvement if the variability associated with that characteristic is high. As an example, consider volumetric growth rate,

Table 12.4.   Heritability of various tree and wood properties in pine

Property	Heritability	Remarks
Wood specific gravity	0.5–0.7	Reported by McElwee (1963) as an average of results obtained in a number of studies of pine. Individual findings ranged from 0.2 to 1.0.
	0.5–0.8	Values for southern pine as reported by Barker (1972).
	0.52	*Pinus taeda*—Stonecypher et al. (1973).
	0.5–0.7	*Pinus radiata*—Dadswell et al. (1961).
Fiber length	0.73–0.83	*Pinus radiata*—Dadswell et al. (1961).
Latewood percentage	0.47–0.54	*Pinus radiata*—Dadswell et al. (1961).
	0.80	*Pinus taeda*—Goggans (1962).
Latewood cell wall thickness	0.84	*Pinus taeda*—Goggans (1962).
Earlywood cell wall thickness	0.13	*Pinus taeda*—Goggans (1962).
Growth rate (expressed as volumetric gain)	0.15	*Pinus taeda*—Stonecypher et al. (1973).
Stem straightness	0.14	Stonecypher et al. (1973).
Oleoresin yield	0.55	Squillace and Dorman (1961).
Resistance to disease (fusiform rust)	0.22	Stonecypher et al. (1973).

which has a heritability of only 0.15. Despite this low value, Zobel (1977) indicated that volumetric yield gains of at least 10–20% could be expected in young plantations of southern pine made up of trees from first-generation seed orchards. He further estimated that volume yield gains of 35–45% (over nonimproved stock) could be reasonably expected in plantations established from second-generation orchards. Although these figures were impressive, Zobel pointed out that such estimates were conservative and referred to reports of 30–50% or greater gains in volume yield in established first-generation plantations.

Wood specific gravity is an important determinant of wood quality and dry weight yields per volume of woody material. Because of this, even large increases in volumetric growth might be viewed as undesirable if the result were a significant decrease in specific gravity. Thus breeding programs are generally aimed at controlling specific gravity as well as improving growth rate. Using an example provided by Zobel (1977), an assessment of 8-year-old southern pine trees in North Carolina revealed an average specific gravity for trees in the plantation of 0.425 compared to 0.410 for commercial controls. This meant that the plantation trees had produced about 90 more lb dry wt/l00 ft³ (or about 15 kg dry wt/m³) wood than the controls. Translated to an area basis for a 25-year rotation, the difference amounts to about 4300–4500 lb additional dry wood/acre (or 4820–5040 kg/ha), even assuming equal volumetric growth rates of plantation and control trees. This estimated large increase was described by Zobel as conservative, since genetic differences in specific gravity among tree families generally increase with age.

A recent study of genetic selection, growth rate, and wood density in Douglas-fir (Abdel-Gadir et al. 1993) found that fast growth is genetically associated with low density in earlywood but with high density in latewood. This finding suggests that although selection to increase growth rate may have little or no effect upon wood density, wood quality may suffer because of the effect on wood uniformity. Further study of this issue is needed.

Estimates of the first-generation gains possible in other characteristics are presented in Table 12.5. While these figures refer only to pine, estimates of similar magnitude have been obtained for other softwoods and a variety of hardwood species as well.

Table 12.5.   Gains from mass selection of loblolly pine based on 280 open-pollinated families from random parents

Characteristic	Gain, as percent of mean
Height	14
Basal area	18
Straightness	7
Crown	4
Volume	25
Specific gravity	10
Dry weight	26
Fusiform rust resistance	18–42

Source: Stonecypher et al. (1973).

In summary, by identifying trees in the natural forest with the most-desirable characteristics and then selectively breeding their offspring to combine into one tree the best features of the superior parents, fast-growing new trees are being developed that will be more suitable for product conversion than their ancestors. Based upon initial experience, it appears that benefits from this kind of activity will be enormous.

Intensive culture ■

A relatively new concept in forestry is *intensive culture*. The idea here is that forestland that has the highest productive capacity can be intensively farmed to achieve high yields, thereby easing pressure on less-productive lands. In intensive culture plantations, genetically superior trees are ideally spaced and then fertilized and irrigated over optimally selected rotations. Under these conditions, growth rates are quite high. The main application of such plantations appears to be for production of wood for reconstituted products such as paper and flakeboard or for energy generation. In these plantations, short rotations will be selected to maximize the production of biomass per unit time. As an example of what is possible, yields as high as 6.0 dry tons/acre/yr (13.6 m^3/ha/yr) have been reported for intensively cultured hybrid aspen stands in northern Wisconsin. This compares to an average yield in natural aspen stands within the same region of just 0.31 dry tons/acre/yr (0.70 m^3/ha/yr) and as much as 1.0 ton/acre/yr on the best sites. Attainment of even higher rates of growth is thought possible with development of improved genotypes and cultural practices.

Tree plantation growth in regions of the world where rainfall is evenly distributed and temperatures moderate can be spectacular (Fig. 12.5). The Aracruz project on the northeast coast of Brazil has achieved growth rates as high as 11.5 dry tons/acre/yr (25.8 m^3/ha/yr) using various species of eucalyptus.

(Photos by Jim Bowyer)

Fig. 12.5

Spectacular growth in Aracruz plantation in northeastern Brazil

These eucalypts, photgraphed at the Aracruz plantation in northeastern Brazil, are 2 months old (*top*), 6 months old (*middle*), and 3
years old (*bottom*). The intensive management of these plantation
trees produces this dramatic growth.

REVIEW

A. Terms to define or explain:
   1. Silviculture
   2. Rotation age
   3. Epicormic branching
   4. Biotechnology
   5. Intensive culture
   6. Heritability

B. Questions and concepts to explain:
   1. What is meant by wood quality?
   2. What is the general relationship between growth rate and wood density? In soft-woods? In diffuse-porous hardwoods? Why have many investigators incorrectly associated rapid growth with decreased wood density?
   3. How is wood quality affected by spacing? Thinning? Fertilizing and irrigating? Pruning of dead branches? Pruning of green branches?
   4. How might silvicultural practices differ when raising pulpwood versus raising sawlogs?
   5. Why is timing of silvicultural treatments important?
   6. What characteristics of wood can be modified by genetic selection?

REFERENCES

Abdel-Gadir, A.Y.; Krahmer, R.L.; and McKimmy, M.D. 1993. Relationships between in-tra-ring variables in mature Douglas-fir trees from provenance plantations. Wood Fiber Science 25(2):182–191.

Aldridge, F., and Hudson, R.H. 1958. Growing quality softwoods. I. Q.J. For. 52(2):107–114.

———. 1959. Growing quality softwoods. II. Q.J. For. 53(3):210–219.

Allchin, P.C. 1960. The I.G.T. vessel picking test. Appita 13(6):186–190.

Anderson, E.A. 1951. Healing time for pruned Douglas-fir. Timberman 52(12):74–80.

Barger, R.L., and Ffolliott, P.F. 1976. Factors affecting occurrence of compression wood in individual ponderosa pine trees. Wood Sci. 8(3):201–208.

Barker, J. 1972. Location effects on heritability estimates and gain predictions for ten-year-old loblolly pine. Ph.D. diss., N.C. State Univ., School of Forest Resources.

Barrett, J.W. 1968. Pruning of ponderosa pine—Effect on growth. USDA For. Serv. Pac. Northwest For. Range Exp. Stn. Res. Pap. PNW-68.

Barrett, J.D., and Kellogg, R.M. 1984. Strength and stiffness of second-growth Douglas-fir dimension lumber. Forintek Canada Corp. Rep. FR22.

Bendtsen, B.A. 1978. Properties of wood from improved and intensively managed trees. For. Prod. J. 28(10):69–72.

Bissett, I.J.W.; Dadswell, H.E.; and Wardrop, A.B. 1951. Factors influencing tracheid length in conifer stems. Aust. For. 15(1):17–30.

Boyce, S.G. 1965. Improved hardwoods for increased utilization. Proc. 8th Conf. Forest Tree Improvement, pp. 1–6.

Boyd, J.D. 1968. Effect of plantation conditions on wood properties and utilization. FAO World Symp. Manmade Forests and Their Industrial Importance, pp. 789–822.

Brazier, J.D. 1977. The effect of forest practices on quality of the harvested crop. Forestry 50(1):49–66.

Briggs, D.G., and Smith, W.R. 1986. Effects of silvicultural practices on wood properties of conifers—A review. In Douglas-fir: Stand management for the future, C. Oliver, D. Hanley, and J. Johnson, eds. Seattle: Univ. of Washington Press.

Brinkman, K.A. 1955. Epicormic branching on oaks in sprout stands. U.S. For. Serv. Cent. States For. Exp. Stn. Tech. Pap. 146.

Brown, G.S. 1965. The improvement of the quality of the timber from coniferous planta-tions in New Zealand by silvicultural means. Presented at IUFRO Sect. 41 (For. Prod.) Meet., Melbourne, Aust.

Bryant, P.A.V. 1984. The impact of fast growth in plantations on wood quality and utilization. Proc. Symp. Site Quality and Productivity of Fast Growing Plantations. IUFRO, Pretoria, S. Africa.

Cahill, J.M. 1991. Pruning young-growth ponderosa pine: Product recovery and economic evaluation. For. Prod. J. 41(11/12):67–73.

Cahill, J.M.; Snellgrove, T.A.; and Fahey, T.D. 1988. Lumber and veneer recovery from pruned Douglas-fir. For. Prod. J. 38(9):27–32.

Calvert, W.W., and Brace, L.G. 1969. Pruning and sawing eastern white pine. Can. For. Serv. Dep. Fish. For. Publ. 1262.

Carmean, W.H., and Boyce, S.G. 1974. Hardwood log quality in relation to site quality. USDA For. Serv. North Cent. For. Exp. Stn. Res. Pap. NC-103.

Cave, I.D., and Walker, J.C.F. 1994. Stiffness of wood in fast-grown plantation softwoods: The influence of microfibril angle. For. Prod. J. 44(5):43–48.

Chalk, L. 1951. Water and growth of Douglas-fir. Q. J. For. 45(3):237–242.

Choong, E.T., and Fogg, P.J. 1989. Effect of cultural treatment and wood-type on some physical properties of longleaf and slash pine wood. Wood Fiber Science 21(2):193–206.

Ciesler, A., and Janka, G. 1902. Studien uber die Qualitat Rasch erwachsenen Fichten-holzes. Centralbl. Gesamt. Forstwes. 28:337–416.

Clark, A., and Saucier, J.R. 1989. Influence of initial planting density, geographic location, and species on juvenile wood formation in southern pine. For. Prod. J. (7/8):42–48.

Clark, A., Saucier, J.R.; Baldwin, V.C.; and Bower, D.R. 1994. Effect of initial spacing and thinning on lumber grade, yield, and strength of loblolly pine. For. Prod. J. 44(11/12):14–20.

Crist, J.B., and Dawson, D.H. 1975. Anatomy and dry weight yields of two *Populus* clones grown under intensive culture. USDA For. Serv. North Cent. For. Exp. Stn. Res. Pap. NC-113.

Crist, J.B.; Dawson, D.H.; and Nelson, J.A. 1977. Wood and bark quality of juvenile jack pine and eastern larch grown under intensive culture. Proc. Tech. Assoc. Pulp and Paper Ind. For. Biol. Wood Chem. Conf., pp. 211–216.

Dadswell, H.E. 1958. Wood structure variations occurring during tree growth and their influence on properties. J. Inst. Wood Sci 1:11–32.

Dadswell, H.E.; Fielding, J.M.; Nicholls, J.W.P.; and Brown, A.G. 1961. Tree to tree variations and the gross heritability of wood characteristics of *Pinus radiata*. TAPPI 44(3):174–179.

Dimock, E.J., and Haskell, H.H. 1962. Veneer grade yield from pruned Douglas-fir. USDA For. Serv. Pac. Northwest. For. Range Exp. Stn. Res. Pap. PNW-48.

Dobie, J., and Wright, D.W. 1978. Economics of thinning and pruning—A case study. For. Chron. 54(1):34–38.

Einspahr, D.W.; Benson, M.K.; and Harder, M.L. 1972. Influence of irrigation and fertilization of growth and wood properties of quaking aspen. Proc. Symp. Effect of growth acceleration on the properties of wood. USDA For. Serv. For. Prod. Lab.

Erickson, H.D., and Arima, T. 1974. Douglas-fir wood quality studies. II. Effects of age and stimulated growth on fibril angle and chemical constituents. Wood Sci. Technol. 8:255–265.

Erickson, H.D., and Lambert, G.M.G. 1958. Effects of fertilization and thinning on chemical composition, growth, and specific gravity of young Douglas-fir. For. Sci. 4(4):307–315.

Fight, R.; Snellgrove, T.; Curtis, R.; and Debell, D. 1986. Bringing timber quality considerations into forest management decisions: A conceptual approach. In Douglas-fir: Stand Management for the Future, C. Oliver, D. Hanley, and J. Johnson, eds. Seattle: Univ. of Washington Press.

Fukazawa, K. 1984. Juvenile wood of hardwoods judged by density variation. IAWA Bull. 5(1):65–73.

Ganchev, P. 1971. Studies on wood anatomical structure in several Euro-American poplar species. Gorskostop Nauk. 8(4):15–22.

Gladstone, W.T., and Gray, R.L. 1973. Effects of forest fertilization on wood quality. For.

Fertil. Symp. Proc. USDA For. Serv. Gen. Tech. Rep. NE-3.

Gladstone, W.T.; Barefoot, A.C., Jr.; and Zobel, B.J. 1970. Kraft pulping of earlywood and latewood from loblolly pine. For. Prod. J. 20(2):17–24.

Goggans, J. F. 1961. The interplay of environment and heredity as factors controlling wood properties in conifers with special emphasis on their effects on specific gravity. N.C. State Coll. Sch. For. Tech. Rep. 11.

_____. 1962. The correlation, variation, and inheritance of wood properties in loblolly pine (*Pinus taeda* L.). N.C. State Coll. Sch. For. Tech. Rep. 14.

Gooding, J.W., and Smith, W.H. 1972. Effects of fertilization on stem, wood properties, and pulping characteristics of slash pine (*Pinus elliottii* var. eliottii Engelm.). Proc. Symp. Effect of Growth Acceleration on the Properties of Wood. USDA For. Serv. For. Prod. Lab.

Gray, R.L., and Kyanka, G.H. 1974. Potassium fertilization effects on the static bending properties of red pine wood. For. Prod. J. 24(9):92–96.

Hagner, S.O. 1967. Fertilization as a production factor in industrial forestry. MacMillan Lect. Ser., Univ. B.C. For. Lect. 37.

Harris, J.M.; James, R.N.; and Collins, M.J. 1975. Case for improving wood density in *radiata* pine. N.Z. J. For. Sci. 5(3):347–354.

Hillis, W.E., and Ditchburne, N. 1974. The prediction of heartwood diameter in *radiata* pine trees. Can. J. For. Res. 4:524–529.

Horton, K.W. 1966. Profitability of pruning white pine. For. Chron. 42(3):294–305.

Howe, J.P. 1968. Influence of irrigation on ponderosa pine. For. Prod. J. 18(1):84–92.

Hsu, J.K., and Walters, C.S. 1975. Effect of irrigation and fertilization on selected physical and mechanical properties of loblolly pine (*Pinus taeda*). Wood Fiber 7(3): 192–206.

Isebrands, J., and Bensend, D. 1972. Incidence and structure of gelatinous fibers within rapid-growing eastern cottonwood. Wood Fiber 4(2):61–71.

Isebrands, J., and Hunt, C.M. 1975. Growth and wood properties of rapid-grown Japanese larch. Wood Fiber 7(2):119–128.

Isebrands, J., and Parham, R.A. 1974. Tension wood anatomy of short rotation *Populus* spp. before and after kraft pulping. Wood Sci. 6(3):256–265.

Jane, F.W.; Wilson, K.; and White, D.J.B. 1970. The structure of wood. London: Adam & Charles Black.

Jones, E.P. 1977. Precommercial thinning of naturally seeded slash pine increases volume and monetary returns. USDA For. Serv. Southeast. For. Exp. Stn. Res. Pap. SE-164.

Kellison, R.C.; Lea, R.; and Frederick, D.J. 1982. Effect of silvicultural practices on wood quality of southern hardwoods. Proc. TAPPI R&D Conf., pp. 99–103.

Kellogg, R.M., and Kennedy, R.W. 1986. Practical implications of wood quality relative to end use. In Douglas-fir: Stand management for the future, C. Oliver, D. Manley, and J. Johnson, eds. Seattle: Univ. of Washington Press.

Kennedy, R.W. 1957. Fiber length of fast- and slow-grown black cottonwood. For. Chron. 33(1):46–50.

_____. 1968. Anatomy and fundamental wood properties of poplar. Growth and utilization of poplars in Canada. Can. Dep. For. Rural Dev. Dep. Publ. 1205, pp. 149–168.

Kennedy, R.W., and Smith, J.H.G. 1959. The effects of some genetic and environmental factors on wood quality in poplar. Pulp Pap. Mag. Can. 60:T35–T36.

Klem, G.S. 1964. The effect of fertilization on three quality properties of Norway spruce. For. Comm. Lond. 235. Transl. (1965) by C. Clayre from Nor. Skogbr. 10(18):491–494.

_____. 1967. Some aspects of the qualities of wood from fertilized forests. Proc. 4th Tech. Assoc. Pulp Paper Ind. For. Biol. Conf., Pointe Claire, Quebec, pp.120–130.

_____. 1968. Quality of wood from fertilized forests. TAPPI 51(11):99A–103A.

_____. 1974. Properties of wood from fertilized pine and spruce forests. Nor. Treteknisk Inst. 51.

Koch, P. 1972. The three-rings-per-inch dense southern pine—Should it be developed?

Proc. Symp. Effect of Growth Acceleration on the Properties of Wood. USDA For. Serv. For. Prod. Lab.

Krajicek, J.E. 1959. Epicormic branching in even-aged, undisturbed white oak stands. J. For. 57:372–373.

Krinard, R.M., and Johnson, R.L. 1975. Ten-year results in a cottonwood plantation spacing study. USDA For. Serv. South. For. Exp. Stn. Res. Pap. SO-106.

Kucera, B. 1994. A hypothesis relating current annual height increment to juvenile wood formation in Norway spruce. Wood Fiber Sci. 26(1):152–167.

Larson, P.R. 1967. Silvicultural control of the characteristics of wood used for furnish. Proc. 4th TAPPI For. Biol. Conf., Pointe Claire, Quebec.

_____. 1969. Wood formation and the concept of wood quality. Yale Univ. Sch. For. Bull. 74.

_____. 1973. Evaluating the quality of fast grown coniferous wood. Proc. 63rd West. For. Conf., pp. 146–152.

_____. 1972 Evaluating the quality of fast-grown coniferous wood. Proceeding 1972 Ann. Meet. West. Stand. Mgmt. Comm., Seattle, WA, 7pp.

Lowery, D.P., and Schmidt, W.C. 1967. Effect of thinning on the specific gravity of western larch crop trees. USDA For. Serv. Int. For. Range Exp. Stn. Res. Note INT-70.

McElwee, R.L. 1963. Genetics in wood quality improvement. Proc. 7th Conf. Forest Tree Improvement, pp. 21–24.

McKimmy, M.D. 1986. The Genetic Potential for Improving Wood. In Douglas-fir: Stand management for the future, C. Oliver, D. Manley, and J. Johnson, eds. Seattle: Univ. of Washington Press.

McKimmy, M.D., and Campbell, R.K. 1982. Genetic variation in the wood density and ring width trend in coastal Douglas-fir Silv. Genet. 31(2–3):43–51.

MacPeak, M.D.; Burkhart, L.E; and Weldon, D. 1987. A mill study of the quality, yield, and mechanical properties of plywood produced from fast grown loblolly pine. For. Prod. J. 37(2):51–56.

McQuilkin, R.A. 1975. Pruning pin oak in southeastern Missouri. USDA For. Serv. North Cent. For. Exp. Stn. Res. Pap. NC-121.

Maeglin, R.R.; Hallock, H.; Freese, F.; and McDonald, K.A. 1977. Effect of nitrogen fertilization on black walnut—Growth, log quality, and wood anatomy. USDA For. Serv. Res. Pap. FPL-294.

Manwiller, F.G. 1972. Volumes, wood properties, and fiber dimensions of fast- and slow-grown spruce pine. Proc. Symp. Effect of growth acceleration on the properties of wood. USDA For. Serv. For. Prod. Lab.

Mar: Møller, C. 1960. The effect of pruning on the growth of conifers. Forestry 33 1(1):37–53.

Marton, R.; Stairs, G.; and Schreiner, E. 1968. Influence of growth rate and clonal effect on wood anatomy and pulping properties of hybrid poplars. TAPPI 51(5):230–235.

Megraw, R.A., and Nearn, W.T. 1972. Detailed DBH density profiles of several trees from Douglas-fir fertilizer thinning plots. Proc. Symp. Effect of Growth Acceleration on the Properties of Wood. USDA For. Serv. For. Prod. Lab.

Middleton, G.R.; Jozsa, L.A.; Munro, B.D.; Palka, L.C.; and Sen, P. 1995. Lodgepole pine product yield related to differences in stand density. Abstract, XX IUFRO World Congress, Finland. IAWA J 16(1):13.

Mitchell, H.L. 1972. Effect of nitrogen fertilizer on the growth rate and certain wood quality characteristics of sawlog size red oak, yellow poplar, and white ash. Proc. Symp. Effect of Growth Acceleration on the Properties of Wood. USDA For. Serv. For. Prod. Lab.

Moschler, W.W.; Dougal, E.F.; and McRae, D.D. 1989. Density and growth ring characteristics of *Pinus taeda* L. following thinning. Wood Fiber Sci. 21(3):313–319.

Murphey, W.K., and Bowier, J.J. 1975. The response of aspen to irrigation by municipal waste water. TAPPI 58(5):128–129.

Murphey, W.K., and Brisbin, R.L. 1970. Influence of sewage plant effluent irrigation on crown wood and stem wood of red pine (*Pinus resinosa* Ait.). Pa. Agri. Exp. Stn. Bull. 772.

Nicholls, J.W.P. 1971. The effect of environmental factors on wood characteristics. II. The effect of thinning and fertilizer treatment on the wood of *Pinus pinaster. Silv.* Genet. 20(3):67–73.

Noskowiak, A.F. 1963. Spiral grain in trees—A review. For. Prod. J. 13(7): 266–277.

Parker, M.L.; Hunt, K.; Warren, W.G.; and Kennedy, R.W. 1976. Effect of thinning and fertilization on intra-ring characteristics and kraft pulp yield of Douglas-fir. Proc. 28th Symp. Applied Polymer, pp. 1075–1086.

Paul, B.H. 1957. Second growth is good. South. Lumberman 195(2432):29–30.

_____ .1963. The application of silviculture in controlling the specific gravity of wood. USDA For. Serv. Tech. Bull. 1288.

Paul, B.H., and Marts, R.O. 1931. Controlling the proportion of summerwood in longleaf pine. J. For. 29:784–796.

Peszlen, I. 1995. Juvenile wood characteristics of plantation wood species. Abstract XX IUFRO Wood Congress, Finland. IAWA Journal 16(1):14.

Phelps, J.E. and Chen, P.Y.S. 1991. Wood and drying properties of white oak from thinned and unthinned plantations. For. Prod. J. 41(6):34–38.

Phelps, J.; Isebrands, J.; Einspahr, D.; Crist, J.; and Sturos, A. 1985. Wood and paper properties of vacuum airlift segregated juvenile poplar whole-tree chips. Wood Fiber Sci. l7(4):529–539.

Pillow, M.Y., and Luxford, R.F. 1937. Structure, occurrence, and properties of compression wood. USDA For. Serv. Tech. Bull. 546.

Posey, C.E. 1965. Effects of fertilization upon wood properties of loblolly pine (*Pinus taeda* L.). Proc. 8th Conf. Forest tree improvement, pp. 126–130.

Radcliffe, B.M. 1953. The influence of specific gravity and rate of growth upon the mechanical properties of sugar maple in flexure. Purdue Univ. Agric. Exp. Stn. Bull. 597.

Rendle, F.J., and Phillips, E.W.J. 1957. The effect of rate of growth (ring width) on the density of softwoods. Proc. 7th Conf. Br. Commonw. For.

Saucier, J.R., and Ike, A.F. 1972. Response in growth and wood properties of American sycamore to fertilization and thinning. Proc. Symp. Effect of Growth Acceleration on the Properties of Wood. USDA For. Serv. For. Prod. Lab.

Senft, J. F.; Bendtsen, B. A.; and Galligan, W. L. 1985. Weak wood: Fast grown trees make problem lumber. J. of For. 83 (8):476-484.

Shupe, T.F.; Choong, E.T.; and Yang, C.H. 1995. The effect of cultural treatments on the chemical composition of plantation-grown loblolly pine wood. Abstract XX IUFRO World Congress-Finland. IAWA J. 16(1), p. 18.

Siddiqui, K.M.; Gladstone, W.; and Marton, R. 1972. Influence of fertilization on wood and pulp properties of Douglas-fir. Proc. Symp. Effect of Growth Acceleration on the Properties of Wood. USDA For. Serv. For. Prod. Lab.

Smith, D.; Wahlgren, H.; and Bengtson, G.W. 1972. Effect of irrigation and fertilization on wood quality of young slash pine. Proc. Symp. Effect of Growth Acceleration on the Properties of Wood. USDA For. Serv. For. Prod. Lab.

Snook, S.; Labosky, P.; Bowersox, T.; and Blankenhorn, R. 1986. Pulp and paper-making properties of a hybrid poplar clone grown under four management strategies and two soil sites. Wood Fiber Sci. 18(1):157–167.

Spurr, S.H., and Hsiung, W.Y. 1954. Growth rate and specific gravity in conifers. J. For. 52(3):191–200.

Spurr, S.H., and Hyvarinen, M.J. 1954. Wood fiber length as related to position in the tree and growth. Bot. Rev. 20:561–575.

Squillace, A.E., and Dorman, K.W. 1961. Selective breeding of slash pine for high oleoresin yield and other characters. Proc. Int. Bot. Congr. 2(14):1616–1621.

Staebler, C.R. 1963. Growth along the stems of full-crowned Douglas-fir trees after pruning to specified heights. J. For. 61(2):124–130.

Stonecypher, R.; Zobel, B.; and Blair, R. 1973. Inheritance patterns of loblolly pines from a nonselected natural population. N.C. State Univ. Agric. Exp. Stn. Tech. Bull. 220.

Szopa, P.S.; Tennyson, L.C.; and McGinnes, E.A., Jr. 1977. A note on effects of sewage effluent irrigation on specific gravity and growth rate of white and red oaks. Wood Fiber 8(4):253–256.

Taylor, F.W. 1977. Variation in specific gravity and fiber length in selected hardwoods throughout the mid-South. Forest Sci. 23(2):190–194.

Taylor, F., and Burton, J. 1982. Growth ring characteristics, specific gravity, and fiber length of rapidly grown loblolly pine. Wood Fiber 14(3):204–210.

Thor, E., and Core, H.A. 1977. Fertilization, irrigation, and site factor relationships with growth and wood properties of yellow poplar. Wood Sci. 9(3):130–135.

Timell, T.E. 1986. Compression Wood In Gymnosperms, vol. III. Berlin: Springer-Verlag, p. 1703.

Turnbull, J.M. 1947. Some factors affecting wood density in pine stems. Union South Africa, British Empire For. Conf.

USDA Forest Service. 1976. Intensive plantation culture. North Cent. For. Exp. Stn. Gen. Tech. Rep. NC-21.

Wardrop, A.B. 1951. Cell wall organization and the properties of the xylem. I. Cell wall organization and the variation of breaking load in tension of the xylem in conifer stems. Aust. J. Sci. Res. Ser. B4:391–414.

Weetman, G.F. 1971. Effects of thinning and fertilization on the nutrient uptake, growth, and wood quality of upland black spruce. Woodland Pap. Pulp Pap. Res. Inst. Can. No. 28.

Wellwood, R.W. 1952. The effect of several variables on the specific gravity of second-growth Douglas-fir. For. Chron. 28(3):35–42.

Williams, R.E., and Hamilton, J.R. 1961. The effect of fertilization on four wood properties of slash pine. J. For. 59(9):662–665.

Yang, K.C. 1994. Impact of spacing on width and basal area of juvenile and mature wood in *Picea mariana* and *Picea glauca*. Wood Fiber Sci. 26(4):479–488.

Ying, L.; Kretschmann, D.E.; Bendtsen, B.A. 1994. Longitudinal shrinkage in fast-grown loblolly pine plantation wood. For. Prod. J. 44(1):58–62.

Youngberg, C.T.; Walker, L.C.; Hamilton, J.R.; and Williams, R.F. 1963. Fertilization of slash pine. Ga. For. Res. Counc. Res. Pap. 17.

Zarges, R.; Neuman, R.; and Crist, J. 1980. Kraft pulp and paper properties of *Populus* clones grown under short rotation intensive culture. TAPPI 63(7):91–94.

Zobel, B. 1977. Increasing southern pine timber production through tree improvement. South. J. Appl. For. 1(1):3–10.

Zobel, B., and Talbert, J. 1984. Applied Forest Tree Improvement. New York: John Wiley & Sons, pp. 403–404.

Zobel, B.J.; McElwee, R.L.; and Browne, C. 1961. Interrelationship of wood properties of loblolly pine. Proc. 6th South. Cont. Forest Tree Improvement, pp. 142–163.

Zobel, B.J.; Kellison, R.; and Matthias, M. 1969. Genetic improvement in forest trees— Growth rate and wood characteristics in young loblolly pine. Proc. 10th South. Conf. Forest Tree Improvement, pp. 59–75.

Zobel, B.J.; Kellison, R.C.; and Kirk, D.G. 1972. Wood properties of young loblolly and slash pines. Proc. Symp. Effect of Growth Acceleration on the Properties of Wood. USDA For. Serv. For. Prod. Lab.

The technology of major forest products

PART 3 is intended to provide an understanding of the manufacturing processes involved in producing the major forest products. Emphasis is placed on the relationship between the wood raw material, the processing technology, and the quality and yield of the forest product produced.

Lumber types and technology are discussed first, including techniques for measuring sawlogs. Other forest products covered are plywood, particle-based products (particleboard, waferboard, oriented-strandboard, and composite lumber), and fiber products (paper, fiberboards, and hard-

▶

board). The overview provided for each product includes discussion of the wood raw material requirements, the basic steps in the manufacturing process, and the effect of wood quality on the product. Product classifications and grades and major considerations in the wise selection and use of each product are summarized.

This section makes no attempt to cover all forest products. Only primary products are covered, not secondary products such as furniture or pallets. Two quite old but still very important forest products—poles and pilings—are not covered. Other references are available and adequately cover these topics.

■

13

Lumber

■ **THE CONVERSION** of logs to lumber in its simplest form consists of sawing boards from logs, squaring the edges, and cutting to length. This process is still accomplished by hand power in a few remote areas of the world. Yet today's modern sawmill is a highly technical operation using electronic scanners and computers to control important steps in the process. Economics dictates that as much lumber as possible be obtained from the logs using methods capable of high production rates. This does not mean that modern sawmills are larger than older mills. Old sawmills in the western United States designed to handle large logs could cut over a million board feet (bd ft) per day. New mills must have equipment appropriate for the small logs now available. Today's small-log sawmills produce one-third to one-half the amount of lumber once produced in large mills but must process 5–10 times the number of logs to do so.

In 1991 the approximately 7500 sawmills operating in the United States produced about 56 billion bd ft of lumber products (Phelps and McCurdy 1993). The southern region of the country then had about 2700 mills producing annually an average of about 10 million bd ft of lumber per mill while the West had 690 mills producing about three times as much lumber per mill. Mills in the northeast and north central regions of the country, about 4000 of them, produced an average just slightly over 2 million bd ft per year or only about 7% of the average western mill. These numbers indicate the great difference in the nature of the lumber industry as one looks at different regions of the country.

Almost one-half of the U.S. lumber is produced in the South, an increase from a decade ago when the South contributed only about one-third of the U.S. production. The South has changed places with the West, which today produces about one-third of the U.S. lumber. Some of the reasons for this shift are suggested in the Introduction. The northeast and north central regions of the country are much less important in the lumber industry and together are responsible for only about 16% of U.S. lumber production.

One of the reasons for the large regional differences in the lumber industry is the proportion of the forest inventory in hardwoods versus softwoods. Softwood mills are generally more highly automated using more-advanced technology and designed for a high rate of production. Hardwood mills generally require greater labor input per unit of output and are more conscious of recovering the maximum grade of lumber possible from each log. Hardwood lumber constitutes only about one-fifth of total U.S. lumber production. Production of hardwood lumber is somewhat evenly distributed throughout the eastern half of the United States (Luppold and Dempsey 1994). Only about 3% of hardwood lumber is produced in the West.

One of the interesting challenges when entering the lumber industry or an industry that is a user of lumber is to learn the terminology. *Lumber* is often defined for trade as a product sawn from a log. In more-common usage, however, the term is applied to products sawn to a standard thickness and differentiated from railroad crossties or cants produced by slabbing a log on two or four sides. In North America softwood lumber is classified as boards, dimension, or timbers. These terms apply to thickness categories. When dealing with softwood lumber, the term *boards* indicates lumber less than 2 in. thick, *dimension* is material 2–4 in. thick, and *timbers* are pieces 5 in. or thicker. The terminology of hardwood lumber is in many cases, e.g., size categories, quite different from that of softwood. For example, the term *dimension* when applied to hardwood refers to material that has been cut to size for furniture or pallet manufacture, not at all similar to the meaning used for softwood lumber.

Differences between softwood and hardwood lumber ■

The main uses for the higher grades of hardwood lumber are furniture, high-grade flooring, millwork, and cabinets or case goods. Lower grades are utilized for common flooring, pallet and container manufacture, and miscellaneous industrial applications. The largest single use of hardwood lumber in the United States is for pallets. Nearly 5 billion bd ft of hardwood lumber are used each year for pallets, about 40% of the total hardwood lumber production (Christoforo et al. 1994). Pallet production also utilizes about 2 billion bd ft of softwood lumber, mostly in West Coast pallet plants. Hardwoods find many miscellaneous industrial uses such as timbers for mining, retention walls at construction sites, local agricultural construction, and dunnage for shipping.

Railroad crossties and switchties are another important product of hardwood sawmills. About 25 million ties are produced annually, 60% of them in the southern region (Phelps and McCurdy 1993). Sawmills producing ties also produce lumber, with ties making up only about one-fourth of their production. The dense hardwoods, red and white oak, maple, and hickory are the preferred species and are used for 80% of ties produced. Only about 4% of ties in the United States are produced from softwood.

White oak, red oak, the gums, yellow poplar, the maples, and ash are among the most commonly harvested hardwoods, red oak being the single most important species. Red oak, black walnut, black cherry, hard maple, and yellow birch are the most highly sought-after fine hardwoods in the United States. However, practically every hardwood found in suitable quantity and size is manufactured into lumber for some purpose. Some lumber marketing firms specialize in developing uses for relatively little known species such as sassafras, holly, and honey locust.

Softwood lumber is used principally as a building construction material. Softwoods are used as structural members (as defined in Chapter 10) and for decorative or finishing purposes such as paneling, siding, decking, exterior trim material, and window and door manufacture. The largest single use of softwoods in the United States is as dimension lumber used in light-frame buildings. About 85% of all housing units built are of this type. The construction of single-family homes in the United States utilizes about 17 billion bd ft/yr or about one-third of total U.S. lumber production (McKeever and Anderson 1992).

Douglas-fir, southern yellow pine, ponderosa pine, western white and sugar pines, western hemlock, and the true firs are the most important U.S. softwoods cut for lumber. Douglas-fir and southern yellow pine provide about three-fourths of the softwood sawtimber harvested in the United States. Another 15% of softwood sawlogs are obtained from western hemlock, ponderosa pine, and the true firs. Of the softwood construction lumber consumed in the United States, about one-third is produced in Canada.

The basis for grading and *scaling* (measuring the volume) of hardwood lumber is very different from softwoods. Also, hardwood sawmills generally produce rough lumber of random width, while softwood mills typically surface their lumber to specific sizes, e.g., 2×4, 1×6. As a result, there are significant differences in the manufacturing process for these two types of lumber. Hardwood lumber grades were developed with the assumption that the lumber will be cut into smaller pieces for the manufacture of furniture or millwork parts. Grading is based upon the percent of the board that is usable in smaller clear pieces free of defects on one or both sides. These usable pieces are termed *cuttings*. For instance, the highest grade of hardwood lumber, *firsts and seconds* (FAS), is a board that contains 83% usable cuttings that exceed a certain minimum size. The standard hardwood lumber grades, promulgated by the National Hardwood Lumber Association, are thus not readily adaptable to applications where the entire board will be used as a single piece.

Softwood lumber grades, in contrast, are based principally on either structural uses or uses where the appearance of the board as a whole is important. Therefore, softwood lumber is graded as an entire piece for a combination of strength and appearance or for appearance only. As explained in Chapter 10, knots and slope of the grain are the main characteristics that determine strength. Softwood grading rules contain specifications intended to assure a minimum level of strength while maintaining a reasonably good appearance. The process by which standards and grades are established is discussed later in this chapter.

Lumber designation by species group ∎

To simplify marketing and distribution, lumber is sometimes sold by species group rather than by individual tree species. Appendix Tables A.8 and A.10 list the standard commercial names for hardwood and softwood lumber produced from North American tree species. In most cases, hardwood species are grouped to include woods that are difficult or impossible to separate once they are cut from the tree. For example, all oaks are sold commercially as either red oak or white oak. Foresters may pay a preferential price when purchasing logs of a certain species because of their knowledge of the grade yield that can be expected. For example, they might be willing to pay more per unit volume for northern red oak logs than northern pin oak or for southern red oak than for turkey oak. However, once cut, the lumber becomes simply red oak and its value is determined by the lumber grade.

Inconsistencies between hardwood tree names and lumber names can cause confusion. Some hickories are classed as pecan when cut to lumber. Sweetgum is simply called gum or is classed as red gum if it is heartwood. Lumber from yellow poplar is called poplar, which could be confused with the true poplars, i.e., aspen and cottonwood.

In softwoods the grouping of species for commercial use is slightly different than for hardwoods. Softwood species that can be visually separated are sometimes grouped because of their similar strength properties and to simplify marketing. Examples of such groupings are *Doug Fir-Larch,* which is Douglas-fir and western larch; *Hem-Fir,* which is West Coast hemlock and various true firs; and *Northern Pine,* which is jack pine and Norway pine. *Southern pine* lumber is produced principally from four tree species: longleaf, slash, shortleaf, and loblolly pine. In some instances slash and longleaf pine are exported under the name pitch pine.

Lumber size and measurement standards ∎

In North America and much of the developing world that exports to the United States, lumber is sold on the basis of board feet. A *board foot* is a volume 1 ft square by 1 in. thick. The number of board feet in a piece of lumber is therefore determined by multiplying the nominal thickness in inches times the nominal width in feet times the length in feet. For example, a 1 × 6-in. piece 10 ft long contains $1 \times \frac{6}{12} \times 10 = 5$ bd ft.

Complicating the measurement of lumber when using board feet is the fact that the actual size of a piece often differs from its *nominal size.* A dry, surfaced softwood 2 × 4, for example, measures 1½ × 3½ in. There is a larger standard size for softwoods in the rough green condition to allow for shrinkage and surfacing but this size is less than the nominal size. Sizes of hardwood lumber also take shrinkage and surfacing into account but in hardwoods the nominal and the rough dry size are the same. A nominal 1-in. hardwood board has a standard surfaced thickness of $\frac{26}{32}$ in. and a standard rough dry thickness of a full inch. If sold green, hardwood lumber should be thick enough to allow for shrinkage when dried to the specified rough size.

The board footage of softwood lumber is based upon the nominal size rather than the actual size. Therefore, an 8-ft 2 × 4, which actually measures 1½ in. × 3½ in. × 8 ft, contains $2 × \frac{4}{12} × 8 = 5\frac{1}{3}$ bd ft. Appendix Table A.9 lists nominal and actual sizes for S4S softwood lumber when dry or green.

The board footage of hardwood lumber is based upon the nominal thickness and the actual width. Remember that hardwoods are typically manufactured to random widths. For example, a piece of 2-in. lumber that measures 9¼ in. wide by 10 ft long contains $2 × 9.25/12 × 10 = 15$ bd ft (round 15.4 to the nearest board foot). Hardwood lumber is usually scaled using a scaling stick and the footage of each piece is recorded to the nearest board foot. A hardwood inspector simultaneously measures and grades hardwood lumber as it passes on the green chain. If hardwoods are cut to specified widths, as in the case of material to be used to manufacture pallets, the board footage is measured as with softwoods. The thickness of hardwood lumber is often spoken of in quarters of an inch. For example, 1-in. lumber is referred to as four-quarter and 2-in. lumber as eight-quarter.

In Europe and most countries outside North America, lumber is specified by its actual size. The volume in cubic meters (the unit used for measurement) is based on the actual volume of the material when dry. Therefore, a dry piece measuring 148 mm × 240 mm × 4 m contains $0.148 × 0.24 × 4 = 0.142$ m³. If the lumber is measured when green, a shrinkage factor must be taken into account. A cubic meter of dry lumber contains 424 bd ft as determined from the actual (not the nominal) lumber size. A conversion factor of 450 bd ft/m³ is often used in the international trade of green lumber.

Sawlog scaling and measurement ■

The units of measure used in the sale of sawlogs vary widely depending upon the size of the logs, whether the logs are sold tree length or as individual bolts, and upon the local practices in the region. The same basic methods are used to purchase logs for a plywood plant, although some specifications such as the minimum diameter and the amount of acceptable heart rot may differ from that for sawlogs.

The most commonly used methods of measuring logs are:

1. *Log scaling,* in which the diameter and length of each log is measured. These measurements are converted, by use of a log rule, to board feet or to actual cubic measure (ft³ or m³). Scaling can be done manually or by use of electronic scanners. The procedure for scaling will be described later.

2. *Weight scaling,* in which a load of logs is simply weighed. Weight can then be converted to an equivalent board foot or cord volume, or payment can be made directly on a weight basis. Table 13.1 shows the average weight of 1000 bd ft of logs for the major southern yellow pines measured using three different log rules. The reason for the differences between the log scales will be explained later. Note that even for these similar species there can be as much as a 35% difference in the weight of an equivalent volume of wood. The effect of variability of moisture content and wood density on weight scaling was discussed in Chapters 8 and 9.

Table 13.1.   The average weight of 1000 bd ft of logs as scaled by three log rules

Species of southern pine	Log rules		
	Doyle	Scribner Decimal C	International ¼
		(lb/1000 bd ft)	
Loblolly	17,750	12,800	11,010
Shortleaf	17,920	12,650	10,870
Longleaf	24,230	14,350	12,240
Slash	23,860	14,990	12,730

Source: Page and Bois (1961).

3. *Cord scaling* is sometimes used in the sale of sawbolts but is more commonly applied to pulpwood. A *standard cord* is defined as the volume of stacked wood $4 \times 4 \times 8$ ft, i.e., 128 ft³. There are many variations from this standard. In some regions of the Lake States a cord length of 100 in. is used instead of 8 ft. In areas of the South, a unit with a depth of 63 in. is used. The actual volume of wood in a cord, regardless of its definition, varies with the length, diameter, and straightness of the bolts and with the care used in stacking. Table 13.2 illustrates the relationship between bolt diameter and the volume of wood and bark in a cord of 4-ft-long bolts. Note the dramatic increase in the green weight and the volume of wood per cord as the bolt diameter increases. Various studies have found the solid wood content of a standard cord to vary from 58 to 94 ft³.

Table 13.2.   Volume for stacked standard cords of 4-ft longleaf pine pulpwood

Diameter of average bolt, inside bark	Volume per standard cord		Green weight per cord
	Wood	Bark	
(in.)	*(ft³)*	*(ft³)*	*(lb)*
5	56	23	4840
7	67	22	5430
9	71	21	5590
11	74	20	5760
13	77	20	5893
15	80	20	6100

Source: Williams and Hopkins (1968).

Log rules provide a conversion that relates the diameter and length of the log to an estimate of the lumber yield. Many factors determine how many board feet of lumber will be obtained per cubic foot of round logs. These include the width of saw kerf, diameter of the log (which affects the proportion lost as slabs), taper, and presence of sweep. Various log rules provide estimates of lumber volume based upon different assumptions regarding these factors. Lumber recovery that exceeds the volume estimated by a log rule is called *overrun*. Three commonly used log rules are briefly described:

1. *Doyle rule.* This rule is computed from the equation $V = [(D - 4) \div 4]^2 \times L$, where V = the board foot volume, D = the scaling diameter in inches, and L = the long length in feet. This rule greatly underestimates the volume of lumber

that can be obtained from small logs. Mills purchasing small logs on Doyle may obtain over twice the volume of lumber estimated by the log rule. A mill producing twice as much lumber as the log scale would have a 100% overrun.

2. *Scribner rule.* This rule was devised on the premise of sawing 1-in.-thick boards with ¼-in. kerf from perfectly circular logs based on diameter at the small end of the log and no taper taken into account. This rule underestimates lumber yield on small logs and on long logs with taper. If the volumes are rounded to the nearest 10 bd ft, this rule is called the Scribner Decimal C.

3. *The International ¼ rule.* This rule assumes sawing 1-in.-thick lumber with ¼-in. kerf allowing ½ in. of taper for each 4 ft of length and ¹⁄₁₆ in. of shrinkage in board thickness. The International rule generally provides the closest estimate to actual lumber production of any of these commonly used rules. Thus it allows less overrun than the Doyle or Scribner rules for all but the largest logs.

The scaling of logs, regardless of the log rule used, involves measuring the length and diameter of the log. Strict specifications for length must be met or the log is considered to be of the next shorter standard length. The scaling diameter is the average diameter of the small end inside the bark. Tables can be used to convert the diameter and length to the desired log scale. Electronic scanners can be used for scaling. When done manually, scaling sticks that read directly in bd ft are used.

When selling or purchasing logs, the basis for measurement is not nearly as important as understanding the relationship between the different rules and the actual log volume. Table 13.3 compares the content of 16-ft-long logs as scaled with different log rules. Note that as the logs get larger, the differences become smaller.

Table 13.3. Comparison of board foot volumes as determined by three log rules for 16-ft logs

Scaling diameter	Cubic volume*	Log rule		
		Doyle	Scribner	International ¼
(in.)	*(ft³)*		*(bd ft)*	
6	4.30	4	12	19
8	7.10	16	31	39
10	10.59	36	55	65
12	14.78	64	86	97
14	19.66	100	123	136
16	25.25	144	166	181
18	31.53	196	216	232
20	38.53	256	272	290
22	46.19	324	334	354
24	54.57	400	403	424
26	63.64	484	478	501

*Assumes cone with 2-in. taper per log.

Mills often calculate overrun to monitor the efficiency of their log conversion. Overrun again is the percentage by which lumber output exceeds the log input.

$$\% \text{ overrun (underrun)} = \frac{\text{bd ft lumber tally} - \text{bd ft log scale}}{\text{bd ft log scale}} \times 100$$

It should be apparent that the overrun obtained from a mill will vary greatly depending on the log rule used. Table 13.4 compares typical overrun expectations in the southern pine region. The overrun when using Doyle is by far the greatest for logs 14 in. and smaller in diameter. The International ¼ rule may actually overestimate the amount of lumber that can be produced and thus a negative overrun *(underrun)* may result.

Table 13.4. Predicted percent overrun in southern pine sawmills using three log rules

Scaling diameter	Log rule		
	Doyle	Scribner Decimal C	International ¼
(in.)		*(%)*	
6	172	21	−3
8	95	19	−4
10	59	16	−5
12	39	14	−5
14	25	11	−6
16	16	9	−6
18	8	6	−7
20	2	4	−8

Source: Williams and Hopkins (1968).

Measurement of the actual cubic volume of log input by use of electronic scanners is becoming more common in the softwood lumber industry. This allows monitoring of the true volume input to a mill not possible when using log rules or weight scaling. This information makes significant improvement in process control procedures possible.

Lumber manufacturing ■

The sequence of processing steps in lumber manufacture is illustrated in Figure 13.1. All lumber will not necessarily go through all the steps shown. Some will not be remanufactured in any way (resawn or re-edged) but may go directly from the edger to the trimmer. Some sawmills do not dry lumber but sell it green, while still others produce only rough, unsurfaced lumber. Most modern sawmills, however, have equipment to accomplish all the steps shown in the block diagram.

DEBARKING. Almost all modern sawmills debark logs prior to sawing. This has several advantages, but the main reason for debarking is so that the bark-free slabs can be chipped for use in making pulp. Bark-free wood chips are more valuable and more readily marketable to pulp mills than barky chips (chips with bark). Many pulp mills will not purchase chips containing bark at any price. This situation will change if methods developed to separate bark from chips become economically feasible and are adopted by the pulp industry. Acceptance of barky chips improves when bark-free chips are in short supply.

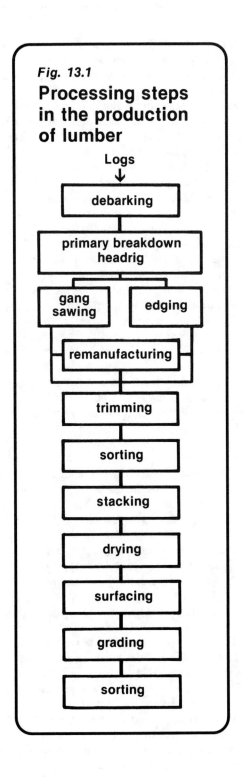

Fig. 13.1

Processing steps in the production of lumber

Logs

debarking

primary breakdown headrig

gang sawing

edging

remanufacturing

trimming

sorting

stacking

drying

surfacing

grading

sorting

There are two other important advantages of debarking. Removal of sand and grit along with the bark greatly decreases the rate at which saws are dulled, reducing downtime in the mill. Second, bark is an economical source of fuel for energy generation.

The most widely used type of debarker in medium to large sawmills is the *ring debarker* (Fig. 13.2). In this machine the log passes through a rotating ring that holds a number of pressure bars. These press against the log and tear off the bark. Large units of this type can debark logs at speeds of up to 200 lineal ft/min. Another type of equipment, a *cambio debarker,* looks similar to a ring debarker but centers the log between three rotating cylindrical heads and rotates it as it passes through a revolving ring holding knife-faced pressure arms.

A *rossing head debarker* is sometimes used in sawmills where high production rates are not needed. A similar machine is also used for peeling posts and poles. The rossing head is a rotating cutterhead, similar to the head on a lumber planer, that rides along the log and cuts off the bark as the log is rotated. This debarker is also suited to situations where crooked or stubby logs must be debarked. With this type of equipment care must be taken to not remove too much wood with the bark. The high value of lumber and pulp chips makes excessive wood fiber removal an expensive mistake.

Hydraulic debarkers were well suited to sawmills designed for large, old-growth logs in species with thick, heavy bark. Jets of high-pressure water directed against the log surface blast the bark loose. These debarkers are now used only rarely as milling of large logs has declined in the western United States and Canada. Hydraulic debarkers are suitable for large tropical hardwoods. Use is diminishing because of the expensive water treatment needed to meet environmental regulations.

PRIMARY BREAKDOWN. The primary breakdown of the log is accomplished by one of two methods. One method is to place the log on a carriage traveling on rails, which conveys the log back and forth through the saw. This is referred to as a *carriage rig.* One piece is cut from the log with each pass by the saw. The thickness of the lumber is determined by moving the log on the carriage. The mechanism that moves the log forward on the carriage is called the *setworks.* Until the 1960s almost all lumber was produced on carriage rigs. Since that time, single-pass headrigs specifically designed for small logs have come into common use. In new softwood sawmills today, carriage rigs are used principally for larger logs (over about 16 in. in diameter) or in mills that require a great deal of flexibility in regard to log and lumber sizes. Most hardwood mills use carriage rigs because of their flexibility and ability to use a variety of sawing patterns.

Two types of saws, the *circular saw* and the *bandsaw,* have been used in conjunction with carriage rigs since the mid-1800s. Figure 13.3 illustrates a typical small carriage rig sawmill utilizing a circular headsaw. In such a mill there are three operators, the head sawyer, the edgerman, and the trimmerman, who are responsible for the decisions that determine the quantity and grade of lumber obtained from each log. Circular headsaws vary in diameter from about 36 to 60 in. (0.9 to 1.5m) and can handle logs up to about 36 in. (0.9m) in diameter. If larger logs are to be cut, a second circular saw located above the main saw can be used.

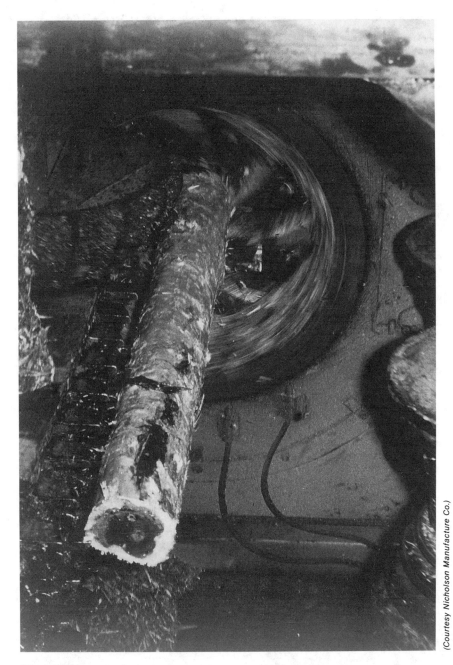

(Courtesy Nicholson Manufacture Co.)

Fig. 13.2
A small pine log passing through a ring debarker. The ring is rotating counterclockwise. The ring and the pressure bars appear here as a blur.

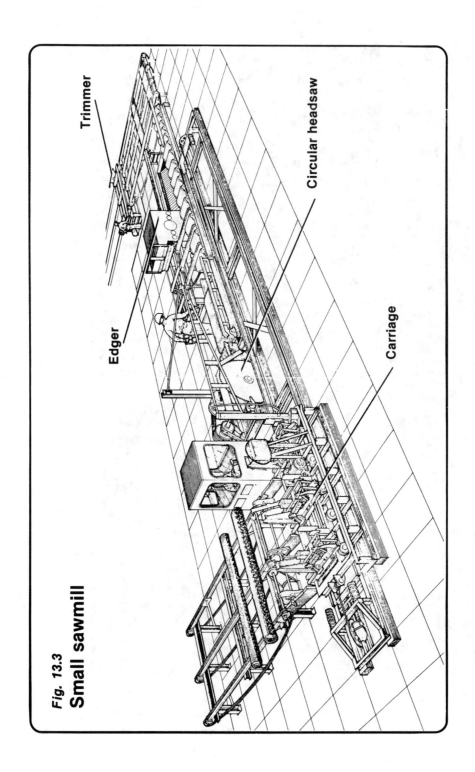

Fig. 13.3
Small sawmill

Trimmer

Edger

Circular headsaw

Carriage

Single-band headsaws have the advantage of being able to cut almost any diameter of log that can be delivered to the saw. They are much more expensive to maintain than circular saws, and the original capital investment is higher. They are used principally where large logs are to be sawn.

Both circular and band headrigs remove a considerable amount of wood with the cut. The width of this cut, called the *kerf*, varies from about $\frac{3}{16}$ to $\frac{3}{8}$ in. in circular saws. Bandsaw kerf is somewhat narrower, typically about $\frac{1}{8}$ to $\frac{3}{16}$ in. As a result, large volumes of sawdust are produced, particularly if boards and dimension are cut on the headsaw. For example, if boards with an actual target green thickness of 1 in. are being cut with a saw kerf of $\frac{3}{8}$ in., $1\frac{3}{8}$ in. of the log is removed each time a board is cut. This does not consider the variability in sawing thickness that inevitably occurs. About $\frac{3}{8} \div 1\frac{3}{8}$, or 27%, of the wood removed in this case becomes sawdust. This does not include the kerf lost in edging the lumber. For this reason, and also to increase the production rate through a mill, headsaws often do not cut the lumber to its final thickness but instead saw the log into thick cants. These *cants* are then cut to final size by resaws or edgers that have higher feed speed and less kerf loss than the headsaw.

The mechanisms that position the log, control the thickness of the cut, and move the log through the saw are actually more critical to good lumber production than the type of headsaw. Williston (1976) points out four primary requirements for breakdown of a log to yield maximum lumber value: (1) means of measuring the geometry and grade of the log including taper and sweep, (2) ability to calculate the correct sawing position for the log and for moving and holding it in that position, (3) ability to hold the log firmly and move it in a straight line, and (4) capability of generating thin, straight saw cuts at suitably high speeds.

The second method of primary breakdown is by a *single-pass headrig*. In equipment of this type, the logs pass through the machine only once, in a more-or-less continuous flow. Further breakdown of the log is accomplished by secondary saws of some type. The three most common types of single-pass headrigs in use are chipper canters, scragg mills, and multiple-band headrigs. The increasing use of small logs for the production of lumber has stimulated the development and improvement of this type of processing equipment. Figure 13.4 shows a twin-band headrig cutting a small log.

The *chipper canter* or chipping headrig is very different from carriage rig headsaws in that a squared or shaped cant is produced by the removal of chips from the sides of the log. The chips are removed with knives mounted on rotating cutterheads, so no sawdust is produced. Typically, these machines operate at from 150 to 200 lineal ft/min. Such a mill can cut over 200 logs per 8-hr shift. Theoretical capacity is nearly double this figure.

Chipping headrigs, developed in the 1960s, are now used throughout North America for small softwoods. Although some models will handle logs up to 24 in. in diameter, most mills using these machines are cutting logs from 6 to 16 in. in diameter. There are several manufacturers of chipper canters of various types. These differ in the way the log is held and transported through the machine, the type of cutterhead used, and the shape of the chipped profile. Some models incorporate a sawing section that cuts the cant into lumber immediately after it has been chipped to shape. Such a machine is shown in Figure 13.5. Some of the pos-

Fig. 13.4

Twin-band headrig cutting a small softwood log. A 4-in. cant and two slabs are produced.

sible configurations of lumber that can be produced on chipping headrigs are shown in Figure 13.6. In chipper canters that do not contain a sawing section, a rectangular cant is produced on the headrig. This cant is then broken down into lumber by a *gang saw,* such as the rotary gang shown in Figure 13.7.

Some sawmills utilize a chipping headrig for their small logs and a carriage rig for larger logs that have the potential of yielding the higher grades of lumber. Chipper canters are also used to convert cores from plywood veneer bolts into 2×4s. In this case, the veneer bolts are peeled down to a certain size, usually about 5⅝ in., and then the core of the bolt is ejected from the veneer lathe and conveyed to the chipper canter.

Scragg mills consists of two or four circular saws on a common arbor (or shaft). The distance between the blades can be adjusted by the operator to produce 4-, 6-, or 8-in.-thick cants. Logs make one pass through this rig, producing a two-sided cant plus two slabs (on a two-saw scragg). The cant is then broken down to boards by a gang resaw. If the slabs are thick enough, they can be resawn to produce a 1- or 2-in. board. The logs in most scragg mills are moved through the saws by a conveyor chain. A more-recent version uses an overhead device that clamps the log at both ends and carries it through the saws.

Multiple-band headrigs usually consist of two or four opposing bandsaws of the same general type but somewhat smaller than the single-band headsaws used with carriage rigs. As with the other single-pass headrigs, multiple-band headrigs were developed to process small logs. Williston (1976) stated that there was no reason they could not also be used for larger logs, as long as there was no

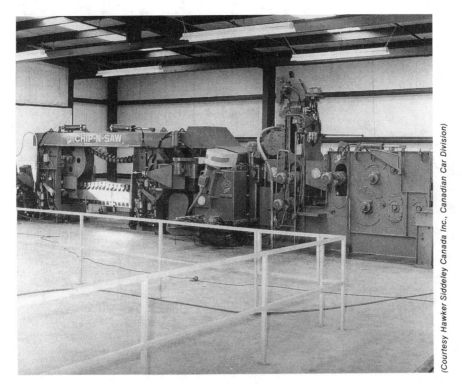

(Courtesy Hawker Siddeley Canada Inc., Canadian Car Division)

Fig. 13.5
Chipping headrig (Chip-N-Saw) showing the log transport and chipping and sawing sections.

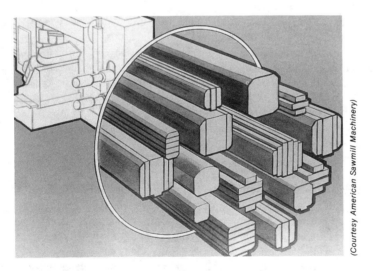

(Courtesy American Sawmill Machinery)

Fig. 13.6
Illustration of the various configurations of cants and lumber that can be produced in a pass through machines of the general type shown in Figure 13.5.

(Courtesy Corley Manufacturing Co.)

Fig. 13.7
**A double-arbor edger that can break down a cant into many boards.
An upper and a lower arbor (shaft) carry circular saws that mesh
perfectly to cut the cant from both faces.**

need to turn the log to recover higher lumber grades. Multiple-band headrigs are
adaptable to electronic scanner and computer control applications.

Multiple-band headrigs are sometimes used in conjunction with *slab chippers* that slab two sides of the log before it reaches the bandsaws. The slab chipper has a cutterhead with knives, which chips flat the portion of the log that
would ordinarily be removed as a slab. The cutting action of a slab chipper is
similar to the cutterheads in some chipper canters. The use of two-slab chippers
with a quad band makes it possible to cut the log into four pieces of lumber plus
one cant as it passes through the rig.

SECONDARY BREAKDOWN. After primary breakdown on the headrig, the
lumber may only require cutting to width (edging) and length (trimming). In
most mills, however, a greater degree of secondary breakdown is required, such
as sawing a cant into boards or resawing a slab to obtain a board. Many types of
saws and chippers are available for secondary breakdown. Gang saws make a series of cuts and so can reduce a cant to boards in one pass. Resaws can split a
plank into two boards or cut a board from the wider side of a slab. A slab chipper can also be used to salvage lumber from slabs. In this process, the excess
wood is chipped away rather than sawn.

Edging and trimming are important operations requiring operators with a
good knowledge of lumber grades. Electronic scanners and control systems that

will allow automatic edging and trimming of boards for maximum volume yield are now available. Development is still needed for systems that will automatically cut to maximize value (grade) rather than volume. The value of a board can often be increased by properly removing a defect from one edge or end. Excessive edging and trimming is costly, of course, as it reduces lumber output.

Figure 13.8 illustrates the importance of properly edging and trimming hardwood lumber. This piece of basswood originally contained 13 bd ft of No. 1 Common grade valued at $340/1000 bd ft (MBF) or $0.34/bd ft. If edged and trimmed as shown, the volume of the piece would decrease to 12 bd ft, but the grade would increase to FAS at $500/MBF. The value of the piece in this example is increased from $4.42 to $6.00, an increase of 36%. Most mills present opportunities to increase lumber value through improved manufacturing.

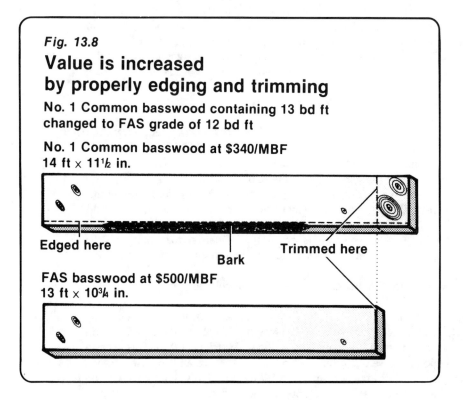

Fig. 13.8

**Value is increased
by properly edging and trimming**

**No. 1 Common basswood containing 13 bd ft
changed to FAS grade of 12 bd ft**

**No. 1 Common basswood at $340/MBF
14 ft × 11½ in.**

Edged here   **Bark**   **Trimmed here**

**FAS basswood at $500/MBF
13 ft × 10¾ in.**

DRYING, SORTING, AND FINISHING. The drying process was discussed in Chapter 8. Before lumber is dried, it is usually sorted by grade, size, and species. To dry lumber uniformly and in a minimum time, it is desirable to dry only one thickness, width, and species per kiln load. Automatic stacking equipment is available to stack the lumber for drying. Lumber packages ready for the kiln consist of alternate layers of lumber and *stickers* (spacer sticks). After drying, the packages are broken down by machine and the stickers removed.

The handling and sorting of lumber typically is done twice. At the green chain (located following the trim saws in the mill) the lumber is sorted by species, size, and grade. Then after it is dried and surfaced it will again be graded, grade-stamped if softwood lumber, sorted, and packaged for shipment. A wide variety of lumber-sorting equipment is available for use at the green or dry end of the mill. The simplest system is to have the lumber manually pulled and sorted as it proceeds down a green or dry chain. The manual handling of lumber is eliminated in modern mills by mechanical sorters that can be controlled by a single grader/operator. Sorters are available to automatically sort lumber by length, width, or thickness.

The portion of a lumber manufacturing plant where cutting to final size and surfacing is done is called the *planer mill*. In hardwood mills shipping only rough lumber, obviously no planer mill is required. Planing equipment commonly used includes surfacers, matchers, and moulders. A *surfacer* is a machine that planes the lumber on two faces only (S2S). High-speed *matchers* used for softwood dimension have four or more heads to surface the lumber on four sides (S4S). Some of these machines can operate at lineal speeds in excess of 1000 ft/min. Matchers may have profile heads for running patterns or splitting wide stock into narrower widths. A *moulder* is similar to a matcher but is designed to run smaller stock to pattern. It usually has both top and bottom profile heads.

Improving sawmill efficiency ■

A mill purchasing wood by log rule can compare total log volume input with lumber volume output to determine overrun. Done over time, this process gives as indication of any change in the performance of the key operators in the mill or in the quality of the logs. A better way to consider the efficiency of a sawmill, however, is to analyze yield in terms of board feet of lumber produced per cubic foot of actual log volume. This ratio is termed the *lumber recovery factor* (LRF). To determine this, the mill must scale the logs being processed for cubic volume.

LRF = board feet lumber tally / cubic feet log volume

Note that if lumber were actually cut to nominal sizes, there were no losses from kerf, and logs were square, the LRF would be 12. In the United States the average LRF among the larger sawmills is about 7.8 (Clapp 1982). This average varies by region because of the size of timber and the size and sophistication of mills. Regional averages range from 8.3 to 5.7 bd ft/ft^3. Individual mills will differ considerably from these averages, but the LRF gives manufacturers a guideline with which to compare their efficiency of log conversion.

There are a number of possible means of improving the LRF of a sawmill. Among the most important are reducing kerf; reducing variability in thickness, which requires that lumber be sawn oversize; and making optimum decisions about how to cut each log and accurately positioning it according to the decision made.

The reduction of kerf losses in a sawmill is accomplished primarily by minimizing the saw cuts made on the headsaw and breaking down cants on smaller secondary saws that have much less kerf. There have been significant advancements in circular saw technology, which has reduced the kerf in saws designed to rip cants. Modern rotary gang saws typically have kerfs of about ⅛ in. and produce smooth, accurately sawn lumber.

Another important means of increasing the LRF is by reducing the variability of lumber thickness. If a headrig has a variability of sawing thickness of ¼ in. (±⅛ in.) and this can be reduced in some way to ⅛ in. (±¹⁄₁₆ in.), there can be a saving of ¹⁄₁₆ in. of wood each time a saw cut is made. This saving results from setting the saw ¹⁄₁₆ in. over the desired thickness rather than ⅛ in., which would be required with the greater variability. Proper selection and maintenance of equipment is very important in attaining this goal.

The greatest advancement in increasing the efficiency of sawmills in recent years has been the application of electronic log scanners and computers for the measurement of logs and for placement of the first saw cut. The results as applied to chipping headrigs are shown in Figure 13.9; they came from a Canadian study of improved sawing decisions made by computer control over manual control with two different models of a Chip-N-Saw, a chipper canter of the type shown in Figure 13.5. Note in Figure 13.9 that the LRF was increased ½ to 1 bd ft/ft³ by using the computer-controlled system.

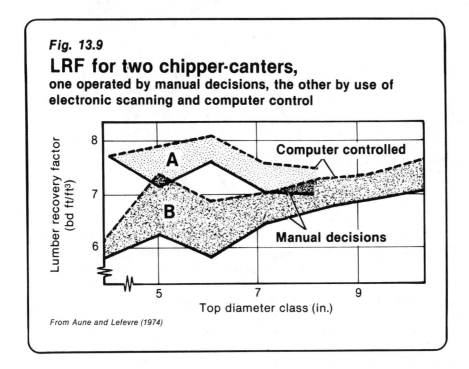

Fig. 13.9

LRF for two chipper-canters,
one operated by manual decisions, the other by use of electronic scanning and computer control

From Aune and Lefevre (1974)

The coupling of an electronic scanner and a computer for operation control has many potential applications within a sawmill (Williston 1976). For example, a computerized optimizing edger measures board geometry, computes the optimum edging decision, positions the board and the saws, and passes the board through the edger to achieve maximum value.

A scanner is a means of measuring the length, diameter, or shape of a log or cant by passing it through a light or laser beam. Some scanners operate with a light receiver that senses the width of the object being placed between the light source and the receiver. Other scanners take measurements from the light reflected from the object being measured, whether it is a log or a cant. Figure 13.10 illustrates the combination of a scanner and a computer to control the relative position of the log and the saw lines.

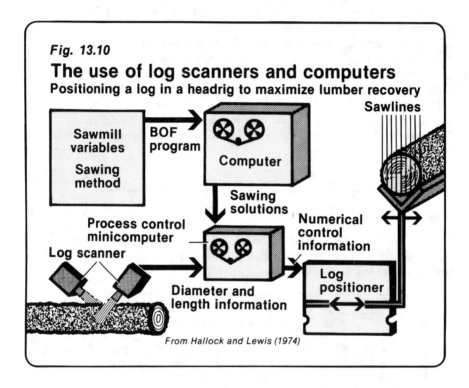

Fig. 13.10

The use of log scanners and computers
Positioning a log in a headrig to maximize lumber recovery

From Hallock and Lewis (1974)

The importance of making the first cut in a log at the proper position may not be apparent. However, once the first saw cut is made, the location of subsequent cuts is already determined. An illustration of how much difference a shift in the first cut can make in lumber yield is shown in Figure 13.11. On this small log the lumber yield could increase from 32 to 40 bd ft by moving the cut to the right only 0.20 in. The data in this figure is from Hallock (1973), who did much work to demonstrate the importance of properly locating the first saw cut on a log. He referred to this as the *best opening face,* or the BOF.

At the present time the application of scanners and computers to sawmills is aimed at maximizing the volume of lumber. Work is under way to extend these methods toward the goal of obtaining lumber of the highest value from the logs, not necessarily the greatest volume. Value is a combination of volume, grade, and size. In Figure 13.8 it is demonstrated that the piece with the highest volume does not necessarily have the highest value. It is very likely that in the next few years significant further advancements will be made in the application of computerized process control of lumber manufacture.

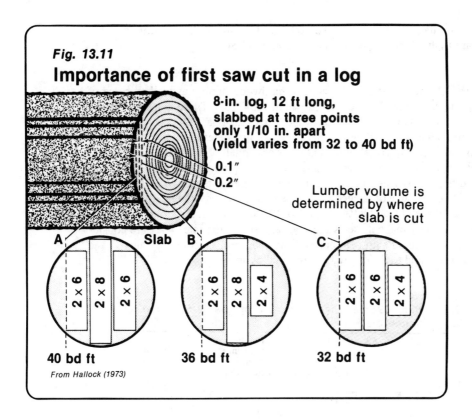

Fig. 13.11

Importance of first saw cut in a log

8-in. log, 12 ft long,
slabbed at three points
only 1/10 in. apart
(yield varies from 32 to 40 bd ft)

0.1″
0.2″

Lumber volume is
determined by where
slab is cut

A

Slab B

C

| 2 × 6 | 2 × 8 | 2 × 6 |

| 2 × 6 | 2 × 8 | 2 × 4 |

| 2 × 6 | 2 × 6 | 2 × 4 |

40 bd ft

36 bd ft

32 bd ft

From Hallock (1973)

Importance of standards and grades
for proper selection and use of lumber ■

Those involved in the manufacture, sale, or use of lumber for secondary products must understand lumber grades if they are to utilize the material in the most-efficient manner. Using the wrong species, grade, or size for a job can be costly to the homebuilder or furniture manufacturer. It can also result in using more lumber than necessary or in unsatisfactory performance of the final product.

The grades used in the United States and Canada for hardwood lumber are written by the National Hardwood Lumber Association (NHLA). These rules are also widely used in other countries exporting lumber to the United States. A number of softwood lumber trade associations are responsible for preparing and administering the grade rules applicable to their particular species. The larger of these organizations are the Western Wood Products Association, Southern Pine Inspection Bureau, West Coast Lumber Inspection Bureau, Redwood Inspection Service, Northeastern Lumber Manufacturers Association, and Northern Softwood Lumber Bureau. The grade rules they have prepared must conform to PS 20-94, a product standard developed under the jurisdiction of the U.S. Department of Commerce and administered by the American Lumber Standards Committee (ALSC). The grades of dimension lumber for all these softwood associations are similar, conforming to the National Grading Rule for Softwood Dimension Lumber prepared under supervision of ALSC.

HARDWOODS. The standard grades of hardwood lumber as well as some of the major requirements for each are shown in Table 13.5. These grades are based upon the percentage of the total area of the face of the board that is usable as furniture parts. When grading, the lumber inspector first determines the poorest side of the board. Then by visual judgment and occasionally by actual measurement, the proportion and size of clear, rectangular cuttings from the piece is estimated. These cuttings must meet the minimum size requirements shown in Table 13.5. If over 83% of the area of a piece is in these usable cuttings, the board is an FAS; if it yields between 66 and 83%, it is a No. 1 Common, etc. Experienced inspectors can accurately make these estimations at a surprising rate. They are considered to have graded a shipment correctly if upon reinspection the value of the lumber is not found to differ from the original by more than 4%.

Table 13.5. Some characteristics of the NHLA hardwood lumber grades

Grade name	Required yield*	Minimum size of cuttings used in calculating yield	Minimum allowed size of board
	(%)	(in. × ft)	(in. × ft)
FAS	83	4 × 5 or 3 × 7	6 × 8
Select†	83	Similar to FAS	4 × 6
No. 1 Common	66	3 × 3 or 4 × 2	3 × 4
No. 2 Common	50	3 × 2	3 × 4
No. 3A Common	33	3 × 2	3 × 4
No. 3B Common†	25	3 × 2	3 × 4

*Percent of board in cuttings that must be free of defects on one side.

†Differs from FAS in that the minimum board size is smaller and the grading is done from the best side of the board rather than from the poorest. Different basis is used to grade pieces less than 6 in. wide.

†Grading from poorest side and yield based upon sound, not clear, areas.

When purchasing hardwood lumber, a furniture plant selects the grade based upon the size of pieces (dimension) they must cut from the lumber. The smaller the pieces they require, the lower the grade of lumber that can be used. Generally, a plant will obtain a much higher yield of *usable cuttings* from the lumber than indicated by the required yield percentages for that grade as shown in Table 13.5. This results from the fact that the plant is not restricted to the size of cutting used in the grading rules and the fact that the required yields for the grades are minimums, not averages.

An inexperienced hardwood lumber buyer will tend to buy a higher grade than necessary and as a result will needlessly increase raw material costs. To approach the use of lumber grades scientifically, many private firms and public research agencies have developed tables of expected yield for various size cuttings obtained from different grades and species. With this information, a firm can calculate which grades to purchase to minimize the total cost. Computer programs to accomplish these calculations are available through private consultants and forestry extension personnel of the U.S. Department of Agriculture.

There is no moisture content standard for hardwood lumber; i.e., there is no specific moisture content maximum for lumber sold as dry or kiln dried. A purchaser should specify the moisture content requirement when buying such lumber. Although there are standard surfaced thicknesses for hardwood lumber, it is a good practice to specify both moisture content and actual thickness when purchasing hardwood lumber surfaced on both sides (S2S).

Many uses of hardwoods do not involve a cut-up operation like those in a furniture or flooring plant. Pallet plants usually purchase lumber already ripped to the width needed. Much of the material used in pallets consists of No. 2 or No. 3 Common or is purchased ungraded. This material is often not sold by species but simply in a group of species of similar density. The higher-density woods are preferred for most pallets where strength and nail-holding power is needed. Low-density woods are selected where ease of nailing and shipping weight are important.

Hardwoods are generally not used for *construction lumber,* e.g., as joists, rafters, studs, and truss members. However, some lower-density hardwoods are suitable for this purpose and may find greater use in the future. Aspen has been used to produce 2×4s graded similarly to softwoods. Poplar was an important construction lumber in the early years of American history.

SOFTWOODS. Most grading of softwood lumber is by visual inspection. Each piece must be inspected on both sides. In a few seconds experienced graders assess the knot size and location, slope of grain, freedom from decay, and other characteristics that determine grade. Some dimension lumber to be used in engineered structures is also graded by machine. This is termed *machine stress-rated* (MSR) *lumber.* The main use of MSR lumber is in floor trusses and trussed rafters. The major components of a machine that stress-grades lumber are shown in Figure 13.12. The machine measures the stiffness of lumber passing through it by flexing it in the two flatwise directions and measuring the force required to do so. The *stiffness* is then related by a computer program to the bending strength and the piece is stamped accordingly. The variability in strength of a grade of MSR lumber is much less than for visually graded lumber, an advantage when high strength is needed. In 1993 over 800 million bd ft of lumber was machine stress-rated, an increase of 23% in only 3 years.

The major use of softwood lumber is for construction. A few grades that are intended for cut-up operations to produce window and door parts are called *shop grades.* The largest portion of construction lumber goes into dimension, i.e., lumber 2–4 in. thick. The grades of softwood dimension assigned allowable stresses are shown in Table 13.6, with the highest grade in each category listed at the top. (Recall that the use of the allowable stress values was discussed in Chapter 10.) The special grade of Stud is somewhat similar to a No. 3 but with stricter re-

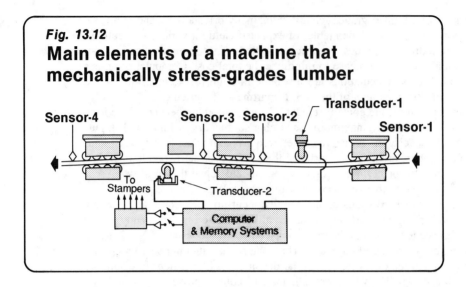

Fig. 13.12
Main elements of a machine that mechanically stress-grades lumber

quirements in regard to warp. The Appearance grade is quite similar to a No. 1 but with greater restrictions as to wane (barky edges) and other appearance factors. Not shown are lower grades usable for blocking, dunnage, etc.

The many grades and species of softwood dimension lumber can cause confusion in selection of building materials. There are 11 grades of softwood 2 × 4s, so if a mill produces lumber from three species groups it would have 33 different categories of material for just this one size. Most manufacturers and building materials dealers restrict themselves to a very limited number of grades and species. This reduces inventory problems and confusion of the customer/builder. It is common practice to sell mixed grades of dimension, for example, No. 2 and Better or Standard and Better. The percentage of the lower grade allowed in such a mix is often specified to assure that the customer does not receive only the lower grade.

Three moisture content levels can be specified for softwood lumber: (1) *S-Grn* or *Grn*—the lumber was green or above 19% MC when surfaced; (2) *S-Dry* or *KD 19*—the lumber was surfaced when at 19% MC or less; and (3) *MC-15* or *KD 15*—the lumber was surfaced when at 15% MC or less. These cat-

Table 13.6. Grades of softwood dimension lumber assigned allowable stresses

Nominal size	Grades	
	General use	Structural use
2–4 in. thick and 2–4 in. wide	Construction Standard Utility Appearance	Select Structural No. 1 No. 2 No. 3 Stud
2–4 in. thick and 6 in. and wider	Select Structural No. 1 No. 2 No. 3 Appearance	Select Structural No. 1 No. 2 No. 3

egories are used for both boards and dimension. Timbers are ordinarily sold only in the green condition. It is not advisable to use green dimension in finished buildings because of the possibility of warp and shrinkage. Nonetheless, green dimension is still used for home construction in some areas. Southern pine is often manufactured to the 15% MC requirement (KD), but other softwood manufacturers produce principally S-Dry material.

Most softwoods lumber, particularly dimension, is grade-stamped at the mill after it has been dried and surfaced. Building codes require the use of grade-stamped lumber for framing. Grade stamps for visually graded lumber indicate the grade, the species or species group, the moisture content category, the association under whose supervision the grader works, and also a number that designates the mill at which the lumber was produced. An example of such a grade stamp is shown in Figure 13.13. A grade stamp for MSR lumber is illustrated in Figure 13.14. The elements in this stamp are similar to those of a visually graded piece. However, the classification of MSR lumber is designated by the allowable bending strength and stiffness values.

The sale of species of softwood lumber in various regions follows traditional marketing patterns developed over many years. Builders and building contractors become accustomed to certain species and grades, and sometimes it is difficult to change their preferences unless significant cost savings are possible. Homebuilders may advertise their use of well-known species such as Douglas-fir or southern pine as indications that their homes are superior, implying that builders using other species are producing inferior homes. Although significant advantages or disadvantages of one species as compared to another do exist,

Fig. 13.13
A grade stamp on a 2 × 4 indicating that the piece is a Stud grade of spruce, pine, or fir (Canadian), surfaced when below 19% MC.

there is no reason that any species of softwood dimension will not do the job for which it is intended if the lumber is properly manufactured and the building is designed with the properties of that species and grade in mind.

In many situations in building construction, it is possible to use the next larger size of dimension rather than changing to a higher grade or a stronger species. Such a change may be less costly and result in a better building than using the smaller size of the higher grade.

When using dimension lumber for construction, it is often helpful to be able to compare the strength and stiffness of different lumber sizes. Two rules of thumb can be very useful in this regard: (1) *the strength of a beam is proportional to the square of its depth* and (2) *stiffness of a beam is proportional to the cube of the depth.* For example, from Table 13.7, the strength of a 2×8 can be compared to a 2×10 by comparing 52.6 to 85.6. The 2×10 can safely support 85.6/52.6 or 1.6 times as great a load as the 2×8. In terms of stiffness, the 2×10 is 791.5/381.1 or 2.1 times as stiff as the 2×8. This means it will deflect 1.0/2.1 or only 48% as much under a given load. Such comparisons assume that the span and allowable stress values for the sizes being compared are the same. The large increases in strength and stiffness often obtained by merely increasing the size of structural members by one increment should be understood.

Table 13.7. *Factors to compare bending strength and stiffness of different lumber sizes*

Nominal size	Depth	Depth squared	Depth cubed
	(*in.*)	(*in.*^{2})	(*in.*^{3})
2×4	3.5	12.3	42.9
2×6	5.5	30.3	166.4
2×8	7.25	52.6	381.1
2×10	9.25	85.6	791.5
2×12	11.25	126.6	1423.8

REVIEW

A. Terms to define or explain:

1. Board foot
2. Hem-Fir
3. Southern yellow pine (or southern pine)
4. Log rules
5. Ring debarker
6. Rossing head debarker
7. Chipper canter
8. Scragg mill
9. Band headsaw
10. Log scanner
11. Overrun
12. Lumber recovery factor
13. Gang saw
14. National Hardwood Lumber Association
15. Standard cord
16. Doyle rule
17. Scribner rule
18. Weight scaling
19. Red oak lumber
20. S-Dry
21. MC 15
22. Construction grade
23. FAS
24. No. 3A Common
25. Cuttings
26. Select Structural
27. Boards
28. Timbers
29. Required cuttings (hardwood grades)
30. Stiffness
31. Nominal size
32. Matcher
33. Planer mill
34. Sticker
35. MSR lumber

B. Questions or concepts to explain:

1. The major processing steps in the manufacturing of lumber.
2. Reasons for debarking logs prior to processing.
3. Types of headsaws and characteristics of each.
4. Basis of grading hardwood lumber as compared to softwood lumber.
5. Procedure for scaling logs.
6. Relationship between three major log rules.
7. The difference between overrun and lumber recover factor.
8. The difference between tree names and lumber species group names.
9. How board footage is calculated for hardwood and softwood lumber.
10. The use of scanners and computers for control systems.
11. The thickness categories of softwood dimension.
12. The moisture content standards for hardwood and softwood lumber.
13. The relationship between the size of a wood beam and its strength and stiffness.
14. Methods of grading softwood lumber.

REFERENCES AND SUPPLEMENTAL READING

American Lumber Standards Committee. 1994. American softwood lumber standard. Vol. Prod. Std. 20–94. ALSC.

Aune, J.E., and Lefevre, E. 1974. Chipping headrigs: Do they achieve maximum recovery? Can. For. Ind. 94(8):70.

Baldwin, R.F. 1984. Operations Management in the Forest Products Industry. San Francisco: Miller Freeman.

Barrett, J.D., and Kellogg, R.M. 1991. Bending strength and stiffness of second-growth Douglas-fir dimension lumber. For. Prod. J. 41(10): 35–43.

Christoforo, J.C.; Bush, R.J.; and Luppold, W.G. 1994. A profile of the U.S. pallet and container industry. For. Prod. J. 44(2):9–14.

Clapp, V.W. 1982. Lumber recovery: How does your mill rate? For. Ind. 109(3): 26–27.

Cohen, D.H., and Sinclair, S.A. 1990. The adoption of new technologies: Impact on performance of producers of softwood lumber and structural panels. For. Prod. J. 40(11/12):67–73.

Denig, J. 1993. Small Sawmill Handbook. San Francisco: Miller Freeman.

Forbes, C.L., Sinclair, S.A., and Luppold, W.G. 1993. Wood material use in the U.S. furniture industry: 1990 to 1992. For. Prod. J. 43(7/8)59–65.

Hallock, H. 1973. Best opening face for second growth timber. Modern Sawmill Techniques, Vol. 1. San Francisco: Miller Freeman.

Hallock, H., and Lewis, D.W. 1974. Best opening face for southern pine. Modern Sawmill Techniques. Vol. 2. San Francisco: Miller Freeman.

Luppold, W.G., and Dempsey, G.P. 1994. Factors affecting regional changes in hardwood lumber production. For. Prod. J. 44(6):8–14.

McKeever, D.B. and Anderson, R.G. 1992. Timber products used to build U.S. single family houses in 1988. For. Prod. J. 42(4):11-18.

McKeever, D.B., and Phelps, R.B. 1994. Wood products used in new single-family houses: 1950 to 1992. For. Prod. J. 44(11/12):66–74.

Meyer, C.J., Michael, J.H., Sinclair, S.A., and Luppold, W.G. 1992. Wood material use in the U.S. wood furniture industry. For. Prod. J. 42(5):28–30.

Page, R., and Bois, P. 1961. Buying and selling southern yellow pine sawlogs by weight. Ga. For. Res. Counc. Rep. 7.

Peak, M.D., Burkart, L.F., and Weldon, D. 1990. Comparison of grade, yield and mechanical properties of lumber from fast-grown and slow-grown slash pine. For. Prod. J. 40(1):11–14.

Phelps, J.E., and D.R. McCurdy. 1993. Raiload tie production in the United States. For. Prod J. 43(3):15–18.

_____. 1993. Sawmill production in the United States—1991. For. Prod. J. 43(3):19–21.

Steele, P.H., and Risbrudt, C.D. 1985. Efficiency of sawmills in the southern United States in relation to capacity. For. Prod. J. 35(7/8):51–56.

Wade, M.W.; Bullard, S.H.; Steele; P.H. and Araman, P.A. 1992. Estimating hardwood sawmill conversion efficiency based on sawing machine and log characteristics. For. Prod. J. 1992. 42(11/12):21–26.

Wagner, F.G.; Steele, P.H., Kumar L.; and Butkovic, D. 1991. Computer grading of southern pine lumber. For. Prod. J. 41(2):27–29.

Williams, D.L., and Hopkins, W.C. 1968. Conversion factors for southern pine products. La. State Univ. Agric Exp. Sta. Bull. 626.

Williston, E.M. 1976. Lumber Manufacturing: The Design and Operation of Sawmills and Planer Mills. San Francisco: Miller Freeman.

———. 1979. State of the art in lumber manufacturing. For. Prod. J. 29(10):45–49.

_____. 1985. Computer Control Systems for Log Processing and Lumber Manufacture. San Francisco: Miller Freeman.

_____. 1981. Small Log Sawmills. San Francisco: Miller Freeman.

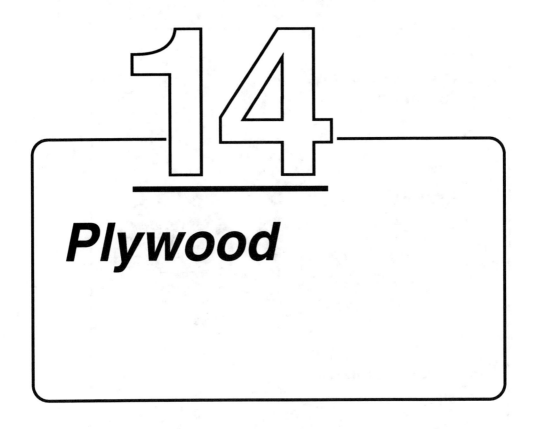

14

Plywood

■ **PLYWOOD** is a panel product of wood veneers glued together so that the grain direction of some veneers run at right angles and others parallel to the long axis of the panel. In most types of plywood, the grain of every other layer is laid parallel to the first. Therefore, to maintain a balance from one side of the panel to the other, an uneven number of veneers is used. Some plywood, however, is produced with an even number of veneers, an example being softwood plywood made up of four or six *plies* (veneers) with two of the veneers laid parallel to form a thick center core. The variety of panel types is illustrated in Figure 14.1.

Plywood takes advantage of the properties of wood in several ways. First, since wood is strongest along the grain, the alternating layers achieve good strength properties in both directions. Since plywood is made from veneer, it lends itself to large panels, typically 4 × 8 ft in North America. Plywood is strongest in the 8-ft direction, the direction of face grain. The alternating veneer layers provide resistance to dimensional change in both dimensions of the panel.

Plywood can be differentiated by whether it is for structural or decorative use. Structural plywood is manufactured primarily from softwood species. Major applications of structural plywood are residential and commercial construction and industrial markets such as pallets, crates, and concrete forms. Decorative plywood generally uses hardwood face veneers and interior resin types. These panels are intended for applications such as wall paneling and furniture manufacture.

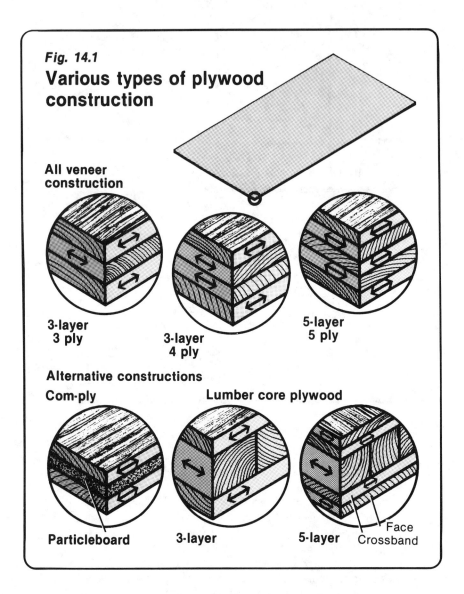

Fig. 14.1

Various types of plywood construction

All veneer construction

3-layer 3 ply

3-layer 4 ply

5-layer 5 ply

Alternative constructions

Com-ply

Lumber core plywood

Particleboard

3-layer

5-layer

Face
Crossband

Although the plywood industry dates back only to about 1905, the product from which plywood is made, *veneer,* has an ancient history. The Egyptians circa 1500 B.C. are credited with producing veneer to decorate furniture. The ancient Greeks and Romans also developed means of cutting veneer. Plywood did not, however, become a major industry until the 1930s. The adoption of the hot press from Europe and the development of synthetic heat-curing resin adhesives provided the technological advances needed to make mass-produced plywood possible.

Most of the technology and production equipment for the softwood plywood industry was developed in the United States. World War II greatly accelerated the technology for efficiently manufacturing phenolic resin–bonded exterior plywood, which was used extensively for small naval craft including the famous PT boats. During the 1960s and 1970s the technology for efficiently cutting softwood veneer from small logs was developed, making possible the use of a much greater portion of the U.S. softwood resource. Resource constraints in the 1980s led to further innovation to increase veneer yields.

The production of plywood at the 137 plants in the United States currently exceeds 30 billion ft². This is enough plywood to form a continuous layer ⅜ in. thick and ½ mile wide all the way from New York City to Los Angeles. Over 95% of this plywood is softwood produced primarily in the South and on the West Coast. The softwood plywood industry originally developed on the West Coast and was concentrated there for several decades because of the availability of large high-quality peeler logs, primarily Douglas-fir. In the 1960s developments in resin technology and manufacturing equipment made it possible to manufacture plywood from relatively small southern pine logs, and the industry began to shift to the South. Production from that region has exceeded production from the West since 1980. Decorative hardwood plywood production is scattered throughout the eastern half of the United States but the South has the major concentration.

The manufacturing processes for production of structural and decorative plywood differ significantly. Although the process of *rotary cutting* the veneer and hot pressing the panels is similar in principle, the equipment developed to produce structural plywood tends to be more automated with less labor input per unit of output, the emphasis being on high rates of production. The decorative plywood industry is very diverse, from small plants that produce custom-ordered plywood for specific architectural applications to large high-capacity plants producing thin panels in production lines similar to those in the structural plywood industry.

Decorative hardwood veneer is used to manufacture plywood for paneling, industrial parts, furniture, cabinets, and case goods. Hardwood veneer is imported from South America, Asia, and Africa, but most hardwood plywood produced in the United States is from domestically produced veneer. A limited amount of hardwood veneer, primarily gum and poplar, is used in structural plywood. Most decorative plywood in the United States is manufactured according to an American National Standards Institute and Hardwood Plywood and Veneer Association Standard ANSI/HPVA HP-1-1994.

Most structural plywood produced in the United States is manufactured to meet the requirements of the U.S. Product Standard PS1-83 or under a performance standard for structural-use panels APA PRP-108 written by APA—the Engineered Wood Association (formerly the American Plywood Association). The purpose of the performance standard is to allow a wider variety of panel technologies by emphasis on the requirements the panel must meet in the application for which it is intended. The principle of APA's Performance Standard has been widely adopted and has evolved into national consensus standards in the United States (U.S. Product Standard PS2-92) and in Canada (CSA 0325).

The major use of structural plywood is for construction of light-frame structures, single-family homes, apartments, and commercial buildings. Roof and wall sheathing, subfloors, underlayment, and siding are the most-common applications. About 10 billion ft² (⅜-in. basis) of structural panels were used in 1992 for the construction of single-family homes (McKeever and Phelps 1994). Note that softwood plywood statistics are always given on a ⅜-in. basis; that is, all thicknesses are converted to an equivalent volume of ⅜-in. panels.

Plywood has become a significant building component because of its unique characteristics that are ideally suited for construction. It is light in weight yet strong. It is a sheet material allowing large areas of a roof or floor to be covered by handling only a few pieces. It can easily be cut to size and nailed, or nailed and glued. It has very high racking strength making it ideally suited for use in manufactured housing.

As sheathing or subflooring, plywood has many advantages over lumber. Since veneer grain runs in both directions, a strip of plywood between two supports will not carry more load than a piece of lumber of the same width and thickness. Plywood, however, has bending strength in both directions. For the most efficient use of plywood in general construction, it should be laid perpendicular to the joists or rafters. Some applications such as wall sheathing plywood can be applied parallel to the studs (wall framing). Another advantage of plywood is its rigid rectangular shape (high racking strength), which makes it almost impossible to deform by a force in the plane of the panel. Figure 14.2 shows a home of light-frame construction and plywood sheathing hit heavily by an earthquake in Anchorage, Alaska, in 1966. The home did not collapse but retained its shape as a rectangular solid because of the racking strength of the plywood nailed to the lumber framing.

Structural panels produced from large flakes called strands rather than veneers are becoming widely used for many of the same purposes as structural plywood. These boards, such as *oriented strandboard* (OSB), now make up about one-fourth of the structural panels used in single-family homes. The properties and use of these products are discussed in Chapter 15. The technology for the manufacture of these panels is very similar to that for particleboard, also covered in Chapter 15.

(Courtesy U.S. Forest Products Laboratory)

Fig. 14.2
A plywood-sheathed home that remained structurally whole during the Alaskan earthquake of 1964.

Species used for manufacture of structural plywood ■

Southern yellow pine (generally termed southern pine in the trade) and Douglas-fir are the two main species used for the manufacture of structural plywood in the United States. However, all major softwoods on the West Coast including the true firs, western hemlock, and western pines are also utilized. Structural plywood is not sold by species name. Instead, it is classified by its intended structural application such as sheathing, siding, concrete form, or marine-grade plywood. In the case of plywood intended for construction, the panels are graded by a *span rating,* which indicates the maximum spacing between framing supports. Other panels are classified by a species group that corresponds to the species of the face and back veneers. The grouping of species according to PS1-83 is shown in Table 14.1.

Note that many hardwood species—both domestic and foreign—are listed in Table 14.1. When used to manufacture plywood according to PS1-83, these products are classified as structural plywood. Apitong and keruing are a group of species from the genus *Dipterocarpus* originating in the Philippines, Malaysia, and Indonesia. *Lauan* is a group of species once marketed as Philippine mahogany, a misnomer since they are not true mahoganies. *Meranti* refers to many of the same species as lauan but originating in Malaysia or Indonesia rather than in the Philippines.

Most of the major hardwood species or species groups, e.g., red oak, white oak, hard maple, and hickory, are used to some extent in the United States for decorative hardwood plywood manufacture. The higher-grade veneer from the fine hardwoods are used primarily for their decorative and aesthetic value. In ad-

Table 14.1.   Grouping of species for structural plywood

Group 1	Group 2	Group 3	Group 4	Group 5
Apitong	Cedar, Port	Alder, red	Aspen	Basswood
Beech, American	Orford	Birch, paper	Bigtooth	Poplar,
Birch	Douglas-fir No. 2*	Cedar, Alaska	Quaking	balsam
Sweet	Fir	Fir, subalpine	Cativo	
Yellow	Balsam	Hemlock, eastern	Cedar	
Douglas-fir No. 1*	California red	Maple, bigleaf	Incense	
Keruing	Grand	Pine	Western red	
Larch, western	Noble	Jack	Cottonwood	
Maple, sugar	Pacific silver	Lodgepole	Eastern	
Pine	White	Ponderosa	Black (west-	
Caribbean	Hemlock, western	Spruce	ern poplar)	
Ocote	Lauan	Redwood	Pine	
Pine, southern	Maple, black	Spruce	Eastern white	
Loblolly	Meranti, red	Engelmann	Sugar	
Longleaf	Pine	White		
Shortleaf	Pond			
Slash	Red			
Tanoak	Virginia			
	Western white			
	Spruce			
	Black			
	Red			
	Sitka			
	Sweetgum			
	Tamarack			
	Yellow poplar			

Source: APA (1985a).

*Douglas-fir from trees grown in the states of Washington, Oregon, California, Idaho, Montana, Wyoming, and the Canadian provinces of Alberta and British Columbia shall be classed as Douglas-fir No. 1. Douglas-fir from trees grown in the states of Nevada, Utah, Colorado, Arizona, and New Mexico shall be classed as Douglas-fir No. 2.

dition to wood grown domestically, logs and veneer are imported for hardwood plywood manufacture. The lower-density hardwoods, gums, poplar, cottonwood, and aspen, are often used for backs and core of plywood that are faced with more-expensive species. These species are still sometimes used in containers.

Basic steps in plywood manufacture ■

Logs delivered to a plywood plant are first debarked and then cut to the length required for the plywood to be produced. A length of 100 in. is often used for manufacture of 8-ft plywood. The sections cut from the logs for cutting on the lathe are referred to as *blocks,* the smaller diameters as *bolts*.

HEATING THE BLOCKS. Almost all hardwood and most softwood blocks are heated prior to cutting veneer. Heating softens the wood and knots, requiring less power to cut and resulting in smoother veneer. Some of the dense hardwoods must be heated to produce satisfactory veneer. Although some softwoods can be satisfactorily cut when cold, there are several definite advantages to heating the blocks. Thus, heating has become a standard practice. Heated blocks result in a higher yield of veneer and in a higher grade of veneer. As the cost of logs has risen, this has become a very important advantage. Also, the amount of resin required to obtain an adequate bond is reduced because of the smoother veneer surface. The ribbon of veneer coming from the lathe has less breakage when the veneer is hot, reducing the labor cost in handling.

A variety of methods are used to heat the logs. Steaming, soaking in hot water, spraying with hot water, or combinations of these methods are all used in various situations to obtain the increased wood temperature required. Dense hardwoods are usually heated by soaking at temperatures of up to 200°F (93°C). The objective is to heat the log to a suitable temperature as deeply into the log as veneer will be cut.

Mills develop their heating schedules based upon trial and error or by measuring the log surface temperature with an optical pyrometer as the block is peeled (as veneer is cut). The heating time required depends upon the density of the wood, diameter of the block, and the temperature required for a satisfactory cut. Fleischer (1965) showed that the higher the wood density the higher the temperature needed to obtain the surface quality expected. For example, basswood may cut well at 60°F (16°C) but white oak requires about 200°F (93°C).

CUTTING VENEER. There are two common methods of cutting veneer: (1) peeling on a *lathe (rotary cutting)* and (2) slicing. Almost all structural and a great deal of decorative veneer is produced on a lathe. Lathes utilize most of the block, leaving only the center core, and are capable of high production rates. Slicing involves greater raw material loss and is a relatively labor-intensive process. The block of wood cut from the log and placed on the slicer is called a *flitch.* Slicing is used for producing decorative veneers from high-quality hardwoods where particular grain patterns are desired. By orienting the flitch properly, it is possible to produce veneer with the grain pattern of flat-sawn, quarter-sawn or mixed-grain lumber.

The cutting action on a lathe and on a slicer are shown in Figure 14.3. In either case the wood is forced under a pressure bar that compresses the wood slightly as it hits the cutting edge of the knife. On the lathe the pressure bar and knife assembly move forward continuously as the block is turned. On the *slicer*

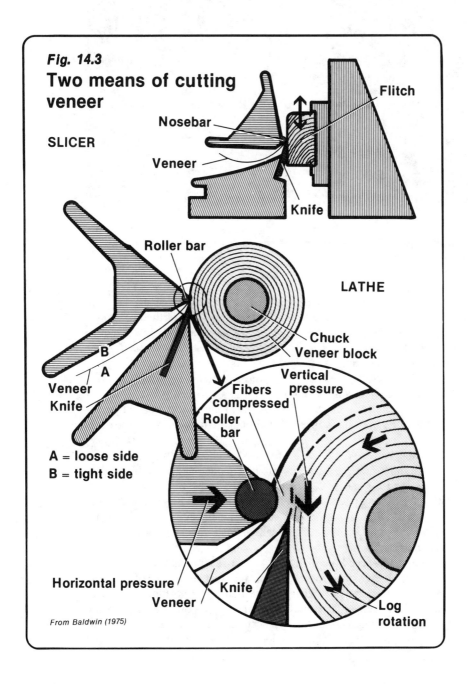

Fig. 14.3

Two means of cutting veneer

SLICER

Nosebar

Veneer

Flitch

Knife

Roller bar

LATHE

Chuck

Veneer block

B

A

Veneer

Knife

A = loose side
B = tight side

Vertical pressure

Fibers compressed

Roller bar

Horizontal pressure

Knife

Veneer

Log rotation

From Baldwin (1975)

(Courtesy Coe Manufacturing Co.)

Fig. 14.4
A small-log veneer lathe and one of many types of lathe chargers.

the knife cuts in one direction, returns, and then advances the distance required for the next cut. For either type of cutting, careful adjustment of the knife angle and the horizontal and vertical gap between the pressure bar and the knife edge is necessary to obtain the proper peel. Proper pressure must be developed by the pressure bar to reduce checking of the veneer as it is severed from the log and to minimize surface roughness. The use of a powered roller on the tip of the *pressure bar* increases veneer quality. The horizontal gap between the pressure bar and the knife is set slightly less than the thickness of the veneer to be cut to allow for veneer compression. The veneer springs back in thickness once the cut is made.

The side of the veneer next to the knife edge is called the loose side. Close examination will show hairline fractures running parallel to the grain, called *lathe checks*. If a sanded grade of plywood is painted and subjected to weathering, these lathe checks may open and appear as checks in the finish. For this reason, plywood to be used as siding or for other exterior finish is generally manufactured to have a rough-textured surface where such checks only add to the textured appearance.

The key to the high-speed production of veneer in a modern plywood plant is a computer-controlled scanner-operated *charger* that automatically centers each block and then quickly loads (charges) the lathe. The positioning devices are called *optimizers*. A veneer lathe and one of many types of lathe chargers are shown in Figure 14.4. Equipment of this type can charge the lathe with a small-diameter block, round the block, peel the block down to a 4- to 5-in. core, and discharge the core in about 10 sec. As soon as the core is discharged, the charger has a bolt ready for the next cycle. Less highly automated means of charging are used in structural plywood mills still cutting large blocks and in many decorative veneer plants.

An innovative peeling method was introduced in the late 1980s. A "spindle-less" lathe using a series of rollers rather than end chucks supports the veneer log during peeling. This allows peeling down to cores of 2 in. or less in diameter. The increased veneer yield is especially important to mills that must rely on small-diameter logs.

VENEER STORAGE AND CLIPPING. In high-speed mills the green ribbon of veneer must be handled gently and rapidly as it comes from the lathe. A series of trays is generally used at structural plywood mills to handle the ribbon of veneer, which is peeled at a rate of 300 to 800 lineal ft/min. The trays are long enough, about 120 ft, to handle the veneer that comes from a 15-in. block. Figure 14.5 shows a *tray storage* system located between the lathe and the clipper. In decorative veneer mills the green veneer is often wound onto a roll and then moved to the clippers. This is called a *reel storage* system. Other hardwood mills use directly coupled conveyors between the lathe and the clipper, but this requires that the clipper speed be as fast as the lathe.

(Courtesy Coe Manufacturing Co.)

Fig. 14.5
A typical veneer tray storage system as seen looking back toward the lathe. The veneer being discharged is moving to the clipper.

Clippers are high-speed knives that chop the veneer ribbons to usable widths. In structural plywood mills, and some decorative plywood mills, lower-grade veneer is clipped automatically at speeds up to 1500 lineal ft/min. These clippers cut the veneer to a width of about 54 in. to provide allowance for trimming the final 48-in.-panel width. Open flaws in the ribbon are detected by the clipper and narrow pieces are cut. Higher-grade veneer, both hardwood and softwood, may be clipped by an operator to obtain optimum yield.

VENEER DRYING. The fundamentals of drying were outlined in Chapter 8. Two types of dryers are used in structural veneer mills: roller-restraint dryers heated by forced air and platen dryers heated by steam (Sellers 1985). The operation of one type of drier is illustrated in Figure 14.6 showing how hot air at speeds up to 4000 ft/min is forced to impinge on the veneer. This removes the boundary layer of moist air that acts as an insulator in dryers with low-velocity air circulation. With some species, the use of high temperature over 400°F (204°C) is avoided due to adverse affects upon gluing.

One problem encountered in veneer drying is the generation of emissions that contain hydrocarbons, some of which can produce a blue haze in the atmosphere. The opacity of these emissions is controlled by the Environmental Pro-

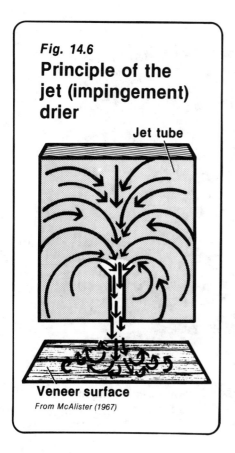

Fig. 14.6
Principle of the jet (impingement) drier

Jet tube

Veneer surface
From McAlister (1967)

tection Agency and local authorities. Baldwin (1975) reported that Douglas-fir and ponderosa pine are the western species producing the greatest opacity under any given drying condition. Softwoods with lower resin contents create less of a problem. Drying temperatures over about 400°F (204°C) produce the greatest emission problem.

LAY-UP AND PRESSING. The process of applying adhesives to the veneers, assembling veneers into a panel, and moving the panels in and out of the press are often the most labor-intensive steps in manufacture. Veneer is highly variable in width, length, and quality, which makes it difficult to handle with automated systems. However, semiautomated systems developed in the 1970s have greatly improved this part of the process.

The application of the adhesive to the veneer is commonly done with a spray or curtain-coater. Both of these methods are well suited to the more-automated lay-up systems now in wide use. In these systems the veneer travels on a belt under the spray or curtain. A *curtain-coater* consists essentially of a box with a slot in the bottom through which adhesive flows in a continuous sheet or curtain. An older method, which uses roller coaters that require the veneer be fed between grooved rubber rollers to apply the glue by contact, is still in use.

Two other methods of application, a foamed resin extrusion and a liquid extrusion, have been successful. These systems lay continuous beads of resin on the veneer, and more coverage with the same amount of glue is reported. Also, the adhesives used contain less water so shorter press times are possible.

The assembly of veneers into plywood panels can be mechanized in larger plants producing standard-size panels. Systems that are nearly automatic are widely used, but the variability in size of veneer makes some manual input necessary. For example, the full-size faces of the panel may be handled by machine, but the narrower strips used to make up the core may be handled manually. Systems are available to connect the strips of veneer used for the core by pressing parallel strings of fiberglass coated with hot-melt adhesive at right angles to the strips. The sheet that is created can then be handled by machine rather than manually. Many different semiautomated lay-up systems are now in use.

Most structural plywood plants prepress the loads of laid-up panels prior to final pressing in the hot press. This is done in a cold press at low pressure. The purpose is to allow the wet adhesive to tack the veneer layers together. This permits easier loading of the hot press and reduces shifting of the veneer, which can result in a down-graded panel.

Pressing of the panels to cure the glueline is done in multiopening presses of the type shown in Figure 14.7. Such presses can produce 20 to 40 4-x-8 ft panels with each press cycle, which may take 2 to 7 min. The purpose of the press is twofold: to bring the layers of veneer tightly together and to heat the resin adhesive to the temperature required for polymerization. The *phenol-formaldehyde resins* used in most structural plywood manufacture typically require temperatures of about 240°F (155°C) in the innermost glueline for approximately 90 sec to cure properly. Resin systems must be carefully tailored to the specific conditions of the plant.

(Courtesy Superior Production Machines, Inc.)

Fig. 14.7
Two 24-opening 4 × 8 ft plywood hot presses. The press openings
are loaded by an elevator seen in front of one of the presses.

The pressing conditions must be designed for adequate pressure to bring the veneer surfaces tightly together without overcompressing the wood. The better the lathe produces smooth veneer of uniform thickness, the less the pressure required. Some mills reduce the pressure during the press cycle to eliminate unnecessary compressing of the plywood. Since the plywood must meet industry standards for thickness, overcompression must be avoided. Pressures used in the press cycles vary from about 110 psi for low-density woods to 200 psi for dense species.

Adhesives ∎

Thermosetting synthetic resins are used almost exclusively for the manufacture of plywood in North America. Phenol-formaldehyde is the primary adhesive type in the structural plywood industry, while urea-formaldehyde resins are used for most decorative plywood. The phenol-formaldehyde resins can form waterproof bonds important to the use of structural panels. Urea-formaldehyde has the advantage for decorative-type plywoods of being less expensive than phenol, about one-half the cost, and being light in color, thus avoiding discoloration of thin decorative veneers. The urea resin does not, however, provide a waterproof bond. The basic components of these resins are formaldehyde derived from methanol, urea, and phenol.

In North America there has been some use of lignin derived from pulping to replace part of the phenol in phenol-formaldehyde resin. Lignosulfonate lignins have been used successfully to replace up to 35% of the resin solids in some adhesives. In 1989 five North American companies were manufacturing lignin-modified resin adhesives using lignosulfonates, and seven were blending lignosulfonates with their thermosetting resins (Sellers 1990). Lignosulfonates are the by-products of the sulfite pulping process. Kraft lignins refined from the black liquor of the kraft pulping process can be used in a similar way but are more expensive to refine than the lignosulfonates. Improvements in these and other technologies may make it possible to use abundant naturally produced materials to reduce the dependence of the wood panel industry on petrochemical resin systems.

The adhesives used in the plywood industry are not pure resins but are mixes of resin with fillers and extenders. *Extenders* are substances with some adhesive value added to reduce the amount of primary binder needed, while *fillers* are additives with little adhesive value in themselves. One extender often used is Furafil, a lignocellulose by-product of furfuryl alcohol production. Fine flour produced from wood, bark, and nutshells is also used. Starch and animal blood are sometimes used to modify the viscosity, control the penetration of the adhesive into the veneer, and control the tack or stickiness.

One adhesive mix for southern pine plywood is shown in Table 14.2. The purpose of caustic soda is to aid in the dispersion of the extender. The rate at which this adhesive is applied to the veneer is in the range of 35 to 45 lb of adhesive/1000 ft^2 of single glueline. Thus, 1000 ft^2 of three-ply plywood (two gluelines) requires 79 to 90 lb of adhesive mix. This is referred to as a spread of 70–90 lb MDGL (1000 ft^2 of double glueline).

Table 14.2. An adhesive mix for southern pine plywood

Component	Weight
	(*kg*)
Phenol-formaldehyde resin (42% solids)	2883
Water	726
Furafil	386
Wheat flour	204
Caustic soda	136
Total mix	4335
Total resin	2883

Source: Sellers (1985).

Factors affecting the efficiency of plywood production ■

In the early years of the softwood (structural) plywood industry in the Pacific Northwest, production depended upon a supply of large high-quality logs. Baldwin (1975) reported that some Douglas-fir mills in the 1920s did not accept logs less than 5½ ft in diameter or with any end defects. Such logs are hard to even imagine today. Many mills in the South are now utilizing southern pine logs averaging 10 to 12 in. in diameter. It would take 44 of these bolts to equal the volume of one 5½-ft block.

Fortunately, as the size of available timber decreased, the technology for producing veneer from small logs developed. Optimizing lathe chargers and high-speed lathes capable of peeling to 3½-in. or smaller cores make it currently possible to utilize much more of this forest resource. In many situations the best logs are not being used for plywood as was the case previously. The sheathing grades (unsanded) of softwood plywood are often produced from logs of intermediate grade and size, while the best logs are used for poles, piling, and lumber production. Mills producing sanded grades of softwood plywood also need to procure these high-quality logs whenever possible.

There are some areas of the world where it is still possible to obtain logs of relatively large size. The supply of such material is limited, however, and production of plywood from large logs seems certain to continue its decline. Figure 14.8 contrasts the size of logs in a log pond at a plywood plant in the Philippines with those in the log yard of a southern pine mill.

Regardless of size, the quality of veneer logs is determined by the absence of knots or other surface defects, by straightness and roundness, and by the absence of defects on the ends. Smaller logs are usually not sold to plywood plants by log grade, the purchase price being established by volume or weight. Large high-quality veneer logs, particularly hardwoods, may be graded individually and sold by log grade. Log grades are usually established based upon straightness, freedom from rot or soft centers (blocks that cannot be chucked), and how many of the four sides are free from knots or other defects.

The quality of logs entering a mill is important as it controls the quality and yield of veneer and also the number of blocks that prove to be defective once in the lathe. Such blocks can seriously reduce the rate of production. The yield of veneer varies with log diameter, core diameter, and the efficiency with which the veneer is clipped and utilized. It is not unusual to encounter yields of less than 50%, i.e., less than half the block volume is converted to usable veneer volume. Table 14.3 shows how the core and block diameters affect the yield from southern pine veneer blocks. The yield in this table is expressed as square feet of ⅜-in. plywood. The student should convert these values to percentage yields, that is, veneer volume as a percent of block volume. Note that in large blocks (18 in.), the increased veneer obtained by reducing the core diameter from 5 to 4 in. is insignificant (3% increase) but if 8-in. blocks were being peeled, the difference would be very important (21% increase).

Table 14.3. *Relationship between block diameter, core diameter, and volume of veneer produced*

Block diameter	Veneer yield*		
	Core diameter		
	3 in.	4 in.	5 in.
(*in.*)	(*ft²*)		
8	46	40	33
10	77	71	63
12	114	108	100
14	157	151	144
16	208	202	194
18	264	259	251

Source: Williams and Hopkins (1968).
* ⅜-in. basis, i.e., 3 ft² of ⅛-in. veneer equals 1 ft² ⅜-in. basis.

Fig. 14.8
Contrast in the size of veneer logs. *(above)* Lauan blocks being floated to a veneer mill in the Philippines. *(below)* Southern pine logs to be sorted for use either in a chipper-canter headrig or a veneer lathe.

Phillips et al. (1980) reported from a study of southern pine that as little as a 1 in. of sweep in an 8-in. block reduced the veneer yield by 44%. Although not as serious in larger blocks, a 2-in. sweep in an 18-in. block (a large diameter in most regions) would reduce the volume of veneer by 23%.

Mills normally monitor their yield on the basis of the particular log-measuring system they use. Thus, they may express yield in terms of 1000 ft^2 of ⅜-in. plywood produced per 1000 bd ft (MBF) of logs scaled by the Doyle or Scribner log rule or as determined by conversion from a weight scale. In some areas of the South, a factor of 5350 lb/cord is used to convert from weight to an approximate volume. The yield of a plant may be expressed in any of these units. For example, a plant may obtain an average yield of 2400 ft^2 of ⅜-in. plywood per MBF Scribner. Mills that measure small veneer logs on the Scribner log rule often consider yields of over 3000 ft^2/MBF to be a good recovery. This is referred to as a *recovery factor* of 3.

Today the expanding use of scanners that measure actual block diameter, and thus volume, is making it possible to avoid the problems associated with the use of log rules and to monitor the true yield of their operation. The next generation of forest products engineers and managers may convert the industry to a uniform and consistent system of measuring the efficiency of their mills. The present systems of measuring by cords, Doyle, Scribner, International, or weight conversions, are confusing to many, not just the new professional in the field.

Plywood selection and use ■

There are four primary considerations when selecting plywood for a specific use: (1) durability of the glueline needed to avoid delamination; (2) strength requirements for panels to be used structurally; (3) quality needed on the faces to accomplish the appearance desired; (4) special requirements such as fire or decay resistance.

Decorative plywood is, of course, selected based upon appearance criteria. The species of the face veneers and the grain pattern as determined by the way the veneer was cut are the major factors. Flat- or quarter-sawn grain patterns are available in the more-expensive plywoods with faces of sliced veneer. In less-expensive plywood with rotary-cut faces, the grain pattern will be highly variable, but different species provide a variety of grain effects. Veneer from the ring-porous species provides a more-distinct pattern, particularly when rotary cut. The color desired in the finished panel is also important when selecting species. Although it is possible to produce a light finish on the darker woods, e.g., walnut, cherry, mahogany, it would be easier to start with a lighter-colored species.

Most decorative plywood is made with a nonwaterproof adhesive so if the panel is to be used where it will be subjected to liquid water, special precautions need be taken. Decorative plywood with a waterproof glueline can be obtained in situations where the additional cost is justified and the quantities involved are adequate. Decorative plywood is designated *Type 1* or *Technical* if it has a waterproof glueline, *Type 2* if it is moisture resistant, and *Type 3* if even less resistant to water. Means of testing to see that the glueline meets these requirements are spelled out in the American National Standard for Hardwood and Decorative Plywood ANSI/HPVA HP-1-1994.

For structural plywood, the durability of the glueline is specified as being either *Exterior* or *Exposure 1*. These two designations indicate not only the durability of the glueline but also the grade of veneers that must be used in laying up the panel. For example, D grade veneers are not used in an Exterior panel. All structural plywood produced today in the United States has an exterior glueline regardless of whether it is classified as Exterior or Exposure 1.

Structural plywood with the Exterior durability classification is intended for applications that may involve permanent exposure to weathering . Such applications include siding and concrete forming. Structural plywood with the Exposure 1 durability classification is intended for uses that may involve temporary exposure to weathering such as during a construction delay. However, Exposure 1 panels should ultimately be protected from permanent exposure to weather.

Panel grades are generally identified in terms of the veneer grades of the two surfaces, e.g., A-B or C-D, or by the an indication of the intended use, e.g., Underlayment or Rated Sheathing. The veneer grades define both the appearance of the growth characteristics (knots and holes) and the amount of veneer repair that may be made. The main grades of veneer and the characteristics are outlined in Table 14.4.

Table 14.4.   Four main grades of softwood veneer

Grade	Description and characteristics
A	Smooth, paintable. Not more than 18 neatly made repairs permitted—synthetic, boat, sled, or router type and parallel to grain. May be used for natural finish in less demanding applications.
B	Solid surface. Shims, various synthetic or wood patches or plugs and tight knots to 1 in. across grain permitted. Some minor splits permitted.
C	Tight knots to 1½ in. Knotholes to 1 in. across grain and some to 1½ in. if total width of knots and knotholes is within specified limits. Synthetic or wood repairs. Discoloration and sanding defects that do not impair strength permitted. Limited splits allowed. Stitching permitted.
D	Knots and knotholes to 2½ in. width across grain and ½ in. larger within specified limits. Limited splits permitted. Stitching permitted. Limited to interior grades of plywood.

Source: APA (1985a).

There is a distinct difference between the grades of sanded structural plywood and the unsanded sheathing/structural panels. The sanded grades are graded by the veneer grades of the faces; thus, one can select a panel to be painted with one side showing by selecting A-C, A-B, B-C, or B-D, depending upon the quality of face needed. If the panel is to be exposed to view on both sides, one would select A-A, A-B, or B-B.

The major use of the unsanded grades of softwood plywood is for subfloors and roof and wall sheathing. The grades of C-C and C-D are commonly used in these applications. *Sturd-I-floor* is a touch-sanded grade suitable as a combination subfloor and underlayment. These panels are designated by the spans over which they can be used as roof sheathing and as subflooring in residential construction, e.g., ¹⁹⁄₃₂ or ³²⁄₁₆. A ³²⁄₁₆ panel can be used as roof sheathing to span rafters up to 32 in. apart or as subfloor over joists with 16-in. spacing. Typical registered grade stamps of APA are shown in Figure 14.9. In addition to the span rating, the stamps indicate the durability classification, the thickness of the panel, the mill number (000 is shown), and the product standard. Only APA member mills participating in their quality inspection and testing program can use these stamps. Other grading agencies have their own grade stamps and quality verification programs.

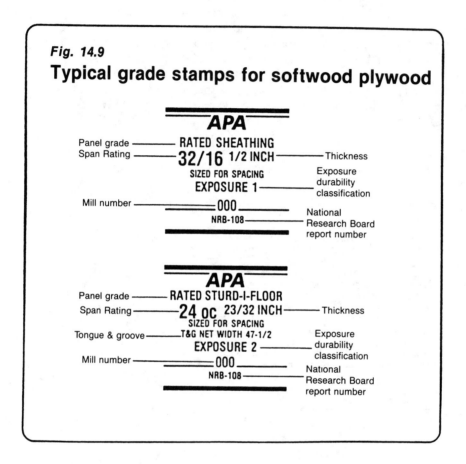

Fig. 14.9
Typical grade stamps for softwood plywood

Many special types of plywood are manufactured to provide the surface properties needed for siding, highway signs, painted cabinets, and commercial case goods. Two approaches are used to overcome surface checking of plywood exposed to exterior conditions. One method is to *overlay* the plywood with a layer of medium- or high-density resin-impregnated wood fiber sheets. These wood fiber overlays hold paint well and provide a check-free base. The second approach is to provide a rough or textured surface that will not be downgraded by the presence of checks. These rough, natural surfaces are very receptive to stains and are popular as exterior siding. Figure 14.10 shows some of the types of softwood plywood surfaces that are manufactured.

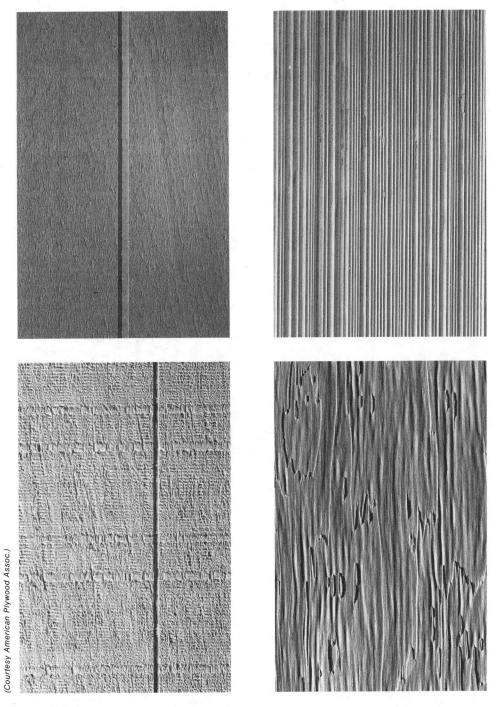

Fig. 14.10
Some of the wide variety of textures and patterns produced for decorative softwood plywood.

Laminated veneer lumber (LVL) ■

Although not a panel product, another product produced from veneer should be mentioned. *Laminated veneer lumber* (LVL), as the name implies, is an alternative to solid-sawn or glue-laminated lumber. It is manufactured by laying all veneers in one grain direction and pressing in either a continuous or a platen press. The billet produced can be up to 50 in. wide and of adequate layers of veneer to produce the thickness of lumber desired. Phenol-formaldehyde resin adhesive is used to achieve a waterproof glueline. Veneer production and glue application is done as in a plywood plant. Often a LVL plant will purchase veneer rather than produce its own. Veneer thicknesses of $\frac{1}{10}$ to $\frac{1}{6}$ in. are typically used. If a continuous press is used, the end joints of the veneer can be randomized, either butt-jointed, overlapped, or scarfed, and thus any length of billet that is practical to handle can be produced. The billets are cross-cut and ripped to produce the length and width of the lumber desired. There is a practical limit to the thickness of lumber that is produced as a result of the longer press times required for thicker material.

LVL is more costly than solid-sawn lumber but it has several technical advantages, which has made it a popular product for some applications where straightness, high strength, and/or long length are needed. One advantage of LVL is the fact that having been made from dry veneers, it has a uniform and well-controlled moisture content. Because of its multiveneer construction, it is less likely to change shape even with moisture content change. The fact that growth characteristics such as knots and slope of grain are not continuous throughout the piece, but randomized in each veneer, results in design strength properties that are higher than most solid-sawn lumber.

The major applications of LVL at this time are for headers over garage doors and large windows, as the flanges in I-beams, and in structural members where safety is critical, such as in scaffold planks. Some is produced with a colorless glueline to be cut up for door and window parts and other millwork (Maloney 1994).

REVIEW

A. Terms to define or explain:

1. Blocks
2. Plies
3. Rotary cut
4. Lathe
5. Slicer
6. Flitch
7. Pressure bar
8. Charger
9. Lathe checks
10. Tray storage
11. Curtain-coater
12. Extender
13. Filler
14. Automatic clipper
15. Sturd-I-floor
16. Exterior plywood
17. Type 1 plywood
18. Phenol-formaldehyde resin
19. B veneer
20. Span rating
21. Lauan
22. Meranti
23. Overlayed plywood
24. Recovery factor
25. LVL

B. Questions or concepts to explain:
  1. Two major methods used to cut veneer.
  2. Differences in use of hardwood versus softwood plywood.
  3. Advantages of plywood as a construction material.
  4. Trends in species used for softwood plywood.
  5. Steps in the manufacture of plywood.
  6. Advantages of heating the blocks before peeling.
  7. Importance of the pressure bar in veneer cutting.
  8. Use of tray storage and reel storage systems.
  9. Adhesives used for hardwood and softwood plywood.
  10. Major veneer and softwood plywood grades.
  11. Speed at which veneer can be cut (softwoods).
  12. How veneer yield is expressed.
  13. Classification of glueline durability (hardwood and softwood).
  14. How core diameter affects the veneer yield of small-diameter blocks.
  15. Factors that determine the grade of veneer logs.
  16. Factors that determine the yield of veneer from a block.
  17. Technical advantages of LVL as compared to solid lumber.

REFERENCES AND SUPPLEMENTAL READING

American National Standards Institute (ANSI). 1994. American national standard for hardwood and decorative plywood. ANSI/HPVA HP-1-1994.

APA. (The Engineered Wood Association) 1990. Product guide to grades and specifications. Tacoma, Wash.

_____. 1994. Performance standards and policies for structural-use panels. APA PRP-108. Tacoma, Wash.

_____. 1992. Performance standards for wood-based structural-use panels. PS2-92. Tacoma, Wash.

_____. 1990. Design/construction guide—Residential and commercial. Tacoma, Wash.

_____. 1990. End-use marketing profiles for structural panels. Tacoma, Wash.

Baldwin, R.F. 1975. Plywood manufacturing practices. San Francisco: Miller Freeman.

_____. 1985. Managing the basics in softwood plywood. For. Ind. 112(4):18–20.

Fleischer, H. 1965. Use of small logs for veneer. USDA For. Ser. Res. Note FPL 101.

Fronczak, F.J., and Loehnertz, S.P. 1982. Powered back-up roll: New technology for peeling veneer. USDA For. Serv. Res. Pap. FPL-428.

Fuller, B. 1990. Composite products will increase market share in the '90s. Panel World. 31(2):30–32.

Grantham. J.B., and Atherton, G.H. 1959. Heating Douglas-fir veneer blocks—Does it pay? Oreg. For. Prod. Res. Lab. Bull. 9.

Griffin, G. 1983. Optimizers boost lathe efficiency. Plywood Panel World 24(10):6–9.

Guttenberg, S. 1967. Veneer yields from southern pine bolts. For. Prod. J. 17(12):30–32.

Jokerst, R.W., and Geimer, R.L. 1994. Steam-assisted hot-pressing of construction plywood. For. Prod. J. 44(11/12):34–36.

Koch, P. 1964. Wood Machining Processes. New York: Ronald Press, Chap. 12.

_____. 1972. Utilization of Southern Pines. USDA For. Ser. Agric. Handb. 420. Chap. 19, 23.

Lutz, J.F. 1960. Heating veneer bolts to improve quality of plywood. U.S. For. Prod. Lab. Rep. 2182.

Maloney, T. 1994. The development of wood composite materials. Res. Pap. Wood Mtls. and Eng. Lab. Wash. State Univ.

McAlister, R.H. 1967. Jet veneer dryers: Theory and operation. Woodwork Dig. 69(6):32.

_____. 1983. Case strong for hardwoods in structural panels. Plywood Panel World. 24(10):14.

McKeever, D.B., and Anderson, R.G. 1992. Timber products used to build U.S. single family houses in 1988. For. Prod. J. 42(4):11–18.

McKeever, D.B., and Phelps, R.B. 1994. Wood products used in single-family house construction, 1950–1992. For. Prod. J. 44(11/12):66-74.

National Institute of Standards and Technology. 1983. U.S. Product Standard PS 1-83 for construction and industrial plywood. Washington DC.

O'Halloran, M.R., 1979. Development of performance specifications for structural panels in residential markets. For. Prod. J. 29(12):21–26.

Pease, D.A. 1983. Small logs yield veneer for high-tech pine plywood. For. Ind. 110(4):25–29.

Phillips, D.R.; Schroeder, J.G.; and Clark. A. III. 1980. Reduce pine veneer losses by selecting blocks properly. For. Ind. 107(4):40–42.

Sellers, T., Jr. 1985. Plywood and Adhesives Technology. New York: Marcel Dekker.

_____. 1990. Use of lignin as partial substitute for phenol. Panel World. Sept. 26–30.

Watkins, E. 1980. Principles of Plywood Production. White Plains, New York: Reichold Chemicals.

Woodfin, R.O., Jr. 1973. Wood losses in plywood production. For. Prod. J. 23(9):100–108.

15

Particle-based panels and lumber

■ **THREE PRODUCTS** produced from wood particles are discussed in this chapter: particleboard, waferboard/oriented strandboard (OSB), and composite lumber. Since the technology of manufacture of these products has many similarities, brevity is served by covering them in one chapter. The manufacture of particleboard, waferboard, and oriented strandboard (OSB) is fundamentally the same except for the resins used, the flaking process, and the formation of the mat. OSB is a more-advanced version of waferboard. The manufacture of particleboard is described in some detail in this chapter with the differences for waferboard/OSB noted under that topic. The properties and uses of OSB and particleboard are quite different and are both discussed.

Particleboard ■

Particleboard is a panel product produced by compressing small particles of wood while simultaneously bonding them with an adhesive. The many types of particleboard differ greatly in regard to the size and geometry of the particle, the amount of resin (adhesive) used, and the density to which the panel is pressed. The properties and potential uses of any board depend on these variables.

The major types of particles used for particleboard and OSB are

1. *Shaving*—a small wood particle of indefinite dimensions produced when planing or jointing wood. It is variable in thickness and often curled.
2. *Flake*—a small particle of predetermined dimension produced by specialized equipment. It is uniform in thickness, with fiber orientation parallel to the faces.
3. *Chip*—a piece of wood chopped from a block by a knife or hammer, as in a hammermill.
4. *Sawdust*—produced by sawing, in a wide range of sizes. It is usually further refined.
5. *Sliver*—nearly square cross section, with length at least four times the thickness.
6. *Excelsior*—long, curly, slender slivers.
7. *Strand*—a long and narrow flake, wafer, or veneer strip with parallel surfaces.
8. *Wafer*—similar to a flake but larger. It is wider than a strand—often square. Usually over 0.020 in. thick and over 1 in. long. It may have tapered ends.

The range of particleboard types is shown in Figure 15.1. These boards are visibly different because of the size of particles on the faces. However, even boards that appear similar may be quite different in strength and dimensional stability. The trend today is toward boards from smaller particles. Boards from small particles can compete better with MDF (see Chapter 16) for furniture core markets. One of the advantages of particleboard as an industrial material is that it can be tailored to meet a wide variety of use requirements.

The particleboard industry in Europe and North America has shifted during its development back and forth between an emphasis on the use of roundwood to the use of mill *residues*. In Europe the first plants used wood chips and plywood plant residues. However, as technology improved it was shown that flakes of uniform thickness, which could be cut from bolts or sawmill lumber scrap, produced a superior product. Many plants were then built with roundwood as the raw material. In the United States most of the earliest plants relied upon mill residues, principally planer shavings and sawdust; this trend has continued.

The development of particleboard in the United States has been of great benefit to the forest products industry in that it has provided a strong market for mill residue. When particleboard emerged as a major segment of the industry in the late 1950s and early 1960s, it was based upon the use of mill residues then available at $2 or $3/ton, almost the cost of hauling them away. Now the situation has changed dramatically. In most parts of the country, few clean wood residues remain unutilized. Since dry residue is also valuable as an energy source (see Chapter 17), the particleboard industry faces stiff competition for this raw material.

Presently about one-half of the raw material used for particleboard in the United States is from planer shavings, four-tenths is from other mill residues, and one-tenth is from roundwood. When producing particles from roundwood, it is possible to control the size and shape of the flakes and thus improve the strength and dimensional properties of the panels. In the United States the cost of the wood raw material now makes up one-fourth to one-third of the total production cost, a dramatic increase over the situation a decade ago. In the future we may

Fig. 15.1
Typical particleboard types
Boards appear different because of color, density, and particle size.

see whole-tree chips and logging residues used for particleboard. Increased attention is now being given to the use of recycled or "urban wood."

The idea for the product now called particleboard dates back to a number of U.S. and European patents issued between 1905 and 1937. Nevertheless, the first commercial plant was not built until 1941 in Germany. About that same time, a small-scale pilot plant was operating in Dubuque, Iowa. The development of the industry was stimulated in Europe by lumber shortages and in the United States by large quantities of unused softwood mill residues. In the late 1940s and early 1950s, a number of particleboard plants were built in Europe and the United States, but the product was crude and the industry struggled to capture new markets (Carlyle et al. 1956). But by 1960 the particleboard industry was established and growing rapidly. World production increased from 0.02 million m³/yr in 1950, to 3 million m³/yr in 1960, to 20 million m³/yr in 1970, to 62 million m³/yr in 1990. Kollmann et al. (1975) and Maloney (1977) provide interesting histories of the development of this industry.

A number of factors were responsible for the time lag between the early patents and the realization of the particleboard industry. The lack of equipment to cut particles, apply resin, and form particles into a mat was certainly a deterrent. Equally important was the fact that the technology of manufacture was not developed. The effect of processing variables such as species, particle geometry, resin level, moisture content, pressing cycles (pressures and press times), and board density had to be understood before rapid progress could be made. Kollmann et al. (1975) estimated that by the mid-1970s about 2500 research papers had been published in the world literature regarding particleboard technology. Haygreen et al. (1985) identified more than 1200 research papers dealing with structural particleboard technology.

U.S. production of particleboard grew rapidly during the 1960s and 1970s, doubling from 1965 to 1975. Since that time there has been a slow increase in U.S. particleboard with capacity in mid-1996 at about 5.04 billion ft²/yr (¾-in. basis). This represents about 17% of world particleboard capacity. As of 1996, about 47 plants in the United States were producing particleboard. Note that in the United States softwood plywood statistics are normally expressed in square feet of ⅜-in. panels, particleboard in ¾-in., hardboard in ⅛-in., and insulation board in ½-in.

VARIABLES IN PARTICLEBOARD PRODUCTION. The types of particleboard could be classified by particle size and geometry, particle size differentiation between face and core, board density, type of resin, or method of manufacture. The American National Standards (ANSI, 1993) for particleboard categorize it under three variables: board density, quality class, and resin type. The Canadian standards recognize 11 grades of particleboard differentiated principally on the basis of physical properties.

Particle size and geometry. All the types of particles listed earlier are used, singly or in combination, for the production of particleboard. Figure 15.2 shows a number of these types used as furnish. At the lower end of the size range are particles so small that they approach the wood fiber bundles used to produce

Fig. 15.2
**Some of the many types of particles used as
furnish for particleboard.**

fiberboards. At the upper end are flakes over 0.5 in. long. Much longer strands
are used for OSB.

The ideal particle for developing strength and dimensional stability is a thin
flake of uniform thickness with a high length-to-thickness ratio. For example, a
flat uniform particle 0.5–1.0 in. long and 0.010–0.015 in. thick produces an excellent board. However, such flakes are difficult to produce. Most equipment designed to make thin flakes actually produces a variety of particles, including
some ideal flakes but also considerable amounts of finer granular material. Generally, the larger the size of the material entering the flaking machine, the higher
the proportion of nearly ideal flakes produced. Thus, it is better to start the
process with pulp chips than with planer shavings, but even better to produce
flakes from roundwood. In practice, the industry starts with the most-economical
form of raw material that is suited for the type of particleboard being produced.
Any raw material from pulpwood to sawdust may be used.

Particle distribution between face and core. Surface properties are of concern when the boards are used in furniture manufacture or are to be overlaid or painted. Small, fiberlike particles are best for the surface layer if a smooth face is needed. Many boards are made in three or five distinct layers, with smaller particles on the surface and larger ones in the core. The purpose is to develop adequate strength plus good surface smoothness. Figure 15.3 illustrates particle distributions that can be achieved.

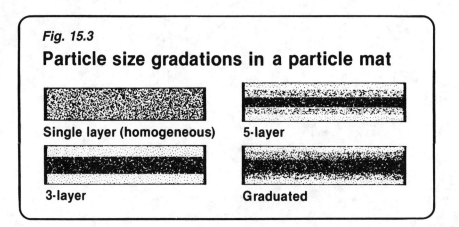

Fig. 15.3

Particle size gradations in a particle mat

Single layer (homogeneous)   **5-layer**

3-layer   **Graduated**

Few particleboards of the single-layer (homogeneous) type are being produced today. One of the reasons that multilayer boards are technically superior is that layering makes it possible to increase the bending strength and stiffness of the boards by altering the relative properties of the face and core.

Board density. The standard of the American National Standards Institute for particleboard (ANSI 1993) includes three board-density classifications; high density, 50 lb/ft^3 or over; intermediate density, 40–50 lb/ft^3; and low density, less than 40 lb/ft^3.

Most particleboard produced in the low-density category is used for door core, which has only minimal strength requirements. It is not possible to develop strength adequate for most uses at such low density. Most conventional particleboards range from 42 to 50 lb/ft^3. One of the goals in the production of any board is to maintain as low a density as possible while developing the strength properties required by the standards or the purchaser. Reduced density decreases manufacturing and shipping costs while increasing the ease of handling and fabrication.

Resin type. Urea-formaldehyde adhesives are the most commonly used resins for conventional particleboard manufacture in Europe and the United States. Relatively low cost and short curing cycles are two advantages of this binder. Boards produced with this type of resin are intended for interior use only. In northern Europe, particleboards produced with urea resins have been widely used in home construction for floors and interior wall surfaces. In North America, however, such boards are not considered suitable for structural subflooring or sheathing in residential construction. Urea-bonded boards have been used as mobile home decking (a combination of subfloor and underlayment) in the United States.

Phenol-formaldehyde resin, without the extenders and fillers used in exterior plywood, is most commonly used for the small volume of particleboard intended for exterior or structural applications as manufactured housing floor deck or siding products. Phenolic-bonded board is marked with the designation "exterior glue."

Other resin systems are in limited use for particleboard. Combinations of urea resin and melamine resin are used in Europe to produce a board with greater water resistance than that produced using only urea resin. A relatively new but potentially important binder, *MDI* (*diphenylmethane-diisocyanate*), is now used in several plants in Europe. It has been used to some degree in the United States although currently it provides only 1% of U.S. particleboard binders. Although expensive, it can be used in smaller quantities than phenolic resins and provides bonds and water resistance superior to urea binders. Advantages also cited for this resin are faster press cycles and increased dryer throughput. MDI is reported to be tolerant of higher moisture content in the furnish, up to 22% MC, than urea or phenolic binders (Youngquist et al. 1982).

Manufacturing process. Most particleboard is produced by forming the *furnish* (the particles used to make the board) into a low-density mat. This mat is then moved into a press as a unit, where it is compressed and heated, and the resin cured. Such material is termed *platen-pressed particleboard*. Multiopening presses of the type shown in Figure 15.4 are generally used for platen-pressed boards, although large, single-opening presses are also in operation. Multiopening presses are usually equipped with push-and-pull rods that close all openings (between the platens) simultaneously as the press closes. This permits each mat to be pressed under the same pressure-time cycle. Without such a device (Fig. 15.5) the mat in the bottom opening would be under pressure for the longest time and at the highest stress level.

A manufacturing system fundamentally different from the platen process is the *extrusion* process in which particles are compressed between two fixed platens by an oscillating ram. Many of the earliest particleboard plants were of this type but its use has been largely discontinued. With each stroke the ram compresses a few particles between the fixed heated platens. As the particles are compressed at the end of the panel, the cured portion of the panel is slowly driven out of the extruder. The properties of this type of board are inferior to platen-pressed board because the particles orient themselves in a plane perpendicular to the plane of the panel. This results in relatively low bending strength and dimensional stability.

BASIC STEPS IN MANUFACTURING. Raw material brought to a plant in the form of roundwood, shavings, chips, mixed mill residue, or sawdust is segregated where possible on the basis of its form, species, and moisture content. It is advantageous to maintain a uniform mix of species and moisture contents entering the mill. If this is achieved, adjustments to the process are minimized, simplifying quality control. However, it is often impossible to maintain this uni-

Fig. 15.4

Multiopening particleboard press
Particleboard presses are typically much larger and more complex than plywood presses because of the need to load the mats carefully into the press and maintain a uniform pressure.

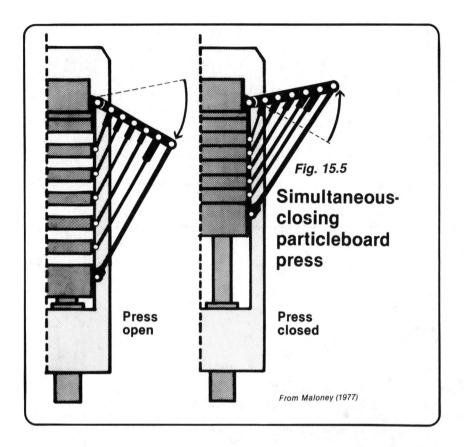

Fig. 15.5

Simultaneous-closing particleboard press

Press open

Press closed

From Maloney (1977)

form flow. One week the raw material may be shavings from sawmills planing green softwood lumber, while the next week it may be from kiln-dried softwood lumber or a furniture plant producing hardwood shavings. If large storage facilities are available and an adequate inventory can be maintained, these material types can be stored and constantly mixed as they enter the process. In plants that use roundwood exclusively, the problem of uniformity of raw material is simplified since all material is green and often of just a few species.

Most raw material is purchased on the basis of weight, and payment is usually determined by weight and material type. Some mills buy roundwood by the cord. Dry planer shavings are usually the most highly valued type of residue, and sawdust is valued the least. The price paid for roundwood or chips is often dictated by the price paid by pulp and paper mills in the area. It would be possible to sample incoming particles or chips for moisture content and make payment based upon the ovendry weight, but this is rarely done.

Preparation of the particles. Some type of milling is required for almost all types of raw material. Chips must be cut into flakes or smaller and finer particles. Roundwood bolts are usually debarked and then cut into shorter lengths before being reduced to flakes. Lumber trim and other types of solid wood residues are often chipped prior to the final breakdown into particles. Even planer shavings and sawdust may have to be further milled to obtain the size of particle desired and to reduce size variation.

A variety of machines including refiners, hammermills, and flakers can be used to produce the type of furnish desired. These machines grind, cut, or tear the wood into a range of particle sizes. Figure 15.6 illustrates the operation of a *ring flaker*. This machine has knives that cut thin particles from chips. A *disk refiner* of the general type shown in Figure 15.7 is sometimes used to prepare small fiberlike particles. The rotating disk plates are grooved. As wood particles move from the center to the outer edges of the disk, they are ground to fiber bundles. The closer the disks are set together, the finer the particles produced. Disk refiners are also used to produce fiber for the fiberboard and paper industries.

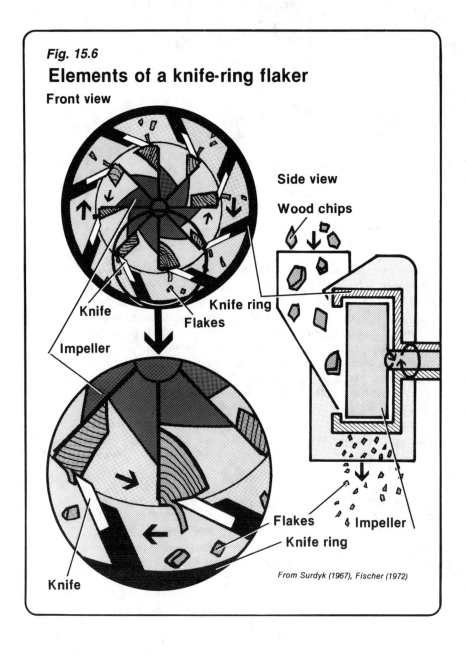

Fig. 15.6

Elements of a knife-ring flaker

Front view

Knife

Knife ring

Flakes

Impeller

Side view

Wood chips

Flakes　Impeller

Knife ring

Knife

From Surdyk (1967), Fischer (1972)

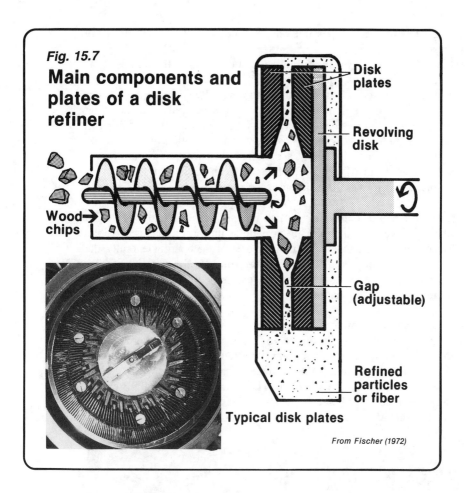

Fig. 15.7

Main components and plates of a disk refiner

Disk plates

Revolving disk

Wood→ chips

Gap (adjustable)

Refined particles or fiber

Typical disk plates

From Fischer (1972)

The drying of particles was discussed briefly in Chapter 8. Most types of particleboard are made with resins which contain water and are applied in liquid form. In this case the particles are dried to 2–5% MC and with the addition of 4–6% MC from the resin have a final moisture content near 10%.

Once particles are dried, they are often screened to remove fine dustlike material (fines). If such material is not removed, it tends to absorb much of the resin, thus lowering the strength of the boards. Fines contribute little but weight to the properties of a board. Screening may also be used to separate finer components from the coarser ones so that these two fractions can be used to form the face and core layers of the board respectively.

Blending. The process of adding the resin adhesive and *wax* or other sizing to particles is called *blending*. The wax (ranging from about 0.25 to 2% by weight) is added to provide some water repellency to the board. The amount of resin solids (ranging from 5 to 10% by weight) used to produce particleboard is very low considering the very large surface area of the small particles. When lumber or plywood is glued, a continuous layer or film of adhesive is laid down between the two surfaces. In particleboard, however, the adhesive coverage is far from continuous; it consists of droplets of resin with large gaps between them. This has been compared to spot welding. It is desirable that the distribution of the resin droplets be as uniform as possible and that all sides of the particles have some coverage.

Blending of the furnish for the surface and core layers of the boards is often done separately. In this way more resin, wax, and moisture can be added to the surface layers if desired. The resin and wax are usually added to the blender through spray nozzles or simple tubes or on rotating centrifugal applicators that atomize the materials. Some blenders mix and blend the furnish and resins in large containers at rather low speeds; however, short retention-time blenders, used in many new large-capacity plants, accomplish their work in just a few seconds and with greater resin efficiency. Rubbing between particles in the short retention-time blender improves distribution of the resin.

Forming. The process of depositing furnish into the form of a mat is termed *forming*. The objective of formation is to provide as uniform a mat as possible, i.e., to produce a uniform mat weight across the area of the board. Generally, the finer the furnish, the easier it is to obtain mat uniformity. In the particleboard industry, all formation is dry, using air as the conveying medium. The particles are dropped or thrown into an air chamber above the cauls or belts and float down to their position.

Many different types of formers have been developed. These are often rather large machines, as shown in Figure 15.8. The way some of them operate is shown in Figure 15.9. The former in Figure 15.9A uses air currents to produce a gradation of particle sizes from surface to core to surface. The smaller, lighter particles are carried farther in the airstream. The former in Figure 15.9B can be used to produce a three-layer board by using a series of heads to lay down the bottom face, the core, and then the top face.

Fig. 15.8
Large forming machine
Forming (depositing the particles to form a mat) is one of the most critical steps in the production of particleboard.

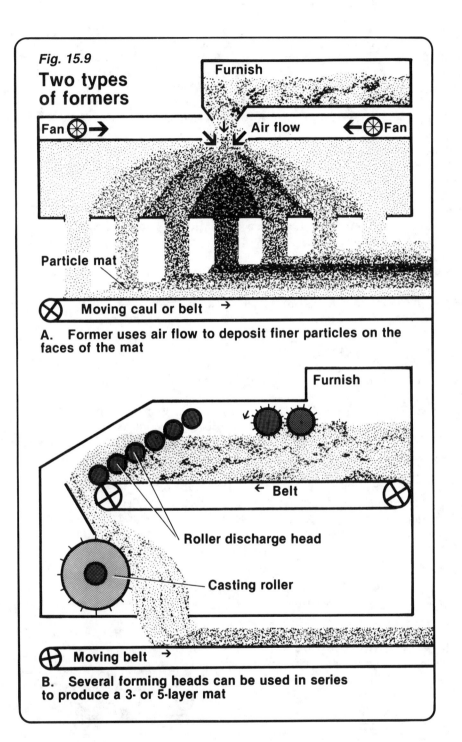

Fig. 15.9

Two types of formers

Furnish

Fan → | Air flow | ← Fan

Particle mat

⊗ Moving caul or belt →

A. Former uses air flow to deposit finer particles on the faces of the mat

Furnish

← Belt

Roller discharge head

Casting roller

⊕ Moving belt →

B. Several forming heads can be used in series to produce a 3- or 5-layer mat

Pressing. Once the mats are formed, they are moved into a press loader, which will simultaneously load all openings in the press. Since they are not consolidated, care must be taken so that material is not lost from the edges. The particle mats are formed either on metal cauls or on belts. In the belt (caulless) system, the mat must be strong enough to be moved into the press without a caul plate to carry it. To accomplish this the mats are prepressed prior to moving them into the hot press.

The multiopening presses (Fig. 15.4) used in most plants in North America have platen sizes ranging from 4×8 ft to 8×28 ft. Large single-opening presses are also used in some plants, primarily in Europe. In either case, the keys to a high production rate are how rapidly the press can be loaded and closed and how quickly the adhesive can be cured.

The rate of cure of particleboard resins has been increased greatly since the early days of the industry. For instance, the press time for a ½-in. urea resin board has been reduced from around 10 min to less than 3 min. Press times are somewhat longer and temperatures often higher (over 360°F, 182°C) when using phenolics.

The manufacturing of particleboard is a semicontinuous process—from the forming stage through the pressing. The speed of the formers and the press are synchronized so that the elevators loading the press are filled by the time a press cycle is completed. Since the press is the most-expensive equipment in the plant, the process is designed to keep the press operating continuously. Also, the forming process is difficult to start and stop, so once the forming line is running well it is best to keep it going. Thus, most mills prefer to operate 7 days/wk, 24 hr/day, with scheduled shifts for maintenance. The relationship of the formers and press is shown in Figure 15.10. Note the weighing station between the formers and the press. If the mat is below or above target weight limits, it will be dumped and the furnish recycled.

The thickness of the boards can be controlled in several ways. Metal stops are used along the edge of the platens in some presses. These presses are closed until the platens come to rest on the stops. When the thickness of the board is changed, the stops must be changed. Many multiopening presses control the distance from the bottom to the top of the press when in the closed position. This in essence controls the total thickness of all the panels in the press. A few presses

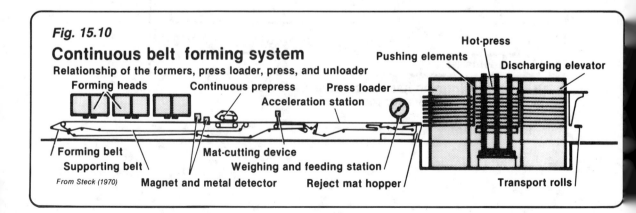

Fig. 15.10

Continuous belt forming system

Relationship of the formers, press loader, press, and unloader

Forming heads — Continuous prepress — Press loader — Hot-press — Pushing elements — Discharging elevator — Acceleration station — Forming belt — Mat-cutting device — Supporting belt — Weighing and feeding station — Magnet and metal detector — Reject mat hopper — Transport rolls

From Steck (1970)

rely entirely upon the pressure cycle to give the board thickness desired. In this way, boards are compressed to a uniform density; so if the former has deposited less furnish in a mat than is desired, the resulting board will be too thin.

Primary finishing. After pressing, urea-bonded boards must be cooled prior to stacking. Urea resins are degraded, once cured, by prolonged exposure to high temperatures. Phenolic-bonded boards are sometimes hot-stacked to provide additional cure time. Most particleboard is then sanded. This provides a clean, smooth surface for gluing, finishing, or overlaying. Sanding is also important for thickness control. Some plants cut their panels to the many special sizes desired by furniture manufacturers. Others cut them to 4×8 ft, the standard size in North America for residential and commercial construction.

FACTORS AFFECTING BOARD PROPERTIES

Species. The most important characteristic of a species that affects its suitability for particleboard manufacture is its specific gravity. As a general rule, the lower-density species are preferred, the medium-density woods are used if readily available at a good price, but the highest-density woods are avoided. Although it is technically possible to produce particleboard from wood of any density, heavier boards made from high-density species are less marketable.

It might seem that a strong high-density wood should produce strong particleboard. In fact, the lower the wood density, the higher the board strength at any given particleboard density. For example, if particleboard is produced from aspen, with wood specific gravity (SG) of about 0.38, an adequately strong board can be produced at a board SG of about 0.62. However, if paper birch with a SG of 0.55 is used, the board SG must be raised to about 0.75 to obtain a board equally as strong as the aspen board.

Low-density woods are also preferable because of the reduced variability of density within a mat. Suchsland (1959) developed a statistical model explaining this fact. He demonstrated that because of the variation in density across the face of a board, it is necessary to compress wood furnish beyond the average density of the species to obtain adequate contact between the particles. If a mat containing furnish (wood) with an SG of 0.45 is pressed so the total SG of the mat (particleboard) is 0.45, only about 50% of the mat particles will be under pressure and have intimate contact. To produce satisfactory contact between particles, it is usually necessary to compress the board to a density 1.2–1.6 times that of the furnish. This ratio between board density and wood density is called the *compression ratio*.

Maloney (1977) pointed out that a compression ratio of 1.3 is a good guideline for determining the minimum board density for a medium-density board. Using this guideline, it would be expected that satisfactory particleboard could be produced as shown in Table 15.1. Most commercial boards being produced from Douglas-fir and ponderosa pine exceed the density indicated in Table 15.1 by 3–5 lb/ft³. It should be noted that particleboards are being produced in tropical countries from dense hardwoods; many of these areas do not have low-density species available. Much research has been conducted on the utilization of dense hardwood species. Means to produce medium-density boards from high-density species have been demonstrated experimentally.

Table 15.1.   Guidelines for particleboard specific gravity as related to raw material specific gravity

Raw material	Wood SG	Particle-board SG*	Particleboard density*
Douglas-fir	0.48	0.69	43 lb/ft^3
Hickory	0.72	1.03	64 lb/ft^3
Oak	0.63	0.90	56 lb/ft^3
Ponderosa pine	0.40	0.57	36 lb/ft^3
Southern pine	0.53	0.76	47 lb/ft^3
Yellow poplar	0.42	0.60	37 lb/ft^3

*Including 10% resin and wax at 0% MC.

Other species characteristics having an effect upon particleboard manufacture are the presence of extractives, the pH, and the buffering capacity. Extractives are reported to cause problems in a few woods with high extractive content, such as western redcedar and some tropical species. The difficulties arise in developing proper cure of the resin and in blows in the board. A *blow* is an internal rupturing of the board resulting from internal gas pressure as the press opens. This may result from the internal pressure of volatilized extractives.

The pH and buffering capacity of a species affect the cure of the resin. Thus the adhesive system used in a plant must be tailored to these characteristics of the species. Urea resins are more sensitive to the pH than phenolics, curing well on wood with a pH of 4–5. However, if the wood has a higher pH, a catalyst may be added to aid the cure. Catalysts are also added to speed the curing rate, particularly in the furnish for the core. The greater the buffering capacity of a species, the more catalyst must be added to lower the pH any given amount.

It is possible to use fibrous cellulosic nonwood crops as raw material for particleboard. Bamboo, flax shives, sunflower stalks, bagasse (residue from sugarcane), and kenaf are among materials that could be used to produce a marketable board. Generally the quality of such boards is less than those of wood-based boards (Youngquist and Chow 1993), but these materials can be used in combination with wood with little loss in quality. Bagasse and flax shives are being used in several parts of the world for board products. Most nonwood materials are annual crops and so must be stored for long times between the periods of the harvest. Deterioration during storage is therefore a problem.

Particle geometry. The desirability of flakelike particles for strength and fine particles for a smooth surface has been mentioned. The most important aspects of particle geometry are the length of the particles and the ratio of the thickness to the length. The distribution of different particle geometries in a mat from the face layer to the core is also significant.

The effect of particle size and geometry on the horizontal density distribution in the board can be demonstrated from Suchsland's (1967) theoretical analysis. Figure 15.11 shows an idealized mat of bricklike particles. The total height of the columns of solid wood within the mat is shown, with these columns arranged in order of the areas over which the most wood is stacked to those with the least. When the board is compressed to any thickness, the area of the mat under pressure is as indicated by the darkened portion in the figure. The more the mat is compressed, the greater the area under compression and the more the total available glue line area is utilized. The pressure and density developed within each column depend upon the extent to which it is compressed.

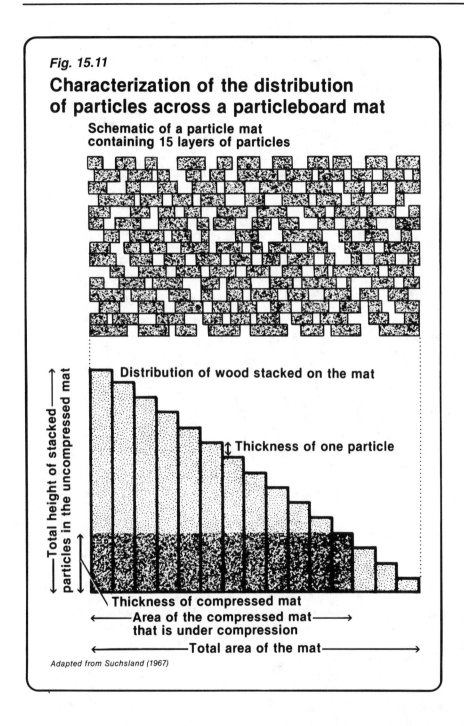

Fig. 15.11

Characterization of the distribution of particles across a particleboard mat

Schematic of a particle mat containing 15 layers of particles

Distribution of wood stacked on the mat

↕ **Thickness of one particle**

Total height of stacked particles in the uncompressed mat

Thickness of compressed mat

←—— Area of the compressed mat ——→ that is under compression

←————— Total area of the mat ————→

Adapted from Suchsland (1967)

The *mat polygon* (total column widths and heights) in Figure 15.11 differs as various particle thicknesses and shapes are used. Thus, when different particle types are compressed, a different distribution of densities occurs. This effect is shown in Figure 15.12 for thick and thin particles, which are wide (square) or slender (narrow). The theoretical density distribution for a mat with long, slender, thick (0.05 in.) particles is broad, while that of a mat with short, wide, thin (0.01 in.) particles is relatively narrow. In the board with long, slender, thick particles, there are very high density areas that would result in excessive thickness swelling. There are also very low density areas where poor adhesion might occur between particles. In the board with short, wide, thin particles, the density is much more uniform across the mat area, and a better board is the result.

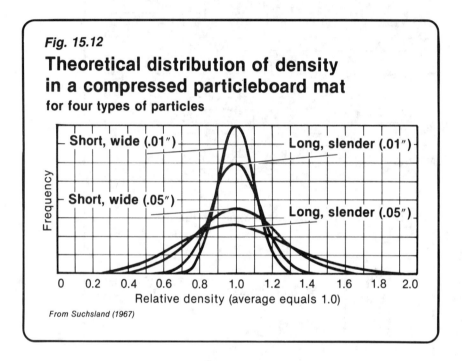

Fig. 15.12

Theoretical distribution of density in a compressed particleboard mat

for four types of particles

From Suchsland (1967)

The form of the raw material (sawdust, shavings, chips, or roundwood) affects the properties of particleboard because it determines the particle sizes and shapes that can be produced in the flakers and refiners. The form of the raw material also influences the amount of drying capacity required in the plant. Most board mills use little bark in the process although some bark may enter on chips or roundwood. Bark in small quantities is not deleterious to the strength of the board, but it adds mostly undesirable weight. Furthermore, bark detracts from the appearance of the board, creating dark flecks or spots on the surface. Bark generally has greater economic value for energy (see Chapter 17) than as a component of the furnish and so is screened out whenever possible.

Board density and density profile. The higher the overall density of the board from a given raw material, the greater the strength. However, other properties such as dimensional stability may be adversely affected by increased density.

To produce a board of the highest possible bending strength, at any given overall board density, the surface layer is made denser than the core. The variation in density throughout the thickness of the board is called the *density profile*. This vertical density variation (profile) should not be confused with the horizontal variation of density in the plane of the board illustrated in Figure 15.12.

It is not possible to produce a board with a truly uniform density profile, i.e., equal face and core density, because as the press is closed the surface layers of the mat heat first and to a higher temperature than the core. This softens the surface particles more and allows them to be densified to a greater degree than the core. The effect is very similar to the densification of solid wood during platen drying mentioned in Chapter 8. The development of steam-injected presses, now in limited use, make it possible to heat the furnish more rapidly and to approach the goal of uniform density.

Other factors also affect the density profile. A higher moisture content in the face layers at the time of pressing will result in greater densification. The effect of a moisture gradient within a mat when producing a ½ in.-thick particleboard is shown in Figure 15.13. The rate at which the press is closed also affects the density profile. The more rapidly it is closed, the greater the relative compression of the face as compared to the core.

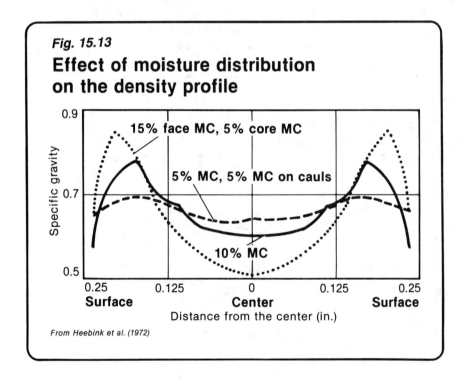

Fig. 15.13

Effect of moisture distribution on the density profile

From Heebink et al. (1972)

Differences in particle geometry between face and core also affect the density profile. More pressure is required to compress a mat of long, slender, thick particles than short, wide, thin particles. Therefore, if the core is made of coarse particles and the surfaces of fine shavings, more densification occurs in the face layers. Experimental boards with densities as low as 46 lb/ft^3 have been successfully produced from high-density hardwoods using this principle.

As indicated, the density profile in a board can be manipulated in many ways. Unfortunately, some properties of a board are improved by a high-contrast density profile, while for other properties a uniform density is best. A uniform density is desirable if a high internal bond strength is needed or if the edges are to be exposed in use. The edge of a uniform-density board will be less porous than one with a high contrast between face and core.

Resin content and distribution. The amount of resin used to manufacture a board is the major factor determining strength and dimensional properties. The more resin used, the stronger and more dimensionally stable the board will be. However, for economic reasons it is undesirable to use a greater amount of resin than necessary to obtain the properties desired. Resin costs can make up to one-fourth the total production cost for particleboard, in some cases as much as the cost of the wood.

Normally, the resin content of urea-bonded boards varies from 6 to 10% based upon the weight of resin solids. Phenolic boards can be made with slightly less resin. Most strength properties are improved by resin increase at a decreasing rate; i.e., the more resin that is added, the less the improvement. Once enough resin is added that particle strength becomes the factor limiting board strength, there is no reason to add still more. Figure 15.14 shows the relationship of resin to strength in pine and spruce boards produced from planer shavings.

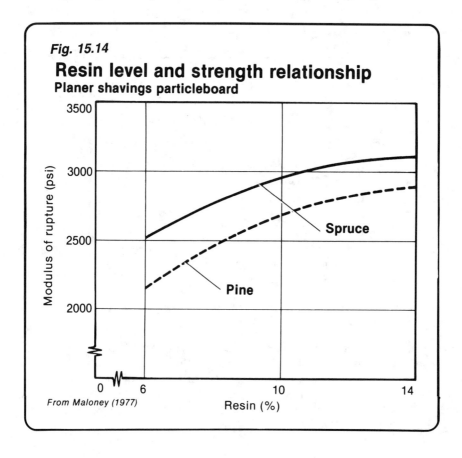

Fig. 15.14
Resin level and strength relationship
Planer shavings particleboard

From Maloney (1977)

PROPERTIES AND USE OF PARTICLEBOARD. The major uses of conventional particleboard in the United States have not changed greatly during the past decade. About one-half of the production of industrial particleboard goes into home or office furniture manufacture and one-third into kitchen and stereo/TV cabinets. Construction applications (classified nonindustrial) such as mobile home decks and underlayment for carpeted floors provide a significant market.

Strength properties. The most important strength properties of particleboard are modulus of elastic (MOE), modulus of rupture (MOR), and internal bond. Screw-holding strength is also critical for uses in furniture and cabinets. Screw-holding strength is determined largely by the density of the board, although resin content has an effect. It is advisable to design particleboard components so that no screws or fasteners are required on the edge in the plane of the panel.

The significance of MOR and MOE was discussed in Chapter 10. For many particleboard applications, these properties are important mainly as an indication of overall board quality. Of course where components are to be loaded in bending, these properties are quite significant. The tendency of particleboard to creep under long-term load needs to be considered in applications such as shelving. The ANSI standard for the top quality of urea-bonded medium-density matformed particleboard (grade M-3) requires a minimum MOR of 2400 psi and an MOE of 400,000 psi.

Internal bond (IB) is the strength in tension perpendicular to the plane of the panel. To determine internal bond, a 2-in. square sample of board is glued between two steel blocks. The blocks are then pulled apart, and the load to failure is recorded. The load to failure divided by the area (4 in.^{2}) gives the IB in psi. The ANSI standards require an IB of about 60 psi for most of the medium-density grades of particleboard. A board with inferior IB could delaminate in service when swelling stresses occur in face laminates. IB is the best single measure of the quality of manufacture because it indicates the strength of the bonds between particles. It is an important test for quality control because it indicates the adequacy of the blending, forming, and pressing processes. Figure 15.15 shows the specimen and blocks for conducting an IB test. A quicker method of assessing internal bond is shown in Figure 10.5.

Dimensional characteristics. Dimensional change of particleboard, both in thickness and in the plane of the panel (known as *linear change*) can be important in many applications. Generally, particleboard is not quite as stable in the linear direction as plywood. *Medium-density particleboard* is allowed (ANSI 1993) a *linear swelling* up to 0.35% in going from 50 to 90% relative humidity. However, for particleboard made from flakes, linear expansion is limited to 0.20%. Although these changes sound small, they are large enough to cause problems if panels are improperly installed with no provision for swelling. When particleboard is used as underlayment, it has been recommended that it be glued to the subfloor to reduce its linear change.

The swelling in thickness of particleboard exceeds the normal swelling of solid wood and can be quite significant, ranging from about 10 to 25% when going from dry to wet conditions. Thus urea-bonded particleboard should generally

Fig. 15.15
The setup for testing the internal bond of particleboard. The specimen is glued between two steel blocks.

not be used where it may be subjected to wetting. *Thickness swelling* is only partially reversible so if particleboard is repeatedly wetted and redried, its thickness will continually grow. The permanent, nonrecoverable component of the swelling is called *springback*. This response of thickness to moisture occurs in all types of particleboard including the phenolic-bonded boards used for structural applications. Therefore, exterior particleboard should be applied in a way that will minimize the pick-up of water.

Despite these dimensional characteristics, some types of particleboard can be successfully used for exterior applications. One phenolic-bonded siding product with an embossed patterned surface is shown in Figure 15.16. An example of exterior use of particleboard under severe moisture conditions is shown in Figure 15.17. This housing development of over 600 units in the wet, tropical climate of Indonesia is constructed with particleboard interior and exterior walls. Urea-melamine–bonded boards produced from wood of rubber tree plantations was used in this project.

Waferboard and oriented strandboard (OSB) ■

The first *waferboard* plant was built in Idaho in the mid-1950s; six years later one was built in Saskatchewan, and in the mid-1970s plants were built in Minnesota and Ontario. These plants primarily utilized aspen because of its low

Fig. 15.16

Particleboard siding product

Here the surface is composed of a layer of secondary fiber produced from reconstituted newsprint.

Fig. 15.17

Housing units in a wet tropical climate that utilize particleboard for walls and partitions. Such an application and climate represent a severe test of board properties. Indonesian wood scientists are seen inspecting the homes after 2 years of service.

(Courtesy G. A. Koenigshof, U.S. Forest Service.)

density and cost. Development of markets for this new product was slow because the competitive product was plywood, which was a proven product and was accepted as the standard panel material for sheathing and subfloor applications. Development of means to orient the strands (wafers refined to narrower widths) made possible an improved product called *oriented strandboard* (OSB). OSB is made of three or five alternate layers of strands oriented at 90 degrees, utilizing the same principle as plywood.

Raw material in the form of roundwood is necessary to produce the large wafers/strands used for waferboard and OSB. A strand length of 3 in. is commonly used for the surface layer of OSB. In older plants special waferizers are used to cut these particles from short, round blocks. Many newer plants have machines that cut the wafers/strands from longwood. For OSB production, the wafers are further broken down in width to produce a strand geometry. Aspen has been the preferred species for these products because of its low density, but other low-density woods such as yellow poplar and sweetgum are also currently being used.

The resin systems for OSB vary from those of particleboard. Phenol formaldehyde is typically used although there is increasing use of isocyanate resins (MDI). A number of plants use a dual resin system with MDI in the core and phenolic resin on the faces. Waferboards have been traditionally manufactured with a powdered form of phenolic resin at a level of about 2.5% of total board weight. Liquid forms of phenolic resins as well as the powdered forms are now being used for OSB.

Figure 15.18 shows one of the machines developed to orient the strands. The spiked roll above throws the strands into the air so they fall between the parallel rotating disks below. A number of machines have been developed to form a layer of oriented strands. The greater the degree of orientation in the surface layer, the stronger the board will be along its long axis. After the mat-formation stage, the manufacture of OSB is essentially the same as for particleboard.

PROPERTIES AND USE OF OSB. Since OSB is formed in layers, it is possible to vary the resin, moisture, and flake geometry throughout the board to provide superior strength properties. The major strength advantage of OSB, however, is derived from the parallel orientation of the strands. Figure 15.19 shows the bending strength of a single layer of OSB which is flexed parallel and perpendicular to the orientation of the strands. Note the 3- or 4-to-1 ratio between parallel and perpendicular orientation. Randomly oriented homogeneous waferboards typically have MORs of about 2500 psi.

New methods of evaluating the strength of structural panels (APA 1994,1992) have made it possible for OSB to compete on a performance basis with softwood plywood. Because of its uniformity, these newer products have compared more favorably than would be expected by evaluating MOR or MOE data. Competition with plywood on a thickness-for-thickness basis has become possible. Because of its lower-strength properties, waferboard must be thicker than OSB to do the same job.

The major use of OSB is for structural panels, primarily roof and wall sheathing and subflooring, in light-frame construction (Figure 15.20). There are over 40 plants now producing OSB, which now makes up over one-fifth of the structural panel production (plywood and OSB) in the United States. APA has projected that OSB will hold a 40% market share by 1998. Some have predicted that within 25 years, one-half of structural panels will be OSB and one-half ply-

Fig. 15.18
One type of former and strand-orienting machine.

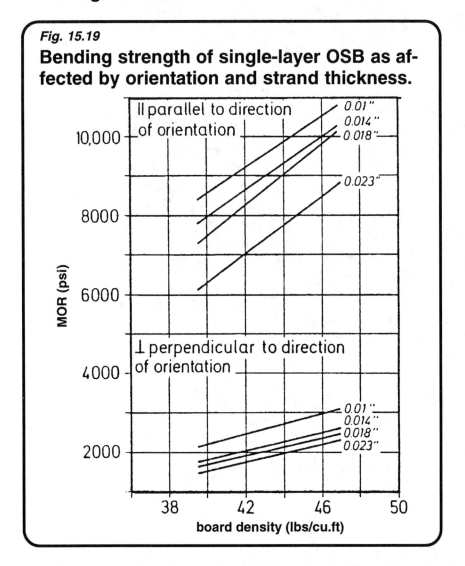

Fig. 15.19
Bending strength of single-layer OSB as affected by orientation and strand thickness.

wood. Canada is also a major producer of OSB and production is planned in Europe and South America.

Cement-bonded wood panels

Mineral binders (mainly Portland cement and gypsum) are used to produce

Fig. 15.20
OSB being used as wall sheathing on a residence.

composite products which combine the characteristics and advantages of wood fiber and the mineral binders. In the United States, gypsum-bonded wood fiber panels are increasingly used in place of gypsum wallboard and ceiling board. A second product combines wood chips or splinters and cement into hollow building blocks which are later filled with concrete. Yet another type of product is a cement/wood fiber shingle that has an appearance similar to a wood shake shingle (Youngquist 1995). A long-established product in the United States is one in which wood excelsior (long, round strands of wood) is combined with Portland cement to make acoustical ceiling tiles for use in commercial and industrial buildings. In international trade this latter product is termed *wood wool.*

Wood wool board is about one-fourth to one-third wood by weight, the remainder being Portland cement or other mineral binder. The product is usually produced in densities from 20 to 25 lb/ft^3. It is well suited to developing countries of the world because it can be produced by very simple hand-forming methods using the mineral binder that is locally available. Figure 15.21 shows a wood wool board and a prototype home in the Philippines with exterior walls of this product.

Species selection is important in the production of wood wool since many species contain wood sugars and other extractives that retard the cure of the cement. This problem can be reduced by long-term storage of the wood bolts prior to shredding and by the addition of chemicals that accelerate the cure rate of the cement. The density of the wood is not critical except as it affects shredding on the excelsior machines.

Particle-based composite lumber products ■

The term *composite* has often been used in forest products literature for products produced from combinations of veneer and particleboard. Maloney (1994) points out that the term composite should properly be applied to any product made from glued-up wood elements. Nonetheless, plywood, particleboard, OSB, MDF (see Chapter 16), and glue-laminated lumber are generally not referred to as composites. Perhaps because of their more-recent origin, LVL and particle-based lumber are often called composite lumber.

Particleboard, oriented flakeboard, and veneer have been used in combination to manufacture composite lumber. Refer to Figure 15.22. The engineering basis behind the combination of veneer and particleboard or oriented flakeboard is to utilize veneers for the edges of framing lumber, e.g., 2 × 8s and 2 × 10s, where the bending stresses are the highest. Recall the discussion of shear and flexural stresses in Chapter 10. This same principle is used to produce a variety of I-beam products with LVL or composite lumber as the flanges and OSB or plywood as the web.

A similar product but with veneer applied to the faces rather than to the edges has been produced to provide lumber for trussed-rafter components. Such components are stressed in tension or compression rather than in bending, and the veneer faces provide good holding power for the metal truss-plate connectors. In either type product, the veneer also acts to limit dimensional change in the grain direction of the veneers.

Several other composite lumber products are now being manufactured.

Fig. 15.21
Board produced from wood excelsior bonded with Portland cement and prototype home. The left-hand side of the wall shows the individual panels in place. The finished wall on the right is produced by application of a cement stucco.

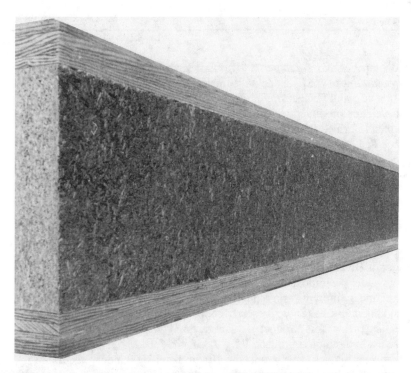

Fig. 15.22

Experimental floor joists

Composed of a particleboard center with edges of parallel laminated veneer. Straightness and availability of long lengths are among the advantages of this product as compared to lumber.

These include *parallel strand lumber* (PSL) made from long strands of veneer, *laminated strand lumber* (LSL) made with smaller strands, and *oriented strand lumber* (OSL) made with furnish similar to that used for OSB. Other alternatives for lumber have been produced in Australia and Japan from small logs that are crushed and then reformed with a resin binder (Maloney 1994). This technology has been purchased by a U.S. firm.

PSL, sold under the trade name Parallam, is produced from oriented strands of Douglas-fir or southern pine veneer up to 1 m long. Thick billets of this product are made by the use of microwave heating to cure the phenolic resin adhesive in a continuous-type press. The billets can then be sawn into lumber of any size and length needed. This composite lumber product provides an alternative for structural softwood lumber of large size in applications where high uniform strength and reliability are essential. The strength of this product is superior to the best grades of Douglas-fir or southern pine lumber.

LSL, sold under the trade name TimberStrand, is similar to PSL except with smaller strands and a different resin binder. Aspen and yellow poplar flakes produced on a modified disk flaker are presently being used. The billets are cured in a steam-injection press. This product is manufactured with MDI (isocyanate) resin to provide a light-colored product. It has been sold for a variety of applications requiring clear lumber to be wrapped with vinyl and for window and door parts. It is also sold as beams for construction.

OSL is the newest of the composite lumber products and markets are still under development. It is produced from oriented flakes, in much the same way as the faces and core of OSB. In this case, of course, all strands are oriented in one direction. To date, this product has been used in furniture, but development of recognized strength properties will allow its use as an alternative to structural lumber.

A major advantage of these composite lumber products is that they allow production of relatively large sizes of lumber from small logs. Also, raw material utilization is high—typically 70% or more ends up in the primary product. Although more costly, composite lumber compares very favorably to solid-sawn lumber in terms of strength, uniformity, and straightness. While the quality of lumber is determined to a great extent by the quality of the raw material, the quality of composite lumber is dependent upon the manufacturing process. It is likely that composite lumber will become a much more important forest product in the future.

REVIEW

A. Terms to define or explain:
1. Furnish
2. Shaving
3. Wafer
4. Flake
5. Blending
6. Forming
7. Density profile
8. Ring flaker
9. Disk refiner
10. Extruded particleboard
11. Platen-pressed particleboard
12. Wax size
13. Buffering capacity
14. Blow (delamination during pressing)
15. Wood wool
16. Composite lumber
17. Internal bond
18. Thickness swell and springback
19. Linear swelling
20. Medium-density particleboard
21. Compression ratio
22. Residues
23. Waferboard
24. OSB
25. PSL, LSL, and OSL

B. Questions or concepts to explain:
1. The basic steps in the manufacture of particleboard and OSB.
2. The relationship between the density of the wood and the density to which a board must be manufactured to obtain adequate properties.
3. How the form of the raw material affects the type of particle that can be produced.
4. Some ways in which particle shape affects the properties of particleboard.
5. How the gluing of particles in particleboard differs from glue joints in solid wood.
6. Ways in which the density profile in the board can be influenced.
7. The types of resin used for particleboard.
8. Some of the ways (machines) used to mill the furnish.
9. Types of particleboard that require the use of roundwood as raw material.
10. The uses of particleboard compared to those of OSB.
11. The importance of internal bond in the quality control of particleboard.
12. The dimensional characteristics of particleboard as compared to plywood.

REFERENCES AND SUPPLEMENTAL READINGS

American National Standards Institute. 1993. Particleboard. Amer. Nat. Stand. ANSI A208.1. Gaithersburg, Md.: National Particleboard Association.

American Society for Testing and Materials. 1987. Standard methods of evaluating wood-base fiber and panel materials. ASTM D 1037-87.

APA (The Engineered Wood Association). 1994. Performance standards and policies for structural-use panels. PRP-108. Tacoma, Wash.

———. 1992. Performance standard for wood-based structural-use panels. PS2-92. Tacoma, Wash.

———. 1992. Grades and specifications: Product guide. Tacoma, Wash.

Carlyle, A.; McGee, L.; and McLean, R. 1956. Wood Particleboard Handbook. School of Eng., N.C. State College. Raleigh, N.C.

Cohen, D.H.; and Sinclair, S. 1990. The adoption of new manufacturing technologies by North American producers of softwood lumber and structural panels. For. Prod. J. 40(11/12):67-73.

Donnell, R. 1990. Highland American starts gypsum fiberboard plant. Panel World. Nov. 8-12.

Fischer, K. 1972. Modern flaking and particle reduction. Proc. Wash. State Particleboard Symp. 6:195-213.

Forest Products Research Society. 1985. Structural wood composites. Proc. Symp. For. Prod. Res. Soc. 7339.

Fuller, B. 1990. Composite products to increase market share in 90s. Panel World. 31(2):30-32.

Griffin, G. 1988. Plant combines LVL and OSB to make dimension. For. Industries. 115(1):12-15.

Haygreen, J.; Gregersen, H.; Hyun, A.; and Ince, P. 1985. Innovation and productivity change in the structural panel industry. For. Prod. J. 35(10):32-38.

Haygreen, J., and Gertjejansen, R. 1972. Influence of the amount and type of phenolic resin on properties of wafer-type particleboard. For. Prod. J. 22(12):30-34.

Haygreen, J. 1973. Use of particleboard for manufactured housing in Sweden and Finland. For. Prod. J. 23(10):14-17.

Kelly, M. 1977. Critical literature review of relationships between processing parameters and physical properties of particleboard. USDA For. Serv. Gen. Tech. Rep. FPL-10.

Kollmann, F.; Kuenzi, E.; and Stamm, A. 1975. Principles of Wood Science and Technology. Vol. 2. Chap. 5. Heidelberg, Germany: Springer Verlag.

Lee, A.W.C.; and Hse, C.Y. 1993. Evaluation of cement-excelsior boards made from yellow-poplar and sweetgum. For. Prod. J. 43(4): 50-52.

Maloney, T. M. 1977. Modern Particleboard and Dry Process Fiberboard Manufacturing. San Francisco: Miller Freeman.

———. 1987. Technology extending the resource. Proc. Expert Consultation on Wood-Based Panels. Rome, Italy.

———. 1994. The development of wood composite materials. Res. Pap. Wood Mtls. and Eng. Lab., Wash. State Univ. Pullman, WA.

Miller, D. P., and Moslemi, A. 1991. Wood-cement composites: Effects on hydration and tensile strength. For. Prod. J. 41(3):9-14.

Parker, D.J. 1987. Parallam parallel strand lumber: Evolution. Proc. International Particleboard/Composite Materials Symp. Wash. State Univ. Pullman, Wash.

Stevenson, J. A. 1984. Structural panel codes and standards. Proc. For. Prod. Res. Soc. 7339.

Suchsland, O. 1959. An analysis of the particleboard process. Mich. State Univ. Agric. Exp. Sta. Bull. 42(2):350-372.

———. 1962. Density distribution in flakeboards. Mich. State Univ. Agric. Exp. Sta. Bull. 45(1):104-21.

———. 1967. Behavior of a particleboard mat during the pressing cycle. For. Prod. J. 17(2):51-57.

White, J.T. 1995. The outlook for worldwide resin supplies. For. Prod. J. 45(3):21-28.

Youngquist, J.A. 1995. The marriage of wood and nonwood materials. For. Prod. J. 45(10):25-30.

Youngquist, J., Carll, C.; and Dickerhoff, H. 1982. U.S. wood-based panel industry: Research and technological innovations. For. Prod. J. 32(8):14-24.

Youngquist, J., and Chow, P. 1993. Agricultural Fibers in Composition Panels. Proc. International Particleboard Symp. Wash State Univ. Pullman, Wash.

16

Paper and other fiber products

■ **WOOD-BASED FIBER PRODUCTS** include paper, paperboard, tissues, hardboard, insulation board, medium-density fiberboard, and a rapidly growing number of wood fiber–plastic composites. All these products are manufactured from wood that has been reduced to individual fibers or fiber bundles, which are then formed into a mat, compressed, and dried. The distinction between paper and paperboard is primarily based upon product thickness with sheets over 0.3 mm thick classified as *paperboard*. The linerboard and corrugating medium used to make corrugated cartons are examples of paperboard. *Tissues* include a wide range of products with low-weight sheets such as facial and bathroom tissues, napkins, and paper toweling. *Hardboard, insulation board,* and *medium-density fiberboard* are products generally 3.0 mm and thicker used in building, furniture, and cabinet construction.

Paper ■

It was not until the late 1800s that wood became an important source of papermaking fiber. Prior to that time cotton and linen rags were the major source. In 1840 the groundwood pulping method was developed in Germany. In 1856 the soda chemical pulping process was developed in England, and in 1884 the kraft pulping process was developed in Germany. These processes were soon adopted in the United States. Today, wood is clearly the dominant raw material for paper manufacture, with wood fiber providing 99+% of the fiber needs in the United States and 90% of fiber used in paper worldwide (FAO 1993). Nonwood fibers in use include cereal and seed flax straws, bamboo, sugarcane bagasse, reeds, abaca, esparto and Sabai grasses, cotton linters, rags, sisal, and kenaf.

Paper (in general usage this category includes paperboard and tissues) has become such a vital element in our daily lives that most people rarely consider its source or its importance. Paper serves as a primary packaging product, communications medium, base for sanitary and disposable products, and industrial sheet material. In the United States the pulp and paper industry is the largest consumer of wood; in 1994 the U.S. production of paper and paperboard was equivalent to 721 lb per person in the entire population. Table 16.1 shows the production of different types of paper in the United States in 1994.

Table 16.1. Production of paper and paperboard in the United States for 1994

Type	Production (million short tons)
Paper	
Newsprint	7.0
Printing/writing	25.7
Packaging paper	4.7
Tissue	6.1
Total paper	43.5
Paperboard	
Unbleached kraft	22.5
Corrugating medium	5.7
Bleached paperboard	5.0
Recycled paperboard	12.5
Total paperboard	45.7
Total U.S. paper and paperboard production	89.2

Source: American Forest and Paper Association (1995).

THE MANUFACTURING PROCESS. In simple terms, the process of paper manufacture involves (1) reduction of wood to constituent fibers (pulping), (2) suspension of fibers in water, (3) beating or refining the pulp, (4) blending of additives (fillers, sizing materials, wet-strength binders, etc.), (5) formation of a fiber mat, (6) drainage of water, and (7) drying of the sheet. Surface treatment to improve printing qualities follows in many types of paper.

Pulp production. A primary difference among various paper manufacturing processes is the method used to break the wood into fibers, i.e., *pulp*. Mechanical, chemical, heat energy, or combinations of these processes are employed to accomplish pulping. The forms of energy used determine to a large extent both pulp yield and pulp properties.

Mechanical pulping. There are two methods of producing mechanical or groundwood pulp. These are the stone groundwood and the refiner groundwood processes. To produce *stone groundwood pulp* (SGW) a large abrasive stone, or a wheel made up of stone segments, is rotated while the tangential surface of wood bolts is pressed against the stone (Fig. 16.1). As the abrasive stone grinds against the wood the fibers are compressed, loosened, and separated. Frictional heat softens the lignin, helping to separate the fibers from the wood mass. Groundwood pulp made from spruce is pictured in Figure 16.2. Note the pieces of fiber and bundles of unseparated fiber in the mixture.

A newer method of manufacturing mechanical pulp involves the use of a machine with opposing serrated steel disks, which accomplish the grinding. One type, called a double-disk refiner, is composed of two fluted metal disks that can be closely spaced and driven in opposite directions. A variation of this machine, called a single-disk refiner, has one fixed disk and one disk that rotates. In both types of refiners, wood chips are moved by a screw-feed mechanism into the center of the machine where they must pass between the two closely positioned disks; the resulting mechanical action reduces the chips to fiber (see Fig. 15.8). Pulp produced in this way is called *refiner mechanical pulp,* or RMP.

Since the wood is physically torn apart, little material is lost in the mechanical pulping process as long as the fibers are flexible enough to avoid the production of fines. Because of the fiber-shattering problem, dense species are generally not pulped by mechanical processes. The short thick-walled fibers and large proportion of vessels and parenchyma in some hardwoods also reduce their usefulness for mechanical pulp. Resinous softwoods can also present a problem, although techniques to overcome such difficulties with highly resinous woods such as southern pine are successfully employed.

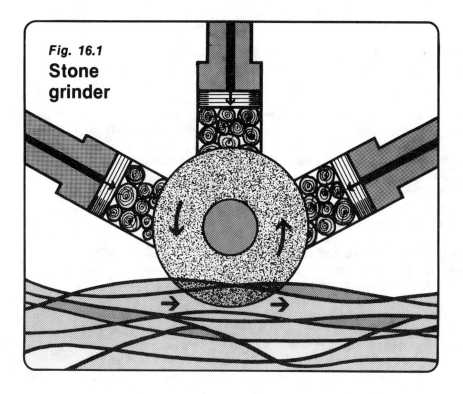

Fig. 16.1
Stone grinder

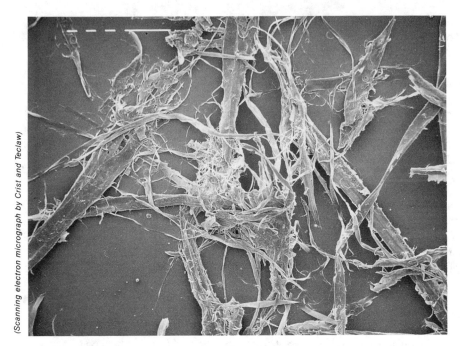

(Scanning electron micrograph by Crist and Teclaw)

Fig. 16.2

Unbeaten groundwood pulp
(Spruce) ×125

In mechanical pulping, the proportion of wood raw material that becomes usable fiber is commonly on the order of 95%, a fact translating to relatively low-cost pulp. Unfortunately, high yield also results in pulp unsuitable for many uses since the cellulose, hemicellulose, and lignin that make up the roundwood are still present. The lignin, which serves to strengthen solid wood through stiffening of fibers, continues to give rigidity to the fibers of mechanical pulp. These rigid fibers have little fiber-to-fiber bond potential and form a coarse, bulky mat. The paper thus formed has low strength and relatively poor surface quality. The presence of lignin in mechanical pulp contributes to yet another problem—long-term durability. Lignin and certain carbohydrates yellow with age, particularly when exposed to ultraviolet rays of sunlight. This is the reason for the yellowing commonly seen in old newspapers.

Semimechanical pulping. Several pulping methods are combinations of mechanical, thermal, and/or chemical processes. One is the *thermomechanical process* (TMP), where chips are subjected to steam as they pass through refiners, generally in two passes. The first stage of thermomechanical pulping is normally done under pressure, with chips subjected to superheated steam at a temperature of 110°–135°C. In some systems steaming is done at atmospheric pressure. The heat serves to soften lignin, allowing fiber separation with less fiber damage than can be obtained by the SGW or RMP process. This improves both strength and absorbency.

Chemi-thermomechanical pulping (CTMP) is a process similar to TMP but with chemicals added to the chips during the process to assist in softening and separating the wood fibers. Alkaline sulfite liquor, kraft black liquor, and sodium sulfite are among the chemicals used. CTMP makes possible the use of denser hardwoods such as oak, birch, and eucalyptus for magazine paper and newsprint.

Semichemical-mechanical pulping (SCMP) process is similar to CTMP with the exception that the chips are refined at atmospheric pressure, thus at a lower temperature. These two processes provide the highest-quality pulp and have been the most widely used in recent pulp mill construction of any of the mechanical pulping processes. The semimechanical processes typically have pulp yields from 80–90%.

Semichemical pulping. Semichemical processes consist of a chemical treatment more severe than used in the semimechanical processes but still requiring some degree of mechanical treatment to complete fiberization. Wood pulped in this way combines the high-yield advantages of mechanical processing with some of the high-quality fiber characteristics of chemical processing. The *cooking liquor* (chemical solution) causes partial degradation of the ligneous bonds and serves basically the same function as heat in the thermomechanical process. Mechanical energy needed for fiber separation is greatly reduced and damage to fibers is decreased. The most widely used process in this category is the *neutral sulfite semichemical process* (NSSC). In this case, sodium sulfite, buffered with sodium carbonate, is used to pretreat the chips. Semichemical pulp yields of 65–75% are common and may occasionally be higher. NSSC makes possible the use of a wide range of hardwoods for products ranging from corrugating medium to newsprint.

Chemical pulping. The use of chemicals to achieve fiber separation is the most widely used pulping method worldwide. About 83–84% of the pulp produced in North America uses processes of this type. Wood chips are placed in a chemical solution (cooking liquor) and heated in a pressurized vat (*digester*). Fiber separation occurs as lignin cementing cell to cell is dissolved. These processes result in low yields, as compared to other pulping methods, varying from 40 to 55% depending upon the severity of the pulping and bleaching processes.

There are two major chemical pulping processes now in use, the sulfite and kraft (sulphate) processes, which differ in the chemicals comprising the cooking liquor. The *sulfite process* makes use of a mixture of sulfurous acid and ammonium, magnesium, calcium, or sodium bisulfites. The sulfurous acid (H_2SO_3) reacts with lignin to form lignosulfonic acid. This relatively insoluble compound is, in turn, reduced to soluble lignosulfonic salts in the presence of the basic bisulfites. The sulfite process yields high-quality pulp of the type desired for fine writing papers.

The calcium-based bisulfite came to be the most commonly used with the sulfurous acid. The calcium compound was cheap and worked quite well in the pulping of long-fibered species such as spruce, hemlock, and true fir. There were, however, several problems associated with the use of the calcium bisulfite–based process. The most serious was that recovery of cooking chemicals and process heat was technically difficult and economically unfavorable. The outcome was that sulfite mills constantly had a used cooking liquor disposal problem—in a volume of approximating 1500 gal/ton of pulp produced. Another problem was that the process did not work well in pulping highly resinous softwoods such as pine. As a result, more recent sulfite installations were designed to use ammonium or magnesium bisulfites. Development of chemical recovery technology has made it possible to achieve complete chemical recovery of magnesium-based cooking liquors through a relatively simple process. Nonetheless, in recent decades sulfite pulp mill capacity has declined steadily while the kraft process has grown rapidly (Table 16.2).

Table 16.2. *Estimated annual wood pulp production in the United States (thousands of short tons)*

Year	Sulfite	% of total	Kraft	% of total	Soda	% of total	Semi-chemical pulping	% of total	Mechanical pulping	% of total	Total pulp from raw wood	Recycled paper	% of raw wood total
1994	1604	2.5	52,639	81.3	...	0.0	4347	6.7	6104	9.4	64,694	29,987	46.4
1983	2877	5.5	40,742	77.5	...	0.0	3851	7.3	5067	9.7	52,537	18,567	35.3
1977	3507	7.1	34,862	70.2	...	0.0	3876	7.8	7417	14.9	49,662	14,015	28.2
1970	4024	9.4	28,670	67.3	218	0.5	3297	7.7	6379	15.0	42,588	11,803	27.7
1960	3711	14.8	14,516	57.9	420	1.7	1970	7.9	4469	17.9	25,086	9,032	36.0
1950	2848	19.4	7,501	51.0	522	3.5	686	4.7	3151	21.4	14,708	7,956	54.1
1940	2608	29.3	3,748	42.1	532	6.0	165	1.9	1843	20.7	8,896	4,668	52.5
1930	2517	*	950	*	474	*	...	*	*	*	*	*	*

Source: Libby (1962), Evans (1978), Lowe (1978), Haas et al. (1979), American Paper Institute (1984), American Forest and Paper Association (1995).

The *kraft (*or sulfate) *process* is based upon use of a cooking liquor made primarily of sodium hydroxide and sodium sulfide. The sodium hydroxide attacks lignin, breaking it down into segments whose sodium salts are soluble in the cooking liquor. The sodium sulfide, when exposed to water, breaks down to sodium hydroxide (increasing the amount of that compound available for pulping) and sodium hydrosulfide, which serves to increase the solubility of lignin.

An interesting part of science history is the explanation of how this process become known as the kraft process. In the course of operating a Swedish soda process mill, a digester full of partially cooked pulp was accidentally blown. The material was about to be thrown away when the mill manager decided to use it in making some low-quality paper; the surprising result was that the paper produced was far stronger than any previously made. The Swedish (and German) word *kraft*, meaning strong, soon became the commonly used name for what is also called the sulphate process.

The recoverability of cooking liquors and process heat means that the kraft process is comparatively free of residual disposal problems. The kraft process is effective in pulping any species, including those that are highly resinous. These factors, plus the fact that high-strength pulp is produced, explain the overwhelming popularity today of the kraft process. One negative aspect is a characteristic rotten cabbage smell caused by volatile sulfur compounds. Costs of eliminating this smell are high. Because the human olfactory system can detect even minute concentrations, virtually 100% of the sulfur compounds must be removed from stack gases to completely solve the odor problem.

Because no mechanical action is needed to achieve cell separation, chemically produced pulp is composed of smooth and largely undamaged fibers (compare Figs. 16.2, 16.3A). Moreover, when a high proportion of the lignin is removed in the process, an important component of age-induced yellowing in bleached paper is eliminated. The penalty paid for high quality is low yield (and therefore high pulp cost). The yield, expressed as dry weight of usable fiber divided by the dry weight of chips placed in the digester, is lower (40–55%) than the lignin content might suggest. The reason is that the conditions that solubilize lignin also degrade both cellulose and the low-molecular-weight hemicellulose.

The advantages of the kraft and sulfite processes can be summarized as follows. The kraft process produces the highest strength pulp, allows efficient recovery of pulping chemicals, utilizes a wide range of species, and tolerates bark in the process. The sulfite process provides a higher yield of bleached pulp, produces pulp that is easy to bleach, and produces pulp that is easier to refine for fine papers.

Fiber recycling. In the United States in 1994, an estimated 40% of all paper consumption was recovered for recycling according to the American Forest and Paper Association, (AF&PA 1995). Also in 1994, recovered paper provided 32.9% of all the raw material fiber used at U.S. paper mills. In Japan, by comparison, the paper reuse rate is about one-half; the highly concentrated Japanese population makes collection of paper for recycling quite economical. It is predicted that by 1997 the recycling rate in the United States will reach 45%, a significant increase from a 26% rate only 20 years earlier (Iyengar and Ackley 1993).

Much of the recycled paper used in the United States goes into the manufacture of corrugating medium, the paper used in the fluted plies of corrugated boxes. Other uses are for newsprint and other printing grades and for structural wood fiber products.

A firm using recycled fiber faces several significant problems, including removal of contaminants from recovered fiber (adhesives, plastics, waxes, latex, asphalt, etc.) and elimination of inks from fiber to be used in making printing papers. In addition, there is a limit to the number of times that fiber can be recycled. With present technology it is considered that 50% represents a practical maximum recycling rate. As explained by Smook (1982), "Significant losses of fiber substance occur during each recycling and at the 50% recycle level, it is apparent that half of the material being recycled has already been through at least one previous recycling process."

Washing and bleaching. It is necessary to clean pulp after it is formed to remove cooking liquor and/or impurities. After chemical pulping, the wood fiber and cooking liquor is blown from the digester into what is known as a *blow pit*. Here fiber is collected and initially separated from spent cooking liquor and gases that have been produced. Fiber is next cleaned in a multistage washing process to remove any residual liquor.

Untreated wood pulp is brown to tan in color, due mainly to the presence of lignin or extractives from heartwood. Unbleached fiber is used for bag paper, linerboard, and other uses where strength, but not color, is important. When manufacturing writing or book papers or other products where whiteness is important, fiber must be bleached. This is usually done by exposure to strong chlorine-based compounds. However, the technology of bleaching chemical pulps is

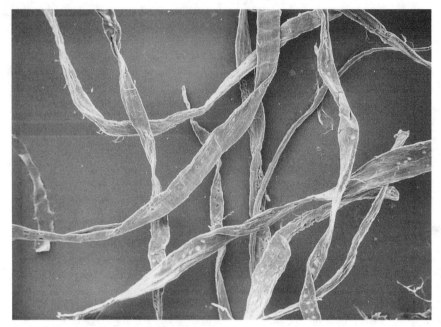

A. Before beating (745 CSf)

B. After beating (145 CSf)

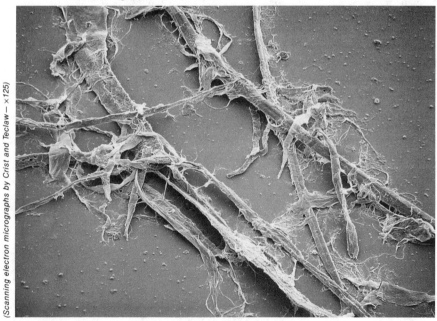

Fig. 16.3
Beating flattens and partially unravels fiber walls (chemically pulped southern yellow pine).

going through rapid technological change in the 1990s and bleaching processes using chlorine are falling out of favor. New processes based upon oxygen-bleaching techniques are gaining commercial acceptance. Pulp referred to as TCF (*totally chlorine-free*) is now being produced in the United States and Europe (Singh 1993).

Bleaching attacks residual lignin and can be carried to the point where lignin is either totally removed, as with the highest-quality writing and printing papers, or simply lightened in color, as in the manufacture of newspaper or catalog quality stock. The latter degree of treatment is less expensive, having little effect upon yield, but it results in only temporary whiteness. Bleaching to achieve removal of essentially all lignin gives virtually permanent whiteness but is expensive. In this case, water use is high and pulp yield is significantly reduced.

Beating and refining. Much of the strength of paper results from hydrogen bonding of cellulose molecules that make up adjacent fibers. To provide the maximum potential for bonding, fibers are pounded or ground to flatten them and to partially unravel microfibrils from the cell walls; the surface area of fibers (and thus the area available for bonding) is greatly increased by even a small degree of such flattening and unraveling (Fig. 16.3).

The mechanical flattening and unraveling of fibers is called *beating* and is accomplished in various types of refining machines. Disk refiners are commonly used for this purpose (see discussion under mechanical pulping). Another common type of machine is the conical refiner (known as a Jordan refiner). In this type of machine (Fig. 16.4) a conically shaped, longitudinally fluted plug rotates inside a similarly shaped and ribbed housing. The location of the plug inside the housing controls the spacing between the flutes and ribs. Fibers are subjected to a mechanical rubbing action as they pass through the conical refiner.

Because fiber-to-fiber bonding has a great deal to do with paper properties, it is desirable to have a quantitative measure of the pulp's bond potential. In North America, bond potential is usually expressed in terms of *Canadian Standard freeness* (CSf). This is measured by suspending a given amount of fiber in water and then determining the rate at which water drains through a wire mesh onto which the fiber has been allowed to settle. Since the rate of drainage is inversely related to the surface area of the fiber, a mat of well-beaten fiber is quite resistant to drainage of water. The freeness of well-beaten fiber is thus low.

The relationship between beating time, freeness, and various strength properties is illustrated in Figure 16.5. Note that freeness is in all cases decreased by extended beating. Burst and tensile strengths tend to be higher with longer beating times. Burst and tensile properties are closely related to interfiber bonding and are thus directly affected by any treatment that increases bond potential (Fig. 16.5A,B). Figure 16.5C shows that tear strength is significantly increased as beating is begun but is reduced rapidly thereafter. The explanation for this is that tear is somewhat influenced by interfiber bonding but is much more influenced by the integrity of individual fibers. Within the first few minutes of beating, flattening of cells and some unraveling of microfibrils occurs, which greatly increases surface area while causing little reduction in either length or strength of fibers. The increased surface area resulting from further beating is offset by the damage to the individual fibers.

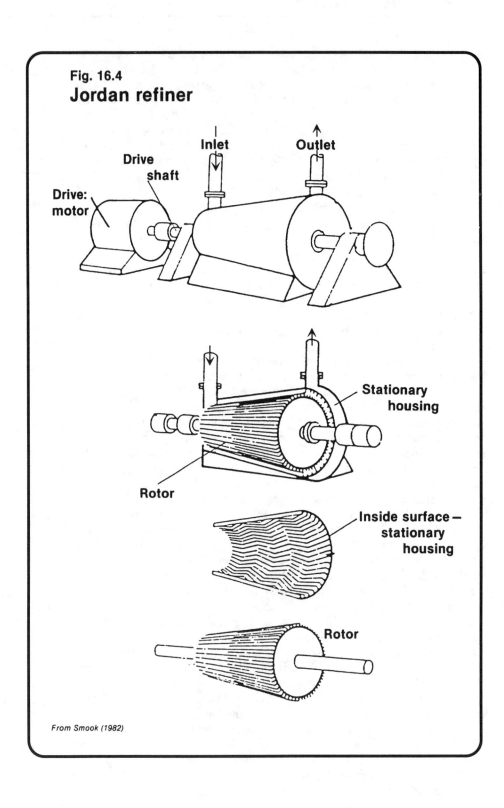

Fig. 16.4
Jordan refiner

Drive shaft

Drive motor

Inlet

Outlet

Stationary housing

Rotor

Inside surface — stationary housing

Rotor

From Smook (1982)

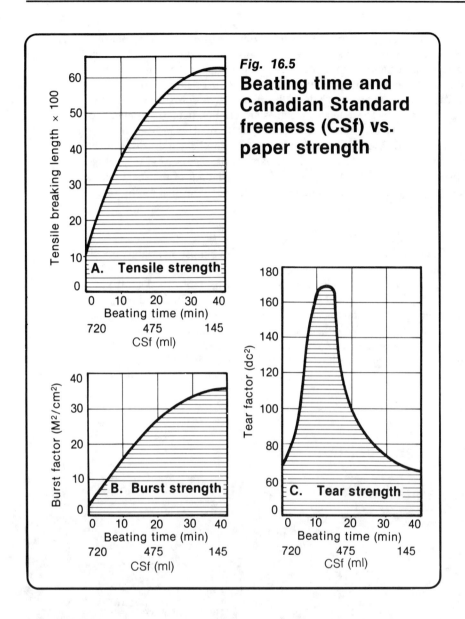

Fig. 16.5
Beating time and Canadian Standard freeness (CSf) vs. paper strength

Sheet formation. Following beating, and in some cases secondary refining, fiber is mixed with water to a consistency of about 1% fiber by weight. It is quite common to mix different types of pulp (i.e., mechanical and chemical) at this stage, with the proportion of each dependent upon the kind of paper to be manufactured. Additives such as starch (for increased bond strength) or wet-strength resin are often added to the mixture at this point as well, as are clays (for brightness and opacity) and rosin size (for decreased liquid absorption). This mixture is then formed into a thin mat.

The most commonly used machine to form the fiber mat is called a *Fourdrinier* (Fig. 16.6). It is basically a rapidly moving horizontal screen fitted with a device called a head box that accurately meters the pulp slurry onto the screen. As pulp flows onto the screen, water drains away with the aid of suction boxes or other drainage-enhancing devices mounted under the wire, leaving a mat of fibers. Another type of paper machine forms a fiber mat on a rotating wire cylinder. Twin-wire machines, in which the fiber mat is formed between two screens, are also in use. These latter machines are used particularly to manufacture multi-ply paperboard. After the fiber mat is formed using one of these machines, it is wet pressed, dried over a series of steam-heated drums, pressed again to desired thickness, and wound into large rolls. Application of coating, sheet polishing operations (known as calendaring), winding of the sheet onto a reel, and slitting of large rolls into smaller rolls are operations that might follow. The entire process is summarized in Figure 16.7.

PAPER COMPOSITION. Certain types of paper are almost invariably associated with specific types of pulps. Brown wrapping paper and grocery bags, for example, are almost always made from high-strength, unbleached kraft pulp, whereas gift wrap, including hard tissue paper, is typically produced from fine sulfite pulp. Though other examples of this kind can be given, most paper products are made from a blend of pulps. Wallpaper, for instance, is often made using a blend of sulfite, sulfate, and mechanical pulps in order to incorporate the advantages of tear strength (sulfate), printability (sulfite), and low cost (mechanical) into the product. Similarly, low-cost newsprint, which is made primarily

Fig. 16.6
Fourdrinier paper machine

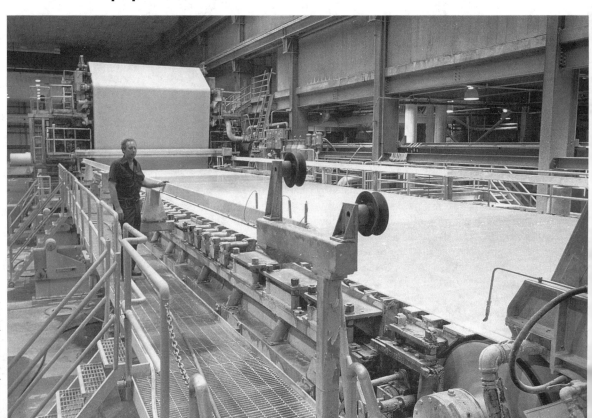

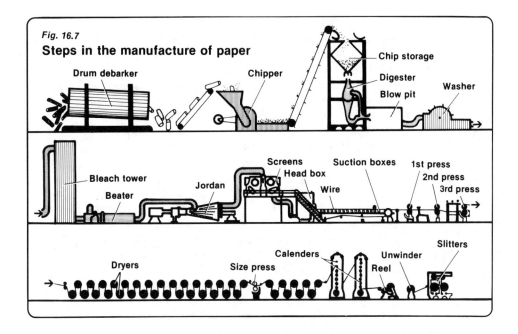

Fig. 16.7
Steps in the manufacture of paper

Chip storage — Digester — Washer — Blow pit — Drum debarker — Chipper

Bleach tower — Beater — Jordan — Screens — Head box — Suction boxes — Wire — 1st press — 2nd press — 3rd press

Dryers — Size press — Calenders — Reel — Unwinder — Slitters

from mechanical or semimechanical pulp, often contains a certain amount of sulfite pulp to improve sheet quality.

Blending of bleached hardwood kraft pulp with that from softwoods is common when making most types of printable papers for periodicals, catalogs, and containers. The hardwood pulp provides a smooth, opaque paper, while the softwood fibers add strength. Mixtures of pulp containing from 50 to 80% hardwoods are commonly used for such products.

PAPER PROPERTIES

Common measures of quality. There are many ways to define paper quality. When making grocery bags, for instance, strength is quite important. As with solid wood, there are many measures of strength. A bag filled with heavy canned goods is often picked up by its sides, so it must have high tensile strength. A bag that contains an exceptionally heavy item such as a large soft drink bottle should be able to resist this kind of concentrated load, a property measured by burst strength. High resistance to tear is another property obviously needed in an all-purpose bag. Moreover, the bag should retain its strength when wet.

When book paper is manufactured, tear strength is obviously critical. But other factors are quite significant as well. The sheet must accept ink, but it must have low absorbency to prevent ink diffusion and development of fuzziness around printed characters. High *opacity* is also necessary so that printing does not show through to the other side. Other important properties might be brightness, permanent whiteness, and surface smoothness. If the paper is to be used in making a product like a restaurant menu, all the properties outlined above would be needed as well as folding endurance.

Paper used for toweling should have an entirely different set of properties. Strength, particularly wet strength, is important in a towel, and such paper should also be highly absorbent. For each of the thousands of paper products, a similar list of important properties might be enumerated. Various test methods have been developed for evaluation of the suitability of different pulps for manufacture of these various kinds of paper. Also, there are dozens of tests that are used to evaluate the strength, surface, and optical properties of the paper. These tests are spelled out in TAPPI (Technical Association of the Pulp and Paper Institute) and CPPA (Canadian Pulp and Paper Association) standards.

Paper properties and fiber characteristics. Knowledge of only one characteristic of wood, i.e., density, allows prediction of the yield of pulp per unit volume of wood as well as a number of paper properties. Density is directly related to cell wall thickness. The general rule is that the lower the density, and thus the lower the proportion of thick-walled latewood cells, the better the wood as a papermaking raw material. It should be noted that this rule does not hold if high tear strength is desired.

Thick-walled fibers result in paper with low burst and tensile strengths but with a high degree of resistance to tear. Paper made primarily of thick-walled cells also tends to have very low folding endurance. The relationship of burst and tensile strengths to cell wall thickness is explained by the fact that these properties are very dependent upon a high degree of fiber-to-fiber bonding. The primary reason for apparently low bond potential of thick fibers is that paper is manufactured on a weight basis, meaning that the number of fibers in a sheet is inversely related to the density of fiber walls. Second, thick-walled fibers have less surface area per unit weight than thin-walled fibers. These two factors lessen opportunities for interfiber bonding.

Tear strength, like burst and tensile strengths, is influenced by the extent of interfiber bonding. More important, however, is the effect that individual fiber strength has upon tear resistance. Thick-walled fibers are obviously stronger than those having thin walls. It has been found that thick-walled cells that provide high tear strength are usually composed of a high proportion of hemicellulose. High levels of hemicellulose are evidently related to rapid hydration of pulp, formation of more and better interfiber bonds, and development of dense mats.

A second characteristic of wood that has an effect upon paper properties is fiber length. Tear strength is the property most affected and the relationship is direct up to a length of 4–5 mm. Generally, the greater the fiber length, the higher the tear resistance. Some reference can be found in the literature to direct relationships between fiber length and other important strength factors such as burst and tensile. Other investigators, however, discount fiber length as a significant influence on these properties.

The proportion of various cell types in wood can affect the quality and quantity of pulp. This is particularly true of the portion of hardwood volume accounted for by vessels. Because of their shape, vessels do not bond readily to fibers, thereby contributing little to strength. Vessels may separate from the surface of the finished sheet in printing. Vessels are also more likely to break up during processing, and thereby woods containing a high proportion of these cells are likely to give lower pulp yields than those with a higher fiber content.

IMPORTANT TYPES OF PAPER

Linerboard. This is a relatively lightweight board typically produced from un-bleached kraft fiber to be used as the outer surface on corrugated containers. The production of linerboard in the United States is very large, exceeding even newsprint in tonnage. Linerboard generally is made from softwood fiber and is produced on a Fourdrinier machine. Its most important properties are stiffness and burst resistance, although some degree of printability is also desired on the outer surface. This latter property may be enhanced by forming a small amount of highly refined fiber on top of the base of coarser high-yield fiber.

Corrugating medium. This lightweight paperboard is used for the fluted in-ner plies of corrugated boxes. Linerboard is glued to both sides of corrugating medium to produce what the public calls "cardboard." Since corrugating medium provides much of the rigidity to corrugated containers, it must have both good stiffness properties and good resistance to crushing. Some is produced from 100% recycled fiber, but most is produced from a mixture of semimechanical and recycled pulp. Since this paper does not require high tensile and tear strength, the use of long-fibered softwood pulp is not necessary.

Newsprint. The primary requirement of newsprint is that it can be run through modern high-speed printing presses and provide a reasonably good printing sur-face. It must also be low in cost. Newsprint is generally produced from a mixture of mechanical, semimechanical, and chemical pulp. Few additives like those used to enhance the printing properties of fine or magazine papers are added to newsprint. In order to develop adequate strength for printing at high speeds, some unbleached sulfite or bleached kraft is usually added to the groundwood pulp. Since mechanical pulp is cheaper than chemical pulp, only enough chemi-cal pulp is used to meet the print-speed requirements.

Publication grades. Papers for high-quality printing purposes must be coated in the papermaking process to improve the gloss, detail, and brilliance that can be obtained in printing. The addition of fillers and coatings at various stages in the process can greatly alter the properties of the paper. Coatings can make up over 30% of total sheet weight in some lightweight grades. There is a trend to lighter-weight printing papers because of increasing postage rates and the tremendous growth in the use of catalogs for home shopping. A higher propor-tion of chemical pulp is usually required as paper weight is reduced. TMP pulp and other semimechanical pulps are used in these papers, as are bleached kraft pulp from both hardwoods and softwoods.

Fine paper. This is the classification for white, uncoated printing and writing paper containing only a small amount of mechanical pulp. Sulphite and highly refined bleached kraft pulp may be used in those cases where wood furnish is in-corporated. Nonwood fibers such as cotton and linen are also used.

Tissue. This category of paper covers a wide variety of facial and bathroom tis-sues, paper napkins, and toweling. Because these are lightweight papers that must have a loose structure, they cannot be produced on conventional paper machines. One of the keys to success in this business is to have an effective proprietary system of producing a low-density sheet. These products generally require a high-quality furnish with long, highly refined fibers since softness is a function of fiber properties and bulk.

Paperboard. This category of thick paper includes linerboard and corrugating medium described above. However, there are a number of other important types of paperboard that usually have a multi-ply construction. Folding boxboard is made from virgin pulp in the outer ply and from secondary fiber for the inner plies. Foodboard, utilizing 100% bleached virgin pulp, is used for food packaging. The paper for the outer layer of gypsum board, i.e., sheetrock, is a paperboard usually made from 100% secondary fiber.

Kraft sack paper. This paper is produced from unbleached softwood kraft pulp. Tear strength and tensile energy absorption are two of the most-important properties. Sizing is often added to the well-refined fibers in the papermaking process to provide additional internal and wet strength.

MEASUREMENT AND SOURCES OF RAW MATERIAL. In the United States, about half of the wood used for the manufacture of paper is in the form of small-diameter pulpwood bolts (Fig. 16.8). Because of the large volume of pulpwood handled at the mill and irregular shapes of individual pieces, pulpwood is measured by cord or other quasi-volume units or by weight as discussed in Chapter 13.

A standard unit of measure for pulpwood in the United States is the cord, which is defined in Chapter 13. It is important to remember that a cord does not contain 128 ft³ of wood but 128 ft³ of space. A cord of 7–10-in. (18–25-cm) diameter undebarked bolts 4 ft (1.2 m) long, for example, contains only about 80 ft³ (2.3 m³) of wood and another 10 ft³ (0.3 m³) or so of bark. A greater amount of wood is contained in cords composed of larger-diameter and/or shorter bolts.

Pulpwood is also purchased by weight. Payment is then made either directly

(Courtesy S. Sinclair)

Fig. 16.8
A load of pulpwood begins the trip to the paper mill.

by weight ($/ton), or the weight is converted to cord equivalents, with payment then made on a cord basis. Elsewhere in the world, pulpwood volume is commonly expressed in cubic meters (m^3). In the United States pulp chips are often purchased on a weight basis (by the green or estimated dry ton), volume basis (by the 200 ft^3 unit), or a combination weight/volume basis (by converting weight measurements to cords).

Hardboard ■

Hardboard is a high-density wood fiber product that is most commonly manufactured to a specific gravity near 1.0. The product is generally in the form of flat sheets ranging from $\frac{1}{16}$ to $\frac{1}{2}$ in. (1.6–12.7 mm) in thickness but it can also be molded to a variety of shapes. Hardboard was developed accidentally in 1924 by William H. Mason who had invented a quick explosion process for transforming chips to pulp and was attempting to make a low-density insulation-type product from such fibers. Having placed a wet fiber mat in a steam-heated press for the purpose of drying the fiber, Mason left his laboratory to eat lunch. When he returned, he found that a small steam valve had failed, causing high and prolonged pressure on the fiber mat, resulting in a hard, dense panel. The product, dubbed "pressed wood" by its discoverer, soon came to be known as hardboard. The invention led to immediate formation of the Mason Fiber Company, a name later changed to Masonite Corporation. The name Masonite is still sometimes used interchangeably with the term *hardboard*. Today, the hardboard industry is sizable, with 23 plants producing 8 billion ft^2 on a $\frac{1}{8}$-in. basis annually in the United States.

MANUFACTURING. An important distinction between hardboard and other fiber products is that in hardboard (of the wet-process type), lignin plays the major role in fiber-to-fiber bonding. Because of this, the kind of pulp suitable for making hardboard is from the RMP or TMP process in which the lignin is retained. A type of refiner widely used in this industry is the Asplund defibrator, invented by a Swedish engineer of that name in 1931. This invention played a major role in the development of the hardboard industry (Suchsland and Woodson 1986).

The basic procedure employed in commercial hardboard manufacture is shown in Figure 16.9. Note that resin and wax are added after the pulping process or during drying of the fiber. Water-compatible resins such as phenol formaldehyde are normally used, with the concentration generally on the order of 1–2% of dry board weight. These small amounts improve board strength, and the resin as well as the wax increases water resistance.

Following production of pulp, fibers are formed into a mat and prepressed. Mat formation can be accomplished using either water or air as a forming medium. The difference in these techniques, known as the wet and the dry processes, is explained below. The manufacturing sequence is concluded with a hot-press operation in which high temperature (190°–235°C) and high pressure (500–1500 psi) are employed to bring the lignin to a thermoplastic condition and thus to densify the fiber mat.

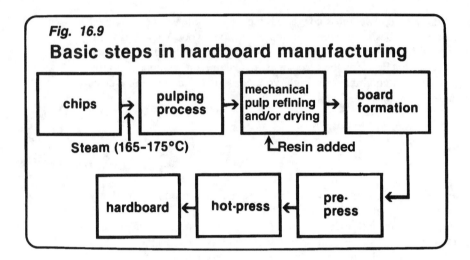

Fig. 16.9
Basic steps in hardboard manufacturing

chips → pulping process → mechanical pulp refining and/or drying → board formation

Steam (165–175°C)

Resin added

hardboard ← hot-press ← pre-press ←

Wet process. As the name suggests, in the wet process, pulp is mixed with water as in the making of paper. This water-fiber mixture is then metered onto a wire screen. Water is drained away with the aid of suction applied to the underside of the wire, and the fiber mat along with the supporting wire is moved to a prepress where excess water is squeezed out. The prepress operation is an important part of the wet process, since the subsequent step involves pressing at high temperatures. Unnecessary vaporization of water and resulting waste of heat would result from omission of this step. Following prepressing, the compressed mat is moved into the hot press along with the wire screen on which it was formed. High levels of pressure and heat serve to form ligneous bonds, squeeze out additional water, and dry the mat. The screen is retained in the hot-pressing operation to allow escape of water vapor.

Wet-process hardboard is typified by evenly distributed density (because water is an efficient forming medium) and one rough side caused by the screen. Several firms do produce a wet-process board with two smooth sides by drying the fiber mat prior to pressing. In this case fiber bonding is entirely of the lignin type since the phenol resins would cure during drying and so are not used.

Dry process. Dry-process hardboard is made using air rather than water as a forming medium. Bonding of the fibers is accomplished with a synthetic resin as it is in the manufacture of particleboard discussed in the previous chapter. Following pulping, the fiber is dried, resin is added, and the furnish is introduced into a forming device that creates a "snowstorm" of the dry, fluffy fiber. The fiber blanket formed in this way is quite thick (4–5 in. for what will eventually be a ¼-in. panel), so a press roll is placed downstream of the former to compress the loosely piled fibers. Hot pressing completes the sequence. The fiber mat is relatively dry when it enters the hot press, and therefore no screen is needed beneath the mat, resulting in panels smooth on both sides (S-2-S).

Dry-process hardboard tends to have less evenly distributed density, has greater linear expansion, and its bending strength is typically lower than the wet-process variety. There is a substantial lowering of lignin bonding as compared to the wet process, and therefore more resin (about 2% resin solids based on dry weight) is used. The major advantage of the dry process is the two smooth sides.

Tempering. Hardboard is sensitive to water. Unless specially treated, it should be used only as an interior product. Moisture causes linear expansion of panels, thickness swelling, and formation of surface blisters. For these reasons, hardboard intended for exterior use should be treated for resistance to moisture. The treated product is known as tempered hardboard.

Traditionally *tempering* has been achieved by soaking finished panels in various oils, followed by baking at high temperature to flash off the volatile fractions. The result is greatly improved water resistance, increased abrasion resistance, improved hardness, and better overall strength. Another process for tempering involves high-temperature treatment without a preliminary oil soak; the purpose of exposure to heat, which may be as great as 200°C, is to increase crosslinking between cellulose and other polymers. Performance under wet conditions can also be improved by simply using more resin in board manufacture. The latter mentioned methods for tempering have become more popular because of the air pollution problems associated with baking oil-soaked panels.

APPLICATIONS. Hardboard in the form of flat panels is used in furniture, for television and radio cabinet backing, drawer bottoms, dust stops, sliding doors, general purpose backing, and tabletops. It is also commonly used for wall paneling, cabinet doors and tops, interior door faces, garage door panels, and store fixture components. Unfinished panels are perforated with holes and used as pegboard for decoration of workshop, laundry room, and garage walls. Smooth-faced hardboard sheets are also often painted or covered with vinyl or other material for use as exterior siding or as decorative paneling for interior use (Fig. 16.10). Appearance-grade panels can be made with contoured or sculptured surfaces by using sculptured platens (or dies) in the hot press. This technique allows reproduction of rough-sawn surfaces, simulated brick, or other textures. Another family of hardboard products is based upon the fact that finished panels can be steamed and molded to various shapes (Fig. 16.11). Molded hardboard products are particularly evident in the auto industry, where they are used as door and roof panels, back window decks, and dashboards. Door skins for production of simulated panel doors are another major use. Three product standards govern the product properties and test specifications for hardboard products: ANSI/AHA A135.4 (1995)—Basic Hardboard; ANSI/AHA A135.5 (1995)—Prefinished Hardboard Paneling; and ANSI/AHA A135.6 (1996)—Hardboard Siding.

Fig. 16.10
Hardboard panels have a variety of uses.

Fig. 16.11
Hardboard can be molded to different shapes.

Insulation board ■

A group of fiber panel products manufactured to specific gravities ranging from about 0.16 to 0.50 are referred to as *insulation board.* These range from low-density acoustical ceiling tile (Fig. 16.12) to a higher-density wall sheathing board used under siding in light-frame construction (Fig. 16.13). There are only about one-half as many insulation board plants in the United States as there were 30 years ago. Most of these are in the South. Competition from both wood and nonwood products, primarily fiberglass, plastic foam, and plywood, has greatly reduced the markets for wood-based insulation board.

Insulation board has been produced in the United States since 1916 when a plant using SGW pulp was built in Minnesota. Another early plant built in 1931 in Louisiana used *bagasse* (waste left after extraction from sugar cane) for insulation board production. At one time there were about 25 insulation board plants in the United States.

MANUFACTURING PROCESSES. The process used to produce insulation board is quite similar to that employed in making wet process hardboard except for the pressing operation. As with hardboard, the insulation board sequence involves TMP or RMP pulping of chips, subsequent refining of fiber, and board formation with water as the forming medium. A hot press is not used in making insulation board. Instead, the mat is simply brought to desired thickness using a press roll and then dried. The omission of hot pressing means that ligneous bond-

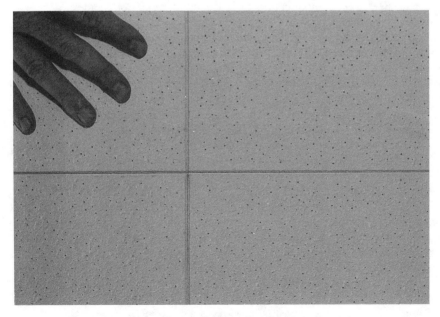

Fig. 16.12
Acoustical ceiling tile is commonly made of wood fiber.

Fig. 16.13
Structural insulation board is applied prior to siding.

ing is not achieved in insulation board. Fiber-to-fiber linkages are provided primarily by hydrogen bonding, although additives such as starch or asphalt are often used for bond enhancement.

Formation of the mat for insulation board is done with a single- or double-cylinder machine or on a Fourdrinier. As compared to the Fourdrinier, the *cylinder machines* are simple and rugged. The pulp slurry is pumped into a trough that surrounds a large cylinder faced with a wire screen. The cylinder rotates slowly as a vacuum inside the cylinder sucks the slurry and fiber against the wire. The fiber mat is thus built up on the wire screen and is transferred to a conveyor as it emerges from the trough. On a double-cylinder machine the two mats formed come together to form one thick mat. This double machine results in a mat that is symmetrical in regard to the fibers on both surfaces. The single-cylinder machine produces a mat with the coarser fibers on the cylinder side.

USES. Traditionally, wall sheathing and ceiling tile were the major products made from insulation board. Insulation board sheathing provides insulation to the wall construction, eliminates the need for corner bracing, and serves to reduce noise transmission through the exterior walls. Nonetheless, only a small portion of the wall sheathing currently used in the United States is insulation board. Also, as a result of competition from more fire-resistant products, little insulation board production currently goes into ceiling tile. Other uses of insulation board include backers for aluminum siding and shingles and panels for use in built-up roof construction and board for a variety of industrial purposes such as sound-deadening board. The product standards ANSI/AHA A194.1 (1996)—Cellulosic Fiberboard, and ASTM C208-95 (1995)—Standard Specifications for Cellulosic Fiber

Insulating Board spell out the property requirements and test methods for insulation board.

One insulation board product made from recycled fiber is enjoying success (Maloney 1994). This structural product sold under the name Homosote is produced from waste newspaper and groundwood paper waste. This product is used as panels and is combined with fiberglass and foams to produce wall and roof components.

Medium-density fiberboard (MDF) ∎

MDF is a dry-formed panel product produced primarily from wood fiber (although some bagasse is used) and bonded with synthetic resins to a density of 31–50 lb/ft³ (500–800 kg/m³). Like dry-process hardboard, MDF is made from wood that has been reduced to individual fibers and fiber bundles with a binder added to accomplish board strength. One of the keys in the production of this product is the use of pressurized refiners which produce pulp of a very low bulk density. Once the mat is formed, the remainder of the manufacturing process for thick MDF is quite similar to that for particleboard. Some thin MDF is manufactured in a continuous process on a large drum press termed a *Mende press*.

Medium-density fiberboard has only been produced for about 30 years. Worldwide there now are about 100 plants with total production capacity of about 10 million m³/yr. About 20% of this capacity is in the United States. The consumption of MDF continues to grow due to its versatility for a range of products from core-stock to a substitute for clear lumber. The consumption of MDF in the United States has increased from 0.5 to 1.5 billion ft² (¾-in. basis) from 1980 to 1995.

MANUFACTURING PROCESS. The first steps in making MDF are very similar to those employed in manufacturing hardboard. Logs are reduced to chips, with these then subjected to a thermomechanical pulping. The process thereafter closely resembles that used in making particleboard (see Chapter 15). Fiber is dried, blended with resin and wax, and formed into a mat that is subsequently hot-pressed to desired thickness and density. Special blending and forming machines are necessary for MDF because of the bulky low-density fiber. Like particleboard, resin solids comprise 6–7% of the dry weight of the product. Urea-formaldehyde resins as in the particleboard industry are typically used as the binder.

A wide variety of raw material types can be used for MDF. Although wood residue such as planer shavings, sawdust, and plywood trim can be used, the input needs to include at least 25% pulp chips to produce the desired quality of furnish (Maloney 1994). Many species can be utilized as long as the interaction between the chemistry of the species and the urea-formaldehyde resin is properly controlled.

USES. The most-significant use (70% in the United States) of MDF is in furniture and kitchen cabinet manufacture where it is used in much the same way as particleboard or lumber-core plywood. The edges of particleboard are too porous to be shaped or finished directly and thus are commonly edge-banded for furniture applications (Fig. 16.14). MDF in contrast has a more-uniform density and smooth, tight edges that can be machined almost like solid wood. MDF can also be finished to a smooth surface and grain-printed, thus eliminating the need for surface veneers or laminates. For these reasons there is a well-defined market for MDF furniture panels. Another increasing use is to simulate clear lumber in applications where the strength of lumber is not required but where a smooth, printable or paintable surface is needed. Interior door skins are commonly made of thin, molded MDF panels.

The product standard ANSI A208.2 (1994) governs product properties and test methods for MDF produced in the United States.

Other wood-fiber products ■

Several products utilizing inorganic binders (gypsum, Portland cement, or magnesite) and wood fiber have been recently commercialized. The fiber provides bending strength and flexibility while the binders provide desireable properties such as high fire and termite resistance. The wood content in these proprietary products is not stated although wood does not appear to be the major component. These products are quite different from the cement-excelsior and cement-particle products described in Chapter 15, which have been on the market for many years (see Fig. 15.20).

One cement-bonded product containing wood fiber is said to be immune to water damage, termites, and decay. The decay and insect immunity are attributed to the high alkalinity. Some of these products contain ground sand as well as the binder and wood fiber. These cement-bonded products are generally character-

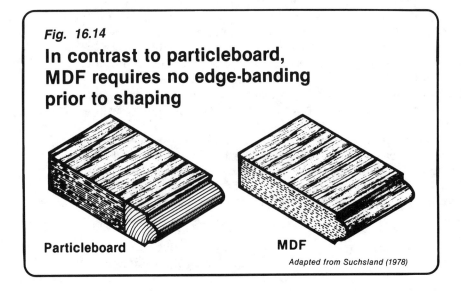

Fig. 16.14

In contrast to particleboard, MDF requires no edge-banding prior to shaping

Particleboard   **MDF**

Adapted from Suchsland (1978)

ized by high density (up to 100 lb/ft^3) and tend to be less flexible than an all wood-fiber product but of comparable or higher bending strength. These products appear well suited for use as lap siding, vertical siding, roof shingles, and shakes.

A gypsum-fiber product utilizing gypsum as the binder and recycled paper has become quite widely used in Europe and is now being produced in at least one plant in North America (Maloney 1994, 1996). This product is an alternative to conventional gypsum board used for walls and ceilings. Conventional gypsum board has gypsum sandwiched between two thick sheets of paperboard. This product has the wood fiber distributed uniformly throughout the thickness of the panel.

Recent years have marked the development of a number of thermoplastic composites made using waste paper or waste wood fiber as a reinforcing filler. As described by Youngquist (1995), "It is possible to assemble a wide variety of wood fibers and synthetic plastic fibers into a random web or mat using air-formed web technology. This technology involves mixing, at room temperature, lignocellulosic fibers or fiber bundles with other long fibrous materials. This process can accommodate a wide range of wood-based and synthetic fibers and can be used to produce a variety of products of varying densities.

Wood fibers can also be combined with plastics such as polyethylene, polypropylene, and comingled thermoplastics using melt-blending technology, which is an inherently low-cost, high-production rate process in which wood and paper are mixed with molten plastic. These blends can then be formed into products using conventional plastics processing techniques such as extrusion or injection molding. The plastic acts as a means to convey the wood/paper during processing and the wood/paper fiber bears the load in the final composite, offering an effective balance between processability and strength of the end product."

REVIEW

A. Terms to define or explain:

1. RMP	12. Kraft pulp
2. TMP	13. Opacity
3. NSSC process	14. Tempering
4. Cooking liquor	15. Insulation board
5. Digester	16. MDF
6. Pulp	17. Linerboard
7. Tissue	18. Dry-process hardboard
8. Beating	19. Canadian Standard freeness
9. Jordan refiner	20. Cylinder machine
10. Fourdrinier	21. Bagasse
11. Paperboard	

B. Questions or concepts to explain:
1. What are the primary processes used to produce pulp? What kind of pulp yields are realized when these various processes are employed?
2. Mechanical pulp is used in making certain kinds of paper and paperboard. Why is it a favored material for production of newsprint? Why is mechanical pulp avoided when making high-quality papers?
3. What are the two chemical pulping processes most commonly used? What are the advantages and disadvantages of each?

4. What is the meaning of the term "freeness"? How is freeness related to properties of paper?
5. How is hardboard made? What is the difference between wet- and dry-process hardboard and what are the advantages of each?
6. What has been the trend in the production of insulation board? Why?
7. Describe some of the semimechanical pulping methods.
8. In what ways is MDF different from wet-formed hardboard and insulation board?

REFERENCES AND SUPPLEMENTAL READINGS

American Forest and Paper Association. 1995. Paper, Paperboard, and Wood Pulp, 1995. Washington, D.C.

American Paper Institute (API). 1984. Wood pulp and fiber statistics. 47th ed. New York.

Dadswell, H.E., and Watson, A.J. 1962. Influence of the morphology of wood-pulp fibers on wood properties. In The Formation and Structure of Paper, Vol. 2. Tech. Sec. British Paper and Board Makers Association. Oxford Symp. Trans.

Ellwood, E.L.; Hitchings, R.G.; and Barefoot, A.C. 1965. Wood characteristics and kraft paper properties of four selected loblolly pines. For. Prod. J. 15(8):313–320.

Evans, J.C.W. 1978. Wastepaper: Use increasing faster than paper production in the U.S. Pulp Pap. 52(7):124–125.

Food and Agriculture Organization (FAO). 1993. Forestry Statistics, 1961–1991. Rome.

Haas, L.; Kalish, J.; and Bayliss, M. 1979. World review. Pulp Pap. 53(9):62–70.

Iyengar, S., and Ackley, K. 1993. Paper producers should consider options for secondary fiber use. Pulp and Paper. 67(8):45–47.

Kauppi, P.K. 1984. High-yield pulping brightens industry future. Paper Trade J. Nov.:46–50.

Krzysik, A.M., Younquist, J.A.; Rowell, R.M.; Muehl, J.H.; Chow, P.; and Shook, S.R. 1993. Feasibility of recycled newspapers for dry-process hardboard. For. Prod. J. 43(7/8):53–58.

Libby, C.E., ed. 1962. Pulp and Paper Science and Technology. Vol. 1. New York: McGraw-Hill.

Lowe, K.E. 1978. U.S. profile. Pulp Pap. 52(7):21–30.

Lynn, E.S. 1985. Global perspective of the pulp and paper industry. TAPPI J. 68(1):42–47.

Maloney, T.M. 1994. Development of wood composite materials. Res. Pap. Pullman,Wash.:Wash. State Univ. Wood Mtl. Lab.

Maloney, T.M. 1996. The family of wood composite materials. For. Prod. J. 46(2):19–26.

McGovern, J.N. 1982. Fibers used in early writing papers. TAPPI J. Dec.:57–58.

Quicke, H.E.; Caulfield, J.P.; and Duffy, P.A. 1990. The production structure of the U.S. paper industry. For. Prod. J. 40(9):44–48.

Saltman, D. 1978. Paper Basics. New York: Van Nostrand Reinhold.

Singh, R.P. 1993. Technological approaches to TCF pulp. Pulp and Paper. 67(10):35–36.

Smook, G.A. 1982. Handbook for Pulp and Paper Technologists. Joint Textbook Committee of the Paper Industry of the United States and Canada.

Suchsland, O. 1978. Markets and applications of MDF. In Complete Tree Utilization of Southern Pine. Proc. For. Prod. Res. Soc. Symp.

Suchsland, O. and Woodson, G.E. 1986. Fiberboard Manufacturing Practices in the United States. USDA For. Ser. Agric. Handbk. 640.

Youngquist, J.A. 1995. The marriage of wood and nonwood materials. For. Prod. J. 45(10):25–30.

4

Wood as a fuel and industrial raw material

THE LAST PART of this book provides a glimpse of some of the trends in the use of the world's wood resources and examines environmental implications of periodic forest harvest and wood use.

Fuelwood has been the most important use of wood in most of the developing countries of the world. However, in the developed world, wood for energy was rediscovered as a result of the 1970s energy crisis. The forest products industry suddenly found energy at its waste burners, debarkers, and logging sites and initiated programs to make maximum use of what had previously been

▶

waste. The forest products industry today has the enviable potential of becoming energy self-sufficient, or nearly so, by converting its manufacturing residues and the low-grade timber on its lands to heat and power.

Wood for energy is also increasingly interesting to nonforest industries and to those who generate commercial power. The value of wood as a fuel has made complete utilization of the harvested forest biomass not only possible but a reality in many sections of the United States. Continuing economic and technological developments in forest products and other fields will determine how various components of the tree are to be used in the future—whether for solid wood, particles, fiber, or fuel. Looking further to the future, wood has potential as a raw material for production of many industrial chemicals. Here again, the rate of development will be affected by technological change, availability of alternate raw materials, and economic factors.

One other factor that will influence the future use of wood is public policy regarding forest management. In view of current contentiousness over periodic forest harvesting in the United States, the role of domestic forests in providing for future needs of U.S. citizens remains unclear. What is clear is that wood, whether from the United States or elsewhere, will remain a critically important raw material for the United States for a very long time to come. ■

17

Wood for energy

■ **WHEN REFERRING** to forest products, one generally thinks of lumber, panel products, and paper. In the past three decades, however, energy has become a significant product of forest biomass. The use of woody residues to provide industrial processing, heat, and electricity has become very important to the economic viability of the forest products industry. In some communities in North America and throughout many developed and developing countries worldwide, wood in solid, pellet, or powdered form is important for heating and cooking in homes and businesses. Today, energy should be considered as one of the major products from the forest.

In North America the emergence of *woody biomass* (wood and bark) as a vital source of energy for industry came about because of the rapidly escalating cost of petroleum and natural gas during the 1970s, when the cost of imported oil increased abruptly from $3 to $30 per barrel. Prior to 1973 energy was cheap, and energy efficiency was not a major concern in the design of industrial equipment for manufacturing processes. As a result, the capital cost of equipment for manufacturing was more important than its energy efficiency. It made economic sense, for example, to install an inexpensive natural gas–fired boiler for a lumber dry kiln rather than to spend several times as much for a combustion system capable of using the bark and wood residue available. Even though residue was available at little or no cost, the high capital cost of wood-burning equipment often made its use uneconomical. The cost of liquid and gas fuels has declined since those peak years, but energy conservation and use of "alternative" fuels has become both a public and political concern. Wood has become an economically desirable source of energy for the forest products industry and the only affordable source of energy for many people throughout the world.

An illustration of the value of wood fuel compared to alternative industrial fuels is shown in Table 17.1. For example, if fuel oil costs $1.50/gal it would cost $102 to purchase enough fuel oil to produce the same amount of heat as one ton of wet (60% MC) sawdust. Note that the amount of heat obtained from wood depends upon the moisture content, so dry wood fuels are more valuable than wetter wood residues. The value of wood fuel shown in the table does not take into account the additional cost of the equipment to store, handle, and burn wood as compared to the fossil fuels. Nevertheless, the equivalent value of wood fuel is much higher than most realize, and the added cost of handling it can often be justified.

Table 17.1.   Equivalent value of wood fuel at alternative fossil fuel prices

	Cost of fossil fuel required to produce the same amount of heat as 1 ton wood fuel*								
	Natural gas (per 1000 ft^3)			#2 Fuel oil (per gal.)			Bituminous coal (per ton)		
Type of wood fuel	$2	$4	$6	$1	$1.50	$2	$50	$75	$100
					($)				
Ovendry wood	36	70	106	120	181	240	30	45	60
Dry planer shavings									
15% MC	30	60	90	102	153	204	26	38	51
Sawdust and bark									
30% MC	26	52	78	88	132	176	22	33	44
60% MC	20	40	60	68	102	136	17	25	34
90% MC	16	32	48	54	81	108	13	20	27

*These values assume normal combustion efficiencies for each fuel type. They do not include the additional costs for wood fuel resulting from handling, storage, maintenance, and capital costs. Value of wood fuel is thus considered to be the cost of the fossil fuel required to produce the same amount of heat as 1 ton of wood.

The value of wood as a fuel can present problem for some types of manufacturing plants. Serious wood procurement problems can result for firms dependent on low-cost wood residue for product raw material when there is a high value on that raw material if used as a fuel. As an example, consider a particleboard plant using oil for energy and purchasing $30/ton planer shavings for board furnish. Suppose the oil it is using for heating the driers and hot presses increases to $1.50/gal. In this situation, one ton of shavings used as fuel will replace $153 worth of fuel oil, so there is obviously a strong economic incentive to use planer shavings for energy. But is this increased amount available and if so what will this added demand do to the price the supplier will ask? The decision to convert to wood for energy will be influenced by the cost of the new combustion and fuel-handling system required, but the major factor in a decision to convert to wood energy may be the adequacy and reliability of the supply of shavings and wood residue.

The importance of woody biomass as a source of industrial energy will continue unless other economical alternatives to petroleum and natural gas are developed. The use of wood for energy by the forest products industry is not likely to decrease. In 1980 the 14 largest forest products companies in the United States reported that they produced 70% of their energy from wood waste. Those companies produced one-fourth of the lumber and one-half of the plywood and particleboard in the United States. Since that time, most new forest products–manufacturing plants have been designed to obtain their process and space heat from combustion of their mill residues. The largest plants also generate much of their electrical demand from residues.

It has been traditional to refer to the portion of the forest biomass not used for primary forest products as residues. *Mill residues* consist of planer shavings, bark, slabs, plywood trim, and saw- and sander dust. Woods or *logging residues* include tops, limbs, and cull trees normally left in the woods. Overall, the use of mill residues as a fuel source is projected to remain steady in the United States over the next several decades (with use in 1990 estimated to be 1939 million cubic feet, or about 55 million cubic meters), while substantial increases in the use of logging resides for this purpose are expected (High and Skog 1989).

The international significance of wood as a home heating and cooking fuel should be recognized. On a worldwide basis, the use of wood for fuel has always been the single largest use of wood and remains so today. It is estimated that 50% of the wood consumed in the world is used for home heating and cooking. Shortage of wood in many developing countries has very serious implications to the maintenance of the remaining forests. Forests are disappearing in many countries where the growing population needs fuel and agricultural land for survival. In the decade of the 1980s, it is estimated that 17 million ha of forests were lost in the world each year (FAO 1992). Clearly, the implications of the use of wood for fuel are quite different in the United States where there is much woody biomass physically, if not economically, available. As discussed in the Introduction, forests in the United States are not in decline as is the case in many tropical regions.

From a study of wood-fuel use, Warsco (1994) concluded that the potential for displacement of conventional space-heating fuels by wood is substantial in the United States. About 23 million households burn wood for main or auxiliary heat, although only about one-fourth of these are using the equipment to near its maximum heat output. This means that 27% of all households in the United States are burning some wood for heating. The greatest wood fuel use is in the Alabama, Tennessee, Kentucky, and Mississippi region where 16% of households rely on wood as their primary source of heat.

Materials available for energy

There are five potential sources of woody material for generating energy. These are roundwood from growing stock, mill residues, logging or woods residues, recycled materials (paper, paperboard, wood pallets, railroad ties, etc.), and so-called *energy plantations*. Roundwood and mill residues are, of course, also in demand to produce fiber and particle products. Logging residues could technically be used for particle and fiber products also, but because of the higher bark and grit content and other contaminants, this material is better suited to the production of energy. Recycled paper is in demand for many types of paper products. Marks (1992) points out the advantages of wood powder from residues as an upgraded wood fuel.

The use of short-rotation intensive forest management to produce biomass in energy plantations caught public attention in the 1970s and 1980s and generated considerable study and controversy. Such plantations have existed in a few former third world countries for some years. In the United States commercial development of energy plantations is in its infancy, although plantations devoted to producing a variety of wood products, including energy, are nothing new. Recent discussions within the U.S. Congress (1993) have focused on the possibility of dedicating large land areas in the United States to tree and other biomass plantations for the purpose of providing energy and sequestering carbon.

Mill residues are a highly desirable wood fuel because they are available at the mills (no transportation cost), and they are often partially dried. Estimates of the volume of mill residues in the United States in 1976 indicated that at that time one-third were unused. The mill residue utilization picture has changed dramatically since then. In the United States today, although residues at some small plants are still not completely utilized, most bark and wood residue available in sufficient quantity has a ready market.

The material left in the woods after logging represents a huge store of potential fuel. Because of its dispersion and small size, however, this material is expensive to collect. Its utilization depends upon the development of cost-effective harvesting systems. Wahlgren and Ellis (1978) estimated that in the United States, about 105 million tons of logging residue could be available for use annually. In 1990, only about 5 million tons of logging residue were being utilized for energy (High and Skog 1989).

It is very difficult to estimate the total annual growth of forest biomass in the United States that might be usable for energy. Forest inventories have traditionally been concerned with estimating the volume of stems of merchantable size rather than the total biomass. Only limited data are available regarding the volume of total tree biomass either by tree or by stand. Much biomass can never be used for energy because of its location, ownership, or environmental concerns. Nevertheless, the limited data available indicate that biomass could contribute in a significant way to U.S. energy needs.

Whole-tree chippers of the type used to harvest stands for pulp chips can be used to produce chips for energy. A number of firms have used whole-tree chippers for this purpose. However, these machines are not well suited for harvesting the small-diameter stems present in most stands or for handling tops and limbs. A major deterrent to the use of the total forest biomass for fuel has been the cost of harvesting.

Specialized equipment to harvest small-diameter stems and collect and transport the material is needed. Several machines to do this job have been developed and tested by equipment manufacturers and forest products firms. Such a machine is shown in Figure 17.1. It appears that wide use of such equipment will only occur when fossil fuel prices again increase significantly.

(Courtesy P. Koch)

Fig. 17.1
An experimental machine designed to harvest total forest biomass.

Nature of wood as fuel

The most-common method of converting wood into energy is by *combustion*. The first stage of combustion is the evaporation of the water present. Next, the volatile components of wood, both combustible and noncombustible, are volatilized at temperatures from 100° to 600°C. From 75 to 85% of the wood can be volatilized. In the last stage of combustion, the carbon is oxidized. A standard test method to evaluate solid fuels, termed *proximate analysis*, provides the percentage of volatile matter and fixed carbon. The proximate analysis of several fuels is shown in Table 17.2.

Table 17.2. Proximate analysis of several fuels

Fuel	Volatile matter	Fixed carbon	Ash
		(%)	
Douglas-fir			
Wood	86.2	13.7	0.1
Bark	70.6	27.2	2.2
Western hemlock			
Wood	84.8	15.0	0.2
Bark	74.3	24.0	1.7
Hardwoods (avg.)			
Wood	77.3	19.4	3.4
Bark	76.7	18.6	4.6
Western coal	43.4	51.7	4.9

Source: Corder (1975), Arola (1976), Pingrey (1976).

The combustion reaction involves the combining of carbon from the wood with oxygen to form carbon dioxide and the combining of hydrogen from the wood with oxygen to form water. The oxygen in these reactions comes partly from the wood but mostly from the air. Wood contains approximately 6% hydrogen, 49% carbon, and 44% oxygen. The amount of oxygen (and thus air) required for the burning process can be theoretically calculated based upon the chemical analysis (termed *ultimate analysis*) of the species involved. However, in practice, more air than this theoretical amount is required to assure complete combustion. This is termed *excess air*. In modern wood furnaces, excess air is carefully controlled to assure efficient burning.

Table 17.3 gives average heating values for wood and bark. Resin has a heating value almost twice as high as wood; therefore, resinous woods have a somewhat higher value than those with no resin. Bark and wood from softwoods tend to be somewhat higher in heat value than those from hardwoods. Heating values also vary by species because of the varying proportion of carbon, oxygen, and hydrogen present. However, in engineering practice, an average heat of 9000 Btu/dry lb for resinous woods and 8300 Btu/dry lb for other woods is sometimes used.

Table 17.3. *Average heating values for wood and bark*

Type of wood	Ovendry heating values (higher heating values)	
	Wood	Bark
	(*Btu/dry lb*)	
Nonresinous	8000–8500	7400–9800
Resinous	8600–9700	8800–10,800

Source: Corder (1975).

The total heat generated by complete combustion under controlled conditions is termed the *higher heating value* (HHV). The actual heat that can be recovered in conventional burners is considerably less than the HHV due to the loss from vaporizing the water in the fuel and from other losses occurring in the process. These other losses include energy to heat the excess air and to heat the water formed during combustion. Figure 17.2 (Ince 1979) illustrates the relationship between the potential and *recoverable heat energy* per pound of wood fuel and the moisture content of the fuel.

The available potential heat at any moisture content, as illustrated in Figure 17.2, is sometimes called the *gross heating value* (GHV). The example shown in the figure is for a fuel with a HHV of 8500 Btu/lb in a combustion system with a 500°F stack gas (i.e., exhaust gas) temperature. Note that the GHV represents the HHV in the portion of fuel composed of dry wood. The GHV of wood can be calculated from the HHV as follows:

GHV = HHV × [1 − % MC (wet basis)/100]

The ratio of the recoverable heat to the available potential heat (see Fig. 17.2) is called the *combustion efficiency*. With wood fuels and current combus-

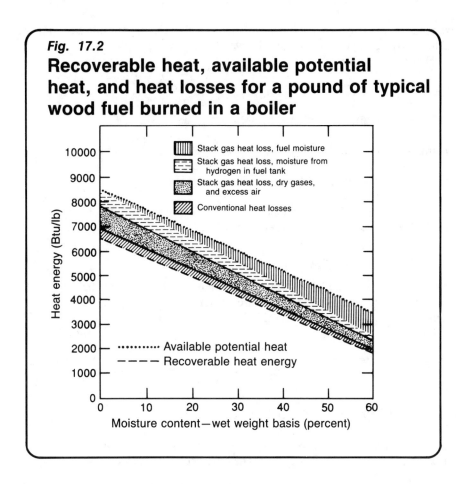

Fig. 17.2

Recoverable heat, available potential heat, and heat losses for a pound of typical wood fuel burned in a boiler

tion equipment, combustion efficiencies range from about 80% for dry fuels to 60% for wet fuels. Unfortunately, green rather than dry fuels are most-commonly available. When comparing the cost of alternative fuels, it is the recoverable heat value that is of most importance. It is this heat energy that produces the steam for industrial processes, or to drive a turbine, or that can be used for space heating.

The terms *net heating value* (NHV) and *lower heating value* (LHV) are sometimes encountered in combustion engineering. NHV and LHV are the net heat released by a fuel after reducing the HHV by the heat of vaporization of the water generated by combustion of the hydrogen in the fuel. LHVs are customarily used in Europe for purchases of fuel, while in America HHV is used as the basis on which fuel is bought and sold (Georgia Institute of Technology 1984).

As discussed in Chapter 8, the moisture content of forest products is normally calculated on a dry weight basis; if moisture content is based upon the wet weight, it should be so indicated. Caution is needed when reading wood fuel literature as the wet basis is often used without reference to its basis. Moisture content on a dry weight basis can be converted to moisture content on a wet basis by the following relationship:

$$\% \text{ MC (wet basis)} = \frac{\% \text{ MC (dry basis)}}{100 + \% \text{ MC (dry basis)}} \times 100$$

An example may aid in understanding the relationship between the moisture content and the recoverable heat. Assume it is known that a species of wood is at 75% MC and has a HHV of 8800 Btu/lb.

1. What will be the gross heating value?

75% MC = 75/(100 + 75) = 43% MC (wet basis)

So the gross heating value is

8800 Btu × (1 − 0.43) = 5016 Btu/wet lb

2. If the combustion efficiency of the boiler is 70%, how much recoverable heat will be obtained per pound of wood fuel at 75% MC?

5016 Btu/lb × 0.70 = 3511 Btu/lb

3. If recoverable heat is valued at \$4/million Btu, how much more could be paid for this fuel without increasing the cost of energy if it were purchased at 15% MC rather than at 75% MC? (At 15% MC the combustion efficiency of the boiler is 78%.)

15% MC = 15/(100 + 15) = 13% MC (wet basis)

8800 (1 − 0.13) = 7656 Btu/lb (gross heat)

7656 Btu/lb × 0.78 = 5972 Btu/lb (recoverable heat)

Therefore, the usable heat is increased by 5972 − 3511 = 2461 Btu/wet lb when using wood at 15% MC rather than 75%. The difference in value would be

(2461 × 4)/1,000,000 = \$0.01/lb or \$19.69/ton

A forest products engineer should know how to estimate the amount of wood fuel required to supply an industrial boiler or an electrical generation plant. Such an estimate requires consideration of the operating characteristics of the boiler system as well as the nature of the fuel to be used.

The energy output of a boiler is commonly expressed in pounds of steam per hour (pounds of water evaporated per hour). The heat required to produce a pound of steam varies depending upon the pressure and temperature, but it is generally in the range of 1100–1300 Btu/lb. Typical boiler sizes in the forest products industry run from 20,000 to 400,000 lb/hr.

The following example will explain the general approach to estimating fuel requirements. Assume a 50,000 lb/hr boiler requires 1250 Btu/lb steam to heat the feed water and generate the steam. This boiler is to be fired with fuel at 75% MC having a gross heat value of 5016 Btu/wet lb (see 1 in example above). The efficiency of the boiler is 67%. Weight of fuel required per hour is estimated as

$$\frac{50{,}000 \text{ lb steam/hr} \times 1250 \text{ Btu/lb steam}}{0.67 \text{ (boiler efficiency)} \times 5016 \text{ Btu/lb fuel}} = 18{,}600 \text{ lb fuel/hr}$$

Calculations for estimating the wood requirements of a wood-fired electric generating plant are discussed by Garrett (1981). The process can be outlined by the following example: 1 kilowatt hour (kWh) is the equivalent of 3412 Btu/hr. Thus, if an electric-generating plant operates with a typical overall efficiency of 25%, it requires a 13,648 Btu input (3412/0.25) to produce 1 kWh. The daily energy requirement for a 20-megawatt (MW) plant would be

$$13{,}648 \text{ Btu/kWh} \times 20{,}000 \text{ kWh} \times 24 \text{ hr} = 6.55 \times 10^9 \text{ Btu/day}$$

If the wood fuel going into the plant has a higher heating value of 8300 Btu/lb and 45% MC (wet basis), then the gross heating value is 8300 $(1 - 0.45)$ = 4565 Btu/wet lb. Thus, the daily wood fuel requirement for the plant is

$$\frac{6.55 \times 10^9 \text{ Btu/day}}{4565 \text{ Btu/wet lb}} = 1.44 \times 10^6 \text{ lb fuel/day}$$

Therefore, even this small power plant requires about 720 tons/per day of green chips for fuel. This is as much wood as required to supply a 200 ton/day pulp mill with fiber.

The gross heat and the usable heat, assuming typical combustion efficiencies, of a hardwood at different moisture contents are shown in Table 17.4. Note that the usable heat per wet pound at 100% MC is less than half that at 15% MC.

Table 17.4. The gross and usable heat of hardwood at different moisture contents and assumed combustion efficiencies

Moisture content, ovendry basis	Gross heat value	Assumed combustion efficiency	Usable or recoverable heat
(%)	(Btu/net lb)	(%)	(Btu/net lb)
0	8300	80	6640
15	7218	78	5630
30	6385	76	4853
60	5188	72	3735
100	4150	67	2780

There are two approaches to reducing the moisture in wood fuels. The most-common means of drying is by supplying heat energy to vaporize the moisture, i.e., by thermal means. The second is by applying mechanical energy to squeeze the free water from the wood or bark. This is referred to as *dewatering* or *compression drying* and is applicable only to very wet fuels.

Thermal drying is the approach generally used to dry wood fuel. The installation of thermal fuel–drying equipment can often be economically justified, particularly if increased boiler capacity is needed. The heat for these fuel dryers is typically supplied by burning dried fines separated from the fuel being processed. Cascade dryers, which utilize waste heat from stack gases, are also available. Such equipment is widely used in Scandinavia, and there are several installations in the United States.

The drying of wood chips or particles by evaporation of moisture in a tube, drum, or cascade dryer makes it possible to dry particles to any moisture content desired; but it has the disadvantage that it requires high energy input, generally greater than 1800 Btu for each pound of water removed. Thermal drying thus requires an energy input that is greater than the increase in heating value resulting from the drying. Nonetheless, drying wood fuels by evaporative means may prove advantageous in those cases where the energy consumed is from flue gas or another low-cost source.

An approach to the drying of wood fuels well above the fiber saturation point is *mechanical compression* or *dewatering*. Although equipment for mechanically dewatering bark and very wet residue has been available to the forest products industry for many years, these existing processes are limited in application because they can reduce the moisture content to only about 50% (wet basis). These mechanical dewatering systems are thus best suited for removing water added in processing, not the water naturally occurring in green biomass. Process water is typically added in log storage, saw cooling, debarking, and fiber processing.

Research has been conducted to develop other less-costly means of reducing the moisture in wood-chip fuels. Methods investigated include drying in the woods after felling but prior to chipping, air drying forest residue in ventilated bins, and high-pressure compression drying of wood chips. The latter method can reduce the moisture content to about 40%, lower than presently available commercial equipment can accomplish (Haygreen 1981, 1982). This method shows economic potential if chips from energy plantations, typically with a high moisture content, are used as fuel.

The use of dry rather than wet wood fuel has advantages in addition to the increased heat value described above. The capacity of a boiler is increased if dry fuel is used rather than green. The greater efficiency of the furnace and the smaller amount of steam generated from wood moisture result in less flue gas volume. This permits an increase in the amount of wood that can be fired, raising total heat production. If fuel at 40% (wet basis) MC is burned rather than fuel at 50%, the steam output of the boiler will typically increase by about 10%. Likewise, a new, smaller boiler can be installed if drier fuels are to be burned. Newby (1980) cites a 7% increase in the rate of steam generation as a result of reducing fuel moisture from 60 to 55% (wet basis).

When drier fuel is burned, the volume of stack gases generated per pound of steam produced is decreased. Thus a boiler designed for a specific steam capacity using dry fuel will have lower capital and operating costs for stack gas emission-control equipment than a boiler designed for wet fuel. In a test to evaluate the effects of fuel moisture on particulate emissions, Johnson (1975) shows that the increase of fuel moisture from 52 to 63% (wet basis) caused a doubling of the rate of particulate emissions. Thus, drier fuels yield savings because of reduction in stack gas volume to be handled by the environmental control equipment and the quantity of particulate emissions that must be collected.

A further advantage of drier fuels is discussed by Vanelli and Archibald (1976). A conventional wood residue boiler requires constant adjustment of controls as fuel moisture fluctuates. As a result, the maximum efficiency for the boiler may not be obtained. A fuel-drying system that provides fuel at a relatively uniform moisture content eliminates this problem.

Gasification and pyrolysis processes also realize benefits from using dried wood fuels, similar to those for combustion systems. The use of fuel at high moisture levels reduces the temperature of combustion products and generally the efficiency of the system. In low-Btu gasifiers, efficiency may be lowered about 15% when burning green wood. In some gasification systems, only dry wood can be used.

Despite the advantages of burning drier fuels, most wood-residue fuels are combusted as received, without the benefit of drying. With wet fuels, the drying is accomplished in the boiler during the first stage of combustion. For very wet fuels, some burning systems include a separate step prior to burning in the boiler or reactor.

One desirable characteristic of wood as an industrial fuel is the fact that it is low in sulfur and nitrogen. This reduces the cost of air-cleansing equipment as compared to fossil fuels that produce significant amounts of sulfur dioxide and nitrous oxide emissions. The major air pollution problem with industrial wood fuels is *particulate emission,* largely unburned carbon particles. Particulate emission can be controlled by mechanical collectors and scrubbers. With large boilers, electrostatic precipitators are suitable for reducing particulate emissions to acceptable levels.

There is a popular belief that dense species such as oak are far better than others for fuel. This is true in the sense of the volume of wood to be handled to obtain a given amount of heat or in terms of the rate at which the wood burns in a stove or fireplace. However, in terms of industrial applications, species is relatively unimportant. Remember that the amount of heat per ovendry pound varies little among species; the moisture content of the wood is much more important. Difficulties do exist, however, in handling and grinding the bark of some species. If extremely low-density woods are burned, the weight of wood in the furnace at any time, and thus heat output, may be reduced.

Chemical wood products

Chemical wood products in use today are made from wood or bark that has been reduced to basic chemical components such as cellulose, hemicellulose, or lignin. The raw material for many of these products is waste liquor, which results from the chemical pulping of wood. Also included in the chemical wood products category are products made from the resins of pines and other softwood species. Chemical products are seldom recognizable as wood based. These include cellulose ethers, lignosulfonates and lignin-based chemicals, modified cellulose, regenerated cellulose, ethyl and methyl alcohol (ethanol and methanol), and naval stores.

CELLULOSE ETHERS are made by treating alkali cellulose with various reagents. The cellulose ethers include carboxymethyl cellulose, which is used in making products as diverse as laundry detergent additives, adhesives, and strengtheners in unfired ceramics. Other cellulose ethers are used as sizing in papers and textiles and as emulsifying agents in paints and foods.

LIGNOSULFONATES originate from used cooking liquors that are employed in the chemical pulping of wood. These versatile compounds are used as dispersing and stabilizing agents in oil well–drilling muds, printing inks, dyes, and concrete and as binders in such things as gravel roads, animal food pellets, and textiles. Artificial vanilla, used widely in products such as ice cream, cookies, and cakes, is also made from lignosulfonates.

MODIFIED CELLULOSE includes the cellulose acetates and cellulose nitrates. Both of these are important ingredients in adhesives and lacquers. Acetylated cellulose is used in the making of rayon acetate, a material from which women's dresses, scarves, and the like are made. In addition, photographic film is made from cellulose acetate, as are a number of extruded and injected molded plastics. Cellulose nitrate is itself an important source of plastics and was, in fact, the primary ingredient in celluloid, the first synthetic plastic made commercially. Molded plastic articles such as table tennis balls and piano keys are made from this material. Cellulose that is highly nitrated is used in making guncotton and cordite, both common ingredients in explosives.

REGENERATED CELLULOSE products are produced by partially breaking down cellulose through chemical treatment and then recombining components to form a synthesized fiber. Products in this category include cellophane and viscose rayon, a colorfast material used extensively for curtains and drapes, clothing, and bedspreads. Rayon fiber is also used in the inner plies of radial tires and in conveyor belts. A new product, known as lyocell or tencel, is made by a process similar to that of rayon, though the product has a softer feel; lyocell is being widely produced as a clothing material.

ETHYL AND METHYL ALCOHOL are produced by very different processes. Ethanol can be produced from wood by hydrolysis and fermentation of the six-carbon sugars. The difficulty of separating and hydrolyzing the crystalline cellulose component has been approached in several ways, but the fact that ethanol can be produced much more easily from petroleum feedstocks or grains has limited the use of wood for ethanol production. Methanol can be produced by thermal decomposition of wood sometimes referred to as *pyrolysis* or *gasification.* Until the 1920s wood pyrolysis was the only source of methanol. Today most methanol is produced from a *synthesis gas* obtained from reformed natural gas.

NAVAL STORES include turpentine and rosin. Both of these materials, along with pine pitch and tar, were once essential to the operation of wooden sailing ships, explaining the term *naval stores.* Almost all naval store products are obtained today from tall oil and from volatile fractions recovered after the chemical pulping of pine wood. Tall oil itself is an ingredient of some lubricants. Turpentine and its derivatives are used in the manufacture of paints and lacquers and various chemicals including insecticides, perfumes, and artificial flavors. One derivative, pine oil, is used in making cleaners and disinfectants. *Rosin,* produced

when turpentine is distilled from pine gum, is a very important industrial chemical. Rosin is not to be confused with *resin,* a common component in epithelial cells and resin canals of some conifers. Used principally in sizing of paper to reduce penetration of liquids, rosin also is employed in making paints, lacquers, varnishes, hot-melt adhesives, printing inks, plastics, and linoleum floor coverings; it is also used as a plasticizing agent in synthetic rubber.

Wood for energy in the forest products industries ■

Wood-based materials range from products that require low-energy inputs for manufacture, e.g., lumber, to those requiring high levels of energy, e.g., pulp and paper. Unfortunately, the low-energy level manufacturing processes generate more residues than do the high-energy level products. The plywood and particleboard industries fall somewhere between these two extremes in terms of energy requirements and residues generated. If a typical sawmill were to burn all the sawdust, bark, and other residues generated, it would produce more energy than is consumed in the manufacturing process. Therefore, it is potentially energy self-sufficient. Pulp and paper mills, by contrast, can only be about 45–50% energy self-sufficient when using all their residues.

The possible use of internal mill residues to supply energy for manufacturing a variety of forest products is shown in Table 17.5. These data show that there is potentially an excess of residues in some industries but a deficit in most. The data do not include the use of residues from logging. If fiber products and particleboard plants are to generate all their energy from wood residue, it generally requires that residue from other plants be purchased.

Arola (1976) estimated that to satisfy the energy needs of a kraft paper mill producing 1000 tons paper/day, about 4000 tons of green wood would be needed. This is in addition to the 4000 tons/day for the paper itself. Supplying such a quantity of wood would not be a reasonable possibility in many mills. Although complete energy self-sufficiency may not be realized in the future, most of the forest products industry will use wood residue for energy to the full extent that it is available.

Most forest products industries use wood combustion to generate energy in the form of heat. Their single largest use of heat is for drying; about 70% of the energy used in lumber manufacture and 40% in papermaking is for this purpose.

In relatively large plants that operate continuously, it is also economically feasible to use wood to generate electricity. In small plants, generating electricity from residues has not been practical because of the high cost of the steam boilers, turbines, and generators that are required. However, pulp and paper mills have large electrical power needs and continuous operations, which can make such installations cost-effective. Independent plywood plants and sawmills, on the other hand, generally rely upon purchased electricity.

Since the energy requirements of the forest products industries are in the form of heat and electricity, they are well suited to the simultaneous generation of electricity and low-pressure steam, a process called *cogeneration.* Cogeneration can be accomplished by special equipment consisting of a high-temperature, high-pressure boiler and a special turbine that generates electricity from the high-

Table 17.5. Energy required to produce selected wood-based and non-wood materials

Commodity	Harvest-ing	Manu-facture	Total	Available from processing residual fuel	Supplementary requirements for manufacture
	(mil Btu/ovendry ton)				
Wood-based					
Softwood lumber	0.9	4.8	5.7	8.3	0 (3.5)
Oak flooring	1.1	5.7	6.8	11.4	0 (5.7)
Lumber laminated from veneer	0.7	6.6	7.3	3.5	3.0
Softwood sheathing plywood	0.7	6.9	7.6	3.7	3.2
Structural flakeboard	1.0	7.5	8.5	8.6	0 (1.1)
Medium-density fiberboard	0.8	9.3	10.1	2.7	6.6
Insulation board	0.6	10.5	11.1	0.7	9.9
Hardwood plywood	1.0	10.2	11.2	10.6	0 (0.4)
Underlayment particleboard	4.6	8.1	12.7	1.5	6.6
Wet-formed hardboard	0.7	19.7	20.4	0.8	18.9
Not wood-based					
Gypsum board	0.1	2.7	2.8		
Asphalt shingles	0.0	5.7	5.7		
Concrete	0.5	7.6	8.1		
Concrete block	0.5	7.6	8.1		
Clay brick	0.6	7.7	8.3		
Carpet and pad	6.6	28.7	35.3		
Steel wall studs	2.5	46.2	48.7		
Steel floor joists	2.5	46.2	48.7		
Aluminum siding	26.8	172.0	198.8		

Source: Jahn and Preston (1976).
Note: In calculations of supplementary requirements it is assumed that energy from processing residual fuel can be used in the manufacturing process but not in harvesting. Values in parentheses are for excess energy from processing residual fuel that would be available for other uses.

pressure steam and exhausts low-pressure steam to use for process heat. In a survey of wood-using plants in the Pacific Northwest, West and Mills (1990) found that 43% were interested in cogeneration if it were cost-effective. For those plants already using cogeneration, they found that the cost of steam was only two-thirds of that in plants not using cogeneration. Figure 17.3 illustrates a cogeneration system for a plant requiring only one pressure of process steam.

Cogeneration is more economical than the generation of electricity by itself because the heat from the exhausted steam is utilized. According to Engelken and Farrell (1979), an efficient steam-turbine power plant requires about 9500 Btu to produce 1 kWh of electrical power. The heat equivalent of 1 kWh is about 3400 Btu. For each kWh generated, about 5000 Btu in process steam can be obtained for the plant. A typical utility company producing only electricity from woody biomass may be only 25% efficient in its energy conversion, but cogeneration could increase that to about 75%.

Some large forest products complexes can utilize wood-fired cogeneration plants to provide their own heat and electrical needs and may in addition sell their excess capacity to public utilities. Tillman (1979) discussed the economic considerations involved in cogeneration. The attitude of the public utilities is important. The National Energy Act of 1978 provided incentives for cogeneration and the use of fuels other than oil and gas.

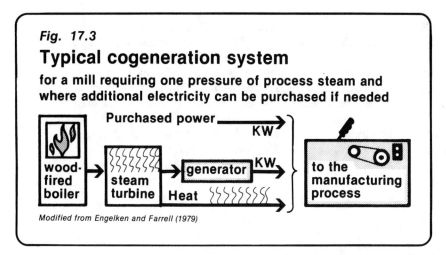

Fig. 17.3
Typical cogeneration system
for a mill requiring one pressure of process steam and where additional electricity can be purchased if needed

Modified from Engelken and Farrell (1979)

Energy use of wood by other industries ∎

It is reasonable to expect that the forest products industry will remain as the major industrial consumer of wood for energy. Although other industries will purchase wood fuels where the local situation makes this feasible, they will generally be at a disadvantage compared to forest products industries because of the additional transportation and handling costs involved and the uncertainty of a continuing supply. Nonforest industries consumed only 2.7% of the wood energy used in the industrial sector in the United States in 1994 according to estimates by the U.S. Department of Energy.

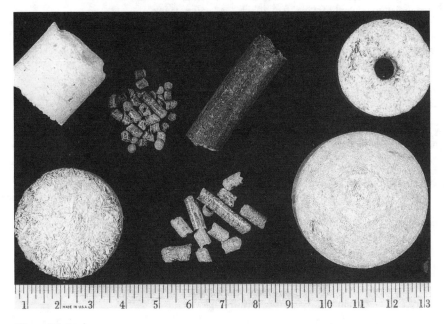

Fig. 17.4
Several types and sizes of wood fuel pellets and briquettes.

One of the disadvantages of wood as a fuel for small commercial firms, public buildings, and homes is that it is bulky and difficult to handle and store. Also, the heating value varies over time as the moisture content changes. One way to reduce these problems is to pelletize the wood residue. Some advantages of wood pellets as fuel are that pellets are dry and therefore of a uniform and high heating value; they have a high bulk density so storage space is minimized; and they can be burned in many systems designed for coal. Because of the cost of *pelletizing,* there will be little use of pelletized fuel within the forest products industry itself. However, it can be an attractive fuel for others where convenience is important and where a reliable supply is available. Several types of wood pellets are shown in Figure 17.4.

REVIEW

A. Terms to define or explain:
   1. Mill residues
   2. Logging residues
   3. Energy plantations
   4. Proximate analysis
   5. Excess air
   6. Higher heating value
   7. Gross heating value
   8. Usable or recoverable heat value
   9. Combustion efficiency
   10. Synthesis gas
   11. Combustion
   12. Cogeneration
   13. Pelletizing
   14. Lignosulfonates
   15. Regenerated cellulose

B. Questions or concepts to explain:
   1. Reasons the forest products industry relied heavily upon fossil fuels for energy until the 1970s.
   2. How the value of wood fuels is related to the cost of oil and natural gas.
   3. How the moisture content of wood fuel affects the heating value.
   4. Importance of wood for home heating and cooking.
   5. Advantages of wood fuel with respect to air pollution problems.
   6. Factors affecting the amount of usable heat obtained when burning wood.
   7. The degree of energy self-sufficiency possible in the forest products industries.
   8. Advantages of cogeneration for the forest products industries as compared to generating electrical energy alone.
   9. Advantages of using dry rather than wet wood fuel for a steam boiler.
   10. How to estimate the fuel requirements for a wood-fired electric generation plant.
   11. How to estimate the fuel requirements for a wood-fired steam boiler.
   12. Methods available to dry wood residue fuel.

REFERENCES AND SUPPLEMENTAL READING

Arola, R.A. 1976. Wood fuels: How do they stack up? Proc. Conf. Energy and the Wood Products Industry. For. Prod. Res. Soc.

Corder, S.E. 1975. Fuel characteristics of wood and bark and factors affecting heat recovery. Proc. Conf. Wood Residue as an Energy Source. For. Prod. Res. Soc.

Ellis, T.H. 1975. Role of wood residue in the national energy picture. Proc. Conf. Wood Residue as an Energy Source. For. Prod. Res. Soc.

Engelken, L.D., and Farrell, R.S. 1979. Cogeneration in plant operation. Proc. Conf. Hardware for Energy Generation. For. Prod. Res. Soc.

FAO. 1992. The forest resources of the tropical zone by main ecological regions. Forest Resources Assessment 1990 Project, FAO, Rome, Italy.

Garrett, L.D. 1981. Evaluating feedstock requirements for a 50-megawatt wood-fired electric generating plant. For. Prod. J. 31(1):26–30.

Georgia Institute of Technology. 1984. The Industrial Wood Energy Handbook. New York: Van Nostrand Reinhold.

Goldstein, I.S. 1978. Chemicals from wood: Outlook for the future. Position Pap. 8th World For. Cong. FAO. Jakarta, Indonesia.

Hall, D.O.; Barnard, G.W., and Moss, P.A. 1982. Biomass for Energy in Developing Countries. New York: Pergamon.

Haygreen, J.G. 1981. Potential for compression drying of green wood chip fuel. For. Prod. J. 31(8):43–54.

_____. 1982. Mechanics of compression drying solid wood cubes and chip mats. For. Prod. J. 32(10):30–38.

High, C. and Skog, K. 1989. Current and projected wood energy use in the United States. In Energy from Biomass and Wastes 23, ed. D. L. Klass, Proceedings of Institute of Gas Technology Conference, New Orleans, La., Feb. 13–17, pp. 229–260.

Ince, P.J. 1979. How to estimate recoverable heat energy in wood or bark fuels. USDA For. Ser. Gen. Tech. Rep. FPL-29.

Jahn, E.C., and Preston, S.B. 1976. Timber: More effective utilization. Science 191:757–61.

Johnson, R.C. 1975. Some aspects of wood waste preparation for use as a fuel. TAPPI 58(7):102–6.

Karchesy, J., and Koch, P. 1979. Energy production from hardwoods growing on southern pine sites. USDA For. Ser. Gen. Tech. Rep. SO-24.

Koch, P. 1978. Harvesting residual biomass and swathe-felling with a mobile chipper. Proc. Conf. Complete Tree Utilization of Southern Pine. For. Prod. Res. Soc.

_____. 1976. Material balances and energy required for manufacture of ten commodities. Proc. Conf. Energy and the Wood Products Industry. For. Prod. Res. Soc.

Lin, F.B. 1981. Economic desirability of using wood as a fuel for steam production. For. Prod. J. 31(1):31–36.

Marks, J. 1992. Wood powder: An upgraded wood fuel. For. Prod. J. 42(9):52–56.

Newby, M.W. 1980. An overview of combustion technology available to the pulp and paper industry. Pap. Trade J. May:30–34.

Office of Technology Assessment (OTA). 1980. Energy from biological processes. U.S. Cong. Rep.

Pingrey, D.W. 1976. Forest products energy overview. Proc. Conf. Energy and the Forest Products Industry. For. Prod. Res. Soc.

Rice, R.W., and Willey, R.M. 1995. Higher heating values for pellets made from wood waste and recycled newsprint. For. Prod. J. 45(1):84–85.

Simonds, J.E.; Bushnell, D.J.; and Wheeler, G.M. 1992. Estimating cogeneration feasibility. For. Prod. J. 42(9):13–20.

Smith, N. 1981. Wood: An ancient fuel with a new future. Worldwatch Inst. Pap. 42.

Society of American Forestry (SAF). 1979. Forest biomass as an energy source. J. For. 77(8):495–502.

Tillman, D.A. 1979. Cogeneration with wood: An introduction Proc. Conf. Hardware for Energy Generation. For. Prod. Res. Soc.

Tillman, D.A.; Rossi, A.J.; and Kitto, W.D. 1981. Wood Combustion Principles, Processes and Economics. New York: Academic Press.

U.S. House of Representatives. 1993. Global Warming (Part 2). Committee on Energy and Commerce, Subcommittee on Energy and Power, Record of Hearings July 29, October 27, and November 16, Serial No. 103–92.

Vanelli, L.S., and Archibald, W.B. 1976. Economics of hog fuel drying. Proc. For. Prod. Res. Soc. P-76-14.

Wahlgren, H.G., and Ellis, T. 1978. Potential resource availability with whole-tree uti-
    lization. TAPPI 61(11):37–40.
Warsco, K. 1994. Conventional fuel displacement by residential wood use. For. Prod. J.
    44(1):68–74.
West, T.M., and Mills, N.L. 1990. Biomass-fueled cogeneration: A survey. For. Prod. J.
    40(3):62–64.
Zerbe, J.I. 1978. Status and feasibility of utilizing forest residues for energy. Invited Pap.
    8th World For. Cong. FAO. Jakarta, Indonesia.

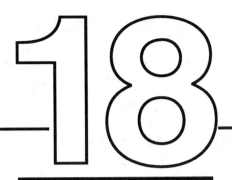

Wood in the global raw materials picture

■ **UNITED STATES**. There is a widespread—and incorrect—perception that wood use is declining in the United States. The fact is that U.S. per capita consumption of wood rose more than 30% between 1972 and 1992 to over 2.26 m³ (80.1 ft³) per person per year. Moreover, U.S. production of forest products in the early 1990s was higher than at any point in history (Fig. 18.1) totaling 18 billion ft³ (510 million m³).

Today, wood is one of the most-important raw materials in the United States. The economic value of wood can be illustrated by examining how much is used relative to other materials. For example, the weight of wood used every year in the United States is roughly equivalent to the weight of all metals, all plastics, and portland cement *combined!* One reason for misperceptions about the magnitude of wood use is that as sophistication of wood products increases, many products are becoming scarcely recognizable as wood. Other products are so common that they are often taken for granted (Bowyer 1992).

You can get an idea of the importance of wood by considering your use of this material. You might, for example, take a look around your home. As described in previous chapters, the structural shell—walls, roof rafters, floor joists—is probably wood. So are the roof and floor decks. The roofing felt is most likely asphalt-impregnated wood fiber. Even the paint on the house may contain rosins and resins traceable to distillation of softwood chips.

431

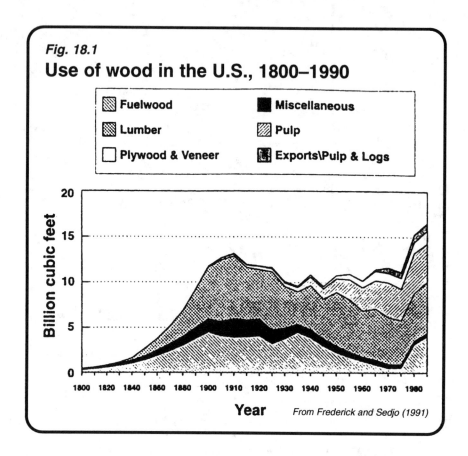

Fig. 18.1

Use of wood in the U.S., 1800–1990

Fuelwood   Miscellaneous

Lumber   Pulp

Plywood & Veneer   Exports\Pulp & Logs

From Frederick and Sedjo (1991)

The wall sheathing is likely wood, in the form of plywood, oriented strand-board, or insulation board. The siding may be lumber, hardboard, or wood shakes. More than likely, the windows have wood frames. The gypsum board that forms the interior walls and ceiling is faced with heavy paper, a wood product. Other common wood features include doors, molding, trim, and kitchen and bathroom cabinets. Countertops of Formica or another high-density laminate cover a wood particleboard core, and the laminate itself is made by impregnating sheets of wood-fiber paper with plastic. The floors may be wood, but if not, the carpet or vinyl floor covering is almost certainly placed over a wood subfloor.

Most of your furniture is probably wood. Your curtains, drapes, and bedspreads could be a rayon blend. *Rayon* is made of regenerated cellulose, usually from wood. In the basement you may have a wood workbench, shelves, and pegboard. The high impact plastic handles of your screwdrivers and chisels likely contain finely ground wood fiber. If you have a Ping-pong table, it probably has a hardboard top, and the faces of the wood paddles are overlaid with natural rubber, made of latex that is tapped from trees in the tropics. The Ping-pong ball itself is made completely of celluloid, derived from wood cellulose.

Next, take a look at the family car. Wood is difficult to recognize, but it's there. The door liners (the interior part of the door covered with cloth or vinyl) are probably thin sheets of hardboard. So too may be the deck between the back seat and back window. The dashboard may be made of molded hardboard. The bucket seats, trunk liner, and interior exposed surfaces may be plastic that contains up to 50% wood, a filler that greatly reduces cost. The roof insulation and the insulation between the engine compartment and the car interior are usually a fire-resistant wood-fiber mat. The steel-belted radial tires contain a rayon inner ply. Even the oil in the crankcase was probably brought to your service station through the aid of wood-based lignosulfonates used in controlling the consistency of oil well–drilling mud.

If you get into the car and head for the supermarket, you will see wood almost everywhere along the way. Even the concrete road surface probably contains about 0.3% lignosulfonates, dispersing agents that help strengthen cured concrete.

At the store you'll see paper boxes, packaging, and labels, almost all made from wood fiber—about one-third of which is recycled. Notebook paper, tablets, pencils, and natural rubber pencil erasers are wood- or forest-based. Photographic film is made of cellulose acetate. The flavoring in vanilla ice cream and cookies may be vanillin, a food additive made as a by-product of wood-pulping operations. At the checkout stand, you'll see wood-fiber books, newspapers, and magazines. Even the check you hand to the clerk is a wood product.

Casual observation through the course of a day or two would reveal many more products made of or derived from wood. In any event, wood plays a principal role in sheltering and meeting a variety of needs of U.S. citizens.

GLOBAL TRENDS. In 1990, global wood harvest approximated 3.5 billion m^3 annually, with slightly over half of that used as fuelwood (Table 18.1). Approximately 63% of the total annual harvest was comprised of hardwoods. The vast majority of the hardwood harvest occurred in developing countries and was used for fuel, while the primary use of softwood was in developed nations for industrial purposes (Figure 18.2). Most of the developed nations, including the United States, were net importers of wood.

Table 18.1. Annual world roundwood consumption in 1990

	(million cubic meters)
Annual roundwood harvest	3,450
Fuelwood	1,770
Industrial roundwood	1,680

Source: FAO (1993).

As noted by Sutton (1993), global per capita consumption of wood is approximately 0.67 m^3 (or 24 ft^3) per year, a figure that has remained largely unchanged since 1960 (Schultz 1993). What this means is that growth in world wood demand is closely following the growth in world population, a very significant trend in view of the fact that world population is expected to more than double within the next century.

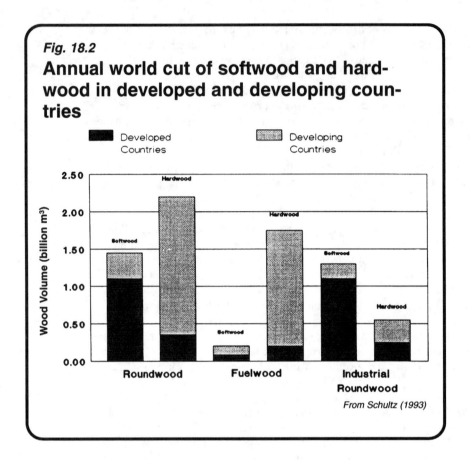

Fig. 18.2

Annual world cut of softwood and hardwood in developed and developing countries

From Schultz (1993)

Forests and their condition ■

U.S. FORESTS. U.S. forests in 1992 covered 737 million acres, or 33% of the total land area of the country. Of this, 488 million acres were potentially harvestable (i.e., sufficiently productive and not in a designated reserve status).

The area covered by forests in the United States in 1992 was slightly larger than in 1986, due to reversion of former farmland to forest, and it amounted to about 70% of the area that was covered by forests in the year 1700. Some 307 million acres of forestland were converted to other uses in the 260 years preceding 1990; most of that conversion was to agricultural uses in the course of the 19th century. Since 1920, the area of U.S. forests has remained quite stable (Powell et al. 1993). MacCleery (1993) recorded a series of observations about U.S. forests that provide a useful overview of the situation in 1900 as compared to today:

1. Following two centuries of decline, the area of forestland has stabilized (see Fig. 18.3). Today the United States has about the same forest area as in 1920.

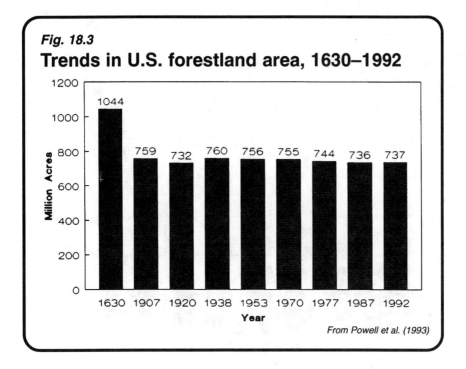

Fig. 18.3

Trends in U.S. forestland area, 1630–1992

From Powell et al. (1993)

2. The area consumed by wildfire each year has fallen 90%; it was between 20 million and 50 million acres in the early 1900s and is between 2 million and 5 million acres today.

3. Nationally, the average volume of standing timber per acre in U.S. forests is about one-third greater today than in 1952; in the East, average volume per acre has almost doubled.

4. Populations of whitetail deer, wild turkey, elk, pronghorn antelope, and many other wildlife species have increased dramatically.

5. The tens of millions of acres of cutovers or *stumplands* that existed in 1900 have long since been reforested. Many of these areas today are mature forests; others have been harvested a second time, and the cycle of regeneration to young forests has started again.

6. Forest growth nationally has exceeded harvest since the 1940s, with each subsequent decade generally showing increasing margins of growth over harvest. By 1991 forest growth exceeded harvest by 31%, and the volume of forest growth was over 350% greater than it had been in 1920 (see Fig. 18.4).

7. The efficiency of wood utilization has improved substantially since 1900. Much less material is left in the woods, many sawmills produce more than double the usable lumber and other products per log input, engineering standards and designs have reduced the volume of wood used per square foot of building space, and preservative treatments have substantially extended the service life of wood. These efficiencies have reduced by millions of acres the area of annual harvest that otherwise would have occurred.

8. American society in the 20th century changed from rural and agrarian to

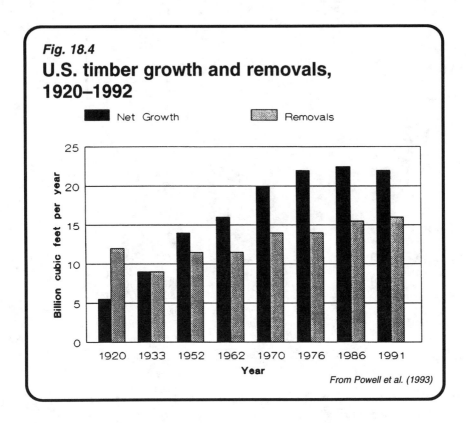

Fig. 18.4
U.S. timber growth and removals, 1920–1992

From Powell et al. (1993)

urban and industrialized. Although this change has been accompanied by a corresponding physical and psychological separation of people from the land and resources, today's urbanized nation is no less dependent on the products of its forests and fields than were the subsistence farmers of America's past.

Despite healthy growth/harvest ratios in most regions of the United States, pressures to reduce harvesting activity mounted greatly in the 1980s and 1990s. Growing concern about the environment has led to an increase in legislative, legal, and other actions designed to protect and enhance environmental quality; the nation's forests have been a major focus of such actions. Activity has centered on issues ranging from biodiversity and ecosystem health to water quality and aesthetics.

GLOBAL FORESTS

Natural forests. Natural softwood forests of the world are found in the Northern Hemisphere. Hardwood forests dominate the tropical and subtropical regions and the Southern Hemisphere, and they occur in extensive regions of the Northern Hemisphere as well. Hardwoods, therefore, are present in greatest volume worldwide (Table 1.2).

Other than in the tropical regions, where deforestation driven primarily by agricultural clearing amounts to 11 million ha annually (Mather 1990), forests worldwide are generally increasing in area coverage or are stable in size (Sedjo and Lyon 1990). Moreover, this is the case even though the majority of the world's natural forests are unmanaged (Fig. 18.5). Estimates of growth/harvest ratios in world forests have been varied. Removals of wood from world forests has been recently estimated to amount to as little as 60% of the annual increment, while others have estimated harvests to exceed net growth (Mather 1990). As in the United States, however, significant concerns about forest health and sustainability of forest use are evident in virtually every nation.

The potential for increased harvest of natural forests is today constrained, by both limitations of growth and by politics, to a relatively few areas of the world. These areas include Siberia, the far eastern region of Russia, northern Europe, and several European nations. Additionally, the vast (mostly hardwood) forests of Brazil and other parts of South America could conceivably support a larger sustainable harvest, but since these are mainly tropical forests, there is considerable pressure to conserve them for their biodiversity values. The potential for large increases in harvest volumes over an extended period appears possible only in Siberia, although economics and environmental concerns may prove to be significant limitations in this area also (Sutton 1993).

Plantations. Tree plantations generally produce much more wood per geographic area than natural forests because they are usually established on highly productive sites, intensive silviculture (including fertilization) is practiced, and

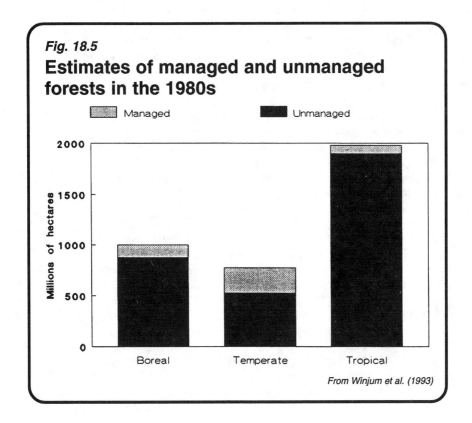

Fig. 18.5
Estimates of managed and unmanaged forests in the 1980s

From Winjum et al. (1993)

genetically selected growing stock is used. Plantations will clearly play a significant role, and perhaps even a dominant role, in providing future wood supplies. Within the near term (the next two to three decades), however, it appears that wood production of plantations will be insufficient to meet anticipated increases in demand for wood and will not make up for expected decreases in harvest levels in the natural forests of some countries.

Sutton reported in late 1993 that there are currently about 100 million ha of plantations worldwide (compared to 3.03 billion ha of natural forests). This figure squares with a 1985 estimate by Postel and Heise (1988) of 92 million ha, excluding fuelwood plantations, and a 1990 estimate by Mather that some 1.0 to 1.2 million ha of plantations are being established annually in the tropics alone. According to Sutton, most existing plantations were established within the past 30 to 35 years. Some 85% of these are located in the Northern Hemisphere (approximately 9 to 10 million ha are in the southeastern United States). Most of these plantations are currently contributing to wood supply needs, or soon will, and their existence has undoubtedly served to take some of the pressure for harvest off natural forests. As noted previously, though, demand for wood is rising at the same time that harvesting in natural forests is declining; and it is therefore unlikely that existing plantations will be productive enough to provide the difference.

Sutton noted that of the 100 million ha of plantations globally, there are only 14 million ha of fast-growing species around the world (i.e., species that produce at least 20 m³/ha/yr on average sites): radiata pine in New Zealand, Australia and Chile; and eucalyptus and southern pines in Brazil, Argentina, Venezuela, Uruguay, and South Africa. In his view, these plantations will produce only relatively modest volumes, and no more than 20 to 25 million m³ of sawlogs, through at least 2010. Moreover, virtually none of this volume will be in the form of hardwood sawlogs. It would clearly benefit the world community if more land were dedicated to tropical plantations that can produce fast-growing species suitable for sawlogs.

The pulpwood picture is brighter. Pulpwood can be produced over rotations as short as 5–7 years; therefore, establishment of added plantations has the potential of significantly impacting pulpwood supplies in the relatively near term. For example, if 1 million ha of subtropical plantations were solely dedicated to pulpwood production each year, available pulpwood volumes could be increased by as much as 300 million m³ annually within a decade, which would double the current pulpwood harvest.

Within the United States, there is considerable potential for establishment of additional areas of tree plantations. It was reported in 1992 that there are about 392 million acres (160 million ha) of U.S. nonfarmed land that are capable of supporting production of wood-producing crops without irrigation (Wright et al. 1992). Over half of these acres (225 million acres, or 91 million ha) are believed capable of supporting a sustained production of 2 short tons/acre (4.5 tonnes/ha or approximately 8–10 m³/ha) per year. But there has been considerable discussion of late about the possibility of using this land to create vast areas of energy crops or, alternatively, large areas of planted tree reserves for the purpose of sequestering carbon (U.S. House of Representatives 1993). Others view lands not now in commercial use as opportunities for creating additional wildlife or wilderness reserves. So, while there is considerable potential for expanding the area of tree plantations in the United States, competing interests are likely to substantially limit the amount of land dedicated to this purpose.

Increased efficiency of wood use ■

The past five decades have brought dramatic technological change to the utilization of timber in the United States. Bingham (1975) provided an example of what was accomplished in utilizing old-growth Douglas-fir timber in western Oregon between 1948 and 1973. The logs harvested on an acre of this timberland typically contained about 17,900 ft^3 of wood. He reported that the extent of utilization was as follows:

In 1948, 17,900 ft^3 of logs produced:
    3600 ft^3 for lumber
                      TOTAL = 3600 ft^3 for products
  14,300 ft^3 of residue (fuel and waste)

In 1963, 17,900 ft^3 of logs produced:
    4600 ft^3 for lumber
    3800 ft^3 for paper
     800 ft^3 for plywood
                      TOTAL = 9200 ft^3 for products
  8700 ft^3 of residue (fuel and waste)

In 1973 17,900 ft^3 of logs produced:
    5000 ft^3 for lumber
    1700 ft^3 for plywood
    5900 ft^3 for paper
    1500 ft^3 for particleboard
                      TOTAL = 14,100 ft^3 for products
  3800 ft^3 of residue (fuel and waste)

In the 25-year period from 1948 to 1973, the usable products obtained from similar acres of Douglas-fir increased nearly four times. Advancements in technology did not cease in 1973. By 1983:

1. *Waferboard,* a new high-strength wood composite panel product was being commercially manufactured in Canada and the United States. This technology made it possible to produce high-strength panels that were fully substitutable for plywood from small-diameter trees.

2. *Wood structural I-beams and laminated veneer lumber* (LVL) were both being sold on the commercial market. The development permitted the use of small-diameter trees in making large-sized structural timbers and dimension lumber.

3. *Centerless lathe technology* for producing veneer had been introduced. This technology allowed the use of logs that previously could not be used in making veneer and thus increased the volume of veneer that could be gleaned from a log.

4. Technologies for producing *lightweight coated papers* had been developed in Europe.

By 1993:

1. *Best Opening Face* (BOF) *technology*, a system developed at the U.S. Forest Products Laboratory for maximizing lumber yield from logs using automated scanners and computer-interfaced production equipment, was used in half of U.S. softwood sawmills, accounting for at least 75% of production.

2. *Parallel strand lumber* (PSL) was commercially available. PSL is another product that allows the use of small trees for production of large-sized lumber and structural timbers.

3. The use of *fingerjointing* to produce softwood studs from small pieces of wood that had previously been wasted or burned for power was common practice.

4. *Veneer overlay technology* allowed the use of thin veneers over complex profiles of substrate materials to produce high-quality moldings, trim, and raised panels.

5. *A wood polymer composite,* made from 100% recycled polyethylene and wood waste, was commercially available for building and landscape applications.

6. *Postconsumer collection of waste paper* in the United States for reuse in paper and fiber products manufacture approximated 40% of domestic paper production.

Many more examples could be given. The point, however, is that ongoing technology improvements, driven by competition and rising costs of raw materials, are serving to continually increase the quantity of useful products that can be obtained from a given quantity of logs. Furthermore, improvements in forestry practices are increasing the yield of raw materials from a given area of land.

Nonwood renewable materials

Research efforts worldwide are beginning to focus on the possibility of utilizing agricultural crops or crop residues as raw materials for production of paper and various structural and nonstructural composite materials. Promotion of houses constructed largely of straw bales even began in the United States in 1994 (Bowyer 1993).

There is clearly potential for the use of agriculturally produced fiber in manufacturing what are now totally wood-based products. Some of this fiber (e.g., corn stalks, straw) is readily available as by-products of current operations. Other fibrous material such as kenaf would come from plantings specifically established for the purpose of producing fiber. Kenaf, in fact, is well on its way to becoming a supplemental papermaking fiber, with one U.S. commercial kenaf paper mill already in operation in 1994.

Should agricultural crops become a viable source of fiber for paper and other products, from both technical and economic perspectives, much of the land earlier discussed as available for establishment of tree plantations would be available alternatively for raising annual crops. Whether the raising of intensively cultured agricultural crops, instead of trees, makes sense from an environmental point of view has yet to be determined.

Nonrenewable raw materials—Trends and outlook ■

DEMAND. Nonrenewable raw materials that can be substituted for wood that is used for structural purposes include steel, aluminum and other metals, plastics, and concrete. Because of growing populations and expanding global economies, demand for all of these materials is increasing significantly. Global demand for plastics and portland and masonry cement is, for example, expanding more rapidly than either population or economic growth, a continuation of a decade-old trend. Demand for metals, on the other hand, is growing, but at variable rates; in the decade of the 80s, markets for primary aluminum and steel expanded at rates of 113% and 93% of the rate of population growth, respectively.

SUPPLY. The *life index values* for many important minerals used worldwide, including fuels, are currently estimated at 20 to 50 years. For example, the 1992 world reserves life indices for tin, copper, and lead were 45, 33, and 18 years, respectively. These estimates are sometimes used to support the contention that the world is on the verge of running out of many of these materials. However, since the life index of a material is based only on the stock of known reserves that are economically available at current technology, it is totally incorrect to forecast resource depletion using the life index value. Low-quality mineral ore is far more abundant than ore of high quality. Therefore, as the ore progressively becomes lower in quality, the quantity of that ore becomes geometrically larger. Thus, for all practical purposes, the earth will never "run out" of most mineral resources, including materials used in making cement.

As is the case with wood, ongoing technology improvements in extraction, processing, conversion to products, and product use are serving to stretch or extend raw material supplies. Automobiles, for example, are today made of thinner metal skins than formerly, and lightweight plastics have substituted for metals in many of the vehicle parts. Advances in rust protection and use of noncorroding materials in key locations have, moreover, extended vehicle life. Similar developments are occurring in virtually all industries. Such advances are largely responsible for raw materials demand trends such as those of Western Europe and as shown in Figure 18.6. Note that when consumption of raw materials is expressed on the basis of consumption per unit of *gross national product*, GNP, the value of all goods and services produced in an economy, a drop in consumption of several key materials can be seen. Similar patterns of raw materials use are in evidence in the United States. Should such trends continue, they will help to moderate population-driven increases in global raw material demand.

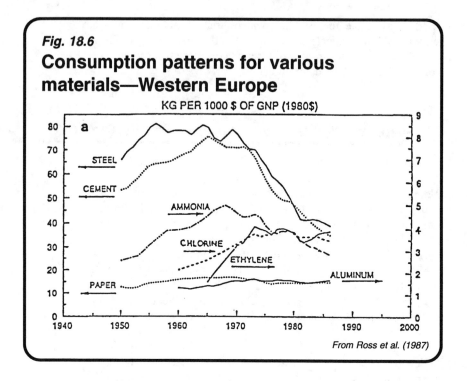

Fig. 18.6
Consumption patterns for various materials—Western Europe

KG PER 1000 $ OF GNP (1980$)

From Ross et al. (1987)

Environmental impacts of forest harvesting and wood use ■

It is clearly essential that forests be managed in such a way as to ensure sustainability not only of wood production but of water, wildlife, and forest biodiversity. It is also critical that actions taken to protect the environment do, in fact, benefit the environment from a global point of view.

Based on environmental concerns, it is often suggested that the harvesting and use of wood in the United States be substantially reduced. The argument is frequently made, for example, that periodic harvesting of forests should be curtailed because harvesting has negative environmental impacts. However, careful consideration of global environmental concerns, given the realities of today's world, leads to a much different conclusion: to protect the environment, forests should be utilized to the maximum extent possible within sustainable limits.

Essential factors to consider when contemplating the proper role of forests include the following:

1. Growing populations worldwide consume vast quantities of raw materials, and those raw materials must come from somewhere.

2. Despite ongoing advances in technology and an increasing focus on recycling, global raw material demand is increasing rapidly.

3. While the production of wood and wood fiber does have environmental impacts, so too does production of potential substitutes for wood—metals, plastics, concrete, and agriculturally derived materials.

4. Environmental impacts associated with production of wood products are

less and, in many cases, substantially less, than those associated with production using other materials.

5. Wood is a dominant raw material in the United States and worldwide. In the United States its use roughly equals that of all metals, all plastics, and portland and masonry cement combined.

6. The United States is a net importer of most categories of raw materials—most metals, petroleum (the basis for plastics), portland and masonry cement, and wood.

One reason for public concern about periodic harvesting of forests is that forest harvest activity occurs over relatively large land areas—on the order of 0.75% of the area of commercially available forests (0.5% of the area of all forests) in the United States are harvested each year. However, environmental impacts associated with harvesting are relatively short term, even though visual impacts immediately following harvest are sometimes dramatic (Figs. 18.7, 18.8).

Despite public perceptions to the contrary, the area covered by U.S. forests is stable; and standing timber volume is increasing each year. To the extent forestland has been lost in recent decades, losses have been due almost exclusively to urban expansion and associated development: widening of highways; construction of housing developments, shopping centers, and industrial complexes; establishment of power line corridors; and creation of reservoirs.

Mining activity, including mining of metals, cements, and fuel resources, impacts a much smaller land area than does forest harvesting. Although 0.1% or

(Photo by John Krantz)

Fig. 18.7
Harvesting in Minnesota aspen-spruce forest.

Forest renewal over a 30-year period following clearcutting. *(Courtesy of Weyerhaeuser Company Archives)*

1940

1945

1950

444

1955

1961

1971

445

less of U.S. land area is affected by mining in any one year, mining activity shifts very slowly from location to location, meaning that the more or less same locations tend to be impacted year after year. Because the United States is a significant net importer of metals and some nonmetallic minerals such as mica, fluorspar, and gypsum, additional land areas outside the U.S. borders are impacted as well.

An effective means of assessing the relative environmental impact of a material is to examine them over the life cycle of the material from raw materials extraction, through processing and conversion, and ultimate use. Examination of energy use is particularly revealing, since a number of serious environmental problems are related to consumption of energy including acid deposition, oil spills, air pollution (SO_2, NO_x), and increasing concentrations of atmospheric carbon dioxide.

In the mid-1970s the National Academy of Sciences, through its Committee on Renewable Resources for Industrial Materials (CORRIM) conclusively established that wood had a substantial advantage in relation to other materials in terms of energy consumption per unit of finished products (National Research Council 1976). Although technologies have changed significantly in all industries since 1976, recent studies have confirmed the advantages of wood (Buchanan 1991; Honey and Buchanan 1992; Marcea and Lau 1992; Meil 1993).

The mid-1970s CORRIM effort examined the energy required to build wall systems for residential homes. Energy use associated with raw material gathering (harvesting or mining), transport, manufacturing, and building construction was considered. Wood-frame construction was found to require the use of far less energy than steel, aluminum, concrete block, or brick (Table 18.2). Because of concerns about the potential for global warming, recent examination of environmental impacts associated with raw materials processing have examined carbon dioxide emissions as well as energy consumption. A 1992 Canadian assessment of alternative materials for use in constructing a 110,000 ft^2 building showed all-wood construction on a concrete foundation to require only 35% as much energy as steel construction on a concrete foundation. Furthermore, the liberation of carbon dioxide associated with building the steel structure was over 3.1 times that when building with wood. In a New Zealand study, Honey and Buchanan (1992) found office and industrial buildings constructed of timber to require only 55% as much energy as steel construction and approximately 66 to 72% as much energy as concrete construction. When residential buildings were considered, wood-frame construction with wood-framed windows and wood fiberboard cladding was found to require only 42% as much energy as a brick-clad, steel-framed dwelling built on a concrete slab and fitted with aluminum-framed windows. Accordingly, large differences in carbon dioxide emission were noted (Fig. 18.9). In another comparison of wood and steel-frame construction for light-frame commercial structures, which examined a wide range of factors in addition to energy, Meil (1993) again showed low environmental impacts of wood construction relative to steel (Table 18.3).

The values shown in Table 18.3 are dramatic, and they show that although wood construction clearly has environmental impacts, these impacts are minuscule compared to those of steel. When use of recycled steel is considered, the differences between wood and steel narrow, but wood retains a significant advantage. As part of the wood vs. steel wall comparison, Meil examined load-bearing

Table 18.2.   Energy required in the manufacture of various wall systems

Type of Wall	Energy to Manufacture 100 ft^2 of Wall (million Btu oil equivalent)[a,b]	
Plywood siding, no sheathing, 2 × 4 frame	1.988	(2.255)
MDF siding, plywood sheathing, 2 × 4 frame	2.541	(2.883)
Concrete building block, no insulation	17.087	(19.385)
Aluminum siding, plywood, insulation board, over 2 × 4 frame	4.953	(5.619)
MDF siding, plywood sheathing, steel studs	5.106	(5.792)
Brick veneer over sheathing	17.887	(20.291)

Source: National Research Council (1976).

[a]These figures include consideration of energy consumed in extraction or harvesting, transportation, processing, and construction.

[b]Figures in parentheses are thousand megajoules oil equivalent per 100 m^2 of wall.

Table 18.3.   Comparative energy use, air emissions, water-borne effluents, and solid wastes for steel and wood wall construction[a,b]

	Wood	Steel[c]
Energy Consumption (GJ)	3.6	11.4
Air Emissions		
Carbon dioxide (kg)	310	980
CO (g)	2,600	11,900
SO$_x$ (g)	400	3,700
NO$_x$ (g)	1,000	1,600
Particulates (g)	200	500
VOCs (g)	350	1,600
CH$_4$ (g)	neg.	100
Water and Effluents		
Water use (L)	2,200	51,000
Suspended solids (g)	12,180	495,640
Nonferrous metals (mg)	62	2,532
Cyanide (mg)	99	4,051
Phenols (mg)	17,715	725,994
Ammonia and ammonium (mg)	1,310	53,665
Hologenated organics (mg)	507	20,758
Oil and grease (mg)	1,421	58,222
Sulfides (mg)	13	507
Iron (mg)	507	20,758
Solid Wastes (kg)	125	95

Source: Meil (1993).

[a]Figures include resource extraction, processing and manufacturing, transportation, and construction of a structural assembly.

[b]Based on construction of nonload-bearing walls 3 m high by 30 m long (or approximately 10 × 100 ft).

[c]100% virgin steel (nonrecycled content).

wood and steel-framed walls in which the steel contained 50% recycled steel content. In this case the steel-framed wall was found to be "some four times as energy intensive, and correspondingly ... at least that much more environmentally damaging, despite its recycled steel content." The point here is not that wood should be used to the exclusion of all other materials, but rather that production and use of all materials have environmental impacts that must be considered when formulating environmental policies. In the future, it can be ex-

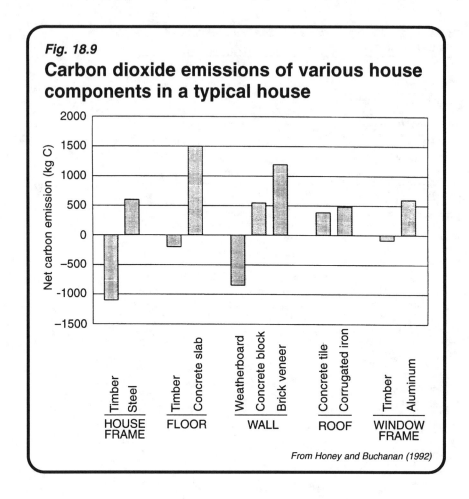

Fig. 18.9

Carbon dioxide emissions of various house components in a typical house

From Honey and Buchanan (1992)

pected that development of building design and construction technology will seek to take maximum advantage of the properties of each raw material, thereby designing buildings so as to minimize the total environmental impact. Wood will clearly play an important role in buildings of the future.

REVIEW

A. Terms to define or explain:
1. Renewable materials
2. Nonrenewable materials
3. World reserves life index (minerals)
4. Tree plantations

B. Questions or concepts to explain:
1. What is the principal cause of tropical deforestation?
2. What was the primary reason for the loss of several hundred million acres of U.S. forestland between 1630 and 1900?
3. True or false—U.S. forests continue to decline in terms of both area coverage and volume of trees standing within them.
4. It is often suggested that sharp reductions in forest harvest activity are needed in

order to protect the environment. However, in view of growing population and associated increases in demand for raw materials, would reduction in forest harvesting activity necessarily benefit the environment? Why or why not?

5. Tree plantations are sometimes viewed as undesirable from an environmental perspective since these plantations sometimes bear more similarity to agricultural enterprises than to natural forested areas. What are the environmental advantages of producing wood in intensively-managed plantations?

6. Cite at least three examples of new or emerging technologies or practices, other than those listed in this chapter, that are intended to extend wood supplies by increasing the quantity of useful products that can be obtained from a given quantity of logs.

REFERENCES

Bingham, C.W. 1975. The keynote. For. Prod. J. 25(9):9–14.

Bowyer, J.L. 1992. How wood dependent are you? The Minnesota Volunteer. March/April, pp. 24–25.

Bowyer, J.L. 1993. Wood and other raw materials for the 21st century: where will they come from? For. Prod. J. 45(2):17–24.

Buchanan, A. 1991. Building materials and the greenhouse effect. New Zealand J. of Timber Construction 7(1):6–10.

Food and Agriculture Organization of the United Nations. 1993. FAO Yearbook: Forest Products 1950–1991. FAO Forestry Series No. 26.

Frederick, K.D., and Sedjo, R.A., eds. 1991. America's Renewable Resources: Historical Trends and Current Challenges. Resources For The Future. Washington, D.C.

Honey, B.G., and A.H. Buchanan. 1992. Environmental impacts of the New Zealand building industry. Research Report 92-2. Dept. Of Civil Engineering, Univ. Of Canterbury-Christchurch, Canterbury, N.Z.

MacCleery, D.W. 1993. American Forests: A History of Resiliency and Recovery. Forest History Society Issues Series.

Marcea, R.L., and K.K. Lau. 1992. Carbon dioxide implications of building materials. J. Forest Engineering 3(2):37–43.

Mather, A.S. 1990. Global Forest Resources. Timber Press, Portland, Oreg., p. 13.

Meil, J.K. 1993. Environmental measures as substitution criteria for wood and nonwood building products. In The Globalization of Wood: Supply, Processes, Products, and Markets, Forest Products Society Proceedings 7319, pp. 53–60.

National Research Council. 1976. Renewable Resources For Industrial Materials. National Academy of Sciences, Washington, D.C. 266 pp.

Postel, S., And L. Heise. 1988. Reforesting the earth. Worldwatch Paper 83, Worldwatch Institute, Washington D.C.

Powell, D.S.; J.L. Faulkner; D.R. Darr; Z. Zhu; and D.W. MacCleery. 1993. Forest resources of the United States, 1992. Gen. Tech. Rept. RM-234. Rocky Mountain Forest and Range Expt. Sta., Fort Collins, Colo.

Ross, M.; Larson, E.D., and Wiliams, R.H. 1987. Energy demand and material flows in the economy. Energy 12(10/11):953–967.

Schultz, H. 1993. The development of wood utilization in the 19th, 20th, and 21st centuries. Forestry Chronicle 69(4):413–418.

Sedjo, R.A., and Lyon, K.S. 1990. The Long Term Adequacy of World Timber Supply. Washington, D.C.: Resources For The Future.

Sutton, W.R.J. 1993. The world's needs for wood. In The Globalization of Wood: Supply, Processes, Products and Markets. Forest Products Society Proceedings 7139, pp. 21–28.

U.S. House of Representatives. 1993. Global warming (Part 2). Committee on Energy and Commerce, Subcommittee on Energy and Power. Report of Hearings, Serial No. 103-92.

Winjum, J.K.; R.A. Meganck; and R.K. Dixon. 1993. Expanding global forest management: An "easy first" proposal. J. Forestry 91(4):38–42.

Wright, L.L.; R.L. Graham; A.F. Turhollow;. and B.C. English. 1992. Growing short-rotation woody crops for energy production. In: Forests and Global Change, Vol. 1. Opportunities for Increasing Forest Cover, R.N. Sampson and D. Hair, eds. American Forestry Association, Washington, D.C.

APPENDIX

Tables in this Appendix are from U.S. Forest Products Laboratory. 1987. Wood Handbook. USDA For. Serv. Agric. Handb. 72.

Table A.1. Moisture content of wood in equilibrium with stated dry-bulb temperature and relative humidity

Temperature, dry-bulb °F	Relative humidity, percent (% MC)																			
	5	10	15	20	25	30	35	40	45	50	55	60	65	70	75	80	85	90	95	98
30	1.4	2.6	3.7	4.6	5.5	6.3	7.1	7.9	8.7	9.5	10.4	11.3	12.4	13.5	14.9	16.5	18.5	21.0	24.3	26.9
40	1.4	2.6	3.7	4.6	5.5	6.3	7.1	7.9	8.7	9.5	10.4	11.3	12.3	13.5	14.9	16.5	18.5	21.0	24.3	26.9
50	1.4	2.6	3.6	4.6	5.5	6.3	7.1	7.9	8.7	9.5	10.3	11.2	12.3	13.4	14.8	16.4	18.4	20.9	24.3	26.9
60	1.3	2.5	3.6	4.6	5.4	6.2	7.0	7.8	8.6	9.4	10.2	11.1	12.1	13.3	14.6	16.2	18.2	20.7	24.1	26.8
70	1.3	2.5	3.5	4.5	5.3	6.2	6.9	7.7	8.5	9.2	10.1	11.0	12.0	13.1	14.4	16.0	17.9	20.5	23.9	26.6
80	1.3	2.4	3.5	4.4	5.3	6.1	6.8	7.6	8.3	9.1	9.9	10.8	11.7	12.9	14.2	15.7	17.7	20.2	23.6	26.3
90	1.2	2.3	3.4	4.3	5.1	5.9	6.7	7.4	8.1	8.9	9.7	10.5	11.5	12.6	13.9	15.4	17.3	19.8	23.3	26.0
100	1.2	2.3	3.3	4.2	5.0	5.8	6.5	7.2	7.9	8.7	9.5	10.3	11.2	12.3	13.6	15.1	17.0	19.5	22.9	25.6
110	1.1	2.2	3.2	4.0	4.9	5.6	6.3	7.0	7.7	8.4	9.2	10.0	11.0	12.0	13.2	14.7	16.6	19.1	22.4	25.2
120	1.1	2.1	3.0	3.9	4.7	5.4	6.1	6.8	7.5	8.2	8.9	9.7	10.6	11.7	12.9	14.4	16.2	18.6	22.0	24.7
130	1.0	2.0	2.9	3.7	4.5	5.2	5.9	6.6	7.2	7.9	8.7	9.4	10.3	11.3	12.5	14.0	15.8	18.2	21.5	24.2
140	.9	1.9	2.8	3.6	4.3	5.0	5.7	6.3	7.0	7.7	8.4	9.1	10.0	11.0	12.1	13.6	15.3	17.7	21.0	23.7
150	.9	1.8	2.6	3.4	4.1	4.8	5.5	6.1	6.7	7.4	8.1	8.8	9.7	10.6	11.8	13.1	14.9	17.2	20.4	23.1
160	.8	1.6	2.4	3.2	3.9	4.6	5.2	5.8	6.4	7.1	7.8	8.5	9.3	10.3	11.4	12.7	14.4	16.7	19.9	22.5
170	.7	1.5	2.3	3.0	3.7	4.3	4.9	5.6	6.2	6.8	7.4	8.2	9.0	9.9	11.0	12.3	14.0	16.2	19.3	21.9
180	.7	1.4	2.1	2.8	3.5	4.1	4.7	5.3	5.9	6.5	7.1	7.8	8.6	9.5	10.5	11.8	13.5	15.7	18.7	21.3
190	.6	1.3	1.9	2.6	3.2	3.8	4.4	5.0	5.5	6.1	6.8	7.5	8.2	9.1	10.1	11.4	13.0	15.1	18.1	20.7
200	.5	1.1	1.7	2.4	3.0	3.5	4.1	4.6	5.2	5.8	6.4	7.1	7.8	8.7	9.7	10.9	12.5	14.6	17.5	20.0
210	.5	1.0	1.6	2.1	2.7	3.2	3.8	4.3	4.9	5.4	6.0	6.7	7.4	8.3	9.2	10.4	12.0	14.0	16.9	19.3
220	.4	.9	1.4	1.9	2.4	2.9	3.4	3.9	4.5	5.0	5.6	6.3	7.0	7.8	8.8	9.9	*	*	*	*
230	.3	.8	1.2	1.6	2.1	2.6	3.1	3.6	4.2	4.7	5.3	6.0	6.7	*	*	*	*	*	*	*
240	.3	.6	.9	1.3	1.7	2.1	2.6	3.1	3.5	4.1	4.6	*	*	*	*	*	*	*	*	*
250	.2	.4	.7	1.0	1.3	1.7	2.1	2.5	2.9	*	*	*	*	*	*	*	*	*	*	*
260	.2	.3	.5	.7	.9	1.1	1.4	*	*	*	*	*	*	*	*	*	*	*	*	*
270	.1	.1	.2	.3	.4	.4	*	*	*	*	*	*	*	*	*	*	*	*	*	*

*Indicates conditions not possible at atmospheric pressure.

Table A.2. Shrinkage values of domestic woods

Species	Shrinkage from green to ovendry moisture content*			Species	Shrinkage from green to ovendry moisture content*		
	Radial	Tangential	Volumetric		Radial	Tangential	Volumetric
	(%)				(%)		
HARDWOODS							
Alder, red	4.4	7.3	12.6	Honeylocust	4.2	6.6	10.8
Ash				Locust, black	4.6	7.2	10.2
Black	5.0	7.8	15.2	Madrone, Pacific	5.6	12.4	18.1
Blue	3.9	6.5	11.7	Magnolia			
Green	4.6	7.1	12.5	Cucumbertree	5.2	8.8	13.6
Oregon	4.1	8.1	13.2	Southern	5.4	6.6	12.3
Pumpkin	3.7	6.3	12.0	Sweetbay	4.7	8.3	12.9
White	4.9	7.8	13.3	Maple			
Aspen				Bigleaf	3.7	7.1	11.6
Bigtooth	3.3	7.9	11.8	Black	4.8	9.3	14.0
Quaking	3.5	6.7	11.5	Red	4.0	8.2	12.6
Basswood, American	6.6	9.3	15.8	Silver	3.0	7.2	12.0
Beech, American	5.5	11.9	17.2	Striped	3.2	8.6	12.3
Birch				Sugar	4.8	9.9	14.7
Alaska paper	6.5	9.9	16.7	Oak, red			
Gray	5.2	...	14.7	Black	4.4	11.1	15.1
Paper	6.3	8.6	16.2	Laurel	4.0	9.9	19.0
River	4.7	9.2	13.5	Northern red	4.0	8.6	13.7
Sweet	6.5	9.0	15.6	Pin	4.3	9.5	14.5
Yellow	7.3	9.5	16.8	Scarlet	4.4	10.8	14.7
Buckeye, yellow	3.6	8.1	12.5	Southern red	4.7	11.3	16.1
Butternut	3.4	6.4	10.6	Water	4.4	9.8	16.1
Cherry, black	3.7	7.1	11.5	Willow	5.0	9.6	18.9
Chestnut, American	3.4	6.7	11.6	Oak, white			
Cottonwood				Bur	4.4	8.8	12.7
Balsam poplar	3.0	7.1	10.5	Chestnut	5.3	10.8	16.4
Black	3.6	8.6	12.4	Live	6.6	9.5	14.7
Eastern	3.9	9.2	13.9	Overcup	5.3	12.7	16.0
Elm				Post	5.4	9.8	16.2
American	4.2	9.5	14.6	Swamp chestnut	5.2	10.8	16.4
Cedar	4.7	10.2	15.4	White	5.6	10.5	16.3
Rock	4.8	8.1	14.9	Persimmon, common	7.9	11.2	19.1
Slippery	4.9	8.9	13.8	Sassafras	4.0	6.2	10.3
Winged	5.3	11.6	17.7	Sweetgum	5.3	10.2	15.8
Hackberry	4.8	8.9	13.8	Sycamore, American	5.0	8.4	14.1

Table A.2. *(continued)*

Species	Shrinkage from green to ovendry moisture content*			Species	Shrinkage from green to ovendry moisture content*		
	Radial	Tangential	Volumetric		Radial	Tangential	Volumetric
HARDWOODS	(%)				(%)		
Hickory, Pecan	4.9	8.9	13.6	Tanoak	4.9	11.7	17.3
Hickory, true				Tupelo			
Mockernut	7.7	11.0	17.8	Black	5.1	8.7	14.4
Pignut	7.2	11.5	17.9	Water	4.2	7.6	12.5
Shagbark	7.0	10.5	16.7	Walnut, black	5.5	7.8	12.8
Shellbark	7.6	12.6	19.2	Willow, black	3.3	8.7	13.9
Holly, American	4.8	9.9	16.9	Yellow-poplar	4.6	8.2	12.7
SOFTWOODS	(%)				(%)		
Baldcypress	3.8	6.2	10.5	Larch, western	4.5	9.1	14.0
Cedar				Pine			
Alaska	2.8	6.0	9.2	Eastern white	2.1	6.1	8.2
Atlantic white	2.9	5.4	8.8	Jack	3.7	6.6	10.3
Eastern red	3.1	4.7	7.8	Loblolly	4.8	7.4	12.3
Incense	3.3	5.2	7.7	Lodgepole	4.3	6.7	11.1
Northern white	2.2	4.9	7.2	Longleaf	5.1	7.5	12.2
Port Orford	4.6	6.9	10.1	Pitch	4.0	7.1	10.9
Western Red	2.4	5.0	6.8	Pond	5.1	7.1	11.2
Douglas-fir†				Ponderosa	3.9	6.2	9.7
Coast	4.8	7.6	12.4	Red	3.8	7.2	11.3
Interior North	3.8	6.9	10.7	Shortleaf	4.6	7.7	12.3
Interior West	4.8	7.5	11.8	Slash	5.4	7.6	12.1
Fir				Sugar	2.9	5.6	7.9
Balsam	2.9	6.9	11.2	Virginia	4.2	7.2	11.9
California red	4.5	7.9	11.4	Western white	4.1	7.4	11.8
Grand	3.4	7.5	11.0	Redwood			
Noble	4.3	8.3	12.4	Old growth	2.6	4.4	6.8
Pacific silver	4.4	9.2	13.0	Young growth	2.2	4.9	7.0
Subalpine	2.6	7.4	9.4	Spruce			
White	3.3	7.0	9.8	Black	4.1	6.8	11.3
Hemlock				Engelmann	3.8	7.1	11.0
Eastern	3.0	6.8	9.7	Red	3.8	7.8	11.8
Mountain	4.4	7.1	11.1	Sitka	4.3	7.5	11.5
Western	4.2	7.8	12.4	Tamarack	3.7	7.4	13.6

* Expressed as a percentage of the green dimension.
† Coast Douglas-fir is defined as Douglas-fir growing in the states of Oregon and Washington west of the summit of the Cascade Mountains. Interior West includes the state of California and all counties in Oregon and Washington east of but adjacent to the Cascade summit. Interior North includes the remainder of Oregon and Washington and the states of Idaho, Montana, and Wyoming.

Table A.3. Shrinkage values of some woods imported into the United States

Species	Shrinkage from green to ovendry moisture content* (%)		Species	Shrinkage from green to ovendry moisture content* (%)	
	Radial	Tangential		Radial	Tangential
Afrormosia (Pericopsis elata)	3.0	6.4	Mahogany, African (Khaya spp.)	2.5	4.5
Albarco (Cariniana spp.)	2.8	5.4	Mahogany, true (Swietenia macrophylla)	3.0	4.1
Andiroba (Carapa guianensis)	3.1	7.6	Manbarklak (Eschweilera spp.)	5.8	10.3
Angelin (Andira inermis)	4.6	9.8	Manni (Symphonia globulifera)	5.7	9.7
Angelique (Dicorynia guianensis)	5.2	8.8	Marishballi (Licania spp.)	7.5	11.7
Apitong (Dipterocarpus spp.)	5.2	10.9	Merbau (Intsia bijuga and palembanica)	2.7	4.6
Azobe (Lophira alata)	8.4	11.0	Mersawa (Anisoptera spp.)	4.0	9.0
Balata (Manilkara bidentata)	6.3	9.4	Mora (Mora spp.)	6.9	9.8
Balsa (Ochroma pyramidale)	3.0	7.6	Obeche (Triplochiton scleroxylon)	3.0	5.4
Banak (Virola spp.)	4.6	8.8	Ocote pine (Pinus oocarpa)	4.6	7.5
Benge (Guibourtia arnoldiana)	5.2	8.6	Okoume (Aucoumea klaineana)	4.1	6.1
Bubinga (Guibourtia spp.)	5.8	8.4	Opepe (Nauclea spp.)	4.5	8.4
Caribbean pine (Pinus caribaea)	6.3	7.8	Parana pine (Araucaria angustifolia)	4.0	7.9
Cativo (Prioria copaifera)	2.4	5.3	Pau Marfim Balfourodendron riedelianum	4.6	8.8
Courbaril (Hymenaea courbaril)	4.5	8.5	Peroba Rosa (Aspidosperma spp.)	3.8	6.4
Cuangare (Dialyanthera spp.)	4.2	9.4	Piquia (Caryocar spp.)	5.0	8.0
Determa (Ocotea rubra)	3.7	7.6	Pilon (Hyeronima spp.)	5.4	11.7
Ebony (Diospyros spp.)	5.5	6.5	Primavera (Cybistax donnell-smithii)	3.1	5.1
Gmelina (Gmelina arborea)	2.4	4.9	Purpleheart (Peltogyne spp.)	3.2	6.1
Greenheart (Ocotea rodiaei)	8.8	9.6	Ramin (Gonystylus spp.)	4.3	8.7
Hura (Hura crepitans)	2.7	4.5	Roble (Quercus spp.)	6.4	11.7
Ipe (Tabebuia spp.)	6.6	8.0	Roble (Tabebuia spp. Roble group)	3.6	6.1
Iroko (Chlorophora excelsa and regia)	2.8	3.8	Rosewood, Brazilian (Dalbergia nigra)	2.9	4.6
Jarrah (Eucalyptus marginata)	4.6	6.6	Rosewood, Indian (Dalbergia latifolia)	2.7	5.8
Kaneelhart (Licaria spp.)	5.4	7.9	Santa Maria (Calophyllum brasiliense)	4.6	8.0
Kapur (Dryobalanops spp.)	4.6	10.2	Sapele (Entandrophragma cylindricum)	4.6	7.4
Karri (Eucalyptus diversicolor)	7.2	10.7	Sepetir (Pseudosindora and Sindora spp.)	3.7	7.0
Kempas (Koompassia malaccensis)	6.0	7.4	Spanish-cedar (Cedrela spp.)	4.2	6.3
Keruing (Dipterocarpus spp.)	5.2	10.9	Teak (Tectona grandis)	2.5	5.8
Lauan (Shorea spp.)	3.8	8.0	Wallaba (Eperua spp.)	3.6	6.9
Limba (Terminalia superba)	4.5	6.2			
Macawood (Platymiscium spp.)	2.7	3.5			

Note: Shrinkage values in this table were obtained from world literature and may not represent a true species average.

*Expressed as a percentage of the green dimension.

Table A.4. Grouping of some domestic woods according to heartwood decay resistance

Resistant or very resistant	Moderately resistant	Slightly or nonresistant
Baldcypress (old growth)	Baldcypress (young growth)	Alder
Catalpa	Douglas-fir	Ashes
Cedars	Honeylocust	Aspens
Cherry, black	Larch, western	Basswood
Chestnut	Oak, swamp chestnut	Beech
Cypress, Arizona	Pine, eastern white	Birches
Junipers	Southern pine	Buckeye
Locust, black*	Longleaf	Butternut
Mesquite	Slash	Cottonwood
Mulberry, red*	Tamarack	Elms
Oak		Hackberry
Bur		Hemlocks
Chestnut		Hickories
Gambel		Magnolia
Oregon white		Maples
Post		Oak (red and black species)
White		Pines (other than longleaf, slash, and eastern white)
Osage-orange*		Poplars
Redwood		Spruces
Sassafras		Sweetgum
Walnut, black		True firs (western and eastern)
Yew, Pacific*		Willows
		Yellow-poplar

* These woods have exceptionally high decay resistance.

Common names of species	Moisture condition	Specific gravity*	Static bending			Impact bending (height of drop causing complete failure)‡	Compression parallel to grain (maximum crushing strength)	Compression perpendicular to grain (fiber stress at proportional limit)	Shear parallel to grain (maximum shearing strength)	Tension perpendicular to grain (maximum tensile strength)	Side hardness (load perpendicular to grain)
			Modulus of rupture	Modulus of elasticity†	Work to maximum load						
			(psi)	(mil psi)	(in.-lb/in.³)	(in.)	(psi)	(psi)	(psi)	(psi)	(lb)
HARDWOODS											
Alder, red	Green	0.37	6,500	1.17	8.0	22	2,960	250	770	390	440
	Dry	0.41	9,800	1.38	8.4	20	5,820	440	1,080	420	590
Ash											
Black	Green	0.45	6,000	1.04	12.1	33	2,300	350	860	490	520
	Dry	0.49	12,600	1.60	14.9	35	5,970	760	1,570	700	850
Blue	Green	0.53	9,600	1.24	14.7	…	4,180	810	1,540	…	…
	Dry	0.58	13,800	1.40	14.4	…	6,980	1,420	2,030	…	…
Green	Green	0.53	9,500	1.40	11.8	35	4,200	730	1,260	590	870
	Dry	0.56	14,100	1.66	13.4	32	7,080	1,310	1,910	700	1,200
Oregon	Green	0.50	7,600	1.13	12.2	39	3,510	530	1,190	590	790
	Dry	0.55	12,700	1.36	14.4	33	6,040	1,250	1,790	720	1,160
White	Green	0.55	9,500	1.44	15.7	38	3,990	670	1,350	590	960
	Dry	0.60	15,000	1.74	16.6	43	7,410	1,160	1,910	940	1,320
Aspen											
Bigtooth	Green	0.36	5,400	1.12	5.7	…	2,500	210	730	…	…
	Dry	0.39	9,100	1.43	7.7	…	5,300	450	1,080	…	…
Quaking	Green	0.35	5,100	.86	6.4	22	2,140	180	660	230	300
	Dry	0.38	8,400	1.18	7.6	21	4,250	370	850	260	350
Basswood, American	Green	0.32	5,000	1.04	5.3	16	2,220	170	600	280	250
	Dry	0.37	8,700	1.46	7.2	16	4,730	370	990	350	410
Beech, American	Green	0.56	8,600	1.38	11.9	43	3,550	540	1,290	720	850
	Dry	0.64	14,900	1.72	15.1	41	7,300	1,010	2,010	1,010	1,300
Birch											
Paper	Green	0.48	6,400	1.17	16.2	49	2,360	270	840	380	560
	Dry	0.55	12,300	1.59	16.0	34	5,690	600	1,210	…	910
Sweet	Green	0.60	9,400	1.65	15.7	48	3,740	470	1,240	430	970
	Dry	0.65	16,900	2.17	18.0	47	8,540	1,080	2,240	950	1,470
Yellow	Green	0.55	8,300	1.50	16.7	48	3,380	430	1,110	430	780
	Dry	0.62	16,600	2.01	20.8	55	8,170	970	1,880	920	1,260
Butternut	Green	0.36	5,400	.97	8.2	24	2,420	220	760	430	390
	Dry	0.38	8,100	1.18	8.2	24	5,110	460	1,170	440	490
Cherry, black	Green	0.47	8,000	1.31	12.8	33	3,540	360	1,130	570	660
	Dry	0.50	12,300	1.49	11.4	29	7,110	690	1,700	560	950
Chestnut, American	Green	0.40	5,600	.93	7.0	24	2,470	310	800	440	420
	Dry	0.43	8,600	1.23	6.5	19	5,320	620	1,080	460	540
Cottonwood											
Balsam poplar	Green	0.31	3,900	.75	4.2	…	1,690	140	500	…	…
	Dry	0.34	6,800	1.10	5.0	…	4,020	300	790	…	…
Black	Green	0.31	4,900	1.08	5.0	.20	2,200	160	610	270	250
	Dry	0.35	8,500	1.27	6.7	22	4,500	300	1,040	330	350
Eastern	Green	0.37	5,300	1.01	7.3	21	2,280	200	680	410	340
	Dry	0.40	8,500	1.37	7.4	20	4,910	380	930	580	430

457

Table A.5. (continued)

Common names of species	Moisture condition	Specific gravity*	Static bending Modulus of rupture (psi)	Static bending Modulus of elasticity† (mil psi)	Static bending Work to maximum load (in.-lb/in.³)	Impact bending (height of drop causing complete failure)‡ (in.)	Compression parallel to grain (maximum crushing strength) (psi)	Compression perpendicular to grain (fiber stress at proportional limit) (psi)	Shear parallel to grain (maximum shearing strength) (psi)	Tension perpendicular to grain (maximum tensile strength) (psi)	Side hardness (load perpendicular to grain) (lb)
Elm											
American	Green	0.46	7,200	1.11	11.8	38	2,910	360	1,000	590	620
	Dry	0.50	11,800	1.34	13.0	39	5,520	690	1,510	660	830
Rock	Green	0.57	9,500	1.19	19.8	54	3,780	610	1,270	...	940
	Dry	0.63	14,800	1.54	19.2	56	7,050	1,230	1,920	...	1,320
Slippery	Green	0.48	8,000	1.23	15.4	47	3,320	420	1,110	640	660
	Dry	0.53	13,000	1.49	16.9	45	6,360	820	1,630	530	860
Hackberry	Green	0.49	6,500	.95	14.5	48	2,650	400	1,070	630	700
	Dry	0.53	11,000	1.19	12.8	43	5,440	890	1,590	580	880
Hickory, pecan											
Bitternut	Green	0.60	10,300	1.40	20.0	66	4,570	800	1,240	...	...
	Dry	0.66	17,100	1.79	18.2	66	9,040	1,680	...	...	...
Nutmeg	Green	0.56	9,100	1.29	22.8	54	3,980	760	1,030	...	...
	Dry	0.60	16,600	1.70	25.1	...	6,910	1,570	...	...	...
Pecan	Green	0.60	9,800	1.37	14.6	53	3,990	780	1,480	680	1,310
	Dry	0.66	13,700	1.73	13.8	44	7,850	1,720	2,080	...	1,820
Water	Green	0.61	10,700	1.56	18.8	56	4,660	880	1,440	...	...
	Dry	0.62	17,800	2.02	19.3	53	8,600	1,550	...	...	...
Hickory, true											
Mockernut	Green	0.64	11,100	1.57	26.1	88	4,480	810	1,280	...	...
	Dry	0.72	19,200	2.22	22.6	77	8,940	1,730	1,740	...	...
Pignut	Green	0.66	11,700	1.65	31.7	89	4,810	920	1,370	...	...
	Dry	0.75	20,100	2.26	30.4	74	9,190	1,980	2,150	...	...
Shagbark	Green	0.64	11,000	1.57	23.7	74	4,580	840	1,520	...	...
	Dry	0.72	20,200	2.16	25.8	67	9,210	1,760	2,430	...	...
Shellbark	Green	0.62	10,500	1.34	29.9	104	3,920	810	1,190	...	...
	Dry	0.69	18,100	1.89	23.6	88	8,000	1,800	2,110	...	...
Honeylocust	Green	0.60	10,200	1.29	12.6	47	4,410	1,150	1,660	930	1,390
	Dry	...	14,700	1.63	13.3	47	7,500	1,840	2,250	900	1,580
Locust, black	Green	0.66	13,800	1.85	15.4	44	6,800	1,160	1,760	770	1,570
	Dry	0.69	19,400	2.05	18.4	57	10,180	1,830	2,480	640	1,700
Magnolia											
Cucumbertree	Green	0.44	7,400	1.56	10.0	30	3,140	330	990	440	520
	Dry	0.48	12,300	1.82	12.2	35	6,310	570	1,340	660	700
Southern	Green	0.46	6,800	1.11	15.4	54	2,700	460	1,040	610	740
	Dry	0.50	11,200	1.40	12.8	29	5,460	860	1,530	740	1,020
Maple											
Bigleaf	Green	0.44	7,400	1.10	8.7	23	3,240	450	1,110	600	620
	Dry	0.48	10,700	1.45	7.8	28	5,950	750	1,730	540	850
Black	Green	0.52	7,900	1.33	12.8	48	3,270	600	1,130	720	840
	Dry	0.57	13,300	1.62	12.5	40	6,680	1,020	1,820	670	1,180
Red	Green	0.49	7,700	1.39	11.4	32	3,280				700

Species	Condition	Sp. gr.	2	3	4	5	6	7	8	9	10
Silver	Green	0.44	5,800	.94	11.0	29	2,490	370	1,050	560	590
	Dry	0.47	8,900	1.14	8.3	25	5,220	740	1,480	500	700
Sugar	Green	0.56	9,400	1.55	13.3	40	4,020	640	1,460	…	970
	Dry	0.63	15,800	1.83	16.5	39	7,830	1,470	2,330	…	1,450
Oak, red											
Black	Green	0.56	8,200	1.18	12.2	40	3,470	710	1,220	…	1,060
	Dry	0.61	13,900	1.64	13.7	41	6,520	930	1,910	…	1,210
Cherrybark	Green	0.61	10,800	1.79	14.7	54	4,620	760	1,320	800	1,240
	Dry	0.68	18,100	2.28	18.3	49	8,740	1,250	2,000	840	1,480
Laurel	Green	0.56	7,900	1.39	11.2	39	3,170	570	1,180	770	1,000
	Dry	0.63	12,600	1.69	11.8	39	6,980	1,060	1,830	790	1,210
Northern red	Green	0.56	8,300	1.35	13.2	44	3,440	610	1,210	750	1,000
	Dry	0.63	14,300	1.82	14.5	43	6,760	1,010	1,780	800	1,290
Pin	Green	0.58	8,300	1.32	14.0	48	3,680	720	1,290	800	1,070
	Dry	0.63	14,000	1.73	14.8	45	6,820	1,020	2,080	1,050	1,510
Scarlet	Green	0.60	10,400	1.48	15.0	54	4,090	830	1,410	700	1,200
	Dry	0.67	17,400	1.91	20.5	53	8,330	1,120	1,890	870	1,400
Southern red	Green	0.52	6,900	1.14	8.0	29	3,030	550	930	480	860
	Dry	0.59	10,900	1.49	9.4	26	6,090	870	1,390	510	1,060
Water	Green	0.56	8,900	1.55	11.1	39	3,740	620	1,240	820	1,010
	Dry	0.63	15,400	2.02	21.5	44	6,770	1,020	2,020	920	1,190
Willow	Green	0.56	7,400	1.29	8.8	35	3,000	610	1,180	760	980
	Dry	0.69	14,500	1.90	14.6	42	7,040	1,130	1,650	…	1,460
Oak, white											
Bur	Green	0.58	7,200	.88	10.7	44	3,290	680	1,350	800	1,110
	Dry	0.64	10,300	1.03	9.8	29	6,060	1,200	1,820	680	1,370
Chestnut	Green	0.57	8,000	1.37	9.4	35	3,520	530	1,210	690	890
	Dry	0.66	13,300	1.59	11.0	40	6,830	840	1,490	…	1,130
Live	Green	0.80	11,900	1.58	12.3	…	5,430	2,040	2,210	…	…
	Dry	0.88	18,400	1.98	18.9	…	8,900	2,840	2,660	…	960
Overcup	Green	0.57	8,000	1.15	12.6	44	3,370	540	1,320	730	…
	Dry	0.63	12,600	1.42	15.7	38	6,200	810	2,000	940	1,190
Post	Green	0.60	8,100	1.09	11.0	44	3,480	860	1,280	790	1,130
	Dry	0.67	13,200	1.51	13.2	46	6,600	1,430	1,840	780	1,360
Swamp chestnut	Green	0.60	8,500	1.35	12.8	45	3,540	570	1,260	670	1,110
	Dry	0.67	13,900	1.77	12.0	41	7,270	1,110	1,990	690	1,240
Swamp white	Green	0.64	9,900	1.59	14.5	50	4,360	760	1,300	860	1,160
	Dry	0.72	17,700	2.05	19.2	49	8,600	1,190	2,000	830	1,620
White	Green	0.60	8,300	1.25	11.6	42	3,560	670	1,250	770	1,060
	Dry	0.68	15,200	1.78	14.8	37	7,440	1,070	2,000	800	1,360
Sassafras	Green	0.42	6,000	.91	7.1	…	2,730	370	950	…	…
	Dry	0.46	9,000	1.12	8.7	…	4,760	850	1,240	…	1,190
Sweetgum	Green	0.46	7,100	1.20	10.1	36	3,040	370	990	540	600
	Dry	0.52	12,500	1.64	11.9	32	6,320	620	1,600	760	850
Sycamore, American	Green	0.46	6,500	1.06	7.5	26	2,920	360	1,000	630	610
	Dry	0.49	10,000	1.42	8.5	26	5,380	700	1,470	720	770
Tanoak	Green	0.58	10,500	1.55	13.4	…	4,650	…	…	…	…

Table A.5. (continued)

Common names of species	Moisture condition	Specific gravity*	Static bending — Modulus of rupture (psi)	Static bending — Modulus of elasticity† (mil psi)	Static bending — Work to maximum load (in.-lb/in.³)	Impact bending (height of drop causing complete failure)† (in.)	Compression parallel to grain (maximum crushing strength) (psi)	Compression perpendicular to grain (fiber stress at proportional limit) (psi)	Shear parallel to grain (maximum shearing strength) (psi)	Tension perpendicular to grain (maximum tensile strength) (psi)	Side hardness (load perpendicular to grain) (lb)
Oak, white											
Bur	Green	0.58	7,200	.88	10.7	44	3,290	680	1,350	800	1,110
	Dry	0.64	10,300	1.03	9.8	29	6,060	1,200	1,820	680	1,370
Chestnut	Green	0.57	8,000	1.37	9.4	35	3,520	530	1,210	690	890
	Dry	0.66	13,300	1.59	11.0	40	6,830	840	1,490	…	1,130
Live	Green	0.80	11,900	1.58	12.3	…	5,430	2,040	2,210	…	…
	Dry	0.88	18,400	1.98	18.9	…	8,900	2,840	2,660	…	…
Overcup	Green	0.57	8,000	1.15	12.6	44	3,370	540	1,320	730	960
	Dry	0.63	12,600	1.42	15.7	38	6,200	810	2,000	940	1,190
Post	Green	0.60	8,100	1.09	11.0	44	3,480	860	1,280	790	1,130
	Dry	0.67	13,200	1.51	13.2	46	6,600	1,430	1,840	780	1,360
Swamp chestnut	Green	0.60	8,500	1.35	12.8	45	3,540	570	1,260	670	1,110
	Dry	0.67	13,900	1.77	12.0	41	7,270	1,110	1,990	690	1,240
Swamp white	Green	0.64	9,900	1.59	14.5	50	4,360	760	1,300	860	1,160
	Dry	0.72	17,700	2.05	19.2	49	8,600	1,190	2,000	830	1,620
White	Green	0.60	8,300	1.25	11.6	42	3,560	670	1,250	770	1,060
	Dry	0.68	15,200	1.78	14.8	37	7,440	1,070	2,000	800	1,360
Sassafras	Green	0.42	6,000	.91	7.1	…	2,730	370	950	…	…
	Dry	0.46	9,000	1.12	8.7	…	4,760	850	1,240	…	…
Sweetgum	Green	0.46	7,100	1.20	10.1	36	3,040	370	990	540	600
	Dry	0.52	12,500	1.64	11.9	32	6,320	620	1,600	760	850
Sycamore, American	Green	0.46	6,500	1.06	7.5	26	2,920	360	1,000	630	610
	Dry	0.49	10,000	1.42	8.5	26	5,380	700	1,470	720	770
Tanoak	Green	0.58	10,500	1.55	13.4	37	4,650	…	…	…	…
	…	…	…	…	…	…	…	…	…	…	…
Tupelo											
Black	Green	0.46	7,000	1.03	8.0	30	3,040	480	1,100	570	640
	Dry	0.50	9,600	1.20	6.2	22	5,520	930	1,340	500	810
Water	Green	0.46	7,300	1.05	8.3	30	3,370	480	1,190	600	710
	Dry	0.50	9,600	1.26	6.9	23	5,920	870	1,590	700	880
Walnut, black	Green	0.51	9,500	1.42	14.6	37	4,300	490	1,220	570	900
	Dry	0.55	14,600	1.68	10.7	34	7,580	1,010	1,370	690	1,010
Willow, black	Green	0.36	4,800	.79	11.0	…	2,040	180	680	…	…
	Dry	0.39	7,800	1.01	8.8	…	4,100	430	1,250	…	…
Yellow-poplar	Green	0.40	6,000	1.22	7.5	26	2,660	270	790	510	440
	Dry	0.42	10,100	1.58	8.8	24	5,540	500	1,190	540	540
SOFTWOODS											
Baldcypress	Green	0.42	6,600	1.18	6.6	25	3,580	400	810	300	390
	Dry	0.46	10,600	1.44	8.2	24	6,360	730	1,000	270	510
Cedar											
Alaska	Green	0.42	6,400	1.14	9.2	27	3,050	350	840	330	440
	Dry	0.44	11,100	1.42	10.4	29	6,310	620	1,130	360	580
Atlantic white	Green	0.31	4,700	.75	5.9	18	2,390	240	690	180	290
	Dry	0.32	6,800	.93	4.1	13	4,700	410	800	220	350

Species	Condition										
Eastern red	Green	0.44	7,000	.65	15.0	35	3,570	700	1,010	330	650
	Dry	0.47	8,800	.88	8.3	22	6,020	920	—	—	900
Incense	Green	0.35	6,200	.84	6.4	—	3,150	370	830	280	390
	Dry	0.37	8,000	1.04	5.4	17	5,200	590	880	270	470
Northern white	Green	0.29	4,200	.64	5.7	15	1,990	230	620	240	230
	Dry	0.31	6,500	.80	4.8	12	3,960	310	850	240	320
Port Orford	Green	0.39	6,600	1.30	7.4	21	3,140	300	840	180	380
	Dry	0.43	12,700	1.70	9.1	28	6,250	720	1,370	400	630
Western red	Green	0.31	5,200	.94	5.0	17	2,770	240	770	230	260
	Dry	0.32	7,500	1.11	5.8	17	4,560	460	990	220	350
Douglas-fir§											
Coast	Green	0.45	7,700	1.56	7.6	26	3,780	380	900	300	500
	Dry	0.48	12,400	1.95	9.9	31	7,230	800	1,130	340	710
Interior West	Green	0.46	7,700	1.51	7.2	26	3,870	420	940	290	510
	Dry	0.50	12,600	1.83	10.6	32	7,430	760	1,290	350	660
Interior North	Green	0.45	7,400	1.41	8.1	22	3,470	360	950	340	420
	Dry	0.48	13,100	1.79	10.5	26	6,900	770	1,400	390	600
Interior South	Green	0.43	6,800	1.16	8.0	15	3,110	340	950	250	360
	Dry	0.46	11,900	1.49	9.0	20	6,230	740	1,510	330	510
Fir											
Balsam	Green	0.33	5,500	1.25	4.7	16	2,630	190	662	180	290
	Dry	0.35	9,200	1.45	5.1	20	5,280	404	944	180	400
California red	Green	0.36	5,800	1.17	6.4	21	2,760	330	770	380	360
	Dry	0.38	10,500	1.50	8.9	24	5,460	610	1,040	390	500
Grand	Green	0.35	5,800	1.25	5.6	22	2,940	270	740	240	360
	Dry	0.37	8,900	1.57	7.5	28	5,290	500	900	240	490
Noble	Green	0.37	6,200	1.38	6.0	19	3,010	270	800	230	290
	Dry	0.39	10,700	1.72	8.8	23	6,100	520	1,050	220	410
Pacific silver	Green	0.40	6,400	1.42	6.0	21	3,140	220	750	240	310
	Dry	0.43	11,000	1.76	9.3	24	6,410	450	1,220	—	430
Subalpine	Green	0.31	4,900	1.05	—	—	2,300	190	700	—	260
	Dry	0.32	8,600	1.29	—	—	4,860	390	1,070	—	350
White	Green	0.37	5,900	1.16	5.6	22	2,900	280	760	300	340
	Dry	0.39	9,800	1.50	7.2	20	5,800	530	1,100	300	480
Hemlock											
Eastern	Green	0.38	6,400	1.07	6.7	21	3,080	360	850	230	400
	Dry	0.40	8,900	1.20	6.8	21	5,410	650	1,060	—	500
Mountain	Green	0.42	6,300	1.04	11.0	32	2,880	370	930	330	470
	Dry	0.45	11,500	1.33	10.4	32	6,440	860	1,540	—	680
Western	Green	0.42	6,600	1.31	6.9	22	3,360	280	860	290	410
	Dry	0.45	11,200	1.63	8.3	23	7,200	550	1,290	340	540
Larch, western	Green	0.48	7,700	1.46	10.3	29	3,760	400	870	330	510
	Dry	0.52	13,000	1.87	12.6	35	7,620	930	1,360	430	830
Pine											
Eastern white	Green	0.34	4,900	.99	5.2	17	2,440	220	680	250	290
	Dry	0.35	8,600	1.24	6.8	18	4,800	440	900	310	380
Jack	Green	0.40	6,000	1.07	7.2	26	2,950	300	750	360	400
	Dry	0.43	9,900	1.35	8.3	27	5,660	580	1,170	420	570
Loblolly	Green	0.47	7,300	1.40	8.2	30	3,510	390	860	260	450
	Dry	0.51	12,800	1.79	10.4	30	7,130	790	1,390	470	690
Lodgepole	Green	0.38	5,500	1.08	5.6	20	2,610	250	680	220	330
	Dry	0.41	9,400	1.34	6.8	20	5,370	610	880	290	480
Longleaf	Green	0.54	8,500	1.59	8.9	35	4,320	480	1,040	330	590
	Dry	0.59	14,500	1.98	11.8	34	8,470	960	1,510	470	870
Pitch	Green	0.47	6,800	1.20	9.2	—	2,950	360	860	—	—
	Dry	0.52	10,800	1.43	9.2	—	5,940	820	1,360	—	—

Table A.5. *(continued)*

Common names of species	Moisture condition	Specific gravity*	Static bending — Modulus of rupture (psi)	Static bending — Modulus of elasticity† (mil psi)	Static bending — Work to maximum load (in.-lb/in.³)	Impact bending (height of drop causing complete failure)‡ (in.)	Compression parallel to grain (maximum crushing strength) (psi)	Compression perpendicular to grain (fiber stress at proportional limit) (psi)	Shear parallel to grain (maximum shearing strength) (psi)	Tension perpendicular to grain (maximum tensile strength) (psi)	Side hardness (load perpendicular to grain) (lb)
Pond	Green	0.51	7,400	1.28	7.5	...	3,660	440	940	...	...
	Dry	0.56	11,600	1.75	8.6	...	7,540	910	1,380	...	...
Ponderosa	Green	0.38	5,100	1.00	5.2	21	2,450	280	700	310	320
	Dry	0.40	9,400	1.29	7.1	19	5,320	580	1,130	420	460
Red	Green	0.41	5,800	1.28	6.1	26	2,730	260	690	300	340
	Dry	0.46	11,000	1.63	9.9	26	6,070	600	1,210	460	560
Sand	Green	0.46	7,500	1.02	9.6	...	3,440	450	1,140	...	...
	Dry	0.48	11,600	1.41	9.6	...	6,920	836	...	...	...
Shortleaf	Green	0.47	7,400	1.39	8.2	30	3,530	350	910	320	440
	Dry	0.51	13,100	1.75	11.0	33	7,270	820	1,390	470	690
Slash	Green	0.54	8,700	1.53	9.6	...	3,820	530	960	...	...
	Dry	0.59	16,300	1.98	13.2	...	8,140	1,020	1,680	...	...
Spruce	Green	0.41	6,000	1.00	...	...	2,840	280	900	...	450
	Dry	0.44	10,400	1.23	...	...	5,650	730	1,490	...	660
Sugar	Green	0.34	4,900	1.03	5.4	17	2,460	210	720	270	270
	Dry	0.36	8,200	1.19	5.5	18	4,460	500	1,130	350	380
Virginia	Green	0.45	7,300	1.22	10.9	34	3,420	390	890	400	540
	Dry	0.48	13,000	1.52	13.7	32	6,710	910	1,350	380	740
Western white	Green	0.35	4,700	1.19	5.0	19	2,430	190	680	260	260
	Dry	0.38	9,700	1.46	8.8	23	5,040	470	1,040	...	420
Redwood											
Old-growth	Green	0.38	7,500	1.18	7.4	21	4,200	420	800	260	410
	Dry	0.40	10,000	1.34	6.9	19	6,150	700	940	240	480
Young-growth	Green	0.34	5,900	.96	5.7	16	3,110	270	890	300	350
	Dry	0.35	7,900	1.10	5.2	15	5,220	520	1,110	250	420
Spruce											
Black	Green	0.38	6,100	1.38	7.4	24	2,840	240	739	100	370
	Dry	0.42	10,800	1.61	10.5	23	5,960	550	1,230	...	520
Engelmann	Green	0.33	4,700	1.03	5.1	16	2,180	200	640	240	260
	Dry	0.35	9,300	1.30	6.4	18	4,480	410	1,200	350	390
Red	Green	0.37	6,000	1.33	6.9	18	2,720	260	750	220	350
	Dry	0.40	10,800	1.61	8.4	25	5,540	550	1,290	350	490
Stika	Green	0.37	5,700	1.23	6.3	24	2,670	280	760	250	350
	Dry	0.40	10,200	1.57	9.4	25	5,610	580	1,150	370	510
White	Green	0.33	5,000	1.14	6.0	22	2,350	210	640	220	320
	Dry	0.36	9,400	1.43	7.7	20	5,180	430	970	360	480
Tamarack	Green	0.49	7,200	1.24	7.2	28	3,480	390	860	260	380
	Dry	0.53	11,600	1.64	7.1	23	7,160	800	1,280	400	590

Note: Results of tests on small, clear, straight-grained specimens. Values in the first line for each species are from tests of green material; those in the second line are from tests of seasoned material adjusted to a moisture content of 12 percent.

*Specific gravity based on weight ovendry and volume at moisture content indicated.

†Modulus of elasticity measured from a simply supported, center-loaded beam, on a span-depth ratio of 14/1. The modulus can be corrected for the effect of shear deflection by increasing it 10 percent.

‡50-pound hammer.

§Coast Douglas-fir is defined as Douglas-fir growing in the States of Oregon and Washington west of the summit of the Cascade Mountains. Interior West includes the State of California and all counties in Oregon and Washington east of but adjacent to the Cascade summit. Interior North includes the remainder of Oregon and Washington and the States of Idaho, Montana, and Wyoming. Interior South is made up of Utah, Colorado, Arizona, and New Mexico.

Table A.6. Mechanical properties of some woods imported into the United States

Common and botanical names of species	Moisture content	Specific gravity*	Static bending — Modulus of rupture	Static bending — Modulus of elasticity†	Static bending — Work to maximum load	Compression parallel to grain (maximum crushing strength)	Shear parallel to grain (maximum shearing strength)	Side hardness (load perpendicular to grain)	Sample origin‡
	(%)		(psi)	(mil psi)	(in.-lb/in.³)	(psi)	(psi)	(lb)	
Afrormosia (*Pericopsis elata*)	Green	0.61	14,800	1.77	19.5	7,490	1,670	1,600	AF
	12		18,400	1.94	18.4	9,940	2,090	1,560	
Albarco (*Cariniana* spp.)	Green	0.48	14,500	1.50	13.8	6,820	2,310	1,020	AM
	12		10,300	1.69	9.8	4,780	1,220	880	
Andiroba (*Carapa guianensis*)	Green	0.54							AM
	12		15,500	2.00	14.0	8,120	1,510	1,130	
Angelin (*Andira* spp.)	Green	0.65							AM
	12		18,000	2.49		9,200	1,840	1,750	
Angelique (*Dicorynia guianensis*)	Green	0.60	11,400	1.84	12.0	5,590	1,340	1,100	AF
	12		17,400	2.19	15.2	8,770	1,660	1,290	
Avodire (*Turraeanthus africanus*)	Green	0.48	12,700	1.49	9.4	7,150	2,030	1,080	AF
	12		16,900	2.16	12.0	9,520	2,040	2,890	
Azobe (*Lophira alata*)	Green	0.87							AM
	12		24,500	2.47		12,600	2,960	3,350	
Balsa (*Ochroma pyramidale*)	Green	0.16							AM
	12		3,140	.49	2.1	2,160	300		
Banak (*Virola* spp.)	Green	0.42	5,600	1.64		2,390	720	320	AF
	12		10,900	2.04	4.1	5,140	980	510	
Benge (*Guibourtia arnoldiana*)	Green	0.65							AF
	12		21,400	2.04	10.0	11,400	2,090	1,750	
Bubinga (*Guibourtia* spp.)	Green	0.71							AM
	12		22,600	2.48		10,500	3,110	2,690	
Bulletwood (*Manilkara bidentata*)	Green	0.85	17,300	2.70	13.6	8,690	1,900	2,230	AM
	12		27,300	3.45	28.5	11,640	2,500	3,190	
Cativo (*Prioria copaifera*)	Green	0.40	5,900	.94	5.4	2,460	860	440	AM
	12		8,600	1.11	7.2	4,290	1,060	630	
Ceiba (*Ceiba pentandra*)	Green	0.25	2,200	.41	1.2	1,060	350	220	AM
	12		4,300	.54	2.8	2,380	550	240	
Courbaril (*Hymenaea courbaril*)	Green	0.71	12,900	1.84	14.6	5,800	1,770	1,970	AM
	12		19,400	2.16	17.6	9,510	2,470	2,350	
Cuangare (*Dialyanthera* spp.)	Green	0.31	4,000	1.01		2,080	590	230	AM
	12		7,300	1.52		4,760	830	380	
Cypress, Mexican (*Cupressus lusitanica*)	Green	0.39	6,200	.92		2,880	950	340	AF§
	12		10,300	1.02		5,380	1,580	460	
Degame (*Calycophyllum candidissimum*)	Green	0.67	14,300	1.93	18.6	6,200	1,660	1,630	AM
	12		22,300	2.27	27.0	9,670	2,120	1,940	
Determa (*Ocotea rubra*)	Green	0.52	7,800	1.46	4.8	3,760	860	520	AM
	12		10,500	1.82	6.4	5,800	980	660	
Ekop (*Tetraberlinia tubmaniana*)	Green	0.60							AF
	12		16,700	2.21		9,010			
Goncalo alves (*Astronium graveolens*)	Green	0.84	12,100	1.94	6.7	6,580	1,760	1,910	AM
	12		16,600	2.23	10.4	10,320	1,960	2,160	
Greenheart (*Ocotea rodiaei*)	Green	0.80	19,300	2.47	10.5	9,380	1,930	1,880	AM
	12		24,900	3.25	25.3	12,510	2,620	2,350	
Hura (*Hura crepitans*)	Green	0.38							AM
	12		6,300	1.04	5.9	2,790	830	440	

Table A.6. (continued)

Common and botanical names of species	Moisture content (%)	Specific gravity*	Static bending — Modulus of rupture (psi)	Static bending — Modulus of elasticity† (mil psi)	Work to maximum load (in.-lb/in.³)	Compression parallel to grain (maximum crushing strength) (psi)	Shear parallel to grain (maximum shearing strength) (psi)	Side hardness (load perpendicular to grain) (lb)	Sample origin†
Ilomba (*Pycnanthus angolensis*)	12	0.40	8,700	1.17	6.7	4,800	1,080	550	AF
	Green		5,500	1.14	...	2,900	840	470	
Ipe (*Tabebuia* spp.—Lapacho group)	12	0.92	25,400	3.14	22.0	13,010	2,120	3,680	AM
	Green		22,600	2.92	27.6	10,350	2,060	3,060	
Iroko (*Chlorophora* spp.)	12	0.54	12,400	1.59	10.5	7,590	1,800	1,260	AF
	Green		10,200	1.29	9.0	4,910	1,310	1,080	
Jarrah (*Eucalyptus marginata*)	12	0.67	16,100	1.88	...	8,870	2,130	1,910	AS
	Green		9,900	1.48	...	5,190	1,320	1,290	
Jelutong (*Dyera costulata*)	15	0.36	7,300	1.18	6.4	3,920	840	390	AS
	Green		5,600	1.16	5.6	3,050	760	330	
Kaneelhart (*Licaria* spp.)	12	0.96	29,900	4.06	17.5	17,400	1,970	2,900	AM
	Green		22,300	3.82	13.6	13,390	1,680	2,210	
Kapur (*Dryobalanops* spp.)	12	0.64	18,300	1.88	18.8	10,090	1,990	1,230	AS
	Green		12,800	1.60	15.7	6,220	1,170	980	
Karri (*Eucalyptus diversicolor*)	12	0.82	20,160	2.60	25.4	10,800	2,420	2,040	AS
	Green		11,200	1.94	11.6	5,450	1,510	1,360	
Kempas (*Koompassia malaccensis*)	12	0.71	17,700	2.69	15.3	9,520	1,790	1,710	AS
	Green		14,500	2.41	12.2	7,930	1,460	1,480	
Keruing (*Dipterocarpus* spp.)	12	0.69	19,900	2.07	23.5	10,500	2,070	1,270	AS
	Green		11,900	1.71	13.9	5,680	1,170	1,060	
Lignumvitae (*Guaiacum* spp.)	12	1.05	...	...	...	11,400	...	4,500	AM
	Green		...	...	...	...	...	...	
Limba (*Terminalia superba*)	12	0.38	8,800	1.01	8.9	4,730	1,410	490	AF
	Green		6,000	.77	7.7	2,780	880	400	
Macawood (*Platymiscium* spp.)	12	0.94	27,600	3.20	...	16,100	2,540	3,320	AM
	Green		22,300	3.02	...	10,540	1,840	3,150	
Mahogany, African (*Khaya* spp.)	12	0.42	10,700	1.40	8.3	6,460	1,500	830	AF
	Green		7,400	1.15	7.1	3,730	931	640	
Mahogany, Honduras (*Swietenia macrophylla*)	12	0.45	11,500	1.50	7.5	6,780	1,240	800	AM
	Green		9,000	1.34	9.1	4,340	1,230	740	
Manbarklak (*Eschweilera* spp.)	12	0.87	26,500	3.14	33.3	11,210	2,070	3,480	AM
	Green		17,100	2.70	17.4	7,340	1,630	2,280	
Manni (*Symphonia globulifera*)	12	0.58	16,900	2.46	16.5	8,820	1,620	1,120	AM
	Green		11,200	1.96	11.2	5,160	1,140	940	
Marishballi (*Lincania* spp.)	12	0.88	27,700	3.34	14.2	13,390	1,810	3,570	AM
	Green		17,100	2.93	13.4	7,580	1,750	2,250	
Merbau (*Intsia* spp.)	15	0.64	16,800	2.23	14.8	8,440	1,810	1,500	AS
	Green		12,900	2.02	12.8	6,770	1,560	1,380	
Mersawa (*Anisoptera* spp.)	12	0.52	13,800	2.28	...	7,370	890	1,290	AS
	Green		8,000	1.77	...	3,960	740	880	
Mora (*Mora* spp.)	12	0.78	22,100	2.96	18.5	11,840	1,900	2,300	AM
	Green		12,600	2.33	13.5	6,400	1,450	1,450	

Table A.6. (continued)

Common and botanical names of species	Moisture content (%)	Specific gravity*	Static bending — Modulus of rupture (psi)	Static bending — Modulus of elasticity† (mil psi)	Static bending — Work to maximum load (in.-lb/in.³)	Compression parallel to grain (maximum crushing strength) (psi)	Shear parallel to grain (maximum shearing strength) (psi)	Side hardness (load perpendicular to grain) (lb)	Sample origin‡
Oak (*Quercus* spp.)	Green	0.76	· · ·	· · ·	· · ·	· · ·	· · ·	· · ·	AM
	12		23,000	3.02	16.5	· · ·	· · ·	2,500	
Obeche (*Triplochiton scleroxylon*)	Green	0.30	5,100	.72	6.2	2,570	660	420	AF
	12		7,400	.86	6.9	3,930	990	430	
Okoume (*Aucoumea klaineana*)	Green	0.33	· · ·	· · ·	· · ·	· · ·	· · ·	· · ·	AF
	12		7,400	1.14	12.2	3,970	970	380	
Opepe (*Nauclea diderrichii*)	Green	0.63	13,600	1.73	12.2	7,480	1,900	1,520	AF
	12		17,400	1.94	14.4	10,400	2,480	1,630	
Ovangkol (*Guibourtia ehie*)	Green	0.67	· · ·	· · ·	· · ·	· · ·	· · ·	· · ·	AF.
	12		16,900	2.56	· · ·	8,300	1,600	· · ·	
Para-angelium (*Hymenolobium excelsum*)	Green	0.63	14,600	1.95	12.8	7,460	1,600	1,720	AM
	12		17,600	2.05	15.9	8,990	2,010	1,720	
Parana-pine (*Araucaria augustifolia*)	Green	0.46	13,500	1.35	9.7	4,010	970	560	AM
	12		14,400	1.61	12.2	7,660	1,730	780	
Pau marfim (*Balfourodendron riedelianum*)	Green	.73	· · ·	· · ·	· · ·	6,070	· · ·	· · ·	AM
	15		18,900	1.66	· · ·	8,190	2,130	· · ·	
Peroba de campos (*Paratecoma peroba*)	Green	0.62	· · ·	· · ·	· · ·	· · ·	· · ·	· · ·	AM
	12		15,400	1.77	10.1	8,880	2,130	1,600	
Peroba rosa (*Aspidosperma* spp.—Peroba group)	Green	0.66	10,900	1.29	10.5	5,540	1,880	1,580	AM
	12		12,100	1.53	9.2	7,920	2,490	1,730	
Pilon (*Hyeronima* spp.)	Green	0.65	10,700	1.88	8.3	4,960	1,200	1,220	AM
	12		18,200	2.27	12.1	9,620	1,720	1,700	
Pine, Caribbean (*Pinus caribaea*)	Green	0.68	11,200	1.88	10.7	4,900	1,170	980	AM
	12		16,700	2.24	17.3	8,540	2,090	1,240	
Pine, ocote (*Pinus oocarpa*)	Green	.55	8,000	1.74	6.9	3,690	1,040	580	AM
	12		14,900	2.25	10.9	7,680	1,720	910	
Pine, radiata (*Pinus radiata*)	Green	.42	6,100	1.18	· · ·	2,790	750	480	AS§
	12		11,700	1.48	8.4	6,080	1,600	750	
Piquia (*Caryocar* spp.)	Green	.72	12,400	1.82	· · ·	6,290	1,640	1,720	AM
	12		17,000	2.16	15.8	8,410	1,990	1,720	
Primavera (*Cybistax donnell-smithii*)	Green	0.40	7,200	.99	7.2	3,510	1,030	700	AM
	12		9,500	1.04	6.4	5,600	1,390	660	
Purpleheart (*Peltogyne* spp.)	Green	0.67	13,700	2.00	14.8	7,020	1,640	1,810	AM
	12		19,200	2.27	17.6	10,320	2,220	1,860	
Ramin (*Gonystylus* spp.)	Green	0.52	9,800	1.57	9.0	5,390	990	640	AS
	12		18,500	2.17	17.0	10,080	1,250	1,300	
Robe (*Tabebuia* spp.—Roble group)	Green	.52	10,800	1.45	11.7	4,910	· · ·	910	AM
	12		13,800	1.60	12.5	7,340	1,450	960	
Rosewood, Brazilian (*Dalbergia nigra*)	Green	0.80	14,100	1.84	13.2	5,510	2,110	2,440	AM
	12		19,000	1.88	· · ·	9,600	2,360	2,720	
Rosewood, Indian (*Dalbergia latifola*)	Green	.75	9,200	1.19	11.6	4,530	1,400	1,560	AS
	12		16,900	1.78	13.1	9,220	2,090	3,170	
Sande (*Brosimum* spp.—Utile group)	Green	0.49	8,500	1.94	· · ·	4,490	1,040	600	AM
	12		14,300	2.39	· · ·	8,220	1,290	900	

Table A.6. *(continued)*

Common and botanical names of species	Moisture content (%)	Specific gravity*	Static bending: Modulus of rupture (psi)	Static bending: Modulus of elasticity† (mil psi)	Static bending: Work to maximum load (in.-lb/in.³)	Compression parallel to grain (maximum crushing strength) (psi)	Shear parallel to grain (maximum shearing strength) (psi)	Side hardness (load perpendicular to grain) (lb)	Sample origin‡
Santa Maria (*Calophyllum brasiliense*)	Green	0.52	10,500	1.59	12.7	4,560	1,260	890	AM
	12		14,600	1.83	16.1	6,910	2,080	1,150	
Sapele (*Entandrophragma cylindricum*)	Green	0.55	10,200	1.49	10.5	5,010	1,250	1,020	AF
	12		15,300	1.82	15.7	8,160	2,280	1,510	
Sepetir (*Pseudosindora palustris*)	Green	. . .	11,200	1.57	13.3	5,460	1,310	950	AS
	12	0.56	17,200	1.97	13.3	8,880	2,030	1,410	
Shorea (*Shorea* spp. – Baulau group)	Green	0.68	11,700	2.10	. . .	5,380	1,440	1,350	AS
	12		18,800	2.61		10,180	2,190	1,780	
Shorea-Lauan-Meranti group, Dark red (*Shorea* spp.)	Green	0.46	9,400	1.50	8.6	4,720	1,110	700	AS
	12		12,700	1.77	13.8	7,360	1,450	780	
Shorea-Lauan-Meranti group, Light red (*Shorea* spp.)	Green	0.34	6,600	1.04	6.2	3,330	710	440	AS
	12		9,500	1.23	8.6	5,920	970	460	
Shorea-White Meranti group (*Shorea* spp.)	Green	0.55	9,800	1.30	8.3	5,490	1,320	1,000	AS
	15		12,400	1.49	11.4	6,350	1,540	1,140	
Shorea-Yellow Meranti group (*Shorea* spp.)	Green	0.46	8,000	1.30	8.1	3,880	1,030	750	AS
	12		11,400	1.55	10.1	5,900	1,520	770	
Spanish-cedar (*Cedrela* spp.)	Green	0.41	7,500	1.31	7.1	3,370	990	550	AM
	12		11,500	1.44	9.4	6,210	1,100	600	
Sucupira (*Bowdichia* spp.)	Green	0.74	17,200	2.27	. . .	9,730	. . .	. . .	AM
	15		19,400			11,100			
Sucupira (*Diplotropis purpurea*)	Green	0.78	17,400	2.68	13.0	8,020	1,800	1,980	AM
	12		20,600	2.87	14.8	12,140	1,960	2,140	
Teak (*Tectona grandis*)	Green	0.55	11,600	1.37	13.4	5,960	1,290	930	AS
	12		14,600	1.55	12.0	8,410	1,890	1,000	
Tornillo (*Cedrelinga catenaeformis*)	Green	0.45	8,400	. . .	. . .	4,100	1,170	870	AM
	12								
Wallaba (*Eperua* spp.)	Green	0.78	14,300	2.33	. . .	8,040	. . .	1,540	AM
	12	. . .	19,100	2.28		10,760		2,040	

Note: Results of tests on small, clear, straight-grained specimens. Property values were taken from world literature (not obtained from experiments conducted at the Forest Products Laboratory). Other species may be reported in the world literature, as well as additional data on many of these species. Some property values have been adjusted to 12 percent moisture content; others are based on moisture content at time of test.

*Specific gravity based on weight ovendry and volume green.

†Modulus of elasticity measured from a simply supported, center-loaded beam, on a span-depth ratio of 14/1. The modulus can be corrected for the effect of shear deflection by increasing it 10 percent.

‡Key to code letters: AF, Africa; AM, Tropical America; AS, Asia.

§Plantation grown.

Table A.7. Mechanical properties of some commercially important woods grown in Canada and imported into the United States

Common names of species	Specific gravity	Static bending		Compression parallel to grain (maximum crushing strength)	Compression perpendicular to grain (fiber stress at proportional limit)	Shear parallel to grain (maximum shearing strength)
		Modulus of rupture	Modulus of elasticity*			
	(psi)	(psi)	(mil. psi)	(psi)	(psi)	(psi)
HARDWOODS						
Aspen						
Quaking	0.37	5,500	1.31	2350	200	720
		9,800	1.63	5260	510	980
Big-toothed	0.39	5,300	1.08	2390	210	790
		9,500	1.26	4760	470	1100
Cottonwood						
Balsam, poplar	0.37	5,000	1.15	2110	180	670
		10,100	1.67	5020	420	890
Black	0.30	4,100	0.97	1860	100	560
		7,100	1.28	4020	260	860
Eastern	0.35	4,700	0.87	1970	210	770
		7,500	1.13	3840	470	1160
SOFTWOODS						
Cedar						
Alaska	0.42	6,600	1.34	3240	350	880
		11,600	1.59	6640	690	1340
Northern white	0.30	3,900	0.52	1890	200	660
		6,100	0.63	3590	390	1000
Western red	0.31	5,300	1.05	2780	280	700
		7,800	1.19	4290	500	810
Douglas-fir	0.45	7,500	1.61	3610	460	920
		12,800	1.97	7260	870	1380
Fir						
Subalpine	0.33	5,200	1.26	2500	260	680
		8,200	1.48	5280	540	980
Pacific silver	0.36	5,500	1.35	2770	230	710
		10,000	1.64	5930	520	1190
Balsam	0.34	5,300	1.13	2440	240	680
		8,500	1.40	4980	460	910
Hemlock						
Eastern	0.40	6,800	1.27	3430	400	910
		9,700	1.41	5970	630	1260
Western	0.41	7,000	1.48	3580	370	750
		11,800	1.79	6770	660	940
Larch, western	0.55	8,700	1.65	4420	520	920
		15,500	2.08	8840	1060	1340
Pine						
Eastern white	0.36	5,100	1.18	2590	240	640
		9,500	1.36	5230	490	880
Jack	0.42	6,300	1.17	2950	340	820
		11,300	1.48	5870	830	1190

Table A.7. (continued)

Common names of species	Specific gravity	Static bending		Compression parallel to grain (maximum crushing strength)	Compression perpendicular to grain (fiber stress at proportional limit)	Shear parallel to grain (maximum shearing strength)
		Modulus of rupture	Modulus of elasticity*			
	(psi)	*(psi)*	*(mil. psi)*	*(psi)*	*(psi)*	*(psi)*
SOFTWOODS						
Pine						
Lodgepole	0.40	5,600	1.27	2860	280	720
		11,000	1.58	6260	530	1240
Ponderosa	0.44	5,700	1.13	2840	350	720
		10,600	1.38	6130	760	1020
Red	0.39	5,000	1.07	2370	280	710
		10,100	1.38	5500	720	1090
Western white	0.36	4,800	1.19	2520	240	650
		9,300	1.46	5240	470	920
Spruce						
Black	0.41	5,900	1.32	2760	300	800
		11,400	1.52	6040	620	1250
Engelmann	0.38	5,700	1.25	2810	270	700
		10,100	1.55	6150	540	1100
Red	0.38	5,900	1.32	2810	270	810
		10,300	1.60	5590	550	1330
Sitka	0.35	5,400	1.37	2560	290	630
		10,100	1.63	5480	590	980
White	0.35	5,100	1.15	2470	240	670
		9,100	1.45	5360	500	980
Tamarack	0.48	6,800	1.24	3130	410	920
		11,000	1.36	6510	900	1300

Note: Results of tests on small, clear, straight-grained specimens. Property values based on ASTM D 2555–70. Information on additional properties can be obtained from Dep. For. Can. publ. 1104.

The values in the first line for each species are from tests of green material; those in the second line are adjusted from the green condition to 12% MC using dry to green clear wood property ratios as reported in ASTM D 2555–70. Specific gravity is based on weight when ovendry and volume when green.

* Modulus of elasticity measured from a simply supported, center-loaded beam, on a span-depth ratio of 14/1. The modulus can be corrected for the effect of shear deflection by increasing it 10 percent.

Table A.8. Nomenclature for some types of hardwood lumber

Commercial name for lumber	Official common tree name	Botanical name
Alder, red	Red alder	*Alnus rubra*
Ash		
Black	Black ash	*Fraxinus nigra*
Oregon	Oregon ash	*F. latifolia*
White	Blue ash	*F. quadrangulata*
	Green ash	*F. pennsylvanica*
	White ash	*F. americana*
Aspen (popple)	Bigtooth aspen	*Populus grandidentata*
	Quaking aspen	*P. tremuloides*
Basswood	American basswood	*Tilia americana*
	White basswood	*T. heterophylla*
Beech	Beech	*Fagus grandifolia*
Birch	Gray birch	*Betula populifolia*
	Paper birch	*B. papyrifera*
	River birch	*B. nigra*
	Sweet birch	*B. lenta*
	Yellow birch	*B. alleghaniensis*
Box elder	Boxelder	*Acer negundo*
Buckeye	Ohio buckeye	*Aesculus glabra*
	Yellow buckeye	*A. octandra*
Butternut	Butternut	*Juglans cinerea*
Cherry	Black cherry	*Prunus serotina*
Chestnut	Chestnut	*Castanea dentata*
Cottonwood	Balsam poplar	*Populus balsamifera*
	Eastern cottonwood	*P. deltoides*
	Plains cottonwood	*F. sargentii*
Cucumber	Cucumbertree	*Magnolia acuminata*
Dogwood	Flowering dogwood	*Cornus florida*
	Pacific dogwood	*C. nuttallii*
Elm		
Rock	Cedar elm	*Ulmus crassifolia*
	Rock elm	*U. thomasii*
	September elm	*U. serotina*
	Winged elm	*U. alata*
Soft	American elm	*U. americana*
	Slippery elm	*U. rubra*
Gum	Sweetgum	*Liquidambar styraciflua*
Hackberry	Hackberry	*Celtis occidentalis*
	Sugarberry	*C. laevigata*
Hickory	Mockernut hickory	*Carya tomentosa*
	Pignut hickory	*C. glabra*
	Shagbark hickory	*C. ovata*
	Shellbark hickory	*C. laciniosa*
Holly	American holly	*Ilex opaca*
Ironwood	Eastern hophornbeam	*Ostrya virginiana*
Locust	Black locust	*Robinia pseudoacacia*
	Honeylocust	*Gleditsia triacanthos*
Madrone	Pacific madrone	*Arbutus menziesii*
Magnolia	Southern magnolia	*Magnolia grandiflora*
	Sweetbay	*M. virginiana*

Table A.8. (continued)

Commercial name for lumber	Official common tree name	Botanical name
Maple		
Hard	Black maple	*Acer nigrum*
	Sugar maple	*A. saccharum*
Oregon	Bigleaf maple	*A. macrophyllum*
Soft	Red maple	*A. rubrum*
	Silver maple	*A. saccharinum*
Oak		
Red	Black oak	*Quercus velutina*
	Blackjack oak	*Q. marilandica*
	California black oak	*Q. kelloggi*
	Cherrybark oak	*Q. falcata var. pagodaefolia*
	Laurel oak	*Q. laurifolia*
	Northern pin oak	*Q. ellipsoidalis*
	Northern red oak	*Q. rubra*
	Nuttall oak	*Q. nuttallii*
	Pin oak	*Q. palustris*
	Scarlet oak	*Q. coccinea*
	Shumard oak	*Q. shumardii*
	Southern red oak	*Q. falcata*
	Turkey oak	*Q. laevis*
	Willow oak	*Q. phellos*
White	Arizona white oak	*Q. arizonica*
	Blue oak	*Q. douglasii*
	Bur oak	*Q. macrocarpa*
	California white oak	*Q. lobata*
	Chestnut oak	*Q. primus*
	Chinkapin oak	*Q. muehlenbergii*
	Emory oak	*Q. emoryi*
	Gambel oak	*Q. gambelii*
	Mexican blue oak	*Q. oblongifolia*
	Live oak	*Q. virginiana*
	Oregon white oak	*Q. garryana*
	Overcup oak	*Q. lyrata*
	Post oak	*Q. stellata*
	Swamp chestnut oak	*Q. michauxii*
	Swamp white oak	*Q. bicolor*
	White oak	*Q. alba*
Oregon myrtle	California-laurel	*Umbellularia californica*
Osage orange (bois d'arc)	Osage-orange	*Maclura pomifera*
Pecan	Bitternut hickory	*Carya cordiformis*
	Nutmeg hickory	*C. myristicaeformis*
	Water hickory	*C. aquatica*
	Pecan	*C. illinoensis*
Persimmon	Common persimmon	*Diospyros virginiana*
Poplar	Yellow-poplar	*Liriodendron tulipifera*
Sassafras	Sassafras	*Sassafras albidum*
Sycamore	American sycamore	*Platanus occidentalis*
Tupelo	Black tupelo	*Nyssa sylvatica*
	Ogeechee tupelo	*N. ogeche*
	Water tupelo	*N. aquatica*
Walnut	Black walnut	*Juglans nigra*
Willow	Black willow	*Salix nigra*
	Peachleaf willow	*S. amygdaloides*

Table A.9. *American Standard lumber sizes for stress-graded and non-stress-graded lumber for construction*

Item	Thickness Nominal	Minimum dressed Dry	Minimum dressed Green	Face width Nominal	Minimum dressed Dry	Minimum dressed Green
			(*in.*)			
Boards	1	$3/4$	$25/32$	2	$1\frac{1}{2}$	$1\frac{9}{16}$
	$1\frac{1}{4}$	1	$1\frac{1}{32}$	3	$2\frac{1}{2}$	$2\frac{9}{16}$
	$1\frac{1}{2}$	$1\frac{1}{4}$	$1\frac{9}{32}$	4	$3\frac{1}{2}$	$3\frac{9}{16}$
				5	$4\frac{1}{2}$	$4\frac{5}{8}$
				6	$5\frac{1}{2}$	$5\frac{5}{8}$
				7	$6\frac{1}{2}$	$6\frac{5}{8}$
				8	$7\frac{1}{4}$	$7\frac{1}{2}$
				9	$8\frac{1}{4}$	$8\frac{1}{2}$
				10	$9\frac{1}{4}$	$9\frac{1}{2}$
				11	$10\frac{1}{4}$	$10\frac{1}{2}$
				12	$11\frac{1}{4}$	$11\frac{1}{2}$
				14	$13\frac{1}{4}$	$13\frac{1}{2}$
				16	$15\frac{1}{4}$	$15\frac{1}{2}$
Dimension	2	$1\frac{1}{2}$	$1\frac{9}{16}$	2	$1\frac{1}{2}$	$1\frac{9}{16}$
	$2\frac{1}{2}$	2	$2\frac{1}{16}$	3	$2\frac{1}{2}$	$2\frac{9}{16}$
	3	$2\frac{1}{2}$	$2\frac{9}{16}$	4	$3\frac{1}{2}$	$3\frac{9}{16}$
	$3\frac{1}{2}$	3	$3\frac{1}{16}$	5	$4\frac{1}{2}$	$4\frac{5}{8}$
	4	$3\frac{1}{2}$	$3\frac{9}{16}$	6	$5\frac{1}{2}$	$5\frac{5}{8}$
	$4\frac{1}{2}$	4	$4\frac{1}{16}$	8	$7\frac{1}{4}$	$7\frac{1}{2}$
				10	$9\frac{1}{4}$	$9\frac{1}{2}$
				12	$11\frac{1}{4}$	$11\frac{1}{2}$
				14	$13\frac{1}{4}$	$13\frac{1}{2}$
				16	$15\frac{1}{4}$	$15\frac{1}{2}$
Timbers	5 and greater		$\frac{1}{2}$ less than nominal	5 and greater		$\frac{1}{2}$ less than nominal

Note: Nominal sizes in the table are used for convenience. No inference should be drawn that they represent actual sizes.

Table A.10. Nomenclature of commercial softwood lumber

Standard lumber name under American Softwood Lumber Standards	Official Forest Service tree name used in this handbook	Botanical name
Cedar		
Alaska	Alaska-cedar	*Chamaecyparis nootkatensis*
Eastern red	Eastern redcedar	*Juniperus virginiana*
Incense	Incense-cedar	*Libocedrus decurrens*
Northern white	Northern white-cedar	*Thuja occidentalis*
Port Orford	Port-Orford-cedar	*Chamaecyparis lawsoniana*
Southern white	Atlantic white-cedar	*C. thyoides*
Western red	Western redcedar	*Thuja plicata*
Cypress, red (coast type), yellow (inland type), white (inland type)	Baldcypress	*Taxodium distichum*
Douglas-fir	Douglas-fir	*Pseudotsuga menziesii*
Fir		
Balsam	Balsam fir	*Abies balsamea*
	Fraser fir	*A. fraseri*
Noble	Noble fir	*A. procera*
White	California red fir	*A. magnifica*
	Grand fir	*A. gandis*
	Pacific silver fir	*A. amabilis*
	Subalpine fir	*A. lasiocarpa*
	White fir	*A. concolor*
Hemlock		
Eastern	Eastern hemlock	*Tsuga canadensis*
Mountain	Mountain hemlock	*T. mertensiana*
West Coast	Western hemlock	*T. heterophylla*
Juniper, western	Alligator juniper	*Juniperus deppeana*
	Rocky Mountain juniper	*J. scopulorum*
	Utah juniper	*J. osteosperma*
	Western juniper	*J. occidentalis*
Larch, western	Western larch	*Larix occidentalis*
Pine		
Idaho white	Western white pine	*Pinus monticola*
Jack	Jack pine	*P. banksiana*
Lodgepole	Lodgepole pine	*P. contorta*
Longleaf yellow*	Longleaf pine	*P. palustris*
	Slash pine	*P. elliottii*
Northern white	Eastern white pine	*P. strobus*
Norway	Red pine	*P. resinosa*
Southern yellow	Longleaf pine	*P. palustris*
	Shortleaf pine	*P. echinata*
	Loblolly pine	*P. taeda*
	Slash pine	*P. elliottii*
	Pitch pine	*P. rigida*
	Virginia pine	*P. virginiana*
Sugar	Sugar pine	*P. lambertiana*
Redwood	Redwood	*Sequoia sempervirens*
Spruce		
Eastern	Black spruce	*Picea mariana*
	Red spruce	*P. rubens*
	White spruce	*P. glauca*
Englemann	Blue spruce	*P. pungens*
	Engelmann spruce	*P. engelmannii*
Sitka	Sitka spruce	*P. sitchensis*
Tamarack	Tamarack	*Larix laricina*
Yew, Pacific	Pacific yew	*Taxus brevifolia*

*The commercial requirements for longleaf yellow pine lumber are that not only must it be produced from the species *Pinus elliottii* and *P. palustris* but each piece must average either on one end or the other not less than 6 annual rings per inch and not less than ⅓ summerwood. Longleaf yellow pine lumber is sometimes designated as pitch pine in the export trade.

INDEX